Baby
Names
That
GO
TOGETHER

Baby Names

That

GO TOGETHER

from **Lily, Rose, and Violet** *to* **Finn and Fay—** *sibling names that mix and match in a perfect way*

Eric Groves, Sr.

Avon, Massachusetts

Published by
Adams Media, a division of F+W Media, Inc.
57 Littlefield Street, Avon, MA 02322. U.S.A.
www.adamsmedia.com

ISBN 10: 1-60550-138-7
ISBN 13: 978-1-60550-138-3
Printed in the United States of America.

J I H G F E D C B A

Library of Congress Cataloging-in-Publication Data
is available from the publisher.

This publication is designed to provide accurate and authoritative information with regard to
the subject matter covered. It is sold with the understanding that the publisher is not engaged
in rendering legal, accounting, or other professional advice. If legal advice or other expert
assistance is required, the services of a competent professional person should be sought.
—From a *Declaration of Principles* jointly adopted by a Committee of the American Bar
Association and a Committee of Publishers and Associations

Many of the designations used by manufacturers and sellers to distinguish their product are
claimed as trademarks. Where those designations appear in this book and Adams Media was
aware of a trademark claim, the designations have been printed with initial capital letters.

This book is available at quantity discounts for bulk purchases.
For information, please call 1-800-289-0963.

Contents

Baby
Names
That
GO
TOGETHER

Name Pairs and Groups
That Begin with the Same Letter

BOYS

🐣 **Abbe** (AH-bay) (French) He Is the Leader of a Catholic Abbey

Alden (ALL-dun) (English) He Is a Trusted Companion

Alphonsus (al-FAHN-sus) (Latin) He Is Aristocratic

Alter (ALL-tur) (Yiddish) He Is a Child Not Yet Ready to Depart

Andel (AHN-jel) (Czech) He Is God's Angelic Messenger

Aristarchus (air-iss-STAR-kus) (Greek) He Is the Source of Greatness

Aristoteles (air-ih-STAH-tuh-leez) (Greek) He Has the Best Ambitions

Armstrong (ARM-strong) (English) He Has Strong Arms

Aston (ASS-tun) (English) He Is the Great Eastern Town

Avery (AY-vur-ree) (English) He Has the Power of the Elfin People

🐣 **Abdul** (ab-DOOL) (Arabic) He Serves the Powerful

Akihiko (ah-kee-HEE-ko) (Japanese) He Is a Majestic Prince

Aleksandr (al-ek-SAN-dur) (Russian) He Protects Humanity

Allen (AL-len) (English) He Is Handsome

Anders (AN-durz) (Norwegian) He Is Powerful

Anderson (AN-dur-sun) (English) He Descends from the Powerful Man

Aleksei (uh-LEK-see) (Russian) He Protects Us

Altman (ALT-mun) (German) He Is Honorable

Anatoli (an-uh-TOH-lee) (Russian) He Is the Bright Sunrise

Arnaldo (ar-NAHL-doh) (Italian) He Is a Soaring Eagle

🐣 **Aegaeon** (EE-jee-yahn) (Latin) He Is Windstorms

Amalcides (uh-MAL-sih-deez) (Latin) He Is the Sacred Soil

> *The giant Hecatoncheires were the sons of Uranus, the Sky, and Gaia, the Earth. Each giant possessed fifty heads and one hundred hands and controlled sea storms.*

🐣 **Agrennon** (AR-guh-non) (Latin) He Is White Sheep's Wool

Aegicorus (ee-juh-KOR-rus) (Latin) He Enjoys Delicious Goat Meat

> *Agrennon and Aegicorus were woodland nature-spirits whom the Romans called "fauns." The fauns, half-human and half-goat, protected shepherds and frequently caroused and fell in love.*

🐣 **Beran** (BAIR-run) (English) He Is a Soaring Bird in Heaven

Birdas (BUR-dus) (English) He Is a Soaring Bird in Heaven

Birky (BUR-kee) (English) He Is a Soaring Bird in Heaven

Brecan (BREK-kun) (English) He Is a Soaring Bird in Heaven

Bredan (BRAY-dun) (English) He Is a Soaring Bird in Heaven

Breed (BREED) (English) He Is a Soaring Bird in Heaven

Breiten (BRYE-tun) (German) He Is a Soaring Bird in Heaven

Brock (BRAHK) (English) He Is a Soaring Bird in Heaven

Broeden (BRO-dun) (Dutch) He Is a Soaring Bird in Heaven

Byre (BYE-yur) (English) He Is a Soaring Bird in Heaven

🐦 **Eridanus** (air-uh-DAY-nus) (Latin) He Is the Eridanus River, Greece

Erymanthus (air-uh-MAN-thus) (Latin) He Is the Erymanthus River, Greece
> *Eridanus and Erymanthus were two of the river-spirits called the "Flumina" by the Romans who personified every river in the world.*

🐦 **Garrett** (GAIR-ret) (English) He Rules with Powerful Weapons

George (JORJ) (English) He Farms the Land
> *Garrett Morgan (1877–1963) was the African-American inventor of an early gas mask; used in 1916 to rescue victims of a tunnel collapse. Garrett was also a member of the Alpha Phi Alpha fraternity, which was cofounded by his friend, George Kelley.*

🐦 **Tim** (TIM) (English) He Is the Little One Who Honors God

Tom (TAHM) (English) He Is Our Precious Little Twin
> *Tim Russert (1950–2008) was a journalist with the National Broadcasting Corporation (NBC) and a moderator of* Meet the Press. *Tim's colleague, journalist Tom Brokaw, said, "This news division will not be the same without his strong, clear voice."*

GIRLS

🐦 **Abby** (AB-bee) (English) Her Father Is Joyful

Ann (ANN) (English) She Is Graceful
> *Twins Abigail Van Buren (1918–) and Ann Landers (1918–2002) penned the two most successful syndicated advice columns in history, "Dear Abby" and "Dear Ann."*

🐦 **Acte** (AK-tee) (Greek) She Is the Meal Hour

Aletris (uh-LEE-triss) (Greek) She Is a Hard-Working Woman

Amaryllis (am-ur-IL-liss) (English) She Shimmers Radiantly

Anemone (uh-NEM-uh-nee) (English) She Is the Refreshing Breeze

Anise (AN-niss, uh-NEESS) (English) She Is a Fragrant Herb

Aristea (ah-ree-STAY-yuh) (French) She Is Supreme

Aster (ASS-tur) (Greek) She Is a Heavenly Star

Aubrieta (aw-bree-ET-tuh) (French) She Is the Flower Who Honors French Artist Aubriet

Averill (AV-ur-il) (English) She Is a Mighty She-Boar

Azalea (uh-ZAYL-yuh) (English) She Is Clean and Perfumed

🐦 **Alanna** (uh-LAH-nuh) (English) She Is a Beautiful Stone

Alannis (uh-LAN-niss) (English) She Is a Beautiful Stone

Alayna (uh-LYE-nuh, uh-LAY-nuh) (English) She Rejoices

Alea (uh-LEE-yuh) (English/Arabic) She Is Magnificently Noble

Alease (uh-LEESS) (English) She Is Aristocratic

Aleesha (uh-LEE-shuh) (English) She Is Aristocratic

Alene (uh-LEEN) (English) She Is Our Little Aristocrat

Aleta (uh-LEE-tuh) (English) She Is Honesty

Alexandrea (al-ex-AN-dree-yuh) (English/Greek) She Protects Humanity

Alexia (uh-LEX-ee-yuh) She Protects Humanity

🐦 **Gayle** (GAYL) (English) Her Father's Name Is Happiness

Gillian (JILL-ee-yun) (English) She Rules Heaven
> *Gayle and Gillian Blakeney (1966–) are Australian-American twins who enjoyed success as Christina and Caroline on the soap opera* Neighbours. *Gayle and Gillian also gained fame as the singing group The Twins, with their 1991 hit "All Mixed Up."*

🐦 **Ianeira** (eye-uh-NEER-ruh) (Greek) She Is Ionia, Greece

Ianthe (eye-AN-thee) (Greek) She Is the Color Violet
> *Ianeira and Ianthe were two of the Oceanides, freshwater nymphs or nature-spirits, who personified Earth's water sources. The Oceanides were the daughters of Oceanus, god of the ocean that surrounded Gaia, the Earth.*

🐾 **Jacqueline** (JAK-kwuh-lin) (French) She Is Divinely Protected

Jill (JIL) (English) She Is the Little One Who Rules Heaven

Canadian twins Jacqueline and Jill Henessy (1968–) are actresses who starred as twin doctors in the 1998 thriller Dead Ringers. *Jacqueline currently hosts the Canadian television show* Medical Intelligence, *while Jill portrayed attorney Claire Kinkaid on* Law and Order.

🐾 **Linda** (LIN-duh) (Spanish) She Is Beautiful

Leslie (LESS-lee) (English) She Is a Fragrant Garden of Holly

Linda and Leslie Hamilton (1956–) are American twin actresses who shared the role of Sarah Connor in the 1991 science-fiction film Terminator 2: Judgment Day. *Linda also gained fame for her portrayal of Catherine Chandler in the television series* Beauty and the Beast *(1987–1990).*

🐾 **Tamera** (TAM-uh-ruh) (English) She Is a Beautiful Palm Tree

Tamia (tuh-MEE-yuh) (English) She Is a Magnificent Palm Tree

Tamika (tuh-MEE-kuh) (English/Japanese) She Is a Beautiful Child, a Thousand Times Over

Tammara (tum-MAH-ruh) (English) She Is a Beautiful Palm Tree

Tamra (TAM-ruh) (English) She Is a Beautiful Palm Tree

Tamsen (TAM-zen) (English) She Is a Precious Twin

Taneka (tuh-NEE-kuh) (English/American) She Is an Infinitely Lovely Child

Tanesha (tih-NEE-shuh) (English/American) She Is a Saint, As Powerful as any Male

Tania (TAHN-yuh) (English/Russian) She Is a Little Saint

Taniqua (tah-NEE-kwah) (English/American) She Is a Little Saint

🐾 **Tamera** (tah-MAIR-rah) (Russian/Hebrew) She Is a Beautiful Palm Tree

Tia (TEE-yah) (Spanish) She Is a Beloved Auntie

Tamera and Tia Mowry (1978–) are African-American twin actresses beloved for their performances as twins Tamera Campbell and Tia Landry on the television series Sister, Sister *(1994–1999).*

BOYS AND GIRLS

🐾 **Aali** (ah-LEE) (Arabic) He Is Supreme

Aaliyah (ah-LEE-yah) (Arabic) She Is Supreme

Aamina (ah-MEE-nah) (Arabic) She Is Our Protector

Abbas (AHB-bahss) (Arabic) He Is Stern

Abd-al-Malik (ahb-dahl-mah-LEEK) (Arabic) He Follows Our Divine God

Abd-al-Rahman (ahb-dahl-rah-MAHN) (Arabic) He Follows Our Merciful God

Abdul-Aziz (ahb-dool-ah-ZEEZ) (Arabic) He Follows Our Mighty God

Abdul-Hamid (ahb-dool-hah-MEED) (Arabic) He Follows Our Revered God

Abdul-Rahman (ahb-dool-rah-MAHN) (Arabic) He Follows Our Merciful God

Afif (ah-FEEF) (Arabic) He Is Pure

🐾 **Aaren** (AIR-ren) (English) She Is a Lofty Mountain

Abbi (AB-bee) (English) She Is the Little One Whose Father Is Joyful

Abegail (AB-eh-gayl) (English) Her Father Is Joyful

Acacia (uh-KAY-shuh) (English) She Is the Thorny but Lovely Acacia Tree

Adair (uh-DAIR) (English/Scottish) He Is a Powerful Weapon

Adamina (ad-uh-MEE-nuh) (English) She Is the First Human to Walk the Earth

Addie (AD-dee) (English) She Is Our Little Aristocrat

Addison (AD-dih-sun) (English) He Descends from the First Man to Walk the Earth

Adela (uh-DEL-luh) (English/Spanish) She Is Aristocratic

Adria (AY-dree-yuh) (English) She Is Hadria, Italy

🐾 **Abe** (AYB) (English) He Is the Little One Who Is the Father of Nations

Abigail (AB-ih-gayl) (Hebrew) She Is Her Father's Joy

Adel (ah-DEL) (Arabic) She Is Truthful and Fair

Adeline (ahd-LEEN) (French) She Is Aristocratic

Adolph (AH-dahlf) (German) He Is a Courageous Wolf

Adrian (AY-dree-yun) (English) He Is Hadria, Italy

Alberto (al-BAIR-toh) (Spanish) He Is Aristocratic

Alma (AHL-muh) (Spanish) She Is Our Soul

Andres (AHN-draysh) (Estonian) He Is Powerful

Axel (AX-sul) (Norwegian) Her Father Is Peaceful

🕭 *Abele* (ah-BAY-lay) (Italian) She Is the Breath of Life

Adalberto (ah-dahl-BAIR-toh) (Italian) He Is Brilliantly Aristocratic

Adamo (ah-DAH-mo) (Italian) He Is the First Person to Walk the Earth

Adolfo (ah-DAHL-fo) (Italian) He Is a Courageous Wolf

Adriano (ah-dree-AH-no) (Italian) He Is Hadria, Italy

Agapito (ah-gah-PEE-toh) (Italian) He Is Adored

Agata (AH-gah-tah) (Italian) She Is Pure and Good

Agnese (ahg-NAY-say) (Italian) She Shimmers with Sunlight

Agostina (ah-go-STEE-nah) (Italian) She Is Absolutely Magnificent

Alberta (ahl-BAIR-tah) (English) She Is Aristocratic

🕭 *Abena* (ah-BAY-nah) (Akan) She Arrived on a Tuesday

Abeni (ah-BAY-nee) (Yoruba) She Is the One for Whom We Prayed

Abidemi (ah-bih-DAY-mee) (Yoruba) She Goes Straight into Her Mother's Arms

Abimbola (ah-beem-BO-lah) (Yoruba) He Is Rich and Successful

Abioye (ah-bee-OH-yay) (Yoruba) He Is Majestic

Adanna (ah-DAHN-nah) (Igbo) She Resembles Her Father

Adannaya (ah-dah-NYE-yah) (Igbo) She Resembles Her Father

Adisa (ah-DEE-sah) (Yoruba) He Sees and Understands

Afia (AH-fee-yah) (Akan) He Arrived on a Friday

Akachi (ah-KAH-chee) (Igbo) He Proves God's Existence

🕭 *Abraham* (AH-brah-hahm) (Dutch) He Is the Father of Nations

Ad (AHD) (Dutch) He Is Hadria, Italy

Adam (ah-DAHM) (Dutch) He Is the First Person to Walk the Earth

Adelbert (AH-del-burt) (Dutch) He Is Aristocratic

Adelheid (AD-ul-hyte) (Dutch) She Is Aristocratic

Adrianus (ah-dree-AH-nus) (Dutch) He Is Hadria, Italy

Aleid (AHL-yet) (Dutch) She Is Our Little Aristocrat

Alida (ah-LEE-duh) (Dutch) She Is Our Little Aristocrat

Alwin (AHL-win) (Dutch) He Is a Loyal Companion

Andries (AHN-dreess) (Dutch) He Is Powerful

🕭 *Acampo* (uh-KAHM-po) (Spanish) He Is a Community of Friends

Acolita (ah-ko-LEE-tuh) (Spanish) She Is a Hard-Working Student

Adelanto (ad-eh-LAN-toh) (Spanish) He Progresses Toward Perfection

Afton (AF-tun) (Scottish) He Is the River Afton, Scotland

Alameda (ah-lah-MAY-duh) (Spanish) She Is a Forest of Poplar Trees

Alamitos (ah-lah-MEE-tohss) (Spanish) He Is the Little One Who Is a Forest of Poplar Trees

Alamo (AHL-uh-mo) (Spanish) He Is a Forest of Poplar Trees

Alcalde (ahl-KAHL-day) (Spanish) He Is an Even-Handed Judge

Almanor (AHL-muh-nor) (American) She Is the Lady from Aliénor, France

Alta (AHL-tuh) (Spanish) She Is the Highest

🕭 *Achille* (ah-KEEL) (French/Greek) He Is Our Nation's Conscience

Adolphe (ah-DAHLF) (French) He Is a Courageous Wolf

Adrien (ah-dree-YAW) (French) He Is Hadria, Italy

Adrienne (ah-dree-YEN) (French) She Is Hadria, Italy

Aimee (em-MAY) (French) She Is Greatly Beloved

Alain (ah-LEN) (French) He Is a Beautiful Little Stone

Albert (ahl-BAIR) (French) He Is Aristocratic

Alderic (ahl-deh-REEK) (French) He Possesses Majestic Strength

Alexandrie (ah-lex-ahn-DREE) (French) She Protects Humanity

Alexandrine (ah-lex-ahn-DREEN) (French) She Is the Little One Who Protects Humanity

🕭 *Addy* (AD-dee) (English) She Is Aristocratic

Adelia (uh-DEL-yuh) (English) She Is Our Little Aristocrat

Adelle (uh-DEL) (English) She Is Aristocratic

Adrianna (ay-dree-AN-nuh) (Italian) She Is Hadria, Italy

Africa (AF-rih-kuh) (English/American) She Is the Great Continent of Africa

Aggie (AG-ghee) (English) She Is the Little One Who Is Pure and Good

Aidan (AY-dun) (English/Irish) He Is the Little One Aflame with Greatness

Aileen (eye-LEEN) (English/Irish) She Is a Radiant Torch

Ainslee (AINZ-lee) (English) She Is a Beautiful Meadow

Alanis (uh-LAN-niss) (English) She Is a Beautiful Stone

 ♫ **Afra** (AH-frah) (Arabic) She Is Beautifully Pink

Afzal (ahf-ZAHL) (Arabic) He Is Supreme

Ahmed (ahk-MED) (Arabic) He Is Praiseworthy

Akeem (ah-KEEM) (Arabic) He Is Intelligent

Ala-al-Din (AH-lah-ahl-DEEN) (Arabic) He Is Our Divine Religion

Alim (ah-LEEM) (Arabic) He Teaches Us All

Alina (ah-LEE-nah) (Arabic) She Is Aristocratic

Aliya (ah-LEE-yah) (Arabic) She Is Supreme

Amal (ah-MAHL) (Arabic) He Labors Mightily

Amani (ah-MAH-nee) (Arabic) She Is Our Fondest Hope

 ♫ **Aileas** (AH-liss) (Scottish) She Is Our Little Aristocrat

Ailpein (AHL-pin) (Scottish) He Is Beautifully Fair

Ailsa (EL-sah) (Scottish) She Is the Fair Isle of the Magical Elfin Nation

Aindrea (AYN-dray) (Scottish) He Is Powerfully Male

Alastair (ahl-ah-STAIR) (Scottish) He Protects Humanity

Alister (AHL-iss-tur) (Scottish) He Protects Humanity

Archie (AR-chee) (Scottish) He Is the Courageous Little One

Arran (AHR-rahn) (Scottish) He Is the Isle of Arran

Artair (AHR-tair) (Scottish) He Is a Courageous Bear

Athol (AH-tahl) (Scottish) He Is the Nation of Ireland

 ♫ **Akseli** (ak-SEH-lee) (Finnish) His Father Is Peaceful

Aku (AH-koo) (Finnish) He Is Absolutely Magnificent

Aleksanteri (ah-lek-SAHN-teh-ree) (Finnish) He Protects Humanity

Aleksi (ah-LEK-see) (Finnish) He Is Humanity's Little Protector

Aliisa (ah-lee-EE-sah) (Finnish) She Is Our Little Aristocrat

Alli (AHL-lee) (Finnish) She Is Our Little Aristocrat

Alpertti (ahl-PAIR-tee) (Finnish) He Is Aristocratic

Altti (AHLT-tee) (Finnish) He Is Aristocratic

Anna-Liisa (ah-nah-lee-EE-sah) (Finnish) She Is the Graceful One Whose God Is Abundant

Anni (AHN-nee) (Finnish) She Is Graceful

 ♫ **Albertina** (ahl-bair-TEE-nah) (Italian) She Is Aristocratic

Alberto (al-BAIR-toh) (Italian) He Is Aristocratic

Albina (AHL-bee-nah) (Italian) She Is Beautifully Fair

Alda (AHL-dah) (Italian) She Is Aristocratic

Alessa (ah-LESS-sah) (Italian) She Is Humanity's Little Protector

Alessia (ah-LESS-see-yah) (Italian) She Is Humanity's Little Protector

Alessio (ah-LESS-see-yo) (Italian) He Is Humanity's Little Protector

Alfeo (ahl-FAY-yo) (Italian) He Is Always Growing

Alfredo (ahl-FRAY-doh) (Italian) He Is a Small but Wise Counselor

Alina (ah-LEE-nah) (Italian) She Is Aristocratic

 ♫ **Alexina** (al-ek-SEE-nuh) (English) She Is the Little One Who Protects Humanity

Alexus (uh-LEX-us) (English) She Protects Humanity

Alfreda (al-FRAY-duh) (English) She Is a Small but Wise Counselor

Algar (AL-ghar) (English) He Is a Weapon of the Magical Elfin Nation

Alger (AL-jur) (English) He Is a Weapon of the Magical Elfin Nation

Aliah (uh-LEE-yuh) (English/Arabic) She Is Noble and Magnificent

Alisha (uh-LEE-shuh) (English) She Is Aristocratic

Alissa (uh-LIS-suh) (English) She Is Aristocratic

Alivia (uh-LIV-ee-yuh) (English) She Is a Beautiful Olive Tree

Allana (uh-LAH-nuh) (English) She Is a Beautiful Stone

🐦 **Alice** (ah-LEESS) (French) She Is Our Little Aristocrat

Alix (ah-LEEX) (French) She Is Our Little Aristocrat

Alphonsine (ahl-fohn-SEEN) (French) She Is Aristocratic

Amandine (ah-mahn-DEEN) (French) She Is Worthy of Love

Amarante (ah-mah-RAHNT) (French) She Is a Fragrant Amaranth Blossom

Ambre (AHM-bruh) (French) She Is Priceless Golden Amber

Amedee (ah-may-DAY) (French) He Is God's Beloved

Anaïs (ah-nah-YEES) (French) She Is Graceful

Anastasie (ahn-nah-stah-ZEE) (French) She Is Reborn to New Life

Anatole (ah-nah-TULL) (French) He Is the Morning Dawn

🐦 **Allegra** (ahl-LAY-grah) (Italian) She Is Happily Energetic

Amadeo (ah-mah-DAY-yo) (Italian) He Is God's Beloved

Amalia (ah-MAH-lee-yah) (Italian) She Works Tirelessly

Amanda (ah-MAHN-dah) (Italian) She Is Worthy of Love

Amando (ah-MAHN-doh) (Italian) He Is Worthy of Love

Amaranta (ah-mah-RAHN-tah) (Italian) She Is an Amaranth Blossom

Ambra (AHM-brah) (Italian) She Is Golden Amber

Ambrogino (ahm-bro-ZHEE-no) (Italian) He Is the Little One Who Lives Forever

Ambrogio (ahm-BRO-zhee-yo) (Italian) He Lives Forever

*Amedea (*ah-may-DAY-yah) (Italian) She Is God's Beloved

🐦 **Altadena** (al-tah-DEE-nah) (Spanish/ English) She Is a Peaceful Valley Nestled Between Mountains

Altamont (AHL-tuh-mahnt) (American/ Spanish) He Is a Lofty Mountain

Altos (AHL-tohss) (Spanish) He Is the Misty Highlands

Altruria (ahl-TROOR-ee-yuh) (American) She Is Lovingly Generous

Andora (an-DOH-ruh) (American/English) She Is a Little Bird Given to Us by God

Arcata (ar-KAY-tuh) (American) She Glows with Golden Light

Arroyo (uh-ROY-yo) (Spanish) He Is a Surging River

Artesia (ar-TEE-zhuh) (English/French) She Is Artois, France

Ashland (ASH-lund) (English) She Is the Land of the Ash Trees

Asilomar (uh-SIL-oh-mar) (Spanish) He Is a Refuge by the Sea

🐦 **Amada** (ah-MAH-dah) (Spanish) She Is Greatly Beloved

Amado (ah-MAH-doh) (Spanish) He Is Greatly Beloved

Amancio (ah-MAHN-see-yo) (Spanish) He Is Love Itself

Amando (ah-MAHN-doh) (Spanish) He Is Worthy of Love

Amaranta (ah-mah-RAHN-tah) (Spanish) She Is an Amaranth Blossom

Ambrosio (ahm-BRO-see-yo) (Spanish) He Lives Forever

Angelita (ahng-hel-EE-tah) (Spanish) She Is God's Angelic Messenger

Anita (ah-NEE-tah) (Spanish) She Is Our Graceful Little One

Anselmo (ahn-SEL-mo) (Spanish) He Is a Divine Helmet of Protection

Antonietta (ahn-toh-nee-YET-tah) (Spanish) She Is Our Lovely Little Flower

🐦 **Amadeo** (ah-mah-DAY-yo) (Italian) He Is God's Beloved

Aminta (ah-MEEN-tah) (Italian) She Protects Humanity

Ampelio (ahm-PAY-lee-yo) (Italian) He Is Sacred Wine

Anancleto (ah-nahn-KLAY-toh) (Italian) He Cares Deeply

Anastasio (ahn-ah-STAH-see-yo) (Italian) He Is Born to New Life

Andreina (ahn-dray-EE-nah) (Italian) She Is as Powerful as any Male

Annabella (ahn-nah-BEL-lah) (Italian) She Is Beautiful and Lovable

Annalisa (ahn-nah-LEE-sah) (Italian) She Is Graceful and Her God Is Abundance

Annetta (ahn-NET-tah) (Italian) She Is Our Graceful Little One
Annunciata (ah-nun-see-YAH-tah) (Italian) She Is Our Blessed Announcement

☙ **Amin** (ah-MEEN) (Arabic) He Is Honest
Amina (ah-MEE-nah) (Arabic) She Is Honest
Aminah (ah-MEE-nah) (Arabic) She Is Honest
Amir (ah-MEER) (Arabic) He Is Our Law-Giver
Amira (ah-MEE-rah) (Arabic) She Is Our Law-Giver
Amna (AHM-nah) (Arabic) She Is Our Protector
Anas (AH-nahss) (Arabic) He Is Affectionate
Anisa (ah-NEE-sah) (Arabic) She Is Affectionate
Anwar (AHN-wahr) (Arabic) He Shimmers with Radiance
Aqil (ah-KEEL) (Arabic) He Is Intelligent

☙ **Angele** (awn-ZHEL) (French) She Is God's Angelic Messenger
Angeline (awn-ZHLEEN) (French) She Is God's Little Angelic Messenger
Annette (ahn-NET) (French) She Is Graceful and Beloved
Anselme (ahn-SELM) (French) He Is a Divine Helmet of Protection
Apollinaire (ah-pah-lee-NAIR) (French/Greek) He Is the Source of All Light
Apolline (ah-pohl-LEEN) (French) She Is the Source of All Light
Arianne (ah-ree-YAHN) (French) She Is Holy
Arienne (ah-ree-YEN) (French/Greek) She Is Holy
Aristide (ah-reess-TEED) (French) He Is the Noblest Sort of Person
Arlette (ahr-LET) (French) She Is Our Soaring Little Eagle

☙ **Angelien** (ahn-zhuh-LEEN) (Dutch) She Is God's Angelic Messenger
Anke (AHN-kuh) (Dutch) She Is Our Graceful Little Princess
Annabel (AHN-nuh-bel) (Dutch) She Is Easy to Love
Anneke (AHN-neh-kuh) (Dutch) She Is Graceful
Annelien (ahn-nuh-LEEN) (Dutch) She Is Our Graceful Little Princess
Annemarie (ahn-nuh-muh-REE) (Dutch) She Is Grace and Love
Anouk (ah-NOOK) (Dutch) She Is Our Graceful Little One

Anselma (ahn-SEL-muh) (Dutch) She Is a Divine Helmet of Protection
Arnoud (ahr-NAWD) (Dutch) He Is a Soaring Eagle
Augustijn (AW-gus-teen) (Dutch) He Is Absolutely Magnificent

☙ **Anniina** (ah-nee-EE-nah) (Finnish) She Is Graceful
Annikki (AHN-nee-kee) (Finnish) She Is Our Graceful Little One
Annukka (AHN-nuh-kuh) (Finnish) She Is Our Graceful Little One
Ansa (AHN-sah) (Finnish) She Is Honorable and Admirable
Anselmi (ahn-SEL-mee) (Finnish) He Is a Divine Helmet of Protection
Anssi (AHNS-see) (Finnish) He Is the Little One Who Is a Divine Helmet of Protection
Antero (AHN-tair-ro) (Finnish) He Is Powerfully Male
Antti (AHNT-tee) (Finnish) He Is Powerfully Male
Armas (AHR-mahss) (Finnish) He Is Adored
Armo (AHR-mo) (Finnish) He Is Compassionate

☙ **Aqila** (ah-KEE-lah) (Arabic) She Is Intelligent
Arij (ah-REEZH) (Arabic) She Is a Heavenly Scent
Arwa (AHR-wah) (Arabic) She Is Sure-Footed and Steady
Asad (ah-SAHD) (Arabic) He Has Good Fortune
Asif (ah-SEEF) (Arabic) He Is Merciful
Asim (ah-SEEM) (Arabic) He Protects Humanity
Atallah (ah-TAHL-lah) (Arabic) He Is Our Divine Blessing
Atiya (ah-TEE-yah) (Arabic) She Is Our Divine Blessing
Atuf (ah-TOOF) (Arabic) He Is Affectionate
Ayda (EYE-dah) (Arabic) She Always Comes Home to Us

☙ **Armel** (ahr-MEL) (French) He Is a Monarch Who Is Rock-Solid
Arnaud (ahr-NO) (French) He Is a Soaring Eagle
Aubert (oh-BAIR) (French) He Is Aristocratic
Aude (ODE) (French) She Is as Powerful as any Male
Aurele (oh-REL) (French) He Is Pure Gold
Aurelie (oh-reh-LEE) (French) She Is Pure Gold

Aurelien (oh-reh-lay-YAN) (French) He Is Pure Gold

Aurore (oh-ROR) (French/Greek) She Is the Rosy-Fingered Dawn

Avril (ahv-REEL) (French) She Is the Springtime Month of April

Axelle (ahk-SEL) (French) Her Father Is Peaceful

Ashlea (ASH-lee) (English) She Is a Meadow in the Ash-Tree Forest

Ashlyn (ASH-lin) (English) She Is a Meadow by a Lake in the Ash-Tree Forest

Auberon (OH-bur-rahn) (English) He Is a Fierce Bear

Aubrie (AW-bree) (English) She Has the Power of the Magical Elfin People

Audie (AW-dee) (English) She Is Our Powerful Little Aristocrat

Audley (AWD-lee) (English) She Is the Eternal War Between Good and Evil

Audra (AW-druh) (English) She Is an Unstoppable Hurricane

Audrea (AW-dree-yuh) (English) She Is a Powerful Aristocrat

Aureole (aw-ree-YOHL) (English) She Is a Golden Crown of Light

Austen (AW-sten) (English) He Is the Little One Who Is Absolutely Magnificent

Asuncion (ah-soon-see-YONE) (Spanish) She Is the Holy Ascension

Atolia (ah-TOL-yuh) (American) She Is a Lovely Chestnut-Brown Horse

Atwell (AT-wel) (English) He Lives by a Freshwater Spring

Atwood (AY-wood) (English) He Lives by the Verdant Woodlands

Auberry (AW-bree) (American/English) He Is the Power of the Magical Elfin People

Auburn (AW-burn) (English) Her Hair Is a Beautiful Reddish Brown

Audrian (AW-dree-yun) (American/English) She Is Hadria, Italy

Avalon (AV-uh-lahn) (English) She Is the Ambrosia of Heaven

Avenal (AHV-nahl) (Spanish) She Is a Field of Golden Oats

Avila (AH-vee-lah) (Spanish) She Is Greatly Beloved

Babs (BABZ) (English) She Is Our Blessed Little Voyager

Beryl (BAIR-ril) (English/Sanskrit) She Is a Priceless Beryl Jewel

Beth (BETH) (English) She Is the Little One Favored by God

Blanca (BLAHNG-kuh) (Spanish) She Is Beautifully Fair

Blas (BLAHSS) (Spanish) His Speech Is Uniquely His Own

Bonny (BAHN-nee) (English/Scottish) She Is Pretty

Boris (BOR-riss) (Russian) He Is a Courageous Wolf

Bret (BRET) (English) He Is Bretagne, France

Bronwyn (BRAHN-win) (Welsh) She Has a Beautiful Bosom

Bud (BUD) (English) He Is a Trusted Friend

Badr (BAH-dur) (Arabic) He Is the Silvery Moon

Baha (BAH-hah) (Arabic) He Is Magnificent

Bahadur (bah-hah-DOOR) (Arabic) He Is Courageous

Bahiga (bah-HEE-gah) (Arabic) He Rejoices

Bahij (bah-HEEZH) (Arabic) He Rejoices

Bahija (bah-HEE-zhah) (Arabic) She Rejoices

Bahiyya (bah-HEE-yah) (Arabic) She Is Lovely

Baki (BAH-kee) (Arabic) He Lives Forever

Bakr (BAH-kur) (Arabic) He Is a Swift, Powerful Camel

Baqir (bah-KEER) (Arabic) He Rends and Destroys

Baldwin (BALD-win) (English) He Is a Courageous Companion

Baptiste (bahp-TEEST) (French) He Is Baptized with Holy Water

Barranca (bah-RAHN-kuh) (Spanish) She Is a Misty Canyon

Barrett (BAIR-ret) (English) He Is Aggressive

Bellota (bay-YO-tuh) (Spanish) She Is the Small Acorn from Which Oaks Grow

Belmont (BEL-mahnt) (French) He Is a Lofty Mountaintop

Benicia (ben-EE-see-yuh) (Spanish) She Is Divinely Blessed

Benton (BEN-tun) (English) He Is a Town near the Bent Trees

Berenda (bair-EN-duh) (Spanish) She Is a Swift-Running Antelope

Berros (BAIR-rohss) (Spanish) He Is the Savory Watercress Herb

🐝 **Baqi** (BAH-kee) (Arabic) He Lives Forever

Barak (bah-RAHK) (Arabic) He Is a Thunderbolt

Batul (bah-TOOL) (Arabic) She Is Chaste and Pure

Bilal (bee-LAHL) (Arabic) He Is Life-Giving Rain

Botros (boh-TROHSS) (Arabic) He Is Rock-Solid

Boulos (BOO-lohss) (Arabic) He Demonstrates Humility

Boutros (BOO-trohss) (Arabic) He Is Rock-Solid

Budur (boo-DOOR) (Arabic) She Is the Silvery Moon

Bulus (BOO-looss) (Arabic) He Demonstrates Humility

Butrus (BOO-trooss) (Arabic) He Is Rock-Solid

🐝 **Barack** (bah-RAHK) (Arabic) He Showers Us with Fortune

Barakat (BAH-rah-kaht) (Arabic) He Showers Us with Blessings

Basim (bah-SEEM) (Arabic) He Flashes a Beautiful Smile

Basima (bah-SEE-mah) (Arabic) She Flashes a Beautiful Smile

Basir (bah-SEER) (Arabic) He Is Intelligent

Basira (bah-SEE-rah) (Arabic) She Is Intelligent

Basit (bah-SEET) (Arabic) His Greatness Increases

Basma (BAHSS-mah) (Arabic) She Flashes a Beautiful Smile

Bassam (bahss-SAHM) (Arabic) He Flashes a Beautiful Smile

Bassem (bahss-SEHM) (Arabic) He Flashes a Beautiful Smile

🐝 **Barbra** (BAR-bruh) (English) She Is Our Divine Voyager

Barnabas (BAR-nuh-bus) (English) He Descends from God's Holy Prophet

Barret (BAIR-ret) (English) He Is Aggressive and Combative

Barrie (BAIR-ree) (English) He Is the Fair-Haired Little One

Baxter (BAX-tur) (English) He Bakes Delicious Bread

Baylee (BAY-lee) (English) She Enforces the Law as a Trusted Bailiff

Beauregard (BO-rih-ghard) (English) He Sees Everything as Beautiful

Becca (BEK-kuh) (English) She Is the Little One Who Brings Us Closer

Becci (BEK-kee) (English) She Is the Little One Who Brings Us Closer

Bee (BEE) (English) She Is a Great Little Voyager

🐝 **Barnabé** (bahr-nah-BEE) (French) He Descends from the Prophet

Bastien (bahss-tee-YEN) (French) He Is the Honorable Little One

Baudouin (bo-DWAN) (French) He Is a Courageous Companion

Béatrice (bay-ah-TREESS) (French) She Is a Great Voyager

Bénédicte (bay-nay-DEEKT) (French) He Is Divinely Blessed

Benjamine (ban-zhah-MEEN) (French/Hebrew) She Is Born in the South

Bernadette (bair-nah-DET) (French) She Is a Courageous She-Bear

Bertrand (bair-TRAW) (French) He Is an Ebony-Black Raven

Blandine (blaw-DEEN) (French) She Is Gracefully Alluring

Brigitte (bree-ZHEET) (French) She Is Knowledge

🐝 **Baron** (BAIR-run) (English) He Is a Free, Invincible Warrior

Baro (BAR-ro) (Latin) He Is a Free, Invincible Warrior

Baroness (BAIR-ruh-ness) (English) She Is a Free, Invincible Warrior

Baronessa (bair-uh-NES-suh) (Italian) She Is a Free, Invincible Warrior

Baroni (bah-RO-nee) (Italian) He Is a Free, Invincible Warrior

Baronin (bar-oh-NEEN) (German) She Is a Free, Invincible Warrior

Barony (BAIR-run-nee) (English) She Is a Free, Invincible Warrior

Baru (BAR-roo) (Latin) He Is a Free, Invincible Warrior

Barun (bah-ROON) (Sanskrit) He Is a Free, Invincible Warrior

Baruni (bah-ROO-nee) (Croatian) He Is a Free, Invincible Warrior

🧒 **Bekki** (BEK-kee) (English) She Is the Little One Who Brings Us Closer

Benj (BENJ) (English) He Is the Little One Born in the South

Benji (BEN-jee) (English) He Is the Little One Born in the South

Benny (BEN-nee) (English) He Is the Little One Born in the South

Bentley (BENT-lee) (English) He Is a Meadow of Bent Grass

Berenice (bair-uh-NEE-see) (English) She Brings Triumph to Humanity

Bernadine (BUR-nuh-deen) (English) She Is a Mighty Bear

Bernetta (BUR-net-tuh) (English) She Is the Little One Who Brings Triumph to Humanity

Berniece (bur-NEESS) (English) She Begins a Golden Age of Triumph

Bertie (BUR-tee) (English) He Is Shimmering Brilliance

🧒 **Bertina** (BUR-tee-nuh) (English) She Is Shimmering Brilliance

Bertram (BUR-trum) (English) He Is a Glistening-Black Raven

Bethanie (BETH-uh-nee) (English) She Is an Estate Full of Figs

Betony (BET-nee) (English) She Is the Fragrant Betony Herb

Bettye (BET-tee) (English) She Is the Little One Favored by God

Bevis (BEE-viss) (English) He Is Beauvais, France

Biff (BIF) (English) He Fights His Way to Victory

Bindy (BIN-dee) (English) She Is the Compassionate Little One

Bishop (BIH-shup) (English) He Is a Bishop of the Holy Church

Blaine (BLAYN) (English/Scottish) He Shimmers with Radiance

🧒 **Blanch** (BLANCH) (English) She Is Beautifully Fair

Blaze (BLAYZ) (English) His Speech Is Uniquely His Own

Boniface (BAHN-uh-fuss) (English) He Is Destined for Greatness

Bonita (bo-NEE-tuh) (English/Spanish) She Is Pretty

Boyce (BOYSS) (English) He Is a Verdant Forest

Braden (BRAY-den) (English/Irish) He Descends from the One as Swift as a Salmon

Brady (BRAY-dee) (English/Irish) He Descends from the Barrel-Chested One

Bram (BRAM) (English) He Is the Little One Who Is the Father of Nations

Brand (BRAND) (English) He Is a Razor-Sharp Weapon

Branda (BRAN-duh) (English) She Is a Razor-Sharp Weapon

🧒 **Braeden** (BRAY-den) (English/Irish) He Descends from the One as Swift as a Salmon

Braelyn (BRAY-lin) (English) She Descends from the One as Swift as Salmon in a Lake

Braidy (BRAY-dee) (English) He Descends from the Barrel-Chested One

Brande (BRAN-dee) (English) She Is Delicious Brandy

Branden (BRAN-den) (English) He Is a Wheat-Covered Hill

Brandt (BRANT) (English) He Is a Razor-Sharp Weapon

Brannon (BRAN-nun) (English/Irish) He Descends from the Glistening-Black Raven

Braxton (BRAX-tun) (English) He Is the City Ruled by Bracca

Breana (bree-AN-nuh) (English) She Is Aristocratic

Breanne (bree-YAN) (English) She Is a Lofty Mountain

🧒 **Brayden** (BRAY-den) (English) He Descends from the One as Swift as a Salmon

Breanna (bree-AN-nuh) (English) She Is Aristocratic

Brenden (BREN-den) (English/Irish) He Is a Majestic Ruler

Brenton (BREN-tun) (English) He Is the City Ruled by Bryni

Brianne (bree-ANN) (English) She Is Aristocratic

Briar (BRY-yur) (English) She Is a Sharp Thorn-Bush

Brice (BRICE) (English) He Is Beautifully Freckled

Bridger (BRIJ-jur) (English) He Builds Enduring Bridges

Bridgette (BRIJ-jet) (English/Irish) She Is Knowledge

Bridie (BRY-dee) (English) She Is Our Wise Little Scholar

⊘ **Brielle** (bree-YEL) (English) She Is God's Little Angelic Messenger

Brigham (BRIG-gum) (English) He Is a Community by a Bridge

Brion (BRYE-yun) (English) He Is Aristocratic

Briony (BRYE-uh-nee) (English) Her Greatness Increases

Briscoe (BRISS-ko) (English) He Is a Grove of Birch Trees

Bristol (BRIS-tul) (English) He Is the Community Where the Bridge Stands

Britanni (BRIT-tuh-nee) (English) She Is Bretagne, France

Brittannia (brit-TAN-yuh) (English) She Is the Nation of Great Britain

Britton (BRIT-tun) (English) She Is Bretagne, France

Brodie (BRO-dee) (English) He Is a Mysterious Abyss

⊘ **Brooklyn** (BROOK-lin) (English) She Is the Ever-Changing Earth

Bryana (brye-AN-nuh) (English) She Is Aristocratic

Bryant (BRY-yunt) (English) He Is Aristocratic

Brynn (BRIN) (English) He Is a Lofty Mountain

Bryson (BRYE-sun) (English) He Descends from the Freckled One

Buck (BUK) (English) He Is a Powerful Deer

Bud (BUD) (English) He Is Our Little Friend

Buffy (BUF-fee) (English) She Is the Little One Favored by God

Buster (BUS-tur) (English) He Destroys

Bysshe (BISH--shee (English) He Is the Beautiful Wilderness

⊘ **Caelan** (KAY-lun) (English/Irish) He Is Wonderfully Slim

Caelie (KAY-lee) (English) She Is the Little Pure-Hearted One Who Is a Meadow

Caetlin (KAYT-lin) (English/Irish) She Is Pure-Hearted

Cairo (KYE-ro) (English) He Is Powerfully Male

Calanthe (kuh-LAN-thee) (English) She Is a Fragrant Blossom

Cale (KAYL) (English) He Is Man's Best Friend—A Faithful, Loyal Dog

Calista (kuh-LISS-tuh) (English) She Is the Most Beautiful

Calla (KAL-luh) (English) She Is a Fragrant Calla-Lily

Callahan (KAL-uh-han) (English/Irish) He Descends from a Great Warrior

Calleigh (KAL-lee) (English) She Is the Little One Who Is the Most Beautiful

⊘ **Callista** (kuh-LISS-tuh) (English/Greek) She Is Supremely Lovely

Camron (KAM-run) (English) Her Nose Goes Its Own Way

Candis (KAN-diss) (English) She Is the Queen Mother

Capricia (kuh-PREE-shuh) (English) She Acts on Her Emotions

Cara (KAIR-ruh) (English) She Is Greatly Beloved

Careen (kuh-REEN) (English) She Is Greatly Beloved

Caren (KAIR-run) (English) She Is Pure-Hearted

Carey (KAIR-ree) (English) He Descends from the Darkly Handsome One

Carina (kuh-REE-nuh) (English) She Is a Ship's Balance and Equilibrium

⊘ **Cam** (KAM) (English) She Is the Little One Whose Nose Goes Its Own Way

Camden (KAM-den) (English) He Is a Peaceful Valley

Camellia (kuh-MEE-lee-yuh) (English) She Is a Fragrant Camellia Flower

Camilla (kuh-MIL-luh) (English) She Observes Sacred Rituals

Cammie (KAM-mee) (English) She Is the Little One Who Observes Sacred Rituals

Camryn (KAM-rin) (English) Her Nose Goes Its Own Way

Candace (KAN-dus) (English/Nubian) She Is the Queen Mother

Candi (KAN-dee) (English) She Is Our Majestic Little Queen

Candida (kan-DEE-duh) (English) She Is Beautifully Fair

Caprice (kuh-PREESS) (English) She Acts on Her Emotions

⊘ **Carine** (kah-REEN) (French/Latin) She Is a Ship's Balance and Equilibrium

Caroline (kah-ro-LEEN) (French) She Is a Powerful Warrior

Catherine (kah-TREEN) (French) She Is Pure-Hearted

Cécile (say-SEEL) (French/Latin) She Sees Deeply Within Herself

Céleste (say-LEST) (French) She Is the Heavenly Blue Sky

Célestine (say-less-TEEN) (French) She Is the Little One Who Is the Heavenly Blue Sky

Cerise (shuh-REEZ) (French) She Is a Sweet Cherry

Cesaire (say-ZAIR) (French) He Is Gloriously Covered with Hair

Charline (shar-LEEN) (French) She Is Our Mighty Little Warrior

Charlot (shar-LO) (French) He Is the Little One Who Is a Mighty Warrior

🕭 **Caris** (KAIR-riss) (English) She Is Elegant and Loving

Carissa (kuh-RISS-suh) (English) She Is Elegant and Loving

Carla (KAR-luh) (English) She Is a Mighty Warrior

Carlene (kar-LEEN) (English) She Is a Mighty Soldier

Carley (KAR-lee) (English) She Is a Mighty Soldier

Carlisa (kar-LEE-suh) (English) She Is the Mighty Warrior Whose God Is Abundance

Carlisle (kar-LYE-yul) (English) He Is the City Ruled by Lugovalos

Carlyn (KAIR-lin) (English) She Is a Powerful Warrior

Carmella (kar-MEL-luh) (English) She Is a Fragrant Garden

Carmen (KAR-mun) (English) She Is a Garden of Melodies

🕭 **Carlotta** (kar-LOT-tuh) (Italian) She Is Our Mighty Little Warrior

Celeste (sel-LEST) (English) She Is the Heavenly Sky

Chantal (shahn-TAHL) (French) She Is Rock-Solid

Charley (CHAR-lee) (English) He Is Our Mighty Little Warrior

Clara (KLAIR-ruh) (Italian) She Shimmers with Fame

Claudette (klo-DET) (French) She Walks a Difficult Path

Connie (KAHN-nee) (English) He Is a Beloved Cornucopia of Abundance

Cora (KOR-ruh) (Greek/American) She Is a Virtuous Maiden

Cosme (KAHZ-may) (Portuguese) He Is Law and Justice

Cristobal (KRIS-toh-bahl) (Spanish) He Follows Christ

🕭 **Carola** (kair-OH-luh) (English) She Is a Mighty Warrior

Carolina (kair-oh-LYE-nuh) (English) She Is a Mighty Warrior

Carry (KAIR-ree) (English) She Is Our Beloved Warrior

Carver (KAR-vur) (English) He Carves Beautiful Sculptures

Caryn (KAIR-rin) (English) She Is Pure-Hearted

Cassarah (kuh-SAR-ruh) (English/Irish) She Descends from the One Who Adores Life

Cate (KAYT) (English) She Is the Little Pure-Hearted One

Catharine (KATH-rin) (English) She Is Pure-Hearted

Cathleen (kath-LEEN) (English/Irish) She Is Pure-Hearted

Cayley (KAY-lee) (English) She Is the Little Pure-Hearted One Who Is a Meadow

🕭 **Ceara** (see-AIR-ruh) (American/Italian) She Is a Range of Lofty Mountains

Cecelia (see-SEEL-yuh) (English) She Sees Deeply Within Herself

Cecil (SEE-sul) (English) He Sees Deeply Within Himself

Cedric (SED-rik) (English) He Is Greatly Beloved

Celandine (say-law-DEEN) (English) She Is the Soaring Swallow

Celestine (SEL-ess-teen) (English) She Is the Heavenly Sky

Celinda (seh-LIN-duh) (English) She Is the Beautiful One Who Sees Deeply Within Herself

Chadwick (CHAD-wik) (English) He Is the Estate Ruled by Chad

Chalice (CHAL-liss) (English) She Is a Costly Drinking-Goblet

Chandler (CHAND-lur) (English) He Crafts Excellent Candles

🕭 **Chanelle** (shuh-NEL) (English/French) She Brings Sparkling Water

Chantel (shahn-TEL) (English) She Is Rock-Solid

Charisma (kuh-RIZ-muh) (English) She Charms Others

Charisse (shur-REESS) (English) She Is the Little Graceful, Elegant One

Charla (SHAR-luh) (English) She Is a Mighty Warrior
Charleen (shar-LEEN) (English) She Is Our Mighty Little Soldier
Charlton (CHARL-tun) (English) He Is the Land of Liberty
Charmain (shar-MAYN) (English) She Is the Little One Who Is the Realm of the Warriors
Charmian (SHAR-mee-yun) (English) She Brings Us Joy
Charnette (shar-NET) (American/English) She Is Our Mighty Little Warrior

🕭 **Chas** (CHAZ) (English) He Is Our Mighty Little Warrior
Chelle (SHEL) (English) She Is the Little One Who Resembles God
Cherette (shur-RET) (English/French) She Is the Little One Who Is Darling and Sweet
Cherice (shur-REESS) (English) She Is the Little Graceful, Elegant One
Cherilyn (SHAIR-ih-lin) (English) She Is Truly Darling and Sweet
Cherish (CHAIR-rish) (English) She Is Greatly Cherished
Chesley (CHEZ-lee) (English) He Is a Fragrant Meadow Near a Campsite
Chet (CHET) (English) He Is the Little One Who Is a Fortress
Cheyanne (shye-YAN) (English/Dakota/American) She Is a Mystical Speaker
Chile (KYLE) (English/Scottish) He Is the Water Between Two Regions of Earth

🕭 **Chip** (CHIP) (English) He Is Our Mighty Little Warrior
Christobel (KRIS-to-bel) (English) She Is Christ's Beautiful Little Follower
Chrystal (KRIS-tul) (English) She Sparkles Like Diamonds
Chyna (CHYE-nuh) (English) She Is China
Cierra (see-AIR-ruh) (English) She Is a Lofty Range of Mountains
Cindi (SIN-dee) (English) She Is Kynthos, Greece
Cindra (SIN-druh) (English) She Is Kynthos, Greece, the One Who Protects Humanity
Cissy (SIS-see) (English) She Is the Little One Who Sees Deeply Within Herself
Clair (KLAIR) (English) She Is Bright and Clear
Clancy (KLAN-see) (English/Irish) He Descends from the Warrior

🕭 **Clarette** (klair-RET) (English/French) She Is the Little One Who Shimmers with Fame
Clarinda (klah-RIN-duh) (English) She Is the Little One Who Shimmers with Fame
Clarity (KLAR-ih-tee) (English) She Thinks Clearly
Claud (KLAWD) (English) He Walks a Difficult Path
Clem (KLEM) (English) He Is the Compassionate Little One
Clemency (KLEM-en-see) (English) She Is Compassion
Cleo (KLEE-yo) (English) She Is the Little One Who Is Her Father's Glory
Cletis (KLEE-tis) (English) He Is Magnificently Renowned
Cleve (KLEEV) (English) He Is the Little One Who Is the Land of Rolling Hills
Clifford (KLIF-furd) (English) He Is a Crossing-Place Near a Lofty Cliff

🕭 **Clint** (KLINT) (English) He Is the Little One Who Is a City on a Mountain
Clotilda (klo-TIL-duh) (English) She Is a Glorious War
Codie (KO-dee) (English) He Descends from the Wealthy One
Coleen (kah-LEEN) (English) She Is Pretty
Collyn (kahl-LIN) (English) He Is Beautiful
Colton (KOLE-tun) (English) He Is the Lovely Town Ruled by Cole
Comfort (KUM-furt) (English) He Gives Us Peace of Mind
Connell (KAHN-nul) (English/Irish) He Is a Mighty Wolf
Conner (KAHN-nur) (English) He Is the Master of Wolves
Constant (KAHN-stunt) (English) He Is Dependably Constant

🕭 **Clotilde** (klo-TEELD) (French) She Is a Renowned Warrior
Coline (kuh-LEEN) (French) She Is Humanity's Little Triumph
Colombe ((ko-LUMB) (French) She Is a Peaceful Dove
Coralie (ko-rah-LEE) (French) She Is Glowing Coral
Corentin (ko-rawn-TAN) (French) He Is an Unstoppable Windstorm
Corin (ko-RAN) (French) He Is a Razor-Sharp Weapon

Cornélie (kor-nay-LEE) (French/Latin) She Is a Cornucopia of Plenty

Cosme (KAHZ-muh) (French/Greek) He Is Fair and Just

Cunégonde (koo-nay-GUND) (French) She Is a Courageous Soldier

Cyrille (sih-REEL) (French/English) He Is Supreme

⚘ **Coreen** (ko-REEN) (English) She Is Chaste and Pure

Cori (KOR-ree) (English/Scottish) He Is a Hillside Teeming with Swift Animals

Corina (ko-REE-nuh) (English) She Is Chaste and Pure

Corwin (KOR-win) (English) He Is Rich-Smelling Leather

Corynn (ko-RIN) (English) She Is Chaste and Pure

Cosmo (KAHZ-mo) (English) He Is Eternal Law and Justice

Coty (KO-tee) (English) He Descends from the Wealthy One

Crawford (KRAW-furd) (English) He Is the Place Where Crows Fly

Cree (KREE) (English/Cree) He Is the Native American Nation of the Cree

Crispian (KRIS-pin) (English) He Has Hair like Fleece

⚘ **Cristal** (KRIS-tul) (English) She Sparkles Like Diamonds

Cristen (KRIS-ten) (English) She Follows Christ

Crofton (KROF-tun) (English) He Is a Farm Surrounded by a Wall

Cybill (SIH-buhl) (English) She Is a Prophetess

Cydney (SID-nee) (English) She Is a Great Island

Cymone (see-MONE) (English) She Hears Everything

Cyndi (SIN-dee) (English) She Is the Little One Who Is the Lofty Source of All Water

Cynthia (SIN-thee-yuh) (English) She Is the Lofty Source of All Water

Cyril (SEER-rul) (English) He Is Supreme

Cyrilla (seer-IL-luh) (English) She Is Supreme

⚘ **Dacre** (DAY-kur) (English) He Is a Swift-Flowing Creek

Daffodil (DAF-fo-dil) (English) She Is a Fragrant Daffodil Flower

Dale (DAYL) (English) He Is a Peaceful Valley

Damian (DAY-mee-yun) (English) He Makes Us Gentle

Dana (DAN-nuh) (English) She Is Denmark

Danette (duh-NET) (English/French) She Is God's Wise Little Judge

Dani (DAN-nee) (English) He Is the Little One Whose God Judges Wisely

Danica (DAN-ih-kuh) (English) She Is the Morning Star

Daniella (dan-YEL-luh) (English) She Is the Little One Whose God Judges Wisely

⚘ **Dakota** (duh-KO-tuh) (Dakota) She Is a Trusted Friend

Danielle (dan-YEL) (French) Her God Judges Wisely

Darcy (DAR-see) (French) She Is Arcy, France

Daryl (DAIR-rul) (English) She Is Airelle, France

Daveigh (duh-VAY, DAY-vee) (American/English) She Is the Beloved Little One

Demi (deh-MEE) (Greek) She Is the Little One Who Is the Blessed Mother Earth

Devon (DEH-vun) (English) She Is a Swift-Running Fawn

Diandra (dee-AN-druh) (American) She Is the Powerful One Who Is the Source of Life

Drew (DROO) (English) He Is the Little One Who Is Powerfully Male

Dylan (DIL-lun) (Welsh) He Is a Mighty Ocean

⚘ **Dalal** (dah-LAHL) (Arabic) She Is Coy and Pretty

Daud (dah-OOD) (Arabic) He Is Greatly Beloved

Dawood (dah-WOOD) (Arabic) He Is Greatly Beloved

Dawud (dah-WOOD) (Arabic) He Is Greatly Beloved

Dema (DAY-mah) (Arabic) She Is Life-Giving Rain

Dima (DEE-mah) (Arabic) He Is Life-Giving Rain

Diya (DEE-yah) (Arabic) He Is Brilliant Radiance

Djamila (jah-MEE-lah) (Arabic) She Is Lovely

Dua (DOO-wah) (Arabic) She Is Our Prayer to God

Duha (DOO-hah) (Arabic) She Is the Bright Dawn

🌸 **Dalila** (dah-LEE-lah) (French) She Spends Money Freely

Darby (DAR-bee) (English) She Is a Swift-Running Deer

Dean (DEEN) (English) He Is a Peaceful Valley

Debby (DEB-bee) (English) She Is Our Busy Little Honeybee

Delia (DEE-lee-yuh) (Greek) She Is Delos, Greece

Delores (del-OR-ress) (English) She Understands Sorrow

Delta (DEL-tuh) (Greek) She Is the Place Where the River Meets the Ocean

Denise (duh-NEES) (French) She Is God's Mountain

Doreen (dor-REEN) (English) She Is the Little One Given to Us by God

Dot (DAHT) (English) She Is Our Little Present from God

🌸 **Danièle** (dahn-YEL) (French) Her God Judges Wisely

Daphné (dahf-NAY) (French/Greek) She Is a Laurel Tree

Débora (DAY-bo-rah) (French) She Is a Busy Honeybee

Delphine (del-FEEN) (French) She Is the Prophetess of Delphi, Greece

Désirée (day-zee-RAY) (French) She Is Greatly Desired

Dianne (dee-YAHN) (French/English) She Is the Heavenly Life Source

Didier (dee-dee-YAY) (French) He Is Greatly Desired

Diodore (dee-oh-DOR) (French) He Is God's Divine Gift

Donat (doh-NAHT) (French) He Is Given to Us as a Sacred Gift

Donatien (doh-nah-tee-YAW) (French) He is Given to Us as a Sacred Gift

🌸 **Danita** (dan-EE-tuh) (English) She Is God's Wise Little Judge

Danni (DAN-nee) (English) He Is God's Wise Little Judge

Daquan (dah-KWAHN) (English/Chinese) He Is the Glorious Warrior

Darby (DAR-bee) (English) He Is the City Where Deer Run Freely

Darcey (DAHR-see) (English) She Is Arcy, France

Darden (DAHR-den) (English) He Is the Arden Forest, France

Darell (DAIR-rel) (English) He Is Airelle, France

Daren (DAIR-ren) (English) He Is Airelle, France

Daria (DAHR-ee-yuh) (English) She Possesses Goodness

Darian (DAIR-ee-yun) (English) He Is Airelle, France

🌸 **Darla** (DAHR-luh) (English) She Is Our Sweet Little Darling

Darlene (dahr-LEEN) (English) She Is Darling and Sweet

Darnell (dahr-NEL) (English) He Is Fields of Verdant Grass

Darrel (DAIR-rel) (English) He Is Airelle, France

Darrin (DAIR-ren) (English) He Is Airelle, France

Dashiell (DASH-shul) (English) He Is a Good-Looking Youth

Davena (dah-VEE-nuh) (English) She Is Greatly Beloved

Davida (dah-VEE-dah) (English) She Is Greatly Beloved

Davie (DAY-vee) (English) He Is the Little One Who Is Greatly Beloved

Davin (DAV-vin) (English/Irish) He Is a Swift-Running Deer

🌸 **Davinia** (duh-VIN-ee-yuh) (English) She Is Greatly Beloved

Dax (DAX) (English) He Is Dax, France

Dayna (DAY-nuh) (English) She Is Denmark

Dayton (DAY-tun) (English) He Is Dairy Products

Deacon (DEE-kun) (English) He Is a Religious Leader

Deana (DEE-nuh) (English) She Is a Religious Leader

Deandre (dee-AHN-dray) (English/French) He Is Powerfully Male

Deangelo (dee-AN-jel-lo) (English/Italian) He Is God's Angelic Messenger

Deanne (dee-YAN) (English) She Is a Religious Leader

Deb (DEB) (English) She Is Our Busy Little Honeybee

🌸 **Debbi** (DEB-bee) (English) She Is Our Busy Little Honeybee

Dedrick (DED-rik) (English) He Is God's Divine Gift

Dee (DEE) (English) She Is Our Busy Little Honeybee

Deeann (dee-YAN) (English) She Is a Religious Leader

Deemer (DEE-mur) (English) He Is a Wise Magistrate

Deena (DEE-nuh) (English) She Is a Religious Leader

Deforest (dee-FOR-rest) (English) He Is a Grove of Forest Trees

Deidra (DEE-druh) (English) She Is All of Womankind

Deitra (DEE-truh) (English) She Is All of Womankind

Delaney (del-LAY-nee) (English) He Is a Forest of Alder Trees

☞ **Delbert** (DEL-burt) (English) He Is Aristocratic

Delia (DEE-lee-yuh) (English) She Is Delos, Greece

Delice (del-LEESS) (English) She Is Delectable

Delicia (deh-LEE-shuh) (English) She Is Delectable

Delma (DEL-muh) (English) She Is Beautiful

Delmar (DEL-mar) (English) He Is a Clear Lake

Delora (deh-LOR-ruh) (English) She Understands Sorrow

Deloris (deh-LOR-riss) (English) She Understands Sorrow

Delroy (DEL-roy) (English) He Is a Majestic King

Demelza (deh-MEL-zuh) (English) He Is the Castle Ruled by Maeldaf

☞ **Den** (DEN) (English) He Is the Little One Who Makes Himself Heard

Dene (DEE-nee) (English) She Is a Peaceful Valley

Denholm (DEN-holm) (English) He Is a Peaceful Valley

Denice (deh-NEESS) (English) She Is God's Mountain

Denton (DEN-tun) (English) He Is a Town in a Peaceful Valley

Denver (DEN-vur) (English) He Is the Crossing-Place of the Danes

Denzil (DEN-zil) (English) He Is Denzell, England

Deon (DEE-yahn) (English) He is God's Mountain

Deonte (dee-AHN-tay) (English) He Is the Steadfast Mountain of God

Derby (DUR-bee) (English) She Is the Town Where Deer Run Freely

☞ **Derick** (DAIR-rik) (English) He Is the Lord of Humanity

Derren (DAIR-run) (English) He Is Airelle, France

Derryl (DAIR-rel) (English) He Is Airelle, France

Deshaun (deh-SHAWN) (English) He Is Truly the One Whose God Is Great

Desirae (dez-ih-RAY) (English) She Is Greatly Desired

Desmond (DEZ-mund) (English/Irish) He Is South Munster, Ireland

Destinee (DES-tih-nee) (English) She Goes Where God Commands

Devan (DEV-van) (English/Irish) He Is a Swift Deer

Devereux (DEV-ur-ro) (English/French) He Is Evreux, France

Dewayne (duh-WAYN) (English) He Is the Little One Who Is Darkly Handsome

☞ **Dexter** (DEX-tur) (English) He Dyes Fabrics Beautifully

Deziree (dez-ih-RAY) (English/French) She Is Greatly Desired

Diane (dye-ANN) (English) She Is the Heavenly Life Source

Diantha (dee-ANN-thuh) (English) She Is a Fragrant Flower and the Highest Source of Life

Digby (DIG-bee) (English) He Is a Peaceful Village near a Dam

Diggory (DIG-guh-ree) (English) He Is the Hopeful Truth-Seeker

Dillon (DIL-lun) (English) He Is a Mighty Ocean

Dina (DEE-nuh) (English) She Has Been Judged and Found Worthy

Dixon (DIX-sun) (English) He Descends from the Powerful Little One

Docia (DO-shuh) (English) She Makes Offerings to God

☞ **Dodie** (DOH-dee) (English) She Is the Little One Given to Us by God

Dollie (DAHL-lee) (English) She Is the Beloved One Given to Us by God

Dolores (doh-LO-russ) (English) She Understands Sorrow

Domenic (dah-mih-NIK) (English) He Comes to Us from God

Dominica (doh-MIN-ih-kuh) (English) She Comes to Us from God

Dominick (dah-mih-NIK) (English) He Comes to Us from God

Dona (DAH-nuh) (English) She Is a Beautiful Lady

Donelle (doh-NEL) (English/French) She Is Our Beloved World Conqueror

Doretta (dor-ET-tuh) (English) She Is the Little One Given to Us by God

Doria (DOR-ee-yuh) (English) She Is God's Divine Gift

🐾 **Dorian** (DOR-ee-yun) (English/Greek) He Is God's Divine Gift

Dorinda (dor-IN-duh) (English) She Is the Pretty One Given to Us by God

Dorine (dor-REEN) (English) She Is the Little One Given to Us by God

Dorris (DOR-russ) (English) She Is Abundance

Dortha (DOR-thuh) (English) She Is God's Divine Gift

Dorthy (DOR-thee) (English) She Is God's Divine Gift

Dory (DOR-ree) (English) She Is the Little One Given to Us by God

Dotty (DAHT-tee) (English) She Is the Little One Given to Us by God

Doug (DUHG) (English) He Is the Little One Who Is a Deep River

Drea (DRAY-yuh) (English) She Is the Powerful Little One

🐾 **Dreda** (DRAY-duh) (English) She Is Powerfully Aristocratic

Drew (DROO) (English) He Is Our Powerful Little Man

Drina (DREE-nuh) (English) She Is Hadria, Italy

Driscoll (DRISS-kull) (English/Irish) He Descends from God's Holy Messenger

Drogo (DRO-go) (English) He Summons Spirits

Drummond (DRUM-mund) (English) He Is a Lofty Ridge

Duana (doo-WAH-nuh, doo-WAY-nuh) (English) She Is Darkly Beautiful

Dulcibella (dul-sih-BEL-luh) (English) She Is the Sweet, Beautiful One

Dulcie (DUHL-see) (English) She Is the Sweet, Beautiful Little One

Dunstan (DUN-stun) (English) He Is a Great Black Stone

🐾 **Durward** (DUR-wurd) (English) He Protects Our Home

Dusty (DUS-tee) (English) He Is the Little One Who Protects Our Home

Dwayne (DWAYN) (English) He Is the Little One Who Is Darkly Handsome

Dyan (dye-YAN) (English) She Is the Heavenly Life Source

Dyson (DYE-sun) (English) He Descends from the One Who Makes His Voice Heard

🐾 **Earle** (URL) (English) He Is an Aristocratic Soldier

Earleen (ur-LEEN) (English) She Is an Aristocratic Soldier

Earnestine (ur-nes-TEEN) (English) She Is Serious

Easter (EES-tur) (English) She Is the Easter Holiday

Ebba (EB-buh) (English) She Is the Rock-Solid Little One

🐾 **Eben** (EB-ben) (English) He Is the Rock-Solid Little One

Edgar (ED-ghur) (English) He Is a Powerful Weapon

Edric (ED-rik) (English) He Is a Wealthy Monarch

Edweena (ed-WEE-nuh) (English) She Is a Wealthy Companion

Edwyn (ED-win) (English) He Is a Wealthy Companion

Edytha (eh-DEE-thuh) (English) She Is a Wealthy Warrior

Edythe (EE-dith) (English) She Is a Wealthy Warrior

Effie (EF-fee) (English) She Is Our Beautiful Little Speaker

Eglantine (EG-lun-tyne) (English) She Is an Eglantine Rose

Eireann (AIR-ran) (English/Irish) She Is the Nation of Ireland

🐾 **Eevi** (ee-EE-vee) (Finnish) She Wants to Live

Eija (ay-EE-zhuh) (Finnish) She Shouts with Joy

Eliina (el-ee-EE-nah) (Finnish) She Is a Radiant Torch

Eliisa (el-ee-EE-sah) (Finnish) She Is the Little One Favored by God

Eljas (EL-yahss) (Finnish) Her God Is the One True God

Elli (EL-lee) (Finnish) She Is Aliénor, France

Ensio (EN-see-yo) (Finnish) He Is First Before All

Erkki (AIRK-kee) (Finnish) He Rules Forever

Esa (AY-sah) (Finnish/Hebrew) Her God Is Our Eternal Hope

Esteri (es-TEH-ree) (Finnish/Hebrew) She Is a Brilliant Star

🐛 **Eileen** (eye-LEEN) (Irish) She Is a Radiant Torch

Elaine (ee-LAYN) (French) She Is a Radiant Torch

Elida (el-LYE-duh) (English) She Is the Little One Who Is a Noble Kind of Person

Ella (EL-luh) (English) She Is Our Radiant Little Torch

Emilia (em-MEEL-yuh) (Italian) She Is Powerfully Competitive

Enrique (en-REE-kay) (Spanish) He Rules Our Home Magnificently

Erika (AIR-ih-kuh) (Swedish) She Rules Forever

Erin (AIR-rin) (Irish) She Is the Nation of Ireland

Ernesto (ur-NES-toh) (Spanish) He Is Serious

Estelle (es-STEL) (French) She Is a Heavenly Star

🐛 **Eldon** (EL-dun) (English) He Is the Beautiful Hill Owned by Ella

Eldred (EL-dred) (English) He Is Wise

Elea (EL-yuh) (English) She Is Aliénor, France

Eleanora (el-ee-uh-NO-ruh) (English) She Is Aliénor, France

Eleanore (el-ee-uh-NOR) (English) She Is Aliénor, France

Elfleda (el-FLAY-duh) (English) She Is Aristocratic

Elfreda (el-FRAY-duh) (English) She Is the Power of the Elfin Nation

Elfrida (el-FREE-duh) (English) She Is the Power of the Elfin Nation

Eli (EE-lye) (English/Hebrew) He Is Divine Greatness

Elicia (el-EE-shuh) (English) She Is Aristocratic

🐛 **Elijah** (ee-LYE-juh) (English/Hebrew) His God Is the True God

Elinor (EL-ih-nor) (English) She Is Aliénor, France

Eliott (EL-ee-yut) (English) His Only God Is God

Elisa (eh-LEE-suh) (English) She Is the Little One Favored by God

Elnora (el-NOR-ruh) (English) She Is Aliénor, France

Eloise (el-oh-WEEZ) (English) She Is Powerful

Elroy (EL-roy) (English) He Is a Majestic King

Elsa (EL-suh) (English) She Is the Little One Favored by God

Elsabeth (EL-sah-beth) (English) Her God Is Abundance

Elsdon (ELZ-dun) (English) He Is the Peaceful Valley Ruled by Elli

🐛 **Elvin** (EL-vin) (English) He Is the Companion of the Elfin People

Elvina (el-VEE-nuh) (English) She Is the Companion of the Elfin People

Elwin (EL-win) (English) He Is the Companion of the Elfin People

Elwood (EL-wood) (English) He Is a Grove of Beautiful Elder Trees

Elyse (el-LEESS) (English) She Demonstrates God's Abundance

Elyzabeth (ee-LIZ-uh-beth) (English) Her God Is Abundance

Em (EM) (English) She Is a Powerful Little Competitor

Emalee (EM-uh-lee) (English) She Is Powerfully Competitive

Emelia (eh-MEEL-yuh) (English) She Works Tirelessly

Emil (em-MEEL) (English) He Is a Powerful Competitor

🐛 **Emilee** (EM-il-lee) (English) She Is Powerfully Competitive

Emmaline (EM-muh-leen) (English) She Works Tirelessly

Emmerson (EM-mur-sun) (English) He Descends from the Industrious Worker

Emmet (EM-met) (English) He Is the Little One Who Is Our Entire Universe

Emmie (EM-mee) (English) She Is the Little One Who Is Our Entire Universe

Emory (EM-uh-ree) (English) He Works Tirelessly

Enola (ee-NO-luh) (English/Cherokee) She Stands Apart

Epiphany (ee-PIH-fuh-nee) (English/Greek) She Is a Divine Revelation

Eppie (EP-pee) (English) She Is Our Beautiful Little Speaker

Erica (AIR-ih-kuh) (English/German) She Rules Forever

🕮 **Erika** (AIR-ih-kuh) (English/German) She Rules Forever

Erle (URL) (English/Norwegian) He Is Aristocratic

Ermintrude (UR-min-trood) (English) She Is Massively Powerful

Ern (URN) (English) He Is the Little One Who Is Serious

Ernestine (ur-nes-TEEN) (English) She Is Serious

Errol (AIR-rul) (English/Scottish) He Is Errol, Scotland

Erskine (UR-skin) (English/Scottish) He Is a Lofty Mountain

Eryn (AIR-rin) (English) She Is the Nation of Ireland

Esmaralda (EZ-mahr-al-duh) (English) She Is a Sea-Green Emerald

Esmond (EZ-mund) (English) He Safeguards Us

🕮 **Essie** (ES-see) (English) She Is Our Heavenly Little Star

Esta (ES-tuh) (English) She Is Our Heavenly Little Star

Estella (es-STEL-luh) (English/Spanish) She Is Our Heavenly Star

Esther (ES-tur) (English/Hebrew) She Is Our Heavenly Star

Ethan (EE-thun) (English/Hebrew) He Is Rock-Solid and Eternal

Ethelinda (eth-uh-LIN-duh) (English) She Is a Fierce Serpent

Ethelred (ETH-ul-red) (English) He Safeguards Us Wisely

Ethelyn (ETH-uh-lin) (English) She Is Our Little Aristocrat

Etta (ET-tuh) (English) She Rules Our Home Magnificently

Eunice (YOO-niss) (English/Greek) She Is Humanity's Triumph

🕮 **Eustacia** (yoo-STAY-shuh) (English) She Produces Greatness

Eva (AY-vuh) (English/Spanish) She Wants to Live

Evaline (EV-uh-lin) (English) She Is Greatly Beloved and Desired

Evan (EV-vun) (English/Welsh) Her God Is Gracious

Evander (ee-VAN-dur) (English/Greek) He Is a Noble Person

Evangelina (ee-van-juh-LEE-nuh) (English) She Is God's Holy Message

Eveleen (ev-uh-LEEN) (English) She Is the Little One Who Wants to Live

Evelina (ev-uh-LEE-nuh) (English) She Is the Little One Who Wants to Live

Everett (EV-uh-ret) (English) He Is a Courageous Boar

Everette (ev-uh-RET) (English) She Is a Courageous She-Boar

🕮 **Fabian** (FAY-bee-yun) (Latin) He Is a Seed from Which Great Things Grow

Fabio (FAH-bee-yoh) (Italian) He Is a Seed from Which Great Things Grow

Fausto (FAH-oo-stoh) (Italian) He Is Favored with Good Fortune

Fay (FAY) (English) She Is a Magical Fairy

Felicia (feh-LEE-see-yah) (Latin) She Is Favored with Good Fortune

Felix (FEE-lix) (Latin) He Is Favored with Good Fortune

Fernanda (fair-NAHN-dah) (Spanish) She Is Peaceful and Brave

Fifi (FEE-fee) (French) She Is the Little One Whose Greatness Increases

Florence (FLOR-renss) (Latin) She Flourishes

Flossie (FLAHSS-see) (English) She Is the Little One Who Flourishes

🕮 **Fabio** (FAH-vee-yoh) (Spanish) He Is a Seed from Which Great Things Grow

Fabiola (fah-vee-OH-lah) (Spanish) She Is a Seed from Which Great Things Grow

Fabricio (fah-BREE-see-yo) (Spanish) He Is a Skilled Artisan

Faustino (fah-oh-STEE-no) (Spanish) He Is Favored with Good Fortune

Fausto (FAH-oh-sto) (Spanish) He Is Favored with Good Fortune

Felicia (fay-LEE-see-yah) (Spanish) She Is Favored with Good Fortune

Feliciana (fay-lee-see-AH-nah) (Spanish) She Is Favored with Good Fortune

Feliciano (fay-lee-see-AH-no) (Spanish) He Is Favored with Good Fortune

Felicidad (fay-lee-see-DAHD) (Spanish) She Is Good Fortune

Felipa (fay-LEE-pah) (Spanish) She Befriends Horses

🐾 **Fadi** (FAH-dee) (Arabic) He Is Our Protector
Fadia (FAH-dee-yah) (Arabic) She Is Our Protector
Fadil (fah-DEEL) (Arabic) He Is Loving and Giving
Fadila (fah-DEE-lah) (Arabic) She Is Loving and Giving
Fadl (FAH-dul) (Arabic) He Is Loving and Giving
Fahd (FAHD) (Arabic) He Is a Powerful Panther
Fahim (fah-HEEM) (Arabic) He Is Wise
Fahima (fah-HEE-mah) (Arabic) She Is Wise
Fairuz (fay-ROOZ) (Arabic) She Is a Priceless Turquoise Jewel
Faiz (fah-YEESS) (Arabic) He Is Humanity's Triumph

🐾 **Faizel** (FYE-suhl) (Arabic) He Judges Humanity
Fahkhriyya (fah-KREE-yah) (Arabic) She Is Respected
Fakhri (FAHK-ree) (Arabic) He Is Respected
Farag (fah-RAHG) (Arabic) He Heals Humanity
Faraj (fah-RAHJ) (Arabic) He Heals Humanity
Farid (fah-REED) (Arabic) He Is a Priceless Treasure
Farida (fah-REE-dah) (Arabic) She Is a Priceless Treasure
Fariha (fah-REE-hah) (Arabic) She Rejoices
Faris (fah-REESS) (Arabic) He Is Our Glorious Cavalier
Farooq (fah-ROOWK) (Arabic) He Understands Justice

🐾 **Fallon** (FAL-lun) (English/Irish) He Descends from the Great Commander
Fancy (FAN-see) (English) She Is Elegantly Beautiful
Farley (FAR-lee) (English) He Is a Meadow Filled with Fern Trees
Faron (fah-RAHN) (English) He Is a Light in the Darkness
Farran (FAIR-run) (English) He Is Tempered Steel
Fawn (FAWN) (English) She Is a Swift-Running Deer
Felicia (fuh-LEE-shuh) (English/Latin) She Is Favored with Good Fortune
Femie (FEE-mee) (English) She Speaks Beautifully

Fenton (FEN-tun) (English) He Is a Town near the Beautiful Wetlands
Ferdie (FUR-dee) (English) He Is the Little One Who Is Peaceful and Brave

🐾 **Ferdy** (FUR-dee) (English) He Is the Little One Who Is Peaceful and Brave
Ferne (FURN) (English) She Is a Living Fern Tree
Finnegan (FIN-ih-gun) (English/Irish) He Descends from the Fair One
Fitzroy (FITZ-roy) (English) He Descends from the Powerful Monarch
Flanagan (FLAN-ih-gun) (English/Irish) He Descends from the Red-Haired One
Flannery (FLAN-nuh-ree) (English/Irish) He Descends from the Red-Blooded Hero
Fleur (FLUR) (English/French) She Is a Fragrant Blossom
Fleurette (flur-RET) (English/French) She Is the Little One Who Is a Fragrant Blossom
Flick (FLIK) (English) She Is the Little One Who Is Good Fortune
Flo (FLO) (English) She Is the Little One Who Flourishes

🐾 **Fermin** (FAIR-meen) (Spanish) He Is Upstanding
Fernando (fair-NAHN-doh) (Spanish) He Is Peaceful and Brave
Fidel (fee-DEL) (Spanish) He Is Devoted
Fidela (fee-DEL-lah) (Spanish) She Is Devoted
Flavia (FLAH-vee-yah) (Spanish) She Is Pure Gold
Flavio (FLAH-vee-yo) (Spanish) He Is Pure Gold
Florencio (flo-REN-see-yo) (Spanish) He Flourishes
Florentina (flo-ren-TEE-nah) (Spanish) She Flourishes
Florinda (flo-REEN-dah) (Spanish) She Is Truly a Lovely Flower
Fortunata (for-too-NAH-tah) (Spanish) She Is Favored with Good Fortune

🐾 **Floella** (flo-EL-luh) (English) She Is Truly a Wealthy, Flourishing Lady
Flora (FLO-ruh) (English/Latin) She Is a Lovely Flower
Floretta (flo-RET-tuh) (English) She Is the Little One Who Is a Lovely Flower
Flower (FLAUW-wur) (English) She Is a Fragrant Flower

Floyd (FLOYD) (English/Welsh) He Is Gray and Wise

Flynn (FLIN) (English/Irish) He Descends from the One with Fiery Red Hair

Forrest (FOR-rest) (English) He Is a Verdant Natural Wilderness

Fortune (FOR-choon) (English) He Is Wealth and Success

Foster (FAHSS-tur) (English) He Cuts Down Mighty Trees in the Forest

Francene (fran-SEEN) (English) She Is the Nation of France

✍ **Francine** (fran-SEEN) (English) She Is the Nation of France

Franklyn (FRANK-lin) (English) He Is a Free Man

Frannie (FRAN-nee) (English) She Is the Little One Who Is the Nation of France

Fraser (FRAY-zur) (English/Scottish) He Is an Adventurous Explorer

Freda (FREE-duh) (English) She Is the Blessed Little One Who Is Beautifully Fair

Frederica (fred-ur-EE-kuh) (English) She Rules Peacefully

Frieda (FREE-duh) (English) She Is Our Peaceful Little Ruler

Frona (FRO-nuh) (English) She Is the Little One Who Is Calm and Collected

Fulke (FULK) (English) He Is Humanity

Fulton (FUL-tun) (English) He Is a Town of Skillful Bird-Hunters

✍ **Gabby** (GAB-bee) (English) She Is the Little One Who Is God's Powerful Angelic Messenger

Gabe (GAYB) (English) He Is the Little One Who Is God's Powerful Angelic Messenger

Gabriella (gab-ree-EL-luh) (English) She Is God's Powerful Angelic Messenger

Gae (GAY) (English) She Is Filled with Joy

Gaenor (GAY-nur) (English) She Is Beautifully Fair

Gage (GAYJ) (English) He Fairly Weighs Priceless Metals

Gaila (GAY-luh) (English) She Is a Mighty Storm

Galen (GAY-lun) (Greek) He Is Tranquil

Garey (GAIR-ree) (English) He Is a Mighty Weapon

Garnett (GAR-net) (English) He Is as Sweet as a Pomegranate

✍ **Gabir** (gah-BEER) (Arabic) She Consoles Humanity

Gafar (gah-FAHR) (Arabic) He Is a Powerful River

Galal (gah-LAHL) (Arabic) He Is Supreme

Galila (gah-LEE-lah) (Arabic) She Is Supreme

Gamal (gah-MAHL) (Arabic) He Is Lovely

Gamil (gah-MEEL) (Arabic) He Is Lovely

Gamila (gah-MEE-lah) (Arabic) She Is Lovely

Gawdat (ghaw-DAHT) (Arabic) He Is Supreme

Ghadir (gah-DEER) (Arabic) She Is a Powerful River

Ghalib (gah-LEEB) (Arabic) He Is Humanity's Triumph

Ghaliya (GHAHL-yah) (Arabic) She Is Priceless

Ghassan (gahss-SAHN) (Arabic) He Lives Forever

✍ **Gabrielle** (French) She Is God's Powerful Angelic Messenger

Gail (GAYL) (English) She Is a Mighty Storm

Gaston (gas-TOW) (French) He Is Gascony, France

Genevieve (zhawn-vee-YEV) (French) She Is Loyal to Her People

Gert (GURT) (German) He Is a Powerful Little Weapon

Gilbert (GIL-burt) (English) He Is a Shining Promise

Ginger (JIN-jur) (English) She Is Peppery Ginger-Spice

Gladys (GLAD-iss) (Welsh) She Is a Mighty Nation

Glenda (GLEN-duh) (Welsh) She Is Decent and Pure-Hearted

Gustav (GOO-stahv) (German) He Is the Great Staff of the Gothic People

✍ **Garnette** (gar-NET) (English) She Is as Sweet as a Pomegranate

Garret (GAIR-ret) (English) He Is a Mighty Weapon

Garrick (GAIR-rik) (English) He Is a Mighty Weapon

Garry (GAIR-ree) (English) He Is a Mighty Weapon

Gavin (GAV-vin) (English) He Is a Snow-White Hawk

Gayelord (GAY-lord) (English) He Is Filled with Energy

Gayla (GAY-luh) (English) She Is a Mighty Storm

Geena (JEE-nuh) (English) She Is Our Little Aristocrat

Geffrey (JEFF-ree) (English) He Is the Land of Peace

Genesis (JEN-uh-sis) (English/Hebrew) She Is Our New Beginning

☙ **Genette** (jeh-NET) (English/French) She Is God's Graceful Little Messenger

Geneva (jeh-NEE-vuh) (English/French) She Is the Little One Who Is Loyal to Her People

Genevra (jeh-NEV-ruh) (English/Italian) She Is Beautifully Fair

Genie (JEE-nee) (English) She Is Aristocratic

Geoff (JEF) (English) He Is Our Little Kingdom of Peace

Geordie (JOR-dee) (English) He Is the Little One Who Farms the Land

Georgeanna (jor-JAN-nuh) (English) She Farms the Land

Georgene (jor-JEEN) (English/French) She Farms the Land

Georgie (JOR-jee) (English) She Is the Little One Who Farms the Land

German (JUR-man) (English) He Is the Nation of Germany

☙ **Gerrard** (jur-RARD) (English) He Is a Powerful Weapon

Gertie (GHUR-tee) (English) She Is the Little One Who Is a Mighty Weapon

Gib (GHIB) (English) He Is the Little One Who Is a Shining Promise

Gid (GHID) (English/Hebrew) He Is the Little One Who Is a Mighty Woodsman

Giffard (GHIF-furd) (English) He Is the Courageous One Given to Us by God

Gil (GHIL) (English) He Is the Little One Who Is a Shining Promise

Ginnie (JIN-nee) (English) She Is the Little One Who Is a Chaste, Pure Maiden

Giselle (jih-ZEL) (English/French) She Is Pledged to Serve Humanity

Githa (GHEE-thuh) (English) She Is the Little One Who Is Divine

Gladwin (GLAD-win) (English) He Is a Brilliant Companion

☙ **Gladwyn** (GLAD-win) (English) He Is a Brilliant Companion

Gladys (GLAD-diss) (English/Welsh) She Is a Mighty Nation

Glanville (GLAN-vil) (English) He Is a Town Ruled by the Famous One Called Gland

Glenda (GLEN-duh) (English/Welsh) She Is Pure-Hearted

Glenna (GLEN-nuh) (English/Scottish) She Is a Peaceful Valley

Gloria (GLO-ree-yuh) (English/Latin) She Is Everlasting Glory

Gloriana (glo-ree-AN-nuh) (English/Italian) She Is Magnificent Glory

Glory (GLO-ree) (English) She Is Everlasting Glory

Godfrey (GAHD-free) (English) He Is God's Own Grace

Goldie (GOL-dee) (English/Yiddish) She Is the Little One Who Is Pure Gold

☙ **Gord** (GORD) (English/Scottish) He Is the Little One Who Is a Lofty Hill

Gorden (GOR-den) (English/Scottish) He Is a Lofty Hill

Gordie (GOR-dee) (English/Scottish) He Is the Little One Who Is a Lofty Hill

Gosse (GAWSS) (English) He Is the Little One Who Is God's Own Child

Grady (GRAY-dee) (English/Irish) He Descends from the Aristocrat

Graeme (GRAY-yum) (English) He Is a Grand Homestead on Gravelly Land

Grahame (GRAM) (English) He Is a Grand Homestead on Gravelly Land

Grant (GRANT) (English/Scottish) He Is Magnificently Great

Granville (GRAN-vil) (English/French) He Is a Town

Greer (GREER) (English/Scottish) He Is Our Little Guardian

☙ **Greta** (GREH-tuh) (English) She Is Our Priceless Little Pearl

Greyson (GRAY-sun) (English) He Descends from the Great Steward

Grier (GREER) (English/Scottish) He Is Our Little Guardian

Griselda (grih-ZEL-duh) (English/Spanish) She Is a Gray-Haired Warrior

Grosvenor (GROVE-nur) (English) He Is a Mighty Warrior

Guendolen (GWEN-doh-len) (English/Welsh) She Is Beautifully Fair

Gussie (GUS-see) (English) She Is the Little One Who Is Absolutely Magnificent

Guy (GYE) (English/French) He Is Magnificently Great

Gwenda (GWEN-duh) (English) She Is Beautifully Fair

Gwenevere (GWEN-uh-veer) (English) She Is Beautifully Fair

🐾 **Hanna** (HAH-nah) (Swedish) She Is Graceful
Harvey (HAR-vee) (English) He Is Battle-Ready
Hattie-Simone (hat-tee-sih-MONE) (French/English) She Rules All and Hears Everything
Hazel (HAY-zul) (English) She Is a Fragrant Hazelnut Tree
Henri (ahn-REE) (French) He Rules Our Home Magnificently
Hermine (hair-MEE-nuh) (German) She Is Aggressively Warlike
Hernan (air-NAHN) (Spanish) He Is the Little One Who Is Peaceful and Brave
Hilda (HIL-duh) (German) She Lives for Combat
Hortense (HOR-tenss) (English/French) She Is a Splendid Garden
Hugo (HYOO-go) (English) He Has a Compassionate Heart

🐾 **Hannelle** (hah-NEL) (Finnish) She Is God's Graceful Little Messenger
Hannes (HAHN-ness) (Finnish) His God Is Gracious
Hannu (HAHN-noo) (Finnish) Her God Is Gracious
Harri (HAHR-ree) (Finnish) He Rules Our Home Magnificently
Heikki (HAY-kee) (Finnish) He Rules Our Home Magnificently
Heino (HAY-no) (Finnish) He Is Our Place of Shelter and Comfort
Heleena (hel-EE-ee-nah) (Finnish) She Is a Radiant Torch
Heli (HEL-lee, HAY-lee) (Finnish) She Is Our Radiant Little Torch
Helka (HEL-kah) (Finnish) She Is Our Little Sacred One
Helmi (HEL-mee) (Finnish) She Is the Little One Who Is a Divine Helmet of Protection

🐾 **Harmony** (HAR-muh-nee) (English) She Is Sweet Harmony
Harriett (HAIR-ree-yut) (English) She Rules the Home

Harrietta (hair-ee-ET-tuh) (English) She Rules the Home

Hartley (HART-lee) (English) He Is the Meadow Where Mighty Harts Run

Harve (HARV) (English) He Is the Little One Who Is Battle-Ready

Harvie (HAR-vee) (English) He Is Battle-Ready

Hatty (HAT-tee) (English) She Is the Little One Who Rules the Home

Haydee (HAY-dee) (English) She Is Obedient and Humble

Haylee (HAY-lee) (English) She Is a Meadow of Hay in the Woodlands

Haywood (HAY-wood) (English) She Is a Sheltered Forest

🐾 **Haydn** (HAY-den) (English) He Is a Peaceful Valley Filled with Sweet Hay
Hailee (HAY-lee) (English) She Is a Meadow of Hay in the Woodlands
Hallam (HAL-lum) (English) He Is a Great Mound of Massive Rocks
Halle (HAL-lee) (English/German) She Is the Great Manor Hall
Hamnet (HAM-net) (English) He Is Our Sacred Homeland
Hamo (HAH-mo) (English) He Is Our Sacred Homeland
Hardy (HAR-dee) (English) He Is Strong and Courageous
Harland (HAR-lund) (English) He Is the Land of Swift-Running Hares
Harmon (HAR-mun) (English) He Is Aggressively Warlike
Harmonie (HAR-muh-nee) (English) She Is Sweet Harmony

🐾 **Haze** (HAYZ) (English) She Is the Little One Who Is a Fragrant Hazelnut Tree
Headley (HED-lee) (English) He Is a Meadow Where Leather-Crafters Work
Heath (HEETH) (English) He Is a Meadow Covered with Fragrant Heather
Hellen (HEL-lun) (English/Greek) She Is a Radiant Torch
Hepsie (HEP-see) (English) She Is the Little One Who Is All Our Joy
Hervey (HUR-vee) (English) He Is Battle-Ready
Hettie (HET-tee) (English) She Is the Little One Who Rules the Home
Hewie (HYOO-wee) (English) He Is the Little One Whose Courage Is Great

Hildred (HIL-dred) (English) She Is a Diplomat and a Warrior

Hiram (HYE-rum) (English/Hebrew) He Is a Respected Sibling

📖 **Hephaestus** (hef-FESS-tus) (Greek) He Shines in the Daytime

Harmonia (har-MO-nee-yah) (Greek) She Is Sweet Harmony

Hephaestus was the Greek god of blacksmiths and volcanoes whose wife was Aphrodite, goddess of love. He forged the gods' weapons, even creating an enchanted necklace for Harmonia, Aphrodite's illegitimate child. But the necklace doomed Harmonia to a life of persecution and challenges.

📖 **Holden** (HOL-den) (English) He Is a Hidden, Peaceful Valley

Hollie (HAHL-lee) (English) She Is the Lovely Red-and-Green Holly Bush

Hollis (HAHL-liss) (English) He Lives in the Holly Tree Forest

Honora (ah-NOR-ruh) (English) She Is Honor Itself

Honour (AH-nur) (English) She Is Honor Itself

Hopkin (HAHP-kin) (English) He Is the Bright One Born in Glory

Howie (HOW-wee) (English) He Is the Little One Whose Heart Is Courageous

Hubert (HYOO-burt) (English/German) His Heart Shines Brightly

Huey (HYOO-wee) (English) He Is the Little One Whose Heart Is Great

Humbert (HUM-burt) (English) He Is a Renowned Fighter

📖 **Ibbie** (IB-bee) (English) She Is the Little One Favored by God

Idella (eye-DEL-luh) (English) She Toils Mightily

Idelle (eye-DEL) (English) She Toils Mightily

Idonea (eye-DOH-nee-yuh) (English) She Is Eternal Compassion

Iesha (eye-EE-shuh) (English/Arabic) She Wants to Live

Iggy (IG-ghee) (English) He Is the Little One Aflame with Greatness

Ilbert (IL-burt) (English) He Is Shimmering Warfare

Ileen (eye-LEEN) (English/Irish) She Is a Radiant Torch

Imogen (IM-uh-jun) (English) She Is Chaste

Imogene (IM-uh-jeen) (English) She Is Chaste

📖 **Ignacio** (ig-NAH-see-yoh) (Spanish) He Is Aflame with Greatness

Ike (IKE) (English) He Is the Little One Who Laughs with Joy

Inez (ee-NESS) (Spanish) She Shimmers with Sunlight

Ingrid (ING-rid) (Swedish) She Is First in Beauty

Inigo (IN-ih-go) (English) He Is a Royal Monarch

Ione (ee-YONE) (Greek) She Is a Fragrant Violet

Irma (EER-mah) (German) She Is Our Universe

Isbell (IZ-bel) (English) Her God Is Abundance

Isidore (IZ-ih-dor) (Greek) He Is a Gift from Isis, the Earth Mother

Ismael (EESS-mah-yel) (Spanish) His God Will Always Hear Him

📖 **Iida** (eye-EE-duh) (Finnish) She Toils Mightily

Iikka (eye-EEK-kuh) (Finnish) He Laughs with Joy

Iines (eye-EE-nuss) (Finnish) She Shimmers with Sunlight

Iiro (eye-EE-ro) (Finnish) He Is the Little One Who Laughs with Joy

Iisakki (eye-ee-SAK-kee) (Finnish) He Laughs with Joy

Ilari (il-AH-ree) (Finnish) He Laughs with Joy

Ilma (IL-mah) (Finnish) She Is the Clear Atmosphere

Ilta (IL-tah) (Finnish) She Is the Beautiful Sunset

Impi (IM-pee) (Finnish) She Is Chaste and Pure

Inka (IN-kah) (Finnish) She Is the Little One Who Is Supreme

📖 **Ina** (EYE-nah) (English/German) She Is the Little One Whose Greatness Increases

Indigo (IN-dih-go) (English) He Is Lovely Indigo-Blue Dye from India

Ingram (ING-rum) (English) He Is a Glistening Ebony-Black Raven

Iona (eye-OH-nuh) (English/Scottish) She Is a Fair, Beautiful Island

Ione (eye-YOWN) (English/Greek) She Is a Fragrant Violet

Ira (EYE-ruh) (English/Greek) He Knows Vengeance

Ireland (EYE-ur-lund) (English/Irish) She Is the Nation of Ireland

Irma (UR-muh) (English/German) She Is Our Universe

Irvine (UR-vine) (English) His Friends Are as Brave as Wild Boars

Isolda (ee-SOUL-duh) (English/Welsh) She Is Exceedingly Beautiful

🕮 *Isolde* (ih-SOUL-duh) (English/Welsh) She Is Exceedingly Beautiful

Issac (EYE-zik) (English/Hebrew) He Laughs with Joy

Issy (ISS-see) (English) He Is the Little One Who Is a Gift from Isis, the Earth Mother

Ivan (EYE-vun) (English/Russian) His God Is Gracious

Ivonette (ee-vuh-NET) (English) She Is the Magnificent, Heart-Stopping Little Yew Tree

Ivor (EYE-vor) (English) He Is the Magnificent Yew Tree

Ivory (EYE-vur-ree) (English) He Is a Beautiful Ivory Color

Ivy (EYE-vee) (English) She Is a Verdant Ivy-Vine

Izabelle (IZ-uh-bel) (English/French) Her God Is Abundance

Izzy (IZ-zee) (English) He Is the Little One Who Is a Gift from Isis, the Earth Mother

🕮 *Jaci* (JAK-kee) (English) She Is the Beloved One Whose God Is Gracious

Jacinda (juh-SIN-duh) (English) She Is a Beautiful Hyacinth Flower

Jacinth (juh-SINTH) (English) She Is a Flaming-Orange Jacinth Gem

Jackalyn (JAK-uh-lin) (English) She Is Divinely Protected

Jacklyn (JAK-lin) (English) She Is Divinely Protected

Jacquetta (juh-KET-tuh) (English) She Is God's Graceful Little Messenger

Jada (JAY-duh) (English) She Is Priceless Jade

Jaden (JAY-den) (English) She Is the Little One Who Is Priceless Jade

Jae (JAY) (English) She Is Our Little Divinely Protected Savior

Jaimie (JAY-mee) (English) She Is Divinely Protected

🕮 *Jacinto* (hah-SEEN-toh) (Spanish) He Is a Beautiful Hyacinth Flower

Jackson (JAK-sun) (English) He Descends from the One Whose God Is Gracious

Jefferson (JEF-ur-sun) (English) He Descends from the Man of Peace

Jenner (JEN-nur) (English) He Is the Engineer Who Builds Great Siege-Engines of War

Jimeno (hee-MAYN-yo) (Spanish) He Hears Everything Clearly

Jones (JONES) (Welsh) His God Is Gracious

Jordan (JOR-dun) (Hebrew) She Is the Mighty Jordan River, Israel

Jovista (jo-VEES-tuh) (American/Spanish) She Sees Her Greatness Increase

Junipero (hoo-NIP-ur-ro) (Spanish) He Is a Fragrant Juniper Tree

Jurupa (hoo-ROO-puh) (Spanish) He Is Peace

🕮 *Jake* (JAYK) (English) He Is Beloved and His God Is Gracious

Jaki (JAK-kee) (English) She Is the Beloved One Whose God Is Gracious

Jalen (JAY-len) (English/American) She Is the Divinely Protected Little Lioness

Jamar (juh-MAHR) (English/Arabic) He Is the Glorious Ocean

Jamey (JAY-mee) (English) He Is the Divinely Protected Little One

Jamison (JAY-mih-sun) (English) He Descends from the One Who Is Divinely Protected

Janae (juh-NAY) (English) Her God Is Truly Gracious

Jancis (JAN-sis) (English) She Is the Nation of France, Whose God Is Gracious

Janeka (juh-NEE-kuh) (English) She Is God's Graceful Little Messenger

Janelle (juh-NEL) (English) She Is God's Graceful Little Messenger

🕮 *Janene* (juh-NEEN) (English) She Is God's Graceful Little Messenger

Janessa (juh-NES-suh) (English) Her God Is Truly Gracious

Janette (JAN-net) (English) She Is God's Graceful Little Messenger

Janie (JAY-nee) (English) She Is the Little One Whose God Is Great

Janis (JAN-niss) (English) Her God Is Truly Great

Janna (JAN-nuh) (English) Her God Is Gracious

Jaquan (juh-KWAHN) (English/Vietnamese) He Is the Divinely Protected Warrior

Jaqueline (JAK-kwuh-lin) (English/French) She Is Divinely Protected

Jarod (juh-RAHD) (English/Hebrew) He Descends from the Mighty Ones

Jaron (juh-RAHN) (English/French) He Descends from the Mighty Ones of Airelle, France

🕊 **Janna** (YAHN-nuh) (Dutch) Her God Is Gracious

Janneke (YAH-neh-kuh) (Dutch) Her God Is Gracious

Jantine (yahn-TEEN) (Dutch) Her God Is Gracious

Jantje (YAHN-tee-yuh) (Dutch) She Is God's Graceful Little Messenger

Jasmijn (yahz-MEEN) (Dutch) She Is Fragrant, Beautiful Jasmine

Jef (YEF) (Dutch) He Is the Little One Whose Greatness Increases

Jeroen (yur-ROON) (Dutch) His Name Is Sacred

Jesse (YES-see) (Dutch) He Is a Gift from God

Jochem (YO-khem) (Dutch) He Is the Little One Who Is Protected by God

Joep (YOOP) (Dutch) He Is the Little One Favored by God

🕊 **Jarred** (JAIR-red) (English/Hebrew) He Descends from the Mighty Ones

Jarrett (JAIR-ret) (English) He Governs with Powerful Weapons

Jarrod (jur-RAHD) (English/Hebrew) He Descends from the Mighty Ones

Jaslyn (JAZ-lin) (English/American) She Is Jazz Music Playing near a Beautiful Lake

Jasmin (JAZ-min) (English/Persian) She Is a Fragrant Jasmine Flower

Jasper (JAS-pur) (English/Persian) He Holds Priceless Wealth

Jaxon (JAK-sun) (English) He Descends from the One Whose God Is Gracious

Jaycob (JAY-kub) (English/Hebrew) He Surpasses Everyone

Jayda (JAY-duh) (English) She Is Priceless Jade

Jayde (JAYD) (English) She Is Priceless Jade

🕊 **Jayden** (JAY-den) (English) She Is the Little One Who Is Priceless Jade

Jaye (JAY) (English) She Is Our Little Divinely Protected Savior

Jayla (JAY-luh) (English) She Is the Divinely Protected Little One

Jaylee (JAY-lee) (English) She Is a Peaceful and Divinely Protected Little Meadow

Jaylen (JAY-len) (English/American) She Is the Divinely Protected Little Lioness

Jayma (JAY-muh) (English) She Is the Divinely Protected Little One

Jayme (JAY-mee) (English) She Is the Divinely Protected Little One

Jaymes (JAYMZ) (English/Hebrew) He Is Divinely Protected

Jayna (JAY-nuh) (English) Her God Is Gracious

Jaynie (JAY-nee) (English) She Is God's Graceful Little Messenger

🕊 **Jayson** (JAY-sun) (English/Greek) He Is a Healer

Jazlyn (JAZ-lin) (English/American) She Is Jazz Music Playing near a Beautiful Lake

Jazmin (JAZ-min) (English/Persian) She Is a Fragrant Jasmine Flower

Jeana (JEE-nuh) (English) Her God Is Gracious

Jeanie (JEE-nee) (English) She Is God's Graceful Little Messenger

Jeanine (jih-NEEN) (English) She Is God's Graceful Little Messenger

Jeannette (juh-NET) (English/French) She Is God's Graceful Little Messenger

Jeb (JEB) (English) He Is Our Little Magnificent One

Jed (JED) (English) He Is the Little One Whom God Adores

Jeffery (JEF-ur-ree) (English) He Is the Great Land of Peace

🕊 **Jeffry** (JEFF-ree) (English) He Is the Great Land of Peace

Jem (JEM) (English) He Is Divinely Protected

Jemma (JEM-muh) (English) She Is a Priceless, Treasured Gemstone

Jemmy (JEM-muh) (English) She Is the Divinely Protected Little One

Jena (JEN-nuh) (English) She Is Our Fair Little Beauty

Jenae (juh-NAY) (English) She Is Our Fair Little Beauty

Jenelle (juh-NEL) (English) She Is God's Graceful Little Messenger

Jenessa (juh-NES-suh) (English) Her God Is Truly Gracious

Jeni (JEN-nee) (English) She Is Our Fair Little Beauty

Jenn (JEN) (English) She Is Our Fair Little Beauty

🕊 **Jennica** (JEN-ih-kuh) (English) She Is Beautifully Fair, a Sight to Behold

Jep (JEP) (English) He Is the Little One Who Is the Land of Peace

Jepson (JEP-sun) (English) He Descends from the Little One Who Is the Land of Peace

Jeptha (JEP-thuh) (English/Hebrew) He Causes Us to See Clearly

Jere (JAIR) (English) He Is the Little One Whom God Exalts

Jeremiah (jair-uh-MYE-yuh) (English/Hebrew) He Is Exalted by God

Jeri (JAIR-ree) (English) He Is the Beloved Little One Whose God Is Uplifting

Jerold (JAIR-ruld) (English) He Rules with Powerful Weapons

Jerome (jur-ROME) (English/Greek) His Name Is Sacred

Jerrard (jur-RARD) (English) He Is a Powerful Weapon

🕭 *Jerred* (JAIR-red) (English/Hebrew) He Descends from the Mighty Ones

Jerrie (JAIR-ree) (English) She Is the Beloved One Whose God Is Uplifting

Jerrod (jur-RAHD) (English/Hebrew) He Descends from the Mighty Ones

Jerrold (JEH-ruld) (English) He Rules with Powerful Weapons

Jervis (JUR-vis) (English) He Is a Mighty Weapon

Jess (JESS) (English) She Is the Little One Who Is a Sight to Behold

Jessalyn (JESS-uh-lin) (English) She Is a Beautiful Lake, a Sight to Behold

Jessamyn (JES-suh-min) (English) She Is a Fragrant Jasmine Flower

Jessi (JESS-see) (English/Hebrew) She Is God's Divine Gift

Jessika (JES-sih-kuh) (English) She Is Lovely to Behold

🕭 *Jesper* (YES-pur) (Danish) He Holds Priceless Wealth

Joakim (YO-uh-keem) (Danish) He Is the Divinely Protected Little One

Johanne (yo-HAH-nuh) (Danish) Her God Is Gracious

Jokum (YO-kum) (Danish) He Is the Divinely Protected Little One

Jonas (YO-nahss) (Danish) He Is a Peaceful Dove

Jonatan (YAHN-uh-tun) (Danish) He Is the One to Whom God Has Given Much

Jonna (YAHN-nuh) (Danish) She Is God's Graceful Little Messenger

Jorck (YORK) (Danish) He Farms the Land

Jorgen (YOR-gun) (Danish) He Farms the Land

Jorn (YORN) (Danish) He Is the Little One Who Farms the Land

🕭 *Jessye* (JESS-see) (English/Hebrew) She Is God's Divine Gift

Jett (JET) (English) He Is Beautifully Black

Jewel (JOO-wul) (English) She Is a Priceless Jewel

Jillie (JIL-lee) (English) She Is the Little One Who Rules Heaven

Jinny (JIN-nee) (English) She Is the Little One Who Is a Chaste, Pure Maiden

Joandra (jo-AN-druh) (English) She Is the Powerful One Whose God Is Gracious

Joanie (JO-nee) (English) She Is God's Graceful Little Messenger

Joanna (jo-ANN-nuh) (English) Her God Is Gracious

Jobeth (JO-beth) (English) She Is the Little One Favored by God

Joby (JO-bee) (English) He Is the Little One Who Understands Sorrow

🕭 *Jesusa* (hay-SOO-sah) (Spanish) Her God Is Salvation

Joaquina (wah-KEE-nah) (Spanish) She Is the Little One Supported by God

Juana (HWAHN-nah) (Spanish) Her God Is Gracious

Juanita (hwahn-EE-tah) (Spanish) She Is God's Graceful Little Messenger

Juanito (hwahn-EE-toh) (Spanish) He Is the Little One Whose God is Gracious

Julia (HOOL-yah) (Spanish) She Is Beautifully Youthful

Juliana (hoo-lee-AH-nah) (Spanish) She Is Julius Caesar's Relative

🕭 *Jocelin* (JAH-suh-lin) (English) She Is the Germanic Nation of the Gauts

Jodene (jo-DEEN) (English) She Is the Magnificent Nation of Judea

Joel (JO-wul) (English/Hebrew) His God Is the True God

Joella (jo-EL-luh) (English) Her God Is the One True God

Joetta (jo-ET-tuh) (English) She Is Truly the Little One Whose Greatness Increases

Johna (JAH-nuh) (English) Her Greatness Increases

Johnathan (JON-uh-thun) (English) He Is the One to Whom God Has Given Much
Johnie (JAHN-nee) (English) His God Is Gracious
Joi (JOY) (English) She Is Great Rejoicing
Joisse (JOYSS) (English) She Is Supreme

🕮 **Joeri** (YOO-ree) (Dutch) He Farms the Land
Johanneke (yo-HAHN-eh-kuh) (Dutch) Her God Is Gracious
Jolanda (yo-LAHN-duh) (Dutch) She Is a Fragrant Violet
Jonathan (YO-nah-tahn) (Dutch) He Is the One to Whom God Gives Much
Joop (YOOP) (Dutch) He Is the Little One Favored by God
Joord (YOORD) (Dutch) He Is the Little One Who Is the Jordan River, Israel
Joos (YOHSS) (Dutch) He Is the Little One Whose Greatness Increases
Joost (YOHST) (Dutch) He Is the Little One Who Is Fair and Just
Jordaan (YOR-dahn) (Dutch) He Is the River Jordan, Israel
Joris (YOR-riss) (Dutch) He Farms the Land

🕮 **Joleen** (jo-LEEN) (English) She Is the Little One Whose Greatness Increases
Jolie (jo-LEE) (English/French) She Is Exceedingly Pretty
Jolyon (JO-lee-yun) (English/Latin) He Is Julius Caesar's Relative
Jonah (JO-nuh) (English/Hebrew) He Is a Peaceful Dove
Jonathon (JON-uh-thun) (English) He Is the One to Whom God Gives Much
Jonie (JAHN-nee) (English) She Is God's Graceful Little Messenger
Jonquil (JAHNG-kwil) (English) She Is a Fragrant Jonquil Flower
Jonty (JAHN-tee) (English) He Is the Little One to Whom God Gives Much
Jools (JOOLZ) (English) She Is the Little One Who Is Lovely and Youthful
Jordan (JOR-dun) (English/Hebrew) She Is the Jordan River, Israel

🕮 **Jordyn** (JOR-din) (English/Hebrew) She Is the Jordan River, Israel
Jorie (JOR-ree) (English/Cornish) He Farms the Land
Jorja (JOR-juh) (English) She Farms the Land

Joscelin (JAH-suh-lin) (English) She Is the Gauts
Josepha (jo-SEE-fuh) (English) Her Greatness Increases
Josephina (jo-seh-FEE-nuh) (English) Her Greatness Increases
Josiah (jo-ZYE-yuh) (English/Hebrew) He Is Favored by God
Joss (JAWSS) (English) She Is the Little One Who Is the Germanic Nation of the Gauts
Josslyn (JAHSS-lin) (English) She Is the Germanic Nation of the Gauts
Joye (JOY) (English) She Is Great Rejoicing

🕮 **Jos** (YOHSS) (Dutch) He Is the Little One Whose Greatness Increases
Jozef (YO-zef) (Dutch) His Greatness Increases
Jozefien (yo-zeh-FEEN) (Dutch) Her Greatness Increases
Jozua (YO-zoo-way) (Dutch) His God Is Eternal Salvation
Julia (YOOL-ee-yuh) (Dutch) She Is Beautifully Youthful
Juliana (yoo-lee-AH-nuh) (Dutch) She Is Julius Caesar's Relative
Jurriaan (YOOR-ee-yun) (Dutch) She Farms the Land

🕮 **Judd** (JUHD) (English) He Is the Little One Who Is the River Jordan, Israel
Jude (JOOD) (English/Hebrew) He Is the One Whom We Praise Highly
Judi (JOO-dee) (English/Hebrew) She Is Judea
Jules (JOOLZ) (English/French) He Rules Heaven
Julianna (joo-lee-AN-nuh) (English) She Is Julius Caesar's Relative
Julyan (JOO-lee-yun) (English/Latin) He Is Julius Caesar's Relative
Junior (JOON-yur) (English) He Is the Namesake of His Illustrious Father
Justice (JUSS-tiss) (English) He Is Law and Justice
Justina (jus-STEE-nuh) (English/Latin) She Is Honest and Just
Justine (jus-TEEN) (English/French) She Is Righteous and Just

🕮 **Kacey** (KAY-see) (English/Irish) He Descends from the Watchful One
Kade (KAYD) (English) He Is the Circle of Life
Kaden (KAY-den) (English/Irish) He Descends from the Warrior

Kae (KAY) (English) She Is the Pure-Hearted Little One

Kaelee (KAY-lee) (English) She Is the Pure-Hearted Little One Who Is a Meadow

Kaety (KAY-tee) (English) She Is the Pure-Hearted Little One

Kailee (KAY-lee) (English) She Is the Pure-Hearted Little One Who Is a Meadow

Kailyn (KAY-lin) (English) She Is the Little One Who Is a Pure, Beautiful Lake

Kaitlyn (KAYT-lin) (English/Irish) She Is Pure-Hearted

Kaleb (KAY-leb) (English) He Is Man's Best Friend—A Faithful, Loyal Dog

☙ **Kai** (KYE) (Danish) He Is the Little One Who Is the Great Earth Itself

Karoline (kah-ro-LEE-nuh) (Danish) She Is a Powerful Warrior

Kasper (KAHSS-pur) (Danish) He Holds Priceless Wealth

Katrine (kah-TREE-nuh) (Danish) She Is Pure-Hearted

Keld (KELD) (Danish) He Is a Warrior's Helmet

Kennet (KEN-net) (Danish) He Is Handsome

Kirsten (KEER-sten) (Danish) She Follows Christ

Klemens (KLEM-menz) (Danish) He Is Compassionate

Knut (NOOT) (Danish) He Is a Complicated, Hard-to-Unravel Knot

Kristian (KREESS-chun) (Danish) He Follows Christ

☙ **Kaito** (KYE-toh) (Japanese) He Is the Ocean Encircling the Earth

Kanon (kan-NONE) (Japanese) She Is a Perfect Flower Blooming in Silence

Kaori (KOR-ree) (Japanese) She Is the Fragrance of Flowers

Kasumi (KAS-soo-mee) (Japanese) She Is the Morning Mist

Kazuki (KAHSS-kee) (Japanese) He Is Golden Sunlight

Kiku (KEE-koo) (Japanese) She Is a Fragrant Chrysanthemum

Kiyoko (kee-OH-ko) (Japanese) She Is Wholesome and Natural

Kohaku (ko-HAH-koo) (Japanese) She Is Golden Amber

Kokoro (KO-ko-ro) (Japanese) She Is the Spirit of Life

Kyou (KYO) (Japanese) He Is a Sweet, Golden Apricot

☙ **Kala** (KAH-lah) (Hawaiian) She Is a Royal Princess

Kalani (kah-LAH-nee) (Hawaiian) She Is the Eternal Sky

Kale (KAH-lay) (Hawaiian/English) He Is a Mighty Warrior

Kalea (kah-LAY-yah) (Hawaiian) She Is a Celebration

Kalena (kah-LAY-nah) (Hawaiian/English) She Is Pure-Hearted

Kaleo (kah-LAY-yo) (Hawaiian) He Speaks Clearly

Kanani (kah-NAH-nee) (Hawaiian) She Is Lovely to Behold

Kapena (kah-PAY-nah) (Hawaiian) He Is Our Commander

Keanu (kee-AH-noo) (Hawaiian) He Is the Refreshing Wind

Kekoa (kay-KO-wah) (Hawaiian) He Is Courage Itself

☙ **Kaleb** (KAH-leb) (Dutch) He Is Man's Best Friend—A Faithful, Loyal Dog

Karin (KAH-rin) (Dutch) She Is the Pure-Hearted Little One

Katelijn (kah-tuh-LEEN) (Dutch) She Is Pure-Hearted

Katrien (kaht-REEN) (Dutch) She Is Pure-Hearted

Kees (KAYSS) (Dutch) He Is the Little One Who Is a Cornucopia of Plenty

Kerneels (kur-NEELSS) (Dutch) He Is a Cornucopia of Plenty

Klaas (KLAHSS) (Dutch) He Is Humanity's Triumph

Klasina (klah-SEE-nuh) (Dutch) She Is Humanity's Little Triumph

Kobus (KO-bus) (Dutch) He Is Our Little Magnificent One

Koen (KOON) (Dutch) He Is Our Wise Little Counselor

☙ **Kali** (KAH-lee) (Sanskrit) She Is Magnificently Dark

Kalyani (kahl-YAH-nee) (Sanskrit) She Is Beautiful

Kama (KAH-mah) (Sanskrit) He Is Divine Love

Kamala (kah-MAH-lah) (Sanskrit) She Is a Beautiful Star in Heaven

Kanti (KAHN-tee) (Sanskrit) She Is Beautiful

Kapila (kah-PEE-lah) (Sanskrit) He Is a Beautiful Terra-Cotta Color

Karna (KAR-nah) (Sanskrit) He Hears Everything

Krishna (KRISH-nah) (Sanskrit) He Is a Beautiful Dark Color

Kumara (koo-MAH-rah) (Sanskrit) He Is Blazing Fire

Kumari (koo-MAH-ree) (Sanskrit) She Is Blazing Fire

✎ **Karaugh** (KAIR-ruh) (English) She Is the Pure-Hearted Little One

Karen (KAIR-run) (English) She Is Pure-Hearted

Karena (kuh-REN-nuh) (English) She Is Truly the Pure-Hearted One

Karenza (kuh-REN-zuh) (English) She Is Truly the One Who Is Pure-Hearted

Karina(kuh-REE-nuh) (English) She Is Truly the One Who Is Pure-Hearted

Karissa (kuh-RISS-suh) (English) She Is Elegant and Loving

Karlee (KAR-lee) (English) She Is a Mighty Soldier

Karlene (kar-LEEN) (English) She Is a Mighty Soldier

Karly (KAR-lee) (English) She Is a Mighty Soldier

Karolyn (KAIR-uh-lin) (English) She Is a Mighty Soldier

✎ **Karrie** (KAIR-ree) (English) She Is Our Beloved Warrior

Karyn (KAIR-rin) (English) She Is Pure-Hearted

Karyna (kuh-REE-nuh) (English/Latin) She Is a Ship's Balance and Equilibrium

Kasandra (kah-SAHN-drah) (English/Greek) She Truly Fills Men's Hearts with Love

Kasey (KAY-see) (English/Irish) He Descends from the Watchful One

Kassia (KASS-see-yuh) (English) She Is the Fragrant Cassia-Spice Tree

Kassidy (KASS-sih-dee) (English/Irish) He Descends from the Fleecy-Haired Man

Kassy (KASS-see) (English) She Truly Fills Men's Hearts with Love

Kat (KAT) (English) She Is the Pure-Hearted Little One

Katelin (KAYT-lin) (English/Irish) She Is Pure-Hearted

✎ **Katelyn** (KAYT-lin) (Irish) She Is Pure-Hearted

Katey (KAY-tee) (English) She Is the Pure-Hearted Little One

Katharine (KATH-uh-rin) (English) She Is Pure-Hearted

Katherina (kath-ur-EE-nuh) (English) She Is Pure-Hearted

Kathi (KATH-thee) (English) She Is the Pure-Hearted Little One

Kathleen (kath-LEEN) (English/Irish) She Is Pure-Hearted

Katrina (kuh-TREE-nuh) (English/Scottish) She Is Pure-Hearted

Katriona (kah-tree-OH-nuh) (English/Scottish) She Is Pure-Hearted

Kaycee (KAY-see) (English/Irish) He Descends from the Watchful One

Kayla (KAY-luh) (English/Yiddish) She Is a Laurel Wreath of Victory

✎ **Kayleah** (KAY-lee) (English) She Is the Little Pure-Hearted One Who Is a Meadow

Kayleen (kay-LEEN) (English) She Is the Pure-Hearted Little One

Kaylin (KAY-lin) (English) She Is a Clean, Beautiful Meadow

Keanna (kee-AH-nuh) (English/American) She Is Soft and Silken

Keara (KEER-ruh) (English) She Is as Ebony-Black as the Night Sky

Keaton (KEE-tun) (English) He Is a Sheltered Town

Keefe (KEEF) (English/Irish) He Descends from the Compassionate One

Keegan (KEE-gun) (English/Irish) He Descends from the One Aflame with Greatness

Keeleigh (KEE-lee) (English/Irish) She Descends from the Thin, Handsome Man

Keila (KEE-luh) (English/Yiddish) She Is a Laurel Wreath of Victory

✎ **Kayleigh** (KAY-lee) (English) She Is the Little Pure-Hearted One Who Is a Meadow

Kalisha (kuh-LEE-shuh) (English) She Is Our Little Aristocrat

Kalla (KAL-luh) (English) She Is a Fragrant Calla-Lily

Kalyn (KAY-lin) (English) She Is the Little One Who Is a Pure, Beautiful Lake

Kalysta (kuh-LISS-tuh) (English/Greek) She Is Supremely Lovely

Kam (KAM) (English) He Is the Little One Whose Nose Goes Its Own Way

Kameron (KAM-ur-run) (English/Scottish) Her Nose Goes Its Own Way

Kamryn (KAM-rin) (English/Scottish) Her Nose Goes Its Own Way

Kandace (KAHN-diss) (English/Nubian) She Is the Queen Mother

Kandi (KAN-dee) (English/Nubian) She Is Our Majestic Little Queen

🕮 **Keir** (KEER) (English/Scottish) He Is the Fresh, Wet Earth

Keiran (KEE-run) (English) He Is the Little One with Beautiful Black Hair

Keitha (KEE-thuh) (English/Scottish) She Is as Solid as Hardwood

Kelcey (KEL-see) (English) She Is an Island of Liberty

Kelia (KEEL-ee-yuh) (English/Irish) She Descends from the Thin, Handsome Man

Kelleigh (KEL-lee) (English/Irish) She Is Conquest

Kendal (KEN-dul) (English/Welsh) He Is the Kent River Valley

Kendrick (KEN-drik) (English) He Is Majestic Strength and Courage

Kenelm (KEN-nulm) (English) He Is a Razor-Sharp Helmet of Protection

Kenith (KEN-nith) (English/Scottish) He Is Handsome

🕮 **Kennard** (KEN-nurd) (English) He Is Our Majestic Protector

Kenny (KEN-nee) (English/Scottish) He Is the Extremely Handsome Little One

Kenrick (KEN-rik) (English) He Is Majestic Courage

Kent (KENT) (English) He Is the Great County of Kent, England

Kenton (KEN-tun) (English) He Is a Majestic Town

Kenzie (KEN-zee) (English) She Is the Little One Descended from the Handsome Man

Kerena (kuh-REN-nuh) (English) She Is Truly the One Who Is Pure-Hearted

Kerensa (kuh-REN-zuh) (English/Cornish) She Is Love

Kermit (KUR-mit) (English) He Descends from the Gracious One

Kerrie (KAIR-ree) (English/Irish) She Descends from the Darkly Handsome One

🕮 **Keshaun** (kuh-SHAWN) (English/Irish/American) His God Is Gracious

Kestrel (KES-trull) (English) She Is the Call of a Bird of Prey

Kevyn (KEH-vin) (English/Irish) He Is Compassionate

Keysha (KEE-shuh) (English/American) She Is a Fragrant Spice Tree

Khloe (KLO-wee) (English/Greek) She Is a Beautiful Maiden

Kian (KEE-yun) (English/Irish) He Is Honorable

Kiana (kee-AH-nuh) (English/American) She Is Silky-Soft

Kiara (kee-AH-ruh) (English/Italian) She Is a Range of Lofty Mountains

Kiaran (KEE-rawn) (English/Irish) He Is the Little One Who Is Beautifully Black

Kiefer (KEE-fur) (English/German) He Crafts Magnificent Beer-Kegs

🕮 **Kierra** (kee-AIR-ruh) (English/Italian) She Is a Range of Lofty Mountains

Kiersten (KEER-stun) (English/Danish) She Follows Christ

Kiki (KEE-kee) (English) She Is the Pure-Hearted Little One

Kiley (KYE-lee) (English/Scottish) She Is the Water Between Two Regions

Kimball (KIM-bul) (English) He Is Majestically Courageous

Kimberlee (KIM-bur-lee) (English) She Is the Realm of the Royal Fortress

Kimberlyn (KIM-bur-lin) She Is the Meadow near the Royal Fortress

Kimbra (KIM-bruh) (English) She Is Our Majestic Little Castle

Kimmie (KIM-mee) (English) She Is Our Majestic Little Castle

Kingsley (KINGZ-lee) (English) He Is the Verdant Forests of the King

🕮 **Kipling** (KIP-ling) (English) He Is the Beautiful House of the Renowned Cybbel

Kirk (KURK) (English) He Is a Magnificent Church

Kisha (KEE-shuh) (English/Hebrew) She Is a Fragrant Cassia-Spice Tree

Kit (KIT) (English) She Is the Pure-Hearted Little One

Kizzie (KIZ-zee) (English) She Is the Little One Who Is a Fragrant Cassia-Spice Tree

Kodey (KO-dee) (English/Irish) He Descends from the Wealthy One

Kolby (KOL-bee) (English) He Is Fragrant, Ebony-Black Charcoal

Kole (KOHL) (English) He Is Fragrant, Ebony-Black Charcoal

Kolleen (kah-LEEN) (English/Irish) She Is a Pretty Girl

Konnor (KAHN-nur) (English/Irish) He Is the Master of Wolves

Korbin (KOR-bin) (English) He Is an Ebony-Black Raven

Korey (KOR-ree) (English) He Is a Hillside Teeming with Swift Animals

Korrine (kor-RIN) (English/French) She Is Chaste and Pure

Kortney (KORT-nee) (English) She Is the One with a Cute Nose

Kris (KRISS) (English/Danish) He Is Christ's Little Follower

Krista (KRIS-tuh) (English) She Is Christ's Little Follower

Kristeen (kris-TEEN) (English/French) She Follows Christ

Kristel (KRIS-tul) (English) She Sparkles Like Diamonds

Kristia (KRIS-tee-yuh) (English) She Is Christ's Little Follower

Kristin (KRIS-tin) (English/German) She Follows Christ

Kristina (kris-TEE-nuh) (English) She Follows Christ

Kristopher (KRIS-tuh-fur) (English) He Follows Christ

Krystelle (KRIS-tel) (English) She Sparkles Like Diamonds

Krysten (KRIS-ten) (English/German) She Follows Christ

Krystine (kris-TEEN) (English/French) She Follows Christ

Kurtis (KUR-tiss) (English) His Courtesy Honors Us

Kyla (KYE-luh) (English/Scottish) She Is a Sparkling Waterway

Kylee (KYE-lee) (English/Scottish) She Is the Water Between Two Regions

Kyler (KYE-lur) (English) He Is a Roof-Tiler, as Beautiful as Sparkling Water

Kym (KIM) (English) She Is Our Majestic Little Castle

Lacy (LAY-see) (English) She Is Lassy, France

Ladonna (luh-DAHN-nuh) (English) She Is the World's Most Beautiful Lady

Lagina (luh-JEE-nuh) (English) She Is the Little One Who Is the Noblest Aristocrat of All

Laila (LAY-luh) (English/Arabic) She Is a Darkly Beautiful Evening

Lainey (LAY-nee) (English) She Is the Little Shining Torch

Laird (LAIRD) (English/Scottish) He Possesses Great Amounts of Land

Lakeisha (luh-KEE-shuh) (English/American) She Is a Fragrant Spice Tree

Lallie (LAL-lee) (English) She Is the Little One Who Giggles Beautifully

Lalo (LAH-lo) (Spanish) He Is Our Wealthy Little Protector

Lamont (luh-MAHNT) (English/Scottish) He Is a Righteous Law-Enforcer

Lana (LAH-nuh) (English/Russian) She Is Radiance

Laivan (luh-VAHN) (American) She Is the Magnificent Yew Tree

LaShawn (luh-SHAWN) (American) Her God Is Gracious

Laura (lah-OO-rah) (Spanish) She Is a Laurel Wreath of Victory

Lauren (LOR-run) (English) She Is a Laurel Wreath of Victory

Laurence (LOR-runss) (English) He Is a Laurel Wreath of Victory

Laurita (lah-oo-REE-tah) (Spanish) She Is Our Little Laurel Wreath of Victory

Layne (LAYN) (English) She Is the Friendly One Who Lives by the Lane

Leonard (LEN-nurd) (English) He Is a Noble Lion

Leonardo (lee-oh-NAR-doh) (Italian) He Is a Noble Lion

Liam (LEE-yum) (Irish) He Is Our Little Protector

Lina (LEE-nah) (Arabic) She Is Our Beautiful Palm Tree

Lukas (LOO-kus) (German) He Is Lucania, Italy

Lance (LANSS) (English) He Is the Good Earth

Landon (LAN-dun) (English) He Dwells Beside the Peaceful Lane

Lane (LAYN) (English) He Is the Friendly One Who Lives by the Peaceful Lane

Laney (LAY-nee) (English) She Is the Friendly One Who Lives by the Peaceful Lane

Lanford (LAN-furd) (English) He Is the Long, Narrow Crossing-Place

Lanny (LAN-nee) (English) He Is the Little One Who Is the Good Earth

Lara (LAR-ruh) (English/Latin) She Is a Laurel Wreath of Victory

Laraine (luh-RAYN) (English/French) She Is Lorraine, France

Larissa (luh-RIS-suh) (English/Greek) She Is Cheerful

Lark (LARK) (English) She Is a Sweetly Singing Lark

🖉 **Larrie** (LAIR-ree) (English) He Is the Little One Who Is a Laurel Wreath of Victory

Laryn (LAHR-rin) (English) She Is a Laurel Wreath of Victory

Lashay (luh-SHAY) (English) She Is Truly the One Who Is Destined

Lashonda (luh-SHAHN-duh) (English) She Is the Gracious One Who Is a Powerful Weapon

Latanya (luh-TAHN-yuh) (English) She Is Our Little Saint

Latisha (luh-TIH-shuh) (English/Spanish) She Is Cheerfulness

Lauraine (luh-RAYN) (English/French) She Is Lorraine, France

Laureen (lo-REEN) (English) She Is Our Little Laurel Wreath of Victory

Laurelle (lo-REL) (English) She Is a Laurel Wreath of Victory

Laurena (lo-REE-nuh) (English) She Is Truly the One Who Is a Laurel Wreath of Victory

🖉 **Lawson** (LAW-sun) (English) He Descends from the One Who Is a Laurel Wreath of Victory

Layton (LAY-tun) (English) He Is a Town Filled with Fragrant Leeks

Laz (LAZ) (English) He Is the Little One Who Is a Laurel Wreath of Victory

Leah (LEE-yuh) (English/Hebrew) She Is Humanity's Queen

Leandra (lee-AN-druh) (English/Greek) She Is the Lioness Who Brings Liberty

Leann (lee-YANN) (English) She Is a Beautiful Meadow, Filled with Divine Grace

Leanna (lee-AN-nuh) (English) She Is Truly a Beautiful Meadow, Filled with Divine Grace

Leanora (le-uh-NO-ruh) (English/Italian) She Is Aliénor, France

Leatrice (LEE-uh-triss) (English) She Is the Great Voyager Who Is the Queen of All

Lecia (LEE-shuh) (English) She Is Our Little Aristocrat

🖉 **Leandro** (lee-AN-dro) (Spanish/Greek) He Is the Lion-Hearted Man Who Brings Liberty

Leocadia (lee-oh-KAH-dee-yah) (Spanish/Greek) She Is Brilliant and Pure

Leocadio (lee-oh-KAH-dee-yo) (Spanish/Greek) He Is Brilliant and Pure

Leoncio (lee-AHN-see-yo) (Spanish) He Is a Noble Lion

Leopoldo (lay-oh-POL-doh) (Spanish) He Is Humanity's Courage and Boldness

Leticia (leh-TEE-shah) (Spanish) She Is Cheerfulness

Liliana (lee-lee-AH-nah) (Spanish) She Is the Little One Whose God Supplies All

Lino (LEE-no) (Spanish/Greek) He Is the Little One Who Is Golden Flax in the Fields

Loida (lo-EE-dah) (Spanish/Greek) She Is Greatly Desired

Lolita (lo-LEE-tah) (Spanish) She Is the Little One Who Is Greatly Desired

🖉 **Leesa** (LEE-suh) (English) Her God Is Abundance

Leighton (LAY-tun) (English) He Is a Town Filled with Fragrant Leeks

Leilah (LAY-luh) (English/Arabic) She Is a Darkly Beautiful Evening

Lela (LEE-luh) (English/Arabic) She Is a Darkly Beautiful Evening

Lemoine (luh-MOYN) (English/French) He Is a Blessed Priest

Lena (LEE-nuh) (English/German) She Is Our Radiant Little Torch

Lenard (LEH-nurd) (English) He Is a Noble Lion

Lennie (LEN-nee) (English) He Is Our Noble Little Lion

Lennox (LEH-nux) (English/Scottish) He Is the Region of Lennox, Scotland

Lenora (luh-NO-ruh) (English) She Is the Little One Who Is Aliénor, France

🖉 **Lenore** (luh-NOR) (English) She Is the Little One Who Is Aliénor, France

Lenox (LEH-nux) (English/Scottish) He Is the Region of Lennox, Scotland

Leola (lee-OH-luh) (English) She Is a Noble Lioness

Leone (lee-YONE) (English/Italian) She Is a Noble Lioness

Leontyne (LEE-un-teen) (English/French) She Is a Noble Lioness

Leopold (lee-uh-POLD) (English/Dutch) He Is Humanity's Courage and Boldness

Leroi (LEE-roy) (English/French) He Is a Majestic King

Lesia (LEE-shuh) (English) She Is Our Little Aristocrat

Lesleigh (LESS-lee) (English/Scottish) She Is a Fragrant Garden of Holly

Lessie (LESS-see) (English/Scottish) She Is the Little One Who Is a Fragrant Garden of Holly

🦋 **Leta** (LEE-tuh) (English/Latin) She Rejoices

Letha (LEE-thuh) (English) She Is the Little Honest One

Letitia (luh-TIH-shuh) (English) She Is Cheerfulness

Lettice (let-TEESS) (English) She Is Cheerfulness

Lettie (LET-tee) (English) She Is the Little One Who Is Cheerfulness

Lewin (LOO-win) (English) He Is a Trusted Companion

Lexa (LEX-suh) (English) She Is the Little One Who Protects Humanity

Lexia (LEX-ee-yuh) (English) She Is Humanity's Little Protector

Lexie (LEX-see) (English) She Is the Little One Who Protects Humanity

Lexine (lex-SEEN) (English) She Is the Little One Who Protects Humanity

🦋 **Lexus** (LEX-suss) (English) He Is Humanity's Little Protector

Lexy (LEX-see) (English) She Is the Little One Who Protects Humanity

Leyla (LAY-luh) (English/Arabic) She Is a Beautiful Dark Night

Leyton (LAY-tun) (English) He Is a Town Filled with Fragrant Leeks

Liana (lee-AN-nuh) (English) She Is Truly a Divinely Beautiful Meadow

Lianne (lee-YAN) (English) She Is the Meadow Filled with God's Grace

Libby (LIB-bee) (English) She Is the Little One Whose God Supplies All

Liberty (LIH-bur-tee) (English) She Is Glorious Liberty

Liddy (LID-dee) (English) She Is the Little One Who Is Lydia

Lilian (LIL-ee-yun) (English) She Is the Little One Favored by God

🦋 **Lies** (LEESS) (Dutch) She Is the Little One Favored by God

Liesbeth (leez-BET) (Dutch) Her God Is Abundance

Liesje (LEE-shuh) (Dutch) She Demonstrates God's Abundance

Lieve (LEEV) (Dutch) She Is the Little One Who Has All of God's Love

Lieven (LEE-ven) (Dutch) She Is a Trusted Companion

Lijsbeth (LEESS-bet) (Dutch) Her God Is Abundance

Lisanne (leess-AHN) (Dutch) Her God Is Abundance and Grace

Liselot (leess-LO) (Dutch) She Is a Dear Little Warrior Whose God Is Generous

Lodewijk (LOH-duh-week) (Dutch) He Is a Renowned Warrior

Loes (LOOSS) (Dutch) She Is a Renowned Warrior

🦋 **Lievin** (LEE-vin) (Dutch) She Is a Trusted Companion

Lotte (LAHT-tee) (Dutch) She Is a Beloved Little Warrior

Louis (LOO-vee) (Dutch) He Is a Renowned Warrior

Louise (loo-VEESS) (Dutch) She Is a Renowned Warrior

Lourens (LOR-renz) (Dutch) She Is a Laurel Wreath of Victory

Lowie (LO-vee) (Dutch) He Is Our Renowned Little Warrior

Lucas (LOO-ee-kahss) (Dutch) He Is Lucania, Italy

Ludger (LUH-jur) (Dutch) He Is the Armada and the Armory of the People

Ludo (LOO-doh) (Dutch) He Is Our Renowned Little Warrior

Luuk (LOO-week) (Dutch) He Is Lucania, Italy

🦋 **Liliana** (lil-lee-AH-nuh) (English) She Is the Little One Favored by God

Lilibeth (LIL-uh-beth) (English) She Demonstrates God's Abundance

Lillia (LIL-ee-yuh) (English) She Demonstrates God's Abundance
Lillie (LIL-lee) (English) She Is a Fragrant Lily
Lina (LEE-nuh) (Arabic) She Is a Gently Swaying Palm Tree
Linden (LIN-dun) (English) He Is a Fragrant Lime Tree on a Lofty Hill
Lindsie (LIN-zee) (English/Scottish) She Is an Island in Lincolnshire, England
Lindy (LIN-dee) (English/German) He Is the Little One Who Is the Lime-Tree Mountain
Linette (lih-NET) (English) She Is Worshipped
Linford (LIN-furd) (English) He Is the Crossing-Place Where Lime Trees Are Found

🕊 **Linnaea** (lin-NAY-yuh) (English/Swedish) She Is a Fragrant Linnea Flower
Linnet (lih-NET) (English) She Is Worshipped
Linnie (LIN-nee) (English) She Is the Little One Who Is Exceptionally Beautiful
Linsay (LIN-zee) (English/Scottish) She Is an Island in Lincolnshire, England
Linton (LIN-tun) (English) He Is a Town Where Lime Trees Are Found
Linwood (LIN-wood) (English) He Is a Forest of Lime Trees
Lisha (LEE-shuh) (English) She Is the Little One Favored by God
Lissa (LISS-suh) (English) She Is the Busy Little Honeybee
Lita (LEE-tuh) (English) She Is the Little One Who Is Honey-Sweet
Livia (LIV-ee-yuh) (English/Latin) She Is the Beautiful Color Blue

🕊 **Livvy** (LIV-vee) (English) She Is the Little One Who Is a Fragrant Olive Tree
Lizbeth (LIZ-beth) (English) She Demonstrates God's Abundance
Lizette (lee-ZET) (English/French) She Demonstrates God's Abundance
Lockie (LAH-kee) (English) He Is the Little One Who Is the Great Land of the Lochs (Lakes)
Logan (LO-gun) (English/Scottish) He Is a Little Valley
Lola (LO-luh) (English/Spanish) She Is the Little One Who Understands Sorrow
Lolicia (lo-LEE-shuh) (English/Spanish) She Is the Little One Who Understands Sorrow
Lon (LAHN) (English/Italian) He Is the Little Aristocrat Who Is Well-Prepared

Lonny (LAHN-nee) (English) He Is the Little Aristocrat Who Is Well-Prepared
Loraine (lor-RAIN) (English/French) She Is Lorraine, France

🕊 **Lou** (LOO) (English) He Is the Renowned Little Warrior
Louella (loo-EL-luh) (English) She Is a Renowned Warrior and a Radiant Torch
Louie (LOO-wee) (English) He Is the Renowned Little Warrior
Lovell (LUH-vul) (English) He Is a Mighty Little Wolf
Lowell (LO-wul) (English) He Is a Mighty Little Wolf
Loyd (LOYD) (English/Welsh) He Is Gray and Wise
Luana (loo-AN-nuh) (English) She Is a Graceful and Renowned Little Warrior
Luann (English) She Is a Graceful and Renowned Little Warrior
Lucas (LOO-kuss) (English/Latin) He Is Lucania, Italy
Lucetta (loo-SET-tuh) (English) She Is the Little One Who Is Radiant Light

🕊 **Lucia** (loo-SEE-yuh) (English/Italian) She Is Radiance
Lucian (LOO-shun) (English/Latin) He Is Radiance
Lucile (loo-SEEL) (English/French) She Is Radiance
Lucius (LOO-shuss) (English/Latin) He Is Radiance
Lucky (LUHK-kee) (English) He Is Fortunate
Luella (loo-EL-luh) (English) She Is a Renowned Warrior and a Radiant Torch
Lula (LOO-luh) (English) She Is the Renowned Little Warrior
Luvenia (loo-VEEN-yuh) (English) She Is Pure-Hearted
Lyall (LYE-yul) (English/Scottish) He Is a Mighty Wolf
Lyle (LYE-yul) (English/French) He Is a Beautiful Island

🕊 **Maarten** (MAHR-ten) (Dutch) He Is Powerfully Male
Maartje (MAHR-tee-yuh) (Dutch) She Is as Powerful as any Male
Maas (MAHSS) (Dutch) He Is a Precious Little Twin
Machteld (mahk-TELD) (Dutch) She Is a Powerful Warrior

Maikel (MAH-ee-kel) (Dutch) He Resembles God

Manfred (MAHN-fred) (Dutch) He Is a Powerful, Handsome Male

Mannes (MAHN-ness) (Dutch) He Is an Aggressive Little Warrior

Margareta (mahr-gah-REH-tuh) (Dutch) She Is Our Priceless Little Pearl

Margriet (mahr-GREET) (Dutch) She Is a Priceless Pearl

Marieke (mah-REE-kuh) (Dutch) She Is Our Little Beloved One

🖉 **Mabella** (may-BEL-luh) (English) She Is the Adorable Little One

Mabelle (MAY-bel) (English) She Is the Adorable Little One

Mable (MAY-bul) (English) She Is the Adorable Little One

Macie (MAY-see) (English) She Is the Land of the Mighty, Tireless Feet

Mack (MAK) (English/Irish) He Is Our Powerful Descendant

Mackenzie (muh-KEN-zee) (English/Irish) She Descends from the Handsome Man

Madalyn (MAD-uh-lin) (English/Hebrew) She Is Magdala, Israel

Maddie (MAD-dee) (English/Hebrew) She Is Magdala, Israel

Maddison (MAD-dih-sun) (English) She Descends from the Powerful Warrior

Maddox (MAD-dux) (English/Welsh) He Descends from the Fortunate One

🖉 **Madelaine** (MAD-uh-layn) (English/Hebrew) She Is Magdala, Israel

Madelina (mad-uh-LEE-nuh) (English/Hebrew) She Is Magdala, Israel

Madeline (MAD-uh-lyne) (English/Hebrew) She Is Magdala, Israel

Madge (MADJ) (English) She Is Our Priceless Little Pearl

Madisyn (MAD-dih-sin) (English) She Descends from the Powerful Warrior

Maegan (MAY-gun) (English/Welsh) She Is Our Priceless Little Pearl

Magdalen (MAG-duh-len) (English/Hebrew) She Is Magdala, Israel

Mahalia (muh-HAYL-yuh) (English/Hebrew) She Is Gentle and Delicate

Makayla (muh-KAY-luh) (English) She Resembles God

Makenna (muh-KEN-nuh) (English/Irish) He Is Created in Heat and Flames

🖉 **Makenzie** (muh-KEN-zee) (English/Irish) She Descends from the Handsome Man

Malakai (MAL-ah-kye) (English/Hebrew) He Is Our Spiritual Guardian

Malandra (muh-LAN-druh) (English) She Is as Powerful as any Male

Malcom (MAL-kum) (English/Scottish) He Obeys the Teachings of Saint Columba

Maleah (muh-LEE-yuh) (English/Hawaiian) She Is Love

Malinda (muh-LIN-duh) (English) She Is Darkly Beautiful

Malone (muh-LONE) (English) He Descends from the Follower of Saint John

Malvina (mal-VEE-nuh) (English) Her Face Is Unwrinkled and Beautiful

Mandi (MAN-dee) (English) She Is the Little One Who Is Worthy of Love

Manny (MAN-nee) (English) He Is the Little One Whose God Is Ever-Present

🖉 **Mami** (MAH-mee) (Japanese) She Is the Golden Flax in the Fields

Manami (MAH-nuh-mee) (Japanese) She Is the Beautiful Sea

Mao (MAH-oh) (Japanese) She Is a Fragrant Cherry Blossom

Mayu (MAH-yoo) (Japanese) She Is the Dark, Peaceful Night

Mei (MAY) (Japanese) She Is a Wholesome, Delicious Bean Sprout

Michi (MEE-chee) (Japanese) He Is a Bright Path through the Wilderness

Midori (mih-DOR-ree) (Japanese) She Is the Verdant Green of the Forest

Miku (MEE-koo) (Japanese) She Is the Heavenly Blue Sky

Mio (MEE-yoh) (Japanese) She Is a Fragrant Cherry Blossom

Misaki (mih-SAH-kee) (Japanese) She Is a Fragrant Flower

🖉 **Mansel** (man-SEL) (English) He Is Le Mans, France

Manuel (MAN-yoo-wul) (English/German) He Is the Little One Whose God Is Ever-Present

Maralyn (MAIR-uh-lin) (English) She Is a Beautiful Lake of Love

Marcelyn (MAR-suh-lin) (English) She Is the Little One Who Is as Powerful as any Male

Marcia (MAR-shuh) (English/Latin) She Is as Powerful as any male

Marcie (MAR-see) (English) She Is the Little One Who Is as Powerful as any male

Maree (MAIR-ree) (English) She Is Love

Margaretta (mar-guh-RET-tuh) (English/Latin) She Is a Priceless Pearl

Margie (MAR-jee) (English) She Is Our Priceless Little Pearl

Maribella (mair-ee-BEL-luh) (English/Latin) She Is a Warrior and Sweet Love Itself

🕭 **Marianna** (mair-ee-AN-nuh) (English) She Is the Graceful, Beloved One

Mariel (MAIR-ee-yul) (English) She Is Our Little Beloved One

Marinda (muh-RIN-duh) (English) She Is Worthy of Love and Respect

Marisa (muh-RISS-suh) (English/Spanish) She Is the Renowned Warrior of Love

Marje (MARJ) (English) She Is Our Priceless Little Pearl

Marjory (MAR-jur-ree) (English) She Is a Priceless Pearl

Marlee (MAR-lee) (English) He Is a Peaceful Forest

Marlena (mar-LEE-nuh) (English) She Is Love

Marlin (MAR-lin) (English/Welsh) He Is a Mighty Fortress by the Sea

Marlowe (MAR-loh) (English) He Is a Lake of Flowing Water

🕭 **Marijana** (mah-ree-YAH-nah) (Croatian) She Is as Powerful as any male

Marko (MAHR-ko) (Croatian) He Is Powerfully Male

Martina (mar-TEE-nah) (Croatian) She Is as Powerful as any male

Matija (mah-TEE-yah) (Croatian) She Is God's Divine Gift

Miho (MEE-ho) (Croatian) He Is God's Little Disciple

Milena (mil-LAY-nah) (Croatian) She Is Graceful

Milica (mil-EE-kah) (Croatian) She Is Graceful

Milos (MEE-lohsh) (Croatian) He Is the Little One Whom God Honors

Mirna (MEER-nah) (Croatian) She Is Peace

Mojca (MOHSH-kah) (Croatian) She Is Our Little Beloved One

🕭 **Marly** (MAR-lee) (English) He Is a Peaceful Forest

Marlyn (MAR-lin) (English/Welsh) He Is a Mighty Fortress by the Sea

Marmaduke (MAR-muh-DOOK) (English) He Follows Saint Maedoc

Marnie (MAR-nee) (English) She Is the Blue Ocean

Marquis (MAR-kiss) (English) He Is an Aristocratic Marquis

Marquita (mar-KEE-tuh) (English) She Is an Aristocratic Marquise

Marshal (MAR-shul) (English) He Is a Law-Enforcer Riding a Horse

Martie (MAR-tee) (English) He Is the Little One Who Is a Powerful Male

Martina (mar-TEE-nuh) (English/Latin) She Is as Powerful as any male

Marva (MAR-vuh) (English) She Is Glorious to the Marrow of Her Bones

🕭 **Marvyn** (MAR-vin) (English) He Is Glorious to the Marrow of His Bones

Maryann (mair-ee-YAN) (English) She Is the Graceful One Who Is Love Itself

Marybeth (mair-ee-BETH) (English) She Is the Beloved One Whose God Is Abundance

Marylou (mair-ee-LOO) (English) She Is a Lover and a Warrior

Marylyn (MAIR-uh-lin) (English) She Is a Beautiful Lake of Love

Maryvonne (mair-ee-VAHN) (English) She Is the Beloved, Heart-Stopping Yew Tree

Masterman (MAS-tur-mun) (English) He Serves Humanity

Mat (MAT) (English) He Is Our Little Present from God

Mathew (MATH-thyoo) (English/Hebrew) He Is God's Divine Gift

Mathilda (mah-TIL-duh) (English) She Is Powerful in War

🕭 **Mathilde** (mah-TEEL-duh) (Dutch) She Is Powerful in War

Matthijs (mah-TYE-yus) (Dutch) He Is God's Divine Gift

Maximiliaan (mahks-ee-MEEL-yahn) (Dutch) He Is Supreme

Mees (MEESS) (Dutch) He Is the Little One with a Furrowed Brow

Meike (MYE-kuh) (Dutch) She Is Our Little Beloved One

Meindert (MAYN-dairt) (Dutch) She Is Powerfully Courageous

Meine (MYE-nuh) (Dutch) He Is the Little One Who Is Forceful

Menno (MEN-no) (Dutch) He Is the Little One Who Is Magnificent Power

Mieke (MEE-kuh) (Dutch) She Is Our Little Beloved One

Miep (MEEP) (Dutch) She Is Our Little Beloved One

🐝 **Mattie** (MAT-tee) (English) He Is God's Divine Gift

Maudie (MAW-dee) (English) She Is Our Powerful Little Warrior

Maura (MAHR-ruh) (English/Irish) She Is Love

Maurene (mo-REEN) (English/Irish) She Is Our Little Beloved One

Max (MAX) (English/German) He Is the Little One Who Is Supreme

Maxine (max-SEEN) (English) She Is Supreme

Maxwell (MAX-wel) (English) He Is the Water-Well Owned by Mack

Maybelle (MAY-bel) (English) She Is the Adorable Little One

Maybelline (MAY-buh-leen) (English) She Is the Adorable Little One

Mayme (MAY-mee) (English) She Is the Beloved One Who Is Love Itself

🐝 **Maynard** (MAY-nurd) (English) He Is Fearless and All-Powerful

Mayra (MYE-ruh) (English) She Is the Fragrant Myrrh Tree

Mayson (MAY-sun) (English) He Is a Skilled Stonecutter

Meade (MEED) (English) He Is Sweet Honey-Liquor

Meadow (MEH-doh) (English) She Is a Fragrant Meadow

Meaghan (MAY-gun) (English/Welsh) She Is Our Priceless Little Pearl

Melantha (mel-AN-thuh) (English/Greek) She Is a Dark, Lovely Blossom

Melany (MEL-ah-nee) (German) She Is Darkly Beautiful

Melicent (MEL-lih-sent) (English) She Is a Tireless, Powerful Worker

Melina (meh-LEE-nuh) (English) She Is the Dark Little One Whose Greatness Increases

🐝 **Mellony** (MEL-luh-nee) (English) She Is Darkly Beautiful

Melva (MEL-vuh) (English) She Is a Good Companion and Advisor

Melville (MEL-vil) (English) He Is a Rough-and-Tumble Frontier Town

Melvyn (MEL-vin) (English) He Is a Good Companion and Advisor

Melyssa (meh-LIS-sah) (Greek) She Is a Busy Honeybee

Mercia (MUR-see-yuh) (English) She Is Compassionate Forgiveness

Mercy (MUR-see) (English) She Is Compassionate Forgiveness

Merideth (MAIR-ih-deth) (English/Welsh) She Is a Powerful Conqueror

Meriel (MAIR-ee-yuhl) (English/Irish) She Is the Shining Ocean

Merilyn (MAIR-uh-lin) (English) She Is a Beautiful Lake of Love

🐝 **Merit** (MEH-rit) (English) She Is Great Worthiness and Merit

Merla (MUR-luh) (English) She Is the Shimmering Ocean

Merletta (mur-LET-tuh) (English) She Is the Little One Who Is the Shimmering Ocean

Merlyn (MUR-lin) (English/Welsh) He Is a Mighty Castle by the Ocean

Merrick (MAIR-rik) (English) He Is Bold and Renowned

Merrilyn (MAIR-uh-lin) (English) She Is a Beautiful Lake of Love

Merton (MUR-tun) (English) He Is a Beautiful Town by the Sea

Merv (MURV) (English) He Is the Little One Who Is Famed to the Marrow of His Bones

Mervin (MUR-vin) (English) He Is the Little One Who Is Famed to the Marrow of His Bones

Meryl (MEH-ril) (English) He Is the Bright Ocean

🐝 **Mia** (MEE-yuh) (English/Italian) She Is Our Little Beloved One

Micah (MYE-kuh) (English/Hebrew) He Resembles God

Michaela (mih-KAY-luh) (English) She Resembles God

Michelle (mih-SHEL) (English/French) She Resembles God

Michelyne (MIH-shul-lin) (English/French) She Is the Little One Who Resembles God

Micky (MIK-kee) (English) He Is God's Little Disciple

Midge (MIDJ) (English) She Is Our Priceless Little Pearl

Milburn (MIL-burn) (English) He Is a River near a Water-Mill

Milford (MIL-furd) (English) He Is a Crossing-Place near a Water-Mill

Mina (MEE-nuh) (English/German) She Is Our Little Protector

🐝 **Minta** (MIN-tuh) (English/Italian) She Is Our Little Protector

Minty (MIN-tee) (English/Italian) She Is Our Little Protector

Mirabelle (MEER-uh-bel) (English) She Is Absolutely Marvelous

Miranda (mur-AN-duh) (English) She Is Absolutely Marvelous

Missie (MISS-see) (English) She Is a Busy Little Honeybee

Mitch (MITCH) (English) He Is God's Little Disciple

Moe (MO) (English) He Is the Little Moor with a Dark Complexion

Mollie (MAHL-lee) (English) She Is Our Little Beloved One

Monday (MUN-day) (English) She Is Monday, the Start of a New Week

Monna (MOHN-nuh) (English/Italian) She Is My Revered Little Lady

🐝 **Montague** (MAHN-tuh-gyoo) (English/French) He Is a Lofty Summit

Monty (MAHN-tee) (English) He Is the Little One Who Is a Mountain of Manly Power

Mordikai (MOR-dih-kye) (English/Hebrew) He Serves God

Moreen (mo-REEN) (English/Irish) She Is Our Little Beloved One

Morgan (MOR-gun) (English/Welsh) She Is the Encircling Ocean

Morgana (mor-GAN-nuh) (English/Welsh) She Is the Encircling Ocean

Moriah (MOR-ee-yuh) (English/Hebrew) She Is Recognized by God

Morley (MOR-lee) (English) He Is a Meadow near the Moors

Morton (MOR-tun) (English) He Is a Town near the Moors

Morty (MOR-tee) (English) He Is the Little One Who Is a Town near the Moors

🐝 **Moss** (MAWSS) (English) He Is the Great Son Who Rescues Us

Murphy (MUR-fee) (English/Irish) He Descends from the Sea-Warrior

Murray (MUR-ree) (English/Scottish) He Is Moray, Scotland

Mya (MYE-yuh) (English/Greek) She Is Love

Myles (MYE-yulz) (English) He Is Graceful

Myra (MYE-ruh) (English) She Is a Fragrant Myrrh Tree

Myranda (meer-AN-duh) (English) She Is Absolutely Marvelous

Myron (MYE-run) (English/Greek) He Is a Fragrant Myrrh Tree

Myrtie (MUR-tee) (English) She Is a Fragrant Little Myrrh Tree

Myrtle (MUR-tul) (English) She Is a Fragrant Myrtle Tree

🐝 **Nana** (NAH-nuh) (Japanese) She Is a Garden of Wholesome Vegetables

Nanami (nah-NAH-mee) (Japanese) She Is the Seven Oceans of the World

Naoki (nah-OH-kee) (Japanese) He Is a Majestic Forest Tree

Naomi (nah-OH-mee) (Japanese) She Is as Pure as Nature Itself

Natsuki (NOT-skee) (Japanese) She Is a Garden of Wholesome Vegetables

Natsumi (NOT-soo-may) (Japanese) She Is the Warm Summer Season

Noa (NO-wah) (Japanese) She Is the Compassion of the Universe

Noboru (NO-buh-roo) (Japanese) He Is as Exalted as the Mountains

Nobu (NO-boo) (Japanese) He Is as Exalted as the Mountains

Nori (NOR-ree) (Japanese) He Is the Immutable Laws of Nature

🐝 **Nanette** (nan-NET) (English/French) She Is the Little One Who Shimmers with Sunlight

Nannie (NAN-nee) (English) She Is the Graceful Little One

Naomi (nay-OH-mee) (English) She Is Cheerfulness

Narelle (nuh-REL) (English) She Is a Majestic Queen

Nash (NASH) (English) He Is a Beautiful Ash Tree

Natalee (NAT-uh-lee) (English/French) She Is Christmas Day

Natasha (nuh-TAH-shuh) (English/Russian) She Is the Little One Who Is Christmas Day

Nate (NAYT) (English/Hebrew) He Is the Generous Little One

Natisha (nuh-TEE-shuh) (English/American) She Is the Little One Who Is Christmas Day

Neely (NEE-lee) (English/Scottish) He Descends from the Singing Bard

🐾 **Nelda** (NEL-duh) (English) She Is Truly the One Who Is a Radiant Torch

Nella (NEL-luh) (English) She Is Truly the One Who Is a Radiant Torch

Nelle (NEL-lee) (English) She Is Our Radiant Little Torch

Nena (NEE-nuh) (English/Italian) She Is a Blossoming Little Flower

Nessa (NES-suh) (English) She Is a Graceful Friend Whose God Is Life

Netta (NET-tuh) (English) She Is the Little One Whose God Is Truly Gracious

Nevada (nuh-VAD-duh) (English/Spanish) She Is a Lofty White Mountain

Nevaeh (neh-VAY-yuh) (English/American) Anyway You Look at It, She Is Heaven

Nevil (NEV-vul) (English) He Is a Shining New City

Nichola (NIK-oh-luh) (English) She Is Humanity's Triumph

🐾 **Nichole** (nih-KOHL) (English/French) She Is Humanity's Triumph

Nickolas (NIK-oh-lus) (English) He Is Humanity's Triumph

Nicola (NIK-oh-luh) (English/Italian) She Is Humanity's Triumph

Nidia (NIH-dee-yuh) (English/Latin) She Is a Safe, Comfortable Nest

Nikeisha (nih-KEE-shuh) (English/Greek) She Is a Victory, a Fragrant Cassia-Spice Tree

Nina (NEE-nuh) (English/Italian) She Is Our Little Blossoming Flower

Noah (NO-wuh) (English/Hebrew) He Is Blessed Tranquility

Noble (NO-bul) (English) He Is Aristocratic

Noelene (no-el-LEEN) (English) She Is the Little One Who Is Christmas Day

Nola (NO-luh) (English) She Is the Little One Who Honors French Naturalist Pierre Magnol

🐾 **Nolan** (NO-lun) (English/Irish) He Descends from the Great Conqueror

Nolene (no-LEEN) (English) She Honors French Naturalist Pierre Magnol

Noll (NAHL) (English) He Is the Little One Who Is a Fragrant Olive Tree

Nonie (NO-nee) (English) She Is the Little One Who Is Honor Itself

Norah (NO-ruh) (English/Irish) She Is the Little One Who Is Honor Itself

Noreen (no-REEN) (English) She Is the Little One Who Is Honor Itself

Norm (NORM) (English) He Is the Little One Who Is a Norse Viking

Norma (NOR-muh) (English/Latin) She Rules Absolutely

Normand (NOR-mund) (English) He Is a Norse Viking

Norwood (NOR-wood) (English) He Is the Lovely Northern Woodlands

🐾 **Ocean** (OH-shuhn) (English) He Is the Blue Ocean

Odelia (oh-DEL-yuh) (English) She Is Prosperity

Odell (oh-DEL) (English) He Is a Beautiful Blue Dye

Odetta (oh-DET-tuh) (English) She Is Prosperity

Ogden (AHG-den) (English) He Is a Valley Filled with Mighty Oaks

Oli (AH-lee) (English) He Is the Little One Who Is a Fragrant Olive Tree

Olyvia (oh-LIV-ee-yuh) (English) She Is a Fragrant Olive Tree

Oneida (oh-NYE-duh) (English/Oneida) She Is a Great Standing Rock

Opaline (oh-puh-LEEN) (English) She Is a Truly Priceless Opal

Ora (OH-ruh) (English/Latin) She Observes Sacred Rituals

🐾 **Octavia** (ahk-TAH-vee-yah) (Spanish/Latin) She Is Eighth

Odalis (oh-dah-LEESS) (Spanish) She Is Rich and Successful

Ofelia (oh-FAY-lee-yah) (Spanish/Greek) She Helps Us All

Olegario (oh-leh-GAH-ree-yo) (Spanish) She Is a Razor-Sharp Weapon of War

Olimpia (oh-LEEM-pee-yah) (Spanish/Greek) She Is the Lofty Summit of the Immortals

Olivia (oh-LEE-vee-yah) (Spanish) She Is a Fragrant Olive Tree

Orfeo (or-FAY-yo) (Spanish/Greek) He Is the Evening

Oscar (OHSS-kar) (Spanish) He Loves to Hunt Deer

Osvaldo (ohss-VAHL-doh) (Spanish) His God Is the Ruler of All

Ovidio (oh-VEE-dee-yo) (Spanish) He Is a Gentle, Harmless Sheep

🐾 **Oralee** (or-uh-LEE) (English) She Is Pure Gold

Orinda (or-IN-duh) (English) She Is Pure Gold

Ormond (OR-mund) (English/Irish) He Descends from the Fiery Red-Haired One

Orpha (OR-fuh) (English) She Has a Beautiful Nape of the Neck

Orrell (OR-rul) (English) He Is a Hillside Filled with Precious Ore

Orval (OR-vul) (English) He Is the Golden City

Osbert (AHZ-burt) (English) He Is Divinely Radiant

Osborn (AHZ-born) (English) He Is a Godlike Bear of a Man

Osmond (AHZ-mund) (English) He Is Our Divine Guardian

Oswin (AHZ-win) (English) He Is Our Divine Companion

🐾 **Paca** (PAH-kah) (Spanish) She Is the Little One Who Is the Nation of France

Palmira (pahl-MEE-rah) (Spanish) She Journeys Far to Seek the Truth

Palmiro (pahl-MEE-ro) (Spanish) He Journeys Far to Seek the Truth

Paloma (pah-LO-mah) (Spanish) She Is a Peaceful Dove

Pancho (PAHN-cho) (Spanish) He Is the Little One Who Is the Nation of France

Paquita (pah-KEE-tah) (Spanish) She Is the Little One Who Is the Nation of France

Paquito (pah-KEE-toh) (Spanish) He Is the Little One Who Is the Nation of France

Pepe (PAY-pay) (Spanish) He Is the Little One Whose Greatness Increases

Pepito (pay-PEE-toh) (Spanish) His Greatness Increases

Pilar (pee-LAHR) (Spanish) She Is a Pillar of Strength

🐾 **Pamila** (PAM-il-luh) (English) She Is Sweetness

Pancras (PAN-kruss) (English) He Demonstrates God's Glory

Parker (PAR-kur) (English) He Protects Nature

Parnel (par-NEL) (English) He Is the Beautiful Countryside

Parris (PAIR-riss) (English) She Is Paris, France

Patience (PAY-shunss) (English) She Is Patience Itself

Patricia (puh-TRIH-shuh) (English) She Is Aristocratic

Patrick (PAT-rik) (English) He Is Aristocratic

Pauleen (paw-LEEN) (English) She Demonstrates Humility

Pauletta (paw-LET-tuh) (English) She Is the Little One Who Demonstrates Humility

🐾 **Paulie** (PAW-lee) (English) He Is the Little One Who Demonstrates Humility

Pauline (paw-LEEN) (English) She Demonstrates Humility

Paxton (PAX-tun) (English) He Is the Town Ruled by Poecc

Payton (PAY-tun) (English) He Is the Town Ruled by Peoga

Pearce (PEERSS) (English) He Is Rock-Solid

Pearle (PURL) (English) She Is a Priceless Pearl

Peers (PEERZ) (English) He Is Rock-Solid

Peg (PEG) (English) She Is Our Priceless Little Pearl

Peggy (PEG-ghee) (English) She Is Our Priceless Little Pearl

Pen (PEN) (English) She Is the Little One Who Weaves Thread

🐾 **Pene** (PEN-nee) (English) She Is the Little One Who Weaves Threads

Perce (PUR-see) (English) He Is Perci, France

Percival (PUR-sih-vul) (English/Welsh) He Ventures Far into the Valley

Perlie (PUR-lee) (English) She Is a Priceless Pearl

Permelia (pur-MEEL-yuh) (English) She Is Sweetness

Pernel (pur-NEL) (English) He Is the Beautiful Countryside

Peronel (pair-oh-NEL) (English) She Is the Beautiful Countryside

Peta (PAY-tuh) (English) She Is Rock-Solid

Petrina (peh-TREE-nuh) (English) She Is the Little One Who Is Rock-Solid

Petula (peh-TOO-luh) (English) She Is a Beautiful Flower Petal

🐾 **Petunia** (peh-TOON-yuh) (English/Tupi) She Is a Fragrant Petunia Flower

Peyton (PAY-tun) (English) He Is the Town Ruled by Peoga

Phebe (FEE-bee) (English) She Is Radiantly Beautiful

Phemie (FEE-mee) (English) She Is the Little One Who Speaks Beautifully

Pheobe (FEE-bee) (English) She Is Radiantly Beautiful

Philander (fil-LAN-dur) (English) He Loves and Respects Humanity

Philbert (FIL-burt) (English) He Is Incredibly Brilliant

Philipa (FIL-ih-puh) (English) She Befriends Horses

Philis (FIL-liss) (English) She Is Beautiful Green Branches

Phillida (FIL-ih-duh) (English) She Is Beautiful Green Branches

🖉 **Philomena** (fil-oh-MEE-nuh) (English) She Is Our Mightiest Companion

Phyllis (FIL-liss) (English) She Is Beautiful Green Branches

Piety (PYE-eh-tee) (English) She Is Piously Religious

Pippa (PIP-puh) (English) She Is the Little One Who Befriends Horses

Placid (PLASS-sid) (English) She Is Placid and Harmonious

Pollie (PAHL-lee) (English) She Is the Beloved One Who Is Love Itself

Porsche (POR-shuh) (English) She Is an Unstoppable She-Boar

Posie (PO-zee) (English) She Is a Fragrant Posy of Flowers

Praise (PRAYZ) (English) She Is Priceless Praise

Precious (PREH-shuhss) (English) She Is Priceless and Precious

🖉 **Presley** (PRESS-lee) (English) He Is a Forest Meadow Owned by the Priests

Primula (PRIM-yoo-luh) (English) She Is First Flower of Dawn

Princess (PRIN-sess) (English) She Is a Majestic Princess

Pris (PRISS) (English) She Is the Little Honorable One

Prissy (PRISS-see) (English) She Is the Little Honorable One

Prosper (PRAHSS-pur) (English) She Is Prosperous

Pru (PROO) (English) She Is the Little One Who Is Careful and Prudent

Prudence (PROO-denss) (English) She Is Careful and Prudent

Prunella (proo-NEL-luh) (English) She Is a Fragrant Plum Blossom

Purdie (PUR-dee) (English) She Lives Her Life by God's Laws

🖉 **Quiana** (kee-AH-nuh) (English/American) She Is Silky Soft

Quanna (KWAH-nuh) (English/Vietnamese) She Is a Graceful Warrior

Queen (KWEEN) (English) She Is a Majestic Queen

Queenie (KWEE-nee) (English) She Is a Majestic Queen

Quentin (KWEN-tin) (English) He Is the Fifth

Quianna (kee-AN-nuh) (English/American) She is Silky Soft

Quin (KWIN) (English/Irish) He Descends from the Great Leader

Quincey (KWIN-see) (English) He Is the Fifth

Quinlan (KWIN-lun) (English/Irish) He Descends from the Lean, Lively One

Quinten (KWIN-ten) (English) He Is the Fifth

🖉 **Rachael** (RAY-chul) (English) She Is a Gentle Mother Ewe

Rachyl (RAY-chil) (English) She Is a Gentle Mother Ewe

Racquel (rah-KEL) (English) She Is a Gentle Mother Ewe

Radcliff (RAD-klif) (English) He Is a Fiery Red Cliff

Raeburn (RAY-burn) (English) He Is a Refreshing River

Raelyn (ray-LIN) (English) She Is a Gentle Mother Ewe and a Sparkling Clear Lake

Rain (RAYN) (English) She Is Refreshing Rain

Rainard (RAY-nurd) (English) He Is the Courageous One Who Gives Wise Counsel

Rainbow (RAYN-bo) (English) She Is Colorful Rainbows

Raleigh (RAH-lee) (English) He Is a Fragrant Meadow of Red Flowers

🖉 **Rachel** (RAY-chul) (Hebrew) She Is a Gentle Mother Ewe

Raviv (rah-VEEV) (Hebrew) She Is Refreshing Rain

Remy (ray-MEE) (French) She Rows the Oars of the Great Ship

Renee (ruh-NAY) (English) She Is Reborn in God

Rheagan (RAY-gun) (American) She Descends from an Impulsive Father

Rider (RYE-dur) (American) He Is a Shining Knight

Robert (RAH-burt) (English) He Is Brilliantly Renowned

Rosanne (ro-ZAN) (English) She Is a Graceful, Fragrant Rose

Roxana (rahk-SAHN-nah) (Spanish) She Is the Radiant Dawn

Rumer (ROO-mer) (English) She Is a Beautiful Marshland

🐾 **Ralf** (RALF) (English) He Counsels Us Like a Crafty Wolf

Ralphie (RAL-fee) (English) He Is the Little One Who Counsels Us Like a Crafty Wolf

Ramona (ruh-MO-nuh) (English) She Counsels Us Wisely

Ramsey (RAM-zee) (English) He Is the Place of Fragrant Garlic

Randall (RAN-dul) (English) He Is a Mighty Wolf Who Shields Us from Harm

Randi (RAN-dee) (English) She Is the Little One Who Is a Mighty Wolf with a Shield

Randolf (RAN-dolf) (English) He Is the Mighty Wolf Who Shields Us from Harm

Raphael (RAY-fee-yul) (English) His God Heals the Sick

Raschelle (rah-SHEL) (English) She Is a Gentle Mother Ewe

Rashaun (rah-SHAWN) (English/Egyptian) He Is the Golden One Whose God Is Gracious

🐾 **Ran** (RAHN) (Japanese) She Is a Fragrant Orchid

Ren (REN) (Japanese) She Is a Fragrant Lotus Flower

Riko (REE-ko) (Japanese) She Is a Fragrant Jasmine Flower

Riku (ree-KOO) (Japanese) She Is the Blessed Earth

Rikuto (REE-koo-toh) (Japanese) He Is the Constellation Ursa Major

Rina (REE-nuh) (Japanese) She Is Fragrant, Beautiful Jasmine

Rio (REE-yoh) (Japanese) She Is a Fragrant Cherry Blossom

Rokurou (ro-KOO-ro) (Japanese) He Is Our Sixth Son

Ryouichi (ree-oo-EE-chee) (Japanese) He Is a Rushing Stream

Ryouta (REE-oo-tuh) (Japanese) He Is Refreshing Spring Rain

🐾 **Rashawn** (rah-SHAWN) (English/Egyptian) He Is the Golden One Whose God Is Gracious

Rastus (RASS-tuss) (English) He Is the Beloved Little One

Ravenna (ruh-VEN-nuh) (English) She Is a Shining Black Bird

Raylene (ray-LEEN) (English) She Is the Little One Who Protects Us with Wise Counsel

Raymund (RAY-mund) (English) He Rules with Wise Counsel

Raynard (RAY-nurd) (English) He Is the One Who Gives Courageous Counsel

Rayner (RAY-nur) (English) He Commands the Military

Read (REED) (English) He Has Fiery Red Hair

Reagan (RAY-gun) (English/Irish) He Descends from a Father Who Favors Action

Reanna (ree-ANN-nuh) (English) She Is the Magnificent Little Ruler

🐾 **Reannon** (ree-AN-nun) (English/Welsh) She Is a Majestic Monarch

Reba (REE-buh) (English) She Is the Little One Who Brings Us Closer

Rebeccah (reh-BEK-kuh) (English) She Brings Us Closer

Reenie (REE-nee) (English) She Is Reborn in God

Regana (reh-GAH-nuh) (English) She Descends from a Father Who Favors Action

Regena (ruh-JEE-nuh) (English) She Is a Majestic Queen

Reilly (RYE-ley) (English/Irish) He Is Supreme

Renie (REE-nee) (English) She Is Reborn in God

Renita (reh-NEE-tuh) (English) She Is Reborn in God

Retha (REE-thuh) (English) She Is a Little Priceless Pearl

🐾 **Reuben** (ROO-ben) (English/Hebrew) Behold, He Is Our Glorious Son

Rex (REX) (English) He Is the Greatest King of All

Rexana (rex-AN-nuh) (English) She Is the Radiant Dawn

Reynold (REH-nuld) (English) He Governs with Wise Advice

Rheanna (ree-ANN-nuh) (English) She Is the Magnificent Little Ruler

Rhett (RET) (English) He Is Who Governs with Wise Advice

Rhetta (RET-tuh) (English) She Governs with Wise Advice

Rhiannon (ree-AN-nun) (English/Welsh) She Is a Majestic Monarch

Rhoda (RO-duh) (English) She Is Our Fragrant Rose

Rhonda (RAHN-duh) (English) She Is a Powerful Weapon

🕊 **Rian** (RYE-yun) (English) He Descends from a Beloved King

Richardine (rih-chur-DEEN) (English) She Is Powerfully Courageous

Richelle (rih-SHEL) (English/French) She Is Powerfully Courageous

Richie (RIH-chee) (English) He Is Powerfully Courageous

Richmal (RISH-mul) (English) He Is the Powerful, Courageous One Who Resembles God

Rickey (RIK-kee) (English) He Is Powerfully Courageous

Ridley (RID-lee) (English) He Is a Meadow Filled with Beautiful Reeds

Rigby (RIG-bee) (English) He Is a Vast Estate near a Ridge of Hills

Rina (REE-nuh) (English) She Is the Pure-Hearted Little One

Ripley (RIP-lee) (English) He Is a Strip of Meadow in the Woodlands

🕊 **Rikki** (RIK-kee) (English) He Is Powerfully Courageous

Rita (REE-tuh) (English) She Is Our Priceless Little Pearl

Ritchie (RIH-chee) (English) He Is Powerfully Courageous

Robby (RAHB-bee) (English) He Is Our Brilliantly Renowned Little Superstar

Robina (rah-BEE-nuh) (English) She Is a Magnificent, Soaring Robin

Robyn (RAH-bin) (English) She Is a Soaring Robin

Rochelle (ro-SHEL) (English) She Is the Little One Who Is Rock-Solid

Roddy (RAHD-dee) (English) He Is the Little One Who Is Mighty and Renowned

Rodge (RAHJ) (English) He Is a Renowned Weapon

Rolf (RAWLF) (English) He Is the Little One Who Is a Mighty Wolf

🕊 **Robin** (RAH-bin) (English) She Is a Soaring Robin

Robinet (rah-bih-NET) (English) She Is a Soaring Robin

Robbi (RAHB-bee) (Icelandic) He Is a Soaring Robin

Roblet (RAHB-lit, ro-BLAY) (English) She Is a Soaring Robin

Robus (RO-bus) (Latin) He Is a Soaring Robin

Ropkarri (rope-KAR-ree) (Icelandic) He Is a Soaring Robin

Ruban (roo-BAW, ROO-bun) (French) He Is a Soaring Robin

Rubienne (roo-bee-YEN) (French) She Is a Soaring Robin

Rubisca (roo-BEES-kuh) (Latin) She Is a Soaring Robin

Ruddock (RUD-duk) (English) He Is a Soaring Robin

🕊 **Rolland** (ROHL-lund) (English) He Is a Mighty, Renowned Nation

Rollo (RAHL-lo) (English) He Is the Little One Who Is a Mighty Wolf

Rolph (RAWLF) (English) He Is the Little One Who Is a Mighty Wolf

Roly (RO-lee) (English) He Is the Little One Who Is a Mighty Nation

Romayne (ro-MAYN) (English) She Is Rome

Romy (ro-MEE) (English) She Is the Little One Who Is a Rose and Who Is Love Itself

Rona (RO-nuh) (English) She Is the Great Island of Rona, Scotland

Ronda (RAHN-duh) (English) She Is a Reliable Weapon

Roni (RAH-nee) (English) She Is the Little One Who Carries Us All to Triumph

Ronnette (rahn-NET) (English) She Rules by Wise Counsel

🕊 **Ronny** (RAHN-nee) (Scottish) He Is Our Wise Little Counselor

Roosevelt (RO-zuh-velt) (English/Dutch) He Is a Meadow of Fragrant Roses

Ros (RAHZ) (English) She Is the Little One Who Is Kind Toward Horses

Rosabel (RO-zuh-bel) (English) She Is the Lovely One Who Is a Fragrant Rose

Rosaleen (ro-zuh-LEEN) (English) She Befriends Horses

Rosalin (RAH-zuh-lin) (English) She Befriends Horses

Rosamond (ro-zuh-MAHND) (English) She Befriends Horses

Rosanna (ro-ZAN-nuh) (English) She Is a Graceful, Beautiful Rose

Rosanne (ro-ZAN) (English) She Is a Graceful, Beautiful Rose

Roscoe (RAHSS-ko) (English) He Is the Forest Where Deer Flourish

🐾 **Rosannah** (ro-ZAN-nuh) (English) She Is the Graceful, Beautiful Rose

Roseanne (ro-ZAN) (English) She Is the Graceful, Beautiful Rose

Roselyn (RAHZ-uh-lin) (English) She Is a Delicate, Beautiful Rose

Roswell (RAHZ-wel) (English) He Is a River Where Horses Come to Drink

Rosy (RO-zee) (English) She Is Our Fragrant Little Rose

Rowanne (ro-WANN) (English) She Is a Tree with Sweet White Berries

Rowena (ro-WEE-nuh) (English) She Is Happy and Renowned

Rowland (RO-lund) (English) He Is a Mighty Nation

Rowley (RAH-oh-lee) (English) He Is the Little One Who Is a Mighty Nation

Roxana (rahk-SAN-nuh) (English) She Is the Radiant Dawn

🐾 **Roxanne** (rahk-SAN) (English) She Is the Radiant Dawn

Roxie (RAHK-see) (English) She Is the Little One Who Is the Radiant Dawn

Royal (ROY-yul) (English) He Is Majestic

Royale (roy-YAL) (English) He Is Majestic

Royce (ROYSS) (English) He Is a Fragrant Rose

Roydon (ROY-dun) (English) He Is the Beautiful Hill Where Rye Grows

Royston (ROY-stun) (English) He Is Royse, England

Roz (RAHZ) (English) She Is the Little One Who Is Kind Toward Horses

Rozanne (ro-ZAN) (English) She Is the Graceful, Beautiful Rose

Rubye (ROO-bee) (English) She Is a Priceless Ruby

🐾 **Roxy** (RAHK-see) (English) She Is the Little One Who Is the Radiant Dawn

Royle (ROYL) (English) He Is the Beautiful Hill Where Rye Grows

Rudyard (RUHD-yurd) (English) He Is a Yard Filled with Red Flowers

Rue (ROO) (English) She Is a Trusted Little Companion

Rupert (ROO-purt) (English) He Is Bright Fame

Russel (RUSS-sul) (English) He Is the Little One Who Has Fiery Red Hair

Ryana (rye-AN-nuh) (English/Irish) She Descends from a Beloved King

Ryanne (rye-ANN) (English/Irish) She Descends from a Beloved King

Ryder (RYE-dur) (English) He Is a Shining Knight Riding a Majestic Steed

Ryker (RYE-kur) (English) He Is Wealthy

🐾 **Saburo** (SAH-boo-roh) (Japanese) He Is Our Third Son

Sachiko (SAH-shee-ko) (Japanese) She Is All the Happiness in the Universe

Saki (SAH-kee) (Japanese) She Is a Fragrant Flower

Sakura (SAH-koo-rah) (Japanese) He Is the Child Who Is a Fragrant Cherry Blossom

Shinju (SHEEN-joo) (Japanese) She Is a Priceless Pearl

Shirou (SHEE-ro) (Japanese) He Is Our Fourth Son

Shizuka (SHEE-zoo-kuh) (Japanese) She Is the Warm Summer

Shou (SHO) (Japanese) He Flies Up to the Blue Sky

Sora (SO-ruh) (Japanese) He Is the Blue Sky

Suzume (SOO-zoo-may) (Japanese) She Is a Delicate Sparrow

🐾 **Sam** (SAM) (English) She Is the Little One Whom God Hears

Samara (suh-MAHR-ruh) (English/Hebrew) She Is Our Sheltering Hillside

Sammie (SAM-mee) (English) She Is the Little One Heard by God

Sampson (SAMP-sun) (English/Hebrew) He Is Born of the Sun

Sandford (SAN-furd) (English) He Is the Place of the Sandy River-Crossing

Sandie (SAN-dee) (English) She Is the Little One Who Protects Humanity

Sara (SAIR-rah) (English/Hebrew) She Is a Royal Princess

Saranna (sah-RAH-nah) (English) She Is the Graceful Royal Princess

Sarina (sah-REE-nah) (English) She Is Peacefully Serene

Sarra (SAHR-rah) (English/Hebrew) She Is a Royal Princess

🐾 **Savanna** (suh-VAN-nuh) (English) She Is a Plain of Fragrant Grass

Saxon (SAK-sun) (English) He Is the Saxons

Scarlett (SKAR-let) (English) She Has a Fiery Red Temperament

Schuyler (SKYE-lur) (English/Dutch) He Is a Scholar and a Gentleman

Scot (SKAHT) (Scottish) He Is the Nation of Scotland

Scout (SKOWT) (English) She Scouts Ahead of Others

Seanna (SHAWN-nuh) (English) Her God Is Gracious

Sebastian (suh-BAS-chun) (English) He Is Honorable

Sefton (SEF-tun) (English) He Is a City Built near a Field of Golden Rushes

Selma (SEL-muh) (English) She Is God's Helmet of Protection

🐾 **Selwyn** (SEL-win) (English) He Is Our Beautiful Home

September (sep-TEM-bur) (English) She Is the Lovely Month of September

Sequoia (seh-KOY-yuh) (English/Cherokee) She Is Our Great Thinker

Seraphina (sair-uh-FEE-nuh) (English) She Is God's Flaming-Bright Angel

Serena (suh-REE-nuh) (English/Greek) She Is Peacefully Serene

Serenity (suh-REN-ih-TEE) (English) She Is Peace and Serenity

Shad (SHAD) (English) He Is an Unstoppable Herd of Bulls

Shae (SHAY) (English) She Is Destined

Shaelynn (shay-LIN) (English) She Is a Beautiful Lake Created by God

Shan (SHAHN) (English/Welsh) Her God Is Gracious

🐾 **Shantel** (shahn-TEL) (English/American) She Is Rock-Solid

Shaquila (shuh-KEE-luh) (English/American) She Is Beautiful

Shaquille (shuh-KEEL) (English/Arabic) He Is Incredibly Beautiful

Sharalyn (SHAIR-uh-lin) (English) She Is Truly Darling and Sweet

Sharise (shuh-REESS) (English) She Is the Little Graceful, Elegant One

Sharla (SHAR-luh) (English) She Is a Mighty Warrior

Sharleen (shar-LEEN) (English) She Is a Mighty Little Soldier

Sharmaine (shar-MAYN) (English) She Is a Little One Who Is the Great Nation of Warriors

Sharon (SHAIR-run) (English/Hebrew) She Is a Fertile Plain

Sharona (shuh-RO-nuh) (English) She Is a Fertile Plain

🐾 **Sharron** (SHAIR-run) (English/Hebrew) She Is a Fertile Plain

Sharyl (SHAIR-rul) (English) She Is Truly Darling and Sweet

Shauna (SHAW-nuh) (English) Her God Is Gracious

Shavonne (shuh-VAHN) (English/Irish) Her God Is Gracious

Shawnda (SHAWN-duh) (English) Her God Is Gracious

Shaye (SHAY) (English) She Is Destined

Shayla (SHAY-luh) (English) She Sees Deeply Within Herself

Shaylyn (shay-LIN) (English) She Is the Divine Lake Created by God

Shayne (SHAYN) (English) Her God Is Gracious

Sheard (SHURD) (English) He Is the Passage Between the Mountains

🐾 **Sheelagh** (SHEE-luh) (English/Irish) She Sees Deeply Within Herself

Sheenagh (SHEE-nuh) (English/Scottish) Her God Is Gracious

Shel (SHEL) (English) He Is the Peaceful Little Valley

Shelby (SHEL-bee) (English) He Is a Farm in the Willow Groves

Shelena (Shel-EE-nuh) (English) She Is a Radiant Little Torch

Shelia (Shel-EE-yuh) (English) She Sees Deeply Within Herself

Shell (SHELL) (English) She Is the Little One Who Resembles God

Shelley (SHEL-lee) (English) She Is a Fragrant Meadow by a Riverbank

Shena (SHEE-nuh) (English/Scottish) Her God Is Gracious

Sheree (shur-REE) (English) She Is Darling and Sweet

🐾 **Sheridan** (SHAIR-ih-den) (English) She Descends from the Truth-Seeker

Sherie (shur-REE) (English) She Is Darling and Sweet

Sherilyn (SHAIR-ih-lin) (English) She Is Truly Darling and Sweet

Sherisse (shur-REESS) (English) She Is the Graceful, Elegant Little One

Sherley (SHUR-lee) (English) She Is a Sunny Clearing in the Woodlands

Sherwood (SHUR-wood) (English) He Is the Sun-Drenched Woodlands

Sheryll (SHAIR-ril) (English) She Is Truly Darling and Sweet

Shevaun (shuh-VAWN) (English) She Is God's Graceful Little Messenger

Shonda (SHAHN-duh) (English) She Is the Gracious One Who Is a Powerful Weapon

Shyla (SHEE-lah) (English/Irish) She Sees Deeply Within Herself

🐾 **Sibilla** (sih-BIL-luh) (English) She Is an All-Seeing Prophetess

Sidony (sih-DOH-nee) (English) She Is Sidon, Lebanon

Siena (see-EN-nuh) (English/Italian) She Is Sienna, Italy

Sierra (see-AIR-ruh) (English/Spanish) She Is a Range of Mighty Mountains

Sigmund (SIG-mund) (English/German) He Is Our Triumphant Defender

Silvester (sil-VES-tur) (English) He Is a Forest of Majestic Trees

Silvia (SIL-vee-yuh) (English/Latin) She Is the Beautiful Woodlands

Simonette (sye-muh-NET) (English) She Hears Everything

Sinclair (sin-KLAIR) (English) He Is Protected by the Blessed Saint Claire

Sindy (SIN-dee) (English) She Is the Beloved Woman from Kynthos, Greece

🐾 **Sinjin** (SIN-jin) (English) He Is Protected by the Blessed Saint John

Sissie (SIS-see) (English) She Is the Little One Who Sees Deeply Within Herself

Skye (SKYE) (English) She Is the Beautiful Blue Sky

Skylar (SKYE-lur) (English) He Is a Scholar and a Gentleman

Slade (SLAYD) (English) He Is a Peaceful Valley

Sloan (SLONE) (English/Irish) He Conquers Other Lands

Sly (SLYE) (English) He Is the Little One Who Is the Beautiful Woodlands

Solomon (SAH-luh-mun) (English/Hebrew) He Is Peace

Sommer (SUM-mur) (English) She Is the Warm Summer Season

Sondra (SAHN-druh) (English) She Is the Little One Who Protects Humanity

🐾 **Sonia** (SOAN-yuh) (English) She Is the Beloved One Who Is Wisdom Itself

Sonnie (SUN-nee) (English) He Is a Devoted Little Son

Sophia (so-FEE-yuh) (English/Greek) She Is Knowledge

Sophie (SO-fee) (English) She Is Knowledge

Sparrow (SPAIR-ro) (English) She Is a Delicate Sparrow

Spike (SPYKE) (English) He Has Beautiful Spiked Hair

Spirit (SPEER-rit) (English) She Is a Divine Spirit

Stacee (STAY-see) (English) She Is Abundantly Productive

Stacia (STAY-shuh) (English) She Is Reborn to New Life

Stafford (STAF-furd) (English) He Is Stafford, England

🐾 **Stan** (STAN) (English) He Is the Little One Who Is a Clearing among the Great Stones

Stanford (STAN-furd) (English) He Is a Crossing-Place Between the Cliffs

Starla (STAR-luh) (English) She Is a Bright Heavenly Star

Ste (STEE) (English) He Is a Shining Little Crown

Steph (STEF) (English) She Is a Shining Little Crown

Stephani (STEF-uh-nee) (English/Greek) She Is a Shining Crown

Stephania (stef-AHN-yuh) (English/Greek) She Is a Shining Crown

Stephen (STEE-vun) (English/Greek) He Is a Shining Crown

Sterling (STUR-ling) (English/Scottish) He Is Absolutely Magnificent

Steven (STEE-ven) (English/Greek) He Is a Shining Crown

🖉 **Stew** (STOO) (English) He Is the Little One Who Safeguards Our Home

Stewart (STOO-wurt) (English/Scottish) He Safeguards Our Home

Storm (STORM) (English) She Is a Mighty Thunderstorm

Sue (SOO) (English) She Is a Fragrant Little Lotus Flower

Suellen (soo-EL-len) (English) She Is a Radiant Torch and a Fragrant Lotus Flower

Sukie (SOO-kee) (English) She Is Our Fragrant Little Lotus Flower

Sullivan (SUL-lih-vun) (English/Irish) He Descends from the Dark-Eyed One

Sunday (SUN-day) (English) She Is Sunday, the Lord's Sacred Day

Sunny (SUN-nee) (English) She Is the Little One Who Is Golden Sunshine

Sunshine (SUN-shyne) (English) She Is Golden Sunshine

🖉 **Suzan** (SOO-zun) (English) She Is a Fragrant Lotus Flower

Suzanna (soo-ZAN-nuh) (English) She Is a Fragrant Lotus Flower

Suzanne (soo-ZAN) (English) She Is a Fragrant Lotus Flower

Suzie (SOO-zee) (English) She Is Our Fragrant Little Lotus Flower

Sybella (sih-BEL-luh) (English) She Is an All-Seeing Prophetess

Sybilla (sih-BIL-luh) (English) She Is an All-Seeing Prophetess

Syd (SID) (English) He Is the Little One Who Is a Great Island

Sydne (SID-nee) (English) She Is a Great Island

Sylvana (sil-VAH-nuh) (English) She Is the Beautiful Woodlands

Symphony (SIM-fuh-nee) (English) She Is a Melodious Symphony

🖉 **Tabatha** (TAB-uh-thuh) (English/Aramaic) She Is a Swift Gazelle

Tacey (TAY-see) (English) She Is Self-Controlled

Taegan (TAY-gun) (English) She Descends from the Eloquent Little Bard

Tahnee (TAH-nee) (English) She Is Tanned and Beautiful

Tajuana (tah-WAH-nuh) (English/American) We Are Thankful That Her God Is Gracious

Talbot (TAL-but) (English) He Carries News of Our Enemy's Destruction

Talisha (tah-LEE-shuh) (English) We Are Thankful That She Is a Little Aristocrat

Tallulah (tuh-LOO-luh) (English/Choctaw) She Is the Rushing River

Tamara (TAM-uh-ruh) (English/Hebrew) She Is a Beautiful Palm Tree

Tamela (TAM-uh-luh) (English) She Is a Beautiful Palm Tree

🖉 **Tafari** (tah-FAH-ree) (Amharic) He Fills Us with Wonder

Tapiwa (tah-PEE-vah) (Shona) She Is God's Divine Gift

Tariro (tah-REE-ro) (Shona) She Is All Our Dreams

Tatenda (tah-TEN-dah) (Shona) He Is the One for Whom We Are Grateful

Tau (TAH-woh) (Tswana) He Is a Noble Lion

Temitope (tem-ee-TOH-pay) (Yoruba) He Is the One for Whom We Are Truly Grateful

Tendai (ten-DYE) (Shona) She Is the One for Whom We Are Truly Grateful

Themba (THAYM-bah) (Zulu) He Is Worshipped

Thulani (thoo-LAH-nee) (Zulu) He Is Easily Soothed

Tinashe (tih-NAH-shee) (Shona) His God Is Ever-Present

🖉 **Taichi** (TYE-chee) (Japanese) He Is as Magnificent as the Earth

Taiki (TYE-kee) (Japanese) He Shimmers More Brightly than the Sun

Takehiko (tah-keh-HEE-ko) (Japanese) He Is a Majestic Bamboo Tree

Takuma (TAH-koo-muh) (Japanese) He Explores the Wilderness

Tamiko (tah-MEE-ko) (Japanese) She Is all the Wonderful Children in the Universe

Tomoko (TO-mo-ko) (Japanese) She Is all the Intelligence in the Universe

Tsubaki (soo-BAH-kee) (Japanese) She Is a Fragrant Camellia

Tsubame (SOO-bah-may) (Japanese) She Is a Soaring Swallow

Tsubasa (soo-BAH-suh) (Japanese) His Wings Let Him Soar

Tsukiko (SOO-kee-ko) (Japanese) She Is the World's Beauty

🖉 **Tanner** (TAN-nur) (English) He Crafts Beautiful Leather Objects

Tanya (TAHN-yuh) (English) She Is a Little Saint

Tanzi (TAN-zee) (English) She Is the Lovely Golden Tansy Flower

Tara (TAIR-ruh) (English/Irish) She Is the Divine Realm

Tarina (tah-REE-nuh) (English) She Is a Realm Ruled by an Aristocrat

Taryn (TAIR-rin) (English) She Is a Realm Ruled by an Aristocrat

Tasha (TAH-shuh) (English/Russian) She Is the Little One Who Is Christmas Day

Tate (TAYT) (English) She Is the Homestead of the Famous Tate

Tatianna (tah-tee-AH-nuh) (English/Bulgarian) She Picks and Chooses

Tatton (TAT-tun) (English) He Is the Homestead of the Famous Tate

☍ **Tatyanna** (tah-tee-AH-nuh) (English/ Bulgarian) She Picks and Chooses

Tawnee (TAW-nee) (English) She Is Tanned and Beautiful

Tayla (TAY-luh) (English) She Sews with Great Skill

Tayler (TAY-lur) (English) She Sews with Great Skill

Teagan (TAY-gun) (English) She Descends from the Eloquent Bard

Teale (TEEL) (English) She Is the Beautiful Color Teal

Tel (TEL) (English) He Is the Little Beginner

Temperance (TEM-pur-runss) (English) She Is Self-Controlled

Tennyson (TEN-nih-sun) (English) He Descends from the One Who Speaks Clearly

Tera (TAIR-ruh) (English/Irish) She Is the Heavenly Realm

☍ **Terance** (TAIR-unss) (English) He Begins Many Things

Teresa (tuh-REE-suh) (English/Polish) She Is a Summer Harvest

Terrell (tur-REL) (English) He Has an Iron Will

Terrie (TAIR-ree) (English) She Is Our Little Gift from God

Tessa (TESS-suh) (English) She Is Our Little Summer Harvest

Tessie (TESS-see) (English) She Is Our Little Summer Harvest

Tetty (TET-tee) (English) She Demonstrates God's Abundance

Thad (THAD) (English) He Is Our Little Gift from God

Thane (THAYN) (English) He Is Aristocratic

Thankful ((English) She Is Grateful for Her Blessings

☍ **Theodoor** (TAY-oh-dor) (Dutch) He Is God's Divine Gift

Theofilus (tay-OH-feel-lus) (Dutch) He Is God's Beloved

Thera (TAY-ruh) (Dutch) She Is the Little One Who Is a Summer Harvest

Theresia (tair-AY-see-yuh) (Dutch) She Is a Summer Harvest

Thirza (TUR-zuh) (Dutch) She Is a Pleasant Nation

Tijn (TINE) (Dutch) He Is the Little Magnificent One

Tijs (TICE) (Dutch) He Is Our Little Gift from God

Tineke (TEE-neh-kuh) (Dutch) She Is Christ's Little Follower

Tjaard (tee-YART) (Dutch) He Studies Humanity

Trees (TRAYSS) (Dutch) She Is Our Little Summer Harvest

☍ **Tia** (TEE-yuh) (English/Haida) She Is a Quiet Departure from this World

Tianna (tee-AHN-nuh) (English) She Is Christ's Little Follower

Tiara (tee-AR-ruh) (English/Greek) She Is a Shining Crown

Tibby (TIB-bee) (English) She Is a Swift Little Gazelle

Tiffiny (TIF-fih-nee) (English) She Proves God's Greatness

Tilda (TIL-duh) (English/Swedish) She Is Our Powerful Little Warrior

Tillie (TIL-lee) (English) She Is Our Powerful Little Warrior

Timotha (TIM-oh-thuh) (English) She Honors God

Tobias (toh-BYE-yuss) (English/Greek) His God Is Goodness

Tobin (TOH-bin) (English) His God Is Goodness

☍ **Tolly** (TAHL-lee) (English) He Is the Little One with a Furrowed Brow

Tommie (TAHM-mee) (English) He Is Our Precious Little Twin

Tonia (TAHN-yuh) (English) She Is a Fragrant Flower

Topaz (TOH-paz) (English) She Is a Priceless Golden Topaz

Topher (TOH-fur) (English) He Is Christ's Little Follower

Topsy (TAHP-see) (English) She Has Reached the Top

Toria (TOR-ee-yuh) (English) She Is Humanity's Little Triumph

Tottie (TOT-tee) (English) She Is Our Beloved Little Warrior

Toya (TOY-yuh) (English) She Is Humanity's Little Triumph

Trace (TRAYSS) (English) She Is the Little One Who Is Thrace

🕮 **Trista** (TRIS-tuh) (English/Welsh) She Is Aggressive

Tristen (TRIS-ten) (English/Welsh) He Is Aggressive

Trixie (TRIK-see) (English) She Is Our Little Voyager

Trudy (TROO-dee) (English) She Is Our Little Weapon

Trueman (TROO-mun) (English) He Is Trustworthy

Twyla (TWYE-luh) (English) She Is the Purple Twilight

Tye (TYE) (English) He Is the Little One Who Is a Field of Green Grass

Tylar (TYE-lur) (English) She Shields Our Roof with Impregnable Tiles

Tyreek (tye-REEK) (English/Arabic) He Is an Aggressive Aristocrat

Tyrell (tye-REL) (English) He Has an Iron Will

🕮 **Ulric** (UL-rik) (English) He Is a Courageous Wolf

Ulrich (UL-rich) (English/German) He Is Wealthy and Strong

Ulyssa (yoo-LISS-suh) (English/Latin) She Is Hatred

Ulysses (yoo-LISS-seez) (English/Latin) He Is Hatred

Unice (YOO-nus) (English/Greek) She Is Humanity's Triumph

Unique (yoo-NEEK) (English) She Is a Unique Masterpiece

Unity (YOO-nih-tee) (English) She Is Unity

Upton (UP-tun) (English) He Is the Upper-Class Part of Town

Ursella (UR-sul-luh) (English/Swedish) She Is a Small but Fierce She-Bear

Ursula (UR-sul-lah) (English/Swedish) She Is a Small but Fierce She-Bear

🕮 **Valary** (VAL-uh-ree) (English/Latin) She Is Powerful

Valda (VAL-duh) (English) She Safeguards Us Courageously

Vaughn (VAWN) (English/Welsh) He Is Petite

Velda (VEL-duh) (English) She Safeguards Us Courageously

Velma (VEL-muh) (English/German) She Protects Humanity

Velvet (VEL-vet) (English) She Is Soft Velvet

Vera (VEER-ruh) (English/Latin) She Is Honest

Vere (VEER) (English) He Is a Mighty Alder Tree

Vergil (VUR-jul) (English/Latin) He Is Pure and Chaste

🕮 **Valencia** (vah-LEN-see-yah) (Spanish) She Is Strong

Valentin (vah-layn-TEEN) (Spanish) He Is Powerful and Energetic

Valeria (vah-LAY-ree-yah) (Spanish/Latin) She Is Powerful

Valerio (vah-LAY-ree-yo) (Spanish/Latin) He Is Powerful

Varinia (vah-REEN-ee-yah) (Spanish/Latin) She Has Many Skills

Victor (VEEK-tor) (Spanish) He Is Victorious

Victorino (veek-toh-REE-no) (Spanish) He Is Victorious

Vidal (vee-DAHL) (Spanish) He Is Life Itself

Vinicio (vee-NEE-see-yo) (Spanish) He Is Delectable Wine

Virgilio (veer-HEE-lee-yo) (Spanish) He Is Pure and Chaste

🕮 **Verity** (VAIR-ih-tee) (English) She Is Our Sacred Truth

Verna (VUR-nuh) (English) He Is a Mighty Alder Tree

Vernon (VUR-nun) (English/French) He Is a Grove of Alder Trees

Veva (VEE-vuh) (English) She Is a Little Woman Who Is Loyal to Her People

Vi (VYE) (English) She Is Our Fragrant Little Violet

Vianne (vye-YAN) (English) She Is Our Graceful Little Violet

Vicky (English) She Is Humanity's Little Triumph

Victor (VIK-tur) (English/Latin) He Is Victorious

Victoria (vik-TOR-ee-yuh) (English/Latin) She Is Humanity's Triumph

Viola (vye-OH-luh) (English/Latin) She Is a Fragrant Violet

& **Warrick** (WAHR-rik) (English) He Is a Strong Fence Across Farmland

Wayland (WAY-lund) (English) He Is the Realm of Warfare

Waylon (WAY-lun) (English) He Is the Realm of Warfare

Weldon (WEL-dun) (English) He Weaves Beautiful Garments

Wenda (WEN-duh) (English) She Is Beautifully Fair

Wendell (WEN-dull) (English/German) He Is the Fierce Nation of the Vandals

Wendi (WEN-dee) (English) She Is Beautifully Fair

Wenona (wen-OH-nah) (English/Dakota) She Is Born First

Westley (WES-lee) (English) He Is a Meadow in the Western Forest

Weston (WES-tun) (English) He Is the Great Western Town

& **Whitaker** (WIT-uh-kur) (English) He Is a Snow-Covered Forest

Wil (WIL) (English) He Is Our Little Protector

Wilbur (WIL-bur) (English) He Shelters Us in His Fortress

Wilburn (WIL-burn) (English) He Shelters Us in His Fortress

Wilda (WIL-duh) (English) She Is Free-Spirited

Wilf (WILF) (English) He Is the Peaceful Little One

Wilford (WIL-furd) (English) He Is a Crossing-Place near Willow Trees

Wilfred (WIL-fred) (English) He Wants Peace

Wilfreda (wil-FRAY-duh) (English) She Wants Peace

Wilhelmina (wil-hel-MEE-nuh) (English/German) She Protects Humanity

& **Wilkie** (WIL-kee) (English) He Protects Humanity

Willoughby (WIL-lo-bee) (English) He Is a Town near Willow Trees

Willy (WIL-lee) (English) He Is Our Little Protector

Wilma (WIL-mah) (English/German) She Protects Humanity

Wilmot (WIL-mut) (English) He Is Our Little Protector

Wilton (WIL-tun) (English) He Is a Town near the Wylye River, England

Windsor (WIN-zur) (English) He Is a River near Beautiful Windmills

Winfred (WIN-fred) (English) She Is Beautifully Fair

Winona (win-OH-nuh) (English/Dakota) She Is Born First

Wisdom (WIZ-dum) (English) She Is Wisdom Itself

Xandra (ZAHN-druh) (Dutch) She Is Humanity's Little Protector

& **Yamato** (yah-MAH-to) (Japanese) He Is in Harmony with the Universe

Yasu (YAH-soo) (Japanese) She Is the Peaceful Plain

Yoko (YO-ko) (Japanese) She Is the Child of Sunlight

Yoshi (YO-shee) (Japanese) He Is all the Good Fortune in the Universe

Youta (YO-tuh) (Japanese) He Is Golden Sunlight

Yuina (YOO-ee-nah) (Japanese) She Is a Garden of Wholesome Vegetables

Yuki (YOO-kee) (Japanese) She Is Snow White

Yuri (YOO-ree) (Japanese) She Is a Fragrant Lily

Yuuna (YOO-nuh) (Japanese) She Is a Garden of Wholesome Vegetables

Yuzuki (yoo-ZOO-kee) (Japanese) She Is Moon-Bright

Zoë (ZO-wee) (Dutch/Greek) She Is Life Itself

Zef (ZEF) (Dutch) He Is the Little One Whose Greatness Increases

Name Pairs and Groups
That Rhyme and Resonate

BOYS

🐾 **Abiel** (AY-bee-yul) (Hebrew) His Father Is Almighty God

Adriel (AY-dree-yul) (Hebrew) He Is the Multitude That Worships God

Ammiel (AM-yul) (Hebrew) He Is of the Holy Family of God

Azriel (AZ-ree-yul) (Hebrew) His God Assists Him

Emmanuel (im-MAN-yul) (Hebrew) His God Is Ever-Present

Ezekiel (ee-ZEE-kee-yel) (Hebrew) His God Gives Him Power

Gamaliel (guh-MAIL-yul) (Hebrew) He Profits from God's Greatness

Ishmael (ISH-may-yul) (Hebrew) His God Always Hears Him

Nathaniel (nuh-THAN-yul) (Hebrew) He Is God's Divine Gift

Remiel (REM-yul) (Hebrew) He Is God's Mercy

🐾 **Aphros** (AF-rohss) (Latin) He Is the Ocean's Depths

Bythos (BYE-thohss) (Latin) He Is the Ocean's Foam
   Aphros and Bythos were Ichthyocentaurs: ocean spirits with the tails of fish, the bodies of horses, and the torsos of humans.

🐾 **Arjuna** (ar-ZHOO-nah) (Sanskrit) He Is Pure and White

Aruna (ah-ROO-nah) (Sanskrit) He Is a Beautiful Terra-Cotta Color

Chyavana (chee-yah-VAH-nah) (Sanskrit) He Is Wisdom

Isana (ee-SAH-nah) (Sanskrit) He Is the Northeast

Karna (KAR-nah) (Sanskrit) He Hears Everything

Krishna (KRISH-nah) (Sanskrit) He Is a Beautiful Dark Color

Mohana (mo-HAH-nah) (Sanskrit) He Is Enchanting

Ramayana (rah-mah-YAH-nah) (Sanskrit) He Journeys to Enlightenment

Vahana (vah-HAH-nah) (Sanskrit) He Accompanies the Divine Ones

Varuna (vah-ROO-nah) (Sanskrit) He Is the Blue Sky

🐾 **Caanthus** (KAN-thus) (Latin) He Is the Caanthus River, Greece

Indus (IN-dus) (Latin) He Is the Indus River, Anatolia
   Caanthus and Indus were two of the river-spirits, called the Flumina by the Romans, who personified every river in the world.

🐾 **Jason** (JAY-sun) (Greek) He Is a Healer

Donovan (DAHN-uh-vun) (Irish) He Descends from the Darkly Handsome One
   Jason Donovan (1968–) is an Australian singer known for such hits as 1988's "Especially for You," performed with Australian songstress Kylie Minogue.

🐾 **Macareus** (muh-KAIR-ree-yus) (Greek) He Is Makaria, Greece

Horus (HOR-rus) (Greek) He Is Horos, Greece
King Lycaon of Arcadia, Greece, had fifty sons.
When Lycaon offended Zeus, high king of the
gods, Zeus transformed Lycaon into a wolf and
slew his sons. Their legacy was fifty magnificent
cities.

Mario (MAH-ree-yoh) (Italian) He Is
Powerfully Male
Aldo (ALL-doh) (Italian) He Is Aristocratic
Mario and Aldo Andretti (both born in 1940) are
twins who won numerous racing champion-
ships, including the Italian Grand Prix and
Indianapolis 500.

GIRLS

Aemilia (ee-MEEL-yah) (Latin) She Is a
Courageous Rival
Aurelia (or-REEL-yah) (Latin) She Is Pure Gold
Aemilia Paulla (c. 230 B.C.–163 B.C.) was the
wife of the Roman conqueror Scipio Africanus.
Aemilia's reputation for compassion influenced
generations of Roman stateswomen, including
Aurelia Cotta, whose son was the legendary
Julius Caesar.

Anjelica (an-JEL-ih-kuh) (English) She
Resembles God's Angels
Annabelle (an-nuh-BEL) (English) She Is
Beautiful and Lovable
Annabeth (AN-nuh-beth) (English) She Is the
Graceful Little One Whose God Is Abundant
Annalee (an-nuh-LEE) (English) She Is Our
Graceful Little Meadow
Anneka (AN-neh-kuh) (English/Swedish) She Is
Beloved and Graceful
Annice (uhn-NEESS) (English) She Shimmers
with Sunlight
Annis (AN-niss) (English) She Shimmers with
Sunlight
Annmarie (AN-muh-ree) (English) She Is the
Graceful Little One Who Is Love Itself
Annora (uhn-NOR-ruh) (English) She Is Honor
Itself
Anona (uh-NO-nuh) (English) She Is the Ninth

Cassie (KASS-see) (English) She Is the
Beloved One Who Enlightens Humanity
Connie (KON-nee) (English) She Is Our
Constant Love
Cassie Powney is a British actress who has
shared acting-parts with her twin sister, Connie
Powney, including a role in the nineties British
soap-opera Hollyoaks.

Lindsay (LIN-zee) (Scottish) She Is an
Island in Lincolnshire, England
Sidney (SID-nee) (English) She Is a Beautiful
Island
Lindsay and Sidney Greenbush (1970–) are
American twin actresses, best remembered for
their sharing of the role of Carrie Ingalls on
the television series Little House on the Prairie
(1974–1983).

Lorainne (lor-RAIN) (English/French) She Is
Lorraine, France
Lorayne (lor-RAIN) (English/French) She Is
Lorraine, France
Loreen (lo-REEN) (English) She Is Our Little
Laurel Wreath of Victory
Lorelle (lo-REL) (English) She Is a Laurel
Wreath of Victory
Loren (LOR-run) (English) She Is a Laurel
Wreath of Victory
Lorena (lo-RAY-nuh) (English/Spanish) She Is
Lorraine, France
Loretta (lo-RET-tuh) (English) She Is Our Little
Laurel Wreath of Victory
Lorn (LORN) (English/Scottish) He Is Lorne,
Scotland
Lorna (LOR-nuh) (English/Scottish) She Is
Lorne, Scotland
Lorri (LOR-ree) (English) She Is Our Little
Laurel Wreath of Victory

Mana (MAH-nah) (Japanese) She Is Pure-
Hearted
Kana (KAH-nah) (Japanese) She Is Powerful
Mana and Kana Mikura (1986–) are Japanese
twin actresses who share the stage name
ManaKana and have appeared in Japanese
soap operas such as Futarikko. *The twins have*
also recorded hit songs such as 2008's "Naite
Waratte."

Serena (seh-REE-nah) (Greek) She Is
Peacefully Serene
Venus (VEE-nus) (Latin) She Is Love and Desire
Serena Williams (1981–) and Venus Williams
(1980–) are African-American sisters who have
dominated the world of professional tennis from
the 1990s to the 2000s.

Shanna (SHAHN-nuh) (English) She Is Our
Fragrant Little Lotus Flower
Shanae (shuh-NAY) (English) Her God Is Gracious
Shanelle (shuh-NEL) (English) She Brings
Sparkling Water

Shanene (shuh-NEEN) (English) She Is God's Graceful Little Messenger

Shania (shuh-NYE-yuh) (English/Ojibwa) She Comes Running to Us

Shanice (shuh-NEESS) (English) She Is God's Graceful Little Messenger

Shanika (shuh-NEE-kuh) (English/American) She Is God's Graceful Little Messenger

Shaniqua (shuh-NEE-kwuh) (English/American)She Is God's Graceful Little Messenger

Shannah (SHAN-nuh) (English) She Is Our Fragrant Little Lotus Flower

Shannen (SHAN-nun) (English/Irish) She Is the Shannon River, Ireland

BOYS AND GIRLS

🌿 **Allannah** (uhl-LAH-nuh) (English) She Is a Beautiful Stone

Allegra (uh-LEG-ruh) (English/Italian) She Is Happily Energetic

Allissa (uh-LIS-suh) (English) She Is Aristocratic

Ally (AL-lee) (English) She Is Our Little Aristocrat

Allycia (uhl-LEE-see-yuh) (English) She Is Aristocratic

Allyn (AL-lin) (English) He Is a Magnificent Stone

Alphonzo (al-FAHN-zo) (English) He Is Aristocratic

Alva (AHL-vuh) (English/Hebrew) He Is Majestic

Alvena (al-VEE-nuh) (English) She Befriends the Elfin People

Alwilda (al-WIL-duh) (English) She Fights as Fiercely as the Elfin People

🌿 **Alyce** (AL-liss) (English) She Is Our Little Aristocrat

Alycia (uhl-LEE-see-yuh) (English) She Is Aristocratic

Alysa (uh-LIS-suh) (English) She Is Aristocratic

Alyx (AL-lix) (English) She Protects Humanity

Amabel (AM-uh-bel) (English) She Is Greatly Beloved

Ambrosine (am-bro-ZEEN) (English) She Lives Forever

Amery (AY-mur-ree) (English) He Works Tirelessly

Amias (ah-MYE-yuss) (English) He Is a Trusted Companion

Amice (uh-MEESS) (English) He Is a Trusted Companion

Amie (AY-mee) (English) She Is Greatly Beloved

🌿 **Amilia** (uh-MEEL-yuh) (English) She Is Powerfully Competitive

Anastacia (an-uh-STAY-see-yuh) (English) She Is Reborn to New Life

Andi (AN-dee) (English) She Is the Little One Who Is as Powerful as any male

Andra (AND-ruh) (English) She Is as Powerful as any male

Andrea (AN-dree-yuh) (English) She Is as Powerful as any male

Andriana (an-dree-AH-nuh) (English) She Is Hadria, Italy, and Is as Mighty as any Male

Andrina (an-DREE-nuh) (English) She Is as Powerful as any male

Angelia (an-jel-EE-yuh) (English) She Is God's Angelic Messenger

Angelle (an-JEL) (English) She Is God's Angelic Messenger

Anissa (uh-NEESS-suh) (English) She Is Graceful

🌿 **Ananta** (ah-NAHN-tah) (Sanskrit) He Is Eternal

Bharata (bah-RAH-tah) (Sanskrit) He Is Eternal

Chitragupta (chee-trah-GOOP-tah) (Sanskrit) He Judges Souls

Lalita (lah-LEE-tah) (Sanskrit) She Is Delightful

Nirta (NEER-tah) (Sanskrit) He Is Above the Law

Revanta (reh-VAHN-tah) (Sanskrit) He Descends from the Sun

Shanta (SHAHN-tah) (Sanskrit) She Is Peaceful

Sita (SEE-tah) (Sanskrit) She Is the Furrows of the Fields

Sunita (soo-NEE-tah) (Sanskrit) She Is Well-Mannered

Vasanta (vah-SAHN-tah) (Sanskrit) He Is the Fresh Spring Season

🌿 **Ansel** (AN-sul) (English) He Is Our Helmet of Divine Protection

Ansley (ANZ-lee) (English) She Is a Hidden Meadow

Anson (AN-sun) (English) He Descends from the One Who Shines with Golden Sunlight

Antonette (an-toh-NET) (English) She Is Our Blossoming Little Flower

Antwan (AN-twahn) (English) He Is Our Blossoming Flower

April (AYP-rul) (English) She Is the Fresh Springtime Month of April

Arabella (air-uh-BEL-luh) (English) She Is Beautiful and Lovable

Ariana (air-ee-AN-nuh) (English) She Is Holy

Aric (AIR-ric) (English) He Rules Forever

Ariella (air-ee-YEL-luh) (English) She Is God's Noble Lioness

☙ **Arleen** (ahr-LEEN) (English) She Is a Free Spirit

Arlen (AR-len) (English) He Is an Oath

Arlie (AR-lee) (English) She Is the Forest Where Eagles Soar

Arline (ar-LEEN) (English) She Is a Free Spirit

Arn (ARN) (English) He Is Our Soaring Little Eagle

Arnie (AR-nee) (English) He Is Our Soaring Little Eagle

Arnold (AR-nuld) (English) He Is Our Soaring Eagle

Arron (AR-run) (English) He Is a Lofty Mountain

Arvel (ar-VEL) (English) He Is Our Soaring Eagle

Aryana (ar-ee-AHN-nuh) (English) She Is Holy

☙ **Ashli** (ASH-lee) (American) She Is a Meadow in the Ash-Tree Forest

Baby (BAY-bee) (English) She Is an Adorable Baby

Landry (LAN-dree) (English) She Is a Powerful Ruler

Lindsey (LIN-zee) (Scottish) She Is an Island in Lincolnshire, England

Mackenzie (mah-KEN-zeh) (Irish) She Descends from the Handsome Man

Nikki (NIK-kee) (English) She Is Humanity's Little Triumph

Scotty (SKAHT-tee) (Scottish) He Is the Little One Who Is the Nation of Scotland

Sherry (SHAIR-ree) (French) She Is Darling and Sweet

Steffani (STEF-fuh-nee) (American) She Is a Shining Crown

Valerie (VAL-eh-ree) (Latin) She Is Powerful

☙ **Ashlie** (ASH-lee) (English) She Is a Meadow in the Ash-Tree Forest

Billi (BIL-lee) (American/English) She Is the Little One Who Is a Helmet of Protection

Corey (KOR-ree) (Scottish) She Is a Hillside Teeming with Swift Animals

Gabi (GAH-bee) (German) She Is God's Little Prophet

Kimberly (KIM-bur-lee) (English) She Is the Realm of the Royal Fortress

Lacey (LAY-see) (English) She Is Lassy, France

Shelley (SHEL-lee) (English) He Is a Meadow by a Riverbank

Sonny (SUN-nee) (English) He Is Our Devoted Little Son

Tiffany (TIF-fuh-nee) (English) She Proves God's Greatness

Zachery (ZAK-uh-ree) (English) His God Remembers Him

☙ **Aubree** (AW-bree) (English) She Has the Power of the Magical Elfin People

Bailee (BAY-lee) (English) She Enforces the Law as a Trusted Bailiff

Josie (JO-zee) (English) She Is the Little One Whose Greatness Increases

Kali (KAH-lee) (Sanskrit) She Is Magnificently Dark

Kelsey (KEL-see) (English) She Is an Island of Liberty

Kristy (KRIS-tee) (English) She Is Christ's Little Follower

Lexi (LEK-see) (English) She Is Humanity's Little Protector

Marki (MAR-kee) (American) She Is the Little One Who Is as Powerful as any male

Marley (MAR-lee) (English) He Is a Peaceful Forest

Reiley (RYE-lee) (Irish) He Is Supreme

☙ **Barnaby** (BAR-nuh-bee) (English) He Descends from the Great Prophet

Buddy (BUD-dee) (English) He Is a Trusted Friend

Cary (KAIR-ree) (English) He Is the Beloved Warrior

Gaby (GAB-bee) (American) She Is God's Little Prophet

Hallee (HAL-lee) (American) She Is the Great Manor Hall

Imani (ih-MAH-nee) (Swahili) She Is Pure Faith

Lily (LIL-lee) (English) She Is a Fragrant Lily

Mikki (MIK-kee) (Japanese) She Is a Beautiful Story

Sammi (SAM-mee) (English) She Is the Little One Heard by God

Teddy (TED-dee) (English) He Is Our Little Present from God

🕊 **Ben** (BEN) (English) He Is the Little One Who Comes from the South

Gwen (GWEN) (Welsh) She Is Beautifully Fair

> *The cartoon television show* Ben 10 *produced by Cartoon Network follows the adventures of young Ben Tennyson, discoverer of an alien device that transforms him into superheroes. The show also stars Ben's adventurous cousin, Gwen Tennyson.*

🕊 **Beverley** (BEV-ur-lee) (English) She Is the River of the Beavers

Courtney (KORT-nee) (English) She Has a Cute Nose

Dickie (DIK-kee) (American) She Is Powerfully Courageous

Gigi (ZHEE-zhee) (French) She Is the Little One Who Farms the Land

Hailey (HAY-lee) (English) She Is a Meadow of Hay in the Woodlands

Jodi (JO-dee) (English) She Is the Little One Whose Greatness Increases

Keke (KEE-kee) (American) She Is the Little Pure-Hearted One

Naelee (NEE-lee) (American) She Descends from the Great Poet

Robbie (RAHB-bee) (English) He Is the Little Brilliantly Renowned One

Rodney (RAHD-nee) (English) He Is a Famous Island

🕊 **Brandon** (English) (BRAN-dn) He Is a Wheat-Covered Hill

Dustin (DUS-tun) (English) He Is the Mighty Rock of Thor, God of Thunder

Dyllan (DIL-lun) (Welsh) He Is the Mighty Ocean

Erin (AIR-run) (Irish) She Is the Nation of Ireland

Evan (EV-vuhn) (Welsh) His God Is Gracious

Jason (JAY-sun) (Greek) He Is a Healer

Jordan (JOR-duhn) (Hebrew) She Is the Jordan River, Israel

Kaitlin (KAYT-lun) (English) She Is Pure-Hearted

Kieran (KEE-ruhn) (Irish) He Is the Little Black-Haired One

Vivien (VIV-ee-yuhn) (French) She Wants to Live

🕊 **Brie** (BREE) (Irish) She Is Lofty and Powerful

Cammie (KAM-mee) (English) She Is the Little One Who Observes Sacred Rituals

Cherie (shur-REE) (French) She Is Darling and Sweet

Davey (DAY-vee) (English) He Is the Little One Who Is Greatly Beloved

Jeffrey (JEFF-ree) (English) He Is the Land of Peace

Joey (JO-wee) (English) He Is the Little One Whose Greatness Increases

Katy (KAY-tee) (English) She Is the Little Pure-Hearted One

Melody (MEL-uh-DEE) (English) She Sings a Sweet Melody

Omri (AHM-ree) (Hebrew) She Is Our Harvest of Abundant Wheat

Staci (STAY-see) (English) She Is Abundantly Productive

🕊 **Brittany** (BRIT-nee) (English) She Is Bretagne, France

Cory (KOR-ree) (Scottish) He Is a Hillside Teeming with Swift Animals

Emmy (EM-mee) (Dutch) She Is the Little One Who Is Our Entire Universe

Kaley (KAY-lee) (English) She Is the Pure-Hearted Little One Who Is a Beautiful Meadow

Macaulay (muh-KAW-lee) (Scottish) He Descends from the Great Ancestor

Macey (MAY-see) (English) She Is the Land of the Tireless Marchers

Maddie (MAD-dee) (English) She Is the Little Town of Magdala, Israel

Mindy (MIN-dee) (English) She Is the Little One Who Is Darkly Beautiful

Rory (ROR-ree) (Scottish) He Is the Monarch with Fiery Red Hair

Stacey (STAY-see) (English) She Is Abundantly Productive

🕊 **Casey** (KAY-see) (Irish) He Descends from the Vigilant One

Courtnee (KORT-nee) (English) She Has a Cute Little Nose

Florrie (FLOR-ree) (English) She Is the Little One Who Flourishes

Haylie (HAY-lee) (English) She Is a Meadow of Sweet Hay in the Forest

Hilary (HIL-uh-ree) (English) She Laughs with Joy

Johnny (JON-nee) (English) He Is the Little One Whose God Is Gracious

Kaylee (KAY-lee) (English) She Is the Little Pure-Hearted One Who Is a Meadow

Lori (LOR-ree) (English) She Is a Laurel Wreath of Victory

Sandy (SAN-dee) (English) She Is Humanity's Little Protector

Temi (TEH-mee) (American/English) She Is Our Beautiful Little Palm Tree

ᣔ *Chrissie* (English) She Is Christ's Little Follower

Christa (KRIS-tuh) (English) She Is Christ's Little Follower

Christabel (KRIS-tuh-bel) (English) She Is Christ's Beautiful Follower

Christabella (kris-tuh-BEL-luh) (English) She Is Christ's Lovely Follower

Christal (KRIS-tul) (English) She Sparkles Like Diamonds

Christiana (kris-tee-AH-nuh) (English/Italian) She Follows Christ

Christianne (kris-tee-YAN) (English) She Follows Christ

Christine (kris-TEEN) (English) She Follows Christ

Christmas (KRIS-muss) (English) He Is Christmas Day

Chrysanta (kris-SAHN-tuh) (English) She Is a Fragrant Chrysanthemum

ᣔ *Delanie* (duh-LAY-nee) (English) She Is a Beautiful Alder-Tree Forest

Fergie (FUR-ghee) (Scottish) She Is the Little One Who Is as Powerful as any Male

Fritzi (FRIT-see) (German) She Is Our Peaceful Little Ruler

Jessie (JESS-see) (English) She Is God's Divine Gift

Kallie (KAL-lee) (English) She Is Our Powerful Little Warrior

Melanie (MEL-uh-nee) (German) She Is Darkly Beautiful

Missy (MISS-see) (English) She Is Our Busy Little Honeybee

Natalie (NAT-ah-lee) (French) She Is Christmas Day

Tory (TOR-ree) (English) She Is the Little One Who Is Triumph for Humanity

Tracey (TRAY-see) (English) She Is Thrace

ᣔ *Fanny* (FAN-nee) (English) She Is the Beloved Little One Who Is the Nation of France

Alexander (al-ex-AN-dur) (Greek) He Protects Humanity

The 1982 Swedish film Fanny and Alexander, directed by famed filmmaker Ingmar Bergman (1918–2007), follows the adventures of two siblings living in early nineteenth-century Sweden.

ᣔ *Faustus* (FAH-oh-stus) (Latin) He Is Favored with Good Fortune

Fausta (FAH-oh-stah) (Latin) She Is Favored with Good Fortune

Faustus Sulla (49 B.C.–A.D. 9) was a Roman conqueror whose first wife, the noblewoman Junia Albina, bore Faustus a beloved daughter, Fausta Sulla.

ᣔ *Geertruida* (ghair-TROO-duh) (Dutch) She Is a Powerful Weapon

Gerben (GHAIR-ben) (Dutch) He Is a Bear Wielding a Spear

Gerd (GHAIRT) (Dutch) She Is Our Powerful Little Weapon

Gerlach (GHAIR-lahk) (Dutch) He Is the One to Whom a Spear Is a Plaything

Gerlof (GHAIR-lawf) (Dutch) He Is a Wolf Wielding a Spear

Gerolf (ghair-RAWLF) (Dutch) He Is a Wolf Wielding a Spear

Gerolt (ghair-RAWLT) (Dutch) He Rules with Powerful Weapons

Gerrit (GHAIR-rit) (Dutch) He Rules with Powerful Weapons

Gert (GHAIRT) (Dutch) He Is Our Powerful Little Weapon

Gerwulf (GHAIR-voolf) (Dutch) He Is a Wolf Wielding a Spear

ᣔ *Lyn* (LIN) (English/Welsh) She Is a Clear Lake

Lynda (LIN-duh) (English) She Is Exceptionally Beautiful

Lyndi (LIN-dee) (English/German) He Is the Little One Who Is a Lime-Tree Mountain

Lyndsay (LIN-zee) (English/Scottish) She Is an Island in Lincolnshire, England

Lynna (LIN-nuh) (English/Welsh) She Is Truly the One Who Is a Clear Lake

Lynton (LIN-tun) (English) He Is a Town of Lime Trees

Lynwood (LIN-wood) (English) He Is a Forest of Lime Trees

Lyric (LEER-rik) (English) He Is a Lyric Poem
Lysette (lih-SET) (English/French) She Demonstrates God's Abundance
Lyssa (LIS-suh) (English/Greek) She Is Fury

⌘ **Marijke** (mah-RYE-kuh) (Dutch) She Is Our Little Beloved One
Marike (MAH-ree-kuh) (Dutch) She Is Our Little Beloved One
Marilou (mahr-ee-LOO) (Dutch) She Is a Lover and a Warrior
Marinus (MAHR-ih-nuss) (Dutch) He Is the Mighty Ocean
Marita (muh-REE-tah) (Dutch) She Is Our Little Beloved One
Marja (MAHR-yuh) (Dutch) She Is Love
Marjan (MAHR-yun) (Dutch) She Is Graceful and Beloved
Marjolein (MAHR-yo-leen) (Dutch) She Is the Fragrant Marjoram Herb
Marleen (MAHR-leen) (Dutch) She Is Our Beloved Tower of Strength
Marloes (MAHR-loos) (Dutch) She Is a Peaceful Warrior

⌘ **Thea** (THEE-yuh) (English/Greek) She Is Divine Inspiration
Thelma (THEL-muh) (English) She Has a Powerful Will
Theo (THEE-yo) (English) He Is Our Little Present from God
Theobald (THEE-uh-bahld) (English) He Has the Courage of Humanity

Theodora (thee-uh-DOH-ruh) (English/Greek) She Is God's Divine Gift
Thomasina (tah-mah-SEE-nuh) (English) She Is a Precious Twin
Thorburn (THIR-burn) (English/Scottish) He Is Thor's Unconquerable Bear
Thorley (THOR-lee) (English) He Is a Meadow Filled with Thorn-Bushes
Thornton (THORN-tun) (English) He Is the Town near the Thorn-Bushes
Thurstan (THUR-stun) (English) He Is Thor's Mighty Stone Cliffs

⌘ **Tracee** (TRAY-see) (English) She Is Thrace
Trafford (TRAF-furd) (English) She Is the Crossing-Place Used by Fish-Trappers
Tranter (TRAN-tur) (English) He Builds Magnificent Carriages
Travers (TRA-vurz) (English) He Gathers Highway Fees from Travelers
Travis (TRA-viss) (English) He Gathers Highway Fees from Travelers
Trecia (TREE-shuh) (English) She Is Our Little Aristocrat
Trenton (TREN-tun) (English) He Is a Town on the Trent River, England
Trev (TREV) (English/Welsh) He Is the Little One Who Is a Glorious City
Trey (TRAY) (English) He Is the Little One Who Is the Holy Trinity
Tricia (TRIH-shuh) (English) She Is Our Little Aristocrat

Name Pairs and Groups
for Classic Boy/Girl Matches

Adonis (ah-DAH-niss) (Greek) He Is the Master
Persephone (pur-SEF-uh-nee) (Greek) She Is a Beautiful Maiden
Adonis was the god of the springtime blooming of Earth's flowers. Persephone, goddess of spring, loved Adonis deeply; but Adonis was tragically slain while hunting.

Aegina (ee-JEE-nuh) (Greek) She Is the One Who Raises Goats
Actor (AK-tur) (Greek) He Is a Bold Leader
Aegina was a wise nymph or nature-spirit who bore a son, Menoetius, to her husband, Actor, son of Azeus. The Greek island-nation of Aegina was named in Aegina's honor.

Bart (BART) (English) He Is the Little One Who Descends from the Serious One
Lisa (LEE-suh) (English) Her God Is Abundance
Bart and Lisa Simpson are two of the title characters in the animated television program The Simpsons, *produced by the Fox Broadcasting Company. The dysfunctional but beloved Simpsons consist of bumbling dad Homer, his loving wife Marge, brainy Lisa Simpson, and her mischievous brother Bart.*

Bijan (bee-ZHAHN) (Persian) He Is the Hero of the Epic of Kings
Manijeh (MAHN-ee-zhay) (Persian) She Is the Heroine of the Epic of Kings
In "Shahnameh" (The Epic of Kings) (c. A.D. 1000), a poem written by the Persian bard Ferdowsi (A.D. 935–A.D. 1020), the warrior Bijan

expresses his adoration for Princess Manijeh. "Shahnameh" is revered by Iranians as the greatest saga in the Persian language.

Bill (BILL) (English) He Is Our Little Protector
Hillary (HIL-luh-ree) (English) She Laughs with Joy
Bill Clinton (1946–) was the forty-second president of the United States (1993–2001). Hillary Clinton, Bill's wife, was the first lady of the United States during the period 1993–2001.

Circe (SUR-see) (Greek) She Is the Circle of Life
Nonnos (NON-nohss) (Greek) He Is the Godfather
Nonnos (c. fourth century A.D.) was a Greek poet who wrote the Dionysiaca, *regarding Dionysus, Greek god of wine. Nonnos also wrote of Circe, the enchantress who tried to keep King Odysseus of Ithaca as her lover, but was forced to release him by Zeus, high king of the gods.*

Frankie (FRANK-kee) (English) He Is the Beloved One from the Nation of France
Johnnie (JAHN-nee) (English) Her God Is Gracious
"Frankie and Johnnie" is the title of an American folk tune performed by numerous recording artists including Elvis Presley. The song relates the poignant story of a tragic love affair.

Gale (GAYL) (Greek) She Is a Mighty Windstorm
Aelianus (ee-lee-AH-nuss) (Latin) He Is Godlike

The Roman grammarian Claudius Aelianus (Aelian) (c. A.D. 175–c. A.D. 235) wrote On the Nature of Animals (De Natura Animalium), *which related the myth of the enchantress Gale.*

🐾 **George** (JORJ) (English) He Farms the Land
Laura (LOR-rah) (Latin) She Is a Laurel Wreath of Victory
George Bush (1946–) was the forty-third president of the United States (2001–2009). Laura Bush, George's wife, was first lady of the United States during the period 2001–2009.

🐾 **Hansel** (HAHN-sul) (German) He Is the Little One Whose God Is Gracious
Gretel (GREH-tul) (German) She Is the Beloved One Who Is a Priceless Pearl
Hansel and Gretel are siblings in the 1812 German fairy tale Hänsel und Gretel, *published in* Grimm's Fairy Tales *by brothers Jacob Grimm (1785–1863) and Wilhelm Grimm (1786–1859). Hansel and Gretel, abandoned in the forest, survive by their wits.*

🐾 **Hero** (HE-ro) (Greek) She Is Our Bold Savior
Leander (lee-AN-dur) (Greek) He Is the Lion-Hearted Man of Liberty
Beautiful Hero lived in a tower in the Greek city-state of Sestos. Each night, Hero's true love, Leander, swam the Hellespont Strait between his home of Abydos and Sestos. But when Leander tragically drowned, Hero leapt from her high tower in grief.

🐾 **Isis** (EYE-sis) (Greek) She Is a Royal Throne
Cadmus (KAD-mus) (Greek) He Is Our Revered Ancestor
Isis, also called Io, was a nymph or nature-spirit of the Argive River in Greece. When Zeus, high king of the Olympian gods, fell in love with Isis, Zeus's wife, Hera, jealously drove Isis into exile. When Isis's descendant Cadmus finally returned to Greece, he established the magnificent city-state of Thebes.

🐾 **Jack** (JAK) (English) He Is Beloved and His God Is Gracious
Jill (JIL) (English) She Is the Little One Who Rules Heaven
The television series Jack & Jill *aired from 1999 to 2001 on the WB Network, and featured American actress Amanda Peet as Jacqueline "Jack" Barrett, and Ivan Sergei as David "Jill" Jillefsky. Amanda Peet was included in the 2000*

listing of People Magazine's *50 Most Beautiful People in the World.*

🐾 **Linus** (LYE-nus) (Greek) He Is the Golden Flax in the Fields
Lucy (LOO-see) (English) She Is Radiance
Linus and Lucy van Pelt are siblings in the classic American comic strip Peanuts, *created in 1950 by artist Charles Schulz (1922–2000). Linus is known for his wit, while Lucy is known for her powerful pragmatism.*

🐾 **Manchester** (MAN-ches-tur) (English) He Is a Town on a Hill
Chelsea (CHEL-see) (English) She Is a Harbor with Chalk Cliffs
The Manchester United Football Club is one of the most successful British soccer teams ever, with 300 million fans globally, and two European Cup victories so far. Another great British team is the Chelsea Football Club, with two Union of European Football Associations Winners' Cup victories currently.

🐾 **Monica** (MAH-nee-kah) (Italian) She Counsels Wisely
Ross (RAWSS) (Scottish) He Is a Lofty Cliff
Monica Geller-Bing is a chef played by actress Courteney Cox Arquette on the television program Friends, *which aired on the National Broadcasting Corporation (NBC) network from 1994 to 2000. Monica's rivalry with her brother Ross—played by actor David Schwimmer—sometimes takes the form of rough-and-tumble football games.*

🐾 **Orpheus** (OR-fee-yus) (Greek) He Is the Dark Evening
Eurydice (yur-ID-ih-see) (Greek) She Is Justice
The demigod Orpheus was one of the most famous harpists in Greece. But when Orpheus's wife Eurydice died, Orpheus gained even greater fame by descending into the underworld of Hades to retrieve Eurydice. Sadly, his quest was unsuccessful.

🐾 **Romeo** (RO-mee-yoh) (Italian) He Journeys to the Eternal City of Rome
Juliet (joo-lee-YET) (English) She Is the Beloved One Who Resembles God
Romeo Montague and Juliet Capulet were the title characters in the tragedy Romeo and Juliet *by the revered English playwright William Shakespeare (1564–1616). Romeo and Juliet hail from two warring families; and their love*

*eventually brings their two warring families
together.*

🌣 **Samia** (SAM-ee-yah) (Greek) She Is Samos
Island, Greece
Maiandros (mye-AN-drohss) (Greek) He Is the
Maiandros River, Greece
*Samia was a nymph or water-spirit embody-
ing the freshwater sources of Samos Island in
Greece. Samia's father was Maiandros, god of
the Maiandros River in Anatolia (Turkey).*

🌣 **Sibyl** (SIH-bul) (Greek) She Is an All-Seeing
Prophetess
Olympius (oh-LIM-pee-yus) (Greek) He Is
Mount Olympus, Greece
*Herophile was a famed Sibyl—a prophetess able
to see the future. The Sibyl's father was Zeus,
high king of the Olympian gods, who was also
known by the title Olympius, the personification
of Mount Olympus, home of the gods.*

🌣 **Timotheos** (tim-ah-THEE-ohss) (Greek) He
Honors God
Leda (LEE-dah) (Greek) She Is Joyful
*Timotheos (fourth century B.C.) was a Greek
sculptor whose genius endeared him to the
Greeks and later to the Romans. His greatest
creation was the statue Leda and the Swan, por-
traying Queen Leda of Sparta, pursued by Zeus,
who had assumed the form of a swan.*

🌣 **Zeno** (ZEE-no) (Greek) He Is Heaven's King
Megara (meh-GAIR-rah) (Greek) She Seeks
Vengeance
*The Cyprian scholar Zeno (334 B.C.–262 B.C.)
invented the philosophy of Stoicism, where people control their destinies by controlling their
emotions. Zeno was influenced by the Megarian
philosophers of the city-state of Megara. Megara
was named after Princess Megara, wife of the
demigod Heracles.*

Name Groupings for Multiple Siblings:
Twins, Triplets, Quads, Quints, and More

BOYS

🐾 **Alamanni** (ahl-uh-MAHN-nee) (German) He Is Powerfully Male

Hanon (HAN-nun) (German) He Is Powerfully Male

Kel (KEL) (Indo-European) He Is Powerfully Male

Kinnus (KIN-nuss) (German) He Is Powerfully Male

Manfred (MAN-fred) (German) He Is Powerfully Male

Manheimar (MAHN-hy-mar) (Icelandic) He Is Powerfully Male

Mannus (MAN-nus) (German) He Is Powerfully Male

Mentis (Latin/German) He Is Powerfully Male

Monn (MAHN) (French) He Is Powerfully Male

Vir (VEER) (Icelandic) He Is Powerfully Male

🐾 **Alan** (AL-lun) (English) He Is a Beautiful Little Stone

Frank (FRANK) (English) He Is the Little One Who Is the Nation of France

Gordon (GOR-dun) (Scottish) He Is a Lofty Hill

Gus (GUS) (Scottish) He Is the Little One Who Is Absolutely Magnificent

Ken (KEN) (English) He Is the Handsome Little One

Rusty (RUS-tee) (English) He Has Fiery-Red Hair

Scott (SKAHT) (Scottish) He Is the Nation of Scotland

Story (STOR-ree) (English) He Is a Legend, Retold Forever

Wally (WALL-lee) (English) He Is Our Little Military Commander

🐾 **Alasdair** (ahl-ahss-DAIR) (Scottish) He Protects Humanity

Beckham (BEK-kum) (English) He Is a Homestead near a River

Bellamy (BEL-luh-mee) (English) He Is a Trusted Friend

Bright (BRITE) (American/English) He Is a Brilliant Genius

Carlson (KARL-sun) (Norwegian) He Descends from the Mighty Soldier

Daley (DAY-lee) (Irish) He Descends from the Magnificent Nation

Ellis (EL-liss) (Welsh) He Is Compassionate

Hanson (HAN-sun) (Danish) He Descends from the Little One Whose God Is Gracious

Siegelman (SEE-gul-mun) (German) He Carries the Official Seal

🐾 **Albertus** (al-BUR-tuss) (Latin) He Is Brilliantly Aristocratic

Bruno (BROO-no) (German) He Is a Chocolate-Brown Color

Clifford (KLIF-furd) (English) He Is a Crossing-Place near a Cliff

Cyril (SEER-reel) (Slovak) He Is Supreme

Dane (DAYN) (English) He Is a Peaceful Valley

Derek (DAIR-rik) (English) He Is God's Divine Gift

Domenico (doh-MEN-ih-ko) (Italian) He Is from God

Ebenezer (eb-uh-NEE-zur) (Hebrew) He Is Rock-Solid

Gautama (go-TAH-muh) (Sanskrit) He Is a Mighty Bull

Gerardo (zhair-AHR-doh) (Italian) He Is a Powerful Weapon

🐾 **Aleksandar** (ahl-ek-SAHN-dahr) (Serbian) He Protects Humanity

Andrej (AHN-dray) (Serbian) He Is Powerful

Danijel (DAHN-yil) (Serbian) His God Judges Wisely

Filip (FIH-lip) (Serbian) He Befriends Horses

Jovan (YO-vahn) (Serbian) His God Is Gracious

Marko (MAR-ko) (Serbian) He Is Powerfully Male

Pavle (PAH-vul) (Serbian) He Has Humility

Petar (PAY-tar) (Serbian) He Is Rock-Solid

Stefan (STEH-fahn) (Serbian) He Is a Shining Crown

Toma (TOH-muh) (Serbian) He Is a Precious Twin

🐾 **Aleksander** (al-ek-SAHN-dur) (Albanian) He Protects Humanity

Bashkim (BAHSH-kim) (Albanian) He Brings Us Together

Behar (bay-HAR) (Albanian) He Is the Warm Summer Season

Besnik (BEZ-nik) (Albanian) He Is Loyal

Dardan (DAR-dun) (Albanian) He Is the Nation of the Dardani

Flamur (flah-MUR) (Albanian) He Is the Proud Banner of Our Family

Gjon (JAHN) (Albanian) His God Is Gracious

Kostandin (ko-stan-DEEN) (Albanian) He Is Dependably Constant

Skender (SKEN-dur) (Albanian) He Is Humanity's Little Protector

Ylli (EE-lee) (Albanian) He Is a Heavenly Star

🐾 **Alonzo** (uh-LAHN-zoh) (Italian) He Is Aristocratic

Casimir (KAZ-ee-meer) (Polish) He Is a Powerful Destroyer

Charles-Augustin (shall-aw-goo-STAN) (French) He Is Magnificent

Cleveland (KLEEV-lund) (English) He Is the Land of Rolling Hills

Coleman (KOL-mun) (Irish) He Is a Peaceful Dove

Colt (KOLT) (English) He Is a Powerful Horse

Eduard (ed-WAHRD) (Czech) He Is a Wealthy Protector

Gaspard (gas-SPAR) (French) He Holds the Priceless Treasure

Gustave (goos-TAHV) (French) He Is the Great Staff of the Gothic People

🐾 **Amedeo** (ahm-eh-DAY-yoh) (Italian) He Is God's Beloved

André-Marie (ahn-dray-mah-REE) (French) He Is the Power of Love

Beaufort (boh-FOR, BO-furt) (French) He Is Beautiful and Strong

Beck (BEK) (English) He Is a Rushing River

Biro (BEER-ro) (Hungarian) He Judges Fairly

Bolivar (BO-lee-var) (Spanish) He Is the Mill by the Stream

Edvard (ED-vard) (Czech) He Is a Wealthy Protector

Elbert (EL-burt) (Dutch) He Is Brilliantly Aristocratic

Gian (jee-YAHN) (Italian) He Is the Little One Whose God Is Gracious

Kaiser (KYE-zur) (German) He Is Covered with Manly Hair

🐾 **Amimitl** (ah-mee-MEE-tul) (Nahuatl) He Is a Clear Lake

Atl (AH-tul, AT-tul) (Nahuatl) He Is Fresh Water

Camaxtli (kuh-MOSH-tlee) (Nahuatl) He Is Fire and Warfare

Mextli (MESH-tlee) (Nahuatl) He Is Thunderstorms and Warfare

Mixcoatl (mish-ko-AH-tul) (Nahuatl) He Is a Star-Dragon

Nanahuatzin (nah-nuh-WAHT-sin) (Nahuatl) He Is the Radiant Sun

Paynal (pay-NAHL) (Nahuatl) He Is God's Messenger

Quetzalcoatl (ket-sul-KWAH-tul) (Nahuatl) He Is a Feathered Dragon

Tlaloc (TLAY-lok) (Nahuatl) He Is Lightning and Rain

Tonatiuh (toh-NAH-tee-yah) (Nahuatl) He Is the Brilliant Sun

🐾 **Andrew** (AN-droo) (Greek) He Is Powerfully Male

Christopher (KRIS-tuh-fur) (English) He
Follows Christ
Daniel (DAN-yul) (Hebrew) His God Judges
Wisely
Ethan (EE-thun) (Hebrew) He Is Rock-Solid
and Eternal
Jacob (JAY-kub) (Hebrew) He Surpasses
Everyone
Joseph (JO-suf) (Hebrew) His Greatness
Increases
Joshua (JAHSH-oo-wuh) (Hebrew) His God Is
Eternal Salvation
Matthew (MATH-yoo) (Hebrew) He Is God's
Divine Gift
Michael (MYE-kul) (Hebrew) He Resembles
God
William (WILL-yum) (English) He Protects
Humanity

& **Archibald** (AR-chih-bald) (Scottish) He Is
Courageous
Barney (BAR-nee) (English) He Is the Little
One Descended from the Prophet
Julio (HOO-lee-yoh) (Spanish) He Rules
Heaven
Lester (LES-tur) (English) He Is Leicester,
England
Manolo (man-OH-loh) (Spanish) His God Is
Ever-Present
Orville (OR-vil) (English) He Is the Golden City
Raj (RAHZH) (Sanskrit) He Is a Majestic Prince
Timothy (TIM-uh-thee) (Greek) He Honors God
Tucker (TUK-kur) (English) He Makes Beautiful
Cloth
Woodrow (WOOD-row) (English) He Is a Row
of Houses in the Woodlands

& **Bias** (BYE-us) (Greek) He Is Human
Strength
Chilon (KYE-lon) (Greek) He Is Green Pastures
Cleobulus (klee-AH-buh-lus) (Greek) He Is
Glorious
Delphi (DEL-fye) (Greek) He Is Delphi, Greece
Pausanias (paw-ZAY-nee-yus) (Greek) He
Grows Olives
Periander (pair-ee-AN-dur) (Greek) He Travels
Amongst the Aegean Islands
Pittacus (PIT-uh-kus) (Greek) He Is Peaceful
Sage (SAYJ) (English) His Wisdom Is Renowned
Solon (SO-lahn) (Greek) He Is Wisdom
Thales (THAY-leez) (Greek) He Is a Blossoming
Flower

Greek historian Pausanias (second cen-
tury A.D.) wrote that the Seven Sages were
humanity's wisest rulers: Bias of Priene, Chilon
of Sparta, Cleobulus of Lindus, Periander of
Corinth, Pittacus of Mytilene, Solon of Athens,
and Thales of Miletus.

& **Bill** (BIL) (English) He Is Our Gleaming
Little Helmet of Divine Protection
Brian (BRYE-yun) (Irish) He Is Aristocratic
Charlie (CHAR-lee) (English) He Is a Mighty
Little Soldier
Chuck (CHUK) (English) He Is Powerfully Male
Darryl (DAIR-rul) (English) He Is Airelle,
France
Dick (DIK) (English) He Is the Powerful Little
One
Ian (EE-yun) (Scottish) His God Is Gracious
Keith (KEETH) (Scottish) He Is Solid
Hardwood
Mick (MIK) (English) He Is God's Little Disciple
Ronnie (RAHN-nee) (Scottish) He Is Our Wise
Little Counselor

& **Bowden** (BO-den) (English) He Is the
Crescent-Shaped Hill
Carmelo (kar-MEL-lo) (Italian) He Is a Fragrant
Garden
Gibson (GIB-sun) (Scottish) He Descends from
the One Who Is a Promise-Keeper
Hammer (HAM-mur) (English) He Is a
Powerful Tool-Maker
Ike (IKE) (English) He Is the Little One Who
Laughs with Joy
Jared (JAIR-red) (Hebrew) He Descends from
the Mighty Ones
Keith (KEETH) (Scottish) He Is Solid
Hardwood
Latrell (luh-TREL) (American/French) He
Holds Flowers
Marion (MAIR-ee-yun) (French) He Is the
Beloved One Who Is Love Itself
Tony (TOH-nee) (English) He Is Our
Blossoming Little Flower

& **Calvin** (KAL-vin) (English) His Head Is
Smooth and Hairless
Chester (CHES-tur) (English) He Is a Fortified
Castle
Gerald (JEH-ruld) (English) He Rules with
Powerful Weapons
Grover (GRO-vur) (English) He Is a Magnificent
Grove of Trees

Herbert (HUR-burt) (English) He Is a Brilliant Conqueror

Lyndon (LIN-dun) (English) He Is a Fragrant Lime Tree on a Lofty Hill

Millard (MIL-lurd) (English) He Safeguards the Mill

Ronald (RAHN-nuld) (Scottish) He Rules by Wise Counsel

Zachary (ZAK-uh-ree) (English) His God Remembers Him

Woodrow (WOOD-row) (English) He Is a Row of Houses in the Woodlands

👬 **Clyde** (KLYDE) (Scottish) He Is the River Clyde, Scotland

Connie (KAHN-nee) (English) He Is a Cornucopia of Abundance

Elgin (EL-jin) (Irish) He Is Aristocratic

Gail (GAYL) (English) He Is a Mighty Storm

Jerry (JAIR-ree) (English) He Is the Beloved Little One Whose God Is Uplifting

Kareem (kuh-REEM) (Arabic) He Is Noble and Giving

Magic (MAJ-jik) (American) He Is Enchanting

Slater (SLAY-tur) (English) He Roofs Houses with Slate

Vern (VURN) (English) He Is the Little One Who Is a Mighty Alder Tree

Wilt (WILT) (English) He Is the Clever Little One

👬 **Cobb** (KAHB) (English) He Is a Beautiful Hillock

Cobio (KO-bee-yoh) (Welsh) He Is a Beautiful Hillock

Cubby (KUB-bee) (English) He Is a Beautiful Hillock

Kekse (KEK-see) (Lithuanian) He Is a Beautiful Hillock

Khaver (kah-VAIR) (Yiddish) He Is a Beautiful Hillock

Kip (KIP) (English) He Is a Beautiful Hillock

Kobbi (KOBE-bee) (Icelandic) He Is a Beautiful Hillock

Koben (KO-ben) (German) He Is a Beautiful Hillock

Koddi (KODE-dee) (Icelandic) He Is a Beautiful Hillock

Schober (SHO-bur) (German) He Is a Beautiful Hillock

👬 **Donald** (DAH-nuld) (Scottish) He Is Humanity's Beloved Ruler

Goldberg (GOLD-burg) (German) He Is a Golden Mountain

Keyes (KEEZ) (English) He Lives Near the Beautiful Waterfront Quays

Larry (LAIR-ree) (English) He Is the Little One Who Is a Laurel Wreath of Victory

Pearson (PEER-sun) (English) He Descends from the Rock-Solid One

Porter (POR-tur) (English) He Guards the Doorway

Quinn (KWIN) (Irish) He Descends from the Great Leader

Robson (ROB-sun) (English) He Descends from the Brilliant One

Schilling (SHIL-ling) (German) He Is Pure Gold

Shields (SHEELDS) (German) He Is the Protector of the People

👬 **Gerolamo** (zhee-RO-lah-mo) (Italian) His Name Is Sacred

Giordano (jee-or-DAH-no) (Italian) He Is the River Jordan, Israel

Guido (GWEE-doh) (Italian) He Is the Forest

Gustav (GOO-stahv) (German) He Is the Great Staff of the Gothic People

Hamid (hah-MEED) (Arabic) He Is Revered

Hannes (HAH-nuss) (German) He Is the Little One Whose God Is Gracious

Hellmut (HEL-moot) (German) His Protective Helmet Is His Genius

Jean-Baptiste (zhaw-bap-TEEST) (French) He Is the Baptized One Whose God Is Gracious

Jing (ZHING) (Chinese) He Is Absolutely Perfect

Kenelm (KEN-nulm) (English) He Wears His Helmet Courageously

👬 **John** (JAHN) (English) His God Is Gracious

Billy (BIL-lee) (English) He Is Our Little Helmet of Protection

Brian (BRYE-yun) (Irish) He Is Aristocratic

Ed (ED) (English) He Is Our Prosperous Little Guardian

Eric (AIR-ric) (Swedish) He Rules Forever

George (JORJ) (English) He Farms the Land

Paul (PAWL) (Latin) He Has Humility

Pete (PEET) (English) He Is the Little Rock-Solid One

Ringo (RING-go) (English) He Wears Many Rings

Stuart (STOO-wurt) (Scottish) He Safeguards Our Home

☺ **Manly** (MAN-lee) (English) He Is Humanity's Meadow in the Woodlands

Mustapha (moo-STAH-fah) (Arabic) He Is Selected by God

Nicolaus (NEE-ko-lohss) (German) He Is Humanity's Triumph

Noel (no-WEL) (French) He Is Christmas Day

Olympiodorus (oh-lim-pee-oh-DOR-rus) (Greek) He Is God's Divine Gift

Philipp (FEE-lip) (German) He Befriends Horses

Pietro (pee-AY-tro) (Italian) He Is Rock-Solid

Porphyry (por-FEER-ree) (Greek) He Is the Royal Purple

Regiomontanus (rezh-ee-oh-mahn-TAN-nus) (Latin) He Is the Mountain King

Reinhold (RYNE-holt) (German) He Rules with Wise Counsel

☺ **Maurice** (mor-REES) (French) He Is a Dark Moor

Don (DAHN) (English) He Is Our Little King

Gary (GAIR-ree) (English) He Is a Mighty Weapon

Greg (GREG) (English) He Is Our Little Guardian

Philip (FIL-ip) (Greek) He Befriends Horses

Reggie (REJ-jee) (English) He Is Our Wise Little Counselor

Ronnie (RAHN-nee) (Scottish) He Is Our Wise Little Counselor

Sheldon (SHEL-dun) (English) He Is a Peaceful Valley

Verdine (vur-DEEN) (American) He Is a Valley of Alder Trees

Wade (WAYD) (English) He Is Always Moving

☺ **Neil** (NEEL) (Irish) He Is a Great Victor

Bob (BAHB) (English) He Is the Glorious Little One

Chris (KRIS) (English) He Is Christ's Little Follower

Deke (DEEK) (American) He Is the Brave Little One

Edwin (ED-win) (English) He Is a Wealthy Companion

Gene (JEEN) (English) He Is Our Little Aristocrat

Guenter (GUN-tur) (German) He Is a Powerful Warrior

James (JAYMZ) (Hebrew) He Is Divinely Protected

Michael (MYE-kul) (Hebrew) He Resembles God

Wernher (VUR-nur) (German) He Guards the Military

Neil Armstrong was the first person to walk on the Moon in 1969; copilot Edwin Aldrin was next; and Michael Collins piloted the Command Module that brought all three men home. The NASA ground crew included Bob Gilruth, Chris Kraft, Deke Slayton, Gene Cernan, Guenter Wendt, James Webb, and Wernher von Braun.

☺ **Primus** (PRYE-mus) (Latin) He Is First

Secundus (seh-KUN-dus) (Latin) He Is Second

Tertius (TUR-shuss) (Latin) He Is Third

Quartus (KWOR-tus) (Latin) He Is Fourth

Quintus (KWIN-tus) (Latin) He Is Fifth

Sextus (SEX-tus) (Latin) He Is Sixth

Septimus (SEP-tih-mus) (Latin) He Is Seventh

Octavius (ahk-TAY-vee-yus) (Latin) He Is Eighth

Nonus (NON-nus) (Latin) He Is Ninth

Decimus (DESS-ih-mus) (Latin) He Is Tenth

☺ **Rui** (roo-WEE) (Portuguese) He Is the Mighty Little One

Sanjay (sahn-JYE) (Indian) He Is Humanity's Triumph

Serge (SAIRZH) (French) He Serves Humanity

Theodor (tay-oh-DOR) (German) He Is God's Divine Gift

Theodosius (thee-uh-DOH-shuhss) (Latin) He Makes Offerings to God

Theophilus (thee-AH-fuh-lus) (Latin) He Is God's Beloved

Tomás (toh-MAHSS) (Portuguese) He Is a Precious Twin

Warren (WAR-run) (English) He Is a Corral for Spirited Horses

Yaqub (yah-KOOB) (Arabic) He Surpasses Everyone

Zev (ZEV) (Hebrew) He Is a Courageous Wolf

☺ **Yi** (YEE) (Korean) He Is a Celebration

Ahpakyun (ah-pahk-YOON) (Korean) He Is a Little White Cloud

Gooeulli (goo-yool-LEE) (Korean) He Is Heaven's Kingdom

Gosiri (go-SEER-ree) (Korean) He Is Our Nation's Virtue

Hwanguk (wahng-GUHK) (Korean) He Is Our Brilliant Nation

Hwanin (wah-NEEN) (Korean) He Is Our Brilliant Nation

Hyukseo (hye-yook-say-YO) (Korean) His Intelligence Rules

Jiwiri (jee-wee-REE) (Korean) He Is Pure Gold

Joowooyang (joo-woo-YANG) (Korean) He Is a Chrysanthemum

Seokjeim (say-oak-jay-EEM) (Korean) He Is Pleasant

Korean scholar Yi Yurip wrote Handan Gogi, *a chronicle of Hwanguk, a fabled Korean kingdom.* Handan Gogi *also details the lives of seven Hwanin or Kings of Hwanguk: Ahpakyun, Hyukseo, Gosiri, Joowooyang, Seokjeim, Gooeulli, and Jiwiri.*

GIRLS

⌘ **Abene** (ah-BAY-nay) (Basque) She Is a Marble Column

Agurne (ah-GUR-nay) (Basque) She Is the One We Welcome into the World

Alaina (ah-LAYN-uh) (Basque) She Rejoices

Alazne (ah-LAHZ-nay) (Basque) She Proves God's Greatness

Amaia (ah-MYE-yuh) (Basque) She Is Our Fondest Hope

Argine (ar-ZHEEN-yuh) (Basque) She Is Radiance

Eider (AY-dur) (Basque) She Is Beautiful

Elixabete (ay-lish-ah-BAY-tay) (Basque) Her God Is Abundance

Erlea (air-LAY-yuh) (Basque) She Is a Busy Honeybee

Esti (ES-tee) (Basque) She Is a Busy Honeybee

⌘ **Abigail** (AB-ih-gayl) (Hebrew) She Is Her Father's Joy

Alexis (uh-LEX-us) (uh-LEK-siss) (Greek) She Protects Humanity

Ashley (ASH-lee) (English) She Is a Meadow in an Ash-Tree Forest

Elizabeth (ee-LIZ-uh-beth) (English) Her God Is Abundance

Emily (EM-uh-lee) (English) She Is Powerfully Competitive

Emma (EM-muh) (English) She Is Our Universe

Hannah (HAN-nuh) (Hebrew) She Is Graceful

Madison (MAD-ih-sun) (English) She Descends from the Powerful Warrior

Olivia (oh-LIV-ee-yuh) (English) She Is a Beautiful Olive Tree

Samantha (suh-MAN-thuh) (English) Her God Hears Her

⌘ **Adrijana** (ah-dree-AH-nuh) (Serbian) She Is Hadria, Italy

Aleksandra (ahl-ex-AHN-druh) (Serbian) She Protects Humanity

Danijela (dahn-YEL-luh) (Serbian) Her God Judges Wisely

Jelena (yel-LAY-nuh) (Serbian) She Is a Radiant Torch

Katarina (kah-tah-REE-nuh) (Serbian) She Is Pure-Hearted

Kristina (kreess-TEE-nah) (Serbian) She Follows Christ

Marija (mah-REE-yuh) (Serbian) She Is Love

Natalija (nah-TAHL-yuh) (Serbian) She Is Christmas Day

Suzana (soo-ZAN-nuh) (Hebrew) She Is a Fragrant Lotus Flower

Teodora (tay-oh-DOR-ruh) (Serbian) She Is God's Divine Gift

⌘ **Agnieszka** (ahg-nee-YESH-kuh) (Polish) She Is a Gentle Child

Alina (ah-LEE-nah) (German) She Is Aristocratic

Breann (bree-YAN) (English) She Is a Lofty Mountain

Jaime (JAY-mee) (English) She Is Divinely Protected

Krisily (kris-suh-LEE) (American/Greek) She Is a Meadow of Golden Blossoms

Lana (LAH-nah) (Russian) She Is Radiance

Linsey (LIN-zee) (American/English) She Is Lincolnshire, England

Myah (MYE-yuh) (Sanskrit) She Is a Lovely Dream

Nadia (NAH-dee-yuh) (English/French) She Is Our Fondest Dream

Nafeesa (nah-FEE-suh) (American/Arabic) She Is a Priceless Jewel

⌘ **Aina** (ah-EE-nuh) (Catalan) She Is Graceful

Anais (ah-nah-YEES) (Catalan) She Is Graceful

Beatriu (bay-ah-TREE-yoo) (Catalan) She Is a Great Voyager

Carme (KAR-may) (Catalan) She Slices and Cuts

Caterina (kaht-eh-REE-nuh) (Catalan) She Is
Pure-Hearted
Clara (KLAH-ruh) (Catalan) She Shimmers
with Fame
Dolors (doh-LORZ) (Catalan) She Understands
Sorrow
Eulalia (yoo-LAY-lee-yuh) (Catalan) She Speaks
Eloquently
Joana (zho-AH-nuh) (Catalan) Her God Is
Gracious
Joaquima (wah-KEE-muh) (Catalan) She Is the
Divinely Protected Little One

🕭 **Albena** (ahl-BAYN-yuh) (Bulgarian) She Is a
Fragrant Peony
Aleksandrina (ahl-ek-SAHN-drih-nuh)
(Bulgarian) She Protects Us
Anastasiya (ahn-nuh-STAH-see-yuh)
(Bulgarian) She Is Reborn to New Life
Anka (AHNG-kah) (Bulgarian) She Is the
Graceful Little One
Bilyana (beel-YAH-nah) (Bulgarian) She Is a
Powerful Medicinal Plant
Bisera (bee-SAIR-ruh) (Bulgarian) She Is a
Priceless Pearl
Bogdana (bahg-DAH-nah) (Bulgarian) She Is a
Present from Our Lord
Boyana (boy-YAH-nah) (Bulgarian) She Is
Aggression and War
Dana (DAH-nah) (Bulgarian) She Is the Little
One Who Is a Present from Our Lord
Darina (dah-REE-nah) (Bulgarian) She Is a
Present from Our Lord

🕭 **Alita** (ah-LEE-tah) (Spanish) She Is Our
Little Aristocrat
Anne-Katherine (ann-KATH-ur-rin) (English)
She Is Pure-Hearted and Graceful
Audra (AW-drah) (Lithuanian) She Is an
Unstoppable Hurricane
Keely (KEE-lee) (Irish) She Descends from the
Thin, Handsome Man
Lanore (luh-NOR) (American/English) She Is
the Little One Who Is Aliénor, France
Latoyia (luh TOY-yuh) (American) She Is
Humanity's Little Triumph
Melana (mel-AH-nuh) (American/Czech) She
Is Graceful
Misti (MIS-tee) (English) She Is the Morning
Mist
Su-Ying (soo-YING) (Chinese) She Is a Gentle
Prophet

Tarah (TAIR-ruh) (English/Irish) She Is a
Divine and Lofty Realm

🕭 **Allyson** (AL-lih-sun) (English) She Is Our
Little Aristocrat
Brenna (BREN-nuh) (English) She Is a Mighty
Sword
Cristin (KRIS-ten) (American/Danish) She
Follows Christ
Danelle (duh-NEL) (American/French) Her God
Judges Wisely
Haleigh (HAY-lee) (English) She Is a Meadow of
Hay in the Woodlands
Jeannine (juh-NEEN) (English) She Is the
Little One Whose God Is Gracious
Katee (KAY-tee) (English) She Is Our Little
Pure-Hearted One
Lacie (LAY-see) (American/English) She Is
Lassy, France
Leeann (lee-YAN) (English) She Is a Graceful
Meadow
Onawa (oh-NAH-wuh) (Diné) She Is Alert

🕭 **Alysha** (uh-LEE-shuh) (English) She Is
Aristocratic
Beckie (BEK-kee) (American/Hebrew) She Is
the Little One Who Brings Us Closer
Casandra (kuh-SAN-druh) (American/Greek)
She Enlightens Humanity
Chelsey (CHEL-see) (American/English) She Is
a Harbor with Chalk Cliffs
Jonelle (juh-NEL) (English) Her God Is
Gracious
Kaetlin (KAYT-lun) (American/English) She Is
Pure-Hearted
Keisha (KEE-shuh) (English/Hebrew) She Is a
Fragrant Cassia-Spice Tree
Shanon (SHAN-nun) (English/Irish) She Is the
Shannon River, Ireland
Tori (TOR-ree) (English) She Is Humanity's
Little Triumph
Vincenza (vin-CHEN-zuh) (Italian) She
Conquers Mightily

🕭 **Amunet** (AH-muh-net) (Egyptian) She Is
the Pure Atmosphere
Anuket (AHN-uh-ket) (Egyptian) She Embraces
Us All
Hathor (HAH-thor) (Egyptian) She Is the
Galaxy
Isis (EYE-sis) (Egyptian/Greek) She Is a
Majestic Throne

Ma'at (mah-HAHT) (Egyptian) She Is the Fair One Who Is the Law

Menhit (MEN-nit) (Egyptian) She Annihilates Enemies

Naunet (naw-NET) (Egyptian) She Is the Primal Ocean

Neith (NEETH) (Egyptian) She Is War

Satis (SAT-tis) (Egyptian) She Is the Life-Giving Flood

Sekhmet (SEK-met) (Egyptian) She Is War

⚘ **Andarta** (an-DAR-tah) (Gaulish) She Is Beloved and Invincible

Andraste (an-DRAHSS-tay) (Proto-Celtic) She Is Beloved and Invincible

Aveta (ah-VAY-tah) (Gaulish) She Is the Mother of Pure-Water Springs

Belisama (bel-ih-SAH-mah) (Gaulish) She Is a Clear Lake

Coventina (kuv-en-TEE-nah) (Latin) She Is the Water-Goddess

Damara (dah-MAR-rah) (Scottish) She Judges Fairly

Divona (dih-VO-nah) (Gaulish) She Is Fertility

Gallia (GAHL-lee-yah) (Gaulish) She Is Gaul

Rosemerta (roze-MAIR-tah) (Gaulish) She Is the Great Provider

Verbeia (vur-BEE-yah) (Proto-Celtic) She Is the Rain and the River

⚘ **Angelique** (awn-zhuh-LEEK) (French) She Is God's Angelic Messenger

Arnica (AR-nik-kuh) (American/Swedish) She Is Graceful and Beloved

Dia (DEE-yuh) (Latin) She Is the Glorious Morning

Doree (DOR-ree) (American/Hebrew) She Is a Woman for all Generations

Michon (mih-SHAWN) (American/English) She Is God's Disciple

Pratima (PRAH-tee-muh) (Sanskrit) She Mirrors the Divine

Shawna (SHAW-nuh) (English) Her God Is Great

Shaynee (SHAY-nee) (American/Yiddish) She Is Lovely to Behold

Trini-Ann (tree-nee-ANN) (American/Spanish) She Is the Blessed, Graceful Trinity

WaLynda (wah-LIN-duh) (American/Polish/English) She Is Beautifully Powerful

⚘ **Angie** (AN-jee) (English) She Is God's Little Angelic Messenger

Denette deh-NET) (American/French) She Is Anet, France

Jensie (JEN-see) (American/Onondaga) She Is a Peaceful Valley

Jina (JEE-nuh) (American/Italian) She Is Our Little Aristocrat

Juel (JOO-wul) (American/English) She Is a Priceless Jewel

Kristal (KRIS-tul) (English) She Sparkles Like Diamonds

Rosalie (RO-sah-lee) (French) She Is Our Fragrant Rose

Sallie (SAL-lee) (English) She Is Our Majestic Little Princess

Tiani (tee-AH-nee) (American/English) She Is Christ's Little Follower

Valarie (VAL-eh-ree) (Latin) She Is Powerful

⚘ **Anna** (AHN-nah) (Breton) She Is Graceful

Annick (AHN-neek) (Breton) She Is Our Graceful Little Princess

Franseza (frahn-SAY-suh) (Breton) She Is the Nation of France

Gaelle (gah-YEL) (Breton) She Is the Sacred One Who Rules Our Hearts

Katarin (kah-tah-REEN) (Breton) She Is Pure-Hearted

Katell (kah-TEL) (Breton) She Is Pure-Hearted

Maelle (mah-YEL) (Breton) She Is the Majestic One Who Rules Our Hearts

Mari (MAH-ree) (Breton) She Is Love

Nolwenn (NOHL-wen) (Breton) She Is the Sacred One from Noyal

Rozenn (ro-ZEN) (Breton) She Is Our Fragrant Rose

⚘ **Apollinariya** (uh-pah-ih-NAR-ee-yuh) (Bulgarian) She Creates all Light

Penka (PEN-kah) (Bulgarian) She Is the Little One Who Is Rock-Solid

Petia (PEH-tee-yah) (Bulgarian) She Is the Little One Who Is Rock-Solid

Polina (po-LEE-nah) (Bulgarian) She Is Our Radiant Little Star

Rada (RAH-dah) (Bulgarian) She Is Endless Rejoicing

Raina (rah-EE-nah, RAY-nah) (Bulgarian) She Is a Majestic Queen

Rositsa (ro-ZEET-sah) (Bulgarian) She Is the Little One Who Is the Morning Mist

Roza (RO-zah) (Bulgarian) She Is Our Fragrant Rose

Silva (SEEL-vah) (Bulgarian) She Is the Little One Who Is the Beautiful Woodlands

Stanislava (stah-nih-SLAH-vuh) (Bulgarian) She Stands Up for Justice

🕭 **Astarte** (ah-STAR-tay) (Phoenician) She Is Motherhood

Eshara (ee-SHAH-rah) (Babylonian) She Is Bountiful Harvests

Ishtar (ISH-tar) (Assyrian) She Is Motherhood

Liluri (lil-OOR-ree) (Syrian) She Is a Lofty Mountain

Nanshe (NAHN-shee) (Sumerian) She Is Motherhood

Nikkal (nik-KAHL) (Phoenician) She Is Sweet, Delectable Fruit

Ninimma (nin-EE-muh) (Sumerian) She Is a Woman's Private Treasure

Shala (SHAH-lah) (Babylonian) She Is War

Sharra Itu (shair-rah EE-too) (Sumerian) She Is Fertility

Tanit (tah-NEET) (Phoenician) She Is the Silvery Moon

🕭 **Bess** (BESS) (English) She Is God's Proof of Prosperity

Juliette (zhool-YET) (French) She Is the Little Relative of Julius Caesar

Manon (man-NAW) (French) She Is Our Little Beloved One

May (MAY) (English) She Is the Fresh Springtime Month of May

Mélisande (may-lee-SAWND) (French) She Works Boldly

Merry (MAIR-ree) (English) She Is Love and Merriment

Nina (NEE-nah) (Italian) She Is Our Little Blossoming Flower

Norma (NOR-mah) (Latin) She Rules Absolutely

Peace (PEESS) (English) She Is Peace

🕭 **Brunhilde** (broon-HIL-duh) (Norwegian) She Is Battle-Armor

Eir (AIR) (Norwegian) She Is Compassionate

Freyja (FRAY-yuh) (Norwegian) She Is Aristocratic

Jorth (URTH, YURTH) (Norwegian) She Is Mother Earth

Nanna (NAH-nah) (Norwegian) She Is Courageous

Saga (SAH-guh) (Norwegian) She Sees Clearly

Sif (SIF) (Norwegian) She Is the Bride of Lightning and Thunder

Sunna (SUN-nuh, SOON-nuh) (Norwegian) She Is the Sun

Syn (SIN) (Norwegian) She Guards Our Sacred Doorways

Verdandi (vair-DAHN-dee) (Norwegian) She Is Absolutely Necessary

🕭 **CaCe** (KAY-see) (American/Irish) She Descends from the Vigilant Man

Endia (IN-dee-yuh) (American/English) She Is India

Ivette (ee-VET) (Spanish) She Is the Magnificent Yew Tree

Jeanette (zhah-NET) (French) She Is God's Graceful Little Messenger

Kandace (KAN-diss) (English) She Is the Ruler of Ethiopia

Kenya (KEN-yuh) (Kikuyu/English) She Is a Majestic Snow-Covered Mountain

Kristie (KRIS-tee) (English) She Is Christ's Little Follower

Liane (lee-AH-nuh) (German) She Is the Little Relative of Julius Caesar

Sujoing (soo-ZHING) (American/Chinese) She Is a Sparkling Jewel

Yanaiza (yah-nah-EE-suh) (Spanish) She Is the Magnificent One Whose God Is Gracious

🕭 **Cari** (KAIR-ree) (English) She Is Our Beloved Warrior

Guerin (GAIR-ren) (American/French) She Safeguards Us All

Jaclyn (JAK-lin) (English) She Is Divinely Protected

Janaye (juh-NAY) (American/English) Her God Is Truly Gracious

Kyla (KYE-lah) (Scottish) She Is a Sparkling Waterway

Molly (MAHL-lee) (English) She Is Our Little Beloved One

Shandi (SHAN-dee) (American/English) She Is a Sweet, Intoxicating Liquor

Steffi (STEF-fee) (German) She Is Our Shining Little Crown

Tara (TAIR-ruh) (Irish) She Is the Divine Realm

Tiara (tee-AR-rah) (Greek) She Is a Shining Crown

🕭 **Carly** (KAR-lee) (English) She Is a Mighty Soldier

Cortney (KORT-nee) (English) She Has a Cute Nose

Ellyn (EL-lun) (American/English) She Is a Radiant Torch

Jeannie (JEEN-nee) (English) She Is God's Graceful Little Messenger

Karla (KAR-luh) (German) She Is a Mighty Warrior

Kasi (KASS-see) (American/English) She Is the Beloved One Who Enlightens Humanity

Kasie (KAY-see) (American/Irish) She Descends from the Alert Man

Kristi (KRIS-tee) (English) She Is Christ's Little Follower

Shauntay (shawn-TAY) (American/French) She Sings Sweet Melodies

Sitania (sih-TAHN-yuh) (American) She Is a Little Saint, Seated on a Glorious Throne

♫ Chanel (shuh-NEL) (French) She Brings Sparkling Water

Despina (des-SPEE-nuh) (Greek) She Is Our Beloved Lady

Geniece (juh-NEES) (American/English) Her God Is Truly Gracious

Jalin (JAY-lin) (American) She Is Our Divinely Protected Little Lioness

Keena (KEEN-nuh) (American/Irish) She Is Honorable and Wise

Meagan (MAY-gun) (English/Welsh) She Is Our Priceless Little Pearl

Mercedes (mur-SAY-deez) (Spanish) She Is Compassionate

Michaé (mih-KAY) (American/English) She Is God's Beloved Little Disciple

Michelle (mee-SHEL) (French) She Resembles God

Sharitha (shur-EE-thuh) (American/English) She Is a Clean Little Field

♫ Charlotte (SHAR-lut) (French) She Is Our Beloved Little Warrior

Cherry (CHAIR-ree) (English) She Is a Sweet Cherry

Clementine (KLEM-un-tyne) (French) She Is Compassionate

Eugénie (yoo-zhay-NEE) (French) She Is Aristocratic

Garden (gar-DEN) (Basque) Her Soul Is Transparent

Margarita (mar-guh-REE-tah) (Spanish) She Is Our Priceless Little Pearl

Melba (MEL-buh) (English) She Is Melbourne, Australia

Nellie (NEL-lee) (English) She Is Our Radiant Little Torch

Princess (PRIN-sess) (English) She Is a Majestic Princess

Theresia (tur-RAY-see-yah) (Italian) She Is the Warm Summer Season

♫ Ebony (EB-uh-nee) (English) She Is the Mighty-Black Ebony Tree

Elle (ELL) (French) She Is the Great Lady Herself

Essence (ESS-sunss) (English) She Is Essential Purity

Grazia (GRAHT-zee-yuh) (Italian) She Is Grace and Beauty

Kuri (KOOR-ree) (Japanese) She Is a Delicious Chestnut

Lilith (LIH-lith) (Assyrian) She Rules the Night

Lucky (LUHK-kee) (English) She Is Fortunate

Mirabella (meer-uh-BEL-lah) (Italian) She Is Astonishingly Magnificent

Sapna (SAHP-nah) (Sanskrit) She Is a Beautiful Dream

Tea (TAY-yah) (German) She Is God's Little Present

♫ Ekaterina (ee-kat-eh-REE-nah) (Bulgarian) She Is Pure-Hearted

Elena (ay-LAY-nah) (Bulgarian) She Is Radiance

Emilya (ee-MEEL-yah) (Bulgarian) She Works Tirelessly

Evangelina (ay-vahn-jah-LEE-nuh) (Bulgarian) She Is God's Holy Message

Evgeniya (ev-GAYN-yah) (Bulgarian) She Is Aristocratic

Galina (gal-EE-nah) (Bulgarian) She Is Tranquil

Gergana (ghur-GAH-nah) (Bulgarian) She Farms the Land

Hristina (riss-TEE-nah) (Bulgarian) She Follows Christ

Irina (ee-REE-nah) (Bulgarian) She Is Springtime

Iskra (EESK-rah) (Bulgarian) She Blazes Like Fire

♫ Eukene (yoo-KAY-nay) (Basque) She Is Aristocratic

Euria (YOOR-ee-yuh) (Basque) She Is Heaven's Refreshing Waters

Frantziska (frahn-SEES-kuh) (Basque) She Is the Nation of France

Garden (gar-DAYN) (Basque) She Sparkles Like Glass

Haizea (hye-ZAY-yuh) (Basque) She Is a Refreshing Breeze

Hirune (hee-ROO-nay) (Basque) She Is the Sacred Trinity

Irati (ee-RAH-tee) (Basque) She Is a Grove of Beautiful Fern-Plants

Izar (ee-ZAR) (Basque) She Is a Heavenly Star

Katalin (kah-tah-LEEN) (Basque) She Is Pure-Hearted

Lore (LOR-ray) (Basque) She Is a Fragrant Flower

& *Fifi* (FEE-fee) (French) She Is the Little One Whose Greatness Increases

Giovanna (gee-oh-VAHN-nah) (Italian) Her God Is Gracious

Gloriana (glo-ree-AH-nah) (Italian) She Is Magnificent Glory

Iolanthe (eye-oh-LAN-thee) (Greek) She Is a Fragrant Violet

Julie (JOO-lee) (English) She Is a Little Relative of Julius Caesar

Lucia (loo-CHEE-yah) (Italian) She Is Radiance

Lucrezia (loo-KREET-zee-yah) (Italian) She Is Wealthy and Successful

Luisa (loo-EE-zah) (Italian) She Is a Renowned Warrior

Lulu (LOO-loo) (Arabic) She Is a Priceless Pearl

Madonna (mah-DAHN-nah) (Italian) She Is Our Noble Lady

& *Hyades* (HYE-uh-deez) (Greek) She Is the Life-Giving Rain

Althaea (al-THEE-yuh) (Greek) She Cures and Heals

Ambrosia (am-BRO-zhah) (Greek) She Is Divine Nectar

Cleea (KLEE-yah) (Latin) She Is Esteemed

Coronis (kuh-RO-nus) (Greek) She Has Beautiful Curves

Eudora (yoo-DOR-rah) (Greek) She Is Well-Blessed

Phaio (FAY-yoh) (Greek) She Is Radiant

Phaislye (FAZE-lee) (Greek) She Shimmers

Pleione (PLEE-uh-nee) (Greek) She Is the Boundless Sky

Polyxo (puh-LIK-soh) (Greek) She Is So Sweet

The Hyades were the radiant star-nymphs (nature-deities) of the Constellation Hyades.

& *Iva* (EE-vah) (Bulgarian) She Is God's Graceful Little Messenger

Ivana (ee-VAH-nah) (Bulgarian) Her God Is Gracious

Ivet (ee-VET) (Bulgarian) She Is the Magnificent Yew Tree

Kalina (kah-LEE-nah) (Bulgarian) She Is the Beautiful Rowan Tree

Katerina (kah-teh-REE-nuh) (Bulgarian) She Is Pure-Hearted

Krasimira (krahss-ee-MEE-rah) (Bulgarian) She Is Lovely and Peaceful

Kristina (kreess-TEE-nah) (Bulgarian) She Follows Christ

Lala (lah-lah) (Bulgarian) She Is a Fragrant Tulip

Lidiya (LIH-dee-yuh) (Bulgarian) She Is the Nation of Lydia

Lilyana (lil-ee-AH-nah) (Bulgarian) She Demonstrates God's Abundance

& *Jenny* (JEN-nee) (English) She Is Fair and Beautiful

Carson (KAR-sun) (Norwegian) He Descends from the Curly Haired One

Eva (AY-vah) (Spanish) She Wants to Live

Evelyn (EV-uh-lin) (English) She Is Greatly Beloved and Desired

Lee (LEE) (English) She Is a Fragrant Meadow

Lou (LOO) (English) She Is Our Renowned Little Warrior

Lucille (loo-SEEL) (French) She Is Radiance

Patti (PAT-tee) (English) She Is the Little One Who Rules the Home

Peggy (PEG-ghee) (English) She Is Our Priceless Little Pearl

Virginia (vur-JIN-yuh) (Latin) She Is Chaste and Pure

Jenny Lou Carson (1915–1978) was the first American female country singer to hit No. 1, with 1945's "You Two-Timed Me Once Too Often." Jenny sang with her sisters Eva and Evelyn Overstake, and wrote songs for singers Patti Page and Peggy Lee.

& *Laia* (LYE-yuh, LAY-yuh) (Catalan) She Speaks Eloquently

Llora (YOR-ruh) (Catalan) She Is a Laurel Wreath of Victory

Mercè (mair-SAY) (Catalan) She Is Compassion

Meritxell (meh-ree-CHEL) (Catalan) She Is Merixtell, Andorra

Mireia (mee-RAY-yuh) (Catalan) She Is Adored

Monica (MO-nee-kah) (Catalan) She Counsels Wisely

Nuria (NOOR-ee-yuh) (Catalan) She Resembles the Virgin Mary

Remei (ray-MAY) (Catalan) She Cures Our Ills

Roser (RO-zur) (Catalan) She Is the Blessed Rosary

Salut (sah-LOO) (Catalan) She Is a Salute to Happiness

𝒷 **Lass** (LASS) (Scottish) She Is Chaste and Pure

Flicka (FLIK-kuh) (Swedish) She Is Chaste and Pure

Gunnhild (goon-HILD) (Swedish) She Is Chaste and Pure

Kona (KO-nuh) (Swedish) She Is Chaste and Pure

Lasah (LAH-suh) (Sanskrit) She Is Chaste and Pure

Lasca (LAHSS-kuh) (Portuguese) She Is Chaste and Pure

Lasikah (lah-SEE-kah) (Sanskrit) She Is Chaste and Pure

Lis (LEESS) (Latin) She Is Chaste and Pure

Polke (POWL-kuh, POLK) (English) She Is Chaste and Pure

Puella (poo-WEL-luh) (Latin) She Is Chaste and Pure

𝒷 **Laurencia** (lo-REN-see-yuh) (English) She Is a Laurel Wreath of Victory

Laurene (lo-REEN) (English) She Is Our Little Laurel Wreath of Victory

Lauressa (lo-RES-suh) (English) She Is Our Little Laurel Wreath of Victory

Laurinda (lo-RIN-duh) (English) She Is the Unique One

Laurissa (luh-RIS-suh) (English/Greek) She Is Cheerful

Lauryn (LO-rin) (English) She Is a Laurel Wreath of Victory

Lavena (luh-VEE-nuh) (English/Latin) She Is Pure-Hearted

Lavern (luh-VURN) (English) She Is a Beautiful Alder Tree

Lavone (luh-VAHN) (English) She Is the Magnificent Yew Tree

Lawanda (luh-WAHN-duh) (English) She Is an Enchanted Wand

𝒷 **Ludmilla** (lood-MEE-luh) (Bulgarian) She Is Beloved by Humanity

Marina (mah-REE-nuh) (Bulgarian) She Is the Blue Ocean

Mariya (MAH-ree-yuh) (Bulgarian) She Is Love

Marta (MAR-tuh) (Bulgarian) She Rules Our Home Magnificently

Milena (mil-LAY-nuh) (Bulgarian) She Is Graceful

Mira (MEE-rah) (Bulgarian) She Is Peaceful

Nedelya (neh-DEL-yuh) (Bulgarian) She Arrived on a Sunday

Nevena (neh-VAYN-yuh) (Bulgarian) She Is a Fragrant Marigold

Nikolina (nee-ko-LEE-nuh) (Bulgarian) She Is Humanity's Triumph

Olga (OL-guh) (Bulgarian) She Is Blessedly Sacred

𝒷 **Maia** (MYE-yah) (Basque) She Is Love

Miren (mee-REN) (Basque) She Is Love

Nagore (nah-GO-ray) (Basque) She Is the Basque Town of Nagore

Nahia (NYE-yuh) (Basque) She Is Greatly Beloved

Nekane (neh-KAH-nay) (Basque) She Understands Sorrow

Nere (NAIR-ray) (Basque) She Is Our Treasure

Oihana (oy-AH-nuh) (Basque) She Is a Beautiful Grove of Trees

Osane (oh-SAH-nay) (Basque) She Is the Panacea for Our Ills

Terese (tair-REZ) (Basque) She Is a Summer Harvest

Udane (oo-DAH-nay) (Basque) She Is the Warm Summer Season

𝒷 **Moira** (MOY-ruh) (Greek) She Is Destiny's Goddess

Aesa (EE-suh) (Latin) She Is Destiny

Atropus (uh-TRO-pus) (Latin) She Cannot Be Turned Back

Clotho (KLO-tho) (Latin) She Spins Destiny's Threads

Decima (DESS-ih-muh) (Latin) She Is Tenth

Heimarmene (hye-MAR-muh-nee) (Latin) She Is Destiny

Lachesis (luh-SHEE-sus) (Latin) She Decides Humanity's Fate

Morta (MOR-tuh) (Latin) She Is the Passing-On to the Next World

Nona (NO-nah) (Latin) She Is the Ninth

Pepromene (peh-PRAH-muh-nee) (Latin) She Shares All

   Aesa, Atropus, Clotho, Decima, Heimarmene, Lachesis, Morta, Nona, and Pepromene were the Parca—the Fates—who determined mortals' lives by giving everyone a portion of good and evil, then punishing those who chose evil.

🖉 **Prima** (PREE-mah) (Latin) She Is First

Secunda (seh-KOON-dah) (Latin) She Is Second

Tertia (TUR-shah) (Latin) She Is Third

Quarta (KWOR-tah) (Latin) She Is Fourth

Quinta (KWIN-tah) (Latin) She Is Fifth

Sextia (SEX-tee-yah) (Latin) She Is Sixth

Septima (SEP-tih-mah) (Latin) She Is Seventh

Octavia (ahk-TAY-vee-yah) (Latin) She Is Eighth

Nona (NO-nuh) (Latin) She Is Ninth

Decima (DESS-ih-mah) (Latin) She Is Tenth

🖉 **Samantha** (suh-MAN-thuh) (English) Her God Hears Her

Bertha (BUR-thuh) (German) She Shines Gloriously

Clara (KLAIR-ruh) (Italian) She Shimmers with Fame

Cornelia (kor-NEEL-yuh) (Latin) She Is a Cornucopia of Abundance

Endora (en-DOH-ruh) (English) She Is God's Sweet Little Bird

Esmeralda (EZ-mur-al-duh) (Spanish) She Is a Priceless Green Emerald

Hepzibah (HEP-zih-buh) (Hebrew) She Is Delightful

Panda (PAN-duh) (English) She Is a Beautiful Panda

Serena (seh-REE-nah) (Greek) She Is Peacefully Serene

Tabitha (TAB-ih-thah) (Aramaic) She Is a Swift Gazelle

🖉 **Svetlana** (svet-LAH-nuh) (Bulgarian) She Is a Sacred Light

Tatiana (tah-tee-AH-nah) (Bulgarian) She Picks and Chooses

Teodora (tay-oh-DOR-ruh) (Bulgarian) She Is God's Divine Gift

Tereza (tair-RAYT-suh) (Bulgarian) She Is a Summer Harvest

Tsveta (SVET-tah) (Bulgarian) She Is a Fragrant Flower

Varvara (VAR-vuh-ruh) (Bulgarian) She Is Our Divine Voyager

Vasilka (wah-SIL-kah) (Bulgarian) She Rules Humanity

Veronika (wair-AH-nee-kah) (Bulgarian) She Is Humanity's Triumph

Viktoriya (wik-TOR-ee-yah) (Bulgarian) She Is Humanity's Triumph

Violeta (wee-oh-LET-tuh) (Bulgarian) She Is a Fragrant Violet

🖉 **Yana** (YAH-nah) (Bulgarian) Her God Is Gracious

Yordan (YOR-dahn) (Bulgarian) She Is the Jordan River, Israel

Yordana (yor-DAH-nah) (Bulgarian) She Is the Jordan River, Israel

Yulia (YOOL-yuh) (Bulgarian) She Is Beautifully Youthful

Yuliana (yool-YAH-nah) (Bulgarian) She Is Julius Caesar's Relative

Zaharina (zah-hah-REE-nah) (Bulgarian) Her God Remembers Her

Zara (ZAH-rah) (Bulgarian) She Is the Little One Remembered by God

Zhenya (ZHEN-yah) (Bulgarian) She Is Our Little Aristocrat

Zhivka (ZHEEV-kah) (Bulgarian) She Is Filled with Energy

Zora (ZOR-ruh) (Bulgarian) She Is the Radiant Dawn

BOYS AND GIRLS

🖉 **Aamu** (ah-AH-moo) (Finnish) She Is the Sunrise

Aapeli (ah-AH-peh-lee) (Finnish) He Is the Breath of Life

Aapo (ah-AH-po) (Finnish) He Is the Father of Nations

Aatami (ah-AH-tah-mee) (Finnish) He Is History's Greatest Man

Aatos (ah-AH-tohss) (Finnish) She Is Spirituality

Aatto (ah-AH-toh) (Finnish) He Is a Courageous Wolf

Aatu (ah-AH-too) (Finnish) He Is a Courageous Wolf

Aimo (ah-EE-mo) (Finnish) She Is Our Portion of Grace

Aina (ah-EE-na) (Finnish) She Is the Universe's Most Important Person

Aki (AH-kee) (Finnish) He Is the Divinely Protected Little One

🐦 **Abigail** (AB-ih-gayl) (English) Her Father Is Joyful

Abram (AY-brum) (Hebrew) He Is the Great Father

Beverly (BEV-ur-lee) (English) He Is the River of the Beavers

Irvin (UR-vin) (Scottish) He Is the Great Friend Who Is a Mighty Wild Boar

Lachlan (LAHK-lun) (Scottish) He Is the Land of the Lochs (Lakes)

Lyon (lee-YO, LYE-yun) (French) He Is a Noble Lion

Marion (MAIR-ee-yun) (French) He Is the Beloved One Who Is Love Itself

Marshall (MAR-shul) (English) He Is a Law-Enforcer Riding a Horse

Millard (MIL-lurd) (English) He Safeguards the Mill

Patsy (PAT-see) (English) She Is the Little One Who Rules the Home

🐦 **Abira** (ah-BEER-rah) (Antioquia) He Is the Creator of All

Chia (CHEE-yah) (Chibcha) She Is the Moon

Kachina (kah-CHEE-nah) (Hopi) She Is the Bringer of Life

Kokopelli (ko-ko-PEL-lee) (Hopi) He Is the Bringer of Life

Manitou (MAHN-ih-too) (Anishinaabe) He Rules Heaven

Nanuq (nah-NUHK) (Inuktitut) He Is a Mighty Polar Bear

Sedna (SED-nah) (Inuktitut) She Is the Sea

Shakuru (shah-KOO-roo) (Pawnee) He Is the Sun

Tia (TEE-yah) (Haida) She Is a Blissful Departure from this World

Wi (WEE) (Lakota) He Is the Sun

🐦 **Adalberto** (ah-dahl-BAIR-toh) (Spanish) He Is Brilliantly Aristocratic

Adelaida (ah-del-AY-dah) (Spanish) She Is Aristocratic

Adelita (ah-deh-LEE-tah) (Spanish) She Is Our Little Aristocrat

Adora (ah-DOH-rah) (Spanish) She Is the Adoration of Christ

Agapito (ah-gah-PEE-toh) (Spanish) He Is Adored

Agata (AH-gah-tah) (Spanish) She Is Pure and Good

Agueda (ah-GWAY-dah) (Spanish) She Is Pure and Good

Alejo (ah-LAY-ho) (Spanish) He Is Humanity's Little Protector

Alfredo (ahl-FRAY-doh) (Spanish) He Is a Small but Wise Counselor

Alondra (ah-LAHN-drah) (Spanish) She Is Humanity's Little Protector

🐦 **Adi** (AH-dee) (Hebrew) He Is a Priceless Gemstone

Cobb (KAHB) (English) He Is a Beautiful Hillock

Cuthbert (KUTH-burt) (English) His Reputation Shines

Davidson (DAY-vid-sun) (English) He Descends from the Beloved Man

Dell (DEL) (English) He Is a Peaceful Valley

Donatello (doh-nah-TEL-lo) (Italian) He Is Our Little Present from God

Harley (HAR-lee) (English) He Is a Fragrant Meadow Filled with Hares

Maverick (MAV-rik) (English) He Is a Trail-Blazer

Melvil (MEL-vil) (Scottish/French) He Is a Rough Community

Temple (TEM-pul) (English) She Is a Warrior Who Fights for the Glory of the Temple

🐦 **Adrijana** (ah-dree-AH-nuh) (Croatian) She Is Hadria, Italy

Andela (AHN-jel-luh) (Croatian) She Is God's Angelic Messenger

Andelko (ahn-JEL-ko) (Croatian) He Is God's Angelic Messenger

Andrej (AHN-dray) (Croatian) He Is Powerfully Male

Antonija (ahn-TOH-nee-yuh) (Croatian) She Is a Lovely Flower

Baldo (BAL-doh) (Croatian) He Is the Divine Protector

Borislav (BOR-ih-slahv) (Croatian) He Gains Renown as a Warrior

Branislav (BRAHN-ih-slahv) (Croatian) He Gains Renown as a Warrior

Branka (BRAHN-kah) (Croatian) She Is the Little One Who Gains Renown as a Warrior

Danica (DAHN-ih-kuh) (Croatian) She Is the Morning Star

🌀 **Aeacus** (EE-uh-kus) (Latin) He Is Lamentation

Cerberus (SUR-bur-rus) (Greek) He Is the Demon of Darkness

Charon (CHAH-rahn) (Greek) He Is Blindingly Bright

Elysium (ee-LEE-zhum) (Latin) She Is the Realm of the Departed

Macaria (muh-KAR-ee-yah) (Greek) She Is a Blessed Release

Minos (MYE-nohss) (Latin) He Is a Labyrinth

Rhadamanthus (rad-uh-MAN-thus) (Latin) His Voyages Are Illustrious

Styx (STIX) (Latin) She Is the Styx River in the Underworld of the Departed

Tenebrae (tuh-NEE-bree) (Latin) They Are the Spirits of Departure

Thanatus (THAN-uh-tus) (Latin) He Is the Soul's Departure

> *The Roman goddess Macaria, the god Thanatus, and the goddesses called the Tenebrae all dispatched mortals to the underworld. There, Aeacus, Minos, and Rhadamanthus judged souls; Charon, the ferryman, led souls across the River Styx; and Cerberus guarded the underworld.*

🌀 **Aedan** (AY-dun) (Irish) He Is the Little One Who Is Blazing Fire

Bridget (BRIJ-jit) (Irish) She Is Knowledge

Cael (KALE) (Irish) His Physique Is Slender and Shapely

Cian (KEEN, KEE-yun) (Irish) He Is Honorable

Connor (KAHN-nur) (Irish) He Is the Master of Wolves

Deirdre (DEER-druh) (Irish) She Is all of Womankind

Fergus (FUR-gus) (Irish) He Is a Man of Magnificent Strength

Lir (LEER) (Irish) He Is the Blue Ocean

Maeve (MAYV) (Irish) She Is Enchanting

Morrigan (MOR-rih-gun) (Irish) She Is the Greatest of all Queens

🌀 **Aeron** (AIR-run) (Welsh) She Is War

Branwen (BRAN-wen) (Welsh) She Is an Ebony-Black Raven

Enid (EE-nid) (Welsh) She Is the Immortal Soul

Galahad (GAL-uh-had) (Welsh) He Is Gallant

Gawain (gah-WAYN) (Welsh) He Is a Snow-White Hawk

Govannon (go-VAN-nun) (Welsh) He Is a Powerful Metal-Worker

Guinevere (GWIN-uh-veer) (Welsh) She Is Beautifully Fair

Lancelot (LAN-suh-lot) (French) He Is the Little One Who Is a Weapon of Power

Myrddin (MUR-thin) (Welsh) He Is a Mighty Fortress Overlooking the Sea

Percival (PUR-sih-vul) (Welsh) He Ventures Far into the Valley

🌀 **Agathe** (ah-GAHT-tah) (Danish) She Is Pure and Good

Aksel (AHK-sel) (Danish) His Father Is Peaceful

Alberte (al-BAIR-tuh) (Danish) He Is Brilliantly Aristocratic

Alf (AHLF) (Danish) He Is the Magical Elfin Nation

Alvilda (al-VIL-dah) (Danish) He Fights with the Fury of the Elfin People

Anders (AHN-durz) (Danish) He Is Powerful

Andrea (AHN-dray-yuh) (Danish) She Is Powerful

Andreas (an-DRAY-us) (Greek) He Is Powerfully Male

Anja (AHN-yah) (Danish) She Is Our Graceful Little Princess

Annelie (AH-nuh-lee) (Danish) She Is the Graceful Little One Whose God Is Abundance

🌀 **Agni** (AG-nee) (Sanskrit) He Is Fire

Brahma (BRAH-mah) (Sanskrit) He Is a Prayer

Kali (KAH-lee) (Sanskrit) She Is Magnificently Dark

Krishna (KRISH-nah) (Sanskrit) He Is Beautifully Dark

Parvati (par-VAH-tee) (Sanskrit) She Descends from the Mountains

Rama (RAH-mah) (Sanskrit) He Is Pleasure

Savitri (sah-VEE-tree) (Sanskrit) She Is the Radiant Sun

Shakti (SHAHK-tee) (Sanskrit) She Is Incredible Power

Shiva (SHEE-vah) (Sanskrit) He Is Compassionate

Vishnu (VISH-noo) (Sanskrit) He Is Omnipresent

🌀 **Agostino** (ah-go-STEE-no) (Italian) He Is Absolutely Magnificent

Arie (AIR-ree) (Dutch) He Is Hadria, Italy

Basile (bah-ZEEL) (French) He Rules Humanity

Faten (fah-TEEN) (Arabic) She Is Endearingly Delightful

Josep (ZHO-sep) (Catalan) Her Greatness Increases
Majed (mah-ZHED) (Arabic) He Is Famous and Honorable
Mayu (MAH-yoo) (Japanese) She Has Integrity
Nuria (NOOR-ee-yuh) (Spanish) She Is Nuria, Spain
Sebastien (say-bahss-CHAW) (French) He Is Honorable
Wasmia (wahz-MEE-yuh) (Arabic) He Is Good-Looking

☙ **Ahti** (AH-tee) (Finnish) He Is the Blue Ocean
Aino (ah-EE-no) (Finnish) She Works Alone
Ilmatar (il-mah-TAR) (Finnish) She Is the Pure Atmosphere
Kyllikki (KIL-ih-kee) (Finnish) She Is Womankind
Louhi (LO-wee) (Finnish) She Is the Passage from this World
Meilikki (KYEL-ih-kee) (Finnish) She Is Determined
Nyyrikki (NEER-ih-kee) (Finnish) He Is a Tireless Hunter
Seppo (SEP-poh) (Finnish) He Is the Greatest Blacksmith of All
Tellervo (tel-LAIR-vo) (Finnish) She Is the Vast Woodlands
Vellamo (vel-LAH-mo) (Finnish) He Grows Ever-Greater

☙ **Akamu** (ah-KAH-moo) (Hawaiian) He Is History's Greatest Man
Akoni (ah-KO-nee) (Hawaiian) He Is Our Blossoming Little Flower
Anakoni (ah-nah-KO-nee) (Hawaiian) He Is Our Blossoming Flower
Haukea (how-KAY-yah) (Hawaiian) She Is Pure Snow
Hokulani (ho-koo-LAH-nee) (Hawaiian) She Is a Heavenly Star
Ikaia (eye-KAY-yah) (Hawaiian) His God Is Our Ever-Present Hope
Iokua (ee-OH-koo-wah) (Hawaiian) His God Is Eternal Salvation
Iolana (ee-oh-LAH-nah) (Hawaiian) She Is a Bird of Paradise
Kai (KYE) (Hawaiian) He Is the Blue Ocean
Kaimana (kye-MAH-nah) (Hawaiian) She Is the Blue Ocean

☙ **Akihiro** (ah-kih-HEE-ro) (Japanese) He Is a Brilliant Student

Eliyahu (el-ee-YAH-hoo) (Hebrew) His God Is the True God
Harald (HAR-rahld) (Norwegian) He Commands the Military
Holt (HOLT) (English) He Is the Vast Woodlands
Llewelyn (loo-EL-lin) (Welsh) He Is the Shimmering Sun
Mara (MAH-ruh) (Czech) She Is the Passage from this World
Meirion (MAIR-ee-yun) (Welsh) He Is Powerfully Male
Sanford (SAN-furd) (English) He Is the Place of the Sandy River-Crossing
Shri (SHREE) (Sanskrit) She Is Brightness
Yoav (yo-WAHV) (Hebrew) His God Is the True God

☙ **Alaska** (uh-LAS-kuh) (Aleut/English) She Is the Magnificent Land of Alaska
Dallas (DAL-luss) (English) He Is a Tranquil Home in a Fragrant Meadow
Hernandez (air-NAHN-dez) (Spanish) He Is Peaceful and Brave
Mir (MEER) (Russian) She Is Peace
Spirit (SPEER-rit) (English) She Is God's Divine Breath

☙ **Alberic** (AL-beh-rik) (German) He Is the Magical Power of the Elfin People
Brunhild (broon-HILD) (German) She Is Mighty Battle-Armor
Donar (doh-NAHR) (German) He Is Thunder and Lightning
Gunther (GOON-tur) (German) He Is an Invincible Army
Lorelei (LOR-uh-lye) (German) She Is the Alluring, Rocky Coastline
Nerthus (NUR-thus) (German) She Is a Healthy Mother
Odin (OH-din) (German) He Rules Heaven
Siegfried (SIG-freed) (German) He Gains Victory and Peace
Sieglinde (sih-GLIN-duh) (German) She Is a Gentle Victory
Wieland (VYE-lund) (German) He Is the Realm of Power and Warfare

☙ **Albina** (AHL-bee-nuh) (Czech) She Is Beautifully Fair
Alena (ah-LEE-nuh) (Czech) She Is Our Radiant Little Torch

Alexandr (ahl-ex-AHN-dair) (Czech) He
Protects Humanity
Alica (AH-lee-kah) (Czech) She Is Our Little
Aristocrat
Alzbeta (ahlz-BAY-tah) (Czech) Her God Is
Great Abundance
Amalia (uh-MAHL-yah) (Czech) She Works
Tirelessly
Aneta (ah-NAY-tah) (Czech) She Is Graceful
Antonie (AHN-toh-nee) (Czech) He Is a
Blossoming Flower
Apolena (ah-PO-lay-nah) (Czech) She Is the Light
Artur (ar-TOOR) (Czech) He Is a Courageous
Bear

⌖ **Alessandra** (ah-lih-SAN-druh) (Italian) She
   Protects Humanity
Andel (AHN-del) (Czech) He Is God's Angelic
Messenger
Eduardo (ed-WAHR-doh) (Spanish) He Is a
Wealthy Protector
Enrique (en-REE-kay) (Spanish) He Rules Our
Home Magnificently
Glenda (GLEN-dah) (Welsh) She Is Decent and
Pure-Hearted
Kansas (KAN-zuss) (American/Kansa) He Is the
Great American State of Kansas
Kingdom (KING-dum) (American/English) He
Is God's Kingdom
Moon (MOON) (English) She Is the Silvery Moon
Viliumas (VEEL-yum-muss) (Lithuania) He
Protects Humanity
Wojciech (VOY-chek) (Polish) He Is the Warrior
Who Protects Us

⌖ **Alf** (ALF) (Norwegian) He Is the Magical
   Elfin Nation
Alvis (AL-vis) (Norwegian) He Is Knowledge
Frea (FRAY-yuh) (Norwegian) She Is
Aristocratic
Gandalf (GAN-dolf, GAN-dalf) (Norwegian) He
Is the Wizard's Wand
Gunnar (GUN-nar, GOON-nar) (Norwegian) He
Is Our Battle-Ready Warrior
Loki (LO-kee) (Norwegian) He Shatters All
Oden (OH-dun) (Swedish) He Rules Heaven
Signy (SIG-nee) (Norwegian) She Is
Humanity's Triumph
Vidar (vih-DAR) (Norwegian) He Is a Warrior of
the Woodlands
Volund (VO-lund) (Norwegian) He Is the Realm
of Warfare

⌖ **Alice** (AL-liss) (English) She Is Our Little
   Aristocrat
Carroll (KAIR-rull) (Irish) He Battles Fiercely
Charles (CHARLZ) (English/French) He Is a
Mighty Warrior
Edith (EE-dith) (English) She Is a Prosperous
Warrior
Henry (HEN-ree) (English) He Rules Our
Home Magnificently
Isis (EYE-sis) (Greek) She Is a Majestic
Throne
John (JAHN) (Hebrew) His God Is Gracious
Lewis (LOO-wiss) (English) He Is a Renowned
Warrior
Lorina (lor-EE-nuh) (English) She Is a Laurel
Wreath of Victory
Pleasance (PLEH-zunss) (English) She Is
Pleasant Enjoyment

*British preacher Charles Dodgson (1832–1898),
also known as Lewis Carroll, wrote his 1865
classic* Alice's Adventures in Wonderland, *illus-
trated by John Tenniel, for Alice Pleasance Liddell, a neighbor-child who lived with her father
Henry, mother Lorina, and sister Edith. Charles
created his story while rowing with Alice on the
Isis River, Oxford.*

⌖ **Alto** (AL-to, ALL-toh) (Spanish) He Is
   Exalted
Angeles (ANJ-uh-lus) (Spanish) She Is a Legion
of God's Angelic Messengers
Berkeley (BURK-lee, BARK-lee) (Scottish) He Is
a Beautiful Birchwood Tree
Corvallis (kor-VAL-lis) (Latin) He Is the Soul of
the Peaceful Valley
Eugene (yoo-JEEN) (Greek) He Is Aristocratic
Palo (PAL-loh) (Spanish) He Is the Branch of a
Sacred Tree
Pullman (PULL-mun) (English) He Pulls Heavy
Loads
Seattle (see-AT-tul) (Suquamish) He Is All the
Ocean's Waters
Tempe (TEM-pee) (Greek) He Is a Peaceful
Valley
Tucson (TOO-sahn) (O'odham) He Is the Great
Black Mountain

⌖ **Alyson** (AL-ih-sun) (English) She Is Our
   Little Aristocrat
Ashley (ASH-lee) (English) She Is a Meadow in
the Ash-Tree Forest
Bart (BART) (Dutch) He Is the Little One Who
Descends from the Serious One

Corbin (KOR-bin) (English) He Is an Ebony-Black Raven

Lucas (LOO-kahs) (Latin) He Is Lucania, Italy

Monique (mo-NEEK) (French) She Is Our Only Advisor

Olesya (oh-LEES-ee-yuh) (Russian) She Is a Brave Protector

Ryne (RHINE) (American) She Is the Rhine River

Vanessa (vuh-NES-suh) (American/English) She Is a Graceful Friend Whose God Is Life

Zac (ZAK) (English) He Is the Little One Whom God Remembers

Amadeus (ah-mah-DAY-yus) (Latin) He Is God's Beloved

Annie (ANN-nee) (English) She Is Our Graceful Little Princess

Ben (BEN) (English) He Is the Little One Who Descends from the Great Southern Land

Bonnie (BAHN-nee) (Scottish) She Is Exceedingly Pretty

Clyde (KLYDE) (Scottish) He Is the River Clyde, Scotland

Eve (EEV) (Hebrew) She Wants to Live

Forrest (FOR-rest) (English) He Is a Verdant Wilderness

Kane (KAIN) (Irish) He Is Ready for War

Lawrence (LO-runss) (English) He Is a Laurel Wreath of Victory

Shane (SHAIN) (Irish) His God Is Gracious

Amanda (uh-MAN-duh) (English) She Is Worthy of Love

Carrie (KAIR-ree) (English) She Is Our Beloved Warrior

Chris (KRIS) (English) He Is Christ's Little Follower

Clay (KLAY) (English) He Is the Little One Who Is the Town Built on Solid Clay

Fantasia (fan-TAY-zhuh) (Italian) She Improvises

Jennifer (JEN-nih-fur) (Welsh) She Is Beautifully Fair

Jordin (JOR-dun) (Hebrew) She Is the River that Flows Forever

Kelly (KEL-lee) (Irish) She Is Conquest and War

Ruben (ROO-bin) (Dutch) Behold, He Is Our Glorious Son

Taylor (TAY-lur) (English) He Sews with Great Skill

Amen (ah-MEN) (Egyptian) He Is the Great One Who Is Eternally Invisible

Ammon (AM-mun) (Egyptian) He Is Hidden from Human Eyes

Anubis (uh-NOO-biss) (Egyptian) He Is Our Majestic Descendant

Aten (AT-tun) (Egyptian) He Is the Golden Disk of the Sun

Iah (EYE-yuh) (Egyptian) He Is the Silver Disk of the Moon

Nephthys (NEF-thiss) (Egyptian) She Rules the Home

Osiris (oh-SYE-rus) (Egyptian) He Judges the Departed

Ra (RAH) (Egyptian) He Is the Golden Disk of the Sun

Seth (SETH) (Egyptian) He Is a Magnificent Pillar

Thoth (THAWTH) (Egyptian) He Keeps the Universe Balanced

An (AHN) (Vietnamese) She Is Harmony

Bao (BAH-wo) (Vietnamese) He Protects Humanity

Bich (BIT) (Vietnamese) She Is Precious Jade

Binh (BING) (Vietnamese) He Is Harmony

Cam (KAHM) (Vietnamese) She Is the Beautiful Color Orange

Chau (CHOW) (Vietnamese) She Is a String of Priceless Pearls

Chi (CHEE) (Vietnamese) She Is an Unbreakable Bough

Cuc (KOOHK) (Vietnamese) She Is a Fragrant Chrysanthemum Flower

Dinh (DEEN) (Vietnamese) He Is a Majestic Mountain

Duc (DOOK) (Vietnamese) He Is Greatly Beloved

Anahera (ah-nah-HEE-rah) (Maori) She Is God's Angelic Messenger

Anaru (AH-nah-roo) (Maori) He Is Powerfully Male

Aroha (ah-RO-hah) (Maori) She Is Love

Ataahua (ah-tah-ah-OO-wah) (Maori) He Is Lovely

Hemi (HEM-mee) (Maori) He Is Divinely Protected

Hine (HEE-nay) (Maori) She Is Our Sacred Flesh and Blood

Hohepa (ho-HAY-pah) (Maori) His Greatness Increases

Huhana (hoo-HAH-nah) (Maori) She Is a Fragrant Lotus Flower

Kiri (KEER-ree) (Maori) She Is the Sweet Covering of a Delectable Fruit

Maata (mah-AH-tah) (Maori) She Rules Our Home Magnificently

⌘ **Anahita** (ah-nah-HEE-tuh) (Avestan) She Is Pure-Hearted

Anu (AH-noo) (Babylonian) He Is the Great Vault of Heaven

Dagon (DAY-gahn) (Ugaritic) He Is an Abundant Grain-Harvest

Hadad (hah-DAHD) (Akkadian) He Is Thunder and Lightning

Inanna (ih-NAH-nah) (Sumerian) She Rules Heaven

Lilith (LIH-lith) (Assyrian) She Rules the Night

Nanaia (nah-NAY-yah) (Babylonian) She Is Pure-Hearted

Shahrivar (SHAH-ree-var) (Avestan) She Has Great Ambitions

Tanis (tah-NEESS) (Greek) She Is the Ruler of Serpents

Tiamat (TEE-ah-maht) (Akkadian) She Is the Blue Ocean

⌘ **Andrus** (AHN-drooss) (Estonian) He Is Powerfully Male

Anu (AH-noo) (Estonian) She Is Graceful

Eliisabet (el-EE-ee-sah-bet) (Estonian) Her God Is Abundance

Heino (HYE-no) (Estonian) He Is the Little One Who Is Our Sacred Homeland

Hillar (HEEL-lahr) (Estonian) He Laughs with Joy

Jaagup (YAH-ah-goop) (Estonian) He Surpasses Everyone

Jaak (YAH-hahk) (Estonian) He Surpasses Everyone

Jaan (YAH-hahn) (Estonian) His God Is Gracious

Joosep (yo-OH-sep) (Estonian) His Greatness Increases

Juhan (YOO-hahn) (Estonian) His God Is Gracious

⌘ **Annette** (ann-NET) (English/French) She Is Graceful and Beloved

Cécile (seh-SEEL) (French) She Sees Deeply Within Herself

Emilie (AY-mee-lee) (French) She Is a Magnificent Competitor

Marie (mah-REE) (French) She Is Love

Yvonne (ee-VUN) (French) She Is the Magnificent Yew Tree

Dionne (dee-AHN, dee-UN) (French) She Is the Little One Who Is God's Holy Mountain

Allan (AL-lun) (English) He Is Magnificently Handsome

Oliva (oh-LEE-vuh) (Portuguese) She Is a Fragrant Olive Tree

Corbeil (kor-BAY) (French) He Is a Charming Little Flower-Basket

Quint (KWINT) (Catalan) He Is the Little One Who Is Fifth

> *Annette, Cécile, Emilie, Marie, and Yvonne Dionne were the first surviving group of quintuplets in Canadian history, born in 1934 in Corbeil, Canada, and delivered by Dr. Allan Dafoe. Oliva Dionne was the mother of these courageous quints.*

⌘ **Anton** (AHN-tahn) (Danish) He Is a Blossoming Flower

Ase (AH-shay) (Danish) He Is a Skilled Physician

Asmund (AHZ-moond) (Danish) His God Safeguards Us

Asta (AHSS-tuh) (Danish) She Is a Radiant Goddess

Bendt (BENT) (Danish) He Is Divinely Blessed

Benedikte (ben-eh-DIK-tuh) (Danish) He Is Divinely Blessed

Berit (BAIR-reet) (Danish) She Safeguards Us

Bertil (bair-TEEL) (Danish) He Is Our Shining Prince

Birgitte (bur-GHEET-tuh) (Danish) She Safeguards Us

Birte (BUR-tuh) (Danish) She Safeguards Us

⌘ **Artturi** (ahr-TOO-ree) (Finnish) He Is a Courageous Bear

Arvo (AHR-vo) (Finnish) He Is a Treasure

Aukusti (aw-KOOSS-tee) (Finnish) He Is Absolutely Magnificent

Aulis (AW-liss) (Finnish) She Assists Humanity

Brita (BRIH-tah) (Finnish) She Is Our Wise Little Scholar

Eemil (ee-EE-meel) (Finnish) He Is a Powerful Competitor

Eerika (ee-EE-rih-kah) (Finnish) She Rules Forever

Eerikki (ee-EE-rik-kee) (Finnish) He Rules Forever

Eero (ee-EE-ro) (Finnish) He Rules Forever

Eeva (ee-EE-vah) (Finnish) She Wants to Live

🎵 **Arvid** (AR-vid) (Norwegian) She Is a Soaring Eagle

Donatella (dahn-uh-TEL-luh) (Italian) She Is Our Little Present from God

Hagop (HAH-gup) (Armenian) He Surpasses Everyone

Jean-Marc (zhaw-MAHK) (French) He Is the Powerful Male Whose God Is Gracious

Jerald (JAIR-ruld) (English) He Rules with Powerful Weapons

Kerry (KAIR-ree) (Irish) She Descends from the Darkly Handsome One

Len (LEN) (English) He Is Our Noble Little Lion

Sharif (shah-REEF) (Arabic) He Is Illustrious

Takeshi (tah-KAY-shee) (Japanese) He Is a Great Warrior

Willibrord (WIL-lih-brart) (Dutch) He Is Our Invincible Weapon

🎵 **Astor** (ASS-tur) (English) He Is a Soaring Hawk

Costa (KOHSS-tuh) (Spanish) He Is the Beautiful Coastline

Domino (DAH-mih-no) (English) She Is the Little One Who Comes to Us from God

Friday (FRY-day) (English) He Is the Glorious Day Called Friday

Kelsey (KEL-see) (English) She Is a Fiercely Independent Island of Liberty

Montana (mahn-TAN-nuh) (American/Latin) She Is a Lofty Mountain

Nando (NAHN-doh) (Spanish) He Is Our Little Peaceful Warrior

Rock (RAHK) (English) He Is Rock-Solid

Roma (RO-muh) (Latin) She Is Rome

Starbuck (STAR-buk) (English) He Is from the Great Starbeck Manor England

🎵 **Aubin** (oh-BAN) (French) He Is Radiance

Burgundy (BUR-gun-dee) (English) She Is Burgundy, France

Charlemagne (SHAU-luh-myne) (French) He Is a Great Soldier

Franc (FRONK) (Slovene) He Is the Nation of France

Julien (zhool-YAW) (French) He Is Julius Caesar's Relative

Margaux (mao-GO) (French) She Is Our Priceless Little Pearl

Maury (MOR-ree) (English) He Is Our Dark Little Moor

Rosette (roh-ZET) (French) She Is Our Fragrant Little Rose

Sherry (SHAIR-ree) (French) She Is Darling and Sweet

Vin (VIN) (English) He Is Our Mighty Little Conqueror

🎵 **Aulay** (AW-lee) (Scottish) He Descends from Our Mighty Ancestors

Beathan (BAY-yahn) (Scottish) He Is the Breath of Life

Beitris (BAY-ih-triss) (Scottish) She Is a Great Voyager

Bhaltair (BALL-tair) (Scottish) He Commands the Military

Cailean (KAY-lin) (Scottish) He Is a Powerful Young Pup

Cairbre (KAIR-brah) (Scottish) He Commands the War-Chariots

Cairistiona (kair-iss-CHEE-nah) (Scottish) She Follows Christ

Caitriona (kay-TREE-nah) (Scottish) She Is Pure-Hearted

Callum (KAL-lum) (Scottish) He Is a Peaceful Dove

Carbrey (KAR-bree) (Scottish) He Commands the War-Chariots

🎵 **Aurel** (oh-REL, AR-rel) (Czech) He Is Pure Gold

Barbora (BAR-bor-rah) (Czech) She Is Our Divine Voyager

Beata (bay-AH-tah) (Czech) She Is Our Blessed Little Voyager

Benedikta (ben-eh-DIK-tah) (Czech) She Is Divinely Blessed

Bohdan (bo-DAHN) (Czech) He Is God's Divine Gift

Branislava (brah-nee-SLAH-vah) (Czech) She Gains Renown as a Warrior

Cecilie (SEH-see-lee) (Czech) She Sees Deeply Within Herself

Cenek (CHEN-nek) (Czech) He Is Our Mighty Little Conqueror

Darina (dah-REE-nuh) (Czech) She Is a Present from God

Denisa (deh-NEE-sah) (Czech) She Is the Goddess Who Speaks Beautifully

🎵 **Avaline** (AV-uh-leen) (English) She Is the Little One Who Wants to Live

Avalina (av-uh-LEE-nuh) (English) She Is the Little One Who Wants to Live

Avis (AY-viss) (English) She Is Greatly Beloved

Aydan (AY-dan) (English/Irish) He Is the Little One Aflame with Greatness

Azura (a-ZHOOR-ruh) (English) He Is the Blue Sky

Azure (AZH-zhur) (English) She Is the Blue Sky

Baldric (BALD-rik) (English) He Rules Us Courageously

Balfour (BAL-for) (English) He Is a Verdant Field in a Beautiful Town

Bambi (BAM-bee) (English/Italian) She Is Our Lovely Little Maiden

Barbie (BAR-bee) (English) She Is Our Sacred Little Voyager

Ayo (AH-yo) (Yoruba) She Is Rejoicing

Hatch (HATCH) (English) He Is a Gate Leading to the Woodlands

Hill (HIL) (English) He Is a Beautiful Hill

Iona (eye-OH-nah) (Scottish) She Is a Beautiful Island

Love (LUV) (English) She Is Love

Mojave (mo-HAH-vee) (Mohave) He Is the Great Mojave Nation

Park (PARK) (Irish) He Is Our Little Aristocrat

Rico (REE-ko) (Spanish) He Is the Little One Who Is Powerfully Courageous

Truth (TROOTH) (American/English) She Is the Truth of Our Lives

Winchester (WIN-chess-tur) (English) He Is Our Shining Fortress

Baako (bah-AH-ko) (Akan) He Was Born Before all Others

Berko (BUR-ko) (Akan) He Was Born Before all Others

Bolanle (bo-LAHN-lay) (Yoruba) His Greatest Treasure Is His Family

Bosede (bo-SAY-day) (Yoruba) He Arrived on a Sunday

Chausiku (shaw-SEE-koo) (Swahili) She Came into this World at Dusk

Chi (CHEE) (Igbo) She Resembles God

Chiamaka (chee-ah-MAH-kah) (Igbo) She Proves God's Magnificence

Chichi (CHEE-chee) (Igbo) She Is the Little One Who Resembles God

Chidi (CHEE-dee) (Igbo) She Demonstrates God's Power

Chidimma (chee-DEE-mah) (Igbo) She Demonstrates God's Compassion

Barry (BAIR-ree) (Irish) He Is Our Little Fair-Haired One

Carter (KAR-tur) (English) He Builds Sturdy Carts

Charlotte (SHAR-lut) (French) She Is Our Beloved Little Warrior

Cheyenne (shye-YAN) (Dakota) He Is a Mystical Speaker in Tongues

Cole (KOHL) (English) He Is Fragrant, Ebony-Black Charcoal

Doyle (DOYL) (Irish) He Descends from the Dark Stranger

Kitty (KIT-tee) (English) She Is Our Little Pure-Hearted One

Mason (MAY-sun) (English) He Is a Skilled Stonecutter

Oscar (AHSS-skur) (Irish) He Loves to Hunt Deer

Whitney (WHIT-nee) (English) She Is a Beautiful White Realm

Bartek (BAR-tek) (Polish) He Descends from the Courageous Man

Cedar (SEE-dur) (English) She Is a Fragrant Cedar Tree

Drago (DRAY-go) (Slovene) He Is a Priceless Treasure

Emancipation (ee-man-sih-PAY-shun) (English) He Is Freedom

Forest (FOR-rest) (English) He Is a Verdant Forest

Life (LIF-ee-yuh) (Irish) She Is the River Liffey, Ireland

Lone (LO-nuh) (Danish) She Is the Light

Maha (mah-HAH) (Arabic) She Is a Beautiful She-Cow

Major (MAY-jur) (English) He Is the Weapon of the Assembly

Tjikko (TEE-ko) (Swedish) He Is Always on Target

Bartel (bar-TEL) (Dutch) He Is the Little One with a Furrowed Brow

Bartholomeus (bar-tah-lo-MAY-yooss) (Dutch) He Has a Furrowed Brow

Bas (BAHSS) (Dutch) He Is Our Honorable Little Prince

Bastiaan (BAHSS-chun) (Dutch) He Is Our Honorable Little Prince

Bonifaas (BO-nee-fahss) (Dutch) He Brings Cheer to All

Bram (BRAHM) (Dutch) He Is the Little One Who Is the Father of Nations

Brecht (BREHKT) (Dutch) He Is the Radiant Sun

Brigitta (brih-GHEET-tuh) (Dutch) She Is Knowledge

Carolien (kahr-oh-LEEN) (Dutch) She Is a Mighty Warrior

Casper (KAHS-pahr, KAS-pur) (Dutch) He Holds Priceless Wealth

🌿 **Belenus** (BEL-uh-nus) (Proto-Celtic) He Is the Radiant Sun

Donwenna (dahn-WEN-nuh) (Welsh) Her Life Is Sacred

Epona (ee-POH-nuh) (Gaulish) She Befriends Horses

Isolde (ee-SOUL-deh) (Welsh) She Is Exceedingly Beautiful

Nyven (NIH-vun) (Welsh) She Rules Heaven

Ocelo (oh-SEL-loh) (Welsh) He Plows the Fields

Olwen (OLE-wen) (Welsh) She Is Beautifully Fair

Tamesis (TAM-ih-sis, tuh-MEE-sis) (Welsh) She Is Deep Waters

Taranis (tuh-RAN-nus) (Proto-Celtic) He Is Lightning and Thunder

Tristan (TRIS-tun) (Welsh) He Is Fiercely Aggressive

🌿 **Benedito** (ben-eh-DEE-toh) (Portuguese) He Is Divinely Blessed

Blake (BLAYK) (English) His Hair Is Ebony Black

Clarke (KLARK) (English) She Is a Wise Scholar

Gal (GAHL) (Hebrew) She Is a Mighty Tidal Wave

Gauri (GAR-ree) (Sanskrit) She Is Beautifully Fair

Gregg (GREG) (English) He Is Our Alert Little Guardian

Jozsef (YO-zhef) (Hungarian) His God Is Abundance

Parnell (par-NEL) (English) He Is from the Farmlands

Ramesh (RAH-mesh) (Sanskrit) He Is the Great and Powerful Deity, Rama

Yoshiro (yo-SHEE-ro) (Japanese) He Is Our Honorable Boy

🌿 **bernarDo** (bur-NAR-doh) (Klingon) He Is a Great and Mighty Bear

ghertlhuD (GUR-trood) (Klingon) She Is a Weapon of Power

Horey'So (hor-RAY-shee-oh) (Klingon) He Is a Man for all Seasons

Khamlet (HAM-let) (Klingon) He Is a Mighty Prince

'ovelya (oh-FEEL-yuh) (Klingon) She Helps Us All

polonyuS (puh-LO-nee-yus) (Klingon) He Is Poland

qornelyuS (kor-NEE-lee-yus) (Klingon) He Is a Cornucopia of Riches

SeQpIr (SHAYK-speer) (Klingon) He Brandishes a Powerful Weapon

tlhaw'DIyuS (KLAW-dee-yus) (Klingon) He Walks with Great Challenges

wIlyam (WILL-yum) (Klingon) He Protects Humanity

🌿 **Bessie** (BES-see) (English) She Is the Little One Favored by God

Chrisette (kris-SET) (American/English) She Is Christ's Little Follower

Eartha (UR-thuh) (English) She Is the Blessed Mother Earth

Illinois (ill-ih-NOY) (Algonquin) He Is of the Great Land Where Women Speak Eloquently

Jimi (JIM-mee) (English) He Is Our Divinely Protected Little Savior

Lolo (LO-lo) (American/Spanish) She Is the Little One Who Understands Sorrow

Phylicia (fil-LEE-shuh) (American/Latin) She Is Favored by Fortune

Redd (RED) (English) He Has Fiery Red Hair

Solange (so-LAWZH) (French) She Is Solemnly Devoted to God

Vivica (American/Swedish) She Is Aggressively Warlike

🌿 **Bijan** (bee-ZHAHN) (Persian) He Is the Hero of the Epic of Kings

Cecil (SEE-sul) (English) He Sees Deeply Within Himself

Corentin (ko-raw-TAN) (French) He Is an Unstoppable Windstorm

Ivette (ee-VET) (Spanish) She Is the Magnificent Yew Tree

Junko (JOON-ko) (Japanese) He Is a Well-Behaved Child

Nolan (NO-lahn) (Irish) He Descends from the Great Conqueror

Ravi (RAH-vee) (Sanskrit) He Is the Golden Sun

Starling (STAR-ling) (Scottish) He Is Absolutely Magnificent

Sweeney (SWEE-nee) (English/Irish) He Journeys Wisely Through Life

Taddeo (tah-DAY-yo) (Italian) He Is a Precious Gift

🌸 **Bill** (BILL) (English) He Is Our Little Protector

Caesar (SEE-zur) (Latin) He Is Covered with Manly Hair

Carlo (KAR-lo) (Italian) He Is a Mighty Soldier

Miracle (MEER-uh-kul) (English) She Is God's Blessed Miracle

Monte (MAHN-tee) (English) He Is the Little One Who Is a Mountain of Manly Power

Paris (PAIR-us) (Greek) He Is a Stone Wall

Royale (roy-YAL) (French) He Is Majestic

Treasure (TREH-zhur) (English) She Is a Gathering of Wealth

Wynn (WIN) (Welsh) He Is the Blessed One Who Is Beautifully Fair

York (YORK) (English) He Is York, England

🌸 **Birthe** (BUR-thuh) (Danish) She Safeguards Us

Bjorn (BYORN) (Danish) He Is a Courageous Bear

Borghild (BORG-heeld) (Danish) She Is Our Castle's Greatest Warrior

Britta (BRIT-tuh) (Danish) She Is Our Little Guardian

Caja (KYE-yuh) (Danish) She Is Our Mighty Little Warrior

Carina (kah-REE-nuh) (Danish) She Is a Ship's Balance and Equilibrium

Christer (KRIS-tur) (Danish) He Is Christ's Little Follower

Christoffer (KRIS-toh-fur) (Danish) He Follows Christ

Claus (KLOWSS) (Danish) He Is Humanity's Little Triumph

Dagmar (DAHG-mahr) (Danish) She Is a Pure Maiden, Fresh as Sunlight

🌸 **Bo** (BO) (American/French) She Is Beautiful

Burrell (bur-REL) (Scottish) He Makes Beautiful Wool Clothing

Bush (BOOSH) (English) He Is the Untamed Wilderness

Condoleezza (kahn-doh-LEEZ-zuh) (American) She Is Truly Sweet

Duffy (DUF-fee) (Scottish) He Is the Little One Who Is Darkly Handsome

Farrell (FAIR-rul) (English) He Descends from the Courageous Warrior

Kelvin (KEL-vin) (English) He Is a Strait of Clear Water

Kushner (KOOSH-nur) (Belorussian) He Makes Lovely Fur-Coats

Perot (pair-RO) (French) He Is Our Rock-Solid Little Fortress

Tyson (TYE-sun) (English) He Is Fiercely Aggressive

🌸 **Bootes** (boo-OH-teez) (Greek) He Farms the Land

Budi (boo-DEE) (Indonesian) He Is Shrewdly Intelligent

Dick (DIK) (English) He Is Powerfully Courageous

Dong (DONG) (Chinese) He Is the Shining East

Hymen (HYE-men) (Greek) He Is the Marriage-Song

Kunto (KOON-toh) (Akan) She Is Third

Lips (LIPS) (Greek) He Is the Mighty Southwest Wind

Lykke (LOO-kuh) (Dutch) She Is Wealth and Success

Suk (SOOK) (Korean) He Is Rock-Solid

Tit (TEET) (Russian) He Is an Honorable Title of Great Respect

🌸 **Bryce** (BRICE) (English) He Is Beautifully Freckled

Forest (FOR-rest) (English) He Is a Verdant Wilderness

Guadalupe (gwahd-ah-LOO-pay) (Spanish) She Is the River That Rushes Like a Wolf

Joshua (JAHSH-oo-wah) (Hebrew) His God Is Eternal Salvation

Rainier (ruh-NEER) (French) He Commands the Military Wisely

Rocky (RAHK-kee) (English) He Is the Little One Who Rests Comfortably

Royale (roy-YAL) (French) He Is Majestic

Sequoia (seh-KWOY-yah) (Cherokee) He Is Our Great Thinker

Theodore (THEE-oh-dor) (Greek) He Is God's Divine Gift

Zion (ZYE-un) (Hebrew) He Is Our Mighty Fortress

🕮 **Carol** (KAIR-rul) (English) She Is Our Powerful Little Warrior

Alice (AL-liss) (English) She Is Our Little Aristocrat

Bobby (BAHB-bee) (English) He Is Glorious and Beloved

Cindy (SIN-dee) (English) She Is the Beloved Woman from Kynthos, Greece

Greg (GREG) (English) He Is Our Little Guardian

Jan (JAN) (English) She Is the Beloved Little One Whose God Is Gracious

Marcia (MAR-shah) (Latin) She Is as Powerful as any male

Mike (MYKE) (English) He Is God's Little Disciple

Oliver (AHL-ih-vur) (English) He Is a Fragrant Olive Tree

Peter (PEE-tur) (Hebrew) He Is Rock-Solid
Mike and Carol Brady, with their children Bobby, Cindy, Greg, Jan, Marcia, and Peter, starred in The Brady Bunch, *the American Broadcasting Corporation (ABC) television series that ran from 1969 to 1974. Alice was the Bradys' maid, and little Cousin Oliver appeared in the show's final season.*

🕮 **Catalina** (kat-uh-LEE-nuh) (Spanish) She Is Pure-Hearted

Concepción (kone-sep-see-YONE) (Spanish) She Is the Immaculate Conception

Cruz (KROOZ, KROOSS) (Spanish) She Is the True Cross of Jesus Christ

Diego (dee-AY-go) (Spanish) He Is Always Teaching

Elena (ee-LAY-nuh) (Spanish) She Is Radiance

José (ho-ZAY) (Spanish) His Greatness Increases

Luz (LOOSS, LOOZ) (Spanish) She Is Radiance

Miguel (mee-GHELL) (Spanish) He Resembles God

Pablo (PAHB-lo) (Spanish) He Shows Great Humility

Pedro (PAY-dro) (Spanish) He Is Rock-Solid

🕮 **Catharina** (kah-thah-REE-nuh) (Dutch) She Is Pure-Hearted

Cato (KAH-toh) (Dutch) She Is Our Little Pure-Hearted One

Cobus (KO-bus) (Dutch) He Is Our Little Magnificent One

Coby (KO-bee) (Dutch) He Is Our Little Magnificent One

Cokkie (KO-kee) (Dutch) She Is the Little One Who Is a Cornucopia of Plenty

Constantijn (KON-stun-teen) (Dutch) He Is Dependably Constant

Coos (KOOSS) (Dutch) He Is Our Little Magnificent One

Corné (kor-NAY) (Dutch) He Is Our Little Cornucopia of Abundance

Daan (DAHN) (Dutch) He Is the Little One Whose God Judges Wisely

Debora (DEB-oh-ruh) (Dutch) She Is a Busy Honeybee

🕮 **Catrina** (kah-TREE-nah) (Scottish) She Is Pure-Hearted

Cinaed (sin-NAYD, shih-NAYD) (Scottish) He Is Bright Flames

Coinneach (KAHN-nik) (Scottish) He Is Handsome

Conall (KAH-nahll) (Scottish) He Is a Courageous Wolf

Cormag (KOR-mahk) (Scottish) He Is Born of Forbidden Lust

Daividh (DYE-veed) (Scottish) He Is Greatly Beloved

Dand (DAHND) (Scottish) He Is the Little One Who Is Powerfully Male

Deoiridh (DOR-ree) (Scottish) She Journeys Far and Seeks Truth

Deorsa (DEER-sah) (Scottish) She Farms the Land

Dermid (DUR-mit) (Scottish) He Is Born in Liberty

🕮 **Catriona** (kah-TREE-nuh) (Scottish) She Is Pure-Hearted

Claudio (KLAW-dee-yoh) (Spanish) He Walks a Difficult Path

Daisuke (DICE-kee) (Japanese) He Greatly Assists Us

Frith (FRITH) (English) He Is Peace

Hakan (hah-KHAN) (Turkish) He Is Our Supreme Ruler

Keita (KYE-tuh) (Japanese) He Rejoices

Lal (LAHL) (Sanskrit) He Touches Gently

Liselotte (LEE-zuh-law-tuh) (Danish) She Is Our Little Warrior Whose God Is Generous

Stefano (steh-FAH-no) (Italian) He Is a Shining Crown

Suzuki (SOO-zoo-kee) (Japanese) She Is a Tree of Musical Bells

Chad (CHAD) (English) He Is a Mighty Herd of Bulls

Dominica (doh-mih-NEE-kuh) (Latin) She Comes to Us from God

France (FRANSS, FRAWSS) (French) She Is the Nation of France

Georgia (JOR-juh) (English) She Farms the Land

India (IN-dee-yuh) (English) She Is India

Leone (lee-OH-nay) (Italian) He Is a Noble Lion

Libya (LIB-ee-yuh) (Greek) She Is the Great Continent of Africa

Rica (REE-kuh) (English) She Is Our Peaceful Little Ruler

Salvador (SAL-vah-dor) (Spanish) He Is Like Our Savior Christ

Sierra (see-AY-rah) (Spanish) She Is a Lofty Range of Mountains

Charles (CHARLZ) (English/French) He Is a Mighty Warrior

Alexandre (al-ex-AWN-druh) (French) He Protects Humanity

Dickens (DIH-kuhnz) (English) He Is Powerfully Courageous

Jacques (ZHAHK) (French) He Is Divinely Protected

Jarvis (JAR-vis) (English) He Is a Mighty Weapon

Jerry (JAIR-ree) (English) He Is the Beloved One Whose God Is Uplifting

Lucie (LOO-see) (English) She Is Radiance

Paris (PAIR-us) (Greek) He Is a Stone Wall

Sydney (SID-nee) (English) He Is a Great Island

Therese (tair-REZ) (French) He Is a Summer Harvest

> In the 1859 novel A Tale of Two Cities by Charles Dickens (1812–1870), banker Jarvis Lorry, clerk Jerry Cruncher, and wastrel Sydney Carton help Frenchman Charles Darnay flee Therese Defarge and her Jacquerie—an army of spies all named Jacques—during the French Revolution. Charles Darnay successfully rejoins his wife Lucie and her father Alexandre.

Chiuta (chee-OO-tah) (Tumbuku) He Rules Heaven

Faro (FAH-ro) (Mande) He Purifies the Earth

Ilomba (ee-LOME-bah) (Lozi) She Is a Great Serpent

Kianda (kee-AHN-dah) (Bantu) She Is the Sea

Kishi (KEE-shee) (Bantu) She Dwells in the Hills

Luanda Magere (loo-AHN-duh mah-ZHAIR-ray) (Luo) He Is a Great Warrior

Nommo (NOME-mo) (Dogon) He Is a Great Ancestor

Oba (OH-bah) (Yoruba) He Is the Thunderstorm

Sasha (SAH-shah) (Swahili) She Is an Ancestor-Spirit

Zamani (zah-MAH-nee) (Swahili) He Is an Ancestor-Spirit

Clark (KLARK) (English) He Is a Wise Scholar

Edward (ED-wurd) (English) He Is a Wealthy Protector

Howard (HOW-wurd) (English) His Heart Is Powerfully Courageous

Miles (MYE-yulz) (English) He Is Graceful

Morgan (MOR-gahn) (Welsh) He Is the Blue Ocean

Morris (MOR-riss) (English) He Is a Dark Moor

Savannah (suh-VAN-nuh) (English) She Is a Plain of Fragrant Grass

Selma (SEL-mah) (German) She Is God's Helmet of Protection

Shelton (SHEL-tun) (English) He Is a Market-Town with Shelves of Goods

Xavier (hah-vee-YAIR) (Portuguese) He Is a Bold New City

Coleman (KOHL-mun) (English) She Is a Peaceful Dove

Dawson (DAW-sun) (English) He Descends from the Beloved One

Della (DEL-luh) (English) She Is Our Little Aristocrat

Edmonia (ed-MO-nee-yuh) (American/English) She Is a Wealthy Protector

Foxx (FOX) (American/English) He Is a Clever Fox

Hendrix (HEN-drix) (English) He Rules Our Home Magnificently

Langston (LANGZ-tun) (English) He Is a Broad Town with Long Streets

Meagan (MAY-gun) (English/Welsh) She Is Our Priceless Little Pearl

Reese (REESS) (Welsh) She Is Powerfully Enthusiastic

Rosario (ro-SAHR-ee-yo) (Spanish) She Is the Blessed Rosary

🕮 **Dakarai** (dah-kah-RYE) (Shona) He Rejoices
Dayo (DYE-yo) (Yoruba) She Rejoices
Desta (DAYSS-tah) (Amharic) She Is Happiness
Dumisani (doo-mih-SAH-nee) (Zulu) She Is Worshipped
Ebele (ay-BAY-lay) (Igbo) She Is Compassionate
Efua (AY-foo-wah) (Akan) He Arrived on a Friday
Ekene (ay-KAY-nay) (Igbo) He Is Worshipped
Emeka (ay-MAY-kah) (Igbo) He Accomplishes Wonders
Eniola (ay-nee-OH-lah) (Yoruba) He Is Rich and Successful
Enitan (ay-nee-TAHN) (Yoruba) He Tells Wondrous Tales

🕮 **Danijel** (dahn-ee-YEL) (Croatian) His God Judges Wisely
Danijela (dahn-YEL-luh) (Croatian) Her God Judges Wisely
Darko (DAHR-ko) (Croatian) He Is God's Divine Gift
Dejan (day-ZHAHN) (Croatian) He Values Swift Action
Dejana (day-ZHAHN-nuh) (Croatian) She Values Swift Action
Dragan (drah-GHAN) (Croatian) He Is Our Priceless Treasure
Dragica (drah-ZHEE-kah) (Croatian) She Is Our Priceless Treasure
Drago (DRAH-go, DRAY-go) (Croatian) He Is Our Priceless Treasure
Dubravka (doo-BRAHV-kah) (Croatian) She Is a Forest of Majestic Oaks
Dunja (DOON-yah) (Croatian) She Is Our Glorious Little One

🕮 **Daveth** (DAH-veth) (Cornish) He Is Greatly Beloved
Eseld (ee-SELD) (Cornish) She Is Exceedingly Beautiful
Jago (YAH-go) (Cornish) He Surpasses Everyone
Jory (YOR-ree, JOR-ree) (Cornish) He Farms the Land
Meraud (mair-RO) (Cornish) She Is the Beautiful Ocean
Merryn (MAIR-rin) (Cornish) She Is a Blessed Saint
Myghal (MYE-kul) (Cornish) He Resembles God
Pasco (PAHSS-ko) (Cornish) He Is Easter and Passover

Piran (peer-RAHN) (Cornish) He Is Darkly Handsome
Steren (STAR-ren) (Cornish) She Is a Heavenly Star

🕮 **Diede** (DEE-dee) (Dutch) She Is Humanity's Little Ruler
Diederick (DEE-dur-rik) (Dutch) He Rules Humanity
Dominicus (doh-MIN-ih-kus) (Dutch/Latin) He Comes to Us from God
Drika (DREE-kuh) (Dutch) She Rules Our Home Magnificently
Elia (EL-yuh) (Dutch) Her God Is the One True God
Elke (EL-kee, EL-kuh) (Dutch) She Is Our Little Aristocrat
Elly (EL-lee) (Dutch) She Is the Little One Favored by God
Elma (EL-ma) (Dutch) She Is Our Little Protector
Els (ELSS) (Dutch) She Is the Little One Favored by God
Evelien (AY-vuh-leen) (Dutch) She Is the Little One Who Wants to Live

🕮 **Domhnall** (doh-NAHL) (Scottish) He Is Our Beloved Ruler of Humanity
Donalda (doh-NAHL-dah) (Scottish) She Is Our Beloved World-Conqueror
Donaldina (doh-nahl-DEE-nah) (Scottish) She Is Humanity's Beloved Ruler
Donella (doh-NEL-lah) (Scottish) She Is Humanity's Beloved Ruler
Dougal (DOO-ghal) (Scottish) He Is the Darkly Handsome Newcomer
Eachann (EE-kahn) (Scottish) She Is a Chestnut-Colored Stallion
Eallair (EL-lair) (Scottish) He Is a Shelter Deep in the Earth
Eanraig (EN-rek) (Scottish) He Rules Our Home Magnificently
Edan (AY-dahn) (Scottish) He Is the Little One Aflame with Greatness
Edme (ED-may) (Scottish) She Is Esteemed

🕮 **Dominik** (DOH-mee-neek) (Czech) He Comes to Us from God
Dorota (dor-OH-tah) (Czech) She Is God's Divine Gift
Edita (ed-EE-tah) (Czech) She Is a Prosperous Warrior

Eliska (el-EES-kah) (Czech) She Is the Little One Favored by God

Estera (es-TAIR-ruh) (Czech) She Is a Heavenly Star

Eugen (OY-gain) (Czech) He Is Aristocratic

Frantiska (frahn-TEES-kuh) (Czech) She Is the Nation of France

Hana (HAH-nah) (Czech) She Is Graceful

Havel (HAH-vul) (Czech) He Is a Fighting Bantam Rooster

Hedviga (hed-VEE-gah) (Czech) She Is Aggressively Warlike

🕊 **Dorete** (dor-ET-tuh) (Danish) She Is God's Divine Gift

Dorit (DOR-rit) (Danish) She Is God's Divine Gift

Ebbe (EB-bee) (Danish) He Is Our Courageous Little Wild Boar

Edvin (ED-vin) (Danish) He Is a Wealthy Companion

Einar (AY-nar) (Danish) He Is Our Greatest Warrior

Elin (EL-lin) (Danish) She Is a Radiant Torch

Elise (ay-LEESS) (Danish) She Is the Little One Favored by God

Ellinor (EL-lih-nor) (Danish) She Is Aliénor, France

Elva (EL-vuh) (Danish) She Is the Magical Elfin Nation

Enok (EE-nahk) (Danish) He Is Loyal

🕊 **Dung** (YUNG) (Vietnamese) He Is Courageous

Duong (YUNG) (Vietnamese) He Is Strong and Aggressive

Hoa (hoo-WAH) (Vietnamese) She Is a Fragrant Blossom

Hong (HAHM) (Vietnamese) She Is Our Fragrant Rose

Hue (hoo-WAY) (Vietnamese) She Is a Fragrant Lily

Hung (HOME) (Vietnamese) His Courage Is Glorious

Huong (HONG) (Vietnamese) She Is Our Fragrant Rose

Kim (KIM) (Vietnamese) She Is Pure Gold

Lan (LAHN) (Vietnamese) She Is a Fragrant Orchid

Lanh (LAHN) (Vietnamese) She Is Tranquility

🕊 **Eagle** (EE-gull) (English) She Is a Soaring Eagle

Fidelia (fee-DAY-lee-yuh) (Spanish) She Is Loyally Devoted

Greenwood (GREEN-wood) (English) He Is Verdant Woodlands

Ishi (EE-shee) (Yahi) He Is Powerfully Male

Jhene (JEEN) (American/English) Her God Is Gracious

Maria (muh-REE-yuh) (Italian) She Is Love

Marigold (MAIR-ih-gold) (English) She Is a Fragrant Marigold

Marjorie (MAR-jur-ree) (English) She Is a Priceless Pearl

Rosella (ro-SEL-luh) (Italian) She Is Our Fragrant Little Rose

Yaya (YAH-yah) (American/Arabic) Her God Is Gracious

🕊 **Eidard** (AY-dahrd) (Scottish) He Is a Wealthy Protector

Eilidh (AY-lee) (Scottish) She Is a Radiant Torch

Eimhir (AY-meer) (Scottish) She Is Swift

Ellar (EL-lahr) (Scottish) He Is a Shelter Deep in the Earth

Elspet (ELZ-bet) (Scottish) Her God Is Abundance

Eoghan (OH-wen) (Scottish) He Is the Magnificent Yew Tree

Ewan (YOO-wahn) (Scottish) He Is the Magnificent Yew Tree

Farquhar (FAR-kwar) (Scottish) He Is Powerfully Male

Fearghas (FEER-ghass) (Scottish) He Is Powerfully Male

Fenella (feh-NEL-lah) (Scottish) She Is Beautifully Fair

🕊 **Ema** (AY-mah) (Croatian) She Is Our Universe

Emilija (em-EEL-yah) (Croatian) She Is Powerfully Competitive

Filip (FIH-lip) (Croatian) He Befriends Horses

Franjo (FRAHN-yo) (Croatian) He Is the Nation of France

Goran (gor-RAHN) (Croatian) He Is a Lofty Mountain

Gordana (gor-DAH-nah) (Croatian) She Is Gordium, Phyrgia

Ilija (EEL-yah) (Croatian) His God Is the True God

Irena (ee-RAY-nuh) (Croatian) She Is Springtime

Isidora (iz-ih-DOR-ruh) (Croatian) She Is a Gift from the Goddess Isis

Iva (EE-vah) (Croatian) She Is God's Graceful Little Messenger

🐾 *Erland* (AIR-lund) (Danish) He Is Our Divine Voyager

Espen (ES-pen) (Danish) He Is a Divinely Powerful Bear

Ester (ES-tair) (Danish) She Is a Heavenly Star

Flemming (FLEM-ming) (Danish) He Is Flanders

Folke (FOLK) (Danish) He Is All of Humanity

Frederikke (fred-ur-EE-kuh) (Danish) She Rules Peacefully

Freja (FRAY-yuh) (Danish) She Is Aristocratic

Frode (FRO-duh) (Danish) He Is Intelligent

Gerda (GUR-duh) (Danish) She Is a Mighty Fortress

Gregers (GREG-ghurz) (Danish) He Is Our Guardian

🐾 *Eshe* (AY-shay) (Swahili) She Arrived on a Sunday

Esi (AY-see) (Akan) She Arrived on a Sunday

Farai (fah-RYE) (Shona) She Is Happiness

Funanya (foo-NAHN-yah) (Igbo) She Is Love

Furaha (fo-RAH-hah) (Swahili) She Rejoices

Gwandoya (gwahn-DOH-yah) (Luganda) He Understands Sorrow

Idowu (ee-DOH-woo) (Yoruba) His Birth Follows Our Sacred Twins

Ife (EE-fay) (Yoruba) She Is Love

Ige (EE-zhay) (Yoruba) Her Feet Preceded Her Head into this World

Ikenna (ee-KEN-nah) (Igbo) She Reflects God's Divinity

🐾 *Everitt* (EV-uh-rit) (English) He Is a Courageous Boar

Evette (ee-VET) (English/French) She Is the Magnificent Yew Tree

Evie (EE-vee) (English) She Is the Little One Who Wants to Live

Evonne (ee-VAHN) (English) She Is the Magnificent Yew Tree

Evvie (EV-vee) (English) She Is the Little One Who Wants to Live

Ewart (YOO-wurt) (English) He Is a Wealthy Protector

Ezekiel (ee-ZEEK-yul) (English/Hebrew) His God Gives Him Power

Ezra (EZ-ruh) (English/Hebrew) He Is Divine Assistance

Fae (FAY) (English) She Is a Magical Fairy

Faithe (FAYTH) (English) She Is All Our Hopes

🐾 *Faas* (FAHSS) (Dutch) He Is the Little One Who Cheers Everybody

Femke (FEM-kee) (Dutch) She Is Our Peaceful Little One

Filibert (FIL-ih-burt) (Dutch) He Shines Brilliantly

Filippus (FIL-ip-pus) (Dutch) He Befriends Horses

Filomena (fil-oh-MEE-nuh) (Dutch) She Is Compassionate

Fleurette (flur-RET) (Dutch/French) She Is Our Fragrant Little Blossom

Flip (FLIP) (Dutch) He Is the Little One Who Befriends Horses

Floris (FLOR-riss) (Dutch) She Flourishes

Fons (FAHNZ, FAHNSS) (Dutch) He Is Aristocratic

Frank (FRAHNK) (Dutch) He Is the Little One Who Is the Nation of France

🐾 *Filib* (FIH-lip) (Scottish) He Befriends Horses

Findlay (FIN-lee) (Scottish) He Is the Soldier Who Is Beautifully Fair

Finella (fih-NEL-lah) (Scottish) She Is Beautifully Fair

Fingal (FIN-gahl) (Scottish) He Is the Newcomer Who Is Beautifully Fair

Finola (fih-NO-lah) (Scottish) She Is Beautifully Fair

Fyfe (FIFE) (Scottish) He Is the Legendary Realm of King Fib of Fife

Gilchrist (GHIL-krist) (Scottish) He Follows Christ

Gillespie (ghil-LES-pee) (Scottish) He Obeys the Holy Church

Gilroy (GHIL-roy) (Scottish) He Descends from the Fiery-Haired Advisor

Graeme (GRAYM) (Scottish) He Is a Grand Homestead on Gravelly Land

🐾 *Flins* (FLINZ) (Polish) He Is the Passage from this World

Mara (MAH-rah) (Czech) She Is the Passage from this World

Morana (mo-RAH-nah) (Czech) She Is the Passage from this World

Porvata (por-VAH-tah) (Polish) He Is the Green Woodlands

Rod (RAHD) (Polish) He Rules Heaven

Siva (SEE-vah) (Polish) She Wants to Live

Triglav (TRIG-lahv) (Bulgarian) He Has Three Divine Faces

Volos (VO-lohss) (Bulgarian) He Is as Powerful as a Team of Oxen

Zaria (ZAHR-ee-yah) (Russian) She Is a Divinely Blessed Bride

Zirnitra (zur-NEE-truh) (Serbian) Her Wizardry Gives Her Power

 Frederik (FRED-ur-reek) (Dutch) He Rules Peacefully

Freek (FRAYK) (Dutch) He Is Our Peaceful Little Ruler

Frits (FREETZ) (Dutch) He Is Our Peaceful Little Ruler

Gabriel (GAH-bree-yel) (Dutch) He Is God's Angelic Messenger

Gilberta (kil-BUR-tuh) (Dutch) She Is a Shining Promise

Gillis (GHIL-liss) (Dutch) He Is a Powerful Young Goat

Gisela (zhee-SEL-luh) (Dutch) She Serves Humanity

Godelieve (go-duh-LEE-vuh) (Dutch) She Has All of God's Love

Godfried (GAHT-freet) (Dutch) He Is God's Sublime Peace

Greet (GRAYT) (Dutch) She Is Our Priceless Little Pearl

 Goyo (GOY-yo) (Spanish) He Is Our Little Guardian

Gracia (GRAH-see-yah) (Spanish) She Is Graceful

Graciana (grah-see-AH-nah) (Spanish) She Is Truly the One Who Is Graceful

Graciano (grah-see-AH-no) (Spanish) He Is Truly the One Who Is Graceful

Graciela (grah-see-EL-lah) (Spanish) She Is Our Graceful Little Princess

Gualterio (gwahl-TAIR-ee-yo) (Spanish) He Commands the Military

Guillermo (gwee-AIR-mo) (Spanish) He Protects Humanity

Hector (EK-tor) (Spanish/Greek) He Stands His Ground

Heliodoro (eel-ee-oh-DOR-roh) (Spanish) He Is Given to Us by the Sun

Heraclio (air-AK-lee-yo) (Spanish) He Resembles Mighty Hercules

 Grahame (GRAYM) (Scottish) He Is a Grand Homestead on Gravelly Land

Gregor (GREG-gur) (Scottish) He Is Our Little Guardian

Greig (GREEG) (Scottish) He Is Our Little Guardian

Hamish (HAY-mish) (Scottish) He Is Divinely Protected

Heckie (HEK-kee) (Scottish) He Is the Little One Who Stands His Ground

Iagan (EE-ghan) (Scottish) He Is the Little One Aflame with Greatness

Iain (EE-yahn) (Scottish) His God Is Gracious

Innes (IN-ness) (Scottish) He Reflects God's Power

Ishbel (ISH-bel) (Scottish) Her God Is Abundance

Isla (EYE-lah) (Scottish) She Is the Isle of Islay, Scotland

 Grete (GRET-tuh) (Danish) She Is a Priceless Pearl

Gudbrand (GHOOD-brahnd) (Danish) He Is God's Weapon

Gudmund (GHOOD-moond) (Danish) He Is Divinely Protected

Gudrun (GHOOD-run) (Danish) She Observes Sacred Rituals

Gunhilda (ghoon-HIL-duh) (Danish) She Is Aggressively Warlike

Haldor (HAHL-dor) (Danish) He Is the Hammer of Thor, God of Thunder

Halvor (HAHL-vor) (Danish) He Is Our Guardian

Helga (HEL-guh) (Danish) She Is Sacred

Hemming (HEM-ming) (Danish) He Can Remake Himself

Henriette (hen-ree-ET-tuh) (Danish) She Rules Our Home Magnificently

 Griet (GREET) (Dutch) She Is Our Priceless Little Pearl

Gusta (GOOS-tuh) (Dutch) She Is the Little One Who Is Absolutely Magnificent

Hadewych (HAHD-vik) (Dutch) He Is Aggressively Warlike

Hannie (HAHN-nee) (Dutch) She Is God's Graceful Little Messenger

Harm (HAHM, HAHRM) (Dutch) He Is Aggressively Warlike

Heike (HYE-kuh) (Dutch) She Rules Our Home Magnificently

Heiko (HYE-ko) (Dutch) He Rules Our Home Magnificently

Hein (HIEN) (Dutch) He Rules Our Home Magnificently

Heintje (HIENT-yuh) (Dutch) She Rules Our Home Magnificently

Heleen (hay-LAYN) (Dutch) She Is Our Radiant Torch

🐣 **Haru** (HAH-roo) (Japanese) He Is the Radiant Sun

Haruto (HAH-roo-toh) (Japanese) He Is Sunlight

Hiroto (HEE-ro-toh) (Japanese) He Commands the Stars

Hoshiko (HO-shee-ko) (Japanese) She Is a Child of the Stars

Rikuto (REE-koo-toh) (Japanese) He Is the Realm of Heaven

Sora (SO-rah) (Japanese) He Is the Heavenly Sky

Youko (YOO-koh) (Japanese) She Is the Radiant Sun

Youta (YOO-tah) (Japanese) He Is the Magnificent Sun

Yuuto (YOO-oo-toh) (Japanese) He Is the Infinite Cosmos

Yuzuki (yoo-ZOO-kee) (Japanese) She Is the Silvery Moon

🐣 **Heleentje** (hay-LAYN-tee-yuh) (Dutch) She Is Our Radiant Little Torch

Helena (hay-LAY-nuh) (Dutch) She Is a Radiant Torch

Hendrika (hen-DREE-kuh) (Dutch) She Rules Our Home Magnificently

Henk (HENK) (Dutch) He Rules Our Home Magnificently

Hennie (HEN-nee) (Dutch) He Rules Our Home Magnificently

Hermanus (hair-MAH-nus) (Dutch/Latin) He Is Aggressively Warlike

Hubrecht (HOO-ee-brekht) (Dutch) His Heart Shines Brightly

Hugo (HOO-ee-go) (Dutch) His Heart Is Compassionate

Ida (EE-duh) (Dutch) She Works Tirelessly

Ignaas (ig-NAHSS) (Dutch) He Is Aflame with Greatness

🐣 **Hellä** (HEL-lah) (Finnish) She Is Compassionate

Henna (HEN-nah) (Finnish) She Rules Our Home Magnificently

Henri (AW-ree) (Finnish/French) He Rules Our Home Magnificently

Henriikka (hen-REE-eek-kah) (Finnish) She Rules Our Home Magnificently

Henrikki (hen-REEK-kee) (Finnish) He Rules Our Home Magnificently

Hermanni (hair-MAHN-nee) (Finnish) He Is Aggressively Warlike

Hesekiel (hez-EE-kee-yel) (Finnish) His God Gives Him Power

Hilja (HIL-yah) (Finnish) She Appreciates Peace

Hillevi (hil-LAY-vee) (Finnish) She Glories in Combat

Kati (KAH-tee) (Finnish) She Is Our Little Pure-Hearted One

🐣 **Henrike** (HEN-rih-kuh) (Danish) She Rules Our Home Magnificently

Hildegarde (HIL-duh-gard) (Danish) She Is a Mighty War-Fortress

Hjalmar (HYAHL-mahr) (Danish) He Is a Soldier's Helmet

Inga (ING-ghuh) (Danish) She Is the Goddess of Motherhood

Ingemar (ING-uh-mahr) (Danish) He Is Our First Little One

Jacob (YAH-kawb) (Danish) He Surpasses Everyone

Jannick (YAHN-nik) (Danish) He Is the Little One Whose God Is Gracious

Jarl (YARL) (Danish) He Is an Aristocratic Earl

Jeppe (YEP-pay) (Danish) He Is Our Little Magnificent One

Jerrik (YAIR-rik) (Danish) He Is an Ever-Powerful Ruler

🐣 **Herberto** (air-BAIR-toh) (Spanish) He Conquers Brilliantly

Heriberto (air-ee-BAIR-toh) (Spanish) He Is Truly a Brilliant Conqueror

Herminia (air-MEEN-yah) (Spanish/Greek) She Is a Pile of Marker-Stones

Herminio (air-MEEN-yo) (Spanish/Greek) He Is a Pile of Marker-Stones

Hilaria (ee-LAH-ree-yah) (Spanish) She Laughs with Joy

Hugo (OO-go) (Spanish) He Is Compassionate

Iliana (il-lee-AH-nah) (Spanish) She Is a
Radiant Torch
Imelda (ee-MEL-dah) (Spanish) She Is a One-
Woman Army Corps
Ines (ee-NESS) (Spanish/Greek) She Shimmers
with Sunlight
Inocencio (ee-no-SEN-see-yo) (Spanish) He Is
Pure-Hearted

🐦 **Horace** (HO-rus) (Greek) He Is the Right
Hour of the Day
Howell (HOWL) (Welsh) He Is Esteemed
Levi (LEE-vye) (Hebrew) He Is Firmly Rooted
Nathan (NAY-thun) (Hebrew) He Is Incredibly
Generous
Pierce (PEERSS) (English) He Is Rock-Solid
Samuel (SAM-yul) (Hebrew) His God Hears
Him
Sandra (SAHN-druh) (Italian) She Is
Humanity's Little Protector
Stanley (STAN-ley) (English) He Is a Clearing
among the Great Stones
Ward (WARD) (English) He Is Our Guardian
Willis (WIL-lus) (English) He Is a Helmet of
Protection

🐦 **Ilona** (ee-LO-nah) (Czech) She Is a Radiant
Torch
Irenka (ee-REN-kah) (Czech) She Is Springtime
Iveta (ee-VET-tah) (Czech) She Is the
Magnificent Yew Tree
Ivona (ee-VO-nah) (Czech) She Is the
Magnificent Yew Tree
Izabela (ee-zah-BEL-lah) (Czech) Her God Is
Abundance
Jarek (YAR-rek) (Czech) He Is Aggressively
Powerful
Jarmila (yar-MIL-lah) (Czech) Her God
Rewards Her Courage
Jirina (yeer-EE-nah) (Czech) She Farms the Land
Johan (yo-HAHN) (Czech) His God Is Gracious
Johana (yo-HAH-nah) (Czech) Her God Is
Gracious

🐦 **Ima** (EE-muh) (Dutch) She Is Our Universe
Iris (EER-ris) (Dutch) She Is Colorful Rainbows
Isa (EE-suh) (Dutch) She Demonstrates God's
Abundance
Ivo (EE-vo) (Dutch) He Is the Magnificent Yew
Tree
Jaap (YAHP) (Dutch) He Is Our Little
Magnificent One

Jacintha (yah-SEEN-tuh) (Dutch) She Is a
Fragrant Hyacinth
Jacoba (yah-KO-buh) (Dutch) She Surpasses
all Others
Jacobina (yah-ko-BEE-nuh) (Dutch) She Is Our
Little Magnificent One
Jacobus (YAH-ko-bus) (Dutch) He Surpasses
Everyone
Jacomina (yah-ko-MEE-nuh) (Dutch) She Is
Divinely Protected

🐦 **Imamu** (ee-MAH-moo) (Swahili) He Helps
Us Understand God
Isingoma (ee-seen-GO-mah) (Luganda) He Is
the Eldest Twin
Jelani (jeh-LAH-nee) (Swahili) He Is Powerful
Jengo (JEN-go) (Swahili) He Constructs
Jumaane (joo-mah-AH-nee) (Swahili) He
Arrived on a Tuesday
Kagiso (kah-GHEE-so) (Tswana) She Is
Tranquility and Harmony
Kamaria (kah-MAH-ree-yah) (Swahili) She Is
the Silvery Moon
Kato (KAH-toh) (Luganda) He Is the Youngest
Twin
Kayode (kah-YO-day) (Yoruba) She Is Happiness
Khamisi (kah-MEE-see) (Swahili) He Arrived
on a Thursday

🐦 **Inkeri** (in-KEH-ree) (Finnish) She Is First
in Beauty
Irina (eye-REE-nah) (Finnish/Greek) She Is
Springtime
Irja (EER-yah) (Finnish) She Is Our Little
Springtime
Jaako (yah-AH-ko) (Finnish) He Is Divinely
Protected
Jaana (yah-AH-nah) (Finnish) She Is Our Little
Beloved One
Jalmari (yahl-MAH-ree) (Finnish) He Is a
Soldier with a Mighty Helmet
Jalo (YAH-lo) (Finnish) He Is Aristocratic
Jani (YAH-nee) (Finnish) His God Is Gracious
Janina (yah-NEE-nah) (Finnish) She Is God's
Graceful Little Messenger
Jari (YAH-ree) (Finnish) He Is a Soldier with a
Mighty Helmet

🐦 **Isandro** (ee-SAHN-dro) (Spanish/Greek) He
Liberates Humanity
Isaura (ee-SAH-oh-rah) (Spanish) She Is
Isauria, Asia

Isidoro (iz-ih-DOR-ro) (Spanish) He Is a Gift from the Goddess Isis

Isidro (ee-SEE-dro) (Spanish) He Is a Gift from the Goddess Isis

Jacinta (hah-SEEN-tah) (Spanish) She Is a Fragrant Hyacinth

Jaime (HYE-may) (Spanish) He Is Divinely Protected

Javier (hah-vee-YAIR) (Spanish) He Builds New Houses

Jeronimo (heh-RAH-nee-mo) (Spanish) His Name Is Sacred

Jessenia (yeh-SEN-ee-yah) (Spanish) She Is a Beautiful Jessenia Tree

Jimena (hee-MAY-nah) (Spanish) She Hears Everything

☙ *Iva* (EE-vah) (Croatian) She Is God's Graceful Little Messenger

Ivanka (ee-VAHN-kah) (Croatian) She Is God's Graceful Little Messenger

Jagoda (yah-GO-dah) (yah-GO-dah) (Croatian) He Is a Sweet Strawberry

Jakov (YAH-kohv) (Croatian) He Surpasses Everyone

Janko (YAHN-ko) (Croatian) He Is the Little One Whose God Is Gracious

Jasna (YAHZ-nah) (Croatian) She Is the Brilliant One Who Thinks Logically

Jelena (yel-LAY-nuh) (Croatian) She Is a Radiant Torch

Josif (YO-seef) (Croatian) His Greatness Increases

Jovan (yo-VAHN) (Croatian) His God Is Gracious

Julija (YOOL-yah) (Croatian) She Is Beautifully Youthful

☙ *Ivy* (EYE-vee) (English) She Is a Verdant Ivy-Vine

Caswell (KAZ-wel) (Scottish) He Lives by a Watercress Field

Brown (BROWN) (English) He Is the Color of the Brown Earth

Columbia (kuh-LUM-bee-yah) (Latin) She Is a Peaceful Dove

Cornell (kor-NEL) (English) He Is a Cornucopia of Abundance

Dartmouth (DART-muth) (English) He Is the Dart River Delta

Harvard (HAR-vurd) (English) He Is a Harbor of Mercy

Princeton (PRINS-tun) (English) He Is the Prince's Town

Penn (PEN) (English) She Is a Needle and Thread

Yale (YAIL) (Latin) He Moves Gracefully

☙ *Jolana* (yo-LAH-nah) (Czech) She Is a Fragrant Violet

Josefa (ho-SEE-fuh) (Czech) Her God Is Abundance

Judita (hoo-DEE-tah) (Czech) She Is a Judean Woman

Kaja (KYE-yuh) (Czech) He Is Our Mighty Little Warrior

Kamila (kah-MEE-lah) (Czech) She Observes Sacred Rituals

Karolina (kah-ro-LEE-nah) (Czech) She Is a Mighty Warrior

Kazimir (kah-zee-MEER) (Czech) He Is the Powerful Destroyer

Klara (KLAH-rah) (Czech) She Shimmers with Fame

Klaudia (KLO-dee-yah) (Czech) She Walks with Difficulty

Klement (KLEM-ment) (Czech) He Is Compassionate

☙ *Jon* (JAHN) (English) He Is the Little One Favored by God

Aaden (AY-dun) (Irish) He Is the Little One Who Is Hot-Tempered

Alexis (uh-LEX-us) (uh-LEX-iss) (Greek) She Is Our Brave Protector

Cara (KAH-ruh) (Italian) She Is Greatly Beloved

Collin (KAHL-lun) (English) He Is Humanity's Little Triumph

Hannah (HAN-nuh) (Hebrew) She Is Graceful

Joel (JO-wel) (Hebrew) His God Is the True God

Kate (KAYT) (English) She Is the Little One Who Is Chaste and Pure

Leah (LAY-yuh) (Hebrew) She Is Humanity's Queen

Mady (MAD-dee) (English) She Is the Little One from Magdala, Palestine

The Gosselin family, seen by millions weekly on The Learning Channel series Jon & Kate Plus Eight, are a multiracial-American family consisting of dad Jon, mom Kate, twins Cara and Mady, and sextuplets Aaden, Alexis, Collin, Hannah, Joel, and Leah.

☙ *Jonas* (JO-nus) (Greek) He Is a Peaceful Dove

Alex (AL-lex) (Greek) He Is Humanity's Little Protector

Greg (GREG) (English) He Is Our Little Guardian

Jack (JAK) (English) He Is Beloved and His God Is Gracious

Joe (JO) (English) He Is the Little One Whose Greatness Increases

John (JAHN) (Hebrew) His God Is Gracious

Kevin (KEH-vin) (Irish) He Is Compassionate

Mandy (MAN-dee) (English) She Is the Little One Worthy of Love

Nick (NIK) (English) He Is Humanity's Little Triumph

Ryan (RYE-yun) (Irish) He Descends from a Beloved King

> The Jonas Brothers are a popular American band consisting of Alex Noyes, Greg Garbowsky, Jack Lawless, Joe Jonas, John Taylor, Kevin Jonas, Nick Jonas, and Ryan Liestman. One of the band's earliest hits was 2006's "Mandy."

🖋 **Jure** (YOO-ree) (Croatian) He Farms the Land

Katarina (kah-tah-REE-nuh) (Croatian) She Is Pure-Hearted

Konstantin (KON-stun-teen) (Croatian) He Is Dependably Constant

Kresimir (KREH-see-meer) (Croatian) He Is Peace

Kristijan (kreess-tee-YAHN) (Croatian) He Follows Christ

Kristina (kreess-TEE-nah) (Croatian) She Follows Christ

Lazar (lah-ZAR) (Croatian) His God Assists Him

Maja (MYE-yah) (Croatian) She Is a Wonderful Mother

Marica (MAHR-eeh-kah) (Croatian) She Is a Fragrant Olive Tree

Marija (mah-REE-yuh) (Croatian) She Is Love

🖋 **Kadri** (KAH-dree) (Estonian) She Is Pure-Hearted

Kaisa (kah-EE-suh) (Estonian) She Is Our Little Pure-Hearted One

Kalev (KAH-LEF) (Estonian) He Is Our Great Hero

Kalju (KAHL-yoo) (Estonian) He Is Rock-Solid

Katariina (kaht-tah-ree-EE-nuh) (Estonian) She Is Pure-Hearted

Koit (KO-weet) (Estonian) He Is the Morning Sunrise

Kristiina (kris-tee-EE-nah) (Estonian) She Follows Christ

Kristjan (KRIST-yahn) (Estonian) He Follows Christ

Leena (LEE-nah) (Estonian) She Is Our Radiant Little Torch

Liisa (lee-EE-sah) (Estonian) She Demonstrates God's Abundance

🖋 **Kanya** (KAHN-yuh) (Thai) She Is a Gentle Young Lady

Klahan (klah-HAHN) (Thai) He Is Courageous

Kulap (koo-LAHP) (Thai) She Is Our Fragrant Rose

Lawan (lah-WAHN) (Thai) She Is Pretty

Malai (mah-LYE) (Thai) She Is a Wreath of Fragrant Blossoms

Mongkut (mong-KOOT) (Thai) He Is a Shining Crown

Pakpao (pahk-PAH-wo) (Thai) He Is a Soaring Kite

Ratree (RAHT-ree) (Thai) She Is Fragrant Jasmine

Suchart (soo-KART) (Thai) He Is Aristocratic

Sukhon (soo-KOHN) (Thai) She Is an Aromatic Fragrance

🖋 **Kiana** (kee-AH-nah) (Hawaiian) She Is the Heavenly Life Source

Kilikina (kil-ih-KEE-nah) (Hawaiian) She Follows Christ

Kimo (KEE-mo) (Hawaiian) His God Is Gracious

Konani (ko-NAH-nee) (Hawaiian) She Is Brilliant

Lani (LAH-nee) (Hawaiian) She Is the Blue Sky

Maile (MYE-lay) (Hawaiian) He Is the Flower Used to Create Colorful Leis

Makaio (mah-KYE-yo) (Hawaiian) He Is God's Divine Gift

Maleko (mah-LAY-ko) (Hawaiian) He Is Powerfully Male

Malia (mah-LEE-yah) (Hawaiian) She Is Love

Malie (MAH-lee-yay) (Hawaiian) She Is Grace under Pressure

🖋 **Kirabo** (KEE-rah-bo) (Luganda) He Is God's Divine Gift

Kobina (ko-BEE-nah) (Akan) He Arrived on a Tuesday

Kojo (KO-zho) (Akan) He Arrived on a Monday

Kwabena (kwah-BAYN-yah) (Akan) He Arrived on a Tuesday

Kwasi (KWAH-zee) (Akan) He Arrived on a Sunday

Kweku (KWAY-koo) (Akan) He Arrived on a Wednesday

Kwesi (KWAY-zee) (Akan) He Arrived on a Sunday

Lekan (lay-KAHN) (Yoruba) He Is the Little One Whose Treasure Increases

Lerato (leh-RAH-toh) (Sesotho) She Is Love

Lesedi (leh-SAY-dee) (Tswana) She Is Brilliant

🐦 **Koenraad** (KOON-rahd) (Dutch) He Rules by Wise Counsel

Koert (KOORT) (Dutch) He Is Our Wise Little Counselor

Koos (KOHSS) (Dutch) He Is Our Little Magnificent One

Lambert (LAHM-bairt) (Dutch) He Is the Bright Land

Lammert (LAHM-mairt) (Dutch) He Is the Bright Land

Laura (LOR-rah) (Dutch) She Is a Laurel Wreath of Victory

Lea (LAY-yuh) (Dutch) She Is Humanity's Queen

Leo (LAY-yo) (Dutch) He Is a Noble Lion

Lieke (LEE-kuh) (Dutch) She Is God's Little Angelic Messenger

Lien (LEEN) (Dutch) She Is Our Little Gently Swaying Palm Tree

🐦 **Konrad** (KAHN-rahd) (Czech) He Rules by Wise Counsel

Kornel (kor-NEL) (Czech) He Is a Cornucopia of Plenty

Kristof (KRIS-toff) (Czech) He Follows Christ

Kristyna (kris-TEE-nah) (Czech) She Follows Christ

Lenka (LEN-kah) (Czech) She Is the Little One Who Is Magdala, Israel

Leos (LEE-wohsh) (Czech) He Is a Noble Lion

Libena (lee-BAYN-yah) (Czech) She Is Sweet Love

Lida (LEE-dah) (Czech) She Is the Little One Who Is Beloved by Humanity

Livia (LEEV-ee-yah) (Czech) She Is the Beautiful Color Blue

Lubomir (LOO-bo-meer) (Czech) He Is Peace and Compassion

🐦 **Kristoffer** (KREESS-toh-fur) (Danish) She Follows Christ

Laurits (LAHR-reetz) (Danish) He Is a Laurel Wreath of Victory

Lene (LAY-nuh) (Danish) She Is a Radiant Torch

Lisbet (LEEZ-bet) (Danish) Her God Is Abundance

Lorens (LOR-renz) (Danish) He Is a Laurel Wreath of Victory

Lotte (LAHT-tuh) (Danish) She Is Our Beloved Little Warrior

Lovise (lo-VEE-suh) (Danish) She Is a Renowned Warrior

Magnus (MAHG-nooss) (Danish) He Is Magnificent

Malene (mah-LAY-nuh) (Danish) She Is Magdala, Israel

Malte (MAHL-tuh) (Danish) She Is the Maiden Who Rules Humanity

🐦 **Lear** (LEER) (Irish) He Is the Blue Ocean

Albany (ALL-buh-nee) (English) He Is Alba Longa, Italy

Cordelia (kor-DEEL-yuh) (English) She Has the Heart of a Lioness

Duke (DOOK) (English) He Is a Renowned Leader

Earl (URL) (English) He Is Aristocratic

Edgar (ED-gur) (English) He Is a Powerful Weapon

Goneril (GAH-nur-rull) (Scottish) Her Name Is Legendary

King (KING) (English) He Is a Majestic Monarch

Regan (RAY-gun) (Irish) She Descends from a Father Who Favors Action

William (WILL-yum) (English) He Protects Humanity

In the 1606 play King Lear *by playwright William Shakespeare (1564–1616), Lear divides his realm between daughters Cordelia, Goneril, and Regan. But only Cordelia, Edgar of Gloucester, and the Duke of Albany remain loyal to Lear.*

🐦 **Lien** (LIN) (Vietnamese) She Is a Fragrant Lotus Flower

Linh (LING) (Vietnamese) He Is Springtime

Mai (MYE) (Vietnamese) She Is a Sweet Apricot

Minh (MING) (Vietnamese) She Is a Genius

Ngai (NYE) (Vietnamese) He Is Fragrant Medicine

Ngoc (NAHP) (Vietnamese) She Is Precious Jade

Nguyen (WIN) (Vietnamese) He Is the Heavenly Life Source

Nguyet (BIHK) (Vietnamese) She Is the Silvery Moon

Nhung (nye-YOONG) (Vietnamese) She Is Velvet

Phuong (FOON) (Vietnamese) She Is the Phoenix

Liisu (lee-EE-soo) (Estonian) She Is the Little One Favored by God

Loviise (lo-vee-EE-suh) (Estonian) She Is a Renowned Warrior

Maarika (mah-AH-rih-kah) (Estonian) She Is Our Little Beloved One

Maarja (mah-ah-REE-yah) (Estonian) She Is Our Little Beloved One

Maret (MAH-ray) (Estonian) She Is a Priceless Pearl

Mihkel (mih-KEL) (Estonian) He Resembles God

Olev (OH-lef) (Estonian) He Descends from Our Ancestors

Paavo (pah-AH-vo) (Estonian) He Demonstrates Humility

Riina (ree-EE-nah) (Estonian) She Is Our Priceless Little Pearl

Triinu (tree-EE-noo) (Estonian) She Is Our Priceless Little Pearl

Lindiwe (lin-DEE-way) (Zulu) She Is the One We Have Awaited

Makena (mah-KAY-nah) (Kikuyu) She Rejoices

Mamadou (MAH-mah-doo) (Akan) He Is Praise-Worthy

Manyara (mahn-YAH-rah) (Shona) She Is Greater than Others

Marjani (mar-ZHAH-nee (Swahili) She Is Beautiful Ocean Coral

Masamba (mah-SAHM-bah) (Yao) She Goes Her Own Way

Masego (mah-SAY-go) (Tswana) She Proves God's Generosity

Masozi (mah-SO-zee) (Tumbuka) She Weeps with Happiness

Melisizwe (mel-ee-SEEZ-way) (Xhosa) She Rules Humanity Wisely

Mirembe (mih-REM-bay) (Luganda) She Is Tranquility

Ludvik (LOOD-vik) (Czech) He Is a Renowned Warrior

Lukas (LOO-kahss) (Czech) He Is the One Who Is Lucania, Italy

Madlenka (mad-LEN-kah) (Czech) She Is Magdala, Israel

Marcela (mar-SEL-lah) (Czech) She Is the Little One as Powerful as any male

Margita (mahr-GHEE-tah) (Czech) She Is a Priceless Pearl

Marika (mahr-EE-kah) (Czech) She Is Our Little Beloved One

Marketa (mahr-KAY-tah) (Czech) She Is a Priceless Pearl

Matylda (mah-TEEL-dah) (Czech) She Is a Powerful Warrior

Maximilian (max-ee-MEEL-yahn) (Czech) He Is Supreme

Melania (mel-LAHN-yah) (Czech) She Is Darkly Beautiful

Lycophron (LYE-kuh-frahn) (Greek) He Howls as Boldly as a Wolf

Alecto (uh-LEK-toh) (Latin) She Is Eternally Wrathful

Apuleius (uh-PYOO-lee-yus) (Latin) He Is Apulia, Italy

Athamas (uh-THAH-mus) (Greek) He Is Athamantia, Greece

Dira (DEER-rah) (Latin) She Is a Dark Avenger

Furia (FYOOR-ee-yuh) (Latin) She Is a Dark Avenger

Megaira (meh-GAIR-ruh) (Greek) She Holds a Grudge

Sorores (sor-ROR-ress) (Latin) She Is One of the Dread Sisters

Tereus (TAIR-ee-yus) (Latin) He Is a Bountiful Harvest

Tisiphone (tye-SIF-uh-nee) (Greek) She Avenges Wrongful Death

Greek poet Lycophron (third century B.C.) and Roman poet Apuleius (second century A.D.) wrote of the avenging Erinyes or Furies—Alecto, Megaira, and Tisiphone--who drove mortals insane, such as King Athamas of Athamantia and King Tereus of Thrace.

Maile (MYE-lay) (Hawaiian) He Is the Flower Used to Create Colorful Leis

Makaio (mah-KYE-yo) (Hawaiian) He Is God's Divine Gift

Mele (MAY-lay) (Hawaiian) She Is God's Melody

Melika (meh-LEE-kah) (Hawaiian) She Is a Busy Honeybee

Mikala (mee-KAH-lah) (Hawaiian) He Resembles God

Nalani (nah-LAH-nee) (Hawaiian) She Is the Blue Sky

Noelani (no-eh-LAH-nee) (Hawaiian) She Is Life-Giving Rain

Peni (PAY-nee) (Hawaiian) He Is Our Glorious Son

Pika (PEE-kah) (Hawaiian) He Is Rock-Solid

Wikolia (wee-KO-lee-yah) (Hawaiian) She Is Humanity's Triumph

🐦 **Maren** (MAIR-ren) (Danish) She Is the Blue Ocean

Margarethe (mar-gah-RET-tuh) (Danish) She Is a Priceless Pearl

Margit (MAR-get) (Danish) She Is a Priceless Pearl

Marius (MAR-ee-yooss) (English) He Is Love Itself

Meta (MAY-tuh) (Danish) She Is Our Priceless Little Pearl

Milla (MEEL-luh) (Danish) She Is the Little One Who Observes Sacred Rituals

Morten (MOR-ten) (Danish) He Is Powerfully Male

Nanna (NAH-nuh) (Danish) She Is Courageous

Nikolaj (NEE-ko-lye) (Danish) He Is Humanity's Triumph

Njord (NYORD) (Danish) He Is Powerfully Healthy

🐦 **Mere** (MAIR-ray) (Maori) She Is Love

Mikaere (mye-kah-AIR-ray) (Maori) He Resembles God

Moana (mo-AH-nah) (Maori) She Is the Blue Ocean

Ngaio (NYE-yo) (Maori) She Is a Beautiful Tree

Ngaire (NYE-ree) (Maori) She Is the Golden Flax of the Fields

Paora (PAH-oh-ruh) (Maori) He Demonstrates Humility

Patariki (pah-tah-REE-kee) (Maori) He Is Aristocratic

Petera (PAY-teh-ruh) (Maori) He Is Rock-Solid

Piripi (PEER-ih-pee) (Maori) He Befriends Horses

Roimata (ro-ee-MAH-tah) (Maori) She Cries Beautifully

🐦 **Michael** (MYE-kul) (Hebrew) He Resembles God

Jackie (JAK-kee) (English) He Is Beloved and His God Is Gracious

Janet (JAN-net) (English) She Is God's Graceful Little Messenger

Jermaine (jur-MAYN) (English) He Is a Beloved Friend

Joseph (JO-suf) (Hebrew) His Greatness Increases

La Toya (luh TOY-yuh) (English/American) She Is Humanity's Little Triumph

Marlon (MAR-lun) (English) He Is a Powerful and Beloved Man

Randy (RAN-dee) (English) He Is Our Little Guardian Wolf

Rebbie (REB-bee) (American/Hebrew) She Is the Little One Who Snares Her Enemies

Tito (TEE-toh) (Spanish) His Name Is Honor
Joseph Jackson molded his sons into the Jackson Five, a popular African-American group who performed from 1966 to 1990. The Jackson Five consisted of Michael, Jackie, Jermaine, Marlon, and Tito. Other talented Jacksons include Janet, La Toya, Randy, and Rebbie.

🐦 **Michal** (mee-KAHL) (Czech) He Resembles God

Michala (mee-KAHL-lah) (Czech) She Resembles God

Mikolas (MEE-ko-lahss) (Czech) He Is Humanity's Triumph

Milada (mee-LAH-dah) (Czech) She Is Graceful

Milana (mee-LAH-nah) (Czech) She Is Graceful

Miloslava (mee-lo-SLAH-vah) (Czech) She Stands Up for Justice

Mirek (MEER-rek) (Czech) He Is the Peaceful Little One

Monika (MO-nee-kah) (Czech) She Counsels Wisely

Noemi (no-AY-mee) (Czech) She Is Hospitable

Oldrich (OLD-rish) (Czech) He Is Wealth and Strength

🐦 **Mies** (MEESS) (Dutch) He Is the Little One with a Furrowed Brow

Minke (MING-kuh) (Dutch) She Is Our Mighty Little Warrior

Mirjam (MEER-yahm) (Dutch) She Is Love

Mirthe (MEER-tuh) (Dutch) She Is a Fragrant Myrtle Tree

Mozes (MO-zess) (Dutch) He Is the Great Son Who Rescues Us

Nicolaas (NEE-ko-lahss) (Dutch) He Is Humanity's Triumph

Nicolet (nee-ko-LET) (Dutch) She Is Humanity's Triumph

Nicoline (nee-ko-LEEN) (Dutch) She Is Humanity's Little Triumph

Niek (NEEK) (Dutch) He Is Humanity's Little Triumph

Norbert (NAHR-boort) (Dutch) He Is the Radiant North

🐦 **Monifa** (mo-NEE-fah) (Yoruba) She Is Favored by Fortune

Munashe (moo-NAH-shay) (Shona) She Is Divinely Protected

Nakato (nah-KAH-toh) (Luganda) She Is the Youngest Twin

Neo (NAY-yo) (Tswana) He Is God's Divine Gift

Nia (NEE-yah, NYE-yah) (Tswana) Her Destiny Is Determined by God

Nomusa (no-MOO-sah) (Ndebele) She Is Compassionate

Nosizwe (no-SEEZ-way) (Xhosa) She Is Our Nation's Great Matriarch

Nuru (NOO-roo) (Swahili) She Is Brilliance

Nyah (NYE-yah) (Tswana) Her Destiny Is Determined by God

Obi (OH-bee) (Igbo) She Is the Majestic One Who Soothes Us

🕮 **Naida** (nah-EE-dah) (Croatian) She Embodies Our Dreams

Natalija (nah-TAHL-yah) (Croatian) She Is Christmas Day

Niko (NEE-ko) (Croatian) He Is Humanity's Little Triumph

Obrad (oh-BRAHD) (Croatian) He Completes Our Joy

Pavao (pah-VAH-wo) (Croatian) He Demonstrates Humility

Pero (PAIR-ro) (Croatian) He Is Rock-Solid

Petar (PAY-tar) (Croatian) He Is Rock-Solid

Radmila (rahd-MEE-lah) (Croatian) She Rejoices

Radomir (RAH-doh-meer) (Croatian) He Is Calmness

Radomira (rah-doh-MEER-rah) (Croatian) She Is Calmness

🕮 **Ogechi** (oh-GAY-chee) (Igbo) He Is Our Little Proof of God's Greatness

Oluchi (oh-LOO-chee) (Igbo) He Is God's Marvelous Creation

Olufeme (oh-loo-FEH-may) (Yoruba) He Is Adored by God

Oni (OH-nee) (Yoruba) She Is Born in God's House

Onyeka (own-YAY-kah) (Igbo) She Is the Little One Who Demonstrates God's Brilliance

Otieno (oh-tee-AY-no) (Luo) She Came into this World at Dusk

Ramla (RAHM-lah) (Swahili) She Speaks of God's Wonders

Rufaro (roo-FAH-ro) (Swahili) She Rejoices

Rutendo (roo-TEN-doh) (Shona) He Is God's Devoted Servant

Sanaa (sah-NAH-hah) (Swahili) She Is an Inspired Masterpiece

🕮 **Ondrej** (AHN-dray) (Czech) He Is Powerful

Patricie (pah-TREE-see-yay) (Czech) She Is Aristocratic

Patrik (PAH-treek) (Czech) He Is Aristocratic

Pavel (PAH-vel) (Czech) He Demonstrates Humility

Pavla (PAHV-lah) (Czech) She Demonstrates Humility

Pavlina (pahv-LEE-nah) (Czech) She Is the Little One Who Demonstrates Humility

Petra (PEH-trah) (Czech) She Is Rock-Solid

Radek (RAH-dek) (Czech) He Is the Little One Who Rejoices

Radim (rah-DEEM) (Czech) He Is the Little One Who Rejoices

Radko RAHD-ko) (Czech) He Is the Little One Who Rejoices

🕮 **Osvald** (AHZ-vahld) (Danish) His God Rules All

Ove (OH-vee) (Danish) He Is Our Little Razor-Sharp Weapon

Peder (PAY-dur) (Danish) He Is Rock-Solid

Pernille (pair-NIL-luh) (Danish) She Is the Little One from the Lovely Countryside

Preben (PRAY-ben) (Danish) He Is Our Courageous Warrior

Ragna (RAHN-yuh) (Danish) She Is the Little One Who Is a Sagacious Counselor

Rakel (rah-KEL) (Danish) She Is a Gentle Mother Ewe

Rasmus (RAHZ-muss) (Danish) He Is Greatly Beloved

Rebekka (reh-BAK-kuh) (Danish) She Brings Us Closer

Rikard (rih-KARD) (Danish) He Is Powerfully Courageous

🕮 **Ottoline** (aht-tuh-LEEN) (English) She Is Our Powerful Little Warrior

Owen (OH-win) (English/Welsh) He Is Aristocratic

Oz (AHZ) (English) His God Rules All

Ozzie (AHZ-zee) (English) He Is the Little One Whose God Rules All

Pacey (PAY-see) (English) He Is Our Tranquil Little Son

Paden (PAY-den) (English/Irish) He Is Aristocratic

Paisley (PAYZ-lee) (English/Scottish) She Is God's Sacred Church

Palmer (PAH-mur) (English) He Is a Fearless Pilgrim

Pamelia (pam-EL-yuh) (English) She Is Sweetness

Pamella (PAM-el-luh) (English) She Is Sweetness

🕮 **Paulien** (po-LEEN) (Dutch) She Demonstrates Humility

Pauwel (POW-wul) (Dutch) He Demonstrates Humility

Peter (PAY-tur) (Dutch) He Is Rock-Solid

Pier (PEER) (Dutch) He Is Rock-Solid

Piet (PEET) (Dutch) He Is Our Rock-Solid Little Fortress

Pietronella (peet-tro-NEL-luh) (Dutch) She Is Our Little Nature-Girl

Radboud (RAHT-boht) (Dutch) He Is Our Brave Counselor

Reinier (rye-NEER) (Dutch) He Wisely Counsels the Military

Reinout (RYE-nowt) (Dutch) He Is Our Wise Counselor

Renate (reh-NAH-tuh) (Dutch) He Is Reborn in God

🕮 **Quan** (WAHN) (Vietnamese) He Is a Courageous Warrior

Thanh (TAHN) (Vietnamese) He Shimmers with Light

Thi (TEE) (Vietnamese) She Is a Melodious Song

Thu (TOO) (Vietnamese) She Is the Beautiful Fall Season

Thuan (TWAHN) (Vietnamese) He Is Obedient

Thuy (TWEE) (Vietnamese) She Is a Dependable Companion

Tien (tee-YEN, tee-YET) (Vietnamese) She Is a Magical Pixie

Trai (TRY) (Vietnamese) He Is as Solitary as an Oyster

Truc (TRUK, TROO) (Vietnamese) He Is the Mighty Bamboo Tree

Tu (TOO) (Vietnamese) She Is a Heavenly Star

🕮 **Quique** (KEE-kah) (Spanish) He Rules Our Home Magnificently

Rafa (RAH-fah) (Spanish) He Is the Little One Whom God Has Rescued

Rafaela (rah-fah-EL-lah) (Spanish) Her God Rescues Her

Raimundo (ray-MOON-doh) (Spanish) He Rules Wisely

Rainerio (ray-NAIR-ee-yo) (Spanish) He Commands the Military

Ramiro (rah-MEE-ro) (Spanish) He Is Renowned for His Wise Counsel

Ramón (rah-MOHN) (Spanish/Latin) He Is a Wise Counselor and Protector

Raul (rah-WOOL) (Spanish) He Advises as Cleverly as a Wolf

Rayen (RAYN) (Spanish/Mapuche) She Is a Beautiful Blossom

Reina (RAY-nah) (Spanish) She Is a Majestic Queen

🕮 **Radmila** (rahd-MEEL-yah) (Czech) She Rejoices in Her Blessings

Romano (ro-MAHN-yo) (Czech) He Is the Great Roman Empire

Ruzena (roo-ZAY-nah) (Czech) She Is Our Fragrant Rose

Sabina (sah-BEE-nah) (Czech) She Is Sabinium

Sara (SAH-rah) (Czech) She Is a Royal Princess

Silvester (seel-VES-tair) (Czech) He Is a Beautiful Forest of Majestic Trees

Simona (see-MO-nah) (Czech) She Hears Everything

Soña (SOHN-yah) (Czech) She Is Wisdom Itself

Stefania (steh-FAHN-yah) (Czech) She Is a Shining Crown

Tatana (tah-TAH-nah) (Czech) She Picks and Chooses

🕮 **Radoslav** (RAH-doh-slahv) (Croatian) He Rejoices in His Great Conquests

Radovan (RAHD-oh-vahn) (Croatian) He Greatly Rejoices

Sava (SAH-vah) (Croatian) He Has the Soul of a Wise, Thoughtful Elder

Silvija (SEEL-vee-yah) (Croatian) She Is the Beautiful Woodlands

Simo (SEE-mo) (Croatian) He Hears Everything

Slavica (SLAH-vee-kah) (Croatian) She Is Eternal Honor

Slobodan (slo-bo-DAHN) (Croatian) He Is Freedom

Sofija (so-FEE-yah) (Croatian) She Is Knowledge

Sonja (SOAN-yuh) (Croatian) She Is the Beloved One Who Is Wisdom Itself

Stanimir (STAHN-ee-meer) (Croatian) He Stands Up for Justice and Peace

🕊 **Raymundo** (ray-MOON-doh) (Spanish) He Rules Wisely

Regulo (RAY-gyoo-lo) (Spanish) He Reigns over all of Us

Reinaldo (ray-NAL-doh) (Spanish) He Governs with Wise Advice

Remedios (ray-MAY-dee-yohss) (Spanish) He Is the Remedy for all Our Ills

Renato (reh-NAH-toh) (Spanish) He Is Reborn in God

Reyna (RAY-nah) (Spanish) She Is a Majestic Queen

Ricarda (ree-KAR-dah) (Spanish) She Is Powerfully Courageous

Ricardo (ree-KAR-doh) (Spanish) He Is Powerfully Courageous

Roberta (ro-BAIR-tah) (Spanish) She Is Brilliantly Renowned

Roberto (ro-BAIR-toh) (Spanish) He Is Brilliantly Renowned

🕊 **Ria** (REE-yah) (Dutch) She Is Our Little Beloved One

Rien (REEN) (Dutch) He Is a Wise Counselor

Rik (RIK) (Dutch) He Rules Our Home Magnificently

Rika (REE-kuh) (Dutch) She Rules Our Home Magnificently

Robbe (RAHB-buh) (Dutch) He Is the Little One Who Is Brilliantly Renowned

Rochus (RO-koos) (Dutch) He Is Peaceful

Rodolf (RO-dahlf) (Dutch) He Is a Courageous Wolf

Roel (ROOL) (Dutch) He Is Our Mighty Kingdom

Roeland (ROO-lund) (Dutch) He Is Our Mighty Kingdom

Rogier (ro-KEER) (Dutch) He Is Our Mighty Kingdom

🕊 **Rikke** (RIK-kee, RIK-kuh) (Danish) She Is Our Peaceful Little Ruler

Rosemarie (rohz-muh-REE) (Danish) She Is Our Fragrant Rose

Runa (ROO-nuh) (Danish) She Observes Sacred Rituals

Sander (SAHN-dur) (Danish) He Is Humanity's Little Protector

Sanna (SAHN-nuh) (Danish) She Is Our Fragrant Little Lotus Flower

Severin (SEV-ur-rin) (Danish) She Is Grimly Determined

Sigrid (SEEG-rid, SIG-rid) (Danish) She Is Humanity's Triumph

Siri (SEER-ree) (Danish) She Is Humanity's Little Triumph

Siv (SIF) (Norwegian) She Is the Bride of the Lightning and Thunder

Soren (SOR-ren) (Danish) He Is Grimly Determined

🕊 **Rocio** (ro-SEE-yo) (Spanish) She Is the Morning Mist

Rodolfo (ro-DAHL-fo) (Spanish) He Is a Courageous Wolf

Rodrigo (ro-DREE-go) (Spanish) He Is Mighty and Renowned

Roldan (roll-DAHN) (Spanish) He Is Our Mighty Kingdom

Romina (ro-MEE-nah) (Spanish) She Is Rome

Roque (RO-kah) (Spanish) He Is Comfort and Healing

Rosalina (ro-sah-LEE-nah) (Spanish) She Befriends Horses

Rosalinda (ro-sah-LEEN-dah) (Spanish) She Befriends Horses

Rosalva (ro-SAHL-vah) (Spanish) She Is a Pure-White Rose

Rosenda (ro-SEN-dah) (Spanish) She Is Priceless

🕊 **Roos** (ROOSS) (Dutch) She Is Our Fragrant Rose

Roosje (ROO-shuh) (Dutch) She Is Our Fragrant Little Rose

Rutger (RUHT-ghur) (Dutch) He Is a Renowned Weapon

Ruud (ROO-weed) (Dutch) He Is a Courageous Wolf

Sabien (sah-BYEN) (Dutch) She Is Sabinium

Sander (SAHN-dair) (Dutch) He Is Humanity's Little Protector

Saskia (SAHSS-kee-yuh) (Dutch) She Is the Mighty Saxon Nation

Sebastiaan (seh-BAHS-tee-yun) (Dutch) He Is Honorable

Servaas (sair-VAHSS) (Dutch) His God Is Salvation

Sjaak (SHAHK) (Dutch) He Is Our Little Magnificent One

🕊 **Rosendo** (ro-SEN-doh) (Spanish) He Is Priceless

Rosita (ro-SEE-tah) (Spanish) She Is Our Fragrant Little Rose
Rubén (roo-BAYN) (Spanish) Behold, He Is Our Glorious Son
Rubina (roo-BEE-nah) (Spanish) She Is a Priceless Ruby
Rufino (roo-FEE-no) (Spanish) He Has Fiery-Red Hair
Ruperta (roo-PAIR-tah) (Spanish) She Is Bright Fame
Ruy (ROO-wee) (Spanish) He Is Our Renowned Little Warrior
Sabas (SAH-bahss) (Spanish) He Is Honorable
Sabina (sah-BEE-nah) (Sabine) She Is Sabinium
Salomón (sah-lo-MOHN) (Spanish) He Is Peace

Ruiha (roo-EE-hah) (Maori) She Is a Helmet of Protection
Tama (TAH-mah) (Maori) He Is Our Sacred Flesh and Blood
Tamati (tah-MAH-tee) (Maori) He Is a Precious Twin
Tane (TAH-nay) (Maori) He Is Powerfully Male
Timoti (TIH-mo-tee) (Maori) He Honors God
Tipene (TEE-peh-nee) (Maori) He Is a Shining Crown
Waitara (wah-ee-TAH-rah) (Maori) She Is a River in the Hills
Waka (wah-KAH) (Maori) He Is Our Magnificent Nation
Whetu (WEH-too) (Maori) She Is a Heavenly Star
Wiremu (WEE-reh-moo) (Maori) He Protects Humanity

Rylan (RYE-lun) (English) He Is the Land Rich with Fields of Golden Rye
Rylee (RYE-lee) (English) She Is a Meadow of Fragrant Rye
Sabella (sah-BEL-luh) (English) She Demonstrates God's Abundance
Sable (SAY-bul) (English) She Glistens with Ebony-Black Beauty
Sabrina (sah-BREE-nuh) (English) She Is the Severn River, Wales
Sachie (SAH-chee) (English) He Is the Little One Who Is Sacheverell, France
Sadie (SAY-dee) (English) She Is a Majestic Princess
Sal (SAL) (English) She Is Our Majestic Little Princess
Salena (sah-LEE-nuh) (English) She Is the Silvery Moon
Salome (SAL-luh-may) (English/Hebrew) She Is Peace

Salud (sah-LOOT) (Spanish) She Is Good Fortune and Many Good Wishes
Sancha (SAHN-chah) (Spanish) She Is Revered
Sancho (SAHN-cho) (Spanish) He Is Revered
Sandalio (sahn-DAHL-yo) (Spanish) He Is a Mighty Wolf to be Feared
Sarita (sah-REE-tah) (Spanish) She Is Our Majestic Little Princess
Saturnina (sah-toor-NEE-nah) (Spanish) She Is Time Itself
Saturnino (sah-toor-NEE-noh) (Spanish) He Is Time Itself
Selena (say-LEE-nah) (Spanish/Greek) She Is the Silvery Moon
Severino (seh-veh-REE-no) (Spanish) He Is Severe
Severo (seh-VEH-ro) (Spanish) He Is Severe

Sauda (sah-OO-dah) (Swahili) She Is Beautifully Black
Sefu (SEE-foo) (Swahili) He Is a Razor-Sharp Weapon
Sekai (see-KYE) (Shona) She Makes Us Laugh
Simba (SEEM-bah) (Swahili) He Is God's Magnificent Lion
Simisola (see-mee-SO-lah) (Yoruba) She Is Rich and Comfortable
Sizwe (SEEZ-way) (Xhosa) He Reflects Our Nation's Greatness
Subira (soo-BEE-rah) (Swahili) She Waits Patiently
Tendaji (ten-DAH-zhee) (Swahili) She Motivates Us to Achieve Greatness
Thabo (TAH-bo) (Tswana) She Rejoices
Thandiwe (tahn-DEE-way) (Xhosa) She Is Compassionate
Silvestre (seel-VEST-ray) (Spanish) He Is a Beautiful Forest of Majestic Trees
Silvio (SIL-vee-yo) (Spanish) He Is the Beautiful Woodlands
Soledad (sohl-eh-DAHD) (Spanish) She Is Peace and Quiet
Susanita (Spanish) She Is Our Fragrant Little Lotus Flower
Tancredo (tahn-KRAY-doh) (Spanish) He Is Wise Deliberation

Telma (TEL-mah) (Spanish) She Reveres the Blessed Saint Elmo

Telmo (TEL-mo) (Spanish) He Reveres the Blessed Saint Elmo

Teobaldo (tay-oh-BAHL-doh) (Spanish) He Has the Courage of Humankind

Teodora (tay-oh-DOH-rah) (Spanish) She Is God's Divine Gift

Teodosio (tay-oh-DOH-see-yo) (Spanish) He Makes Offerings to God

☍ **Simon** (SYE-mun) (Greek) He Hears Everything

Brian (BRYE-yun) (Irish) He Is Aristocratic

Fox (FOX) (English) He Is a Clever Fox

Nigel (NYE-jul) (English) He Is a Towering Champion

Paula (PAW-luh) (English) She Shows Great Humility

Randy (RAN-dee) (English) He Is Our Little Guardian Wolf

Richard (RIH-churd) (English) He Is Powerfully Courageous

Ricky (RIK-kee) (English) He Is Powerfully Courageous

Rupert (ROO-poort) (German) He Is Bright Fame

Ryan (RYE-yun) (Irish) He Descends from a Beloved King

> *Simon Cowell, Paula Abdul, Randy Jackson, and Ryan Seacrest host Fox Broadcasting's singing competition* American Idol *(AI). Other AI luminaries include Fox's owner Rupert Murdoch, producer Nigel Lythgoe, former host Brian Dunkleman, band-leader Ricky Minor, and writer Richard Curtis.*

☍ **Sjakie** (SHAH-kee) (Dutch) He Is Our Little Magnificent One

Sjef (SHEF) (Dutch) He Is the Little One Whose Greatness Increases

Staas (STAHSS) (Dutch) He Is the Little One Who Is Reborn in God

Stef (STEF) (Dutch) He Is Our Shining Little Crown

Stefana (steh-FAH-nuh) (Dutch) She Is a Shining Crown

Stefanie (STAY-fah-nee) (Dutch) She Is a Shining Crown

Stefanus (steh-FAH-nuss) (Dutch) He Is a Shining Crown

Sterre (STUR-ruh) (Dutch) She Is a Heavenly Star

Stijn (STINE) (Dutch) He Is the Little One Who Is Constant

Theo (TAY-yo) (Dutch) He Is Our Little Present from God

☍ **Star** (STAR) (English) She Is a Heavenly Star

Paris (PAIR-iss) (Greek) He Is a Stone Wall

Patton (PAT-tun) (English) He Is Our Little Aristocrat

Rocky (RAHK-kee) (English) He Is the Little One Who Rests Easily

Ryan (RYE-yun) (Irish) He Is Our Small but Powerful King

Sophie (SO-fee) (Greek) She Is Our Wise Little Scholar

Spartacus (SPAR-tuh-kus) (Latin) He Is the Powerful Warrior from Sparta, Greece

Sullivan (SUL-lih-vun) (Irish) He Is the Little One Who Has Beautiful Dark Eyes

Sun (SUN) (Korean) He Is Pure Goodness

Virginia (vur-JIN-yuh) (Latin) She Is Chaste and Pure

☍ **Steffen** (STEF-fen) (Danish) He Is a Shining Crown

Stian (STYAHN) (Danish) He Journeys around the World

Stig (STIG, STEEG) (Danish) He Journeys around the World

Stina (STEE-nuh) (Danish) She Is Christ's Little Follower

Tarben (TAR-ben) (Danish) He Is the Great Bear of Thor, God of Thunder

Tekla (TEK-luh) (Danish) Her God Is All-Powerful

Thora (THOR-ruh) (Danish) She Is Thunder and Lightning

Thorborg (THOR-borg) (Danish) He Is Guarded by Thor, God of Thunder

Thorsten (THOR-sten) (Danish) He Is the Rock of Thor, God of Thunder

Thorvald (THOR-vald) (Danish) He Is Our Monarch Thor, God of Thunder

☍ **Stevan** (STEH-vahn) (Croatian) He Is a Shining Crown

Stojan (STO-zhahn) (Croatian) He Stands Up for Justice

Suzana (soo-ZAHN-nah) (Croatian) She Is a Fragrant Lotus Flower

Svjetlana (SVYET-lah-nah) (Croatian) She Is Radiance

Tatjana (taht-YAH-nah) (Croatian) She Is a Saint

Teodor (TAY-oh-dor) (Croatian) He Is God's Divine Gift

Tihana (tee-YAH-nah) (Croatian) She Is Blissfully Tranquil

Toma (TOH-mah) (Croatian) He Is a Precious Twin

Valerija (vah-LAIR-ee-yah) (Croatian) She Is Powerful

Veca (VAY-kah) (Croatian) She Is Our Little Message of Hope

Teofila (tay-oh-FEE-lah) (Spanish) She Is Beloved of God

Teofilo (tay-oh-FEE-lo) (Spanish) He Is Beloved of God

Tercero (tair-SEH-ro) (Spanish) He Is Third

Tere (TEH-ray) (Spanish) She Is Our Little Summer Harvest

Teresita (teh-reh-SEE-tah) (Spanish) She Is Our Little Summer Harvest

Timoteo (tim-oh-TAY-yo) (Spanish) He Honors God

Tomas (toh-MAHSS) (Spanish) He Is a Twin

Tomasa (toh-MAHSS-sah) (Spanish) She Is a Twin

Trini (TREE-nee) (Spanish) She Is the Holy Trinity

Urbano (oor-BAH-no) (Spanish) He Lives in the Great Metropolis

Thema (TAYM-mah) (Akan) She Is Our Majestic Ruler

Themba (THAYM-bah) (Zulu) She We Believe in and Worship

Thulani (too-LAH-nee) (Zulu) He Rests Peacefully

Thulile (too-LEE-lay) (Zulu) She Knows How to Keep Silent

Tinashe (tee-NAH-shee) (Shona) Her God Is an Ever-Present Help

Tumelo (too-MAY-lo) (Tswana) She Is Devoted to God

Udo (OO-doh) (Igbo) He Is Tranquility and Harmony

Unathi (yoo-NAH-tee) (Xhosa) Her God Is an Ever-Present Help

Uzoma (oo-ZO-mah) (Igbo) She Walks God's Divine Path

Xolani (zo-LAH-nee) (Zulu) He Is Tranquility and Harmony

Thyra (TEER-ruh) (Danish) She Rules Heaven

Tine (TEE-nuh) (Danish) She Is the Little One Who Is a Follower of Christ

Tora (TOR-ruh) (Danish) She Is the Little One Who Honors Thor, God of Thunder

Torben (TOR-ben) (Danish) He Is the Great Bear of Thor, God of Thunder

Torsten (TOR-sten) (Danish) He Is the Rock of Thor, God of Thunder

Tove (TOH-vuh) (Danish) She Is the Little One Who Is the Glorious Thunder and Lightning

Trine (TREE-nuh, TREE-nee) (Danish) She Is Our Little Pure-Hearted One

Ulla (OOL-luh) (Danish) She Is the Little One Who Is Wealth, Success, and Strength

Ulrik (OOL-rikh) (Danish) He Is Wealth, Success, and Invincible Strength

Ulrika (OOL-rik-kuh) (German) She Is Wealth, Success, and Invincible Strength

Tommy (TAHM-mee) (English) He Is the Beloved Little One Who Is a Precious Twin

Angelica (an-JEH-lih-kuh) (Latin) She Resembles God's Angels

Arlene (ar-LEEN) (English) She Is a Free Spirit

Chuckie (CHUK-kee) (English) He Is a Powerful and Beloved Man

Dylan (DIL-lun) (Welsh) He Is a Mighty Ocean

Gabor (guh-BOR) (Hungarian) He Is a Prophet of God

Kimi (KIH-mee) (Vietnamese) She Is Pure Gold

Lil (LIL) (English) She Is the Little One Who Is a Fragrant Lily

Phil (FILL) (English) He Is the Little One Who Befriends Horses

Susie (SOO-zee) (English) She Is the Beloved One Who Is a Fragrant Lotus Flower

Trudie (TROO-dee) (Dutch) She Is the Little One Who Is a Weapon of Power

Valentijn (VAH-lun-tyne) (Dutch) He Is Powerful and Energetic

Viona (vee-OH-nuh) (Dutch) She Is Beautifully Fair

Wendel (VEN-del) (Dutch) He Is the Mighty Nation of the Vandals

Wibo (VEE-bo) (Dutch) He Is the Little One Who Is Aggression and Warfare

Willemijn (vil-leh-MEEN) (Dutch) She Protects Humanity

Willy (VIL-lee) (Dutch) He Is Our Little Protector
Wim (VIM) (Dutch) He Is Our Little Protector
Wouter (VOW-tur) (Dutch) He Commands the Military
Xander (KSAHN-door) (Dutch) He Is Humanity's Little Protector

♨ **Truong** (TRONG) (Vietnamese) He Is a Verdant Field of Fragrant Rice-Stalks
Tuan (TWAHN, TOONG) (Vietnamese) His Genius Is Extraordinary
Tuyen (TOO-yin) (Vietnamese) She Is a Golden Sunbeam
Tuyet (too-WEE) (Vietnamese) She Is Fair and Bright
Van (VAHN, VIN) (Vietnamese) His Intelligence Is Truly Extraordinary
Vien (VIN-nee) (Vietnamese) He Completes Our Lives
Vinh (VIN) (Vietnamese) He Is a Magnificent Coastal Harbor
Vuong (WONG) (Vietnamese) He Is a Majestic Monarch
Xuan (soo-WAHN) (Vietnamese) She Is Springtime
Yen (EE-yun) (Vietnamese) She Is Tranquility and Harmony

♨ **Tyrrell** (teer-REL) (English) His Will Is as Unbendable as Iron
Tyrik (tye-REEK) (English/Arabic) He Is an Aggressive Aristocrat
Tyson (TYE-sun) (English) He Is Fiercely Aggressive and Combative
Ulric (UL-rik) (English) He Has the Fierce Courage of the Mighty Wolf
Ulyssa (yoo-LISS-suh) (English/Latin) She Is Fiery Hatred Itself
Unice (YOO-nus) (English/Greek) She Is Humanity's Triumph
Unique (yoo-NEEK) (English) She Is a One-of-a-Kind Masterpiece
Ursella (UR-sel-luh) (English/Swedish) She Is a Small but Fierce She-Bear
Val (VAL) (English) He Is the Little One Who Is Powerful
Valarie (VAL-uh-ree) (Latin) She Is Powerful

♨ **Ulrike** (OOL-rik-kuh) (German) She Is Wealth, Success, and Invincible Strength
Valdemar (VAHL-deh-mahr) (Danish) He Rules Peacefully

Valentin (val-en-TEEN) (Danish) He Is Powerful and Energetic
Valter (VAHL-tur) (Danish) He Commands the Military
Vanja (VAHN-yuh) (Danish) She Is God's Graceful Little Messenger
Vibeke (vee-BEK-kuh) (Danish) She Is a Mighty War-Fortress
Vidar (vee-DAR) (Danish) He Is a Warrior of the Woodlands
Viggo (VEEG-go) (Danish) He Is the Little One Who Is All-Out Combat
Vilfred (VIL-fred) (Danish) He Wants Peace and Tranquility
Vilhelm (VIL-helm) (Danish) He Protects Humanity

♨ **Vedran** (veh-DRAHN) (Croatian) He Is Happy and Jolly
Vedrana (veh-DRAH-nah) (Croatian) She Is Happy and Jolly
Velimir (VEL-ee-meer) (Croatian) He Is Eternal Peace
Vesna (VAYSS-nah) (Croatian) She Is God's Angelic Messenger
Viktor (VEEK-tohr) (Croatian) He Is Victorious
Vladan (VLAH-dahn) (Croatian) He Is the Little One Who Rules Humanity
Vladislav (VLAH-dee—slahv) (Croatian) He Stands Covered in Greatness
Vukasin (voo-kah-seen) (Croatian) He Is a Mighty Wolf
Zelimir (ZEL-ee-meer) (Croatian) He Works to Achieve Worldwide Peace
Zoran (zo-RAHN) (Croatian) He Is the Radiant Morning Sunrise

♨ **Vendula** (VEN-dyoo-lah) (Czech) Her Fame and Honor Increase Forever
Viktorie (vik-TOR-ee-yay) (Czech) She Is Humanity's Triumph
Vilem (VEE-lem) (Czech) He Protects Humanity
Vilma (VEEL-mah) (Czech) She Protects Humanity
Vincenc (VEEN-sent) (Czech) He Is a Mighty Conqueror
Vladimira (vlad-ee-MEE-rah) (Czech) She Rules Peacefully
Zdenko (zuh-DEN-ko) (Czech) He Is Sidon, Lebanon

Zofia (zo-FEE-yah) (Czech) She Is Knowledge

Zoja (ZOY-yah) (Czech) She Is Life Itself

Zuzana (zoo-ZAH-nah) (Czech) She Is a Fragrant Lotus Flower

🐾 **Viktor** (VEEK-tur) (Danish) He Is Humanity's Triumph

Viktoria (veek-TOR-ree-yuh) (Danish) She Is Humanity's Triumph

Vilmar (VIL-mahr) (Danish) He Is Renowned for His Determination

Vincent (VEEN-sent) (Danish) He Is a Mighty Conqueror

Viola (vee-OH-luh) (Danish) She Is a Fragrant Violet

Virginia (vair-HEEN-yuh) (Danish) She Is Chaste and Pure

Vita (VEE-tuh) (Danish) She Is Life Itself

Ylva (EEL-vuh) (Danish) She Is a Fearless, Mighty Wolf

Yngvar (ING-vahr) (Danish) He Is Our Greatest Warrior

Yngve (ING-vuh) (Danish) He Is Supreme

🐾 **Virgee** (VUR-jee) (English) She Is the Little One Who Is a Chaste, Pure Maiden

Vivian (VIV-ee-yun) (English) She Is Full of Life

Viviette (viv-ee-YET) (English/French) She Is the Little One Who Is Full of Life

Vonda (VAHN-duh) (English/Polish) She Is a Wondrous Enchanted Wand

Waldo (WALL-doh) (English) He Safeguards all of Us

Wallace (WALL-luss) (English/Scottish) He Is a Mysterious Stranger

Walton (WALL-tun) (English) He Is a Town near a Clear Beautiful Brook

Wanda (WAHN-duh) (English/German) She Is a Wondrous, Enchanted Wand

Wardell (wor-DEL) (English) He Is the Summit of the Great Guardians

Warner (WOR-nur) (English) He Protects Our Warriors

🐾 **Wolf** (WULF) (English) He Is the Little One Who Is a Mighty Wolf Blazing New Trails

Wolfe (WULF) (English) He Is the Little One Who Is a Mighty Wolf Blazing New Trails

Wren (REN) (English) She Is a Sweetly Singing Wren

Wynne (WIN) (English) He Is a Loyal and Trusted Companion

Wynona (win-OH-nuh) (English/Dakota) She Is Born Before all Others

Wynter (WIN-tur) (English) She Is the Fresh, Cold Winter Season

Wystan (WIS-tun) (English) He Makes War Even upon the Rocky Cliffs

Xander (ZAN-dur) (English) He Is the Little One Who Is the Protector of Humanity

Xanthia (ZAN-thee-yuh) (English) She Is the Golden Soil in Flowing Rivers

Xavia (ZAY-vee-yuh) (English) She Builds a New House

🐾 **Xaviera** (zay-vee-AIR-ruh) (English) She Builds a New House

Xavior (ZAY-vee-yur) (English) He Builds a New House

Yadira (yah-DEE-ruh) (English/Spanish) She Is Priceless Green Jade

Yancy (YAN-see) (English) He Descends from the One Whose God Is Gracious

Yasmin (YAZ-min) (English/Arabic) She Is a Fragrant Jasmine Flower

Yolonda (yo-LAHN-duh) (English) She Is a Fragrant Violet

Yvette (yih-VET) (English/French) She Is the Magnificent Yew Tree

Yvonne (ee-VAHN) (English/French) She Is the Magnificent Yew Tree

Zack (ZAK) (English) He Is the Little One Whom God Remembers

Zackary (ZAK-uh-ree) (English) His God Remembers Him

🐾 **Zackery** (ZAK-uh-ree) (English) His God Remembers Him

Zak (ZAK) (English) He Is the Little One Whom God Remembers

Zander (ZAN-dur) (English) He Is the Little One Who Is the Protector of Humanity

Zandra (ZAN-druh) (English) She Is the Little One Who Is the Protector of Humanity

Zane (ZAYN) (English) His God Is Gracious

Zanna (ZAN-nuh) (English) She Is Our Fragrant Little Lotus Flower

Zara (ZAHR-ruh) (English) She Is the Little One Whom God Remembers

Zaria (ZAHR-ee-yuh) (English/Russian) She Is a Divinely Blessed Bride

Zavanna (zuh-VAN-nuh) (English) She Is a Vast Plain of Fragrant Grass

Zavia (ZAH-vee-yuh) (English) She Builds a New House

🖎 **Zavier** (ZAY-vee-yur) (English) He Builds a New House

Zechariah (zek-uh-RYE-yuh) (English/Hebrew) His God Remembers Him

Zed (ZED) (English) He Is the Little One Whose God Is Righteous

Zeke (ZEEK) (English) His God Gives Him Power

Zelma (ZEL-muh) (English) She Is God's Great Helmet of Protection

Zena (ZEE-nuh) (English/Greek) She Is Gracious

Zeph (ZEF) (English) His God Shelters and Protects

Zinnia (ZIN-yuh) (English) He Is a Fragrant Zinnia Flower

Zoey (ZO-wee) (English/Greek) She Is Life Itself

Zola (ZO-luh) (English) She Is the Good Rich Soil

Name Pairs and Groups
from Film, Theater, Television, and Recording

BOYS

🐾 **Akira** (uh-KEER-ruh) (Japanese) He Is Radiant and Clear-Sighted

Kon (KAHN) (Japanese) He Is Robust and Powerful

Akira Kurosawa (1910–1998) was one of Japan's greatest filmmakers, crafting such epics as 1954's Seven Samurai (Shichinin No Samurai), *ranked by the Internet Movie Database as one of history's finest films. Akira's brilliant contemporary, Kon Ishikawa, is revered for such pacifist films as 1956's* The Burmese Harp (Biruma No Tategot).

🐾 **Al** (AL) (English) He Is Our Brilliant Little Aristocrat

Blondie (BLAHN-dee) (English) She Has Beautiful Blond Hair

Brian (BRYE-yun) (Irish) He Is Aristocratic

Bruce (BROOSS) (Scottish) He Is Brix, France

Carl (KARL) (German) He Is a Mighty Soldier

David (DAY-vid) (Hebrew) He Is Greatly Beloved

Dennis (DEN-niss) (English) He Makes Himself Heard Clearly

Mike (MYKE) (English) He Is God's Little Disciple

Ricky (RIK-kee) (English) He Is the Little Courageous One

Wilson (WIL-sun) (English) He Descends from the Wearer of the Helmet of Protection

🐾 **Ali** (AL-lee) (English) She Is Our Little Aristocrat

Cameron (KAM-ur-run) (Scottish) Her Nose Goes Its Own Way

Charlize (shar-LEEZ) (English) She Is a Mighty Warrior

Cher (SHAIR) (French) She Is Dear to Our Hearts

Elisha (ee-LYE-shuh) (Hebrew) Her God Is Eternal Deliverance

Hudson (HUD-sun) (English) She Descends from the High-Spirited One

Liu (lee-YOO) (Chinese) She Is a Lovely Weeping Willow

MacPherson (mak-FUR-sun) (Scottish) She Descends from the Holy Parson

Thandie (THAN-dee) (American/Xhosa) She Is Tenderly Affectionate

Tilda (TIL-dah) (Swedish) She Is Our Powerful Little Warrior

🐾 **Arto** (AR-toh) (Finnish) He Is a Courageous Bear

Enver (EN-vur) (Albanian) He Shines with Radiant Light

Fareed (fah-REED) (Arabic) He Is a Priceless Treasure

Henderson (HEN-dur-sun) (English) He Descends from Our Homeland's Great Ruler

Hilton (HIL-tun) (English) He Is a Shining City on a Hill

Lamare (luh-MAR) (English) He Is the Blue Ocean

Lonnie (LAHN-nee) (English) He Is Our Little Aristocrat

Romero (ro-MAIR-ro) (Italian) He Journeys to the Eternal City of Rome

Ryo (REE-yo) (Japanese) He Soothes Us

Toninho (toh-NEEN-yoo) (Portuguese) He Is Our Blossoming Little Flower

🙂 **Babatunde** (bah-bah-TOOn-day) (Yoruba) His Father Will Never Leave Us

Barthelemy (bar-tell-em-MEE) (French) He Has a Furrowed Brow

Femi (FAY-mee) (Yoruba) He Is the Little One Whose God Adores Him

Godwin (GOD-win) (English) He Is Befriended by God

Lokassa (lo-KAHSS-suh) (Swahili) He Is Supreme

Lovemore (LUV-mor) (African/English) He Is More Loving than Others

Mohamed (mo-HAH-med) (Arabic) He Is Praise-Worthy

Mor (MOR) (Scottish) He Is Truly Great

Nico (NEE-ko) (Dutch) He Is Humanity's Little Triumph

Sekou (SAY-koo) (Mandingo) He Is a Noble Warrior

🙂 **Bruce** (BROOS) (Scottish) He Is Brix, France

Danny (DAN-nee) (English) He Is the Little One Whose Judge Is Almighty God

Dawayne (duh-WAIN) (American/English) He Is the Little One Who Is Beautifully Dark

Donnie (DAHN-nee) (English) He Is the Beloved Little One Who Rules the World

Jason (JAY-sun) (Greek) He Is a Healer

Laudir (law-DEER) (Irish) He Is Swift and Strong

Lee (LEE) (English) He Is a Fragrant Meadow

Peter (PEE-tur) (Hebrew) He Is Rock-Solid

Terry (TAIR-ree) (English) He Is the Little One Who Is a Gift from God

Walter (WALL-tur) (English) He Commands the Military

🙂 **Bucky** (BUK-kee) (English) He Is Our Mighty Little Buck

Chielo (chee-EL-lo) (Italian) He Is the Heavenly Blue Sky

Duke (DOOK) (English) He Is a Renowned Leader

Lorne (LORN) (Scottish) He Is Lorne, Scotland

Ray (RAY) (English) He Is the Little One Who Protects Us with Wise Counsel

Roman (RO-mahn) (Ukrainian) He Is the Eternal City-State of Rome

Terje (TAIR-zhuh) (Norwegian) He Is the Weapon of Thor, God of Thunder

Vernon (vair-NO) (French) He Is a Grove of Alder Trees

Wes (WES) (English) He Is the Little One Who Is a Meadow in the Western Forest

🙂 **Cy** (SYE) (English) He Is the Little One Who Is the All-Seeing Sun

Ervin (UR-vin) (Hungarian) He Is the Friend Who Is as Mighty as a Boar

Hal (HAL) (English) He Is Our Home's Magnificent Little Monarch

Hart (HART) (English) He Is a Swift-Running Hart

Lamont (lah-MAHNT) (Scottish) He Is a Great Law-Enforcer

Mack (MAHK) (Irish) He Is Our Powerful Descendant

Mort (MORT) (English) He Is the Little One Who Is the Town by the Moors

Phil (FILL) (English) He Is the Little One Who Befriends Horses

Reginald (REJ-ih-nuld) (English) He Rules by Wise Counsel

Sammy (SAM-mee) (English) He Is God's Little Announcer

🙂 **Deirdre** (DEER-druh) (Irish) She Is all of Womankind

Egberto (eg-BUR-toh) (Portuguese) He Is a Sword's Shining Blade

Elek (EL-ek) (Hungarian) He Protects Humanity

Freddie (FRED-dee) (English) He Is Our Peaceful Little Ruler

Gustavo (goo-STAH-vo) (Portuguese) He Is the Great Staff of the Gothic People

Lenny (LEN-nee) (English) He Is Our Noble Little Lion

Luiz (loo-WEESS) (Portuguese) He Is a Renowned Warrior

Nels (NELZ) (Swedish) He Is Humanity's Triumph

Paco (PAH-ko) (Spanish) He Is the Little One Who Is the Nation of France

Robben (RAH-ben) (American/English) He Is the Beloved One Who Shines Gloriously

🙂 **Denzel** (DEN-ZEL) (English) He Is Denzell, Great Britain

Rubin (ROO-bin) (Hebrew) Behold, He Is Our Glorious Son

> *Denzel Washington (1954–) is an African-American actor noted for playing roles such as the falsely accused boxer Rubin Carter in* The Hurricane, *a role that won him a 1999 Golden Globe Award for Best Actor from the Hollywood Foreign Press Association.*

⚣ **Dylan** (DIL-lun) (Welsh) He Is a Mighty Ocean
Cole (KOHL) (English) He Is Fragrant, Ebony-Black Charcoal
Dylan and Cole Sprouse (1992–) are American twin actors whose fans love their portrayals of Zack and Cody Martin on the Disney Channel television comedy The Suite Life of Zack and Cody.

⚣ **Franco** (FRAH-ko) (Italian) He Is the Little One Who Is the Nation of France
Gianfranco (jee-ahn-FRAHNG-ko) (Italian) He Is France, and His God Is Abundance
Italian filmmaker Franco Zeffirelli (1923-) is best known for Romeo and Juliet *(1968), an adaptation of the play by England's great dramatist, William Shakespeare.*

⚣ **Harrison** (HAIR-uh-sun) (English) He Descends from Our Homeland's Great Ruler
Indiana (IN-dee-an-ah) (English) He Is the Great American State of Indiana
Harrison Ford (1942–) is an American actor famed for his portrayal of archaeologist Indiana Jones in the popular Indiana Jones *film-franchise—including 2008's* Indiana Jones and the Kingdom of the Crystal Skull.

⚣ **Jimmy** (JIM-mee) (English) He Is Our Divinely Protected Little Savior
Cameron (KAM-ur-un) (Scottish) His Nose Goes Its Own Way
Jimmy Buffett (1946–) is a country musician famed for his paean to tropical living, "Margaritaville." Jimmy's businesses include film production and live concerts. Jimmy and his wife Jane have produced beloved offspring Cameron, Savannah, and Sarah.

⚣ **Jon** (YAHN) (Icelandic) His God Is Gracious
Lauri (LOR-ree) (Finnish) She Is a Laurel Wreath of Victory
American actor Jon Voight earned an Academy Award from the Academy of Motion Picture Arts and Sciences for his work in the 1978 film Coming Home. *Jon's ex-wife, actress Lauri Peters, is known for such films as 1968's* For Love of Ivy.

⚣ **Kenny** (KEN-nay) (Scottish) He Is the Handsome Little One
Lionel (LYE-oh-nel) (French) He Is Our Noble Little Lion
Kenny Rogers (1938–) is an American country singer famed for such CDs as 1978's The

Gambler. *Kenny's work with African-American songwriter Lionel Richie produced 1980's hit* Lady.

⚣ **Orson** (OR-sun) (English) He Is a Mighty Bear Cub
William (WILL-yum) (English) He Protects Humanity
Orson Welles (1915–1985) was an American filmmaker whose masterpiece Citizen Kane, *based on the life of newspaper magnate William Hearst, was listed in 2007 by the American Film Institute as the greatest film ever made.*

⚣ **River** (RIV-vur) (English) He Is a Powerful River
Joaquin (wah-KEEN) (Spanish) He Is the Little One Supported by God
River Phoenix (1970–1993) was a young actor nominated for an Academy Award from the Academy of American Motion Picture Arts and Sciences for his role in 1988's Running on Empty. *River's surviving brother, actor-director Joaquin Phoenix, continues the family tradition of filmmaking excellence.*

⚣ **Thespis** (THESS-pis) (Greek) He Issues forth from God
Icarus (ih-KAR-ee-yus) (Greek) He Loyally Follows
Thespis (sixth century B.C.) was perhaps Greece's first actor—hence the word "thespian," meaning actor. Thespis, born in Icaria, was the mortal who was taught how to make wine by Dionysus, god of wine.

⚣ **Walt** (WALT) (English) He Is Our Little Military Commander
Mickey (MIK-kee) (English) He Is God's Little Disciple
Walt Disney (1901–1966) created many beloved cartoon characters, starting with the legendary Mickey Mouse, who starred in scores of cartoons. Walt also conceived the Disneyland and Disney World theme parks, which together draw sixty-three million visitors yearly.

⚣ **Wolf** (WULF) (German) He Is Our Courageous Little Wolf
Ari (AR-ree) (Hebrew) He Is a Noble Lion
Since 1990, Wolf Blitzer (1948–) has worked as an American journalist for the Cable News Network in Atlanta, Georgia. Wolf's potential was recognized in 1973 by Ari Rath, editor of Israel's Jerusalem Post *newspaper. Rath's hiring of Wolf launched a brilliant journalistic career.*

GIRLS

🐣 **Alicia** (uh-LEE-shuh) (English) She Is Aristocratic

Amy (AY-mee) (English) She Is Greatly Beloved

African-American singer Alicia Keys (1981–) earned five Grammy Awards from the National Academy of Recording Arts and Sciences, a record matched only by English singer Amy Winehouse.

🐣 **Allison** (AL-lih-sun) (English) She Is Our Little Aristocrat

Dolph (DAHLF) (German) He Is the Little One Who Is a Courageous Wolf

Francine (fran-SEEN) (French) She Is the Little One Who Is the Nation of France

Ham (HAHM) (Hebrew) He Is Hot-Blooded

Janey (JAY-nee) (English) She Is the Little One Whose God is Gracious

Melissa (meh-LIS-sah) (Greek) She Is a Busy Honeybee

Sherri (SHAIR-ree) (English) She Is Darling and Sweet

Terri (TAIR-ree) (English) She Is God's Little Present

Todd (TAHD) (English) He Is a Cunning Fox

Wendell (VEN-del) (German) He Is the Fierce Nation of the Vandals

🐣 **Amber** (AM-bur) (English) She Is Priceless Golden Amber

Ami (AY-mee) (English) She Is Greatly Beloved

Christy (KRIS-tee) (English) She Is Christ's Little Follower

Colleen (kah-LEEN) (Irish) She Is Pretty

Eliza (ee-LYE-zuh) (English) She Is the Little One Favored by God

Jenna (JEN-nuh) (English) She Is Our Fair Little Beauty

Jerri (JAIR-ree) (English) She Is the Little One Whom God Has Favored

Shii (SHEE) (Chinese) She Is Honest

Tammy (TAM-mee) (English) She Is Our Beautiful Little Palm Tree

Tina (TEE-nuh) (English) She Is Christ's Little Follower

🐣 **Ariel** (ahr-ee-YEL) (French) She Is God's Noble Lioness

Aurora (uh-ROR-ruh) (Greek) She Is the Rosy-Fingered Dawn

Belle (BELL) (French) She Is Beautiful

Cinderella (sin-dur-EL-luh) (English) She Cleans Away every Little Cinder

Giselle (zhee-ZEL) (French) She Serves Humanity

Jasmine (JAZ-min) (Persian) She Is a Fragrant Jasmine Flower

Mulan (moo-LAHN) (Chinese) She Is a Fragrant Orchid

Pocahontas (po-kuh-HAHN-tus) (Algonquin) She Loves to Play

Rapunzel (ruh-PUN-zul) (German) She Is a Beautiful Rapunculus Flower

Tiana (tee-AH-nuh) (English) She Is Christ's Little Follower

🐣 **Avril** (AV-ril) (English/French) She Is the Fresh Springtime Month of April

Wanda (WAHN-dah) (German) She Is an Enchanted Wand

Avril Lavigne (1984–) is a Canadian rocker whose hits include 2002's Complicated. *In the animated film* Over the Hedge *(2006), Avril worked with African-American comedienne Wanda Sykes, winner of 1999's Emmy Award for comedy writing from the Academy of Television Arts and Sciences (ATAS).*

🐣 **Audrey** (AW-dree) (English) She Is Our Powerful Little Aristocrat

Ingrid (ING-rid) (Swedish) She Is First in Beauty

Audrey Hepburn (1929–1993), a Belgian-English actress, is ranked as one of history's greatest actresses for such films as 1964's My Fair Lady *by the American Film Institute (AFI) in Los Angeles. AFI's list also includes the Swedish actress Ingrid Bergman, adored for such films as* Casablanca *(1942).*

🐣 **Beyoncé** (bee-YON-say) (American/English) We Say That She Is Beyond All Others

Destiny (DES-tih-nee) (English) She Goes Where God Commands

Beyoncé Knowles (1981–) is an African-American singer who gained fame with the trio Destiny's Child. Beyoncé, Kelly Rowland, and Michelle Williams sold sixty million CDs from 1997 to 2005—history's best-selling girl group.

🐣 **Britney** (BRIT-nee) (English) She Is from Bretagne, France

Jamie (JAY-mee) (English) She Is Our Little Divinely Protected Savior

Britney Spears (1981–) and her sister Jamie Lynn Spears (1991–) are popular American

singer-actresses who have entertained audiences with hit CDs and television series such as Nickelodeon's Zoey 101.

🐾 **Brooke** (BROOK) (English) She Is a Rushing Brook
Olympia (oh-LIM-pee-yah) (Greek) She Is the Lofty Summit of the Immortals
Brooke Shields (1965–), at six feet in height, is a stunning American actress-model. One of Brooke's half-sisters is Olympia Shields (1989–).

🐾 **Dolly** (DAHL-lee) (English) She Is Our Beloved Gift from God
Stella (STEL-luh) (English) She Is a Heavenly Star
Dolly Parton (1946–) is a shapely country singing star with twenty-six number one singles to her credit. Dolly's sister, Stella Parton, another country-music diva, had a number one hit in 1975 with I Want to Hold You in My Dreams Tonight.

🐾 **Gwen** (GWEN) (Welsh) She Is Beautifully Fair
Stefani (steh-FAH-nee) (German) She Is a Shining Crown
Gwen Stefani (1969–) is an Italian-American singer whose 1995 CD Tragic Kingdom *has sold an astonishing sixteen million copies.*

🐾 **Katie** (KAY-tee) (English) She Is Our Little Pure-Hearted One
Caroline (KAIR-uh-lyne) (English) She Is a Powerful Warrior
American journalist Katie Couric (1957–) anchors the nightly news program for the Columbia Broadcasting System—the first woman to achieve such a position. Katie's daughters are Caroline and Elinor Monahan.

🐾 **Latifah** (luh-TEE-fah) (Arabic) She Is Compassionate
Dana (DAY-nuh) (English) She Is Denmark
African-American singer-actress Queen Latifah (1970–) won a 1995 Grammy Award from the National Academy of Recording Arts and Sciences for her hit U.N.I.T.Y., *plus a 2008 Golden Globe award for her performance in the film* Life Support.

🐾 **Maiara** (mye-AH-rah) (Tupi) She Is Sagacious and Wise
Meena (MEE-nah) (Indian) She Is the Life Within the Seas
Maiara Walsh (1988–) is a Brazilian-American television actress starring in the Disney Channel series Cory in the House. *Maiara plays Meena Paroom, daughter of the Ambassador of the (fictional) country Bahavia.*

🐾 **Mariah** (muh-RYE-yuh) (English) She Is Love
Whitney (WHIT-nee) (English) She Is a Beautiful White Land
Mariah Carey (1970–) is an African-American singer who was named Best-Selling Female Artist of the Millennium at the 2000 World Music Awards in Monaco. Mariah recorded a duet with African-American singer Whitney Houston, 1998's When You Believe.

🐾 **Mary-Kate** (English) She Is the Pure-Hearted Little One Who Is Love Itself
Ashley (ASH-lee) (English) She Is a Meadow in the Ash-Tree Forest
Mary-Kate and Ashley Olsen (1986–) are American twins who began their careers sharing the role of Michelle Tanner on the television comedy Full House *(1987–1995). Since then, they have built a $100 million fashion empire.*

🐾 **Miley** (MYE-lee) (English) She Is the Beloved One Who Resembles God
Hannah (HANN-nuh) (Hebrew) She Is Graceful
Miley Ray Cyrus (1992–) is an American singer-actress who has skyrocketed to fame on the strength of her concert tours and her performances in Walt Disney's hit television series Hannah Montana.

🐾 **Rihanna** (ree-ANN-nuh) (English) She Is Our Majestic Little Princess
Robyn (RAH-bin) (English) She Is a Soaring Robin
In 2008, singer Rihanna (1988–) became the first woman from the Caribbean nation of Barbados to win a Grammy Award from the National Academy of Recording Arts and Sciences for her song Umbrella.

🐾 **Thelma** (TEL-mah) (Norwegian) She Has a Powerful Will
Louise (loo-WEEZ) (French) She Is a Renowned Warrior
The title characters in the hit 1991 movie Thelma and Louise *are played by actresses Susan Sarandon and Geena Davis respectively. Thelma and Louise are dissatisfied American women who cross the country seeking fulfillment.*

🐝 **Tyra** (TYE-rah) (Norwegian) She Rules
Heaven

Heidi (HYE-dee) (German) She Is Our Little
Aristocrat

African-American model Tyra Banks (1973–)
hosts television's Tyra Banks Show. Tyra once
dated English rock-star Seal, who is now mar-
ried to Tyra's modeling colleague Heidi Klum,
host of Project Runway *on the Bravo television*
network.

BOYS AND GIRLS

🐝 **Abdullah** (ab-DOOL-luh) (Arabic) He Serves
Almighty God

Al (AL) (English) He Is Our Brilliant Little
Aristocrat

Bergeron (BAIR-zhur-rahn) (French) He Is a
Lofty Mountain

Freema (FREE-muh) (Persian) She Is
Respectful and Devout

Goodman (GOOD-mun) (English) He Is a
Good-Hearted Guardian

Gore (GOR) (English) He Possesses a Three-
Sided Farmstead

Hawking (HAW-king) (English) He Is an Expert
at Falconry and Hunting

Keyes (KEEZ) (English) He Lives Near the
Beautiful Waterfront Quays

Matt (MAT) (English) He Is Our Little Present
from God

Tom (TAHM) (English) He Is Our Precious
Little Twin

🐝 **Alec** (AL-lek) (English) He Is Humanity's
Little Protector

Barrett (BAIR-ret) (English) He Is Powerfully
Aggressive

Chauncey (CHAWN-see) (English) He Is Great
Fortune and Opportunity

Eben (EB-bun) (English) He Is Rock-Solid

Egbert (EGG-burt) (English) He Is a Sword's
Shining Blade

Jimmie (JIM-mee) (English) He Is Our Divinely
Protected Little Savior

Ned (NED) (English) He Is Our Wealthy Little
Protector

Rida (REE-duh) (Arabic) She Is Great
Happiness

Spencer (SPEN-sur) (English) He Dispenses
Everything We Need to Survive

Stevie (STEE-vee) (English) He Is Our Shining
Little Crown

🐝 **Angelina** (an-juh-LEE-nuh) (Italian) She Is
God's Beloved Angel

Brad (BRAD) (English) He Is a Fragrant
Meadow in the Forest

Jolie (zho-LEE) (French) She Is Exceedingly
Pretty

Knox (NOX) (Scottish) He Is a Lofty Hill

Maddox (MAHD-dux) (Welsh) He Descends
from the Fortunate One

Pax (PAX) (Latin) She Is Peaceful

Pitt (PIT) (Scottish) He Is a Great Abyss
Leading to the Unknown

Shiloh (SHYE-lo) (Hebrew) She Is Peaceful

Vivienne (viv-ee-YEN) (French) She Wants to
Live

Zahara (zuh-HAIR-rah) (Arabic) She Is a
Fragrant Flower

🐝 **Benson** (BEN-sun) (English) He Descends
from the Blessed Man

Byrd (BURD) (English) He Is a Soaring Bird

Carlton (KARL-tun) (English) He Is the Nation
of Boldly Independent Folks

Cliff (KLIF) (English) He Is the Little One Who
Is a Crossing-Place Near a Lofty Cliff

Durham (DUR-rum) (English) He Is a Lofty
Island of Mountains and Cliffs

Garland (GAR-lund) (English) He Is a Vast
Three-Sided Farmer's Field

Grant (GRAHNT) (Scottish) He Is Magnificently
Great

Leni (LEN-nee) (German) She Is Our Radiant
Little Torch

Ronaldo (ro-NAHL-doh) (Portuguese) He Rules
by His Wise Counsel

Tal (TAHL) (Hebrew) He Is the Morning Mist

🐝 **Bo** (BO) (American/French) He Is
Handsome

Maureen (mo-REEN) (Irish) She Is Our Little
Beloved One

African-American singer Bo Diddley (1928–2008)
was an influential early rocker. "I don't have
any idols I copied after," Bo once said. Drummer
Maureen Tucker of the band Velvet Underground
cites Bo Diddley as her greatest idol.

🐝 **Bradley** (BRAD-lee) (English) He Is a
Meadow in the Woodlands

Leroy (LEE-roy) (English/French) He Is a
Majestic King

Lizzy (LIZ-zee) (English) She Is the Little One
Favored by God

Lola (LO-lah) (Spanish) She Is the Little One Who Understands Sorrow

Mandy (MAN-dee) (English) She Is the Little One Who Is Worthy of Love

Millie (MIL-lee) (English) She Is Our Tireless Little Worker

Nelly (NEL-lee) (English) She Is Our Radiant Little Torch

Terrance (TAIR-runss) (English) He Begins Many Things

Timmy (TIM-mee) (English) He Is God's Honorable Little Servant

Wendy (WEN-dee) (English) She Is Beautifully Fair

♪ **Bud** (BUD) (English) He Is a Trusted Friend

Curtis (KUR-tiss) (English) His Courtesy Honors Us

Ellie (EL-lee) (English) She Is Our Radiant Little Torch

Ernesto (ur-NES-toh) (Spanish) He Is Serious

Ethelbert (ETH-ul-burt) (English) He Is Brilliantly Aristocratic

Gerry (JAIR-ree) (English) He Is Our Powerful Little Sword-Wielding Conqueror

Haven (HAY-ven) (English) He Is a Peaceful Fortress

Herb (HURB) (English) He Is Our Brilliant Little Conqueror

Van (VAN) (English) He Is the Little One Whose God Is Gracious

Vernon (vair-NO) (French) He Is a Grove of Alder Trees

♪ **Chris** (KRIS) (English) He Is Christ's Little Follower

Keshia (KEE-shuh) (English/American) She Is a Fragrant Spice Tree

Chris Brown (1989–) is a beloved African-American singer whose hits include 2007's With You. *In 2006, Chris starred with African-Canadian singer Keshia Chanté in a video of the song by* Bow Wow, Shortie Like Mine.

♪ **Clarence** (KLEH-runss) (English) He Is Majestic

Gervase (JUR-vus) (English) He Is a Mighty Weapon

Jeff (JEF) (English) He Is Our Little Kingdom of Peace

Lex (LEX) (English) He Is Humanity's Little Protector

Rafe (RAFE) (English) He Counsels Us Like a Courageous Wolf

Rob (RAHB) (English) He Is Our Brilliantly Renowned Little Superstar

Rodger (RAH-jur) (English) He Is a Renowned Weapon

Rudy (ROO-dee) (English) He Is a Courageous Wolf

Sean (SHAWN) (Irish) His God Is Gracious

Shane (SHAYN) (Irish) His God Is Gracious

♪ **Donny** (DAHN-nee) (English) She Is Our Beloved World-Conqueror

Marie (mah-REE) (French) She Is Love

Donny Osmond (1957–) and sister Marie Osmond (1959–) comprised the teen duo on the Donny & Marie *television series (1976–1979). Marie, whose song* Paper Roses *hit number one in 1973, and Donny, a national teen idol, were the youngest TV emcees ever.*

♪ **Dylan** (DIL-lun) (Welsh) He Is a Mighty Ocean

Baez (bah-YEZ) (Spanish) She Is Swift

Bob Dylan (1941–) has been an American singer-activist for fifty years. One of Dylan's friends, singer Joan Baez, helped introduce such Dylan hits as Blowin' in the Wind.

♪ **Elton** (EL-tun) (English) He Is the Town Founded by the Legendary Ella

Marilyn (MAIR-uh-lin) (English) She Is a Beautiful Lake of Love

Elton John (1947–) is one of the greatest rock singers ever, having sold 200 million CDs, including such hits as 1973's Candle in the Wind—*a tribute to actress Marilyn Monroe, famed for such films as 1955's* The Seven Year Itch.

♪ **Elvis** (EL-vis) (English) He Has Absolute Wisdom

Gladys (GLAD-diss) (Welsh) She Is a Mighty Nation

Elvis Presley (1935–1975) was an American rocker adored by millions worldwide. Elvis was intensely devoted to his mother, Gladys Presley.

♪ **Herbie** (HUR-bee) (English) He Is a Brilliant and Beloved Army

Aung San (awng SAHN) (Burmese) She Honors Her Father and Mother

Herbie Hancock (1940–) is an African-American musician who has revolutionized jazz by utilizing classical music, rock, and so forth. In

1997, Herbie wrote Aung San Suu Kyi, *honoring Burmese Nobel Peace Prize winner Aung San Suu Kyi.*

🕭 **Humphrey** (HUM-free) (English) He Is a Peaceful Warrior

Lauren (LOR-run) (English) She Is a Laurel Wreath of Victory

Humphrey Bogart (1899–1957) was an American actor who starred in many tough-guy films such as 1948's Key Largo. *Humphrey's frequent costar was Lauren Bacall, winner of the 1993 Golden Globe Cecil B. DeMille Award for distinguished acting.*

🕭 **Ingmar** (ING-mar) (Swedish) He Is Our First Little One

Liv (LEEV) (Swedish) She Protects all Life

Swedish director Ingmar Bergman (1918–2007) delved into human psychology in films such as The Seventh Seal *(1957). Ingmar's Muse was actress Liv Ullman, winner of the British Academy of Film and Television Arts award for 1977's* Face to Face.

🕭 **Keira** (KEER-rah) (English) She Is the Ebony-Black Nighttime Sky

Orlando (or-LAN-doh) (Italian) He Is from a Renowned Land

Keira Knightley (1985–) is an English actress noted for her portrayal of adventurer Elizabeth Swann in the Pirates of the Caribbean *films of the 2000s. Keira's love-interest in the films was Will Turner, played by English idol Orlando Bloom.*

🕭 **Maurice** (mo-REESS) (French) He Is a Dark Moor

Mimi (MEE-mee) (Italian) She Is the Beloved One Who Is Love Itself

Maurice Chevalier (1888–1972) was a French-Belgian entertainer who won the hearts of millions with his romantic crooning and debonair acting. Many considered Maurice's greatest performance to be his rendition of 1932's Mimi.

🕭 **Miyoshi** (mee-YO-shee) (Japanese) She Is Beautiful and Good

Red (RED) (English) He Has Fiery Red Hair

Miyoshi Umeki (1929–2007) was a Japanese-American actress who won an Academy Award for Best Supporting Actress from the Academy of Motion Picture Arts and Sciences for playing Katsumi, wife of airman Joe Kelly, in 1957's Sayonara. *Joe was played by American character-actor Red Buttons.*

🕭 **Quincy** (KWIN-see) (English) He Is the Fifth

Simone (sih-MONE) (French) She Hears Everything

Quincy Jones (1933–) is an African-American composer who created such hits as 1962's Soul Bossa Nova *and has worked with legends such as Frank Sinatra and Brazilian singer Simone Bittencourt de Oliveira.*

🕭 **Roy** (ROI) (Scottish) He Is a Fiery Red King

Dale (DAYL) (English) She Is a Peaceful Valley

Roy Rogers (1911–1998) was a beloved American cowboy-actor who not only starred in classic Western films, but had his own television series, The Roy Rogers Show, *from 1951 to 1957. He and Dale Evans were married for fifty-one years.*

🕭 **Scully** (SKUL-lee) (Irish) She Heralds What Is to Come

Mulder (MUL-dur) (Dutch) He Mills Grain

Fox Mulder investigated paranormal activity for the Federal Bureau of Investigation (FBI) on the Fox Broadcasting Company television series The X-Files. *Mulder's fellow-agent Dana Scully assisted him in a search for the truth.*

🕭 **Shirley** (SHUR-lee) (English) She Is a Clearing in the Woodlands

Warren (WAR-ren) (English) He Is a Corral for Spirited Horses

Shirley MacLaine (1934–) is an actress who won an Academy Award for best actress in 1983's Terms of Endearment, *given by the Academy of Motion Picture Arts and Sciences. Shirley's brother is famed actor-director Warren Beatty.*

🕭 **Suzette** (soo-ZET) (French) She Is a Fragrant Little Lotus Flower

Jojo (JO-jo) (English) He Is the Beloved One Who Glorifies the World

Suzette Ranillo is a Filipina actress who has won numerous awards for her powerful performances. Suzette's brother Jojo Ranillo is an accomplished actor in his own right.

🕭 **Trisha** (TRISH-shuh) (English) She Is Our Noble Little Aristocrat

Garth (GARTH) (English) He Is a Glorious Garden

Patricia Yearwood (1964–) is a country singer best known for She's In Love with the Boy. *Trisha's career has exploded under the tutelage of country legend Garth Brooks, whose hits include 1990's* Friends in Low Places.

🖉 **Woody** (WOOD-dee) (English) He Is the
Little One Who Is a Row of Houses in the
Woods
Judy (JOO-dee) (English) She Is the Little One
Who Is Judea
*Judy Collins (1939–) has been an American
singer-activist for fifty years, recording such
hits as Joni Mitchell's 1967 Both Sides Now.
Judy has said that American folksinger Woody
Guthrie, creator of This Land Is Your Land
(1940), was a major influence.*

Name Pairs and Groups
from the World of Sports

BOYS

Alexei (ah-LEX-say) (Russian) He Protects Humanity

Andras (AHN-drahss) (Welsh) He Is Powerful

Evgeny (yev-GAY-nee) (Russian) He Is Aristocratic

Jude (ZHOOD) (Hebrew) His Is the One We Praise Highly

Leonardas (lee-oh-NAR-dahss) (Lithuanian) He Is a Noble Lion

Lev (LEV) (Hebrew) He Is Our Sacred Heart

Mohamad (mo-HAHM-mahd) (Arabic) He Is Praise Worthy

Ralf (RAHLF) (Swedish) He Counsels Us like a Courageous Wolf

Weaver (WEE-vur) (English) He Weaves with Great Artistry

Zoltan (ZOWL-tahn) (Hungarian) He Is a Mighty Ruler

Ali (AH-lee) (Arabic) He Is Magnificently Noble

Frazier (FRAY-zhur) (Scottish) He Is an Adventurous Explorer

African-American boxer Muhammad Ali (1942–) was history's greatest World Heavyweight Boxing Champion, with fifty-six wins in sixty-one bouts. Ali's greatest win was against then-champion Joe Frazier, during 1971's Fight of the Century in New York.

Bo (BO) (Swedish) He Wants to Live

Gene (JEEN) (English) He Is Our Little Aristocrat

Guy (GHEE) (French) He Is Magnificently Great

Matsutaro (MAHT-soo-tuh-ro) (Japanese) He Is Humanity's Triumph

Moshé (mo-SHAY) (Hebrew) He Is Our Mighty Son and Savior

Pierre (pee-YAIR) (French) He Is Rock-Solid

Simon (SYE-mun) (Greek) He Hears Everything Clearly

Terence (TAIR-unss) (English) He Begins Many Things

Vladimir (VLAD-ih-meer) (Russian) He Rules Peacefully

Yves (EEV) (French) He Is the Magnificent Yew Tree

Bromus (BRO-mus) (Latin) He Roars

Elymus (EL-uh-mus) (Latin) He Rocks the World

Bromus and Elymus were two of the Centauri, as the Romans called them—whose upper torsos were human and whose lower bodies were those of horses. The Centauri treated war as a sport—similar to medieval jousting—but instead of lances, they used tree trunks.

Clinton (KLIN-tun) (English) He Is a Town on a Lofty Mountain

Darren (DAIR-run) (English) He Is Airelle, France

Fulton (FUL-tun) (English) He Is a Town of Skillful Bird-Hunters

Hendrik (HEN-drik) (Dutch) He Rules Our Home Magnificently

Michiel (MYE-kul) (Dutch) He Resembles God

Sid (SID) (English) He Is the Little One Who Is a Great Island

Trevor (TREH-vur) (Welsh) He Is a Glorious City

Vaughn (VAHN) (Welsh) He Is Petite

Wayne (WAYN) (English) He Builds Sturdy Chariots

Werner (VUR-nur) (Dutch) He Protects Our Warriors

🖉 **Eddie** (ED-dee) (English) He Is Our Wealthy Little Protector

Willie (WILL-lee) (English) He Is Our Little Protector

African-American football coach Eddie Robinson (1919–2007) of the Grambling State University Tigers in Grambling, Louisiana, led his teams to 408 victories. Eddie trained many players who later enjoyed distinguished pro careers, including Oakland Raiders cornerback Willie Brown.

🖉 **Hank** (HANK) (English) He Is Our Home's Magnificent Little Monarch

Babe (BAYB) (English) He Is Our Sweet Little Baby

Hank Aaron (1934–) was an African-American Major League Baseball player for the Atlanta Braves, who hit home-run number 715 in 1974 to surpass the record of the "Sultan of Swat," Babe Ruth.

🖉 **Jack** (JAK) (English) He Is Beloved and His God Is Gracious

James (JAYMZ) (Hebrew) He Is Divinely Protected

Jack Johnson (1878–1946) was an African-American Heavyweight Champion (1908–1915). Jack's greatest bout came in 1910 against former champ James Jeffries, who left retirement to prove his theory of genetic superiority. Jack defeated him in fifteen rounds.

🖉 **Jesse** (JESS-see) (Hebrew) He Is God's Divine Gift

Berlin (bur-LIN) (German) He Is Berlin, Germany

Jesse Owens (1913–1980) was an African-American athlete who defeated Nazi German opponents during the 1936 Olympics in Berlin, Germany, under the auspices of the supremacist Nazi leader, Adolf Hitler.

🖉 **Clemens** (KLEM-munz) (Latin) He Descends from the Compassionate One

Delgado (del-GAH-doh) (Spanish) He Is Slender and Handsome

Griffey (GRIF-fee) (Welsh) He Is Our Noble and Beloved Prince

Hampton (HAMP-tun) (English) He Is a Protected Area Within a Town

Maddux (MAD-dux) (English) He Descends from the Lucky Little One

Martinez (mahr-TEE-nez) (Spanish) He Is Powerful and Beloved

Ramirez (rah-MEE-rez) (Spanish) He Is Our Beloved Advisor and Protector

Rodriguez (ro-DREE-ghez) (Spanish) He Is Mighty and Renowned

Sheffield (SHEF-feeld) (English) He Is the River Dividing the Woodlands

Walker (WAH-kur) (English) He Walks Powerfully

🖉 **Nahuel** (nah-hoo-EL, nah-WEL) (Mapuche) He Is a Noble Jaguar

Federico (fed-eh-REE-ko) (Spanish) He Rules Peacefully

Nahuel Costabile is a member of the Argentina National Rugby League team, formed in 2005 as the newest member of the Rugby League International Federation. The Argentine team's captain is star player Federico Astoreca.

🖉 **Roger** (RAH-jur) (English) He Is a Renowned Weapon

Drew (DROO) (English) He Is Our Powerful Little Man

Roger Staubach (1942–) is a legendary American football quarterback. In a 1975 game against the Minnesota Vikings, Roger threw a fifty-yard pass to receiver Drew Pearson, who caught it and won the game. Because Roger whispered "Hail Mary" Before passing, such passes are now called Hail Marys.

🖉 **Roger** (RAH-jur) (English) He Is a Renowned Weapon

Sydney (SID-nee) (English) He Is a Great Island

The great track star Roger Bannister was the first person to run one mile in under four minutes (3:59:4) at an Oxford University track meet. Roger's inspiration was famed runner Sydney Wooderson.

🖉 **Sergio** (SAIR-zhee-yoh) (Spanish) He Serves Humanity

Alejandro (al-eh-HAHN-dro) (Spanish) He Protects Humanity

Sergio Garcia (1980–) is a Spanish golf champion who is ranked number eight on the Official World Golf Rankings created by the Royal and Golf Club of St. Andrews, Scotland. Sergio's compatriot, Spanish golfer Alejandro Cañizares, has won the 2006 Imperial Collection Russian Open tournament.

🌿 **Tiger** (TYE-gur) (English) He Is a Noble Tiger

Arnold (AR-nahld) (German) He Is a Soaring Eagle

Tiger Woods (1975–) is a multiracial American golf champion whose winnings may top $1 billion dollars by 2010, according to Golf Digest magazine. In 2006, California's Governor Arnold Schwarzenegger announced that Tiger would be inducted into the California Hall of Fame in Sacramento.

🌿 **Tom** (TAHM) (English) He Is Our Precious Little Twin

Bob (BAHB) (English) He Is Our Gloriously Radiant Little Prince

Mel (MEL) (English) He Is the Little One Who Is a Fiercely Competitive City

Michael (MYE-kul) (Hebrew) He Resembles God

Randy (RAN-dee) (English) He Is Our Little Guardian Wolf

Rayfield (RAY-feeld) (English) He Is the Little One Who Protects the Land

Roger (RAH-jur) (English) He Is Our Legendary Weapon

Tex (TEX) (English) He Is the Little One Who Is the Great American State of Texas

Tony (TOH-nee) (English) He Is Our Blossoming Little Flower

Troy (TROY) (English) He Is from the Legendary City of Troy

🌿 **Troy** (TROY) (English) He Is from the Legendary City of Troy

Michael (MYE-kul) (Hebrew) He Resembles God

Legendary American football quarterback Troy Aikman (1966–), working with receiver Michael Irvin, won three Super Bowl championships in 1993, 1994, and 1996.

GIRLS

🌿 **Adrienne** (ah-dree-EN) (French) She Is Hadria, Italy

Chantelle (shahn-TEL) (American/French) She Is Rock-Solid

Charel (SHAIR-rul) (English) She Is Truly Darling and Sweet

Corissa (kuh-RISS-suh) (American/English) She Is Truly Compassionate

Dena (DEE-nuh) (English) She Is the Heavenly Life Source

Korie (KOR-ree) (Scottish) She Is a Hillside Teeming with Swift Animals

Margo (MAR-go) (English) She Is Our Priceless Little Pearl

Shyra (SHY-ruh) (American/Hebrew) Her Voice Is Musically Sweet

Tammi (TAM-mee) (English) She Is Our Beautiful Little Palm Tree

Ticha (TISH-shuh) (American/English) She Is Our Magnificent Celebration

🌿 **Ai** (AH-ee) (Japanese) She Is Love

Ayako (EYE-uh-ko) (Japanese) She Is the Child Who Is a Beautiful Kimono

Brittany (BRIT-nee) (English) She Is Bretagne, France

Catrin (KAH-treen) (German) She Is a Priceless Pearl

Dottie (DAHT-tee) (English) She Is Our Little Present from God

Estelle (es-STEL) (French) She Is a Heavenly Star

Gwladys (GLAD-iss) (Welsh) She Is a Mighty Nation

Jodie (JO-dee) (English) She Is Judea

Lorena (lo-RAY-nah) (Spanish) She Is Lorraine, France

Mhairi (VAHR-ree) (Scottish) She Is Love

🌿 **Alana** (uh-LAH-nuh) (English) She Is a Beautiful Stone

Cass (KASS) (English) She Is Our Adored Little Queen of Love

Cathrine (kahth-REEN) (Norwegian) She Is Pure-Hearted

Coco (KO-ko) (French) She Is the Little One Who Is Fragrant Chocolate

Janel (juh-NEL) (English) She Is God's Graceful Little Messenger

Kisha (KEE-shuh) (American/English) She Is a Fragrant Spice Tree

Leilani (lay-LAH-nee) (Hawaiian) She Is a Garden of Divine Blossoms

Loree (American/English) She Is a Laurel Wreath of Victory

Tari (TAIR-ree) (American/English) She Is Our Beloved Little Present from God

Vickie (VIK-kee) (English) She Is Humanity's Little Triumph

🕊 *Alena* (ah-LAY-nuh) (German) She Is Our Radiant Little Torch

Alexa (uh-LEX-suh) (English) She Is Humanity's Little Protector

Ana (AH-nuh) (Spanish) She Is Graceful

Ashleigh (ASH-lee) (English) She Is a Meadow in an Ash-Tree Forest

Charlotta (shar-LOT-tuh) (Swedish) She Is Our Beloved Little Warrior

Denise (duh-NEES) (French) She Is God's Holy Mountain

Hollis (HAHL-liss) (English) She Lives in the Holly-Tree Forest

Marilynn (MAIR-uh-lin) (English) She Is a Beautiful Lake of Love

Stacy (STAY-see) (English) She Is Abundantly Productive

Violeta (vee-oh-LAY-tah) (Spanish) She Is a Fragrant Violet

🕊 *Alise* (uh-LEESS) (Latvian) She Is Our Little Aristocrat

Cheri (shur-REE) (French) She Is Darling and Sweet

Cindy (SIN-dee) (English) She Is the Beloved Woman from Kynthos, Greece

Corine (kor-REEN) (French) She Is Chaste and Pure

Deanna (dee-AN-nuh) (English) She Is the Heavenly Life Source

Debbie (DEB-bee) (English) She Is a Busy Little Honeybee

Jamie (JAY-mee) (English) She Is Divinely Protected

Kim (KIM) (English) She Is Our Majestic Little Castle

Melanie (MEL-ah-nee) (German) She Is Darkly Beautiful

Shanaze (shu-NAHZ) (Arabic) She Is the One Who Makes Our King Proud

🕊 *Amaya* (ah-MYE-yuh) (Spanish) She Fulfills All Our Dreams

DeLisha (duh-LEE-shuh) (American/English) She Is Our Little Aristocrat

Kiesha (KEE-shuh) (American/English) She Is a Fragrant Spice Tree

Latasha (luh-TAH-shuh) (American/Russian) She Is the Little One Who Is Christmas Day

Mistie (MIS-tee) (American/English) She Is the Little One Who Is the Morning Mist

Murriel (MYOOR-ee-yuhl) (American/Irish) She Is the Shining Ocean

Polina (po-LEE-nah) (Russian) She Is Our Radiant Little Star

Raffaella (rahf-fah-EL-luh) (Italian) Her God Heals the Sick

Sheryl (SHAIR-rul) (English) She Is Truly Darling and Sweet

Tamecka (tuh-MEE-kuh) (American) She Is a Child Who Is Lovely a Thousand Times Over

🕊 *Anabel* (AN-nuh-bel) (Spanish) She Is Treasured

Brandi (BRAN-dee) (English) She Is Well-Prepared Brandy

Chante (shahn-TAY) (American/French) She Sang When She Was Born

Christen (KRIS-ten) (Danish) She Follows Christ

Jenni (JEN-nee) (English) She Is Our Fair Little Beauty

Joy (JOY) (English) She Is Great Rejoicing

Katia (KAHT-yuh) (Russian) She Is Pure-Hearted

LaKeysia (luh-KEE-shuh) (American/Hebrew) She Is a Fragrant Cinnamon Tree

Sissi (SIS-see) (American/English) She Is the Little One Who Sees Deeply Within Herself

Tisha (TIH-shuh) (American/English) She Is Our Magnificent Celebration

🕊 *A'Quonesia* (ah-kwuh-NEE-shuh) (American/Latin) She Is Deep, Dark Water

Ashjha (AY-zhuh) (American/Greek) She Is Famous Forever

Barb (BARB) (English) She Is Our Blessed Little Voyager

Charde (shah-DAY) (American/Finnish) She Is a Golden Sunbeam

Erica (AIR-ee-kah) (Swedish) She Rules Forever

Kedra (KED-ruh) (American/English) She Is the Little One Who Has Majestic Authority

Kristi (KRIS-tee) (English) She Is Christ's Little Follower

Merlakia (mur-luh-KEE-yuh) (American/English) She Is the Little One Who Is Christ's Sea

Nykesha (nih-KEE-shuh) (American/Igbo) She Is Our Little Present from God
Semeka (suh-MEE-kuh) (American/Igbo) Her God Performs Miracles

🐾 **Ariane** (ah-ree-YAHN) (French) She Is Most Holy
Emmelie (EM-el-lee) (Swedish) She Is Powerfully Competitive
Frida (FREE-duh) (Swedish) She Is Peace
Hanna (HAH-nah) (Swedish) She Is Graceful
Linnea (lee-NAY-yuh) (Swedish) She Is a Fragrant Linnea Flower
Lotta (LOT-tuh) (Swedish) She Is Our Little Warrior
Marit (mah-REET) (Norwegian) She Is a Priceless Pearl
Marta (MAR-tuh) (Portuguese) She Rules Our Home Magnificently
Nadine (nah-DEEN) (French) She Is the Little One Who Is Our Greatest Hope
Sofia (zo-FEE-yuh) (Swedish) She Is Knowledge

🐾 **Arielle** (ahr-ee-YEL) (French) She Is God's Noble Lioness
Belinda (beh-LIN-duh) (English) She Is Beautifully Compassionate
Calista (kah-LEESS-tah) (Spanish) She Is the Most Beautiful of All
Faye (FAY) (English) She Is a Magical Fairy
Jamie (JAY-mee) (Scottish) She Is Our Little Divinely Protected Savior
Kirstie (KUR-stee) (Scottish) She Is Christ's Little Follower
Lynda (LIN-duh) (English) She Is Exceptionally Beautiful
Reese (REESS) (Welsh) She Is Powerfully Enthusiastic
Ruth (ROOTH) (Hebrew) She Is a Trusted Companion
Teri (TAIR-ree) (English) She Is Our Little Gift from God

🐾 **Ashlee** (ASH-lee) (English) She Is a Meadow in the Ash-Tree Forest
Brianna (bree-AN-nuh) (English) She Is Aristocratic
Callie (KAL-lee) (English) She Is Our Powerful Little Warrior
Jesyca (JES-sih-kuh) (American/English) She Is Lovely to Behold

Keri (KAIR-ree) (English/Irish) She Descends from the Darkly Handsome One
Laure (LOR) (French) She Is a Laurel Wreath of Victory
Marcy (MAR-see) (English) She Is as Powerful as any male
Rachael (RAY-chul) (Hebrew) She Is a Gentle Mother Ewe
Rebekah (ruh-BEK-kuh) (Hebrew) She Is the One Who Brings Us Closer
Tonya (TAHN-yuh) (English) She Is a Lovely Little Flower

🐾 **Ayana** (eye-AH-nuh) (American/Russian) She Is God's Graceful Little Messenger
Doneeka (duh-NEE-kuh) (American/English) She Is the Early Dawn Light
Janell (juh-NEL) (English) She Is God's Graceful Little Messenger
Kamila (kah-MEEL-lah) (Polish) She Observes Sacred Rituals
Shalonda (shuh-LAHN-duh) (American/English) She Is the Flower Who Ponders Deeply
Swintayla (swin-TAY-luh) (American/Irish) She Is the Friendly and Helpful Little Tailor
Tangela (TAN-juh-luh) (American/English) She Is the Saint Who Is a Messenger from God
Tanisha (tah-NEE-shuh) (American/English) She Is a Saint, as Powerful as any male
Tully (TUH-lee) (Latin) She Is a Great Speaker
Tye'sha (tye-EE-shuh) (American/Russian) She Is the Little One Who Is Christmas Day

🐾 **Bea** (BEE, BEE-yuh) (English) She Is Our Blessed Little Voyager
Brandie (BRAN-dee) (English) She Is Delectable Brandy
Glenna (GLEN-nah) (Scottish) She Is a Peaceful Valley
Jocelyne (JAH-suh-lin) (English) She Is the Great Germanic Nation of the Gauts
Jody (JO-dee) (English) She Is Judea
Lottie (LOT-tee) (English) She Is Our Little Warrior
Lynnette (lih-NET) (English) She Is Worshipped
Marisa (mah-REE-sah) (Spanish) She Is a Renowned Warrior of Love
Raquel (rah-KEL) (Spanish) She Is a Gentle Mother Ewe

Shi (SHEE) (Chinese) She Is the True History of Humanity

⚘ Bernadette (bur-nuh-DET) (English/French) She Is a Courageous She-Bear

Candice (KAN-diss) (English) She Is the Great Ruler of Ethiopia

Chasity (CHASS-ih-tee) (English) She Is Chaste and Pure

Chioma (chee-OH-muh) (Igbo) She Is Divine Greatness

Jolene (jo-LEEN) (English) She Is the Little One Whose Greatness Increases

Kasha (KAH-shuh) (American/English) She Truly Loves Herself

Ketia (KEE-shuh) (American/English) She Is a Fragrant Spice Tree

Quianna (kee-AHN-nuh) (American/English) She Is Silky-Soft

Sandrine (sawn-DREEN) (French) She Truly Is Humanity's Protector

Temeka (tuh-MEE-kuh) (American) She Is a Child Who Is Lovely a Thousand Times Over

⚘ Bernice (bur-NEESS) (Greek) She Is Our Little Golden Age of Triumph

Dawn (DAWN) (English) She Is the Radiant Dawn

Edwige (ed-VEEZH) (French) She Is Aggressive

Fran (FRAN) (English) She Is the Little One Who Is the Nation of France

Kendra (KEN-druh) (English) She Has Majestic Authority

Krystal (KRIS-tul) (English) She Sparkles Like Diamonds

Sonja (SOAN-yuh) (Serbian) She Is Our Wise, Beloved One

Tiffani (TIF-fuh-nee) (American/English) She Proves God's Greatness

Tynesha (tih-NEE-shuh) (American/Shona) Her God Is with Us

Yolanda (yuh-LAHN-duh) (English) She Is a Fragrant Violet

⚘ Birgit (bur-GHEET) (Norwegian) She Safeguards Us

Briana (bree-AN-nuh) (English) She Is Aristocratic

Cheryl (SHAIR-ril) (English) She Is Truly Darling and Sweet

Gro (GRO) (Norwegian) She Grows Stronger Every Day

Hege (HAY-guy) (Swedish) She Is the Little One Who Is Spiritual

Kylie (KYE-lee) (Scottish) She Is the Water Between Two Regions

Maite (mah-ee-TAY) (Basque) She Is Treasured

Marci (MAR-see) (English) She Is as Powerful as any male

Maribel (mah-ree-BEL) (Spanish) She Is the Beloved One Whose God Is Abundance

Tiffeny (TIF-fuh-nee) (American/English) She Proves God's Greatness

⚘ Candie (KAN-dee) (English) She Is Our Majestic Little Queen

Christa (KREES-tah) (German) She Is Christ's Little Follower

Jang (JANG) (Korean) She Is a Gentle, Beautiful Child

Juli (YOO-lee) (Hungarian) She Is the Little Relative of Julius Caesar

Karine (kah-REEN) (French) She Is Truly and Greatly Beloved

Kelli (KEL-lee) (English/Irish) She Is Conquest and War

Lorie (LO-ree) (English) She Is Our Little Laurel Wreath of Victory

Ludivine (loo-dih-VEEN) (French) She Befriends Humanity

Trish (TRISH) (English) She Is Our Noble Little Aristocrat

Virginie (veer-zhee-NEE) (French) She Is Chaste and Pure

⚘ Carolin (KAH-ro-leen) (German) She Is a Powerful Warrior

Elin (EL-leen) (Swedish) She Is a Radiant Torch

Erle (UR-luh) (Norwegian) She Is Aristocratic

Josefine (yo-zeh-FEE-nuh) (German) Her Greatness Increases

Pernilla (pur-NIL-luh) (Swedish) She Is an Honest Little Farmer

Petra (PEH-truh) (Swedish) She Is Rock-Solid

Sofie (SO-fee) (German) She Is Our Wise Little Scholar

Susanne (soo-ZAH-nuh) (Swedish) She Is a Fragrant Lotus Flower

Ulrica (ool-REE-kuh) (Swedish) She Is Power and Wealth

Veronica (vur-AH-nih-kuh) (English) She Is Humanity's Triumph

Ⓐ **Charmaine** (shar-MAYN) (English) She Is a
Nation of Warriors

Daniela (dahn-ee-EL-luh) (Portuguese) Her
God Judges Wisely

Ester (ESH-tair) (Portuguese) She Is a Brilliant
Star

Grazielle (grah-zee-YEL-ih) (Portuguese) She
Is Our Peaceful Little Beauty

Isabell (ees-sah-BEL) (Swedish) Her God Is
Abundance

Kari (KAH-ree) (Norwegian) She Is Pure-Hearted

Michele (mee-SHEL-ih) (Portuguese) She
Resembles God

Renata (reh-NAH-tah) (Portuguese) She Is
Reborn in God

Silvi (SIL-vee) (Swedish) She Is the Glorious
Woodlands

Solveig (SOUL-vay) (Swedish) She Is the
Radiant Sun

Ⓐ **Christi** (KRIS-tee) (American/English) She
Is Christ's Little Follower

Kathrin (KAHT-reen) (German) She Is Pure-
Hearted

Marlies (mar-LEESS) (German) She Is the
Beloved Little One Whose God Is Abundance

Maylana (may-LAH-nuh) (American/English)
She Is the Little One Who Is Hard and Soft

Nicky (NIK-kee) (English) She Is Humanity's
Little Triumph

Noelle (no-WEL) (English/French) She Is
Christmas Day

Ruthie (ROO-thee) (English) She Is Our
Trusted Little Companion

Shanele (shun-NEL) (American/French) She
Allows Clear Water to Flow

Shona (SHO-nuh) (Scottish) Her God Is
Gracious

Yuko (YOO-ko) (Japanese) She Is a
Compassionate Child

Ⓐ **Corie** (KOR-ree) (Scottish) She Is a Hillside
Teeming with Swift Animals

Fatima (FAH-tee-muh) (Arabic) She Is Modest

Jen (JEN) (English) She Is Our Fair Little
Beauty

Jillian (JILL-ee-yun) (English) She Rules
Heaven

Kati (KAH-tee) (Finnish) She Is Our Little
Pure-Hearted One

Kele (KEL-lee) (American/Irish) She Is
Conquest and War

Lena (LEE-nah) (German) She Is Our Radiant
Little Torch

Marie-Eve (mur-REE-eev) (American/French)
She Is the Beloved One Who Wants to Live

Meghan (MAY-gun) (Welsh) She Is Our
Priceless Little Pearl

Ria (REE-yuh) (German) She Is Our Little
Beloved One

Ⓐ **Dakoda** (duh-KO-tuh) (American/Dakota)
She Is a Trusted Friend

Flory (FLOR-ree) (English) She Is the Little
One Who Flourishes

Hisako (hee-SAH-ko) (Japanese) She Is the
Child Who Brings Good Fortune

Julieta (hoo-lee-ET-tuh) (Spanish) She Is the
Beloved One Who Resembles God

Lora (LOR-ruh) (Italian) She Is a Laurel Wreath
of Victory

Meaghan (MAY-gahn) (Welsh) She Is Our
Priceless Little Pearl

Meg (MEHG) (English) She Is Our Priceless
Little Pearl

Opal (OH-pul) (English) She Is a Priceless Opal

Tammie (TAM-mee) (English) She Is Our
Beautiful Little Palm Tree

Yuri (YOO-ree) (Japanese) She Is a Fragrant
Lily

Ⓐ **Felisia** (fuh-LEE-shuh) (American/English)
She Is the Fortunate One

Kahdijah (kah-DEE-zhuh) (Arabic) She Comes
to Us Early

Kara (KAIR-ruh) (English) She Is Our Little
Pure-Hearted One

Nell (NEL) (English) She Is Our Radiant Little
Torch

Olayinka (oh-lah-YIN-kuh) (Yoruba) Her
Wealth Is all Around Us

Shay (SHAY) (Greek) She Is Destined

Sheri (SHAIR-ree) (French) She Is Darling and
Sweet

Sherill (SHAIR-rul) (English) She Is Truly
Darling and Sweet

Tameka (tuh-MEE-kuh) (English/Japanese) She
Is a Beautiful Child a Thousand Times Over

Tasha (TAH-shah) (Russian) She Is the Little
One Who Is Christmas Day

Ⓐ **Gertrude** (GUR-trood) (German) She Is a
Mighty Weapon

Esther (ES-tair) (Hebrew) She Is a Brilliant Star

American swimmer Gertrude Ederle (1905–2003) was the first woman to swim the English Channel in 1926. Gertrude was a product of the Women's Swimming Association, which also produced swimmer and film-star Esther Williams.

☙ **Isabelle** (EES-ah-bel) (French) Her God Is Abundance

Lucienne (loo-see-YEN) (French) She Is Brilliant Light

Lynette (lih-NET) (English) She Is Worshipped

Pollyanna (pah-lee-AN-nuh) (English) She Is the Graceful, Lovely Little One

Raegon (RAY-gun) (American/Irish) She Descends from an Impulsive Father

Rushia (RUSH-shuh) (American/Russian) She Is Russia

Seimone (sih-MUN) (American/French) She Hears Everything Clearly

Shanna (SHAN-nuh) (English) She Is Our Fragrant Little Lotus Flower

Suzie (SOO-zee) (English) She Is Our Fragrant Little Lotus Flower

Val (VAL) (English) She Is Our Powerful Little Warrior

☙ **Kerri** (KAIR-ree) (English/Irish) She Descends from the Darkly Handsome One

Dominique (doh-mih-NEEK) (French) She Is God's Divine Gift

Kerri Strug (1977–) was a member of the U.S. Women's Gymnastics Team at the 1996 Atlanta Olympics. When teammate Dominique Moceanu suffered mishaps during her floor program, Kerri—in agony from ankle injuries—stepped in and performed brilliantly to clinch her team's gold medal.

☙ **Laila** (LAY-lah) (Arabic) She Is a Darkly Beautiful Evening

Jackie (JAK-kee) (English) She Is the Beloved One Whose God Is Gracious

Laila Ali (1977–), daughter of heavyweight boxing champion Muhammad Ali, is a middleweight boxer undefeated in twenty-four bouts. Laila's greatest victory was over Jackie Frazier-Lyde, daughter of former heavyweight champion Joe Frazier.

BOYS AND GIRLS

☙ **Amikam** (AHM-mee-kahm) (Hebrew) His People Fight for Their Honor

Anatoly (an-uh-TOH-lee) (Ukrainian) He Is the Bright Sunrise

Anjelina (ahn-yeh-LEE-nah) (Ukrainian) She Is God's Angelic Messenger

Curt (KURT) (English) He Is the Little One Who Advises Us Boldly

Gedeon (GED-ay-yohn) (Hungarian) He Is a Mighty Woodsman

Hristos (REES-towss) (Greek) He Follows Christ

Janos (YAH-noosh) (Hungarian) His God Is Gracious

Liudmila (lood-MEE-lah) (Russian) She Earns Our Nation's Gratitude

Olaf (OH-lahf) (Norwegian) He Descends from Our Mighty Ancestors

Zsigmond (ZIG-moond) (Hungarian) He Is Our Triumphant Defender

☙ **An** (AHN) (Chinese) She Is Peace

Bassem (bah-SEM) (Arabic) He Laughs with Joy

Farrukh (fah-ROOK) (Arabic) He Can Distinguish Between Good and Evil

Fricis (FREE-sis) (Latvian) He Rules Peacefully

Izak (EET-zahk) (Polish) He Laughs with Joy

Oskar (AHSS-kar) (German) He Loves to Hunt Deer

Rogelio (ro-HEL-yo) (Spanish) He Is God's Answer to Our Prayers

Ulf (OOLF) (Swedish) He Is a Courageous Wolf

Yoel (yo-WEL) (Hebrew) His God Is the True God

Zaven (ZAY-ven) (Armenian) He Is a Shining Crown

☙ **Annie** (ANN-nee) (English) She Is Our Graceful Little Princess

Doyle (DOYL) (Irish) He Descends from the Dark Stranger

Feldman (FELD-mahn, FELD-mun) (German) He Farms the Fields

Hansen (HAN-sen) (Danish) He Descends from the One Whose God Is Gracious

Hellmuth (HEL-moot) (German) His Genius Is His Protective Helmet

Hoyt (HOYT) (English) He Is Slender and Agile

Kanter (KAHN-tur) (German) He Sings God's Beautiful Hymns

Raymer (RAY-mur) (English) He Is a Courageous Warrior Who Advises Us Boldly

Sexton (SEX-tun) (English) He Is the Saxon People

Vinny (VIN-nee) (English) He Is Our Mighty Little Conqueror

🐝 **Bela** (BEL-luh) (Hungarian) He Is Beautifully Fair

Clarice (klair-REES) (French) She Is Our Radiant Little Superstar

Ivar (EE-vahr) (Norwegian) He Is an Archer with a Yew-Wood Longbow

Karlis (KAR-leess) (Latvian) He Is a Mighty Warrior

Ossip (OH-seep) (Ukrainian) His God Is Abundance

Pál (PAHL) (Hungarian) He Demonstrates Humility

Sergey (sair-GAY) (Russian) He Serves Humanity

Teodors (TAY-oh-dorsh) (Latvian) He Is God's Divine Gift

Vinay (vee-NYE) (Sanskrit) He Rules with Humility

Zdzislaw (ZHEE-swahf) (Polish) He Is Eternally Magnificent

🐝 **Boston** (BOSS-tun) (English) He Is the Little One Who Is Saint Botolph's Town, England

Cedar (SEE-dur) (English) She Is a Fragrant Cedar Tree

Craig (KRAYG) (Scottish) He Is a Mighty Crag

Glen (GLEN) (Scottish) He Is a Peaceful Valley

Greg (GREG) (English) He Is Our Little Guardian

Lutz (LUTZ) (German) He Is Our Gleaming Little Helmet of Divine Protection

Myrtle (MUR-tul) (English) She Is a Fragrant Myrtle Tree

Norman (NOR-mun) (English) He Is a Norse Viking

Pete (PEET) (English) He Is Our Rock-Solid Little Fortress

Tampa (TAM-puh) (Calusa) She Is Bright Lightning

🐝 **Dagur** (dah-GOOR) (Icelandic) He Is a Sunny Day

Ekaterina (ee-kat-ah-REE-nah) (Russian) She Is Pure-Hearted

Etienne (eh-tee-YEN) (French) He Is a Shining Crown

Hipolito (ee-POH-lee-toh) (Spanish) He Befriends Horses

Izaak (EET-zahk) (Polish) He Laughs with Joy

Konstantin (KON-stun-teen) (Russian) He Is Dependably Constant

Lajos (LAH-yohsh) (Hungarian) He Is a Renowned Warrior

Levon (leh-VAHV) (Armenian) He Is a Noble Lion

Romanas (ro-MAH-nahss) (Lithuanian) He Is the Great Roman Empire

Rosendo (ro-SEN-doh) (Spanish) He Is the Shining Road to Glory

🐝 **Laird** (LAY-yurd) (Scottish) He Possesses Much Land

Gabrielle (French) She Is God's Angelic Messenger

Laird Hamilton (1964–) is an American surfer and the inventor of tow-in surfing, where boats tow surfers out to waves. Gabrielle, Laird's wife, is a champion volleyball player, having competed with the Fédération Internationale de Volleyball Beach Volleyball World Tour in 2000.

🐝 **Paul** (PAHL) (Latin) He Demonstrates Humility

Penny (PEN-nee) (English) She Is the Beloved One Who Weaves Threads

Paul Westhead (1939–), coach of the Phoenix Mercury basketball team, led his Women's National Basketball Association team to a 2007 championship. Paul's victory was due in large part to the offense of star forward Penny Taylor-Gil.

Name Pairs and Groups
from the Bible

BOYS

🐦 **Abaddon** (uh-BAD-dun) (Hebrew) He Conquers Every Enemy

Abana (uh-BAHN-nuh) (Hebrew) He Is a Rock-Solid Fortress

Abdeel (ahb-DEEL) (Hebrew) He Devotes His Life to God

Ahiram (ah-hee-RAHM) (Hebrew) He Glorifies God

Akan (ah-KAHN) (Hebrew) He Brings Calamity to His Enemies

Alvan (AHL-vuhn) (Hebrew) He Stands Tall and Speaks Eloquently

Amzi (AHM-zee) (Hebrew) He Is Powerful

Areli (ah-REL-lee) (Hebrew) He Is the Lord's Majestic Lion

Becher (BECK-kur) (Hebrew) He Is a Fleet-Footed Camel

Beriah (bur-RYE-yuh) (Hebrew) He Stands by His Companions

🐦 **Achim** (ah-KEEM) (Hebrew) He Is Well-Prepared

Adar (uh-DAR) (Hebrew) He Is Aristocratic

Addon (AD-dun, ad-DAHN) (Hebrew) He Is God's Solid Foundation

Adlai (AD-lay) (Hebrew) He Demonstrates God's Greatness

Adoram (ah-dor-RAHM) (Hebrew) His Beauty Overwhelms Us

Aenon (EE-nun) (Hebrew) He Is the Source of Wisdom

Agar (AY-ghar) (Hebrew) He Travels to Distant Lands

Ahab (AY-hab) (Hebrew) He Is Called "Adored Uncle"

Ahira (ah-HEE-ruh) (Hebrew) He Is Called "Adored Brother"

Alemeth (AL-eh-meth) (Hebrew) He Is Eternally Young

🐦 **Allon** (AL-lun, al-LAHN) (Hebrew) He Is a Magnificent Oak

Alvah (AL-vuh) (Hebrew) He Is Exalted

Amad (ah-MAHD) (Hebrew) He Deserves Our Praise

Amal (ah-MAHL) (Hebrew) He Works Tirelessly

Aman (ah-MAHN) (Hebrew) He Embodies Our Hopes

Ananias (an-uh-NYE-yuss) (Hebrew) His God Is Graceful

Antioch (AN-nee-yahk) (Hebrew) He Is as Swift as Horses

Antipas (AN-tih-puhss) (Hebrew) He Does Everything for Us

Aphiah (ah-FYE-yuh, AHF-fee-yuh) (Hebrew) He Converses Eloquently

Apollos (ah-PAHL-lohss) (Hebrew) He Rains Destruction on His Enemies

🐦 **Amos** (AY-mus) (Hebrew) He Courageously Carries Heavy Burdens

Judah (JOO-duh) (Hebrew) He Is Highly Praised

Amos, a prophet of God, wrote in the book of Amos of his sacred visions of universal fairness. Amos was from the nation of Judah, which was named in honor of its founder, the warrior-statesman Judah.

🐾 **Apollyon** (ah-PAHL-yun) (Hebrew) He Rains Destruction on His Enemies

Arad (ah-RAHD) (Hebrew) He Is a Fire-Breathing Serpent

Archelaus (ar-kel-AY-yus) (Hebrew) He Rules Over Our Nation

Arcturus (ARK-tur-russ) (Hebrew) He Unites Our Family and Our Nation

Ardon (AR-dahn) (Hebrew) He Brings a Harsh Verdict to Evil-Doers

Arimathea (air-ih-muh-THEE-yuh) (Hebrew) He Is a Noble Lion

Arnon (AR-nun) (Hebrew) He Stands Joyfully in the Sunlight

Artemas (AR-teh-mus) (Hebrew) He Is Healthy and Powerful

Asher (ASH-shur) (Hebrew) He Is Rejoicing

Askelon (ASS-keh-lahn) (Hebrew) He Is Even-Handed and Fair

🐾 **Asriel** (AHZ-ree-yel) (Hebrew) He Is God's Ever-Present Help

Azzan (ahz-ZAHN) (Hebrew) He Is Powerful

Baara (BAHR-ruh) (Hebrew) He Is a Blazing Fire

Birsha (BUR-shuh) (Hebrew) He Blesses Us a Thousand Times Over

Carmi (KAR-mee) (Hebrew) He Is a Sacred Grape-Vine

Dalphon (dal-FAHN, DAL-fun) (Hebrew) He Loves and Pities Himself

Elidad (el-ih-DAHD) (Hebrew) He Is Truly Beloved by God

Elishama (el-ih-SHAH-muh) (Hebrew) His God Hears Him

Elon (ee-LAHN) (Hebrew) He Is a Majestic Oak Tree

Enan (ee-NAHN) (Hebrew) He Sees More than Others

🐾 **Attalus** (AT-tuh-luss) (Greek) He Is Our Savior

Aven (AH-ven) (Hebrew) He Is Prosperous

Baalim (BAY-lim) (Hebrew) He Is Worshipped

Bamah (BAH-mah) (Hebrew) He Is God's Sacred Mountain

Barjesus (bar-JEE-zuss) (Hebrew) He Is Jesus's Son

Barnabas (BAR-nah-buss) (Hebrew) He Comforts Us

Belshazzar (bel-shah-ZAR) (Hebrew) He Safeguards Our Wealth

Ben (BEN) (Hebrew) He Is Our Glorious Son

Benaiah (ben-NYE-yah) (Hebrew) He Is God's Son

Benhadad (ben-hah-DAHD) (Hebrew) He Descends from Thunder

🐾 **Beno** (BEN-no) (Hebrew) He Is His Father's Glorious Son

Berachiah (bair-ruh-KYE-yah) (Hebrew) He Praises God Eternally

Beri (BAIR-ree) (Hebrew) He Is Our Glorious Son

Bithron (BITH-run) (Hebrew) He Is Invincible

Blastus (BLAS-tuss) (Hebrew) He Is a Blossoming Flower

Boaz (BO-wazz) (Hebrew) He Runs Faster than Wind

Bohan (Bo-hahn) (Hebrew) He Is the One Who Gives Us Immortality

Buz (BUZZ) (Hebrew) He Is Feared by His Enemies

Cabul (kah-BOOL) (Hebrew) He Will Do Anything to Win

Caiphas (KYE-uh-fuss) (Hebrew) He Is a Truth-Seeker

🐾 **Cain** (KAIN) (Hebrew) He Takes Possession

Abel (AIB-ul) (Hebrew) He Is the Breath of Life
In the book of Genesis, the first chapter of the Holy Bible, Cain and Abel are the sons of Adam and Eve, the first people created by God. Cain slays Abel due to sheer jealousy.

🐾 **Caleb** (KAY-leb) (Hebrew) He Is Man's Best Friend—A Faithful, Loyal Dog

Calno (KAL-no) (Hebrew) He Is Our Greatest Achievement

Calvary (KAL-vuh-ree) (Hebrew) He Has an Aristocrat's Skull

Camon (KAY-mun) (Hebrew) He Rises to Glory

Capernaum (kuh-PUR-num) (Hebrew) He Is the Brave Realm

Cedron (SED-drun) (Hebrew) His Soul Is Darkly Dangerous

Cephas (SEE-fuss) (Aramaic) He Is Rock-Solid

Cleophas (klee-OH-fuss) (Hebrew) He Follows Jesus Christ

Corinth (KOR-rinth) (Greek) He Completes Us Beautifully

Cozbi (KAHZ-bee) (Hebrew) He Skillfully Bends the Truth

✐ **Eleazar** (el-ee-uh-ZAR) (Hebrew) His God Is Ever-Present Help

Amariah (ah-MAR-ee-yah) (Hebrew) His God Speaks Clearly

Eleazar appears in the first book of the Chronicles as a high priest of Israel who survived the Jewish people's desert wanderings, after their liberation from Egypt by the prophet Moses. Amariah, Eleazar's son, also became a high priest of Israel.

✐ **Ephron** (EF-rahn) (Hebrew) He Will Father Many Offspring

Eran (air-RAHN) (Hebrew) He Guards Us Forever

Eri (AIR-ree) (Hebrew) He Is a Noble Lion

Gaddi (GAD-dee) (Hebrew) He Is Prosperity

Gera (GAIR-ruh) (Hebrew) He Is a Seed from which a Mighty Tree Grows

Hamor (HAY-mor) (Hebrew) He Is a Tireless Beast of Burden

Hamul (HAM-mul) (Hebrew) He Reflects God's Greatness

Heber (HEE-bur) (Hebrew) He Is a Community of Faith

Helek (HEL-lek) (Hebrew) He Is Our Portion of Greatness

Hezron (HEZ-run) (Hebrew) He Is an Impregnable Fortress

✐ **Hymeneus** (him-EN-ee-yus) (Greek) He Holds Chastity as Sacred

Ibri (IB-ree) (Hebrew) He Is Filled with Fury

Ichabod (IK-uh-bahd) (Hebrew) He Desires Honor

Iram (ee-RAHM) (Hebrew) He Is a Lofty Summit

Isaiah (eye-ZAY-yuh) (Hebrew) His God Is Ever-Present

Issachar (ISS-suh-kar) (Hebrew) He Serves Humanity

Ivah (EYE-vuh) (Hebrew) He Is the Ivah Region of Babylon

Jaakan (JAY-kun) (Hebrew) He Works Tirelessly

Jabez (JAY-bez) (Hebrew) He Understands Sacrifice

Jabin (JAY-bin) (Hebrew) He Is Wisdom

✐ **Jachin** (JAY-kin) (Hebrew) He Builds a Solid Foundation

Jahleel (jah-LEEL) (Hebrew) His God Prepares a Place for Him

Jahzeel (jah-ZEEL) (Hebrew) His God Gives Him Treasure

Jairus (JAIR-rus) (Latin) He Is Brilliant

Japheth (JAY-feth) (Hebrew) His Greatness Increases

Jareb (JAIR-reb) (Hebrew) He Avenges Us

Jarmuth (JAR-muth) (Hebrew) He Battles Death

Jedaiah (jeh-DYE-yuh) (Hebrew) His God Is All-Wise

Jemuel (JEM-yoo-wull) (Hebrew) His God Brings the Bright Morning

Jerahmeel (jair-uh-MEEL) (Hebrew) He Is Compassionate

✐ **Jered** (JAIR-red) (Hebrew) He Descends from the Mighty Ones

Jesiah (jah-SYE-yuh) (Hebrew) He Sparkles with God's Light

Jimnah (JIM-nuh) (Hebrew) He Is God's Strong Right Hand

Joab (JO-wab) (Hebrew) His Heavenly Father Is God

Joah (JO-wuh) (Hebrew) He Is Close to God

Johanan (jo-HAH-nun) (Hebrew) His God Is Gracious

Jonan (JO-nun) (Hebrew) He Is a Peaceful Dove

Joram (JOR-rum) (Hebrew) His God Glorifies Him

Jubal (JOO-bul) (Hebrew) He Is a Beautiful River

Justus (JUS-tuss) (Latin/Hebrew) He Is Fair and Just

✐ **Joshua** (JAHSH-oo-wuh) (Hebrew) His God Is Eternal Salvation

Jericho (JAIR-ih-ko) (Hebrew) He Is the Moon-God

Joshua (c. 1200 B.C.), whose story is told in the book of Exodus, commanded Israel's armies after the passing of the prophet Moses, who led the Jewish people from Egyptian slavery. Joshua's greatest victory was his capture of the Canaanite city of Jericho.

✐ **Matthew** (MATH-thyoo) (Hebrew) He Is God's Divine Gift

Augustine (AW-gus-teen) (Latin) He Is Absolutely Magnificent

Saint Matthew (1 B.C.–?) was one of four early Christians, along with Mark, Luke, and John, who chronicled Jesus Christ's life. Matthew's writings, found in the book of Matthew, were said by Saint Augustine of Hippo to be the earliest of the four canons.

🕮 **Moses** (MO-zuss) (Hebrew) He Is the Son Who Rescues Us

Aaron (AIR-run) (Hebrew) He Is the Lofty Mountain

Moses was a prophet of God, who led the Jewish people from slavery in Egypt. Moses's brother was Aaron, the founding patriarch of a great Jewish family.

🕮 **Saul** (SALL) (Hebrew) He Is the One for Whom We Prayed

Abner (AB-nur) (Hebrew) His God Is Radiant Light

The books of Samuel relate that Saul (eleventh century B.C.) was a warrior whose victory over the Ammonite nation caused his people to proclaim him King of Israel. Saul's cousin was the warrior Abner, mentioned in the book of Samuel.

GIRLS

🕮 **Abigail** (AB-ih-gayl) (Hebrew) She Is Her Father's Joy

Carmel (kar-MEL) (Hebrew) She Is a Fragrant Garden

Abigail appears in the books of Samuel as the wife of Nabal, a farmer near Mount Carmel. Nabal denied the young David—who would one day be King of Israel—food and drink. David's fury mounted, but Abigail fed David and his men, calming him.

🕮 **Channah** (HAHN-nah) (Hebrew) She Is Graceful

Peninnah (peh-NEE-nuh) (Hebrew) She Is a Priceless Jewel

In the books of Samuel, Channah and Peninah were the wives of Elkanah of Zuph. Channah eventually became the mother of Saul, a future King of Israel.

🕮 **Dinah** (DYE-nah) (Hebrew) She Has Been Found Worthy

Leah (LEE-uh) (Hebrew) She Is Humanity's Queen

In the book of Genesis, Dinah was the daughter of Leah, matriarch of six of Israel's Twelve Tribes. Dinah's father was Jacob, founder of

Israel. After a foreign prince insulted Dinah, she rallied her brothers Levi and Simeon, who exacted terrible revenge.

🕮 **Joanna** (jo-AN-nuh) (Hebrew) Her God Is Gracious

Susanna (soo-ZAN-nah) (Hebrew) She Is a Fragrant Lotus Flower

In the Gospel according to Luke, Joanna and Susanna were part of Jesus's entourage. After Jesus's crucifixion, Joanna anointed Jesus's body with oil for burial. Three days later, Joanna told the disciples that Jesus's tomb was miraculously empty.

🕮 **Lydia** (LIH-dee-yah) (Greek) She Is Lydia

Thyatira (thy-ah-TEE-rah) (Greek) She Is the Source of all Light

In the Acts of the Apostles, the merchant Lydia of Thyatira (Akhisar, Turkey) was described as an early Christian. Lydia gave food and shelter to one of Jesus Christ's evangelists, Saint Paul the Apostle, until he left to preach the gospel worldwide.

🕮 **Makeda** (mah-KAY-duh) (Ethiopic) She Is Greatness

Sheba (SHEE-buh) (Hebrew) She Is a Sacred Promise

In the book of Kings, Makeda (tenth century B.C.) was the African ruler known as the Queen of Sheba (Ethiopia). Makeda brought riches to Israel's King Solomon in exchange for proofs of his wisdom. Solomon complied, and he and Makeda later produced a child whom Makeda carried back to Ethiopia, founding an Ethiopian-Judean dynasty.

🕮 **Martha** (MAR-thuh) (Hebrew) She Rules Our Home Magnificently

Magdalene (mag-duh-LAYN) (Hebrew) She Is Magdala, Israel

In the Gospel according to Luke, Mary Magdalene and Martha were sisters of wealthy Lazarus of Bethany, who sheltered Jesus Christ. Later, after Lazarus died of an illness, Jesus resurrected Lazarus from his tomb—a miracle which Martha witnessed.

🕮 **Miriam** (MEER-ee-yahm) (Hebrew) She Is Love

Bithiah (BIH-thee-yah) (Hebrew) She Is God's Daughter

In the book of Exodus, Miriam was the sister of the infant Moses, a future prophet of Israel.

Miriam accompanied Moses as he floated down the Nile River in a basket, where he had been placed to protect him from the Egyptian Pharaoh's death decree against Jewish boys. Moses was discovered and raised by Bithiah, Pharaoh's daughter.

⚭ **Priscilla** (prih-SIL-luh) (Latin) She Is the Honored Little One
Angela (AN-juh-luh) (Italian) She Is God's Messenger
In the Acts of the Apostles, Priscilla is the earliest Christian evangelist in the Bible, after Paul of Tarsus. And, although English actress Angela Morant is not an apostle, she nonetheless portrayed Priscilla beautifully in the 1985 television miniseries A.D.

⚭ **Ruth** (ROOTH) (Hebrew) She Is a Trusted Companion
Mara (MAH-rah) (Hebrew) She Understands Sorrow
In the book of Ruth, Ruth was the loyal daughter-in-law of the respected Jewish woman Naomi. Naomi changed her name to Mara after enduring many trials from God.

⚭ **Salome** (SAH-lo-may) (Hebrew) She Is Peace
Sarah (SAIR-ruh) (Hebrew) She Is a Royal Princess
In the Gospel according to Mark, Salome was Jesus Christ's loyal follower. In The Legend of the Saintes-Maries *(1521) by Vincent Philippon, Sarah the Egyptian gave Salome shelter.*

BOYS AND GIRLS

⚭ **Ahava** (ah-HAH-vah) (Hebrew) She Is Life Itself
Ami (AH-mee) (Hebrew) She Is Dependable
Atarah (ah-TAR-ruh) (Hebrew) She Is a Shining Crown
Athaliah (ath-ALL-yuh) (Hebrew) She Proves God's Glory
Bashan (bah-SHAHN) (Hebrew) He Is Beautiful Ivory
Bethesda (beh-THEZ-duh) (Hebrew) She Is Compassionate
Beulah (BYOO-lah) (Hebrew) She Marries and Starts a Family
Kedar (keh-DAR) (Hebrew) He Is a Darkly Beautiful Night

Kemuel (KEM-yoo-wel) (Hebrew) His God Uplifts Him
Kenan (KEE-nun) (Hebrew) He Gives Himself to God

⚭ **Alpha** (AL-fah) (Greek) She Is the Beginning
Omega (oh-MAY-gah) (Greek) He Is the Completion
In the book of Revelation 1:8 by John of Patmos (second century A.D.), John says of God, "I am Alpha and Omega, the first and the last."

⚭ **Deborah** (DEB-uh-rah) (Hebrew) She Is a Busy Honeybee
Barak (bah-RAHK) (Hebrew) He Is a Thunderbolt
Deborah was a judge and prophetess in Israel, as described in the book of Judges. Deborah correctly foretold that the Israelite general Barak would vanquish his enemies.

⚭ **Esther** (ES-tur) (Hebrew) She Is a Brilliant Star
Mordecai (MOR-duh-kye) (Hebrew) He Serves God
The Jewish maiden Esther, whose story is told in the book of Esther, was sent by her cousin Mordecai to meet King Xerxes of Persia. Xerxes instantly loved Esther and married her. Esther became queen of Persia and secured freedom for all Persian Jews.

⚭ **Hagar** (HAY-ghar) (Hebrew) He Soars to Heaven
Halah (HAH-luh) (Hebrew) She Is a Fragrant Lily
Hammon (HAM-mun) (Hebrew) He Masters the Winds
Hanan (hah-NAHN) (Hebrew) She Is Compassionate
Hara (HAR-ruh) (Hebrew) She Rejoices
Hashem (hah-SHEM) (Hebrew) He Destroys His Enemies
Havilah (HAH-vee-lah) (Hebrew) She Is the Beautiful Coastline
Hebron (HEB-run) (Hebrew) He Is a Trusted Companion
Hena (HEN-nuh) (Hebrew) She Is Graceful
Hermas (HUR-muss) (Greek) He Is a Marker-Stone, Guiding Travelers

⚭ **Hermon** (Hebrew) He Is Aggressively Warlike
Herod (HAIR-rud) (Hebrew) He Sings of Courage

Hezekiah (hez-uh-KYE-yuh) (Hebrew) He Is God's Power

Hezron (HEZ-run) (Hebrew) He Is an Unconquerable Fortress

Hillel (hil-LEL) (Hebrew) He Honors God

Hosanna (ho-ZAN-nuh) (Hebrew) She Is Our Savior

Ibhar (EE-bar) (Hebrew) He Is Selected by God

Illyricum (il-LEER-ih-kum) (Latin) She Is Rejoicing

Ishma (ISH-muh) (Hebrew) She Is God's Miracle

Jedidiah (jed-ih-DYE-yuh) (Hebrew) His God Adores Him

Jesús (hay-SOOSS) (Spanish) His Salvation Is Almighty God

Mary (MAIR-ree) (English) She Is Love Jesus Christ (c. A.D. 1–A.D. 36) *is revered by two billion Christians worldwide as God's Son. Jesus's mother was Mary, the virgin who miraculously bore Jesus.*

Joelah (jo-EL-luh) (Hebrew) Her God Is the One True God

Kanah (KAH-nuh) (Hebrew) She Is a Lake Filled with Reeds

Keros (KAIR-rohss) (Hebrew) He Is the All-Seeing Sun

Keturah (keh-TOO-ruh) (Hebrew) She Has a Heavenly Scent

Kezia (keh-ZYE-yuh, KEZ-yuh) (Hebrew) She Is a Fragrant Cassia Tree

Kinah (KEE-nuh) (Hebrew) She Sings Funeral-Songs

Kishon (KEE-shahn) (Hebrew) He Is Rock-Solid

Laban (LAY-bun) (Hebrew) He Is Beautifully Fair

Lael (lay-YEL) (Hebrew) He Comes to Us from God

Lazarus (LAZ-ur-russ) (Hebrew) His God Assists Him

Lod (LAHD) (Hebrew) He Is the Voice of His Generation

Lubin (LOO-bin) (Hebrew) He Is Humanity's Greatness

Lydda (LID-duh) (Hebrew) She Is Clear Water

Lysanias (lye-SAYN-ee-yus) (Hebrew) He Replaces Sadness with Joy

Lysimachus (lye-SIM-uh-kuss) (Hebrew) He Conquers His Enemies

Lystra (LEES-truh) (Hebrew) She Conquers Her Enemies

Madai (mah-DYE) (Hebrew) He Is the Persians

Magdala (MAG-dah-lah) (Hebrew) She Is Magdala, Israel

Mahala (mah-HAH-lah) (Hebrew) She Is Compassion

Malachi (MAL-ah-kye) (Hebrew) He Is Our Spiritual Guardian

Noah (NO-wah) (Hebrew) He Is Tranquility

Ararat (AR-uh-raht) (Hebrew) He Is Mount Ararat

Canaan (KAY-nun) (Hebrew) He Is the Father of the Canaanites

Ham (HAHM) (Hebrew) He Is Hot-Tempered

Japheth (JAY-futh) (Hebrew) He Grows Eternally Greater

Judi (ZHOO-dee) (Arabic) She Is the Nation of Gordyae

Lamech (LAY-mik) (Hebrew) He Demonstrates Humility

Naamah (NAH-muh) (Hebrew) She Is Comforting

Nu (NOO) (Arabic/Hebrew) He Is Tranquility

Shem (SHEM) (Hebrew) His Name Is Sacred

Samson (SAM-sun) (Hebrew) He Is Born of the Sun

Delilah (duh-LYE-luh) (Hebrew) She Spends Money Freely

In the book of Judges, the Israeli warrior Samson divulged the secret of his power to the temptress Delilah—that his strength lay in his hair. Delilah cut Samson's hair while he slept and betrayed him to her masters the Philistines, who enslaved him. But when Samson's hair grew back, he destroyed the Philistines' temple.

Name Pairs and Groups
from World Literature and Mythology

BOYS

🐍 **Aladdin** (uh-LAD-in) (Arabic) He Follows the True Faith

Sinbad (SIN-bad) (Arabic) He Is Powerfully Male
The Book of One Thousand and One Nights follows the Arab princess Scheherazade as she beguiles her husband King Shahryar with stories. Two memorable characters in these stories are Aladdin, a wastrel who becomes wealthy with aid of a genie and a magic lamp; and Sinbad, an adventurous sea-captain.

🐍 **Alfie** (AL-fee) (English) He Is a Small but Wise Counselor

Budd (BUD) (English) He Is a Trusted Friend

Elric (EL-rik) (English) He Is the Ruler of the Magical Elfin People

Enoc (EE-nuk) (Welsh) He Is Faithful

Israel (IZ-ray-yul) (Hebrew) His God Triumphs Forever

Lestat (American/French) He Is Our Nation's Soul

Mort (MORT) (English) He Is the Little One Who Is the Town near the Moors

Rhys (REESS) (Welsh) He Has Dynamic Emotions

Santiago (sahn-tee-AH-go) (Spanish) He Is the Blessed Saint James

Wintersmith (WIN-tur-smith) (English) In Winter, He Smites Metal Powerfully

🐍 **Anansi** (a-NAHN-see) (Akan) He Is a Cunning Spider

Nyame (nye-AH-may) (Akan) He Resembles God

Anansi—an African deity who sometimes takes the form of a spider and sometimes walks as a man—is the originator of all stories. Anansi's father is Nyame, or God.

🐍 **Azrael** (AZ-rah-el) (Hebrew) He Assists God

Baltazar (BAHL-tuh-zahr) (Hebrew) He Is Divinely Protected

Barlaam (bar-LAHM) (Hebrew) He Descends from the Great One

Dismas (DIZ-muss) (Hebrew) He Is the Evening

Israfil (IZ-rah-fill) (Hebrew) He Is God's Angel

Jasper (JAHS-pur) (Persian) He Holds Priceless Wealth

Joachim (JO-uh-keem) (Hebrew) He Is the Divinely Protected Little One

Melchior (MEL-kee-yor) (Hebrew) He Is the King of the City

Remiel (REM-yul) (Hebrew) He Is God's Mercy

Zerachiel (zair-AKH-ee-yel) (Hebrew) He Is Commanded by God

🐍 **Barrington** (BAIR-ing-tun) (English) He Is a Town of Bearlike Men

Berryman (BAIR-ree-mun) (English) He Is an Unconquerable Fortress

Carleton (KARL-tun) (English) He Is a Town of Free Persons

Ferguson (FUR-ghuss-sun) (English/Irish) He Descends from the Powerful Man

Hewitt (HYOO-wit) (Scottish) He Is the Great-Hearted Little One

Kavanagh (KAV-uh-naw) (Irish) He Descends from the Compassionate One

131

O'Connell (oh-KAHN-nul) (Irish) He Descends from the Mighty Wolf

O'Donovan (oh-DAHN-uh-vun) (Irish) He Descends from the Darkly Handsome One

O'Shaughnessy (oh-SHAW-ness-see) (Irish) He Descends from the Wily One

Padraic (PAH-drik) (Irish) He Is Aristocratic

Beau (BO) (American/French) He Is Handsome

Candide (kaw-DEED) (French) He Is Beautifully Fair

Esmond (EZ-mund) (English) He Safeguards Us

Henderson (HEN-dur-sun) (English) He Descends from Our Homeland's Great Ruler

Molloy (mul-LOY) (Irish) He Is a Powerful Aristocrat

Orlando (or-LAN-doh) (Italian) He Is from the Renowned Land

Otto (AHT-toh) (German) He Is Powerful and Successful

Phineas (FIN-ee-yus) (Hebrew) He Is a Magnificent Nubian

Stuart (STOO-urt) (Scottish) He Safeguards Our Home

Watt (WAHT) (Scottish) He Commands the Military

Bede (BEED) (English) He Is Our Fervent Prayer

Copperfield (KAHP-pur-feeld) (English) He Is a Field of Copper

Hadon (HAY-dun) (English) He Is a Valley Filled with Hay

Jurgen (YUR-ghen) (Dutch) He Farms the Land

Ras (RAZ) (American/Latin) He Is the Little Beloved One

Robinson (RAH-bin-sun) (English) He Descends from the Soaring Robin

Tyger (TYE-gur) (American/English) He Is a Ferocious Tiger

Vanya (VAHN-yuh) (Russian) He Is the Little One Whose God Is Gracious

Wieland (VYE-lund) (German) He Is the Dark One from the Realm of War

Zorro (ZOR-ro) (Spanish) He Is a Cunning Fox

Burke (BERK) (Irish) He Is a Beautiful Fortress

Lover (LUH-vur) (English) He Is a Lover of Humanity

MacKenna (muh-KEN-nuh) (Irish) He Is Created in Flames

Moran (mo-RAN) (Irish) He Is Massive

O'Brien (oh-BRYE-yun) (Irish) He Descends from the One Who Is a Lofty Mountain

O'Casey (oh-KAY-see) (Irish) He Descends from the Vigilant One

O'Keefe (oh-KEEF) (Irish) He Descends from the Compassionate One

Sheridan (SHAIR-ih-den) (English) He Descends from the Truth-Seeker

Sterne (STURN) (English) He is the One Who Is a Heavenly Star

Wilde (WILD) (Irish) He Is Wild and Unstoppable

Catlow (KAT-lo) (English) He Is a Magnificent Cat Singing on a Hill

Faust (FAH-wohst) (German) He Is Favored with Good Fortune

Holborn (HOL-born) (English) He Is a Muscular Bear

Peer (PEER) (Norwegian) He Is Rock-Solid

Riddley (RID-lee) (English) He Is a Meadow of Reeds in the Forest

Starman (STAR-mun) (American/English) He Journeys among the Stars

Tam (TAM) (Scottish) He Is a Precious Little Twin

Taras (tah-RAHSS) (Russian) He Is Taras, Italy

Tonio (TOH-nee-yoh) (Italian) He Is a Blossoming Little Flower

Warburton (WOR-bur-tun) (English) He Is Werburg, England

Chinua (CHEEN-wah) (Igbo) He Is Divinely Protected

James (JAYMZ) (Hebrew) He Is Divinely Protected

> *Chinua Achebe (1930–) is a Nigerian author whose 1958 novel* Things Fall Apart *is an acclaimed work of African folklore. In 1980, Chinua befriended African-American author James Baldwin.*

Conor (KAHN-nur) (Irish) He Is the Master of Wolves

Curran (KUR-run) (Irish) He Descends from the Mighty Warrior

Eamon (AY-mun) (Irish) He Is Our Wealthy Protector

Frazer (FRAY-zhur, FRAY-zur) (Scottish) He Is an Adventurous Explorer

Gerson (GUR-sun) (English) He Travels to Distant Lands

Giraldus (jih-RAHL-dus) (Latin) He Rules with Powerful Weapons

Goldsmith (GOLD-smith) (English) He Smites Gold with Great Power

MacManus (mak-MAN-nus) (Irish) He Descends from the Magnificent One

O'Reilly (oh-RYE-lee) (Irish) He Descends from the Supreme One

Yeats (YAYTS) (Scottish) He Guards the Gates of Our City

🖉 **Everard** (EV-uh-rard) (English) He Is as Courageous as a Wild Boar

Grandison (GRAND-ih-sun) (English) He Descends from the Magnificent One

Launcelot (lawss-LO) (French) He Is Our Mighty Little Weapon

Mannering (MAN-ur-ring) (English) He Is Warin, Germany

Nigel (NYE-jul) (English) He Is a Towering Champion

Peregrine (PAIR-ih-grin) (English) He Journeys Everywhere

Quentin (KWEN-tin) (English) He Is the Fifth

Roderick (RAHD-rik) (English) He Is Mighty and Renowned

Tristram (TRIS-trum) (English) He Is Aggressive

Waverley (WAY-vur-lee) (English) He Is the Swaying Aspen Tree

🖉 **Fyodor** (fee-YO-dor) (Russian) He Is God's Divine Gift

Nikolai (NIK-oh-lye) (Russian) He Is Humanity's Triumph

Russian author Fyodor Dostoevsky (1821–1881) explored the human psyche in works such as The Brothers Karamazov. Fyodor was influenced by another great Russian writer, Nikolai Gogol, a dramatist who wrote the fiery play The Inspector-General.

🖉 **Guillaume** (ghee-YOHM) (French) He Protects Humanity

André (awn-DRAY) (French) He Is Powerful

Guillaume Apollinaire (1880–1918) was a Polish-French poet who combined traditional verse with uninhibited symbolism, as in 1913's Alcools. One of Guillaume's colleagues was the legendary French poet André Breton.

🖉 **Hans** (HAHNZ) (Danish) He Is the Little One Whose God Is Gracious

Uriah (yoor-EYE-yuh) (Hebrew) His God Is a Guiding Light

Hans Christian Andersen (1805–1875) was the Danish writer of such tales as The Little Mermaid. Andersen's 1857 visit to the home of English author Charles Dickens inspired Charles to base the character of Uriah Heep in David Copperfield on Hans's personality.

🖉 **Johann** (YO-hahn) (German) His God Is Gracious

Georg (GAY-yorg) (German) He Farms the Land

Johann Wolfgang von Goethe (1749–1832) is Germany's greatest writer, dramatist, and philosopher. Johann influenced the German philosopher Georg Hegel, whose ideas on freedom continue to guide philosophers.

🖉 **Jules** (ZHOOL) (French) He Rules Heaven

Pierre (pee-YAIR) (French) He Is Rock-Solid

Jules Gabriel Verne (1828–1905) was the French author who wrote such works as the 1873 science-fiction novel Twenty Thousand Leagues Under the Sea, about a mysterious submarine and the scientist who penetrated its secrets, Pierre Aronnax.

🖉 **Kamil** (kah-MEEL) (Arabic) He Is Absolutely Perfect

Hayy (hye-YAH) (Arabic) He Has a Higher Consciousness

Literature's feral children—kids raised by noble beasts—include Kamil, a child sage in The Treatise of Kamil on the Prophet's Biography by the thirteenth-century Arab writer Ibn al-Nafis; and Hayy, the philosopher raised by a gazelle in Hayy Ibn Yaqzan by twelfth-century Arab writer Ibn Tufail.

🖉 **Omar** (OH-mar) (Arabic) He Is a Flourishing Community

Malik (mah-LEEK) (Arabic) He Is a Magnificent Ruler

Omar Khayyam (A.D. 1048–A.D. 1122) was a Persian poet whose masterwork Rubaiyat of Omar Khayyam is beloved for lines such as, "A Jug of Wine, a Loaf of Bread—and Thou. . . ." Omar built an observatory for the Persian warrior-monarch Malik Shah I.

🖉 **Roland** (RO-lund, ro-LAW) (French) He Is a Mighty Nation

Oliver (AH-lih-vur) (English) He Is a Fragrant Olive Tree

In the twelfth-century French poem The Song of Roland (La Chanson de Roland), the valiant

knight Roland and his comrade Oliver, along with 20,000 soldiers, perish heroically fighting the Saracens of Spain.

GIRLS

🙂 **Aimée** (em-MAY, AIM-mee) (French) She Is Greatly Beloved

Audre (AW-dree) (American/English) She Is a Powerful Aristocrat

Grazyna (grah-ZHEE-nah) (Lithuanian) She Is Absolutely Gorgeous

Harryette (American/English) She Rules the Home

Hedvig (HED-vigg) (Swedish) She Is Aggressive

Lale (LAH-luh) (German) She Is a Fragrant Tulip

Lisel (LEE-zul) (American/German) She Is the Little One Favored by God

Lorine (lo-REEN) (American/English) She Is a Little Laurel Wreath of Victory

Máire (MOY-ruh) (Irish) She Is Love

Mirabai (meer-uh-BYE) (Indian) She Is God's Handmaiden

🙂 **Alejandra** (ah-leh-HAHN-drah) (Spanish) She Protects Humanity

Amrita (ahm-REE-tuh) (Indian) She Lives Forever

Dalia (DAHL-yuh) (Hebrew) She Is an Unbreakable Branch

Dipti (DEEP-tee) (Sanskrit) She Is Shimmering Radiance

Josefina (ho-seh-FEE-nah) (Spanish) Her Greatness Increases

Marge (MARJ) (English) She Is Our Priceless Little Pearl

Muriel (MYOOR-ee-yuhl) (English/Irish) She Is the Shining Ocean

Nettie (NET-tee) (English) She Is the Graceful Little One

Pauline (po-LEEN) (German) She Demonstrates Humility

Stevie (STEE-vee) (English) She Is a Shining Little Crown

🙂 **Alfonsina** (ahl-fone-SEE-nah) (Italian) She Is Aristocratic

Ania (AHN-yuh) (Russian) She Is Graceful

Celia (SEEL-yuh) (Latin) She Is the Blue Sky

Chase (CHAYSS) (English) She Is the Thrilling Hunt

Elinor (EL-ih-nor) (English) She Is Aliénor, France

Janine (juh-NEEN) (English) She Is God's Graceful Little Messenger

Natasha (nah-TAH-shah) (Russian) She Is the Little One Who Is Christmas Day

Phillis (FILL-luss) (English) She Is Lovely Green Branches

Wislawa (vee-SWAH-vah) (Polish) She Is Brilliant

Yelizaveta (yeh-lee-zah-VAY-tah) (Russian) Her God Is Abundance

🙂 **Allie** (AL-lee) (English) She Is Our Little Aristocrat

Béatrix (bay-ah-TREEX) (French) She Is a Great Voyager

Chao (CHA-oh) (Chinese) She Excels in Everything

Faith (FAYTH) (English) She Is all Our Hopes

Gioconda (zhee-oh-KAHN-duh) (Italian) She Rejoices

Juliana (joo-lee-AH-nuh) (English) She Is Julius Caesar's Relative

Lynne (LIN) (Welsh) She Is a Clear Lake

Malorie (MAL-luh-ree) (American/English) She Meets Life's Challenges

Marthe (MAR-tuh) (German) She Rules Our Home Magnificently

Vicki (VIK-kee) (English) She Is a Glorious Little Victory

🙂 **Ama** (AH-muh) (Akan) She Came into this World on a Saturday

Anne-Marie (ahn-mah-REE) (French) She Is the Graceful Little One Who Is Love Itself

Eleanor (EL-uh-nor) (English) She Is Aliénor, France

Freda (FREE-duh) (English) She Is Our Fair Little Beauty

Harriette (HAIR-ee-yet) (English) She Rules the Home

Ilse (IL-suh) (German) She Is the Little One Favored by God

Ingeborg (ING-ghuh-borg) (Norwegian) She Assists God

Kelley (KEL-lee) (Irish) She Is Conquest

Laurie (LOR-ree) (English) She Is Our Little Laurel Wreath of Victory

Marilou (mair-ee-LOO) (English) She Is a Lover and a Warrior

🙂 **Amma** (AHM-muh) (Akan) She Arrived on a Saturday

Antoinette (ahn-twah-NET) (French) She Is a Blossoming Little Flower
Dymphna (DIMF-nuh) (Irish) She Is a Gentle Doe
Elsa (EL-sah) (German) She Is the Little One Favored by God
Henriette (aw-ree-YET) (French) She Rules Our Home Magnificently
Isak (EE-sahk) (Swedish) She Laughs with Joy
Kiran (kee-RAHN) (Sanskrit) She Is Golden Sunlight
Marceline (mauss-LEEN) (French) She Is as Powerful as any male
Rosemary (ROZE-mair-ree) (English) She Is a Rose, and She Is Love
Shobhaa (SHOWB-hah) (Sanskrit) She Is Shimmering Radiance

Anita (uh-NEE-tuh) (English/Spanish) She Is the Graceful Little One
Bebe (beh-BAY) (French) She Is an Adorable Infant
Erma (UR-muh) (English) She Is Our Entire Existence
Fredrika (fred-REE-kuh) (Swedish) She Rules Peacefully
Geraldine (jair-ul-DEEN) (English) She Rules with Powerful Weapons
Hortense (or-TAWSS) (French) She Is a Splendid Garden
Lan (LAHN) (Vietnamese) She Is a Fragrant Orchid
Marita (mah-REE-tah) (German) She Is Our Little Beloved One
Minna (MIN-nuh) (German) She Is Our Little Protector
Rhoda (RO-dah) (Greek) She Is Our Fragrant Rose

Arlette (ah-LET) (French) She Is a Soaring Little Falcon
Caryl (KAIR-rul) (English) She Is a Powerful Little Warrior
Colette (kuh-LET) (French) She Is Humanity's Little Triumph
Daina (dah-EE-nuh) (Lithuanian) She Is a Beautiful Melody
Ismat (EEZ-maht) (Arabic) She Protects Humanity
Leonora (lee-ah-NO-rah) (Italian) She Is Aliénor, France
Marvel (MAR-vul) (English) She Is a Miracle

Mei (MAY) (Chinese) She Is a Fragrant Plum Tree
Pema (PAY-muh) (Sanskrit) She Is a Fragrant Lotus Flower
Willa (WIL-luh) (English) She Protects Humanity

Aspasia (uh-SPAY-zhuh) (Greek) She Is the One to Whom We Open Our Hearts
Bell (BELL) (American/French) She Is Beautiful
Fannie (FAN-nee) (English) She Is the Little One Who Is the Nation of France
Gloria (GLO-ree-yah) (Latin) She Is Everlasting Glory
Ida (EYE-duh) (English) She Toils Productively
Margery (MAR-jur-ree) (English) She Is a Priceless Pearl
Minh (MIN) (Vietnamese) Her Wisdom Shines
Nomy (NO-mee) (American/Hebrew) She Is Courteous
Sojourner (so-ZHURN-nur) (English) She Seeks Truth
Zora (ZOR-ruh) (Slovak) She Is the Radiant Dawn

Ava (AY-vuh) (English) She Wants to Live
Claribel (KLAIR-uh-bel) (English) She Is the Radiant, Beautiful One
Eavan (EE-uh-vuhn) (Irish) She Shimmers Magnificently
Elisaveta (el-ees-uh-VEH-tuh) (Bulgarian) Her God Is Abundance
Ethel (EH-thul) (English) She Is Aristocratic
Fleur (FLOO-woor) (French) She Is a Fragrant Blossom
Karin (KAH-reen) (Swedish) She Is the Pure-Hearted Little One
Léonie (lay-oh-NEE) (French) She Is a Noble Lioness
Rae (RAY) (English) She Is the Little One Who Is a Gentle Mother Ewe
Rosalia (ro-suh-LEE-yuh) (Italian) She Is Our Fragrant Rose

Babette (bab-BET) (French) She Is the Little One Favored by God
Dani (DAN-nee) (English) Her God Judges Wisely
Erinna (uh-RIN-nuh) (Greek) She Is Tranquil and Poetic
Ina (EE-nah) (German) She Is the Little One Whose Greatness Increases

Jayne (JAYN) (English) Her God Is Gracious

Kamala (kuh-MAH-luh) (Sanskrit) She Is a Heavenly Star

Lynn (LIN) (Welsh) She Is a Clear Lake

Nathalie (NAH-tah-lee) (German) She Is Christmas Day

Tess (TEHSS) (English) She Is the Little One Who Is a Summer Harvest

Vénus (vay-NOOS) (French) She Is Love and Desire

Charlene (shar-LEEN) (English) She Is Our Mighty Little Soldier

Else (EL-suh) (German) She Is the Little One Favored by God

Gayleen (gay-LEEN) (Greek) She Is the Little Peaceful One

Hilde (HIL-duh) (German) She Lives for Combat

Jolan (yo-LAHN) (Hungarian) She Is a Fragrant Violet

Mari (MAIR-ree) (Welsh) She Is Love

Nora (NO-rah) (Irish) She Is the Little Honorable One

Sia (SEE-yuh) (Samoan/Polish) She Is Full of Life

Ursula (UR-syoo-lah) (Swedish) She Is a Fierce She-Bear

Winnifred (WIN-uh-fred) (Welsh) She Is Beautifully Fair

Gina (JEE-nuh) (Italian) She Is Our Little Aristocrat

Justine (zhooss-TEEN) (French) She Is Righteous

Mahnaz (mah-NAHSS) (Persian) She Is the Moon's Serene Beauty

Mahsati (mah-SAH-tee) (Persian) She Is the Beautiful Moon-Goddess

Parvin (PAR-vin) (Persian) She Is the Constellation Pleiades

Rabe'e (rah-BEE-yay) (Persian) She Is Springtime

Rosie (RO-zee) (English) She Is Our Fragrant Little Rose

Sheema (SHEE-muh) (Persian) She Has a Sacred Nature

Tahirih (tah-HEER-ree) (Persian) She Is Chaste and Pure

Zoya (ZOY-yuh) (Russian) She Is Life Itself

Ixchel (ik-SHEL, ee-SHEL) (Mayan) She Is the Colorful Rainbow

Toci (TOH-kee) (Nahuatl) She Cares for Us

In the mythology of the Mayans of Mesoamerica, Ixchel was the goddess of medicine. Ixchel was called Toci by the Aztecs of Mexico.

Pippi (PIP-pee) (Swedish) She Is the Beloved One Who Befriends Horses

Annika (AHN-nih-kuh) (Swedish) She Is Graceful and Beloved

In the Pippi Longstocking series of books by Swedish writer Astrid Lindgren (1907–2002), Pippi is a super-powerful girl befriended by her loyal neighbor Annika Settergren.

Rabia (ROO-bee-yah) (Persian) She Is the Fresh Season of Springtime

Persia (PUR-zhah) (Persian) She Is Persia

Rabia Balkhi (tenth century A.D.) is the greatest woman poet in Persian literature. Rabia's doomed love-affair with the servant Baktash has been immortalized in Baktash Nameh by the nineteenth-century poet Reza Qolikhan Hedayat.

Sadako (sah-DAH-ko) (Japanese) She Is an Innocent Child

Fujiko (FOO-jee-ko) (Japanese) She Is a Fragrant Wisteria Flower

The 1961 German classic Sadako Wants to Live (Sadako Will Leben) *tells of Sadako Sasaki (1943–55), a Japanese girl who died ten years after the 1945 nuclear bombing of Hiroshima from leukemia. Sadako's mother Fujiko wrote a fond memoir,* Come Back to Me Again, Sadako.

Su (SOO) (Chinese) She Honors Us

Ming (MING) (Chinese) Her Name Is Inscribed in Our Hearts

Su Xiaoxiao (?–c. A.D. 501) was a Chinese poetess who wrote of romantic love in such works as Song of the Same Heartbeat. *Su's poems inspired Chinese authors well into the fabled Ming Dynasty (1368–1644).*

Véronique (vair-oh-NEEK) (French) She Is Humanity's Triumph

Ivory (EYE-vuh-ree) (American/English) She Is the Color Ivory

Véronique Tadjo (1955–) is a poetess from Côte d'Ivoire, and the winner of 1983's L'Agence de Cooperation Culturelle et Technique Literary Prize for such works as 1990's La Chanson de la Vie. *Véronique's homeland, Côte d'Ivoire, translates into Ivory Coast.*

⊘ **Xue** (SOO) (Chinese) She Is Snow-White and Intelligent

Li (LEE) (Chinese) She Is the Radiant Dawn
Xue Tao (A.D. 768–A.D. 831), Li Zhi, and Yu Xu-anji were Chinese poetesses of the Tang Dynasty (A.D 618–A.D. 907). Their verses are summed up in this line from Xue's poem Sending Old Poems to Yuan Zhen: "Only I know the delicacy of wind and light."

BOYS AND GIRLS

⊘ **Alonso** (ah-LAHN-zo) (Spanish) He Is Honorably Well-Prepared

Antonia (an-TOH-nee-yuh) (Spanish) She Is a Fragrant Flower
In his classic 1605 novel Don Quixote, Spanish author Miguel de Cervantes (1547–1616) tells of the mad squire Alfonso Quixano, who reads so much history that he dons armor and claims he is a knight. His niece Antonia tries to restore his sanity and his honor.

⊘ **Ella** (EL-luh) (English) She Is a Radiant Little Torch

Maud (MAWD) (English) She Is a Powerful Warrior
Ella Young (1867–1956) was an Irish poet who befriended many artists, including Maud Gonne, muse of the famed Irish poet William Butler

Yeats. William dedicated He Wishes for the Cloths of Heaven to Maud.

⊘ **Miriam** (MEER-ee-yahm) (Hebrew) She Is Greatly Beloved

Yehudah (yeh-HOO-dah) (Hebrew) He Is Highly Praised
Miriam Talan-Shteklis (1900–1984) was an Israeli children's-literature author, and the recipient of the 1956 Israeli Prize for Literature. Miriam added Yalan to her last name to honor her father, writer Yehuda Leib Nissan.

⊘ **Nguyen** (WIN) (Vietnamese) He Is Unique

Thuy (TWEE) (Vietnamese) She Is Steadfast and Loyal
Nguyen Du (1765–1820) is Vietnam's greatest writer, having penned the national saga The Tale of Kieu (Doan Truong Tan Thanh), the story of the pure-hearted Thuy Kieu, who renounces her chastity to save her loved ones.

⊘ **Ping** (PING) (Chinese) She Is Peaceful

Sun (SUN) (Chinese) He Is Good-Hearted
Ping Lu (1953–) is a Taiwanese writer famed for her 1995 novel Love and Revolution based on the life of Sun Yat-Sen, first president of the Republic of China (now the People's Republic of China).

Name Pairs and Groups
from English Literature

BOYS

🐣 **Charles** (SHAHL) (French) He Is a Mighty Warrior

Sydney (SID-nee) (English) He Is a Great Island

In the 1859 novel A Tale of Two Cities *by Charles Dickens (1812–1870), French nobleman Charles Darnay is rescued from the French Revolution and from death at the guillotine by the reformed sinner Sydney Carton.*

🐣 **Draco** (DRAY-ko) (Greek) He Is a Fire-Breathing Dragon

Lucius (LOO-shee-yuss) (Latin) He Is Brilliant Light

Draco Malfoy is a conniving student of witchcraft at the Hogwarts School of Witchcraft and Wizardry, in the Harry Potter novel series by J. K. Rowling (1965–). Lucius Malfoy is Draco's father, a powerful warlock.

🐣 **Edmund** (ED-mund) (English) He Is Our Wealthy Protector

Tudor (TOO-dur) (Welsh) He Is a Ruler of Men

Edmund Spencer (1552–1599) was a brilliant English poet who wrote The Faerie Queene, *lauding England's Queen Elizabeth I, daughter of Henry VIII.*

🐣 **Harry** (HAIR-ree) (English) He Is Our Homeland's Great Ruler

Ron (RAHN) (English) He Is Our Wise Little Counselor

The orphan Harry Potter and his friend Ron Weasley become powerful wizards after studying witchcraft at the Hogwarts School of Witchcraft and Wizardry, in the Harry Potter novel series by J. K. Rowling (1965–).

🐣 **Jonathan** (JON-uh-thun) (English) His God Gives Him Abundance

Lemuel (LEM-yoo-wull) (Hebrew) He Is Possessed by God

Jonathan Swift (1667–1745) was a brilliant Irish-English satirist who mocked his era's prejudices. His masterwork was the 1726 novel Gulliver's Travels, *detailing the globe-spanning exploits of Lemuel Gulliver.*

🐣 **Puck** (PUHK) (English) He Is a Mischievous Demon

Oberon (OH-buh-rahn) (English) He Is the Noble Elfin Nation

In the play A Midsummer Night's Dream *(c. 1590) by the revered dramatist William Shakespeare, Puck is the mischievous sprite who uses enchantment to serve the mystic forest monarch Oberon.*

GIRLS

🐣 **Amelia** (ah-MEEL-yuh) (German) She Works Tirelessly

Dorothea (dor-uh-THEE-yah) (Latin) She Was Given to Us by God

Eliza (ee-LYE-zuh) (English) She Is the Little One Favored by God

Felicia (feh-LEE-see-yah) (Latin) She Is Greatly Favored

Frances (FRAN-siss) (English) She Is the Nation of France

Grizel (grih-ZEL) (Scottish) She Is a Wise Warrior

Henrietta (hen-ree-ET-tuh) (English) She Is the Little One Who Rules the Home

Hester (HESS-tur) (English) She Is a Brilliant Star

Mariana (mair-ee-AN-nuh) (Latin) She Is as Powerful as any Male

Matilda (mah-TIL-dah) (Swedish) She Is a Powerful Warrior

🕮 **Aphra** (AF-rah) (Hebrew) She Is the Land

Astrea (ah-STRAY-yah) (Greek) She Is a Brilliant Star

Aphra Behn (1640–1689) was a legendary spy for King Charles II. Aphra's undercover name was Astrea, a name she also used as a literary pseudonym. English author Virginia Woolf declared, "All women together ought to let flowers fall upon . . . Aphra Behn."

🕮 **Beatrix** (BEE-uh-trix) (Latin) She Is a Great Voyager

Renée (reh-NAY) (French) She Is Reborn in God

Beatrix Potter (1866–1943) was the English writer-illustrator of such children's classics as The Tale of Peter Rabbit. *And, though not an author, American actress Renée Zellweger gave a beautiful portrayal of Beatrix in the 2006 film* Miss Potter.

🕮 **Becky** (BEK-kee) (English/Hebrew) She Is the Little One Who Brings Us Closer

Amelia (uh-MEEL-yuh) (English) She Works Tirelessly

Becky Sharp is the cunning heroine of the 1847 satirical novel Vanity Fair *by William Makepeace Thackeray (1811–1863). Amelia Sedley is Becky's pure-hearted friend.*

🕮 **Clarissa** (kluh-RISS-suh) (Italian) She Is the Little One Who Shimmers with Fame

Darrell (DAIR-rel) (English) She Is Airelle, France

Felicity (fel-LISS-ih-tee) (English) She Is Good Fortune

Georgina (jor-JEE-nuh) (English) She Farms the Land

Gwendoline (GWEN-duh-lin) (Welsh) She Surrounds Us with Beauty

June (JOON) (English) She Is the Warm Summer Month of June

Maureen (maw-REEN) (Irish) She Is Our Little Beloved One

Mavis (MAY-vis) (English) She Is the Beautiful Song-Thrush

Molly (MAHL-lee) (English) She Is Our Little Beloved One

Wilhelmina (vil-hel-MEE-nah) (German) She Protects Humanity

🕮 **Gwyneth** (GWIH-neth) (Welsh) She Is Great Rejoicing

Gillian (JILL-ee-yun) (English) She Rules Heaven

Gwyneth Lewis (1959–) was the first National Poet for Wales, a position created in 2005 by the Welsh National Literature Promotion Agency. The current National Poet is Welsh poetess Gillian Clarke, known for 1971's Snow on the Mountain.

🕮 **Joumana** (joo-MAH-nah) (Arabic) She Is a Priceless Pearl

Elfriede (el-FREE-duh) (German) She Has the Powers of the Elfin People

Joumana Haddad (1970–) is the Lebanese author of such works as 1995's Time for a Dream. *Joumana is also a reporter for the An Nahar newspaper and has interviewed such writers as Austrian feminist Elfriede Jelinek, winner of 2004's Nobel Prize in Literature.*

🕮 **Li** (LEE) (Chinese) She Is Dawn's Beauty

Zhou (JOE) (Chinese) She Is Our Ship of Dreams

Li Qingzhao (A.D. 1084–c. A.D. 1151) is the greatest woman writer in the annals of Chinese literature, famed for such works as Jin Shi Lu. *Li's poems include paeans to the Zhou Dynasty (1122 B.C.–256 B.C.).*

🕮 **Lucy** (LOO-see) (English) She Is Radiance

Susan (SOO-zun) (English) She Is Our Fragrant Little Lotus Flower

Lucy Pevensie and her siblings Susan, Peter, and Edmund enter a wardrobe and discover the magic world of Narnia in the 1950 novel The Lion, the Witch, and the Wardrobe, *part of* The Chronicles of Narnia *series by C.S. Lewis (1898–1963).*

🕮 **Ophelia** (oh-FEEL-yah) (Greek) She Helps Us All

Gertrude (GUR-trood) (German) She Is a Powerful Weapon

Ophelia is the daughter of Danish statesman Polonius, in dramatist William Shakespeare's magnificent 1601 play Hamlet. *When Hamlet, the vengeful prince of Denmark, kills Ophelia's*

father, Ophelia drowns herself. Gertrude,
Hamlet's mother, fears her son almost as much
as she loves him.

BOYS AND GIRLS

🕊 **Alice** (AL-liss) (English) She Is Our Little
Aristocrat
Lewis (LOO-wiss) (English) He Is a Renowned
Warrior
  British mathematician Charles Lutwidge
  Dodgson (1832–1898), writing under the pseud-
  onym Lewis Carroll, debuted his masterpiece
  of children's literature, Alice's Adventures in
  Wonderland, *in 1865.*

🕊 **Iris** (EYE-ris) (Greek) She Is the Colorful
Rainbow
Elias (ee-LYE-yus) (Greek) His God Is the True
God
  Iris Murdoch (1919–1999) was an Irish-English
  writer noted for such books as 1954's Under the
  Net. *Iris's friend was English writer Elias Ca-*
  netti, winner of 1981's Nobel Prize in Literature.

🕊 **Jane** (JAIN) (English) Her God Is Gracious
Edward (ED-wurd) (English) He Is Our
Wealthy Protector
  Jane Eyre is the title character in Charlotte
  Brontë's 1847 masterpiece about an orphan who
  grows into a talented yet lonely woman. When
  she takes a position as governess to nobleman

Edward Rochester's ward Adèle, Jane discovers
redemptive love.

🕊 **Wilfrid** (WIL-frid) (English) He Wants Peace
Rebecca (reh-BEK-kuh) (Hebrew) She Brings
Us Closer
  In the 1819 novel Ivanhoe, *Scottish author Wal-*
  ter Scott (1771–1832) tells of Wilfrid of Ivanhoe,
  a Saxon knight who battles Norman conquerors
  in twelfth-century England. Rebecca is the
  beautiful Jewish healer whom Wilfrid adores.

🕊 **William** (WILL-yum) (English) He Protects
Humanity
Andronicus (an-DRAH-nih-kus) (Latin) He Is
Humanity's Triumph
Cressida (KRES-sih-duh) (Greek) She Is Pure
Gold
Hamlet (HAM-let) (Danish) He Is a Mighty
Prince
Macbeth (mak-BETH) (Scottish) He Descends
from the One Whose God Is Abundance
Othello (oh-THEL-lo) (Italian) He Is the
Renowned Little One
Tempest (TEM-pest) (English) She Is an
Unstoppable Storm
Timon (TYE-mun) (Greek) He Is the Illustrious
One
Titus (TYE-tus) (English) He Is a Title of Honor
Winter (WIN-tur) (English) She Is the Brisk
Winter Season

Name Pairs and Groups
from American Literature

BOYS

🖐 **Algernon** (AL-jur-nahn) (French) He Is the One with a Handsome Moustache
Auguste (oh-GHOOST) (French) He Is Absolutely Magnificent
Gray (GRAY) (English) He Is the Wise Gray-Haired One
Harrison (HAIR-uh-sun) (English) He Descends from Our Homeland's Great Ruler
Harry (HAIR-ree) (English) He Is Our Homeland's Great Ruler
King (KING) (English) He Is a Royal Monarch
Lincoln (English) He Is a Community Near a Lake
Mortimer (MOR-tih-mur) (English) He Is a Place of Peaceful Waters
Randy (RAN-dee) (English) He Is the Little Wolf with a Shield
Wolf (WULF) (German) He Is Our Courageous Little Wolf

🖐 **Faulkner** (FAWK-nur) (English) He Is the Master of Falcons
Anderson (AN-dur-sun) (English) He Descends from the Powerful Man
William Faulkner (1897–1962) was a great American novelist, winner of 1949's Nobel Prize in Literature for such works as 1926's The Sound and the Fury. *Faulkner's idol was writer Sherwood Anderson, author of the short-story collection* Winesburg, Ohio *(1919).*

🖐 **Herman** (HUR-mun) (Norwegian) He Is Aggressively Warlike

Nathaniel (nuh-THAN-yul) (Hebrew) He Is God's Divine Gift
Herman Melville (1819–1891) was one of the greatest writers in American literature, famed for his book Moby-Dick *about Captain Ahab and his manic quest for the gigantic white whale* Moby-Dick. *Herman befriended another great American writer, Nathaniel Hawthorne, author of* The Scarlet Letter.

🖐 **Ray** (RAY) (English) He Is the Little One Who Protects Us with Wise Counsel
Forrest (FOR-rest) (English) He Is a Verdant Wilderness
Ray Bradbury (1920–) is an American author whose powerful stories span many literary genres. In the 1930s, Ray's friend, Forrest Ackerman, introduced Ray to a larger audience for his now-beloved works such as The Martian Chronicles.

🖐 **Tom** (TAHM) (English) He Is Our Precious Little Twin
Huck (HUK) (English) He Is Our Sweet Little Huckleberry
Tom Sawyer and his friend Huckleberry Finn are mischievous Southern boys in the beloved 1876 novel The Adventures of Tom Sawyer, *written by famed American satirist Mark Twain (1835–1910).*

🖐 **Upton** (UP-tun) (English) He Is the Upper-Class Part of Town
Jurgis (YUR-ghiss) (Lithuanian) He Farms the Land
American author Upton Sinclair (1878–1968) is famed for his courageous 1906 novel The

Jungle, *which tells of immigrant Jurgis Rudkis's struggle for survival in nineteenth-century Chicago. The* Jungle *spurred passage of Congress's 1906 Pure Food and Drug Act.*

GIRLS

🕮 **Anne** (ANN) (English) She Is Graceful

Evelyn (EV-uh-lin) (English) She Is Beloved
The adored 1908 American novel Anne of Green Gables *tells of the orphan Anne Shirley, a fiery redhead. Author Lucy Montgomery (1874–1942) used a magazine photograph of dancer Evelyn Nesbit as a model for her heroine Anne.*

🕮 **Edna** (ED-nuh) (Hebrew) She Rejoices

Marianne (mair-ee-ANN) (French) She Is Graceful and Beloved
Edna St. Vincent Millay (1892–1950) was an American poetess known for such works as Renascence. *In 1943, Edna became the second female winner of the American Poetry Society's Frost Medal. Another Frost Medal recipient was the poetess Marianne Moore.*

🕮 **Emily** (EM-ih-lee) (English) She Is Powerfully Competitive

Mabel (MAY-bul) (English) She Is Adorable
Emily Dickinson (1830–1886) was a nineteenth-century American poetess whose heartfelt stanzas distinguished her work from much of the era's florid verse. Emily's poetry was published posthumously by her friend Mabel Loomis Todd.

🕮 **Gertrude** (GUR-trood) (German) She Is a Powerful Weapon

Mina (MEE-nah) (Sanskrit) She Is a Divine Helmet of Protection
Gertrude Stein (1874–1946) was an American writer known for The Autobiography of Alice B. Toklas. *Gertrude's tutelage of writers such as poetess Mina Loy, author of* Lunar Baedecker, *helped foment a golden era of American literature.*

🕮 **Louisa** (loo-EE-zuh) (English) She Is a Helmet of Protection

Jo (JO) (English) She Is the Little One Whose Greatness Increases
Louisa May Alcott (1832–1888) was an American author revered for her 1868 book Little Women *about a family trying to survive the Civil War. The book's heroine is Jo March, who conquers her temper and learns wisdom.*

🕮 **Sara** (SAIR-rah) (Hebrew) She Is a Majestic Princess

Becky (BEK-kee) (Hebrew) She Is the Little One Who Brings Us Closer
In the 1905 novel A Little Princess *by Frances Hodgson Burnett (1849–1924), little Sara Crewe's father dies in India. Sara becomes a maid in Miss Minchin's school, where she befriends the servant-girl Becky. Together they learn that every girl is a princess.*

🕮 **Toni** (TOH-nee) (English) She Is Our Little Blossoming Flower

Oprah (OPE-ruh) (American) She Is the Beautiful Nape of the Human Neck
Toni Morrison (1931–) is an African-American winner of the 1993 Nobel Prize for Literature, for such novels as Beloved—*made into a 1998 film by Oprah Winfrey, the popular African-American host of television's* The Oprah Winfrey Show.

BOYS AND GIRLS

🕮 **Atticus** (AT-tih-kus) (Latin) He Is Attica, Greece

Jean (JEEN) (English) Her God Is Gracious
Atticus Finch is the Depression-era attorney whose Southern town is rocked by race hatred in the revered American novel To Kill a Mockingbird, *by Harper Lee. Jean Louise Finch is Atticus's daughter, whom everyone calls Scout; together, Atticus and Jean begin a journey of profound moral discovery.*

🕮 **Carrie** (KAIR-ree) (English) She Is a Mighty Warrior

Charles (CHARLZ) (English) He Is a Mighty Warrior
Carrie Meeker leaves Wisconsin for Chicago, moving from a factory job to a high-society marriage, in the 1900 novel Sister Carrie *by Theodore Dreiser (1871–1945). Charles Drouet is Carrie's first love, a man she ultimately betrays.*

🕮 **Conan** (KO-nan) (Irish) He Is a Courageous Wolf

Sonja (SOWN-yuh) (German) She Is Wise and Beloved
Conan the Barbarian is the most recognized warrior in the annals of fantasy literature. Robert Howard (1906–1936), an American pulp-fiction writer, debuted Conan in 1932, along with the beautiful sword-wielding Red Sonja in 1934.

𝒫 **Edgar** (ED-gur) (English) He Is a Powerful
Weapon
Raven (RAY-ven) (English) She Is an Ebony-
Black Raven
*Edgar Allan Poe (1809–1849) was a complex
American author who penned suspenseful
stories such as* The Tell-Tale Heart. *Edgar also
penned brilliant poems such as* The Raven,
about an unexpected midnight visitor.

𝒫 **Gwendolyn** (GWEN-doh-lin) (Welsh) She Is
Beautifully Fair
Langston (LANGZ-tun) (English) He Is a Town
with Long Streets
*Gwendolyn Brooks (1917–2000) was an African-
American poet whose works delved into black
life-experiences, such as 1945's* A Street in
Bronzeville. *Gwendolyn's mother introduced
her to the great Harlem Renaissance poet
Langston Hughes, creator of such works as
1943's* Freedom's Plow.

𝒫 **Harper** (HAR-pur) (English) She Plays the
Harp Beautifully
Truman (TROO-mun) (English) He Is
Trustworthy

*American author Harper Lee (1926–) wrote a
twentieth-century masterpiece, 1960's* To Kill
a Mockingbird, *tracing Jean Louise "Scout"
Finch's extraordinary story of race relations
in 1930s America. Harper's dear friend was
novelist Truman Capote, known for* In Cold
Blood *(1966).*

𝒫 **Horatio** (hor-RAY-shee-oh) (Latin) He Is a
Man for all Seasons
Pearl (PURL) (English) She Is a Priceless Pearl
*Horatio Alger (1832–1899) was the prolific
American author of rags-to-riches novels. The
Horatio Alger Society, founded in Horatio's
honor in 1947, has assisted the careers of such
luminaries as Pearl S. Buck, winner of the 1932
Nobel Prize in Literature.*

𝒫 **Maya** (MYE-yuh) (Sanskrit) She Is Our
Dream-Girl
Bill (BILL) (English) He Is Our Little Protector
*Maya Angelou (1928–) is a lauded African-
American poetess who was asked to read her
poem* On the Pulse of Morning *at the 1993
inauguration of President Bill Clinton.*

Name Pairs and Groups
from Greek Literature, Mythology, and History

BOYS

🖋 **Achilles** (uh-KILL-leez) (Greek) He Is the Nation's Conscience

Hector (HEK-tor) (Greek) He Stands His Ground
Achilles was the war-hero whom the Greek poet Homer (eighth century B.C.) wrote of in his epic The Iliad. *Achilles slew Hector, a prince of Troy, during the Trojan War.*

🖋 **Aeschylus** (ES-kuh-lus) (Greek) He Has a Burning Conscience

Chronos (KRO-nohss) (Greek) He Is Time Itself
The Greek playwright Aeschylus (c. 525 B.C.-c. 455 B.C.) wrote in his tragedy Prometheus Bound *about self-created Chronos, god of time, who "teaches all things."*

🖋 **Aesop** (EE-sup) (Greek) He Is the African with a Dark Complexion

Phaedrus (FEE-drus) (Latin) He Is Radiant
Aesop (620 B.C.-560 B.C.), who may have been African, was history's greatest teller of fables, many involving African animals little-known in Greece. The Roman writer Phaedrus wrote down Aesop's fables in Latin in the first century A.D. Since then, the fables have been translated into countless languages.

🖋 **Agamemnon** (ag-uh-MEM-non) (Greek) He Is Mightily Determined

Orestes (or-ES-teez) (Greek) He Is a Mountain
The Greek warrior King Agamemnon returned from the ten-year-long Trojan War as a conqueror. But because Agamemnon had slain his daughter Iphigenia before the war, Agamem-
non's son Orestes slew Agamemnon upon his return to Greece.

🖋 **Akron** (AK-rahn) (Greek) He Is a Mountain

Simonides (sye-MAHN-ih-deez) (Greek) He Has a Prominent Nose
Akron (fifth century B.C.) was a respected Greek physician. The poet Simonides wrote Akron's final epitaph, commenting on Akron's service to humanity.

🖋 **Alexander** (al-ex-AN-dur) (Greek) He Protects Humanity

Philip (FIL-ip) (Greek) He Befriends Horses
Alexander the Great of Macedon (356 B.C.-323 B.C.) conquered much of the world in the fourth century B.C. Alexander's father, Philip II, taught his son to be a wise ruler.

🖋 **Antiochus** (an-TYE-uh-kus) (Greek) He Surpasses all Our Ancestors

Timarchus (tim-AR-kus) (Greek) He Is Honor
Antiochus II Theos (286 B.C.–246 B.C.) ruled the Seleucid Empire, which arose after the Macedonian conqueror Alexander the Great died in 323 B.C. Antiochus gained his subjects' respect after defeating the conqueror Timarchus, ruler of Miletus.

🖋 **Apollodorus** (uh-pah-luh-DOH-rus) (Greek) He Is Apollo's Gift

Pontus (PAHN-tus) (Greek) He Is the Blue Ocean
Greek historian Apollodorus (c. 180 B.C.–c. 120 B.C.) wrote in his Library (Bibliotheca) *that the god Pontus personified the ocean encircling the world.*

🄰 **Archilochus** (ar-KIL-uh-kus) (Greek) He Leads the People

Alcman (ALK-mun) (Greek) He Is the Silvery Moon

Archilochus (c. 680 B.C.–c. 645 B.C.) was a Greek warrior-poet. Instead of writing about heroes, Archilochus wrote about common people, as did his contemporary, Alcman, who specialized in writing hymns to be sung by women's choirs.

🄰 **Archimedes** (ar-kuh-MEE-deez) (Greek) He Is a Genius

Isidore (IZ-ih-dor) (Greek) He Is a Gift from Isis, the Earth Mother

Archimedes (c. 287 B.C.–c. 212 B.C.) was a Greek scientist whose inventions—such as the Archimedes Screw that carried water uphill—gained him eternal fame. Archimedes's achievements were chronicled by the scientist Isidore of Miletus.

🄰 **Ares** (AIR-reez) (Greek) He Is Powerfully Male

Deimos (DAY-mohs) (Greek) He Scatters His Enemies

Ares was Greek god of war, who raced onto countless bloody battlefields drawn in his war-chariot by meat-eating horses. Accompanied by his two generals, Deimos (Terror) and Phobos (Rout), Ares was one of the most dreaded of all the gods.

🄰 **Arion** (AIR-ee-yon) (Greek) He Is Superior

Terpander (tur-PAN-dur) (Greek) He Is Delightful

Arion (seventh century B.C.) was the Greek poet who created the song known as a dithyramb, a religious hymn to Dionysus, god of wine. One of Arion's contemporaries was Terpander, another famed poet.

🄰 **Aristophanes** (air-uh-STAH-fuh-neez) (Greek) He Is Obviously Best

Cleon (KLEE-yon) (Greek) He Is Eternal Glory

Aristophanes (c. 456 B.C.–386 B.C.) was a Greek playwright who is acknowledged as the greatest of all Greek comedy-writers. Aristophanes came from the same region as the Athenian general Cleon, a character often portrayed in Aristophanes's plays.

🄰 **Aristotle** (air-ih-STAH-tul) (Greek) He Has the Best Ambitions

Pythias (PITH-ee-yus) (Greek) He Is from Pythia

Aristotle (384 B.C.–322 B.C.) was one of the greatest of all Greek philosophers. A student of legendary Plato, Aristotle arguably influenced medieval Europe more than any other scholar. Aristotle married Princess Pythias of Atarneus.

🄰 **Athos** (ATH-ohss) (Greek) He Is Mount Athos

Alexandros (al-ex-AN-drohss) (Greek) He Protects Humanity

The god Athos personified Mount Athos in Thrace (present-day Bulgaria). Mount Athos was once considered by Alexandros—Alexander the Great—as a perfect site for a monument to his own glory. Instead, a Christian monastery stands there.

🄰 **Callicrates** (kuh-LIK-kruh-teez) (Greek) He Is Beautifully Powerful

Ictinus (IK-tih-nus) (Greek) He Is Loyal

Callicrates and Ictinus (both fifth century B.C.) were architects who designed one of humanity's greatest monuments, the Parthenon, located on the Acropolis in Athens.

🄰 **Careteron** (CAR-tur-rahn) (Greek) He Is Carteron, Greece

Melaineus (muh-LAY-nee-yus) (Greek) He Is Melaineai, Greece

King Lycaon of Arcadia, Greece, had fifty sons. among them the proud warrior Melaineus. However, when Lycaon offended Zeus, high king of the gods, Zeus transformed Lycaon into a wolf and slew his sons. Their legacy was the fifty magnificent Greek cities they founded.

🄰 **Clement** (KLEM-ment) (Greek) He Is Compassionate

Charmus (CHAR-mus, SHAR-mus) (Greek) He Is Happiness

Saint Clement (c. A.D. 150–c. A.D. 215) was a Greek who rose through the ranks of Egypt's Christian church to become a noted moralist. In his Exhortation to the Greeks Clement condemned the warrior Charmus for erecting a temple to Eros, god of love.

🄰 **Corethon** (KOR-uh-thahn) (Greek) He Is Korethon, Greece

Physios (FIZ-ee-yohss) (Greek) He Is Physios, Greece

King Lycaon of Arcadia, Greece, had fifty sons, among them the proud warriors Corethon and Physios. However, when Lycaon offended Zeus, high king of the gods, Zeus transformed Lycaon

into a wolf and slew his sons. Their legacy was the fifty magnificent Greek cities they founded.

🕊 **Croesus** (KREE-sus) (Greek) He Is Masterful
Cyrus (SYE-rus) (Greek) He Is the All-Seeing Sun
Croesus (595 B.C.–c. 547 B.C.) was the wealthy ruler of Lydia (present-day Turkey). Croesus made war on the Persian armies of Cyrus the Great, but was defeated.

🕊 **Daedalus** (DED-uh-lus) (Greek) He Is Ingenious
Icarus (IK-uh-rus) (Greek) He Is Loyal
Daedalus was a Greek engineer who built the Labyrinth, a stone maze, for King Minos of Crete to hold the monstrous Minotaur. Minos then imprisoned Daedalus and his son Icarus, but Daedalus crafted feathered wings, and he and Icarus flew off. Sadly, Icarus flew too close to the sun despite his father's warnings, and fell to his death.

🕊 **Damocles** (DAM-uh-kleez) (Greek) He Is the Nation's Glory
Timaeus (tih-MAY-yus) (Greek) He Is Magnificent Honor
Greek historian Timaeus (c. 345 B.C.–250 B.C.) told of the Sword of Damocles. Damocles persuaded King Dionysius II of Syracuse to make him king for a day. Damocles enjoyed his role, but when he looked up and saw a sword hanging by a thread, he abandoned his royal ambitions.

🕊 **Damon** (DAY-mun) (Greek) He Causes Others to Become Gentle
Pythias (PITH-ee-yus) (Greek) He Is from Pythia, Greece
Damon and Pythias were students of the Greek philosopher Pythagoras. When the two visited Sicily, King Dionysus I imprisoned Pythias on fraudulent charges. Damon rescued Pythias, then Pythias rescued him in turn.

🕊 **Damysus** (DAM-uh-sus) (Latin) He Is The Mighty Conqueror
Enceladus (Latin) He Leads the Charge
Mimas (MYE-mus) (Latin) He Imitates Marvelously
Mylinus (MYE-lin-nus) (Latin) He Is a Mighty Rock
Olympus (oh-LIM-pus) (Latin) He Is Mount Olympus
Orion (oh-RYE-yun) (Greek) He Is the Water of a Man

Pallas (PAL-lus) (Greek) He Brandishes a Weapon
Polybotes (puh-LIB-uh-teez) (Latin) He Is Fertility
Porphyrion (por-FIH-ree-yun) (Greek) His Strength Surges On
Theodamas (thee-uh-DAY-mus) (Latin) He Submits to God's Power
The Gigantes—including Damysus, Enceladus, Mimas, Mylinus, Olympus, Orion, Pallas, Polybotes, Porphyrion, and Theodamas—were the hundred monstrous giants who, despite their strength, failed in their rebellion against Zeus, high king of Greek gods.

🕊 **Democles** (DEM-uh-kleez) (Greek) He Is the Nation's Glory
Lycurgus (lye-SUR-jus) (Greek) He Is a Courageous Wolf
Democles (fourth century B.C.) was a Greek orator whose chief fame was his defense of the family of the statesman Lycurgus against slander.

🕊 **Democritus** (duh-MAH-krih-tus) (Greek) He Judges the People
Epicurus (ep-ih-KYOO-rus) (Greek) He Is a Trusted Ally
Democritus (c. 460 B.C.–c. 370 B.C.) was a Greek philosopher who invented the atomic theory, that matter is made of tiny units called atoms. Democritus was influenced by Epicurus, a philosopher who counseled moderation in the pursuit of happiness.

🕊 **Demetrius** (duh-MEE-tree-yus) (Greek) He Is Like Demeter, the Earth Mother
Antigonus (an-TIG-uh-nus) (Greek) He Surpasses Our Ancestors
Demetrius II (276 B.C.–229 B.C.) was a king of Macedon, the Greek-influenced nation which produced the military conqueror Alexander the Great, Demtrius's ancestor. Indeed, Demtrius's father, Antigonus, had been one of Alexander's most trusted generals.

🕊 **Deucalion** (doo-KAY-lee-yun) (Greek) He Is Our Voyager Who Brings Back New Wines
Endymion (en-DIM-mee-yun) (Greek) He Enters Boldly
Deucalion ruled Thessaly, a Greek province. Endymion was Deucalion's descendant, a prince who gained immortality from Zeus, high king of Greek gods.

🎭 **Dinocrates** (dye-NAH-kruh-teez) (Greek) He Is Fiercely Powerful

Arrian (AIR-ree-yun) (Greek) He Is Supremely Blessed

The Greek writer Arrian wrote of the architect Dinocrates (fourth century B.C.), a genius who erected a temple in Babylon for the Macedonian conqueror Alexander the Great.

🎭 **Dion** (DEE-yahn) (Greek) He Is God's Little Mountain

Dionysius (di-oh-NYE-see-yus) (Greek) He is God's Mountain

Dion I (408 B.C.–354 B.C.) ruled the island of Sicily and was a student of the Greek philosopher Plato. Dion's father was King Dionysius I.

🎭 **Dionysus** (dye-uh-NYE-sis) (Greek) He Speaks Clearly

Pentheus (PEN-thee-us) (Greek) He Understands Sorrow

Dionysus was the god of wine, born from the thigh of his father, King Zeus of the Olympian gods. Pentheus was Dionysus's cousin, king of the Greek city-state of Thebes.

🎭 **Elisson** (EL-ihss-sun) (Greek) He Is the Elisson River, Greece

Selemnus (suh-LEM-nus) (Greek) He Is the Selemnus River, Greece

Elisson personified the Elisson River in the town of Akhaia, Greece. Elisson's parallel river in Akhaia was the Selemnus, personified by the god Selemnus.

🎭 **Euclid** (YOO-klid) (Greek) He Is Glory

Proclus (PRO-klus) (Latin) He Understands Sorrow

Euclid (fourth century B.C.) founded geometry, the study of shapes and volume. Euclid's works were critiqued by the Roman philosopher Proclus (A.D. 412–A.D. 485), known for his maxim, "Where there is number, there is beauty."

🎭 **Euphronius** (yoo-FRO-nee-yus) (Greek) He Is Delightful

Antaeus (an-TAY-yus) (Greek) He Is Aggressive

Euphronius (c. 535 B.C.–470 B.C.) was an Athenian ceramicist famous for his methods of firing red clay. One of Euphronius's greatest works was his chalice depicting the giant Antaeus battling the warrior Heracles.

🎭 **Euripides** (yoo-RIP-puh-deez) (Greek) He Swings Mightily

Sophocles (SAHF-uh-kleez) (Greek) His Genius Brings Glory

Euripides (c. 480 B.C.–406 B.C.) was one of the greatest dramatists of his age, whose play The Trojan Women (Troades) attests to his genius. Euripides shared the spotlight with Sophocles, author of Oedipus the King (Oedipus Rex), another masterpiece.

🎭 **Galen** (GAY-len) (Greek) He Is Peaceful

Aesculapius (es-kyoo-LAY-pee-yus) (Latin) He Performs Surgery with a Scalpel

Galen (A.D. 129–c. A.D. 200) was Greece's greatest medical practitioner. Galen studied for years in Pergamon's Temple of Aesculapius, god of medicine.

🎭 **Griffin** (GRIF-fin) (Greek) He Is a Noble Prince

Alpheus (AL-fee-yus) (Latin) He Is the Alpheus River

Greek historian Strabo (c. 63 B.C.–c. 24 A.D.) wrote in The Geography (Geographica) that near the Alpheus River in Arcadia, fierce Griffins—part lion, part eagle—were depicted in paintings in the Temple of Artemis.

🎭 **Haimon** (HAY-mun) (Greek) He Is Haimoniai, Greece

Kromos (KRO-mohss) (Greek) He Is Kromoi, Greece

King Lycaon of Arcadia, Greece, had fifty sons, including the warriors Haimon and Kromos. However, when Lycaon offended Zeus, high king of the gods, Zeus transformed Lycaon into a wolf and slew his sons. Their legacy was the fifty magnificent Greek cities they founded.

🎭 **Helios** (HEE-lee-ohss) (Greek) He Is the Radiant Sun

Hyperion (hye-PEER-ee-yun) (Greek) He Safeguards Us from Above

Helios was the Sun, pulled in a golden chariot across Heaven each day by the fiery steeds of Apollo, god of prophecy. Hyperion, god of light, was Helios's father.

🎭 **Heracles** (HAIR-uh-kleez) (Greek) He Is Hera's Glory

Theseus (THEE-soos) (Greek) He Builds a Foundation

Heracles (Hercules to the Romans) was Greece's greatest demigod hero. Heracles's friend, King Theseus of Athens, convinced Heracles to perform the Twelve Labors, among them slaying

the evil Hydra, and battling Cerberus, Hound of Hades.

🖎 **Herodotus** (hur-RAH-duh-tus) (Greek) His Heart Is Heroic

Anacreon (uh-NAK-kree-yon) (Greek) He Speaks for the Nobility

Herodotus (c. 484 B.C.–c. 425 B.C.), a historian from the Greek city of Halicarnassus, gathered information about the known world. In The Histories (Historiae), *Herodotus tells of the Greek lyric poet and philosopher Anacreon.*

🖎 **Homer** (HO-mur) (Greek) He Pledges Loyalty

Hesiod (HEZ-ee-yud) (Greek) He Spreads Songs Among Us

Homer (ninth century B.C.) was the poet who wrote The Iliad, *about the ten-year war between the Greeks and Trojans; and* The Odyssey, *the story of King Odysseus's ten-year voyage from Troy back to his wife and son. The next great poet to follow Homer was Hesiod, who wrote* The Theogony, *about divine lineages.*

🖎 **Hyginus** (HYE-jih-nus) (Latin) He Is Robust

Cygnus (SIG-nus) (Greek) He Is a Graceful Swan

Hyginus (c. 64 B.C.–A.D. 17) was the Roman author of the Fables (Fabulae), *a book of myths such as that of Cygnus, outlaw of Pagasia, who perished in a duel with the demigod Heracles and was transformed into a swan.*

🖎 **Leonidas** (lee-uh-NYE-dus) (Greek) He Is the Son of the Lion

Simonides (sih-MAH-nuh-deez) (Greek) He Has a Magnificent Nose

King Leonidas I of Sparta (fifth century B.C.) and his 300 Spartans died at the Battle of Thermopylae, repelling Persian invaders. The poet Simonides later wrote, "Go tell the Spartans, stranger passing by, that here, obedient to their laws, we lie."

🖎 **Lycius** (lye-SEE-yus) (Greek) He Is Lykios, Greece

Phineus (FIN-ee-yus) (Greek) He Is Phineus, Greece

King Lycaon of Arcadia, Greece, had fifty sons, including the warriors Lycius and Phineus. However, when Lycaon offended Zeus, high king of the gods, Zeus transformed Lycaon into a wolf and slew his sons. Their legacy was the fifty magnificent Greek cities they founded.

🖎 **Lysander** (lye-SAN-dur) (Greek) He Liberates Humanity

Cornelius (kor-NEE-lee-yus) (Latin) He Is a Cornucopia of Plenty

Lysander (?–395 B.C.) was a Spartan commander who defeated the Athenians at the Battle of Aegospotami in 405 B.C. Lysander's exploits were chronicled in The Life of Eminent Greeks *by Roman historian Cornelius Nepos (c. 100 B.C.–24 B.C.).*

🖎 **Matton** (MAT-tun) (Greek) He Kneads Bread Dough

Athenaeus (uh-THEE-nee-yus) (Greek) He Shows Wisdom

Matton was a demigod, the Spartan deity of baking. The Greek historian Athenaeus, in his chronicle Deipnosophistae, *describes statues being erected in Spartan dining halls to honor Matton.*

🖎 **Memnon** (MEM-nahn) (Greek) He Is Loyal

Mentor (MEN-tor) (Greek) He Is Marvelously Spirited

Memnon (380 B.C.–333 B.C.) was a Greek mercenary employed by Emperor Darius III of Persia. In 334 B.C. Memnon led his forces to victory at the Granicus River in present-day Turkey. Memnon's brother Mentor was a great soldier in his own right.

🖎 **Morpheus** (MOR-fee-yus) (Greek) He Shapes Our Dreams

Ovid (AH-vid) (Latin) He Is a Gentle Sheep

Morpheus was the god of dreams, who placed divine messages in people's minds. He is lauded in the Metamorphoses *of the Roman poet Ovid (43 B.C.–A.D. 17) as the god who brought dreams to Agamemnon, hero of the Trojan War.*

🖎 **Myron** (MYE-rahn) (Greek) He Is a Fragrant Myrrh Tree

Callimachus (kuh-LIM-uh-kus) (Greek) He Is a Beautiful Warrior

Myron (c. 480 B.C.–440 B.C.) was the Greek sculptor responsible for such bronze statues as the Discus Thrower (Discobolos). *Myron's contemporary was the sculptor Callimachus, creator of the* Venus Genetrix.

🖎 **Nephalion** (neh-FAYL-yun) (Greek) He Is White Clouds

Khryses (KRYE-seez) (Greek) He Is Pure Gold

Prince Nephalion of Crete, an island near Greece, joined his brothers Khryses, Eurymedon, and Philolaus in an unsuccessful battle against the demigod Heracles.

🖉 **Nestor** (NES-tur) (Greek) He Always
Returns Home
Poseidon (po-SYE-dun) (Greek) He Is the King
of the Oceans
*Nestor ruled the city of Pylos. Nestor's grand-
father was Poseidon, god of the oceans, and
brother of Zeus, high king of Greek gods.*

🖉 **Odysseus** (oh-DIS-soos) (Greek) He Is
Hatred
Ulysses (yoo-LEESS-seez) (Latin) He Is Hatred
*King Odysseus of Ithaca won the Trojan War by
conceiving of the Trojan Horse. The Greeks built
a huge horse, symbol of Troy, then pretended to
flee. When the Trojans pulled the horse inside
Troy's walls, soldiers emerged by night and
burned Troy.*

🖉 **Orontes** (or-AHN-teez) (Greek) He Is the
Orontes River
Euphrates (yoo-FRAY-teez) (Greek) He Is the
Euphrates River
*Orontes was the river-god who personified the
Orontes River in the city-state of Antioch. The
nearby Euphrates River was personified by the
god Euphrates.*

🖉 **Paris** (PAIR-us) (Greek) He Is a Stone Wall
Troy (TROY) (English) He Is the Legendary City
of Troy
*Paris was a Prince of Troy, a walled city-state.
After Paris visited King Menelaus of Sparta,
he seduced Menelaus's wife Helen, the world's
loveliest woman. Helen fled with Paris to Troy,
sparking the ten-year Trojan War that destroyed
the city.*

🖉 **Parmenion** (par-MEN-ee-yun) (Greek) He
Is Loyal
Bryaxis (brye-AX-siss) (Greek) She Is Heaven
*Parmenion (fourth century B.C.) was a Greek
engineer hired by the conqueror Alexander the
Great to design the city of Alexandria, Egypt.
Bryaxis (c. 372 B.C.–c. 312 B.C.) was Parmeni-
on's colleague, an architect who designed the
Mausoleum of Maussollos at Halicarnassus, one
of the Seven Wonders of the World.*

🖉 **Patrocles** (PAT-tro-kleez) (Greek) He Is His
Father's Glory
Sarpedon (SAR-peh-dahn) (Greek) His Flesh Is
Made from Earth
*During the Trojan War between Greece and
Troy, the Greek hero Achilles stopped fighting
because he was furious with Agamemnon,
the Greeks' leader. Achilles's friend Patrocles*

*donned Achilles's armor, but was slain by Prince
Hector of Troy.*

🖉 **Pelops** (PEL-lups) (Greek) He Has Beautiful
Dark Eyes
Neptunus (NEP-tyoon-nus) (Latin) He Rules
the Oceans
*King Pelops of the Greek city-state of Pisa gave
his name to Greece's Peloponnesian Peninsula.
Pelops was slain by his father Tantalos, yet was
divinely resurrected. Eventually, Neptunus, god
of the seas, became Pelops's benefactor.*

🖉 **Periander** (pair-ee-AN-dur) (Greek) He
Travels among the Aegean Islands
Lucian (LOO-shee-yin) (Latin) He Is Radiance
*Periander ruled the city of Corinth and was one
of the Seven Sages, the wisest men of antiquity.
Periander's life is chronicled in the Dialogues of
the Sea Gods, by the Roman scholar Lucian (c.
A.D. 125–A.D. 180).*

🖉 **Pericles** (PAIR-uh-kleez) (Greek) He Is
Incredibly Glorious
Plutarch (PLOO-tark) (Greek) He Is the Source
of Good Fortune
*Plutarch (A.D. 46–A.D. 120) was a Greek biogra-
pher whose book Pericles honored the life of the
Athenian ruler Pericles, founder of the Athenian
Empire.*

🖉 **Phales** (FAY-leez) (Greek) He Is a Mighty
Masculine Organ
Tychon (TYE-kahn) (Greek) He Produces
Much
*Phales was a deity of Greece's woodlands. He
carried a representation of a male member
during parades dedicated to Dionysus, god
of wine. Tychon was another nature-deity
who carried statues of the god of travelers,
Hermes.*

🖉 **Phidias** (FID-ee-yus) (Greek) He Is Devoted
Paulus (PAWL-lus) (Latin) He Demonstrates
Humility
*Phidias (fifth century B.C.) was a legendary
Greek sculptor who created one of the Seven
Wonders of the World, the giant statue of Zeus
in Olympia. When Roman general Lucius
Aemilius Paulus saw the monument, he was
"moved to his soul."*

🖉 **Philo** (FYE-lo) (Greek) He Loves with all
His Heart
Vitruvius (vih-TROO-vee-yus) (Latin) He Is a
Mighty Weapon

Vitruvius (c. 80 B.C.–70 B.C.) was a Roman engineer who wrote On Architecture (De Architectura)*, detailing the lives of great men such as the architect Philo of Athens, who designed the Hall of the Mysteries in Eleusis.*

Pindar (PIN-dahr) (Greek) He Is from Mount Pindos, Greece

Alcaeus (al-KEE-us) (Greek) He Is Powerful
Of all the Greek lyric poets whose works were meant to reproduce the power of music, the greatest was Pindar (c. 522 B.C.–443 B.C.). Pindar's contemporary was Alcaeus, whose poetry glorified combat.

Polichus (PAH-lih-kus) (Greek) He Is Polikhos, Greece

Acontes (ah-KAHN-teez) (Greek) He Is Akontes, Greece
King Lycaon of Arcadia, Greece, had fifty sons, including the warriors Polichus and Acontes. However, when Lycaon offended Zeus, high king of the gods, Zeus transformed Lycaon into a wolf and slew his sons. Their legacy was the fifty magnificent Greek cities they founded.

Praxagoras (prax-uh-GOR-rus) (Greek) He Practices among the People

Diocles (DYE-uh-kleez) (Greek) He Is the Glory of Heaven's King
Praxagoras (c. 340 B.C.–?) was a Greek physician who followed the teachings of the great Greek physician Hippocrates. Praxagoras's contemporary was the physician Diocles of Carystus.

Pythagoras (pih-THAG-uh-rus) (Greek) He Is from the Pythian Marketplace

Milo (MYE-lo) (Latin) He Is a Great Warrior
Pythagoras (c. 580 B.C.–500 B.C.) was the mathematician remembered for the Pythagorean Theorem, describing the properties of right triangles. Pythagoras's devoted disciple was Milo of Croton, Greece's most admired wrestler.

Quintus (KWIN-tus) (Latin) He Is Fifth

Diomedes (dye-AH-muh-deez) (Greek) He Is the King of Thrace
Quintus Smyrnaeus (fourth century A.D.) was a Greek poet who wrote epics such as the Posthomerica, *about the Trojan War. Quintus also wrote about the legendary King Diomedes of Thrace.*

Rufus (ROO-fus) (Latin) He Has Fiery Red Hair

Ephesus (EF-uh-sus) (Greek) He Is the Cayster River, Greece

Rufus (first century A.D.) was a Greek physician born in Ephesus, which was named after Ephesus, son of the river god Cayster.

Satyrus (SAT-ur-rus) (Greek) He Is the Spirit of Nature

Pytheos (PIH-thee-ohss) (Greek) He Is Pythias, Greece
Greek builders Satyrus and Pytheos (both fourth century B.C.) erected the Mausoleum of Maussollos at Halicarnassus, one of the Seven Wonders of the World.

Sauros (SOR-rohss) (Greek) He Is a Powerful Serpent

Alpheus (AL-fee-yus) (Greek) He Is the Alpheus River, Greece
Sauros was an outlaw who robbed travelers near the Alpheus River. The warrior-hero Heracles ended Sauros's career.

Scylax (SKYE-lax, SIL-lax) (Greek) He Is an Aggressive Fighter

Indus (IN-dus) (Greek) He Is the Indus River, India
Scylax (sixth century B.C.) was a Greek navigator dispatched by Persian Emperor Darius I to survey the Indus River, which was personified by the River-god Indus.

Shai (SHAY) (Greek) She Is Destined

Zeus (ZOOS) (Greek) He Rules Heaven
The Greeks appropriated Shai, Egyptian god of destiny, calling him Agathodaemon, or the Excellent God. The historian Pausanias (second century A.D.) wrote in Description of Greece *that Agathodaemon was a title for Zeus, high king of the gods.*

Simmias (SIM-mee-yus) (Greek) He Listens Intently

Phaedo (FAY-doh) (Greek) He Is Radiant
Simmias (fifth century B.C.) was a Greek philosopher who followed the teachings of his master Socrates. Another of Socrates's students, Plato, wrote in his book Phaedo *about Phaedo of Elis, a student who witnessed Socrates's demise.*

Socrates (SAH-kruh-teez) (Greek) He Is Powerful

Plato (PLAY-toh) (Greek) He Has Broad Shoulders
Socrates (469 B.C.–399 B.C.) was the greatest of all Greek philosophers. His ideas on morality influenced philosophers for centuries. Socrates's greatest disciple was Plato.

Strabo (STRAH-bo) (Greek) His Eyes See Differently

Sostratus (SAHSS-truh-tus) (Greek) He Is the Greatest Warrior

Strabo (c. 63 B.C.–c. A.D. 24) was a Greek historian who chronicled Greece's greatest legends, including the story of Sostratus, a soldier who assisted the demigod warrior Heracles during his battles.

Straton (STRA-ton) (Greek) He Is a Mighty Army

Maximus (MAX-ih-mus) (Latin) He Is Supreme

Straton (third century A.D.), a poet from the Greek city-state of Sardis, was famed for his love-poems. Centuries later, the fourteenth-century Greek scholar Maximus Planudes included Straton in his anthology Florilegium Diversorum Epigrammatum.

Theocritus (thee-AH-krih-tus) (Greek) He Is a Divine Judge

Corydon (KOR-ih-dun) (Greek) He Wears the Helmet of Victory

The Greek poet Theocritus (c. 310 B.C.–250 B.C.) wrote poems about shepherds. Theocritus often used the name Corydon in his poems to refer to a shepherd boy, tending his flocks while surrounded by nature.

Theodorus (thee-uh-DOR-rus) (Greek) He Is God's Divine Gift

Rhoecus (REE-kus) (Greek) He Is a Slayer of Fierce Bulls

Theodorus and Rhoecus (both sixth century B.C.) were Greek engineers from the Ionian island of Samos. These geniuses were the first Greeks to melt and refine bronze.

Theodosius (thee-uh-DOH-shuhss) (Latin) He Makes Offerings to God

Libanius (lye-BAY-nee-yus) (Latin) He Is an Offering to the Gods

Libanius (c. A.D. 314–A.D. 394) was a Greek educator from a noble family of the city-state of Antioch. Libanius counted among his friends Emperor Theodosius I, ruler of the Byzantine Empire from A.D. 378–A.D. 392.

Troilus (TROY-lus) (Latin) He Is the Little One Who Brings an End to Troy's Glory

Priam (PRYE-yum) (Greek) He Is Blessed Redemption

Troilus (seventh century B.C.) was a hero of the Trojan War, a son of King Priam and Queen Hecuba of Troy. Troilus perished fighting Achilles, Greece's greatest warrior.

Xenophon (ZEE-nuh-fahn) (Greek) He Speaks with other Men's Voices

Clinias (KLIN-ee-yus) (Greek) He Inclines and Is Flexible

Xenophon (c. 431 B.C.–c. 355 B.C.) was a warrior who wrote treatises on metaphysics. Late in life, Xenophon gained a friend, Clinias, whose assistance Xenophon treasured.

GIRLS

Actaea (AK-tee-yah) (Greek) She Is the Sandy Shoreline

Agave (ah-GAH-vay) (Greek) She Is Majestic

Amphitrite (am-FIH-trih-tee) (Greek) She Embraces the Three

Cymothoe (SIM-uh-thee) (Greek) She Runs along the Waves

Doris (DOR-riss) (Greek) She Is Abundance

Dynamene (dye-NAM-uh-nee) (Greek) She Is Powerful

Erato (air-RAH-toh) (Greek) She Is Beautiful

Eucrante (yoo-KRAHN-tay) (Greek) She Is Prosperity and Victory

Eudora (yoo-DOR-rah) (Greek) She Is Generosity

Eulimine (yoo-LIM-ih-nee) (Greek) She Is a Safe Harbor

Eunice (YOO-neess) (Greek) She Is Humanity's Triumph

Eupompe (yoo-POM-pee) (Greek) She Is a Beautiful Voyage

Evagora (ay-vuh-GOR-rah) (Greek) She Brings Everyone Together

The Nereides—including Actaea, Agave, Amphitrite, Cymothoe, Doris, Dynamene, Erato, Eucrante, Eudora, Eulimine, Eunice, Eupompe, and Evagora—were the nymphs of the seas. Their father was Nereus, god of fishing.

Aeginaea (ee-JEEN-yah) (Greek) She Wields the Mighty Javelin

Agoraia (ah-GOR-ree-yah) (Greek) She Protects Assemblies

Agrotera (ag-ruh-TAIR-ruh) (Greek) She Hunts

Alphaea (al-FEE-yuh) (Greek) She Loves the River God Alphaeus

Aricina (air-uh-SEE-nuh) (Greek) She Is from Aricia, Italy

Aristo (uh-RIS-toh) (Greek) She Is the Absolute Best

Daphnaea (DAF-nee-yuh) (Greek) She Is the Holy Laurel Wreath

Delia (DEE-lee-yah) (Greek) She Is the Sacred Island of Delos

Delphinia (del-FEEN-yuh) (Greek) The One Who Is Delphi, Greece

Hymnia (HIM-nee-yuh) (Greek) The One Who Is Beautiful Hymns

> *Artemis, called Diana by the Romans, was Greek goddess of hunting and was honored with many titles of respect. Artemis loved to dash through the woodlands without clothing; when mortals espied her, she shot them with her bow.*

💛 **Agatha** (AG-uh-thuh) (Greek) She Is Pure and Good

Demeter (DEM-eh-tur) (Greek) She Is the Blessed Mother Earth

> *Agatha Tykhe was the Greek goddess of fortune. She was associated with her mother Demeter, goddess of grain harvests.*

💛 **Aithre** (EE-thur) (Greek) She Is Heavenly

Akaste (ah-KAS-tah) (Greek) Her Father Is the Sea

Althaia (al-THEE-yah) (Greek) She Is Mount Ida, Crete

Amatheia (am-ah-THEE-yah) (Greek) She Is Sparkling Water

Daulis (DAH-liss) (Greek) She Is Daulis, Greece

Eido (AY-doh) (Greek) She Is Wisdom

Euthemia (yoo-THEE-mee-yah) (Greek) She Is Clean

Himalia (him-AHL-yah) (Greek) She Is Generosity

Hippe (HIP-pee) (Greek) She Is Hippe, Greece

Kabeiro (kah-BEE-ro) (Greek) She Is Beyond Human Comprehension

> *The beautiful Naiades—including Aithre, Akaste, Althaia, Amatheia, Daulis, Eido, Euthemia, Himalia, Hippe, and Kabeiro—were nymphs or nature-spirits of Earth's water sources, who guarded maidenly honor.*

💛 **Akraia** (AK-ree-yah) (Greek) She Dominates the Hills

Aphrodite (af-ro-DYE-tee) (Greek) She Is Born of the Sea-Foam

Areia (AIR-ree-yah) (Greek) She Is Warlike

Cypris (SYE-pris) (Greek) She Is the Island of Cyprus

Cythera (SIH-thur-rah) (Greek) She Is Cythera, Crete

Eros (EH-rohss) (Greek) He Is Love

Idalia (eye-DAY-lee-yah) (Greek) She Is Idalion, Cyprus

Melaenis (muh-LEE-nus) (Greek) She Is Meline, Greece

Pandemos (pan-DAY-mohss) (Greek) He Is Accessible to Everyone

Zerynthia (zur-RIN-thee-yah) (Greek) She Is Zerinthus, Thrace

> *Aphrodite, called Venus by the Romans, was the Greek goddess of love and was given many titles of honor. She encouraged Eros, her son, to flit about on his delicate wings and shoot mortals and immortals with love-arrows. In this way, Aphrodite and Eros spread universal love.*

💛 **Alcyone** (al-SEE-uh-nee) (Greek) She Is a Wondrous Helper

Kelaino (kel-LAY-no) (Greek) She Is as Black as Night

Celaeno (suh-LEE-no) (Greek) She Is as Black as Night

Maia (MYE-yah) (Greek) She Is Love

> *The Pleiades—including Alcyone, Kelaino, and Celaeno—were the radiant star-nymphs (nature-deities) of the Constellation Pleiades.*

💛 **Alexandra** (al-ex-AN-drah) (Greek) She Protects Humanity

Helen (HEL-lun) (Greek) She Is a Radiant Torch

> *When Helen of Sparta fled with Paris of Troy, the Trojan War between Greece and Troy began. It ended a decade later when Odysseus of Ithaca had the Greeks build the huge Trojan Horse. The Trojans pulled the horse into Troy, while the seer Alexandra (Cassandra) protested vainly. Greeks later emerged from the horse and destroyed Troy.*

💛 **Algea** (al-JEE-yah) (Greek) She Understands Sorrow

Lethe (LEE-thee) (Greek) Her Memory Is Playful

Makhai (muh-KYE) (Greek) She Is Warfare

Neikea (neh-KEE-yah) (Greek) She Is Argumentation

> *The Amphilogiai—including Algea, Lethe, Makhai, and Neikea—were demon goddesses whose sole parent was Eris, goddess of conflict.*

✍ **Amphiro** (am-FEE-ro) (Greek) She Is Flowing Water

Calliroe (kuh-LEER-ree) (Greek) She Is Beautifully Flowing Water

Calypso (kuh-LIP-so) (Greek) She Hides Her Face

Capheira (kuh-FEER-rah) (Greek) Her Breath Is Thunderstorms

Consolatio (kahn-so-LAH-tee-yoh) (Latin) She Is Consolation

Daeira (DEER-rah) (Greek) She Is a Wise Teacher

Dione (dee-YAHN) (Greek) She Is a Celestial Goddess

Electra (ee-LEK-truh) (Greek) She Is Golden Amber

Ephyra (eh-FEE-rah) (Greek) Her Temper Is Fiery

Europe (YOO-rup) (Greek) She Is Europe

The Oceanides—including Amphiro, Calliroe, Calypso, Capheira, Consolatio, Daeira, Dione, Electra, Ephyra, and Europe—were nymphs or nature-spirits who personified Earth's water sources. They were the daughters of Oceanus, god of the ocean.

✍ **Anatolia** (ann-uh-TOH-lee-yah) (Greek) She Is the Dawn

Auge (AW-ghee) (Greek) She Is the Hour of First Light

Dysis (DYE-sis) (Greek) She Is the Evening

Gymnastica (jim-NAS-tih-kah) (Greek) She Is the Gym Hour

Hesperia (hes-PAIR-ee-yah) (Greek) She Is the Approaching Night

Mesembria (meh-SEM-bree-yah) (Greek) She Is the Noon Hour

Musica (MYOO-zih-kah) (Greek) She Is the Music Hour

Nympha (NIM-fah) (Greek) She Is the Bath Hour

Sponde (SPAHN-day) (Greek) She Is the Wine Hour

Elete (ee-LEE-tee) (Greek) She Is the Flour-Grinding Hour

The Horai or Hours—including Anatolia, Auge, Dysis, Gymnastica, Hesperia, Mesembria, Musica, Nympha, Sponde, and Elete—were the Greek goddesses of the hours. They tended Apollo's horses each night, after the steeds had pulled the Sun across Heaven.

✍ **Antheia** (an-THEE-yah) (Greek) She Blossoms Beautifully

Auxo (AWK-so) (Greek) She Brings Greater Abundance

Eudaimonia (yoo-duh-MO-nee-yah) (Greek) She Is Happiness

Euphrosyne (yoo-FRAH-zuh-nee) (Greek) She Is Cheerfulness

Euthymia (yoo-THIM-ee-yah) (Greek) She Is Happiness

Hegemone (heh-ZHEM-uh-nee) (Greek) She Is Supreme Power

Kalleis (kuhl-LAY-yiss) (Greek) She Is Great Beauty

Kharis (KAIR-riss) (Greek) She Is Magnificently Beautiful

Kleta (KLEE-tah) (Greek) She Is Aristocratic and Renowned

Paidia (pah-DEE-yah) (Greek) She Is Wonderful Playfulness

The Kharites—including Antheia, Auxo, Eudaimonia, Euphrosyne, Euthymia, Hegemone, Kalleis, Kharis, Kleta, and Paidia— were the Greek goddesses of contentment. The Kharites faithfully served Hera, Queen of the Olympian gods, and Aphrodite, goddess of love.

✍ **Aria** (AR-ee-yah) (Greek) She Is a Lilting Melody

Deione (dee-YAHN) (Greek) She Is Heaven-Sent

Aria was a lovely mortal from the island of Crete. Apollo, god of prophecy, loved Aria, and together they produced the warrior Miletos, who eventually ruled a city that bore his name. Another of Aria's names was Deione.

✍ **Asia** (AY-zhah) (Greek) She Is Famous Forever

Clymene (KLIM-uh-nee) (Greek) She Is Famous Forever

Asia, goddess of glory, was a Titan, one of the original deities who ruled in Heaven before being deposed by King Zeus and his Olympian gods. The continent of Asia bears the name of this legendary goddess. Another of Asia's names was Clymene.

✍ **Athena** (uh-THEE-nah) (Greek) She Is Intelligence

Minerva (mih-NUR-vah) (Greek) She Is Wisdom and Virtue

Athena, goddess of wisdom, was unique among the immortals because she protected humanity

and took a loving interest in their welfare. *Athena was called Minerva by the Romans, who appropriated the goddess after conquering Greece.*

🐾 **Atlantea** (at-LAN-tee-yah) (Greek) She Is from Mount Atlas, Greece
Daphnis (DAF-niss) (Greek) She Is a Laurel Crown of Victory
Karya (KAIR-ee-yah) (Greek) She Is the Spreading Chestnut Tree
Clea (KLEE-yah) (Greek) She Is a Singing Cavern
Cyllene (sil-LEEN) (Greek) She Is Mount Cyllene, Greece
Claea (KLEE-yah) (Greek) She Is a Singing Cavern
Morea (mo-RAY-yah) (Greek) She Is the Beautiful Mulberry Tree
Nomia (NO-mee-yah) (Greek) She Is Cool Green Pastures
Penelopeia (puh-nel-uh-PEE-yah) (Greek) She Is a Needle and Thread
Phoebe (FEE-bee) (Greek) She Is Radiant
The Dryades—including Atlantea, Daphnis, Karya, Clea, Cyllene, Claea, Morea, Nomia, Penelopeia, and Phoebe—were nymphs or nature spirits who lived in the forests of Gaia—Earth. Each nymph inhabited a tree; yet even these deities could perish, if their trees were cut down.

🐾 **Aura** (OR-ruh) (Greek) She Is the Fresh Morning Breeze
Cynthia (KIN-thee-yuh) (Greek) She Is the Lofty Source of all Water
Aura was Greek goddess of morning breezes, and the purest virgin in Greece—or so she boasted to Cynthia (Artemis), goddess of hunting. Cynthia asked Nemesis, god of vengeance, to punish Aura for her boasts, and Aura was transformed into a manic slayer.

🐾 **Aurora** (uh-ROR-ruh) (Greek) She Is the Rosy-Fingered Dawn
Terra (TAIR-ruh) (Greek) She Is Mother Earth
Aurora, also called Eos, was the goddess of the beautiful dawn. Aurora's mother was Terra, also called Gaia, or Mother Earth.

🐾 **Bronte** (BRAHN-tay) (Greek) She Is Rolling Thunder
Astrape (ah-STRAH-pay) (Greek) She Is Flashing Lightning

Bronte and Astrape were sister goddesses— Bronte was the personification of thunder and Astrape personified lightning.

🐾 **Calliope** (kuh-LYE-uh-pee) (Greek) She Possesses a Beautiful Voice
Clio (KLEE-yoh) (Greek) She Is a Celebration
Euterpe (yoo-TUR-pee) (Greek) She Gives Delight
Terpsichore (TURP-sih-kor) (Greek) She Loves to Dance
Polyhymnia (pah-lee-HIM-nee-yah) (Greek) She Sings many Hymns
Melpomene (mel-PAH-muh-nee) (Greek) She Celebrates by Singing
Urania (yoor-RAIN-yah) (Greek) She Is Heaven
Eupheme (yoo-FEE-mee) (Greek) She Is Extremely Well-Spoken
Helikon (HEL-ih-kahn) (Greek) She Is Mount Helikon
The Mousai, or Muses—including Calliope, Clio, Euterpe, Terpsichore, Polyhymnia, Melpomene, Urania, Eupheme, and Helikon—were lovely and talented Greek goddesses of inspiration who gave mortals ideas for poems, music, dance, and more.

🐾 **Calliste** (kuh-LIS-tee) (Greek) She Is the Island of Calliste, Greece
Eidothea (ee-DOH-thee-yuh) (Greek) She Is a Wise Goddess
The Haliades—including Calliste and Eidothea—were ocean-nymphs who rode dolphins through Earth's seas. The Haliades blessed and protected sailors.

🐾 **Chloe** (KLO-wee) (Greek) She Is a Beautiful Maiden
Averna (ah-VUR-nah) (Latin) She Is the Queen of the Underworld
When Hades, lord of the underworld, spied Averna (Persephone), he kidnapped her for his bride. Averna's mother Chloe (Demeter), goddess of grain, made the Earth barren in grief. To save humanity, Zeus, high king of Greek gods, ordered that Averna be allowed to come aboveground—and whenever she does so, springtime appears.

🐾 **Chloris** (KLOR-riss) (Greek) She Is Lovely Flowers and Plants
Flora (FLO-rah) (Latin) She Is Lovely Flowers and Plants
Chloris was a Greek nymph or nature-spirit who cared for all the flowers of Gaia, Mother Earth.

Chloris's Roman name was Flora, goddess of blossoms.

🌿 **Corinna** (ko-RIN-nuh) (Greek) She Is Chaste and Pure
Tanagra (tuh-NAH-gruh) (Greek) She Who Is Tanagra, Greece
Corinna (sixth century B.C.) was a Greek lyric poetess whose fragmentary poems hint at her love of her hometown, Tanagra, named after the Naiad nymph Tanagra.

🌿 **Damia** (DAY-mee-yah) (Greek) She Nourishes the Earth
Thallo (THAL-lo) (Greek) She Is Blossoming Flowers
Euporia (yoo-POR-ree-yah) (Greek) She Is Abundance
Theros (THEH-rohss) (Greek) She Is The Warm Summer Season
Irene (eye-REEN) (Greek) She Is Springtime
Eunomia (yoo-NO-mee-yah) (Greek) She Is a Peaceful Meadow
The Horae—including Damia, Thallo, Euporia, Theros, Irene, and Eunomia—were Greek goddesses of annual climate-changes and the hours of the day. The Horae kept the rotations of the stars and planets orderly and brought rain for crops.

🌿 **Diotima** (dee-oh-TEE-mah) (Greek) She Honors the Ruler of Heaven
Aspasia (uh-SPAY-zhah) (Greek) She Is Most Welcome
Diotima (fourth century B.C.) was a prophetess in the Symposium, a treatise written by the philosopher Plato. However, Plato may have invented the character of Diotima based on the life of the poetess Aspasia, consort of Pericles, ruler of Athens.

🌿 **Eirene** (eye-REEN) (Greek) The One Who Is Tranquility and Springtime
Eleusis (el-OO-sis) (Greek) The One Who Is Eleusis, Greece
Eirene was a Greek painter appearing in a book by Italian renaissance author Boccaccio (1313–1375) titled On Famous Women (De Mulieribus Claris). Eirene's greatest painting was of a young girl, and was displayed in Eleusis, a city named for the nymph Eleusis.

🌿 **Erinna** (uh-RIN-nuh) (Greek) She Is Tranquil and Poetic
Baucis (BAHK-us) (Greek) The One Who Makes Her Voice Heard

Erinna (fourth century B.C.) was a Greek poetess and a contemporary of the poetess Sappho of Lesbos. Erinna's greatest poem is the Distaff, written to honor fellow poetess Baucis.

🌿 **Eris** (AIR-iss) (Greek) The One Who Is Conflict and Contention
Thetis (THEE-tus) (Greek) The One Who Is the Beginning of All
Eris was the goddess of conflict, delighting in stirring up brawls among humanity and gods alike. When the nymph Thetis married King Peleus of the Myrmidons, Thetis neglected to invite Eris, and Eris fomented a war as a result.

🌿 **Gaia** (GYE-yuh, gah-EE-yuh) (Greek) The One Who Is Mother Earth
Eurybia (yur-RIH-bee-yuh) (Greek) The One Who Is Majestic Power
Gaia, called Terra by the Romans, was Mother Earth, one of the four elements that sprang into being when time began. Eurybia was Gaia's daughter, goddess of the world's oceans.

🌿 **Galatia** (gal-ah-TEE-yah) (Greek) She Is the Deity of Quiet Seas
Lampetia (lam-PEE-shah) (Greek) She Is Radiant
The Epimelides—including Galatia, and Lampetia—were nymphs or nature-deities who guarded shepherds' flocks. The hair of the Epimelides was made of hyacinths, and their dancing was "dedicated to beauty."

🌿 **Hermes** (HUR-meez) (Greek) He Is a Marker-Stone to Guide Travelers
Iris (EYE-ris) (Greek) She Is Colorful Rainbows
Hermes was the messenger of the gods and the god who helped souls "cross over." Iris, goddess of rainbows, had similar duties as an envoy between the gods and humanity.

🌿 **Hestia** (HES-tee-yuh) (Greek) The One Who Is the Warm Center of the Home
Rhea (RAY-yuh) (Greek) The One Who Moves with Great Ease
Hestia was the goddess of warm, loving homes. Hestia's mother was Rhea, a Titan, one of the deities who ruled in Heaven before being overthrown by Zeus and his Greek gods.

🌿 **Imbrasia** (im-BRAY-zhah) (Greek) She Is the Imbrasus River, Greece
Issoria (is-SOR-ree-yah) (Greek) She Is Mount Issorion, Greece

Kolainis (ko-LAY-nus) (Greek) She Resembles King Coleanus of Attica

Kranaia (KRAY-nee-yah) (Greek) She Is the Temple of Youth

Limenia (lih-MEEN-yah) (Greek) She Is the Harbor's Protector

Limnaea (LIM-nee-yah) (Greek) She Dominates the Marshlands

Lyceia (lye-SEE-yah) (Greek) She Is Education

Melissa (meh-LIS-sah) (Greek) She Is a Busy Honeybee

Mysia (mye-SEE-yah) (Greek) She Is the Sanctuary of Sparta

Parthenia (par-THEE-nee-yah) (Greek) She Is the Parthenius River

Phosphoros (FOS-fur-rohs) (Greek) She Is Radiant

Saronia (suh-RONE-yah) (Greek) She Is a Royal Princess

Artemis, called Diana by the Romans, was Greek goddess of hunting and was honored with many titles of respect, including Imbrasia, Issoria, Kolainis, Kranaia, Limenia, Limnaea, Lyceia, Melissa, Mysia, Parthenia, Phosphoros, and Saronia. Artemis loved to dash through the woodlands without clothing; when mortals beheld her loveliness, she shot them with her bow.

℘ **Keto** (KEE-toh) (Greek) She Is the Ocean Leviathan

Khryseis (krih-SAY-yus) (Greek) She Is the Golden Dusk

Leuce (LOO-see) (Greek) She Is a Beautiful Poplar Tree

Libya (LIB-ee-yah) (Greek) She Is Africa

Melia (meh-LEE-yah) (Greek) She Is Honey-Sweet

Neda (NEE-duh) (Greek) She Is the Neda River, Greece

Nephele (NEF-eh-lee) (Greek) She Is a Beautiful Cloud

Ourania (oo-RAHN-yah) (Greek) She Is Heavenly

Perseis (pur-SAY-yiss) (Greek) She Is a Mighty Conqueror

Phaino (FAY-no) (Greek) She Is Consolation

Polydora (pahl-ee-DOR-rah) (Greek) She Is a Wealth of Gifts

Rhodeia (ro-DEE-yah) (Greek) She Is a Garden of Fragrant Roses

Xanthe (ZAN-thee) (Latin) She Is the Golden River Soil

The Oceanides—including Keto, Khryseis, Leuce, Libya, Melia, Neda, Nephele, Ourania, Perseis, Phaino, Polydora, Rhodeia, and Xanthe—were nymphs, or nature-spirits, who personified Earth's water sources. They were the daughters of Oceanus, god of the ocean.

℘ **Merope** (MEH-ro-pee) (Greek) Her Face Turns Away

Lampetia (lam-PEE-shah) (Greek) She Is Radiant

The beautiful Heliades—including Merope and Lampetia—were the goddess-daughters of Helios, god of the Sun.

℘ **Nausicaä** (naw-zih-KAY-yuh) (Greek) She Sets Warships Aflame

Agallis (ah-GAL-lis) (Greek) She Is a Fragrant Iris

Princess Nausicaä of Phaeacia, daughter of King Alcinous, was mentioned in the Odyssey *by the Greek poet Homer. Nausicaä was also mentioned by the poetess Agallis, who said that Nausicaä created many of the athletic games the Greeks revered.*

℘ **Pandaisia** (pan-DAY-zhah) (Greek) She Is Banquets and Feasting

Pannykhis (PAN-ih-kus) (Greek) She Is Evening Celebrations

Pasithea (puh-SIH-thee-yah) (Greek) She Is Restful Sleep

Peitho (PAY-tho) (Greek) She Is Seductive

Phaenna (fay-EN-nah) (Greek) She Is Radiant

Thalia (THAL-ee-yah) (Greek) She Blooms with Loveliness

The Kharites—including Pandaisia, Pannykhis, Pasithea, Peitho, Phaenna, and Thalia—were the Greek goddesses of contentment. The Kharites served Hera, Queen of the Olympian gods, and Aphrodite, goddess of love.

℘ **Sappho** (SAF-fo) (Greek) She Is a Blue Sapphire

Cleis (KLEE-yis) (Greek) She Is Radiant

Sappho (sixth century B.C.) was a Greek poetess from the island of Lesbos, famed for her invention of Sapphic Stanza poetry. Many of Sappho's poems address "my darling Cleis," who may have been Sappho's daughter. [Note: "Sappho" may refer to lesbians.]

℘ **Thebe** (THEE-bee) (Greek) She Is Thebes, Greece

Antiope (an-TYE-oh-pee) (Greek) Her Eyes Focus on the Prize
>*Thebe was a Naiad nymph, a Greek nature-spirit who personified the world's water sources. Another of Thebe's names was Antiope.*

BOYS AND GIRLS

⏣ **Aesara** (ee-SAH-rah) (Greek) She Rests Comfortably
Pythagoras (pih-THAG-oh-rus) (Greek) He Is Pythia, Greece
>*Pythagoras (c. 580 B.C.–500 B.C.) was the mathematician known for the Pythagorean Theorem, describing right triangles. Aesara was Pythagoras's lovely daughter.*

⏣ **Aethra** (EE-thrah) (Greek) She Is the Blue Sky
Ouranos (oor-AH-nohss) (Greek) She Is Heaven
>*Aethra, goddess of the blue sky, was a Titan, one of the original deities who ruled in Heaven before being deposed by Zeus and his Greek gods. Aethra's father was Ouranos, or Heaven, and her mother was Gaia, or Mother Earth.*

⏣ **Agamemnon** (ag-uh-MEM-nahn) (Greek) He Never Gives Up
Cassandra (kah-SAHN-drah) (Greek) She Fills Men's Hearts with Love
>*King Agamemnon of Mycenae led the victorious Greeks during the Trojan War. The Trojan seer Cassandra warned the Trojans that Greeks were hiding inside the huge Trojan Horse, but the Trojans brought it inside the city walls regardless, hastening their doom.*

⏣ **Agatha** (AG-ah-thah) (Greek) She Is Great
Plouton (PLOO-tahn) (Greek) He Is Wealthy
>*Agatha Tykhe was the goddess of fortune. Statues of Agatha often depicted her carrying the boy Plouton, god of wealth.*

⏣ **Aigle** (AY-glee) (Greek) She Is Radiant
Arethusa (air-eh-THOO-sah) (Greek) She Is Swiftly Moving War
Drakon (drah-KAHN) (Greek) He Is a Majestic Dragon
Asterope (ah-STAIR-ah-pee) (Greek) Her Face Is Starlight
Chrysothemis (krih-SAH-thuh-miss) (Greek) She Is Tradition
Erythea (ur-RIH-thee-yah) (Greek) She Is the Red-Orange Sunset

Hespera (HES-pur-rah) (Greek) She Is the Evening
Lipara (lih-PAH-rah) (Greek) She Is Determined
>*The Hesperides—including Aigle, Arethusa, Asterope, Chrysothemis, Erythea, Hespera, and Lipara—were the goddesses of sunsets. They guarded the tree of golden apples entrusted to them by Gaia, or Mother Earth. The Hesperides's protector was the Drakon, also called the Dragon of the West.*

⏣ **Alala** (ah-LAH-lah) (Greek) She Is the War-Cry
Polemos (po-LEH-mohss) (Greek) He Is War
>*Alala, "to whom soldiers are sacrificed," personified soldiers' war-cries. Alala's only parent was Polemos, Greek god of warfare.*

⏣ **Antoninus** (an-toh-NYE-nus) (Latin) He Is a Blossoming Flower
Carme (KAR-may) (Greek) She Slices and Cuts
>*Antonius Liberalis (c. third century A.D.) was a Greek educator who wrote* Collection of Transformations (Metamorphoses), *telling of Carme, the Greek demigoddess of abundance, who invented fishing-nets.*

⏣ **Apollo** (uh-PAHL-lo) (Greek) He Is the Source of all Light
Artemis (AR-teh-miss) (Greek) She Is the Lofty Source of all Water
>*Apollo was the god of poetry and prophecy, who pulled the Sun, Helios, across the sky each day. Artemis, goddess of the hunt, was Apollo's swift-running sister.*

⏣ **Asia** (AY-zhah) (Assyrian) She Is Everlasting Glory
Prometheus (pro-MEE-thee-yuss) (Greek) He Considers the Future
>*Asia was the Titan goddess of fame, before she and the other Titans were deposed by Zeus and his Olympians. Prometheus, Asia's son, brought the gift of fire to humanity.*

⏣ **Attalus** (AT-ah-lus) (Greek) He Is Our Savior
Appolonis (ahp-puh-LO-nis) (Greek) She Is Powerful
>*King Attalus I of Pergamon (269 B.C.–197 B.C.) conquered present-day Turkey. His wife was Queen Appolonis, memorialized by a monument in Pergamon which reads, "She always considered herself blessed and gave thanks to the gods."*

🙂 **Chrysippus** (KRIS-ip-pus) (Greek) He Is a Golden Stallion

Danais (dah-NAY-yiss) (Greek) She Lives Forever
Chrysippus was a Prince of Pisa, a Greek city-state. When Chrysippus was kidnapped by the Theban Prince Laios, war ensued between Pisa and Thebes, and Chrysippus perished. Chrysippus's mother was the nymph Danais, personification of Pisa's water sources.

🙂 **Cleopatra** (klee-oh-PAT-trah) (Greek) She Is Her Father's Glory

Cassander (kuh-SAN-dur) (Greek) He Fills Humanity with Love
Princess Cleopatra of Macedonia (c. 356 B.C.– c. 308 B.C.) was the sister of the Macedonian conqueror Alexander the Great. When Alexander passed on, his general Cassander proposed to Cleopatra, but he eventually had to settle for Alexander's half-sister Thessalonica instead.

🙂 **Danae** (duh-NAY) (Greek) She Is a Golden Shower

Argos (AR-gohss) (Greek) He Is all Eyes
Princess Danae of the Greek city-state of Argos, and her infant son Perseus, were exiled to an island due to a prophecy that Danae would depose Argos's ruler, Akrisios. But when Perseus matured, he returned to Argos and restored his mother's honor. The city of Argos was named for the mythic hundred-eyed giant, Argos.

🙂 **Darius** (DAIR-ee-yus) (Greek) He Possesses Great Goodness

Mandana (mahn-DAH-nah) (Persian) She Lives Forever
Darius I (c. 549 B.C.–485 B.C.) was the Persian emperor whose realm was conquered by Alexander the Great of Macedon. Mandana of Media was one of Darius's daughters.

🙂 **Diogenes** (dye-AH-juh-neez) (Greek) He Descends from Heaven's King

Cybele (SIH-beh-lee) (Greek) She Is Dynamic
Diogenes the Cynic (404 B.C.–323 B.C.) was a Greek philosopher who believed that people should abandon civilization for a more natural life. Diogenes lived in a large clay tub near the temple of Cybele, the Earth-goddess.

🙂 **Evander** (ee-VAHN-dur) (Greek) He Is Aristocratic

Arcadia (ar-KAY-dee-yuh) (Latin) She Is the Land of the Bears

King Evander led his people as refugees from Arcadia, and founded a new kingdom, Latium, in Italy. Latium was besieged by the giant Cacus, but when the demigod Heracles slew Cacus, Evander built a temple in his honor.

🙂 **Evarne** (ee-VAR-nee) (Greek) She Possesses many Lambs

Galene (gay-LEEN) (Greek) She Is Peace

Galateia (gal-uh-TEE-yuh) (Greek) She Is Milk-White

Halia (HAL-ee-yuh) (Greek) She Is the Ocean Brine

Leagora (lee-ah-GOR-rah) (Greek) She Brings Everyone Together

Lysianassa (lis-see-uh-NAH-sah) (Greek) She Is Our Majestic Deliverer

Melite (muh-LEE-tee) (Greek) She Is Honey-Sweet

Menippe (MEN-ip-pee) (Greek) She Is the Power of the Horse

Nemertes (neh-MUR-teez) (Greek) She Is Perfect

Nereus (NAIR-ee-yus) (Greek) He Is the Old Man of the Sea
The Nereides—including Evarne, Galene, Galateia, Halia, Leagora, Lysianassa, Melite, Menippe, and Nemertes—were the nymphs of the seas. Their father was Nereus, god of fishing.

🙂 **Helene** (hel-LEEN) (Greek) She Is a Radiant Torch

Menelaus (men-uh-LAY-yus) (Greek) He Assists Humanity
Helene was another name for Queen Helen of Sparta, wife of King Menelaus. When Prince Paris of Troy convinced Helene to run away with him, the decade-long Trojan War between the Greeks and Trojans ensued, resulting in Troy's destruction.

🙂 **Hermione** (hur-MYE-uh-nee) (Greek) She Is a Pile of Marker-Stones

Peleus (PEL-loos) (Greek) He Is Chaste and Pure
Hermione was the daughter of King Menelaus and Queen Helen of Sparta. When Helen ran off with Prince Paris of Troy, the Trojan War ensued, resulting in Troy's annihilation. Hermione eventually wed the warrior Neoptolemus, son of the warrior Peleus.

🙂 **Jason** (JAY-sun) (Greek) He Is a Healer

Medea (meh-DEE-yah) (Greek) She Uses Her Mind

Jason, Prince of the Greek city-state of Iolcus, equipped the ship Argo, brought together a crew of Argonauts, and sailed in search of the Golden Fleece. Medea, daughter of King Aeëtes of Colchis, used her magic to help Jason perform three mighty tasks, so he could gain possession of the Fleece.

Kore (KO-ree) (Greek) She Is Virtuous
Kronos (KRO-nohss) (Greek) He Is Time
Kore was a title of honor the Greeks bestowed on Persephone, daughter of Demeter, goddess of harvests. Once, Kore played with river-mud and fashioned a living creature. Zeus, high king of Greek gods, allowed Kronos, god of time, to name the being, and Kronos called it "man."

Larissa (luh-REESS-sah) (Greek) She Is Cheerful
Pythios (PIH-thee-ohss) (Greek) He Is Pythia, Greece
Larissa was a princess of the Greek city-state of Argos. When Poseidon, god of the sea, loved Larissa, they produced a son, Pythios, who later gained fame as a warrior.

Leucippus (loo-SIP-pus) (Greek) He Is a White Stallion
Daphne (DAF-nee) (Greek) She Is a Fragrant Laurel Tree
Leucippus was a Prince of Pisa, a Greek city-state. Leucippus adored fair Daphne, a nymph who personified the Peneios River in Greece.

Libra (LEE-brah) (Greek) She Weighs and Balances
Astraeus (ASS-stree-yus) (Greek) He Is Heaven
Libra was the Greek goddess of justice. Her father was Astraeus, god of constellations and a primordial Titan, one of the deities who ruled in Heaven before being deposed by Zeus and his Greek gods.

Lotus (LO-tus) (Greek) She Is a Fragrant Lotus Flower
Dionysos (dye-uh-NYE-sohss) (Greek) He Makes His Voice Heard
Lotus was the "snow-white" nymph or nature-deity personifying the Sperkheios River in Greece. After a feast honoring Dionysos, god of wine, Lotus and the other guests slept. But when Priapus, god of produce, tried to molest Lotus, she changed into a lotus flower.

Melita (meh-LEE-tah) (Greek) She Is Honey-Sweet
Herakles (HAIR-uh-kleez) (Greek) He Is the Glory of Hera
Melita was a Naiad nymph, a mountain-spirit personifying mount Melite, Greece. Melita loved the legendary Herakles (also called Hercules), "and she bore him the mighty Hyllos," who later became a warrior like his father.

Narcissus (nar-SIS-sus) (Greek) He Is a Fragrant Daffodil
Echo (EK-ko) (Greek) She Returns all Sounds
Narcissus was a handsome boy from Thespiai who rejected the affections of the nymph Echo. Thereafter, Echo could only repeat what others said, becoming the echoes of the world. Narcissus, in turn, was enchanted by Nemesis, god of revenge, and died while gazing at his reflection in a pool.

Neso (NES-soh) (Greek) She Is a Perfect Island
Panopeia (pan-OH-pee-yah) (Greek) She Is a Beautiful Vista
Pasithea (puh-SITH-thee-yah) (Greek) She Brings Everyone Together
Pherusa (fair-OO-zah) (Greek) She Carries with Great Strength
Ploto (PLO-toh) (Greek) She Is the Joy of Sailing
Proto (PRO-toh) (Greek) She Is First among Equals
Protomedea (pro-toh-MEE-dee-yah) (Greek) She Is Our First Queen
Psamathe (SAM-uh-thee) (Greek) She Is Earth's Limitless Sands
Themisto (theh-MIS-toh) (Greek) She Is the Prophetess's Voice
Thetis (THEE-tiss) (Greek) She Is the Beginning
Triton (TRYE-tun) (Greek) She Is Three in Number
The Nereides—including Neso, Panopeia, Pasithea, Pherusa, Ploto, Proto, Protomedea, Psamathe, Themisto, and Thetis—were sea-nymphs whose father was Nereus, god of fishing. The Nereides worked with the Triton, sea-spirits who were half-fish and half-divine, to serve the sea-god Poseidon.

Niobe (nye-OH-bee) (Greek) She Is Refreshing
Argus (AR-gus) (Greek) He Is All Eyes

Queen Niobe was the first mortal whom Zeus, high king of Greek gods, loved. A son was produced, great Argus (also called Argos), the hundred-eyed warrior.

Nyssa (NIS-sah) (Greek) She Is from Mount Nysa, Greece

Stephanos (steh-FAH-nohss) (Greek) He Is a Radiant Crown
Nyssa was one of the Nysiades, the nymphs or nature-deities who personified Mount Nysa, Greece. Nyssa raised Stephanos (also called Dionysos or Dionysus), god of wine.

Pandora (pan-DOR-ruh) (Greek) The One Who Gives all Gifts

Areius (AIR-ee-yus) (Greek) The One Who Is Warlike
Zeus, high king of Greek gods, was also called Areius. One day, Areius asked the gods to create the first woman, Pandora. Afterwards, Areius gave Pandora a jar filled with every evil. Pandora released the evils, but she also released Hope, to aid humanity.

Parthenia (par-THEEN-ee-yah) (Greek) She Is the Parthenius River, Greece

Kleitos (KLAY-tohss) (Greek) He Is Marvelously Renowned
Parthenia was a nymph or river-spirit who personified the Parthenius River in Anatolia (present-day Turkey). After marrying the warrior-hero Agamestor, a son was produced, Kleitos, who later became a hero in his own right, during the Trojan War.

Penthos (PEN-thos) (Greek) He Understands Sorrow

Ira (EYE-rah) (Greek) She Understands Vengeance
Penthos was the god of sorrow, who rose from the underworld to stand near mourners at funerals and intensify their grief. Penthos's sister was Ira, goddess of revenge.

Perseus (PUR-see-yus) (Greek) He Is the Destroyer

Andromeda (an-DRAH-meh-dah) (Greek) She Rules Humanity
Perseus was a demigod who slew the demon Medusa—her hideous face could turn onlookers to stone—by spying her reflection in his bright shield and beheading her. Andromeda was the Ethiopian princess whom Perseus rescued from a sea-dragon.

Philemon (FIL-eh-mahn) (Greek) He Is Compassionate

Baucis (BAH-kus) (Greek) She Makes Her Voice Heard
Philemon and Baucis were an elderly couple who dwelt in Phyrgia (present-day Turkey). They were the only mortals who fed two strangers—who later turned out to be the gods Zeus and Hermes. In gratitude, the gods saved Philemon and Baucis from a lethal flood.

Philostratus (phil-AH-strah-tus) (Greek) He Loves Comfort

Palaestra (puh-LESS-trah) (Greek) He Loves Wrestling
Philostratus III (c. A.D. 190–?) was a Greek philosopher who wrote the Images (Imagines)*, chronicles of deities such as Palaestra, goddess of wrestlers. These wrestlers honored Palaestra by "bending toward her in one wrestler's posture after another."*

Phyllis (FIL-liss) (Greek) She Is Beautiful Green Branches

Ascanius (uh-SKAIN-yus) (Greek) He Is the Ascanius River, Greece
Phyllis personified the Phyllis River in Anatolia (present-day Turkey). A nearby watercourse was the Ascanius River, personified by the river-spirit Ascanius.

Poseidon (po-SYE-dun) (Greek) He Shakes the World

Athena (ah-THEE-nah) (Greek) She Is Intelligence
One of the brothers of Zeus, high king of Greek gods, was the world-shaker Poseidon, god of oceans and earthquakes. Poseidon was jealous of Zeus's position as King of Heaven and plotted with Athena, goddess of wisdom, to overthrow Zeus. But in the end, cowed by Zeus's power, Poseidon relented.

Prax (PRAX) (Greek) He Constantly Practices

Arcadia (ar-KAY-dee-yah) (Latin) She Is the Land of She-Bears
The Greek historian Pausanias (second century A.D.) wrote in Description of Greece *that near the city-state of Arcadia stood a temple dedicated to Achilles, hero of the Trojan War. Pausanias says that mighty Prax, another hero, built the magnificent temple.*

🕭 **Praxilla** (prax-IL-lah) (Greek) She Practices the Ways
Zenobius (zeh-NO-bee-yus) (Greek) He Is Like Heaven's King
Praxilla (fifth century B.C.) was a Greek poetess from the city-state of Sicyon. The lines, "Finest of all the things I have left is the light of the sun, / Next to that the brilliant stars and the face of the moon" were quoted by the Greek philosopher Zenobius.

🕭 **Propertius** (pro-PUR-shuhs) (Latin) He Is Blessed
Tyro (TYE-ro) (Greek) She Is as Beautifully Fair as Milk
Propertius (c. 50 B.C.–c. 15 B.C.) was the Roman author of Elegies, which tell of Princess Tyro of Thessaly, who bore the hero Jason, discoverer of the Golden Fleece.

🕭 **Proteus** (PRO-tee-yus) (Greek) He Is First
Cyrene (sye-REEN) (Greek) She Is Cyrene, Greece
The nymph Cyrene of Thessaly bore a demigod son, Aristaios. When Aristaios needed to consult a prophet, Cyrene sent him to Proteus, the prophetic son of Poseidon, god of the seas. Proteus counseled Aristaios to gain the gods' favor by making holy sacrifices.

🕭 **Pyramus** (PEER-ah-mus) (Greek) He Is the Pyramus River
Thisbe (THIZ-bee) (Greek) She Is a Flock of Gentle Doves
The fable of Pyramus and Thisbe is told by the Roman poet Ovid (43 B.C.–A.D. 17) in Metamorphoses. *Pyramus and Thisbe were friends who spoke through a crack in the wall separating their families. Pyramus and Thisbe ended their lives tragically because of their love for each other, which was forbidden by their families.*

🕭 **Talos** (TAL-lohss) (Greek) He Is the Radiant Sun

Europa (yoo-RO-pah) (Greek) She Has All-Seeing Eyes
Talos was the bronze robot built by Hephaestus, god of blacksmiths. Zeus, high king of Greek gods, gave Talos to his friend Europa, a beautiful nymph or nature-spirit.

🕭 **Telesilla** (tel-eh-SIL-lah) (Greek) She Sees Deep Within Herself
Cleomenes (klee-AH-muh-neez) (Greek) He Is Magnificent Power
Telesilla of Argos (sixth century B.C.) was a Greek poetess from the city-state of Argos. When Sparta's King Cleomenes conquered Argos and killed every male defender, Telesilla commanded women in defense of the city. When the Spartans realized that victory or defeat would be equally disgraceful, they withdrew.

🕭 **Thaumas** (TAH-mus) (Greek) He Is Miraculous
Iris (EYE-rus) (Greek) She Is Colorful Rainbows
Thaumas was the god of the ocean's marvels. Iris, the multicolored goddess of rainbows, was Thaumas's daughter, acting as an envoy between the gods and humanity.

🕭 **Thea** (THEE-yah) (Greek) She Is Divine Inspiration
Acmon (AK-mun) (Greek) He Is the Shimmering Upper Atmosphere
Thea was a Titan, one of the deities who ruled in Heaven until being deposed by Zeus and his Greek gods. Thea was the goddess of the brilliance of the blue sky. Thea's male counterpart was Acmon, or Aether, god of the sky.

🕭 **Zeus** (ZOOS) (Greek) He Is Heaven's King
Hera (HEH-rah) (Greek) She Has Beautiful Eyes
Zeus was the high king of Greek gods who lived on Mount Olympus and directed humanity's affairs. Queen Hera, goddess of motherhood, ruled at Zeus's side.

Name Pairs and Groups
from Roman Literature, Mythology, and History

BOYS

🖎 **Abas** (ah-BAHS) (Latin) The One Who Is Fatherly

Argeus (AR-jooss) (Latin) The One Who Has Hair of Silver

Asbolus (AZ-nul-lus) (Latin/European) The One Who Is Dark and Dusky

Demeleon (deh-MEEL-yun) (Latin) The One With the Body of a Noble Lion

Dryalus (dri-AL-lus) (Latin) He Is the Groves of Oak Trees

Orneus (OR-nee-yus) (Latin) He Is the Mixing of Wine

Perimedes (pur-IM-uh-deez) (Latin) He Walks about and Plans

Petraeus (peh-TRAY-yus) (Latin) The One Who Is as Solid as the Rocks

Phobas (FO-bus) (Latin) The One Who Is Fear Itself

Pholus (FO-lus) (Latin) The One Who Is Mammoth Caverns

Rhoecus (REE-kus) (Latin) His Legs are Bow-Legged but Powerful

Ripheus (RIF-ee-yus) (Latin) He Throws Powerfully

Thereus (THAIR-ee-yus) (Latin) The One Who Like the Wild Beasts

Ureus (YOOR-ee-yus) (Latin) He Is a Lofty Mountain

The wise and powerful Centauri, as the Romans called them—including Abas, Argeus, Asbolus, Demeleon, Dryalus, Orneus, Perimedes, Petraeus, Phobas, Pholus, Rhoecus, Ripheus, Thereus,

and Uresu—were creatures whose upper bodies were human and whose lower bodies were those of horses. Some Centauri gained fame as warriors, while others became great teachers.

🖎 **Africus** (AF-rih-kus) (Latin) He Is the Warm West Wind from Africa

Aquilo (uh-KEE-lo) (Latin) He Is the Bracing North Wind

Eurus (YOO-rus) (Latin) He Is the East Wind

Notus (NO-tus) (Latin) He Is the Stormy South Wind

The Venti (Anemoi in Greek)—including Africus, Aquilo, and Notus—were the Roman wind-gods who blew across the globe.

🖎 **Agrius** (AG-gree-yus) (Latin) He Is a Farmer

Alcyoneus (al-see-OWN-ee-yus) (Latin) He Is Powerful

Aristaeus (air-us-STEE-yus) (Latin) He Is Absolutely Excellent

Azeus (AY-zoos) (Latin) He Is Powerful

Clytius (KLYE-tee-yus) (Latin) He Is Glorious

Eurymedon (yoor-IM-muh-dahn) (Latin) He Dominates

Hippolytus (hip-PAH-luh-tus) (Latin) He Releases His Powerful Horses

Hyperbius (hye-PUR-bee-yuss) (Greek) He Possesses Astonishing Strength

Iapetus (ee-AP-puh-tus) (Latin) He Pierces

Leo (LEE-yoh) (Latin) He Is a Noble Lion

The Gigantes—Agrius, Alcyoneus, Aristaeus, Azeus, Clytius, Eurymedon, Hippolytus, Hyperbius, Iapetus, and Leo—were the 100 monstrous giants who, despite their strength, failed in their rebellion against Zeus, high king of Greek gods.

🖎 **Amnisus** (am-NEE-sus) (Latin) He Is the Amnisus River, Greece

Arno (AR-no) (Latin) He Is the Arno River, Italy

Amnisus and Arno were two of the river-spirits, called the Flumina by the Romans, who personified every river in the world.

🖎 **Amphion** (AM-fee-yon) (Latin) He Is Powerful Wine

Amphythemis (am-fih-THEE-mus) (Latin) His Traditions Surround Us

Antimachus (an-TIM-ih-kus) (Latin) He Fights Back Forcefully

Aphidas (AY-fih-dus) (Latin) He Is Wide-Open Fields

Arctus (ARK-tus) (Latin) He Is a Ferocious Bear

Areus (AIR-ee-yus) (Latin) He Is Warlike

Aristaeus (uh-RIS-tee-yus) (Greek) He Is Absolutely Excellent

Chiron (KYE-rahn) (Greek) He Is Masterful with His Hands

Clanis (KLAN-nus) (Latin) He Pours Forth Emotions

Crenaeus (creh-NEE-yus) (Latin) He Is a Beautiful Color

The Centauri, as the Romans called them—including Amphion, Amphythemis, Antimachus, Aphidas, Arctus, Areus, Aristaeus, Chiron, Clanis, and Crenaetus—were beings whose upper bodies were human and whose lower bodies were those of horses. Many Centauri were renowned as warriors, while others gained fame as teachers.

🖎 **Antonius** (an-TOH-nee-yus) (Latin) He Is a Blossoming Flower

Octavian (ahk-TAY-vee-yun) (Latin) He Is the Eighth

Marcus Antonius (Mark Antony) (83 B.C.– 30 B.C.) was one of three corulers of Rome in 44 B.C., along with the legendary Octavian and Marcus Aemilius Lepidus.

🖎 **Arctinus** (ARK-tih-nus) (Latin) He Is a Ferocious Bear

Proclus (PRO-klus) (Latin) He Is Filled Gloriously

Arctinus (seventh century B.C.) was a Greek poet who wrote Aethiops, among other great

works. Scholars have now restored Arctinus to a place of honor, because some of his works had been mistakenly credited to the Greek philosopher Proclus (A.D. 412–A.D. 85).

🖎 **Arges** (AR-gus) (Latin) He Is a Flash of Lightning

Acmonides (ak-MAH-nih-deez) (Latin) He Descends from the Anvil

Argilipus (ar-GIL-uh-pus) (Latin) He Is Brilliant Light

Pyracmon (peer-AK-mun) (Latin) He Is the Flashing Anvil

The giant, one-eyed Cyclopes—including Arges, Acmonides, Argilipus, and Pyracmon—were the sons of the Roman sea-god Neptune and forged arms for the Titans, the gods who ruled in Heaven prior to Zeus and his Olympians.

🖎 **Arion** (AIR-ee-yahn) (Latin) He Is the Bravest and the Greatest

Balius (BAY-lee-yus) (Latin) He Is Decorated with Markings

Pegasus (PEG-uh-sus) (Latin) He Springs Forth Courageously

Podarces (po-DAR-seez) (Latin) He Is Sure-Footed and Swift

Phlogeus (FLO-zhus) (Latin) He Is Aflame with Greatness

Harpagus (HARP-uh-gus) (Latin) He Is a Sturdy Grappling-Hook

The Immortal Horses—including Arion, Balius, Pegasus, Podarces, Phlogeus, and Harpagus—served the gods courageously, spiriting them away from danger. These horses were the children of the Venti, the divine winds that blew across the world.

🖎 **Augustus** (aw-GUS-tus) (Latin) He Is Absolutely Magnificent

Tiberius (tye-BEER-ee-yus) (Latin) He Is the River Tiber, Rome

Augustus (63 B.C.–A.D. 14) was Rome's first emperor, and Tiberius, his son, was a famed military conqueror.

🖎 **Axius** (AX-ee-yuss) (Latin) He Is the Axius River, Greece

Helicon (HEL-ih-kahn) (Latin) He Is the Helicon River, Greece

Axius and Helicon were two of the river-spirits, called the Flumina by the Romans, who personified every river in the world.

꙳ **Briareus** (bree-AH-rooss) (Latin) He Is
Enormously Powerful
Cottus (KO-tus) (Latin) He Is Conflict
Gyes (GUY-yus) (Latin) He Is the Land
Obriareus (oh-bree-AH-rooss) (Latin) He Is
Magnificently Powerful
The giant Hecatoncheires—including Briareus,
Cottus, Gyes, and Obriareus--were the sons of
Uranus, the Sky, and Gaia, the Earth. The Heca-
toncheires each possessed fifty heads and 100
hands and controlled the storms at sea.

꙳ **Castor** (KAS-tur) (Greek) The One Who Is a
Hard Worker
Pollux (PAHL-lux) (Greek) The One Who Is
Sweet
Castor and Pollux were the Roman names for
the twin brothers Kastor and Polydeuces, whom
the Greeks called the Dioscuri, or the bright
Constellation Gemini.

꙳ **Chrysus** (KRYE-sus) (Latin) He Is Pure
Gold
Jupiter (JOO-pih-tur) (Latin) He Is Heaven's
King
Chrysus was the Roman name for the Greek
god of gold, Khrysos, whose father was Jupiter,
or Zeus to the Greeks. As the Greek poet Pindar
(c. 522 B.C.–443 B.C.) said in a surviving
poetry fragment, "Khrysos is a child of Zeus;
neither moth nor rust devoureth it; but the
mind of man is devoured by this supreme
possession."

꙳ **Cithaeron** (sith-THEER-run) (Latin) He Is
Mount Cithaeron, Greece
Nysus (NYE-sus) (Latin) He Is Mount Nysa,
Greece
Oreus (OR-ee-yus) (Latin) He Is Mount Othrys,
Greece
Timolus (TIM-oh-lus) (Latin) He Is Mount
Timolus, Greece
The gods called the Numina Montanum by the
Romans—including Cithaeron, Nysus, Oreus,
and Timolus—personified the mountains of
Terra, the Earth. Each mountain had its own
god, who stood guard over each summit.

꙳ **Cladeus** (CLAD-ee-yus) (Latin) He Is the
Cladeus River, Greece
Cytherus (SITH-ur-rus) (Latin) He Is the
Cytherus River, Greece
Cladeus and Cytherus were two of the river-
spirits, called the Flumina by the Romans, who
personified every river in the world.

꙳ **Constantine** (KAHN-stun-teen) (Greek) He
Is Dependably Constant
Licinius (luh-SIN-ee-yus) (Latin) He Helps to
End Warfare
Constantine I (c. A.D. 272–A.D. 337) was the
first Byzantine emperor to embrace Christian-
ity. Constantine's coemperor was the legendary
Licinius.

꙳ **Corybas** (KOR-ih-bus) (Latin) He Is the
Sacred Dance
Cyllenus (sye-LEE-nus) (Latin) He Is the
Avenger
Delas (DAY-lus) (Latin) He Entices and
Ensnares
Epimedes (ep-uh-MEE-deez) (Latin) He Smiles
Joyfully
Prymneus (PRIM-nee-yus) (Latin) He Is the
Navigator
Pyrrhichus (PEER-ih-kus) (Latin) He Dances
the Fiery War Dance
The nature-spirits called the Dactylii by the
Romans—including Corybas, Cyllenus, Delas,
Epimedes, Prymneus, and Phyrrhichus—were
the servants of Opis, the Titan Queen of Heaven,
before she was deposed by Jupiter and his new
gods. The Dactylii had raised Jupiter, but he re-
belled against the Titans and conquered Heaven.

꙳ **Elisson** (EL-iss-sun) (Latin) He Is the
Elisson River, Greece
Erasinus (ur-RAZ-nus) (Latin) He Is the
Erasinus River, Greece
Elisson and Erasinus were two of the river-
spirits, called the Flumina by the Romans, who
personified every river in the world.

꙳ **Eosphorus** (ee-AHSS-fur-rus) (Latin) He Is
the Bright Planet Venus
Hesperus (STIL-bun) (Latin) He Is the Bright
Planet Venus
Phaenon (FAY-nun) (Latin) He Is the Bright
Planet Saturn
Phaethon (FAY-uh-tun) (Latin) He Is the Bright
Planet Jupiter
Pyroeis (peer-RAY-yiss) (Latin) He Is the Bright
Planet Mars
Stilbon (STIL-bun) (Latin) He Is the Bright
Planet Mercury
The Romans considered the planets of the Solar
System to be gods, called the Astra Planeta, or
Wandering Stars. The Romans and Greeks did not
identify Neptune, Pluto, and Uranus because they
were unaware these heavenly bodies existed.

🌣 **Eugenius** (yoo-JEEN-yus) (Latin) He Has an Excellent Beard

Philamnus (fil-AM-nus) (Latin) He Is Gentle with Little Lambs

Eugenius and Philamnus belonged to that group of nature-spirits whom the Romans called fauns. The fauns, half-human and half-goat, protected shepherds while at the same time enjoying life by carousing and falling in love.

🌣 **Eurotas** (yoor-RO-tus) (Latin) He Is the Eurotas River, Greece

Ganges (GAHN-jeez) (Latin) He Is the Ganges River, India

Eurotas and Ganges were two of the river-spirits, called the Flumina by the Romans, who personified every river in the world.

🌣 **Eurybios** (yur-RIB-ee-yohss) (Latin) He Lives Forever

Eurynomous (yur-IN-uh-mus) (Latin) He Is Wide-Open Fields

Eurytion (yur-RIH-shun) (Latin) He Is Rock-Solid

Eurytus (YOO-rih-tus) (Latin) He Is a Beautiful Libation-Cup

Faunus (FAW-nus) (Latin) He Is a Trusted Companion

Gleneus (GLEN-yus) (Latin) He Is Merriment

Hylaeus (hye-LEE-yuss) (Latin) He Is the Vast Woodlands

Hyles (HYE-leez) (Latin) He Is the Vast Woodlands

Imbreus (IM-bree-yus) (Latin) He Is a Beautiful Color

Iphinous (IF-uh-nus) (Latin) His Intelligence Is Swift

The Centauri, as the Romans called them—including Eurybios, Eurynomous, Eurytion, Eurytus, Faunus, Gleneus, Hylaeus, Hyles, Imbreus, and Iphinous—were creatures whose upper bodies were human and whose lower bodies were those of horses. Many Centauri were renowned as warriors, while others gained fame as teachers.

🌣 **Eurymedon** (yoo-RIM-eh-dahn) (Latin) He Has Many Resources

Alcon (AL-kahn) (Latin) He Is Powerful

Eurymedon and Alcon were two of the Cabeiri, gods who supervised the Greeks' sacred dances on the island of Samothrace to honor Demeter, goddess of grain, and her daughter, Queen Persephone of the underworld.

🌣 **Evenus** (EV-uh-nus) (Latin) He Is the Evenus River, Greece

Euphrates (yoo-FRAY-teez) (Latin) He Is the Euphrates River, Assyria

Evenus and Euphrates were two of the river-spirits, called the Flumina by the Romans, who personified every river in the world.

🌣 **Granicus** (GRAN-ih-kus) (Latin) He Is the Granicus River, Anatolia

Halys (HAL-liss) (Latin) He Is the Halys River, Anatolia

Granicus and Halys were two of the river-spirits, called the Flumina by the Romans, who personified every river in the world.

🌣 **Hadrian** (HAY-dree-yun) (Latin) He Is Hadria, Italy

Trajan (TRAY-zhun) (Latin) He Is an Emperor

The Roman Emperor Hadrian (A.D. 76–A.D. 138) built Hadrian's Wall, a stone barrier in northern Britain, to hold back the fierce Caledonians or Scots. Trajan, another builder of monumental public works, was Hadrian's predecessor.

🌣 **Hebrus** (HEE-brus) (Latin) He Is the Hebrus River, Greece

Hermus (HUR-mus) (Latin) He Is the Hermus River, Anatolia

Hebrus and Hermus were two of the river-spirits, called the Flumina by the Romans, who personified every river in the world.

🌣 **Icelus** (EYE-suh-lus) (Latin) He Creates Resemblances

Morpheus (MOR-fee-yus) (Latin) He Shapes and Creates

Phantasus (FAN-tah-sus) (Latin) He Brings Dreams to the Mind

Phobetor (FO-beh-tor) (Latin) He Is Feared

The Romans called their dream-giving gods Somnium. The Somnium—including Icelus, Morpheus, Phantasus, and Phobetor—were winged spirits who flew each night from Erebus, the dark realm, to impart dreams to mortals.

🌣 **Ilissus** (IL-iss-sus) (Latin) He Is the Ilissus River, Greece

Inachus (In-uh-kus) (Latin) He Is the Inachus River, Greece

Ilissus and Inachus were two of the river-spirits, called the Flumina by the Romans, who personified every river in the world.

🔖 **Julian** (JOO-lee-yun) (Latin) He Is Julius Caesar's Relative

Gregory (GREG-ree) (Latin) He Is Always Alert
Julian II (A.D. 331–A.D. 363) was a Roman emperor who tried to lead Rome back to its pagan religion; this, despite having studied with the Christian scholar Gregory Nazianzus.

🔖 **Julius** (JOO-lee-yus) (Latin) He Is Youthful

Marcus (MAR-kus) (Latin) He Is Powerfully Male
Julius Caesar (100 B.C.–44 B.C.) was the supreme ruler of Rome, the man who changed Rome from a republic into an empire. During Caesar's military campaigns, Marcus Antonius (Mark Antony) was one of Caesar's ablest generals.

🔖 **Ladon** (luh-DAHN) (Latin) He Is the Ladon River, Greece

Lamus (LAM-mus) (Latin) He Is the Lamus River, Anatolia
Ladon and Lamus were two of the river-spirits, called the Flumina by the Romans, who personified every river in the world.

🔖 **Latinus** (LAT-ih-nus) (Latin) He Is a Latin

Aeneas (ee-NEE-yus) (Latin) He Is Praise-Worthy
Latinus was the king of the Latins in Italy. King Latinus welcomed the Trojan hero Aeneas and his war-refugees, who were fleeing the devastation of the Trojan War. Aeneas eventually helped establish the Eternal City of Rome.

🔖 **Latreus** (LAY-trooss) (Latin) He Is a Public Servant

Lycabas (lye-KAY-bus) (Latin) He Is the Entire Year

Lycas (LYE-kus) (Latin) He Is Like a Wolf

Lycidas (LIS-uh-dus) (Latin) He Is a Young Wolf

Lycopes (LYE-ko-peez) (Latin) He Has the Eyes of the Wolf

Medon (muh-DAHN) (Latin) He Is Planning and Cleverness

Melaneus (mel-LAYN-yus) (Latin) He Wears Black Garments

Monychus (MAHN-ih-kus) (Latin) He Is a Fierce Wild Boar

Nessus (NES-sus) (Latin) He Is a Wild Fowl

Oreius (OR-ee-yus) (Latin) He Is a Lofty Mountain
The Centauri, as the Romans called them— including Latreus, Lycabas, Lycas, Lycidas, Lycopes, Medon, Melaneus, Monychus, Nessus, and Oreius—were beings whose upper bodies were human and whose lower bodies were those of horses. Many Centauri were renowned as warriors, while others gained fame as teachers.

🔖 **Letus** (LEE-tus) (Latin) He Conquers Life

Somnus (SAHM-nus) (Latin) He Conquers Wakefulness
Letus was the Roman god of crossing-over into the next world. Somnus was Letus's twin brother, the god of sleep.

🔖 **Lycus** (LYE-kus) (Latin) He Is a Mighty Wolf

Actaeus (AK-tee-yus) (Latin) He Is the Shoreline
Lycus and Actaeus were members of the group of ocean-spirits the Romans called the Telchines. Inhabiting the island of Rhodes, Greece, the Telchines forged the trident of the sea-god Poseidon, and many other fearsome weapons.

🔖 **Maron** (MEH-run) (Latin) He Is Maroneia, Greece

Leneus (leh-NEE-yus) (Latin) He Is the Grape-Trough for Wine-Making
Maron and Leneus were part of the honor-guard called the Silenus, who served Bacchus, god of wine, by helping mortals and immortals to stomp on grapes and make wine.

🔖 **Maximian** (max-IM-ee-yun) (Latin) He Is Greater than all Others

Galerius (gah-LAIR-ee-yus) (Latin) He Comes from Gaul
When the Roman Emperor Maximian (c. A.D. 250–A.D. 310) left the throne, Galerius Maximianus became emperor. Galerius built the Felix Romuliana palace to honor Romula, his mother.

🔖 **Montanus** (mon-TAN-nus) (Latin) They Are the Mountains

Athos (ATH-thohss) (Greek) He Is Mount Athos
The Montanus were Roman gods who personified Earth's mountains—such as Athos, god of Mount Athos in Thrace (Bulgaria). Alexander once called Mount Athos the perfect site for a monument to his glory. Instead, a Christian monastery stands there today.

🔖 **Mythra** (MITH-rah) (Persian) He Is the Radiant Sun

Antaea (an-TEE-yah) (Greek) He May Be Supplicated with Prayers

Mythra, or Mithra, originally a warlike Persian sun-god, was later adopted by Roman soldiers. Mythra's followers observed the Eleusinian Mysteries, the rituals which were also used to honor Ceres—called Demeter, or Antaea, by the Greeks.

☙ **Nilus** (NYE-lus) (Latin) He Is the Nile River, Egypt
Nessus (NES-sus) (Latin) He Is the Nessus River, Greece
Nilus and Nessus were two of the river-spirits, called the Flumina by the Romans, who personified every river in the world.

☙ **Numicius** (noo-MISH-shuhss) (Latin) He Is the Numicius River, Greece
Nymphaeus (NIM-fee-yus) (Latin) He Is the Nymphaeus River, Anatolia
Numicius and Nymphaeus were two of the river-spirits, called the Flumina by the Romans, who personified every river in the world.

☙ **Orontes** (or-AHN-tez) (Latin) He Is the Orontes River, Syria
Pactolus (PAK-toh-lus) (Latin) He Is the Pactolus River, Anatolia
Orontes and Pactolus were two of the river-spirits, called the Flumina by the Romans, who personified every river in the world.

☙ **Parthenius** (par-THEEN-yus) (Latin) He Is the Parthenius River, Anatolia
Rhodius (RO-dee-yus) (Latin) He Is the Rhodius River, Anatolia
Parthenius and Rhodius were two of the river-spirits, called the Flumina by the Romans, who personified every river in the world.

☙ **Plinius** (PLIN-ee-yus) (Latin) He Is Complete
Yale (YAIL) (Latin) He Moves with Grace
Pliny the Elder (A.D. 23–A.D. 79) was a Roman scientist who studied the natural world. His textbook The Natural History (Naturalis Historiae) describes many wonders, including the Yale, an African beast with large, movable horns.

☙ **Romulus** (RAHM-yoo-luss) (Latin) He Is of Rome
Remus (REE-muss) (Latin) He Is from Rome
Romulus and his twin brother Remus (both c. 771 B.C.–c. 717 B.C.) were the mythic Roman demigods who founded the Eternal City of Rome, making Romulus and Remus the progenitors of the thousand-year Roman Empire.

☙ **Sangarius** (san-GAIR-ree-yus) (Latin) He Is the Sangarius River, Anatolia
Selemnus (suh-LEM-nus) (Latin) He Is the Selemnus River, Greece
Sangarius and Selemnus were two of the river-spirits, called the Flumina by the Romans, who personified every river in the world.

☙ **Severus** (SEV-eh-rus) (Latin) He Is Severe
Galerius (gah-LAIR-ee-yus) (Latin) He Is from Gaul
Flavius Valerius Severus (?–A.D. 307), who began life as a peasant in Illyria (the present-day Balkans) rose through the ranks of the Roman military and gained the friendship of Emperor Galerius Maximus, to eventually become emperor of Rome.

☙ **Silvanus** (SIL-vah-nus) (Latin) He Is the Beautiful Woodlands
Faunus (FAW-nus) (Latin) He Is a Trusted Companion
Silvanus was the Roman name for the woodland god who appeared to mortals as a goat with the tail of a fish. He was the companion of Faunus, the fun-loving god of shepherds, whose upper half was human, while his lower half was goat-like.

☙ **Tacitus** (TAS-ih-tus) (Latin) He Knows How to Keep Silent
Domitian (doh-MEE-shun) (Latin) He Dominates
Tacitus (c. A.D. 56–c. A.D. 117) was a Roman historian who wrote the Annals (Annales), chronicling the lives of various Roman emperors, including Domitian (A.D. 51–A.D. 96), one of the longest-reigning emperors in Roman history.

☙ **Thermodon** (THUR-muh-dahn) (Latin) He Is the Thermodon River, Anatolia
Tigris (TYE-griss) (Latin) He Is the Tigris River, Assyria
Thermodon and Tiigris were two of the river-spirits, called the Flumina by the Romans, who personified every river in the world.

☙ **Valerius** (vuh-LAIR-ee-yus) (Latin) He Is Valorous
Sirius (SEER-ee-yus) (Latin) He Is the Radiant Dog Star
The Roman cleric Gaius Valerius Flaccus (?–A.D. 90) warned in his epic poem, the Argonautica, of the power of Sirius, god of the Dog Star, in the

constellation Canis Major, of overheating the "already heated waters of the streams."

🐾 **Virgil** (VUR-jil) (Latin) He Is Pure and Chaste
Aeneas (ee-NEE-yus) (Latin) He Is Praise-Worthy
Virgil (70 B.C.–19 B.C.) is a Roman poet famed for the Aeneid, published c. 25 B.C. The Aeneid tells the story of Prince Aeneas of Troy, who led refugees from the Trojan War to safety in Italy, thereby helping to establish Rome.

🐾 **Vitruvius** (vih-TROO-vee-yus) (Latin) He Is a Mighty Weapon
Publius (PUB-lee-yus) (Latin) He Is a Very Public Person
Vitruvius (c. 80 B.C.–70 B.C.) was a Roman engineer who authored the treatise On Architecture (De Architectura), which detailed the deeds of men such as the Roman Emperor Publius Septimus.

🐾 **Xanthus** (ZAN-thus) (Latin) He Is Golden-Haired and Radiant
Balius (BAY-lee-yus) (Latin) He Is a Beautiful Color
Xanthus and Balius were the Roman names for two immortal horses owned by Neptune, god of the seas. Neptune presented Xanthus and Balius to the young hero, Peleus, and his new bride, Thetis, goddess of the seas.

GIRLS

🐾 **Albia** (AL-bee-yuh) (Latin) She Is the Radiant Dawn
Marina (muh-REE-nuh) (Latin) She Is the Blue Ocean
Albia Dominica (c. A.D. 337–c. A.D. 378) was empress of Rome, wife of the Roman Emperor Valens. Albia's predecessor was Marina Severa, Roman empress and wife of Valentinian I.

🐾 **Anastasia** (an-ah-STAY-zhah) (Latin) She Is Reborn to New Life
Olga (OL-gah) (Russian) She Is Sacred
Anastasia (fourth century A.D.) was the daughter of Emperor Constantinus Chloris. However, much later in history, the Roman name Anastasia was also given to the lovely Grand Duchess Anastasia Romanova of Russia (1901–1918). One of Anastasia's sisters was the Grand Duchess Olga Romanova.

🐾 **Andarta** (an-DAR-tah) (Gaulish) She Is Invincible

Brigantia (brih-GAHN-tee-yah) (Gaulish) She Is a Town with a Sturdy Bridge
Damona (dah-MOH-nah) (Latin) She Is a Sacred Calf
Epona (ee-PO-nah) (Gaulish) She Is a Magnificent Mare
Levana (leh-VAH-nah) (Irish) She Is a Sacred Calf
Rosmerta (rose-MAIR-tah) (Gaulish) She Is a Great Provider
Sequana (seh-KWAH-nah) (Gaulish) She Is God's Divine Presence
Sirona (sih-RO-nah) (Gaulish) She Is a Radiant Star

🐾 **Anna** (AN-nah) (Latin) She Is Graceful
Dido (DYE-doh) (Latin) She Is Chaste and Pure
Anna, or Anna Perenna, was the Roman goddess of the calendar year. Anna's celebration was held on March 15, and gifts were offered to her in hopes that the year would be bountiful. Anna's sister was Dido, Queen of Carthage, Africa—the woman who loved Aeneas, the Trojan warrior who founded Rome.

🐾 **Annia** (ANN-yah) (Latin) She Is Supportive
Lucilla (loo-SIL-lah) (Latin) She Is Our Beloved Light
Annia (A.D. 147–A.D. 165) was the daughter of Faustina Minor, a Roman empress. Annia's sister was Lucilla, portrayed by actress Connie Nielsen in the 2000 film Gladiator, directed by Ridley Scott.

🐾 **Anthe** (AN-thee) (Latin) She Is all the Blossoming Flowers
Asteria (ah-STEER-ee-yah) (Latin) She Is Bright Starlight
Drimo (DREEM-moh) (Latin) She Is a Razor-Sharp Weapon
Pallene (pal-LEEN) (Latin) She Wields Powerful Weapons
The Alcyonides, daughters of the giant Alcyone—including Anthe, Asteria, Drimo, and Pallene—romped happily until Alcyone perished. Then, they leapt into the sea and became colorful fish.

🐾 **Argyra** (ar-ZHEER-rah) (Latin) She Is Pure Silver
Cabiro (kuh-BEER-roh) (Latin) The One Who Is the Sacred Religious Ritual
Doris (DOR-ris) (Latin) She Is a Pure Gift

Evarne (ee-VAR-nee) (Latin) She Is Rich in Flocks of Sheep

Ino (EYE-no) (Latin) She Is the White Goddess

Psamathea (sam-uh-THEE-yah) (Latin) She Is the Goddess of the Sands

Salacia (sah-LAY-shah) (Latin) She Is the Encircling Trinity

Tritia (TRISH-shah) (Latin) She Is the Daughter of the Sea-Divinity Triton

The Nereids—including Argyra, Cabiro, Doris, Evarne, Ino, Psamathea, Salacia, and Tritia—were nymphs or nature-spirits born to the sea-god Nereus and the river-goddess Doris. Artists painted the Nereids as girls riding on the backs of sea-serpents.

🕊 **Arria** (AHR-ree-yah) (Latin) He Is a Beautiful Melody

Fannia (FAHN-yah) (Latin) She Is a Revered Preacher

Arria was the wife of the Roman warrior Caecina Paetus, whose failed rebellion against Rome resulted in an edict to end his life. When Paetus failed to do so, Arria took his dagger and used it on herself, saying, "Non dolet, Paete," or, "It doesn't hurt, Paetus." Fannia, Arria's descendant, told Arria's story to the Roman poet Pliny the Younger.

🕊 **Atia** (AH-tee-yuh) (Latin) She Is a Precious Gift

Polly (PAHL-lee) (English) She Is Love

The son of Atia (85 B.C.–43 B.C.) would one day become the Roman Emperor Augustus (63 B.C.–A.D. 19). And, although British actress Polly Walker is not Roman, she gave a fine portrayal of Atia in the Home Box Office (HBO) television show Rome (2005–2007).

🕊 **Aurelia** (or-REEL-yah) (Latin) She Is Pure Gold

Julia (JOOL-yuh) (Latin) She Is Beautifully Youthful

Aurelia (120 B.C.–54 B.C.) was the mother of Julius Caesar, the most famous Roman emperor of them all. Aurelia's other children were Julia Caesaris Major and Julia Caesaris Minor. Aurelia was considered by Romans to be the perfect mother.

🕊 **Averna** (ah-VUR-nah) (Latin) She Is the Queen of the Underworld

Persephone (pur-SEF-uh-nee) (Greek) She Is a Beautiful Maiden

The queen of the underworld and goddess of springtime, called Averna by the Romans and Persephone by the Greeks, spent the winter in the underworld with her husband, Hades, and in spring went aboveground to join her mother Demeter, goddess of grain.

🕊 **Bella** (BEL-lah) (Latin) She Is a Warrior

Dino (DEE-no) (Latin) She Inspires Fear

Enyo (EN-yo) (Greek) She Is Warlike

Pemphredo (pem-FRAY-doh) (Latin) She Shows the Way

Persis (PUR-sis) (Latin) She Is the Destroyer

The "saffron-robed" Graeae—including Bella, Dino, Enyo, Pemphredo, and Persis—were the goddesses of the angry sea-foam. They were often shown on Greek pottery as having the heads of women and the bodies of swans.

🕊 **Britannia** (brih-TAN-yah) (Gaulish) She Is the Nation of Great Britain

Satiada (sah-tee-AH-dah) (Gaulish) She Is Abundance

Britannia and Satiada were goddesses of the Gallo-Roman religion, a blending of Roman divinities with Gaulish (French) divinities. Britannia personified the island nation of Great Britain and Satiada was the goddess of abundance.

🕊 **Calpurnia** (kal-PUR-nee-yuh) (Latin) She Is a Beautiful Chalice

Haydn (HAY-dun) (Welsh) She Has Her Own Sacred Beliefs

Calpurnia Pisonis (first century B.C.) was the wife of the Roman conqueror Julius Caesar. Calpurnia had a dream that Caesar would be assassinated, yet she could not save him. And, although not Roman, British actress Haydn Gwynne played Calpurnia beautifully in the 2005–2007 HBO television series Rome.

🕊 **Camilla** (kah-MEEL-lah) (Latin) She Observes Sacred Rituals

Lavinia (lah-VIN-ee-yah) (Latin) She Is Pure-Hearted

When King Metabus of the Italian nation of Volsci was deposed, he fled with his infant daughter Camilla. When a river blocked him, he tied Camilla to a lance, prayed to the goddess Diana, and hurled Camilla safely across. Years later, the warrior Camilla fought in a great battle that would decide which suitor would marry Princess Lavinia of Latium.

🌿 **Carya** (KAIR-ee-yah) (Latin) She Is a Fragrant Nut Tree

Morea (mo-RAY-yah) (Latin) She Is the Fragrant Mulberry Bush

In Roman mythology, Carya and Morea were part of the sorority of forest-spirits called the Hamadryads, the protectors of trees.

🌿 **Claudia** (KLAW-dee-yah) (Latin) She Walks a Difficult Path

Poppaea (po-PAY-yah) (Latin) She Is of the People

Claudia Augusta (A.D. 63–A.D. 63) was the daughter of the Roman Emperor Nero and the Empress Poppaea Sabina. Claudia did not live long after entering this world, and after her passing was proclaimed a goddess.

🌿 **Clementia** (kleh-MEN-tee-yah) (Latin) She Is Forgiving

Anaidea (ah-NAY-dee-yah) (Latin) She Is Unforgiving

Clementia was the Roman goddess of mercy, "of all divinities the most useful," said the Greek poet Pausanias. Clementia's friend was Anaidea, goddess of the unforgiving heart.

🌿 **Clodia** (KLO-dee-yah) (Latin) She Is Vibrantly Glorious

Fulvia (FUL-vee-yah) (Latin) She Is Golden

Clodia Pulchra (c. 57 B.C.–?), wife of the Roman statesman Publius Clodius Pulcher, was the daughter of the famous Fulvia, who received a tribute no other Roman woman had ever received: Fulvia was the first living woman to have coins struck in her honor.

🌿 **Cloelia** (klo-EEL-yah) (Latin) She Is Blossoming

Florence (FLOR-renss) (Latin) She Is a Wealthy and Flourishing Lady

Cloelia was part of a group of Roman teens given to the invader King Lars Porsenna of Clusium, an Italian city, in exchange for peace. But Cloelia escaped by swimming across the Tiber River. Porsenna asked Cloelia to return and when she did, he honored her. Porsenna's city of Clusium is today's Florence, Italy.

🌿 **Concordia** (kun-KOR-dee-yah) (Latin) She Is Peace and Concord

Venus (VEE-nus) (Latin) She Is Love and Beauty

Concordia was the Roman goddess of marriages and peace. Concordia's mother was Venus, the Roman goddess of love.

🌿 **Cornelia** (kor-NEEL-yah) (Latin) She Is a Cornucopia of Plenty

Valeria (vah-LAIR-ee-yah) (Latin) She Is Powerful

Cornelia Sulla (c. 109 B.C.–?), daughter of Consul Lucius Sulla, survived her father's numerous marriages. Cornelia served as Sulla's secretary after his marriage to his fourth spouse, Valeria Messala. Thereafter, Cornelia was honored as an elder stateswoman.

🌿 **Diana** (dye-AN-nah) (Latin) She Is the Heavenly Life Source

Artemis (AR-teh-miss) (Greek) She Is the Heavenly Life Source

Diana was the Roman goddess of hunting, called Artemis by the Greeks. Diana loved to hunt wearing no clothing; if any mortal chanced to see her, she shot him with arrows.

🌿 **Dimale** (DIM-ah-lee) (Latin) She Is the Earth Mother

Apollonia (ap-ah-LO-nee-yah) (Greek) She Is the Light

Dimale was a city-state in Illyria, a nation now called Albania. Dimale lay not far from another important city-state, Apollonia, which in 229 B.C. was conquered by Rome. The name Apollonia honors Apollo, god of prophecy.

🌿 **Dodona** (doh-DAH-nah) (Latin) She Is Dodone, Greece

Dione (dee-YAHN) (Greek) She Is a Celestial Goddess

Dodona was the Roman name for a nymph or nature-spirit who personified the city of Dodone, Greece. Dione was one of the Oceanides, a guardian of Earth's water sources.

🌿 **Domitia** (doh-MEE-shah) (Latin) She Is a Comfortable Home

Messalina (mess-suh-LEE-nah) (Latin) She Is from the Messala Family

Domitia Lepida Major (c. 19 B.C.–A.D. 59) was the daughter of the Roman nobleman Lucius Ahenobarbus and the beautiful Antonia Major. Domitia's niece Messalina eventually became a Roman empress.

🌿 **Endeis** (en-DAY-yis) (Latin) She Loves Her Nation

Aegina (ee-JEE-nah) (Greek) She Tends Goats

Endeis was the Roman name for the nymph or nature-spirit wed to King Aeacus of the island of

Aegina. Aegina was named in honor of Aeacus's mother, the nymph Aegina.

🕭 **Ersa** (UR-sah) (Latin) She Is Morning Dew
Nemea (neh-MEE-yah) (Latin) She Is Nemeia, Greece
Ersa was the Roman goddess of mists, which sustained the forests of the world. Ersa's other name was Nemea, protector of the water sources of Nemea, Greece.

🕭 **Eugenia** (yoo-JEEN-yah) (Greek) She Is Aristocratic
Cecilia (seh-SEEL-yah) (Latin) She Sees Deeply Within Herself
Saint Eugenia (third century A.D.) was a Roman who converted to Christianity and performed miracle cures. Another early Christian, Saint Cecilia, became a holy martyr.

🕭 **Eutropia** (yoo-TRO-pee-yah) (Latin) She Is Multitalented
Galeria (gah-LAIR-ee-yah) (Latin) She Is from Gaul
Roman Empress Eutropia (?–c. A.D. 325) was the Syrian-born spouse of the Roman Emperor Maximian. Eutropia was succeeded on the throne by Empress Galeria Valeria.

🕭 **Fabia** (FAH-bee-yah) (Latin) She Is a Sweet Bean
Orestilla (or-ess-TEE-yah) (Latin) She Is from the Mountains
Fabia Orestilla's ancestor was the Roman Emperor Antoninus Pius. Later, the Augustan History (Historia Augusta) *recorded that Fabia married the Roman Emperor Gordian I.*

🕭 **Fauna** (FAW-nah) (Latin) She Is all Creation
Marica (mah-REE-kah) (Latin) She Is a Fragrant Olive Tree
Fauna was the Roman goddess of childbirth. Fauna was also called Marica. She was beloved under both names because she healed the sick and gave liberty to slaves.

🕭 **Galla** (GAL-lah) (Latin) She Fights like a Bantam Rooster
Placidia (plah-SID-ee-yah) (Latin) She Is Peaceful
Galla (A.D. 392–A.D. 450) was married to the Roman Emperor Constantius III. From A.D. 425, Galla served as Regent of Rome, acting on behalf of her child, Emperor Valentinian, until he came of age in A.D. 437. Galla was often called Placidia.

🕭 **Junia** (JOON-ee-yah) (Latin) She Resembles the Queen of Heaven
Servilia (sur-VILL-yah) (Latin) She Is a Member of the Servilianus Family
Junia (first century B.C.) was the daughter of the seductress Servilia Caepionis, who had been the concubine of the Roman Emperor Julius Caesar.

🕭 **Juno** (JOO-no) (Latin) She Has Beautiful Eyes
Xenia (ZEEN-yuh) (Greek) She Is Gracious and Hospitable
Juno was the Roman name for Hera, queen of Mount Olympus, who ruled beside Jove, her husband, high king of the Olympian gods. In many legends, Juno rejoiced at the birth of Athena Xenia (Athena the Hospitable), goddess of wisdom, who sprang as an adult from Jove's head.

🕭 **Laetitia** (leh-TISH-shah) (Latin) She Is a Delight
Fama (FAH-mah) (Latin) She Is Glory and Fame
Laetitia was the Roman goddess of joy. She would gather with other deities at the Earth's center, a huge chamber with many doors, and tell stories about gods and mortals. Fama, goddess of stories, would listen carefully, then spread these stories around the world.

🕭 **Lalla** (LAHL-lah) (Greek) She Is the Beloved One Who Speaks Much
Faustina (fah-oh-STEE-nah) (Latin) She Is Fortunate
Lalla (c. A.D. 80–c. A.D. 100), a pious nun, was the wife of the Roman aristocrat Diotomos. She tended the sacred Anatolian temples devoted to Romans who had been made into gods by the Senate. One of these deities was the Roman Empress Faustina.

🕭 **Lara** (LAH-rah) (Latin) She Is a Laurel Wreath of Victory
Juturna (joo-TUR-nah) (Latin) She Is the Nymph of the Fountains
The Roman poet Ovid (43 B.C.–A.D. 17) told in his Fasti *of the nymph Lara, sister to the nymph Juturna. When Jove, high king of Greek gods, told Juturna to make love to him, Lara tattled to Juno, Jove's wife. Jove then unfairly removed poor Lara's tongue.*

🕭 **Larenta** (lah-REN-tah) (Latin) She Is the Earth Goddess
Lupa (LOO-pah) (Latin) She Is a Fierce She-Wolf

The Roman shepherd Faustulus found the twins Romulus and Remus in the forest being raised by the wolf Lupa. Faustulus took the boys to Larenta, his wife, who raised these sons of Mars, god of war, to manhood. Romulus and Remus later founded Rome.

🐦 **Larina** (lah-REE-nah) (Latin) She Is the Soaring Sea-Gull

Casmilla (kaz-MIL-lah) (Latin) She Observes Sacred Rituals

Larina was the bodyguard of Princess Camilla, daughter of Queen Casmilla and King Metabus of the Italian nation of the Volsci.

🐦 **Laverna** (lah-VUR-nah) (Latin) She Is Springtime

Naevia (NEE-vee-yah) (Latin) She Is from the Family of Naevius

Laverna was a Roman deity of the underworld. Her devotees made sacrifices to her near the beautiful Porta Neavia gate in Rome's Servian Wall.

🐦 **Licinia** (lih-SIN-ee-yah) (Latin) She Is from Lycia, Anatolia

Eudocia (yoo-DOH-shah) (Latin) She Is Glorious

Licinia Eudoxia (A.D. 422–A.D. 462) was an empress of Rome, ruling beside her first husband, Valentinian III, and her second husband, Petronius Maximus. Licinia's mother was the Roman Empress Eudocia Augusta.

🐦 **Livia** (LIV-ee-yah) (Latin) She Is the Beautiful Color Blue

Agrippina (ag-grip-PEE-nah) (Latin) She Possesses Much Land

Livia Augusta (58 B.C.–29 B.C.) was a Roman empress married to Rome's first emperor, Augustus (63 B.C.–A.D. 14). Livia was Augustus's confidante, even taking official actions on his behalf. Her descendants included the powerful Agrippina Minor.

🐦 **Livilla** (lih-VIL-lah) (Latin) She Is the Little One Who Is the Beautiful Color Blue

Patricia (pah-TRISH-shah) (Latin) She Is Aristocratic

Livilla (c. 13 B.C.–A.D. 31) was the daughter of the Roman Emperor Nero (38 B.C.–9 B.C.). And, although British actress Patricia Quinn is not Roman, she played Livilla brilliantly on the 1976 BBC series I, Claudius.

🐦 **Lucilia** (loo-SEEL-yah) (Latin) She Is the Sacred Light

Alyson (AL-ih-sun) (English) She Is a Noble Sort of Person

Lucilia was the wife of the Roman poet Lucretius. Lucilia's name appears in the story told by Alyson, the Wife of Bath, in Canterbury Tales *by English poet Geoffrey Chaucer.*

🐦 **Lucina** (loo-SEE-nah) (Greek) She Has Beautiful Eyes

Silvia (SIL-vee-yah) (Latin) She Is the Beautiful Woodlands

Lucina was a Roman name for the goddess Hera, who ruled beside Jove, high king of the gods. Lucina's sacred site was Rome's Esquilline Hill, tended by holy Vestal Virgins. The greatest Vestal Virgin was Rhea Silvia, mother of Romulus and Remus, Rome's founders.

🐦 **Lucretia** (loo KREE-shah) (Latin) She Is Pure Gold

Virginia (vur-JIN-yah) (Latin) She Is Chaste and Pure

The Roman maiden Virginia (fifth century B.C.) was violated by King Appius Claudius. Outraged, the Roman people deposed Appius. Similarly, another Roman maiden, Lucretia (sixth century B.C.) was violated by Prince Sextus Tarquinius. Again the people deposed the tyrant, this time establishing the democratic republic of Rome.

🐦 **Maera** (MEE-rah) (Latin) She Sparkles with Light

Melita (meh-LEE-tah) (Greek) She Is Honey-Sweet

Roman mythology tells of the nymphs Maera and Melita, river-goddesses who joined their sisters, the Erasinides, to protect the River Erasinos in Greece.

🐦 **Marcella** (mar-SEL-lah) (Latin) She Is as Powerful as any male

Selanaia (sel-AYN-yah) (Greek) Her Light Always Shines

Saint Marcella (A.D. 325–A.D. 410) was an early Roman Christian. Marcella's family manor stood on Rome's Aventine Hill, a site that also held a temple to the moon goddess Luna, or Selanaia. After Marcella's conversion, her house became a haven for Christians.

🐦 **Moneta** (mo-NEE-tuh) (Latin) The One Who Is Blessed Memory

Melete (muh-LEE-tee) (Latin) The One Who Is Patient Practice

Moneta was the Roman name for Greek goddess of memory Mnemosyne, who bore the Musa (Muses), creative spirits who bestowed inspiration on humanity. One of Moneta's sisters was Melete, goddess of the patient practice that perfects one's art.

🐷 **Nona** (NO-nah) (Latin) She Is the Ninth
Decima (DES-ih-mah) (Latin) She Is Tenth
Nona, Decima, and Morta were the Roman names for the avenging goddesses called the Parcae, or Fates, who decided every aspect of the lives of mortals. The Fates gave every human portions of good and evil, then punished anyone who chose evil.

🐷 **Octavia** (ahk-TAY-vee-yah) (Latin) She Is Eighth
Angela (AN-jay-lah) (Italian) She Is God's Angelic Messenger
Octavia Thurina Minor (69 B.C.–11 B.C.) was a member of the Julio-Claudian Dynasty and wife of Mark Antony, one of three corulers of Rome in 44 B.C. Octavia was portrayed in the 1976 television series I, Claudius by British actress Angela Morant.

🐷 **Panacea** (pan-ah-SEE-yah) (Latin) She Heals All
Salus (SAL-lus) (Latin) She Is Robust Good Health
Panacea was the goddess of healing. Her father was Asclepius, god of medicine, and her mother was Epione, goddess of comfort. Panacea and her sister Salus, goddess of health, knew every medicine that could cure disease.

🐷 **Paulina** (po-LEE-nah) (Latin) She Is Modesty and Humility
Vibia (VIB-ee-yah) (Latin) She Is Movement and Life
Paulina was the niece of Hadrian (A.D. 76–A.D. 138), one of the "Five Good Emperors," who enriched Rome. One of Paulina's relatives was the Roman Empress Vibia Sabina.

🐷 **Porcia** (POR-shah) (Latin) She Is a Powerful Tusked Boar
Jessica (JES-sih-kah) (English) She Is a Sight to Behold
Porcia (c. 95 B.C.–c. 45 B.C.) was the sister of the Roman leader Cato. Centuries later, the name Porcia was applied to the eloquent Portia in The Merchant of Venice *by William*

Shakespeare. Another character in the play is Jessica, daughter of the merchant Shylock.

🐷 **Prima** (PREE-mah) (Latin) She Is First
Hersilia (hur-SEEL-yah) (Latin) She Is a Glorious Sabine Woman
Prima was history's first Princess of Rome. Her mother was Hersilia, first queen of Rome, and her father was Romulus, one of the twins who founded Rome.

🐷 **Procia** (PRO-shah) (Latin) She Is the One Who Lives far from Her Father
Charlotte (SHAR-lut) (French) She Is a Beloved Little Warrior
Procia is a name scholars give to the wife of the Roman governor of Judea, Pontius Pilate, who condemned Jesus Christ. In the Holy Bible, Pontius's wife tells of a dream that warns that Christ must be spared, but Pilate ignores her. And, although British author Charlotte Brontë was not Roman, her poem Pilate's Wife's Dream honors Procia.

🐷 **Proserpina** (pro-SUR-pih-nah) (Latin) She Emerges Wonderfully
Hecate (heh-KAH-tee) (Latin) She Is Far Distant
When Pluto, god of the underworld, kidnapped Proserpina (Persephone), her mother Ceres (Demeter), goddess of grain, grieved terribly. Hecate, goddess of sorcery, helped Ceres by walking beside her through dark nights, holding a torch, looking for Proserpina.

🐷 **Prosymna** (pro-SIM-nah) (Latin) She Is Honored with Sacred Songs
Acraea (ah-KREE-yah) (Latin) She Is a Lofty Summit
In Roman mythology, Acraea and Prosymna belonged to the sorority of nature-deities called the Asteronides by Greek poets. The Asteronides were children of the river-god Asterion.

🐷 **Regina** (reh-JEE-nuh) (Latin) She Is a Majestic Queen
Deorum (dee-OR-rum) (Latin) She Is Godly
Regina was a Roman title given to goddesses and queens—e.g., Regina Deorum, a title given to Juno, Queen of the Olympian gods, and the wife of Jove, high king of the gods.

🐷 **Sextia** (SEX-tee-yah) (Latin) She Is Sixth
Aemilia (ee-MEEL-yah) (Latin) She Is a Courageous Rival

Sextia was the wife of Mamercus Aemilius
Scarus (first century A.D.), a Roman teacher,
consul, and statesman. Scarus's first wife had
been the noblewoman Aemilia Lepida.

🕊 **Tatia** (TAH-tee-yah) (Latin) She Is the
Daughter of King Tatius
Sabina (sah-BEE-nah) (Latin) She Is Sabinium
Princess Tatia was the daughter of King Tatius
of Sabinium, who fought Rome after Rome's
soldiers kidnapped Sabine women. After many
years, the women negotiated peace between the
two nations. Many Sabine women proudly bore
the name Sabina.

🕊 **Terentia** (teh-REN-chuh) (Latin) She Is
Delicate and Gentle
Tullia (TOOL-lee-yah) (Latin) She Is Fine Silk
Terentia (98 B.C.–4 A.D.) was the wife of Rome's
greatest orator, Marcus Cicero. Terentia's advice
helped Cicero achieve his career ambitions,
including becoming Consul of Rome. Terentia's
daughter was Tullia Ciceronis, whom Terentia
and Cicero adored.

🕊 **Triaria** (tree-AHR-ee-yah) (Latin) She Is
Sweet and Elegant
Margherita (mar-geh-REE-tah) (Italian) She Is
a Priceless Pearl
The tale of Triaria (first century A.D.) is told by
Italian author Giovanni Boccaccio in his 1361–
1362 work On Famous Women. He lauds the fact
that Triaria accompanies her husband Lucius Vi-
tellius the Younger into battle and fights bravely.
Boccaccio's own wife was the illustrious Italian
noblewoman Margherita del Mardoli.

🕊 **Veturia** (veh-TOO-ree-yah) (Latin) She Is
Victory
Camilla (kah-MIL-lah) (Latin) She Observes
Sacred Rituals
Veturia was an illustrious woman of the Italian
nation of the Volsci. Veturia's son Coriolanus
became a Roman military conqueror. Another
great Volsci woman was Princess Camilla, who
in adulthood achieved the ability to run at
superspeed.

🕊 **Victoria** (vik-TOR-ee-yah) (Latin) She Is
Humanity's Triumph
Pallas (PAL-lus) (Greek) She Is Chaste and
Pure
In Roman mythology, Victoria was the coun-
terpart of the Greek divinity Nike, goddess of
victory. Victoria's father was Pallas, the war-god
of the Titans, the deities who ruled in Heaven

before being overthrown by Zeus and his
Olympian gods.

🕊 **Zenobia** (zeh-NO-bee-yah) (Greek) She Is
God's Life-Force
Mavia (MAH-vee-yah) (Arabic) She Is a Sacred
Herb
Zenobia (c. A.D. 240–c. A.D. 274) was the Syrian
warrior-empress whose forces defeated Rome's
armies in Egypt. But by A.D. 274, a defeated
Zenobia was taken to Rome, where the Emperor
Aurelian gave her property and riches. A cen-
tury later, the lovely Arab ruler Mavia likewise
defeated Rome's Egyptian armies.

BOYS AND GIRLS

🕊 **Abundantia** (ah-bun-DAHN-tee-yah) (Latin)
She Is Abundance
Thor (THOR) (Norwegian) He Is Thunder and
Lightning
Abundantia was the Roman goddess of bounty.
Over the centuries, Scandinavians placed
Abundantia in their own Norse pantheon, which
included the thunder-god Thor.

🕊 **Agnes** (AG-ness) (Greek) She Shimmers
with Sunlight
Anastasios (ahn-ah-STAH-see-yohss) (Greek)
He Is Born to New Life
Anastasius (ahn-ah-STAY-zhuhs) (Latin) He Is
Born into a New Life
Andreas (an-DRAY-yahss) (Greek) He Is
Powerfully Male
Ariadne (air-ee-AHD-nee) (Greek) She Is Most
Holy
Basil (BAY-zil) (Greek) He Rules Humanity
Caterina (kat-ur-REE-nah) (Latin) She Is Pure-
Hearted
Chapelle (shah-PEL) (French) She Is a Holy
Chapel
Claire (KLAIR) (French) She Is Bright and
Clear
Constantina (kahn-stun-TEE-nah) (Latin) She
Is Loyal and Constant

🕊 **Andreas** (an-DRAY-yus) (Greek) He Is
Powerfully Male
Bertha (BUR-thah) (German) She Shimmers
Gloriously
Charles (CHARLZ) (English/French) He Is a
Mighty Warrior
Constans (KAHN-stunz) (Latin) He Is
Dependably Constant

Leontia (lee-AHN-tee-yah) (Latin) She Is a Noble Lioness
Manuel (MAHN-yoo-wel) (German) His God Is with Us
Phocas (FO-kus) (Greek) He Is a Noble Sea-Lion
Victor (VIK-tor) (Latin) He Is Victorious
Vittoria (vit-TOR-ee-yah) (Latin) She Is Glorious Victory
Zoe (ZO-wee) (Greek) She Is Life Itself

Angita (an-JEE-tah) (Latin) She Is Marked for Greatness
Servius (SUR-vee-yus) (Latin) He Rescues and Preserves
Angita was the Roman deity who changed into a serpent and cured diseases. Angita's story is told in In Tria Virgilii Opera Expositio by the writer Servius (fourth century A.D.).

Apollonius (ahp-pah-LO-nee-yus) (Latin) He Is the Source of all Light
Alexandria (al-ex-AN-dree-yah) (Greek) She Protects Humanity
Apollonius Rhodius (third century B.C.) supervised the Royal Library of Alexandria, Egypt—history's greatest storehouse of knowledge. Tragically, fire destroyed the library.

Arcadius (ar-KAY-dee-yus) (Latin) He Is from the Land of the Bears
Aelia (EEL-yah) (Latin) He Is the Whirlwind
Arcadius (c. A.D. 377–A.D. 408) was the Roman emperor from A.D. 383–A.D. 395 who crafted the statutes titled Corpus Juris Civilis. Arcadius's mother was Aelia Flaccilla.

Arminius (ar-MIN-ee-yus) (Latin) He Has Aquamarine-Blue Eyes
Rhenus (REE-nus) (Latin) She Is the Rhine River
Arminius was the Roman name for the ruler of the Cherusci, a Teutonic nation in present-day Germany. Arminius destroyed several Roman armies and established the Rhine River—which the Romans called the Rhenus—as the Empire's western limit.

Aurelius (or-REE-lee-yus) (Latin) He Is Pure Gold
Alissar (AL-lis-sar) (Arabic) She Is a Wanderer
Saint Aurelius (fifth century A.D.) was the bishop of the city of Carthage in Africa (Tunisia). One of Carthage's legendary rulers was Alissar, also called Dido.

Autumnus (aw-TUM-nus) (Latin) She Is the Colorful Autumn Season
Phoebus (FEE-bus) (Latin) He Is the Sun
Autumnus was the Roman name for the fall season—one of the Horae, goddesses of Earth's seasons. The Horae served bright Phoebus, god of the Sun.

Avitus (AV-ih-tus) (Latin) He Honors His Ancestors
Cypria (SIP-ree-yah) (Latin) She Is Cyprus
Avitus (second century A.D.) was an aristocrat from Roman Syria. He eventually became governor of Cyprus, an island that was also called Cypria, according to the Roman poet Ovid in his poem Metamorphoses.

Bellona (bel-LO-nah) (Latin) He Is Prepared to Go to War
Mars (MARZ) (Latin) He Is Powerfully Male
Bellona was the Roman goddess of war, perhaps even older than Ares, the Greek war-god whom the Romans renamed Mars. The Romans considered Bellona and Mars to be siblings who strode into warfare together, fearless and invincible.

Bromius (BRO-mee-yus) (Latin) He Is Fearsome Thunder
Lenaeus (leh-NEE-yus) (Latin) He Is the Grape-Crushing Tub for Wine-Making
Bromius and Lenaeus were two of the names the Romans gave to Bacchus, god of wine.

Candace (KAHN-dahss) (Nubian) She Is the Queen Mother
Petronius (peh-TRON-ee-yus) (Latin) He Is from the Farmlands
Queen Candace (first century B.C.) ruled the African city-state of Meroë—renowned for its iron-workers—in Nubia, or present-day Sudan. Candace enjoyed military victories in Egypt, but the Roman Governor Petronius eventually defeated Candace's armies.

Carmanor (KAR-muh-nor) (Latin) He Shears the Harvest
Ceres (SEE-reez) (Latin) She Is the Blessed Mother Earth
Carmanor was the god of wheat-shearing in the island-nation of Crete. Carmanor helped Apollo, god of prophecy, complete his purification rites after Apollo slew the serpent Python. Carmanor dearly loved Ceres, goddess of harvests.

🐝 **Carmenta** (kar-MEN-tah) (Latin) She Is a Poem and a Melody

Evander (ee-VAN-dur) (Latin) He Is a Good-Hearted Man

Carmenta was one of the Camenea, Roman nature-spirits who guarded the water sources of Terra, the Earth. Carmenta invented the Latin letters used by the Romans and by our own culture. Carmenta's son was Evander, who later became the ruler of Latium.

🐝 **Cassius** (KASH-shuhs) (Latin) He Truly Loves Himself

Nikaia (nih-KAY-yah) (Greek) She Is Glorious Victory

Cassius Dio (c. A.D. 155–c. A.D. 229) was a Roman biographer whose encyclopedia Roman History *detailed the lives of Roman emperors and other historic personages. Cassius was born in the Greek city-state of Nikaia, in Anatolia (Turkey).*

🐝 **Charito** (CHAIR-uh-toh) (Latin) She Is Charitable

Constantius (kahn-STAN-tee-yus) (Latin) He Is Constant and True

Gregoria (greh-GOR-ee-yah) (Latin) She Is Always Watchful and Alert

Helena (HEL-leh-nah) (Latin) She Is a Radiant Torch

Herakleios (hair-AK-lee-ohss) (Greek) He Is the Glory of the Queen of Heaven

Jacobus (JAY-kuh-bus) (Latin) He Surpasses Everyone

Jovian (JO-vee-yun) (Latin) He Resembles Jove, Heaven's King

Justin (JUS-tin) (Latin) He Is Righteous and Just

Ravenna (rah-VEN-nah) (Latin) She Is a Shining Black Bird

Sophia (so-FEE-yah) (Greek) She Is Knowledge

Tribonian (trih-BO-nee-yahn) (Latin) He Is Three Times Greater than Others

🐝 **Cicero** (SIH-seh-ro) (Latin) He Is a Chickpea

Caecilia (see-SEEL-yah) (Latin) She Sees Deeply Within Herself

Marcus Cicero (106 B.C.–43 B.C.) was Rome's greatest lawyer, winning cases against the rich and powerful. Cicero befriended Caecilia Pomponia Attica, daughter of Titus Pomponius Atticus.

🐝 **Claudius** (KLAW-dee-yus) (Latin) He Walks a Difficult Path

Nero (NEE-ro) (Latin) He Is Hearty and Powerful

Claudius (10 B.C.–A.D. 54) was a Roman emperor famed for monumental building projects. Nero (A.D. 37–A.D. 68) was Claudius's son.

🐝 **Constantine** (KON-stun-teen) (Greek) He Is Dependably Constant

Euphemia (yoo-FEE-mee-yah) (Greek) She Speaks Beautifully

Evelyn (EV-eh-lin) (Latin) She Is Greatly Desired

Giacomo (jee-AH-ko-mo) (Italian) He Is Divinely Protected

Giovanni (jee-oh-VAHN-nee) (Italian) His God Is Gracious

Justinian (just-IN-ee-yun) (Latin) He Is Fair and Just

Katherine (KATH-rin) (English) She Is Pure-Hearted

Kiranna (keer-AHN-nah) (Armenian) She Is Graceful

Magna (MAG-nah) (Latin) She Is Exceedingly Great

Marguerite (mar-guh-REET) (French) She Is a Priceless Pearl

🐝 **Coriolanus** (kor-ee-uh-LAY-nus) (Latin) He Is a Victor

Veturia (veh-TOO-ree-yah) (Latin) She Is Humanity's Triumph

Coriolanus (fifth century B.C.) was a Roman general who defeated the Italian tribe of the Volsci, but later joined them after being exiled from Rome. However, when he led the Volsci against Rome, Coriolanus's mother Veturia tearfully persuaded him to withdraw.

🐝 **Devera** (deh-VEER-rah) (Latin) He Is Made of Honesty

Silvanus (sil-VAN-nus) (Latin) He Is the Great Forest

Devera was the Roman goddess of birth. With her sisters Intercidona and Pilumnus, Devera protected newborns from the god Silvanus, who personified danger. Devera and her sisters represented civilization by personifying the ax, pestle, and broom.

🐝 **Dia** (DEE-yah) (Latin) She Is the Glorious Morning

Eioneus (EE-oh-nus) (Greek) He Is King of Mount Nysa, Greece

In Roman mythology, Dia was the daughter of the warrior Eioneus. When Dia married the mortal Prince Ixion, Eioneus offended Ixion so badly that Ixion took Eioneus's life.

🔗 **Discordia** (dis-KOR-dee-yah) (Latin) She Is Conflict and Aggression

Lyssa (LIS-sah) (Greek) She Is Fury and Rage

Discordia was the Roman goddess of conflicts. A related goddess was Greek goddess Lyssa, called Ira by the Romans, goddess of rage.

🔗 **Drusilla** (droo-SIL-lah) (Latin) She Is the Beloved One Who Is Powerful

Caligula (kah-LIG-yoo-lah) (Latin) He Is the Little Pair of Boots

Drusilla (A.D. 16–A.D. 38) had seven royal siblings, one of whom was the infamous Roman Emperor Caligula, a feared monarch. Drusilla and Caligula shared a close relationship, which many historians have seen as unstable and mysterious.

🔗 **Egeria** (ee-ZHEER-ree-yah) (Latin) She Is Wisdom

Caracalla (kar-ah-KAHL-lah) (Latin) She Moves Slowly and Majestically

Egeria was a Roman river-nymph who personified the hot-springs called the Baths of Caracalla. The Baths derived their name from the Roman Emperor Caracalla, who built the beautiful structures surrounding the springs.

🔗 **Evander** (ee-VAN-dur) (Greek) He Is a Noble Person

Arcadia (ahr-KAY-dee-yah) (Latin) She Is the Land of Bears

The great warrior of Arcadia, King Evander, established the city of Latium, which found itself besieged by the giant Cacus. When the demigod hero Heracles arrived and slew Cacus, Evander built a temple in his honor.

🔗 **Faunus** (FAW-mus) (Latin) He Is a Trusted Companion

Penelope (peh-NEL-oh-pee) (Greek) She Weaves Threads

Faunus was the fun-loving god of shepherds. The upper half of his body was human, while the lower half was goatlike. Faunus's mother was Penelope, a woodland nymph.

🔗 **Felicitas** (feh-LIS-sih-tus) (Latin) She Is Great Happiness

Luca (LOO-kah) (Italian) He Is From Lucania, Italy

Felicitas was the Roman goddess of good fortune. The ruins of a temple dedicated to Felicitas were found beneath the present-day Church of Santi Luca e Martina, raised in A.D. 625 to honor Saint Martina, an early Christian, and Saint Luke, Christ's Apostle.

🔗 **Ferentina** (fair-un-TEE-nah) (Latin) She Is Ferentium, Italy

Euandros (yoo-AN-drohss) (Greek) He Is a Noble Person

The deity Ferentina personified the city of Ferentium, in the Italian region once called Latium. Latium was founded by King Euandros of Arcadia.

🔗 **Flavius** (FLAY-vee-yus) (Latin) He Is Pure Gold

Flavia (FLAY-vee-yah) (Latin) She Is Pure Gold

Flavius Liberalis (first century A.D.) was a Roman knight whose daughter, Flavia Domitilla, married the man who would one day become the Emperor Vespasian.

🔗 **Gaius** (GUY-yus) (Latin) He Is Like the Great Earth Itself

Sophonisba (so-fo-NEES-buh) (Punic) She Is a Beautiful Princess

Gaius Laelius (third century B.C.) was a Roman general who assisted the conqueror Scipio Africanus during his invasions of Carthage, Africa. When Scipio defeated the Carthaginians, the Carthaginian Princess Sophonisba took her own life.

🔗 **Galla** (GAL-lah) (Latin) She Is Gaul (France)

Honorius (ahn-OR-ee-yus) (Latin) He Is Honor Itself

Galla (?–A.D. 394) was a Roman empress, wife of Theodosius I. Galla's stepson Honorius eventually became emperor from A.D. 393–A.D. 395.

🔗 **Herennia** (hur-REN-yah) (Latin) She Is a Magnificent Hero

Decius (DES-ee-yus) (Latin) He Is the Tenth

Herennia (A.D. 249–A.D. 253) was the Roman empress from A.D. 249 to A.D. 251. Her husband was the illustrious Roman Emperor Decius.

🔗 **Honoria** (ah-NOR-ree-yah) (Latin) She Is Honor Itself

Valentinian (val-un-TIN-ee-yun) (Latin) He Is Extremely Powerful

Honoria was the sister of Valentinian III, emperor of Rome. When Honoria's family tried to force her to marry involuntarily, she wrote to the Mongol ruler Atilla the Hun for help. Atilla interpreted the letter as a marriage proposal and sacked several Italian cities.

✏ **Hortensia** (hor-TEN-see-yah) (Latin) She Is a Splendid Garden
Lepidus (LEP-uh-dus) (Latin) He Is Agreeable and Charming
Hortensia (first century A.D.) was a Roman rhetorician who gave eloquent political speeches. In 42 B.C., Hortensia fearlessly delivered an antitax oration before the Second Triumvirate, which included the dreaded warrior Lepidus.

✏ **Inuus** (IN-yoo-wuss) (Latin) He Is Love and Human Contact
Alba (AL-bah) (Latin) She Is the Radiant Dawn
Inuus was the Roman god of loving physical contact. The city-state named the Fortress of Inuus, or in Latin the Castrum Inui, was located in the Alba Longa region of Italy.

✏ **Invidia** (in-VID-ee-yuh) (Latin) She Is Passionate Jealousy
Erebus (AIR-eh-bus) (Latin) He Is the Darkness
Invidia was the Roman name for the goddess of jealousy. Invidia's father was Erebus, the god who personified the darkness that existed at the beginning of time.

✏ **Justina** (jus-STEE-nah) (Latin) She Is Honest and Just
Magnentius (mag-NEN-tee-yus) (Latin) He Is Charming
Justina (?–A.D. 388) was a Roman empress, the wife of Valentinian I, in the fourth century A.D. Justina had married the usurper Magnentius, but the marriage was dissolved and Justina wed Valentinian. Justina's son, Valentinian II, succeeded his father as emperor.

✏ **Juventas** (joo-VEN-tus) (Latin) She Is Fresh and Youthful
Ganymede (GAN-ih-meed) (Latin) He Gladdens Princes
Juventas was the Roman goddess of youth. Juventas and her friend Ganymede carried nectar, the gods' drink, and ambrosia, the gods' food, to Olympus during celebrations.

✏ **Laelia** (LEEL-yah) (Latin) She Is a Fragrant Orchid

Africanus (af-rih-KAH-nus) (Latin) He Is Africa's Greatness
Laelia (first century B.C.), daughter of Roman orator Laelius, was noted for being as eloquent as her father's friend Africanus, the Roman conqueror of Carthage, in Africa.

✏ **Laeta** (LEE-tah) (Latin) She Is Joyful
Gratian (GRAY-shun) (Latin) He Is Graceful
Laeta (fourth century A.D.) was married to the Roman Emperor Gratian, noted for his tolerance of Christianity throughout the Empire. Laeta is noted for feeding starving Romans during a famine caused by the sacking of Rome in A.D. 410.

✏ **Larentina** (lahr-en-TEE-nah) (Latin) She Is the Earth Goddess
Muta (MYOO-tah) (Latin) She Maintains Her Silence
The nymph Larentina was the sister of the nymph Juturna. When Jove, ruler of the gods, commanded Juturna to make love to him, Larentina tattled to Jove's wife Hera. Jove then unfairly removed Larentina's tongue, and she was thereafter known as Muta.

✏ **Leontius** (lee-AHN-tee-yus) (Latin) He Is a Noble Lion
Nika (NEE-kah) (Latin) She Brings Glorious Victory
Leontius was an emperor of Byzantium, the city-state that became the seat of the Eastern Roman Empire after Rome fell in A.D. 410. Leontius perished in the Hippodrome, a horse-racing track famed for its riots, including the Nika Revolt, which nearly brought down Emperor Justinian I.

✏ **Lollia** (LAHL-yah) (Latin) She Is a Mighty Wolf
Saturninus (sat-ur-NYE-nus) (Latin) He Is Time Itself
Lollia Paulina (?–A.D. 49) was an accomplished Roman aristocrat whose ancestry traced back to the Roman Emperor Tiberius. Lollia's uncle was the Roman statesman and political leader Lucius Volusius Saturninus.

✏ **Manlius** (MAN-lee-yus) (Latin) He Is a Man of the People
Elissa (eh-LIS-sah) (Latin) She Is a Wanderer
Manlius (third century B.C.) was a Roman admiral who gained great victories in Rome's First Punic War against the African city of Carthage (Tunisia). One of Carthage's greatest rulers was

Elissa, also called Dido, praised in the Aeneid by Roman poet Virgil.

🖘 **Maria** (mah-REE-yah) (Italian) She Is Love
Martina (mar-TEE-nah) (Latin) She Is as Powerful as any male
Rita (REE-tah) (Latin) She Is a Little Priceless Pearl
Roma (RO-mah) (Latin) She Is Rome
Thecla (THEEK-luh, THEK-luh) (English) She Is God's Glory
Theodora (thee-ah-DOR-rah) (Greek) She Is God's Divine Gift
Theophilus (thee-AH-fih-lus) (Latin) He Is God's Beloved
Thomas (TAH-mahss) (Greek) He Is a Precious Twin
Tiberios (tye-BEER-ee-yohss) (Latin) He Is the River Tiber, Rome
Verina (vur-EE-nah) (Latin) She Is Multitalented

🖘 **Nonia** (NO-nee-yah) (Latin) She Is Ninth
Macrinus (MAK-rih-nus) (Latin) He Is Joyfully Blessed
Roman Empress Nonia Celsa (third century A.D.) was the wife of Macrinus, emperor of Rome from A.D. 217 to A.D. 218.

🖘 **Novius** (NO-vee-yus) (Latin) He Is Refreshing
Colombina (ko-lum-BEE-nah) (Italian) She Is a Peaceful Dove
Novius (first century B.C.) was a Roman playwright specializing in Atellan Fables, comedies that presaged the Commedia dell'arte in Renaissance Italy, which was a form of comedic theatre utilizing stock characters such as Colombina, a free-spirited clown.

🖘 **Philaenis** (fil-LEE-nus) (Greek) She Is a Graceful Feline
Ovid (AH-vid) (Latin) He Is a Gentle Sheep
The Greek concubine Philaenis (third century B.C.) wrote a book on seduction. Later, the Roman Poet Ovid (43 B.C.–A.D. 17) wrote the Art of Love (Ars Amatoria), a more light-hearted commentary on seduction.

🖘 **Pomponia** (pahm-PONE-yah) (Latin) She Is Among the Five Greatest
Aulus (ALL-lus) (Latin) He Is a Shining Palace
The Roman aristocrat Pomponia (first century A.D.) was the wife of the conqueror Aulus

Plautius (?–A.D. 65), who invaded the lands that would one day be called Great Britain.

🖘 **Quietus** (KWYE-eh-tus) (Latin) He Is Tranquil and Quiet
Augusta (aw-GUS-tah) (Latin) She Is Absolutely Magnificent
Augusta was a Roman title equivalent to empress. The noblewoman Iunius became Augusta when her husband Macrianus seized power in A.D. 260. But Iunius's son Titus (?–A.D. 261) never reigned, because the rightful heir, Gallienus, eventually seized power.

🖘 **Rex Superum** (REX soo-PEER-rum) (Latin) He Is the King of Kings
Vesta (VES-tah) (Latin) She Is Hearth and Home
Rex Superum was a Roman title for Zeus, high king of the Olympian gods. Rex Superum's sister was Vesta, goddess of warm, loving households.

🖘 **Saturn** (SAT-turn) (Latin) He Is Eternal Time
Rheia (RAY-yah) (Greek) She Is the Flowing of Time
Saturn was the Roman name for Kronos, Greek god of time. Saturn was also King of the Titans, the deities who ruled in Heaven before being deposed by Jupiter and his Olympian gods. Saturn's wife, the Titan mother of many subsequent deities, was Rheia.

🖘 **Scribonia** (skrih-BO-nee-yah) (Latin) She Writes Beautifully
Pompey (POM-pee) (Latin) He Is One of the Magnificent Five
The Roman noblewoman Scribonia (68 B.C.–A.D. 16) was descended from Pompey the Great, the Roman conqueror who ruled Rome as part of the First Triumvirate, a sharing of power between Pompey, Julius Caesar, and Marcus Crassus.

🖘 **Seneca** (SEN-eh-kah) (Latin) He Lives Many Years
Marcia (MAR-shah) (Latin) She Is as Powerful as any Male
The Roman playwright Seneca (4 B.C.–A.D. 65) preached Stoicism, where people control their fate by controlling their emotions. Seneca's great treatise was Ad Marciam de Consolatione, written to console a woman he called Marcia, whose son had perished.

🕊 **Sol** (SOUL) (Latin) He Is the Radiant Sun
Erythea (ur-RIH-thee-yah) (Latin) She Is the
Red-Orange Sunset
*Sol was the Roman name for the Sun. Each
day, Apollo, god of prophecy, would pull Sol
across the sky in a golden chariot. At day's end,
Erythea, goddess of the sunset, and her sisters,
the Hesperides, would welcome radiant Sol.*

🕊 **Statius** (STAY-shuhss) (Latin) He Is
Powerfully Built
Abbey (AB-bee) (English) Her Father Is Joyful
*Statius (c. A.D. 45–A.D. 96) was a Roman poet
critiqued in the book* Purgatory (Il Purgatorio),
part of The Divine Comedy (Il Divina Commedia) *by Italian poet Dante (1265–1321). A copy
of Statius's work* Thebiad *is found in the Abbey
of Corbie, France.*

🕊 **Suetonius** (suh-TOH-nee-yus) (Latin) He
Persuades Gracefully
Plautia (PLAW-tee-yah) (Latin) She Has
Beautiful Shoulders
*The Roman scholar Suetonius (c. A.D. 69–A.D.
130) wrote* De Vita Caesarum, *detailing the lives
of Roman emperors. One of Suetonius's subjects
was Plautia Urgulanilla, who married Claudius,
the man who later became emperor in A.D. 41.*

🕊 **Valens** (VAY-lenz) (Latin) He Is Powerful
Carosa (kuh-RO-sah) (Latin) She Has a Great
Vision
*Valens (A.D. 328–A.D. 378) was the Roman
emperor from A.D. 364–A.D. 375, a ruler who
began Rome's slide toward conquest by bowing
before Germanic tribes under King Athanaric.
Valens's dearest daughter was the fair Carosa.*

🕊 **Veritas** (VAIR-ih-tahss) (Latin) She Is
Blessed Truth

Hopkins (HAHP-kinz) (English) He Is Born in
Radiant Glory
*Veritas was the Roman goddess of truth, who
lived in deep ponds, because truth is always
hard to find. Veritas's name appears in the
motto of Johns Hopkins University in Baltimore,
Maryland: "Veritas vos liberabit," meaning, "The
truth shall set you free."*

🕊 **Vespasian** (ves-PAY-zhuhn) (Latin) He Is
from the West
Domitilla (doh-mih-TIL-lah) (Latin) She Is
Beloved and Civilized
*Vespasian (A.D. 9–A.D. 79) was emperor of
Rome from A.D. 69 to A.D. 79. Vespasian wed
Domitilla the Elder, daughter of a Roman
knight, in A.D. 38, whereupon Domitilla became
the empress of Rome.*

🕊 **Vipsania** (vip-SAHN-yah) (Latin) She Is as
Formidable as a Viper
Asinius (uh-SIN-yus) (Latin) He Ascends
Higher
*The Roman noblewoman Vipsania (36 B.C.–A.D.
20) was descended from Marcus Licinius
Crassus, a member of the First Triumvirate
that ruled Rome from 60 B.C. to 53 B.C. After
Vipsania married the noble Gallus, she bore a
great son, Asinius Saloninus.*

🕊 **Volturnus** (vol-TUR-nus) (Latin) He Is
Sparkling Water
Italia (ih-TAL-yah) (Latin) She Is Italy
*Volturnus was the Roman god who personified
the Volturnus River in the town of Linternum,
Italy. Romans referred to the Italian Peninsula
as Italia; and the modern nation of Italy is still
called Italia by its inhabitants.*

Name Pairs and Groups
Inspired by Adventurers and Explorers

BOYS

🖉 **Afanasiy** (ah-fah-NAH-see) (Russian) He Lives Forever

Alvaro (al-VAH-ro) (Portuguese) He Protects Humanity

Bartolomeu (bar-tah-lo-MAY-yoo) (Portuguese) He Has a Furrowed Brow

Fridtjof (FREED-yawff) (Norwegian) He Replaces Peace with War

Joaquim (wah-KEEM) (Portuguese) He Is God's Little Protected One

Lancelotto (lahn-sel-LOH-toh) (Italian) He Is Our Powerful Little Weapon

Lourenço (loor-REN-soh) (Portuguese) He Is a Laurel Wreath of Victory

Nicholai (NEE-ko-lye) (Russian) He Is Humanity's Triumph

Tenzing (TEN-zing) (Nepalese) He Obeys the Sacred Scriptures

Zebulon (ZEB-yoo-lahn) (Hebrew) He Praises God

🖉 **Alfons** (al-FAWNSS) (German) He Is Aristocratic

Dionisio (dee-oh-NEE-see-yoh) (Spanish) He Speaks Clearly

Estevão (es-teh-VAH-woh) (Portuguese) He Is a Shining Crown

Gonzalo (gone-SAH-lo) (Spanish) He Is Our Warrior-Protector

Marc-Joseph (mowk-ZHO-sef) (French) He Is the Mighty Male Whose Greatness Increases

Pierre-Jean (pee-air-ZHAW) (French) He Is the Rock-Solid One Whose God Is Gracious

Ranulph (RAH-nulf) (Scottish) He Is Our Mighty Wolf

Romolo (RO-mo-lo) (Italian) He Is Rome

Tristão (tree-STAH-woh) (Portuguese) He Is Aggressive

Vivian (VIV-ee-yun) (English) He Is Full of Life

🖉 **Alvar** (AHL-vahr) (Swedish) He Is a Warrior from the Magical Elfin Army

Alvise (ahl-VEE-say) (Italian) He Is a Renowned Warrior

Étienne (ay-tee-YEN) (French) He Is a Shining Crown

Fletcher (FLEH-chur) (English) He Skillfully Crafts Arrows

Gaspar (gah-SPAR) (Spanish) He Holds Priceless Wealth

Gonçalo (gone-SAH-lo) (Portuguese) He Is Our Great Warrior-Protector

Hermenegildo (air-men-eh-GHEEL-do) (Spanish) He Gives Us Everything

Jim (JIM) (English) He Is the Divinely Protected Little One

Nicolau (nee-ko-LAH-woh) (Portuguese) He Is Humanity's Triumph

René-Robert (ruh-NAY-ro-BAIR) (French) He Is the Brilliant One Who Is Born Again

🖉 **Bjarni** (BYAR-nee) (Icelandic) He Is an Invincible Bear

Cornelis (kor-NEL-liss) (Dutch) He Is a Cornucopia of Abundance

Dragutin (drah-GHOO-tin) (Croatian) He Is
Our Dear One
Emil (ay-MEEL) (Czech) He Is a Powerful
Competitor
Grigori (gri-GOR-ree) (Russian) He Is Always
Alert
Helge (HEL-gur) (Norwegian) He Is Divinely
Protected
Hong (HAWNG) (Chinese) He Is Limitless
Jean-François (zhaw-faw-SWAH) (French) He
Is France, and His God Is Gracious
Roberto (ro-BAIR-toh) (Spanish) He Is
Brilliantly Renowned
Teoberto (tay-oh-BAIR-toh) (Italian) His God
Shines Brightly

✎ **Brendan** (BREN-dun) (Irish) He Is a
    Majestic Ruler
Diogo (dee-OO-go) (Portuguese) He Is Always
Teaching
Fernão (fair-NAH-woh) (Portuguese) He Is
Peaceful and Brave
Henryk (HEN-rik) (Polish) He Is the Powerful
Ruler of the Home
Moric (MOR-reetz) (Hungarian) He Is a Dark
Moor
Pero (PAIR-ro) (Spanish) He Is Our Rock-Solid
Little Fortress
Roald (ro-AHLD) (Norwegian) He Is a
Renowned Monarch
Salomon (SAH-lo-mawn) (Swedish) He Is Peace
Väinö (vah-EE-noh) (Finnish) He Is a Tranquil
River
Vittorio (vit-TOR-ree-yoh) (Italian) He Is
Humanity's Triumph

✎ **Burton** (BUR-tun) (English) He Is a Mighty
    Fortress
Cass (KASS) (English) He Descends from the
Curly Haired One
Cordell (kor-DEL) (English) He Braids Strong
Rope
Drummond (DROOM-mund) (Scottish) He Is a
Lofty Ridge
Glenn (GLEN) (Scottish) He Is a Peaceful
Valley
Lake (LAYK) (English) He Is a Clear Lake
Norris (NOR-riss) (English) He Is from the
Great Northern Land
Pat (PAT) (English) He Is Our Little Aristocrat
Percy (PUR-see) (English) He Is the Town of
Perci, France

Walter (WALL-tur) (English) He Commands
the Military

✎ **Candido** (kahn-DEE-doh) (Portuguese) He
    Is Beautifully Fair
Hernando (air-NAHN-doh) (Spanish) He Is
Peaceful and Brave
Matteo (mah-TAY-yoh) (Italian) He Is God's
Divine Gift
Mirko (MEER-ko) (Croatian) He Is the Peaceful
Little One
Pawel (PAH-vuh) (Polish) He Demonstrates
Humility
Rabban (rah-BAHN) (Arabic) Behold, He Is Our
Glorious Son
Sandor (SAHN-dor) (Hungarian) He Protects
Humanity
Scylax (SKYE-lax, SIL-lax) (Greek) He Is
Aggressive
Stjepan (STAY-fahn) (Croatian) He Is a Shining
Crown
Tibor (TYE-bor) (Croatian) He Is Tibur, Italy

✎ **Chromis** (KRO-mus) (Latin) He Is the
    Sound of Horses
Aphareus (uh-FAIR-ee-yus) (Latin) He Is Rapid
Chromis and Aphareus were two of the Cen-
tauri, as the Romans called them—creatures
with human torsos and the lower bodies of
horses. The Centauri battled many nations,
notably India, where they fought for Bacchus,
god of wine, against Orontes, India's ruler.

✎ **Estevanico** (es-teh-VAH-nih-ko) (Spanish)
    He Is a Shining Crown
Álvar (ALL-vahr) (Spanish) He Is a Warrior
from the Elfin People
Estevanico (c. 1500–1539), or Stephen the Black,
was an African servant of Spanish conquistador
Álvar Núñez Cabeza de Vaca. In 1539, while
exploring American deserts for golden cities, Es-
tevanico survived while his companions perished.
Continuing on, he became the first non-Indian
discoverer of Arizona and New Mexico.

✎ **Ferdinand** (FUR-dih-nahnd) (Spanish) He Is
    Peaceful and Brave
Juan (WAHN) (Spanish) His God Is Gracious
Ferdinand Magellan (1480–1521) was a
Portuguese navigator who led the first suc-
cessful circumnavigation (round trip) of the
Earth. Ferdinand perished prior to the voyage's
completion, but his navigator Juan Sebastián
Elcano led Ferdinand's men safely home.

Henry (HEN-ree) (English) He Rules Our Home Magnificently
David (DAY-vid) (Hebrew) He Is Greatly Beloved
Henry Stanley (1841–1904) was a British-American explorer who reached the interior of Africa and found Dr. David Livingstone, who until then had been lost to the world.

Jean (ZHAW) (French) His God Is Gracious
Jacques (ZHAHK) (French) He Is Divinely Protected
The black Haitian-Frenchman Jean Baptiste Pointe du Sable (c. 1745–1818) was the first non-Indian settler in the region that became the city of Chicago, Illinois. One of Jean's oldest friends was pioneer Jacques Clamorgan.

Leif (LAYF) (Norwegian) He Is a Noble Descendant
Erik (AIR-ik) (Norwegian) He Is an Ever-Powerful Ruler
Leif Ericson (c. A.D. 970–A.D. 1020) was an Icelandic seaman who is acknowledged as the first European to reach the North American mainland, in A.D. 1003. Leif's father was Erik the Red, the first European settler of the island of Greenland.

Lewis (LOO-wiss) (English) He Is Renowned as a Warrior
Clark (KLARK) (English) He Is a Wise Scholar
From 1804–1806, American explorers Meriwether Lewis (1774–1809) and William Clark (1770–1838) crossed North America to survey exactly what President Thomas Jefferson had bought when he made his famed Louisiana Purchase from France in 1803.

Marco (MAR-ko) (Italian) He Is Powerfully Male
Niccolò (NIK-ko-lo) (Italian) He Is Humanity's Triumph
Marco Polo (1254–1324) and his father Niccolò were the first Italians to cross Asia and see the wonders of Chinese civilization under the Mongol Emperor Kublai Khan. Marco recorded his astonishing experiences in his book The Travels of Marco Polo.

Neil (NEEL) (Irish) He Is a Great Victor
Edwin (ED-win) (English) He Is a Wealthy Companion
Neil Armstrong (1930–) was the first American and first person to walk on the Moon. Neil landed the Lunar Excursion Module in Tranquility Bay on July 20, 1969. Neil's

copilot, Edwin Aldrin, was the second person to walk on the Moon.

Pytheas (PITH-ee-yus) (Greek) He Is Pythia, Greece
Polybius (puh-LIB-ee-yus) (Greek) He Lives Forever
Pytheas (c. 380 B.C.–310 B.C.) was a Greek navigator from the city-state of Massilia who reportedly sailed so far north he encountered icebergs. Later, the geographer Polybius found Pytheas's account of a northern realm of ice somewhat unbelievable.

Robert (RAH-burt) (English) He Is Brilliantly Renowned
Matthew (MATH-thyoo) (Hebrew) He Is God's Divine Gift
Robert Peary (1856–1920) is hailed by many as the discoverer of the Geographic North Pole, on April 6, 1909. But Peary's African-American companion in exploration, Matthew Henson, records that he arrived at the Pole minutes before Peary.

Steve (STEEV) (English) He Is a Shining Little Crown
Russell (RUS-sul) (English) He Is Our Little Red One
Steve Irwin (1962–2006) was an Australian zoologist whose television series The Crocodile Hunter *from Alliance Atlantis Communications was an international hit. Steve perished when a stingray attacked during filming in Australia. Fellow Australian, actor Russell Crowe, said, "We've all lost a friend."*

Vasco (VAHSS-ko) (Spanish) He Is an Ebony-Black Raven
Francisco (frahn-SEES-ko) (Spanish) He Is the Nation of France
Spanish conquistador Vasco Nuñez de Balboa (1475–1519) penetrated the interior of Panama and became the first European to see the Pacific Ocean. But Vasco was later arrested for various crimes by another conquistador, Francisco Pizarro, who was destined to conquer Peru's Inca Empire in 1532.

GIRLS

Amelia (uh-MEEL-yuh) (English) She Works Tirelessly
Grace (GRAYSS) (English) She Is Graceful and Beautiful
American aviator Amelia Earhart (1897–1937) completed a nonstop flight in 1928 across the

Atlantic Ocean, the first woman to accomplish such a feat. Amelia's sister Grace Earhart was Amelia's devoted companion.

🕊 **Chiaki** (chee-AH-kee) (Japanese) She Is a Thousand Autumns

Eileen (eye-LEEN) (Irish) She Is a Radiant Torch

Kathryn (KATH-rin) (English) She Is the Pure-Hearted Little One

Marsha (MAR-shuh) (English) She Is as Powerful as any Male

Millie (MIL-lee) (English) She Is Our Powerful Little Laborer

Roberta (ro-BUR-tuh) (English) She Is Brilliantly Renowned

Shannon (SHAN-nun) (Irish) She Is the Shannon River, Ireland

Tamara (tah-MAH-rah, TAM-ah-rah) (Hebrew) She Is a Beautiful Palm Tree

Yelena (yuh-LAY-nuh) (Russian) She Is a Radiant Torch

Wendy (WEN-dee) (English) She Is Beautifully Fair

🕊 **Mae** (MAY) (English) She Is the Springtime Month of May

Nichelle (nih-SHEL) (American/French) She Is the Little One Who Triumphs

    Mae Jemison (1956–) was the first African-American woman to trek into space, aboard the shuttle Endeavor in 1992. Mae decided to become an astronaut after seeing African-American actress Nichelle Nichols in the 1960s television series Star Trek.

🕊 **Valentina** (val-en-TEE-nah) (Italian) She Is Powerful

Svetlana (svet-LAH-nah) (Russian) She Is Radiance

    Russian cosmonaut Valentina Tereshkova (1937–) was the first woman to journey into space, piloting the Vostok 6 spacecraft in 1963. Valentina was followed in 1982 by the second woman in space, Svetlana Savitskaya.

BOYS AND GIRLS

🕊 **Ace** (AYSS) (English) He Is the Supreme Military Commander

Genesis (JEN-eh-sis) (Hebrew) She Is Our New Beginning

Giotto (jee-AHT-toh) (Italian) He Is the Little One Who Lives Forever

Lander (LAN-dur) (Basque) He Is the Lion-Hearted Man of Liberty

Mir (MEER) (Russian) She Is Peace

Reuven (ROO-vun) (Hebrew) Behold, He Is Our Glorious Son

Rosetta (roh-ZET-tuh) (Italian) She Is a Fragrant Little Rose

Sky (SKYE) (English) She Is the Beautiful Blue Sky

Spirit (SPEER-rit) (English) She Is the Spirit of Love

Trace (TRAYSS) (English) He Is the Little One Who Is Thrace

🕊 **Andrés** (AHN-drayss) (Spanish) He Is Powerfully Male

Cayetano (kye-eh-TAH-no) (Spanish) He Is Gaeta, Italy

Eiriksdottir (air-ix-DAW-teer) (Icelandic) She Descends from the Powerful Ruler

Ignacije (ig-NAH-see-yay) (Croatian) He Is Blazing-Hot Fire

Jean-Frédéric (zhaw-fay-deh-REEK) (French) He Is a Calm Ruler Whose God Is Gracious

Langdon (LANG-dun) (English) He Is Beautiful Rolling Hills

Nuno (NOON-yo) (Portuguese) He Is the Ninth

Ruy (ROO-wee) (Spanish) He Is the Powerful Little One

Willem (VIL-lum) (Dutch) He Protects Humanity

Zheng (ZHENG) (Chinese) He Rules with Wisdom and Justice

🕊 **Cho** (CHO) (Chinese) She Is a Beautiful Butterfly

Chomolonzo (cho-mo-LAHN-zo) (Sanskrit) She Is the Goddess of Birds

Devi (DEH-vee) (Sanskrit) She Is a Goddess

Dhaulagiri (doll-ah-GHEER-ree) (Sanskrit) She Is the White Mountain

Ismail (ISS-ma-eel) (Arabic) His God Hears Him

Kamet (KAHM-met) (Tibetan) She Is Mountain Snow

Manaslu (mah-NAHSS-loo) (Sanskrit) He Is a Spiritual Mountain

Nanda (NAHN-dah) (Sanskrit) He Is Divine

Nanga (NAHN-gah) (Sanskrit) She Reveals the World

Parbat (par-BAHT) (Sanskrit) He Is a Lofty Mountain

Rimo (REE-mo) (Sanskrit) She Is a Colorful Mountain

⚘ **Christopher** (KRIS-tuh-fur) (English) He Follows Christ

Isabella (iz-uh-BEL-luh) (Spanish) Her God Is Abundance

Italian navigator Christopher Columbus (1451–1506) sailed his fleet across the Atlantic Ocean in 1492 trying to reach Asia, and became the first European to discover several New World islands. Queen Isabella of Spain funded Columbus's historic voyages.

⚘ **Claudie** (klo-DEE) (French) She Walks a Difficult Path

Clayton (KLAY-tun) (English) He Is a Community Built on Clay

Kalpana (kal-PAH-nuh) (Sanskrit) She Is Enchanting

Laurel (LOR-rul) (English) She Is a Laurel Wreath of Victory

Leland (LEE-lund) (English) He Is Peaceful Farmland

Musa (MOO-suh) (Arabic) He Is the Great Son Who Rescues Us

Nicole (nee-KUL) (French) She Is Humanity's Triumph

Pamela (PAM-ul-luh) (English) She Is Sweetness

Piers (PEERZ) (English) He Is Rock-Solid

Stephanie (STEF-uh-nee) (English) She Is a Shining Crown

⚘ **Jacques** (ZHAHK) (French) He Is Divinely Protected

Calypso (kah-LIP-so) (Greek) She Hides Her True Face

French scientist Jacques-Yves Cousteau (1910–1997) was the world's greatest undersea explorer, as well as the coinventor of the Self-Contained Underwater Breathing Apparatus (SCUBA). Calypso was Jacques's famous high-tech research vessel.

⚘ **Janice** (JAN-us) (English) She Is the Magnificent One Whose God Is Gracious

Daniel (DAN-yul) (Hebrew) His God Judges Wisely

Jan Meek (1944–) is a polar explorer who, accompanied by her son Dan Byles, reached the North Magnetic Pole in 2007.

Name Pairs and Groups
from the Ranks of Warriors
and Great Leaders

BOYS

🦋 **Afonso** (uh-FAHN-so) (Portuguese) He Is Aristocratic

Amado (ah-MAH-doh) (Spanish) He Is Greatly Beloved

Amerigo (ah-MAIR-ih-go) (Italian) He Is a Powerful Worker

Bradley (BRAD-lee) (English) He Is a Meadow in the Woodlands

Eugenio (yoo-JEEN-yo) (Spanish) He Is Aristocratic

Forbes (FORBZ) (Scottish) He Is a Vast Field

Johan (YO-hahn) (German) His God Is Gracious

Khalid (kah-LEED) (Arabic) He Lives Eternally

Léopold (LAY-oh-pold) (French) He Is Our Nation's Lion

Mitchell (MIH-chul) (English) He Resembles God

🦋 **Ahmed** (AH-med) (Arabic) He Is Praise-Worthy

Akbar (AHK-bar) (Arabic) He Is Absolutely Magnificent

Hamid (hah-MEED) (Arabic) He Is Revered

Mirza (MEER-zah) (Persian) He Is a Majestic Prince

Mohammad (mo-HAHM-mahd) (Arabic) He Is Praise-Worthy

Nur (NOOR) (Arabic) He Is Radiance

Sharbat (shar-BAHT) (Arabic) He Feeds Our Souls

Sher (SHAIR) (Persian) He Is a Noble Lion

Timur (tee-MOOR) (Persian) He Is as Strong as Steel

Zaman (zah-MAHN) (Arabic) He Lives Eternally

🦋 **Arthur** (AR-thur) (English) He Is a Courageous Bear

Merlin (MAIR-lin) (Welsh) He Is a Mighty Castle near the Ocean

King Arthur may have been a British monarch who, wielding his sword Excalibur, repelled a sixth-century Saxon invasion. Merlin was Arthur's powerful wizard.

🦋 **Attila** (ah-TIL-lah) (Hungarian) He Is the Little Leader of His Nation

Chin (CHIN) (Chinese) He Is Pure Gold

Attila the Hun (A.D. 406–A.D. 453) ruled the Huns, a nomadic people whose armies swept out of Asia and conquered much of Europe. Chin Shih-Huang, emperor of China, feared the Huns so much that he erected the Great Wall to keep them out

🦋 **Benito** (ben-EE-toh) (Spanish) He Is Blessed by God

Porfirio (por-FEER-ee-yoh) (Spanish) He Is the Royal Color Purple

Benito Juárez (1806–1872), a Mexican-Indian statesman sometimes called Mexico's Abraham Lincoln, served as Mexico's president more often than any other leader. Juárez's army commander was Porfirio Díaz, who also attained the presidency in 1876.

🦋 **Beowulf** (BAY-oh-wulf) (English) He Is a Stinging Bee and a Mighty Wolf

Hrothgar (ROTH-ghar) (English) He Is a
Renowned Weapon
*Beowulf (c. eighth century A.D.) was the warrior
lauded in the eighth-century English poem
Beowulf. When Beowulf slew the dread monster
Grendel for King Hrothgar of the Thanes,
Beowulf gained immortal glory.*

⚡ **Brontes** (BRAHN-tez) (Latin) He Is Thunder
Steropes (STAIR-uh-peez) (Latin) He Is
Lightning
*Brontes and Steropes were one-eyed Cyclopes,
sons of the sea-god Posedion. The Cyclopes
made weapons for the Titans, the gods who
preceded Zeus and his Olympians. After Zeus
deposed the Titans, the Cyclopes crafted Zeus's
lethal thunderbolts.*

⚡ **Douglas** (DUG-lus) (Scottish) He Is a Deep,
Dark Stream
Harry (HAIR-ree) (English) He Rules Our
Home Magnificently
*Douglas MacArthur (1880–1964) rose through
the ranks of the United States Army to com-
mand the forces that defeated Japan in World
War Two. But in 1951, during the Korean War,
President Harry Truman dismissed Douglas for
insubordination.*

⚡ **Edmund** (ED-mund) (English) He Is a
Wealthy Protector
Alfred (AL-fred) (English) He Is a Small but
Wise Counselor
*Edmund Barton (1849–1920) was Australia's
first prime minister, who served honorably from
1901–1903. Australia's second prime minister
was Alfred Deakin, elected in 1903.*

⚡ **Frederick** (FRED-rik) (English) He Rules
Peacefully
Raymond (RAY-mund) (English) He Rules
Wisely
*Frederick Douglass (1818–1895) was a multi-
racial American who escaped from slavery to
become a revered abolitionist, women's-rights
advocate, and statesmen. Frederick was por-
trayed by African-American actor Raymond St.
Jacques in the 1989 film Glory.*

⚡ **George** (JORJ) (English) He Farms the Land
Cincinnatus (sin-sin-NAT-tus) (Latin) He Has
Curly Hair
*George Washington (1732–1799) commanded the
armies of the United States from 1775 to 1783,
eventually gaining independence from Britain.
In 1783, Washington retired in the manner of the*

*Roman conqueror Cincinnatus, who in 460 B.C.
relinquished political power. In 1789, George was
elected the first president of the United States.*

⚡ **Goyathlay** (goy-AHTH-lay) (Apachean) He
Opens His Mouth Wide
Geronimo (heh-RAH-nee-mo) (Spanish) His
Name Is Sacred
*Goyathlay (1829–1909) was a Chiricahua
Apache Native American warrior whose people
fought the United States Army for decades
before capitulating. Goyathlay is more widely
known by the name given to him by the Mexi-
can military—Geronimo.*

⚡ **Hannibal** (HAN-nih-bul) (Punic) His God
Bestows Grace
Hamilcar (HAM-il-kar) (Punic) He Is God's
Friend
*Hannibal (c. third century B.C.–c. second
century B.C.) was the military strategist of the
African city-state of Carthage, who marched
war-elephants over the Alps and threatened
Rome before his defeat in 146 B.C. Hannibal's
father Hamilcar Barca was another Carthagin-
ian general.*

⚡ **Hernán** (air-NAHN) (Spanish) He Brings
Peace Through Strength
Cuauhtémoc (KWAH-teh-mahk) (Nahuatl) He
Is Heaven's Eagle
*From 1519 to 1521, Hernán Cortés (1485–1547),
with his band of Spanish soldiers and legions
of Native American allies, defeated the Aztec
Empire. The last Aztec emperor was Cuauhté-
moc, who defended the doomed capital city of
Tenochtitlan courageously.*

⚡ **Hiawatha** (hye-ah-WAH-thah) (Iroquois) He
Searches Thoroughly
Deganawida (deh-gahn-ah-WEE-dah)
(Iroquois) He Is the Great Peacemaker
*Hiawatha (c. sixteenth century A.D.) was a revered
leader of the Iroquois, or Haudenosaunee, as the
Iroquois call themselves. Hiawatha was a disciple
of the legendary Native American leader Degana-
wida, founder of the Haudenosaunee nation.*

⚡ **Kennedy** (KEN-neh-dee) (Irish) His Head Is
Protected by Armour
King (KING) (English) He Is a Majestic
Monarch
*John Kennedy (1917–1963) was the thirty-fifth
president of the United States (1961–1963) until
his assassination. Kennedy supported the efforts
of African-American civil rights leader Martin*

Luther King, Jr., to guarantee equal rights for all Americans.

☺ **Konrad** (KAHN-rad) (German) He Rules by Wise Counsel

Lambert (LAM-burt) (English) He Is the Bright Land

Logan (LO-gahn) (Scottish) He Is a Little Valley

Manley (MAN-lee) (English) He Is the Community's Meeting-Place

Merrill (MAIR-rul) (English) He Is the Shining Ocean

Montgomery (mahnt-GUM-ur-ree) (English) He Is a Mountain of Manly Power

Preston (PRESS-tun) (English) He Is the Priests

Rafik (rah-FEEK) (Arabic) He Is a Loyal Companion

Rajiv (rah-JEEV) (Sanskrit) He Is a Fragrant Lotus Flower

Rick (RIK) (English) He Is the Powerful Little One

☺ **Kwame** (KWAH-may) (Akan) He Arrived on a Saturday

Marcus (MAR-kus) (Latin) He Is Powerfully Male

From 1952 to 1966, African statesman Kwame Nkrumah (1909–1972) was president of Ghana and a proponent of the creed of Pan-Africanism. Kwame was influenced by African-American leader Marcus Garvey, who advocated resettlement of Africa.

☺ **Mansa** (MAHN-sah) (Mandingo) He Is the King of Kings

Sundiata (soon-dee-YAH-tah) (Mandingo) He Is a Hungry Lion

When King Mansa Musa of Mali (fourteenth century A.D.) made his hajj or pilgrimage to the holy Arab city of Mecca, he bestowed legendary quantities of gold on its inhabitants. Mansa's father was Sundiata, who first established the great family dynasty.

☺ **Santos** (SAN-tohss) (Spanish) He Is the Spirit of the Saints

Sawyer (SOY-yur) (English) He Saws Wood with Determination

Sultan (SUL-tun) (Arabic) He Is a Mighty Ruler

Ted (TED) (English) He Is Our Little Present from God

Toussaint (too-SANT) (French) He Is the Spirit of the Saints

Traian (TRAY-yun) (Romanian) He Is a Military Leader

Trent (TRENT) (English) He Is the Trent River, England

Vincenzo (vin-CHEN-zo) (Italian) He Is a Mighty Conqueror

Will (WILL) (English) He Is Our Little Protector

Yasser (YASS-sur) (Arabic) He Is Wealthy

☺ **Shaka** (SHAH-kah) (Zulu) He Is a Clever Beetle

Nandi (NAHN-dee) (Zulu) She Rejoices

Shaka (c. 1787–c. 1828) once ruled the Zulu Kingdom in southern Africa. Shaka's military innovations created a soldiery that, years later, prevailed against British soldiers during the 1879 Anglo-Zulu War. Shaka's mother Nandi protected her son during his formative years, allowing him to develop into a legend.

☺ **Thomas** (TAH-mus) (English) He Is a Precious Twin

Aaron (AIR-run) (Hebrew) He Is a Lofty Mountain

Thomas Jefferson (1743–1826) was America's greatest statesman—the author of the Declaration of Independence, which dissolved the ties between America and Britain. When Thomas was elected America's third president, his friend Aaron Burr was elected on the same ticket as America's third vice president.

☺ **Winston** (WIN-stun) (English) He Is Rock-Solid Happiness

Neville (NEV-vul) (English) He Is a Shining New City

Winston Churchill (1874–1965), the "British Bulldog," was prime minister of Great Britain during World War Two, when his leadership helped secure victory for the Allies against Nazi Germany and the Axis powers. Winston's predecessor Neville Chamberlain resigned in 1940, after appeasing the Nazi leader Adolf Hitler with multiple concessions.

GIRLS

☺ **Ada** (AY-dah) (English) She Is Our Little Aristocrat

Aine (AWN-yuh) (Irish) She Is Graceful Love

Breeda (BREE-duh) (Irish) She Is Knowledge

Caitlin (KAYT-lin) (Irish) She Is Pure-Hearted

Deirdre (DEER-druh) (Irish) She Is all of Womankind

Lucinda (loo-SIN-duh) (English) She Is Radiance

Nora (NO-rah) (Irish) She Is the Little One Who Is Honor Itself

Olwyn (OHL-win) (Irish) She Leaves Beautiful Footprints

Roisin (ro-SHEEN) (Irish) She Is Our Fragrant Little Rose

Sheila (SHEE-lah) (Irish) She Sees Deeply Within Herself

♫ **Agathe** (ah-GAHT) (French) She Is Pure and Good

Benazir (ban-ah-ZEER) (Indian) She Is Supreme

Claudette (klo-DET) (French) She Walks a Difficult Path

Édith (ay-DEET) (French) She Is a Prosperous Warrior

Golda (GOLD-duh) (Yiddish) She Is Pure Gold

Irena (ee-RAY-nuh) (Lithuanian) She Is Springtime

Kazimira (kah-zee-MEE-ruh) (Lithuanian) She Is the Great Destroyer

Khaleda (khah-LEE-dah) (Arabic) She Lives Forever

Mame (MAYM) (English) She Is the Beloved One Who Is Love Itself

Milka (MIL-kah) (Serbian) She Is Graceful

♫ **Agustina** (ahg-oo-STEE-nah) (Spanish) She Is Absolutely Magnificent

Vitória (vee-TOR-ee-yah) (Portuguese) She Is Humanity's Triumph

Agustina de Aragón (1786–1857) was the Spanish Jeanne d'Arc, who, during the Peninsular War (1807–1814) against Napoleon Bonaparte, fired a cannon at the French after Spanish soldiers had fled. Her example rallied the Spaniards to fight on. Agustina later commanded Spanish soldiers at the Battle of Vitória, Portugal.

♫ **Anneli** (ah-NEL-lee) (Finnish) She Is Graceful

Beatriz (bee-ah-TREESS) (Spanish) She Is a Great Voyager

Eugenia (yoo-JEEN-yah) (Greek) She Is Aristocratic

Luisa (loo-EE-zah) (Italian) She Is a Renowned Warrior

Portia (POR-shuh) (English) She Is a Mighty She-Boar

Radmila (rahd-MEE-lah) (Serbian) She Rejoices

Reneta (reh-NEH-tuh) (Czech) She Is Reborn in God

Stella (STEL-lah) (English) She Is a Heavenly Star

Yulia (YOOL-yah) (Russian) She Is Beautifully Youthful

Zinaida (zin-NYE-dah) (Russian) She Rules Heaven

♫ **Ashbrook** (ASH-brook) (English) She Is a Grove of Ash Trees by a Brook

Cecil (SEE-sul) (English) She Sees Deeply Within Herself

Coya (KOY-yuh) (American/Latin) She Is Our Little Cornucopia of Plenty

Effiegene (ef-fee-JEEN) (American/Portuguese) She Is Aristocratic

Gracie (GRAY-see) (English) She Is the Graceful Little One

Ileana (il-lee-AH-nah) (Romanian) She Is a Radiant Torch

Lera (LEER-ruh) (American/Greek) She Is a Beautiful Harp

Millicent (MIL-lih-sent) (English) She Is a Tireless Worker

Nita (NEE-tuh) (English) She Is the Graceful Little One

Reva (REE-vuh) (Sanskrit) She Is Always Moving

♫ **Atalanta** (at-uh-LAN-tuh) (Greek) She Is Equality and Justice

Belphoebe (bel-FEE-bee) (English) She Shimmers with Loveliness

Britomartis (brit-oh-MAR-tiss) (Greek) She Is Chaste and Pure

Durga (DUR-guh) (Sanskrit) She Is Supreme

Ethelfleda (eth-ul-FLAY-duh) (English) She Is a Beautiful Aristocrat

Gwendolen (GWEN-duh-lin) (Welsh) She Is Beautifully Fair

Hervor (HUR-vur) (German) Behold, She Has Arrived

Oya (OY-yuh) (Yoruba) She Is the Supreme Mother

Sarka (SAR-kuh) (Czech) She Is Chaste and Pure

Trinity (TRIN-ih-tee) (English) She Is the Divine Trinity

♫ **Blanche** (BLAWSH) (French) She Is Beautifully Fair

Dianne (dye-YAN) (English) She Is the Heavenly Life Source

Dixie (DIK-see) (English) She Is the Daughter of the Courageous One

Hattie (HAT-tee) (English) She Is the Little One Who Rules the Home

Hazel (HAY-zul) (English) She Is a Hazelnut Tree

Hillary (HIL-luh-ree) (English) She Laughs with Joy

Jocelyn (JAH-suh-lin) (English) She Is the Great Germanic Nation of the Gauts

Maryon (MAIR-ee-yun) (American/English) She Is the Beloved One Who Is Love Itself

Maurine (mor-REEN) (Irish) She Is Our Little Beloved One

Muriel (MYOOR-ee-yuhl) (English/Irish) She Is the Shining Ocean

☯ **Boudicca** (BOO-dih-kuh) (English) She Is Humanity's Triumph

Siân (SHAHN) (Welsh) Her God Is Gracious *Queen Boudicca (?–c. A.D. 60) of the ancient British nation of Iceni rebelled against the Romans after they insulted her daughter. And, although Welsh actress Siân Phillips is no warrior, she nonetheless portrayed Boudicca brilliantly in the 1978 film Warrior Queen.*

☯ **Brigid** (BREE-yid) (Irish) She Is Knowledge

Eithne (ET-nuh) (Irish) She Is a Seed from Which Great Trees Grow

Gemma (JEM-muh) (English) She Is a Priceless Gemstone

Honor (AHN-nur) (English) She Is Honor Itself

Kathleen (kahth-LEEN) (Irish) She Is Pure-Hearted

Myra (MYE-ruh) (English) She Is a Fragrant Myrrh Tree

Niamh (NEEV) (Irish) She Shimmers with Radiance

Nuala (NOO-luh) (Irish) She Is the Little One Who Has Lovely Shoulders

Sile (SHEE-luh) (Irish) She Sees Deeply Within Herself

Theresa (tur-EE-suh) (English) She Is a Summer Harvest

☯ **Chandrika** (SHAHN-drih-kuh) (Sanskrit) She Is the Silvery Moon

Edda (ED-dah) (Italian) She Is the Aggressive Little One

Ertha (UR-thuh) (English) She Is Mother Earth

Mireya (mee-RAY-yuh) (Spanish) She Is Adored

Sabine (sah-BEAN) (French) She Is Sabina, Italy

Soong (SOONG) (Chinese) She Completes Our Lives

Sylvie (sil-VEE) (French) She Is the Beautiful Woodlands

Tarja (TAR-ee-yuh) (Finnish) She Possesses Goodness

Vaira (vah-EE-ruh) (Latvian) She Is Honest

Vigdis (VEEG-diss) (Icelandic) She Is the War-Goddess

☯ **Cristina** (kree-STEE-nuh) (Spanish) She Is Christ's Little Follower

Eveline (ev-LEEN) (French) She Is the Little One Who Wants to Live

Fausta (FOW-stuh) (Latin) She Is Favored with Good Fortune

Lidia (LEED-yah) (Spanish) She Is Lydia

Megawati (meg-uh-WAH-tee) (Indonesian) She Is Divine

Micheline (mish-LEEN) (French) She Is the Beloved One Who Resembles God

Nataša (nah-TAH-shuh) (Serbian) She Is the Little One Who Is Christmas Day

Nino (NEE-no) (Assyrian) She Is Our Little Blossoming Flower

Pratibha (PRAH-tee-bah) (Sanskrit) She Is Wisdom

Rosalia (ro-suh-LEE-yuh) (Italian) She Is Our Fragrant Rose

☯ **Gabriela** (gah-vree-EL-lah) (Spanish) She Is God's Angelic Messenger

Liza (LYE-zuh) (English) She Is the Little One Favored by God

Gabriela Silang (1731–1763) was a Philippine freedom-fighter against Spanish oppressors. To honor Gabriela, the women's organization GABRIELA works to advance women's rights, under the leadership of Congresswoman Liza Largoza-Maza.

☯ **Hua** (WAH) (Chinese) She Is a Fragrant Flower

Mulan (moo-LAHN) (Chinese) She Is a Fragrant Orchid

Hua Mulan (sixth century) was the heroine of the Chinese epic Ballad of Mulan—a woman who dressed in men's clothing, joined the Chinese military in her father's place, and fought so valiantly that her name will endure forever.

🕊 **Joan** (JOAN) (English) Her God Is Gracious
Margaret (MAR-gret) (English) She Is a
Priceless Pearl
*Joan of Arc (Jeanne d'Arc) (c. 1412–1431) rose
from poverty to become France's greatest
warrior. Joan received aid from spirits such as
medieval dragon-slayer Saint Margaret.*

🕊 **Marcela** (mar-SEL-luh) (Spanish) She Is the
Little One Who Is as Powerful as any Male
Gregoria (greh-GOR-ee-yuh) (Latin) She Is
Always Alert
*Marcela Agoncillo (1860–1946), the Filipina
Betsy Ross, sewed the first flag of the Philip-
pines, depicting a rising sun befitting the Land
of the Morning. Marcela's daughter Gregoria
was the first Filipina to graduate from Britain's
Oxford University.*

🕊 **Nancy** (NAN-see) (English) She Is the Little
One Who Shimmers with Sunlight
Constance (KAHN-stunss) (English) She Is
Loyal and Constant
*American Nancy Langhorne became Nancy
Astor, Viscountess Astor (1879–1964) after
marrying British aristocrat Waldorf Astor. In
1919, Nancy became the first woman to serve as
an elected member of Parliament. Irishwoman
Constance Markiewicz had been elected to
Parliament in 1918, but never served.*

🕊 **Qiu** (CHO, CHOO) (Chinese) She Is the
Colorful Autumn Season
Jin (JIN) (Chinese) She Is Pure Gold
*Qiu Jin (1875–1907) was a Chinese freedom
fighter who battled the Manchu Dynasty that
had ruled China since 1644—and which finally
came to an end in 1912. The Chinese love
Qiu Jin as a national heroine, calling her the
Woman Warrior of the Lake of Mirrors.*

🕊 **Sri** (SHREE) (Sanskrit) She Is Shimmering
Brightness
Sirikit (SEER-ih-keet) (Sanskrit) She Is the
Glory of the Kitiyakara Dynasty
*Queen Sri Suriyothai of Siam (Thailand)
(sixteenth century A.D.) joined her husband
Maha Chakapat in battle against Burmese
armies. In the twenty-first century, Thailand's
Queen Sirikit continues Sri's tradition of
service, as the current president of Thailand's
Red Cross.*

🕊 **Tomoe** (TOH-moh-yeh) (Japanese) She Is
Earth's Eternal Rotation

Marisha-Ten (muh-ree-shuh-TEN) (Japan) She
Rules Heaven
*Japanese noblewoman Tomoe Gozen (c. 1157–c.
1247) was a samurai whose bravery was lauded
in the poem* Tale of the Heike. *Tomoe was "especially beautiful," and worshipped Marisha-Ten,
goddess of protection for all samurai.*

BOYS AND GIRLS

🕊 **Abraham** (AY-bruh-ham) (Hebrew) He Is the
Father of Nations
Harriet (HAIR-ree-yut) (English) She Rules
the Home
*Abraham Lincoln (1809–1865), president of the
United States from 1861–1865, is regarded as
the nation's greatest president. Lincoln's forces
preserved the Union by defeating secessionist
slaveholding states. In 1862, Abraham met
abolitionist Harriet Beecher Stowe, author of
the antislavery novel* Uncle Tom's Cabin, *and
remarked, "So you're the little lady who started
this great war."*

🕊 **Acusa** (uh-KOO-suh) (English) She Is the
Warrior's Mighty Battle-Ax
Adehsa (uh-DAY-shuh) (English) She Is the
Warrior's Mighty Battle-Ax
Adesa (uh-DES-suh) (English) She Is the
Warrior's Mighty Battle-Ax
Addis (AD-dis) (English) He Is the Warrior's
Mighty Battle-Ax
Ador (AY-dor) (Latin) He Is the Warrior's
Mighty Battle-Ax
Adusa (uh-DOO-suh) (English) She Is the
Warrior's Mighty Battle-Ax
Arcia (AR-shuh, ar-SEE-yuh) (Italian) She Is
Sharp-Witted and Cuttingly Clever
Atch (ATCH) (English) He Is the Warrior's
Battle-Ax
Azuela (ah-ZWAY-lah) (Spanish) She Is the
Warrior's Battle-Ax
Azza (AHT-zuh) (Italian) She Is the Warrior's
Battle-Ax

🕊 **Alberta** (al-BUR-tuh) (English) She Is
Aristocratic
Bernardo (bur-NAR-doh) (Spanish) He Is a
Mighty Bear
Duarte (doo-AHR-tay) (Portuguese) He Is a
Wealthy Protector
Fife (FIFE) (Scottish) He Is the Realm of King
Fib of Fife

Hamilton (HAM-ul-tun) (English) He Is a Lofty Hill

Ignacio (ig-NAH-see-yoh) (Spanish) He Is Aflame with Greatness

Paget (PAJJ-jit) (English) He Is the Little Servant of the King and the Queen

Rich (RICH) (English) He Is the Courageous Little One

Vicente (vih-SEN-tay) (Italian) He Is a Mighty Conqueror

Wallis (WALL-liss) (English) He Is the Nation of Wales

🕊 **Albion** (AL-bee-yun) (English) He is Great Britain

America (uh-MAIR-ih-kuh) (German) She is the United States of America

Aquila (AK-kwil-luh) (Latin) He Is a Soaring Eagle

Archer (AR-chur) (English) He Is an Archer with a Mighty Longbow

Belleau (BEL-loh) (French) She Is the Place of Beautiful Lakes

Bennington (BEN-ning-tun) (English) He Is the Benning Clan

Essex (ES-ex) (English) He Is the Great Eastern Land of the Saxons

Langley (LANG-lee) (English) He Is a Long Meadow in the Forest

Lexington (LEX-ing-tun) (English) He Is the Estate of Leaxa

Washington (WASH-ing-tun) (English) He Is the Wassa Clan

🕊 **Alecia** (uh-LEE-shuh, uh-LEE-see-yuh) (English) She Is a Noble Sort of Person

Ciara (see-AIR-ruh) (American/Italian) She Is a Range of Lofty Mountains

Heloise (hel-oh-WEEZ, el-oh-WEEZ) (French) She Is Powerfully Great

Joelle (jo-EL) (French) Her God Is the One True God

Kris (KREESS) (Danish) He Is Christ's Little Follower

Mia (MEE-yah) (Dutch) She Is Our Little Beloved One

Newt (NOOT) (English) He Is the Little One Who Is the New Town

Pam (PAM) (English) She Is the Little One Who Is Absolute Sweetness

Ronda (RAHN-dah) (Welsh) She Is a Reliable Weapon

Shawnee (shaw-NEE) (Algonquin) She Is the South

🕊 **Ashanti** (ah-SHAHN-tee) (Akan) She Is the Great Ashante Nation, Africa

Bolivar (BO-lee-var) (Spanish) He Is the Mill by the Stream

Cherokee (CHAIR-oh-kee) (Cherokee/English) He Is the Great Cherokee Nation

Darien (DAIR-ee-yun) (English) He Is Airelle, France

Domingo (doh-MEEN-go) (Spanish) He Comes to Us from God

Fante (FAHN-tay) (Fante) She Is the Great Fante Nation, Africa

Gustav (GOO-stahv) (German) He Is the Great Staff of the Gothic People

Jenkins (JENK-kinz) (Scottish) He Has Beautiful Curled Hair

Santo (SAHN-toh) (Spanish) He Is Blessed

Tecumseh (teh-KUM-zee) (Shawnee) He Is a Powerful Panther

🕊 **Barnes** (BARNZ) (English) He Is a Legion of Fierce Bears

Bogue (BOWG) (Scottish) He Is a Powerful Longbow

Bonaventure (bo-nah-vaw-TYOO) (French) He Is Magnificent Luck

Cabot (KAB-but) (French) He Is a Small Cabot Boat

Chakri (SHAHK-ree) (Sanskrit) He Is the Circle of Life

Jacinto (hah-SEEN-toh) (Spanish) He Is a Fragrant Hyacinth Flower

Long (LAWNG) (Chinese) He Is a Fire-Breathing Dragon

Melbourne (MEL-burn) (English) He Is the Mill by the Brook

Randolph (RAN-dolf) (English) He Is a Mighty Wolf Who Shields Us from Harm

Valley (VAL-lee) (English) She Is a Peaceful Valley

🕊 **Bay** (BAY) (English) She Is a Blue-Water Bay

Day (DAY) (English) She Is a Glorious Day

Honey (HUN-nee) (English) She Is Honey-Sweet

Italo (ee-TAH-lo) (Italian) He Is Italy

July (joo-LYE) (English) She Is the Warm Summer Month of July

Pacifica (puh-SIF-ih-kuh) (Spanish) She
Brings Peace
Sahara (suh-HAIR-ruh) (Arabic/English) She Is
the Warm Desert
Spring (SPRING) (English) She Is Springtime
Texas (TEX-suss) (Caddoan/English) He Is a
Friend from the Great State of Texas
Winter (WIN-tur) (English) She Is the Brisk
Winter Season

🌸 **Blair** (BLAIR) (Scottish) He Dominates the
Battlefield
Glen (GLEN) (Scottish) He Is a Peaceful Valley
Jerri (JAIR-ree) (English) She Is the Beloved
One Whose God Uplifts
Julianne (joo-lee-YAN) (English) She Is Julius
Caesar's Relative
Kathie (KATH-thee) (English) She Is the Little
Pure-Hearted One
Mary-Louise (mair-ee-loo-WEEZ) (English)
She Is Our Beloved Warrior
Myra (MYE-ruh) (English) She Is a Fragrant
Myrrh Tree
Shaquille (shah-KEEL) (Arabic) He Is
Incredibly Beautiful
Sharon (SHAIR-rahn) (Hebrew) She Is a Fertile
Plain
Toby (TOH-bee) (English) His God Is Great

🌸 **Brandenburg** (BRAN-den-burg) (German)
He Is the State of Brandenburg, Germany
Breton (BRET-tun) (English/Breton) He Is
Brittany, France
Franco (FRAN-ko) (Italian) He Is the Little One
Who Is the Nation of France
Kiev (kee-YEV) (Ukrainian) He Is Kyi, the
Founder of Kiev, Ukraine
Peach (PEECH) (English) She Is a Sweet
Peach
Peru (pair-ROO) (Basque) He Is Rock-Solid
Sancho (SAHN-cho) (Spanish) He Is Revered
Somalia (so-MAHL-yuh) (Somali) She Is
Somalia, Africa
Sung (SUNG) (Chinese) He Is Human
Perfection
Timur (tih-MOOR) (Russian) He Is as Strong
as Steel

🌸 **Brent** (BRENT) (English) He Is a Beautiful
Hill
Cathy (KATH-thee) (English) She Is Our Little
Pure-Hearted One

Clinton (KLIN-tun) (English) He Is a Town on a
Lofty Mountain
Denny (DEN-nee) (English) He Is the Little
One Who Speaks Clearly
Emanuel (im-MAN-yul) (Hebrew) His God Is
Eternal
Fitz (FITZ) (English) He Descends from the
Great Ancestors
Hatch (HATCH) (English) He Is a Gate Leading
to the Woodlands
Mark (MARK) (English) He Is Powerfully
Male
Walley (WALL-lee) (English) He Is Our Little
Military Commander
Woods (WOODZ) (English) He Is the Verdant
Woodlands

🌸 **Cas** (KASS) (Dutch) She Is Our Adored
Little Queen of Love
Feba (FAY-buh) (Croatian) He Is Radiantly
Beautiful
Gen (JEN) (Japanese) He Puts Down Roots in
His Homeland
Kia (KEE-yuh) (Swedish) She Is Christ's Little
Follower
Moab (MO-wab) (Hebrew) He Descends from
His Mighty Father
Raf (RAHF) (Dutch) His God Rescued Him
Sam (SAM) (English) He Is God's Little
Announcer
Sol (SOUL, SOLL) (Latin) He Is the Radiant
Sun
Tad (TAD) (English) He Is Our Little Present
from God
Tu (TOO) (Vietnamese) She Is a Heavenly Star

🌸 **Cho** (CHO) (Chinese) She Is a Beautiful
Butterfly
Dean (DEEN) (English) He Is a Peaceful
Valley
Ernie (UR-nee) (English) He Is the Little One
Who Is Serious
Lavender (LAV-en-dur) (English) She Is
Fragrant Lavender
Marietta (mair-ee-ET-tuh) (Italian) She Is Our
Little Beloved One
Neville (NEV-vul) (English) He Is a Shining
New City
Padma (PAD-muh) (Sanskrit) She Is a Fragrant
Lotus Flower
Parvati (par-VAH-tee) (Sanskrit) She Descends
from the Mountains

Seamus (SHAY-mus) (Irish) He Is Divinely Protected

Zacharias (zak-uh-RYE-yus) (Hebrew) His God Remembers Him

⚥ **Dixy** (DIX-see) (American/English) She Descends from the Courageous One

Ella (EL-luh) (English) She Is Our Radiant Little Torch

Jeanne (ZHAHN) (French) Her God Is Gracious

Linda (LEEN-dah) (Spanish) She Is Exceptionally Beautiful

Madeleine (mad-LEN) (French) She Is Biblical Land of Magdala

Olene (oh-LEEN) (American/Ukrainian) She Is a Radiant Torch

Shaheen (shah-HEEN) (Persian) He Is a Soaring Eagle

Sila (SEE-lah) (Spanish) She Is the Little One Who Is the Beautiful Woodlands

Vesta (VES-tuh) (Latin) She Is Hearth and Home

Walker (WAH-kur) (English) He Walks Powerfully

⚥ **Dwight** (DWITE) (English) He Is the Ruler of the Sky and the Fabled Mountain

Mamie (MAY-mee) (English) She Is the Beloved One Who Is Love Itself

Dwight Eisenhower (1890–1969) led the Allied forces of the United States, Britain, and other nations to victory over the Axis powers, which included Nazi Germany. Mamie Eisenhower was Dwight's wife of thirty-seven years.

⚥ **Napoleon** (nah-POH-lee-yahn) (Italian) He Is Descended from the Clouds

Josephine (JO-suh-feen) (English) Her Greatness Increases

Napoleon Bonaparte (1769–1821) became the emperor of France, subsequent to the 1789 French Revolution. Joséphine de Beauharnais was Napoleon's empress.

⚥ **Rafael** (rah-fah-EL) (Spanish) His God Rescues Him

Karen (KAH-ren) (Danish) She Is Pure-Hearted

Rafael Peralta (1979–2004) was an Iraq War veteran and recipient of the United States Medal of Honor for "gallantry at the risk of his life." Karen is one of Rafael's siblings.

Name Pairs and Groups
from Peacemakers, People of Faith and Vision, and Healers

BOYS

Abreham (ah-bray-HAHM) (Amharic) He Is the Father of Nations

Bartalomewos (bar-tah-luh-MAY-yohss) (Amharic) He Has a Furrowed Brow

Daniel (DAN-yul) (Hebrew) His God Judges Wisely

Marqos (MAR-kohss) (Amharic) He Is Powerfully Male

Mikael (mih-kah-YEL) (Amharic) He Resembles God

Paulos (PAW-lohss) (Greek) He Demonstrates Humility

Petros (PEH-trohss) (Greek) He Is Rock-Solid

Theophilos (thee-AH-fuh-lohss) (Greek) He Is Beloved of God

Yaqob (YAK-kub) (Amharic) He Surpasses Everyone

Yohannes (yo-HAHN-ness) (Amharic) His God Is Gracious

Adolfo (ah-DAHL-fo) (Spanish) He Is a Courageous Wolf

Aloysius (al-uh-WIH-shuhss) (English) He Is a Renowned Warrior

Ballard (BAL-lurd) (English) His Head Is Smooth and Hairless

Baltasar (BAHL-tah-zar) (Spanish) He Is Divinely Protected

Campion (KAMP-ee-yun) (English) He Is a Champion Warrior

Faber (fah-BAIR, FAY-bur) (French) He Shapes and Creates

Hurtado (hur-TAH-doh) (Spanish) He Takes What He Wants

Ignatius (ig-NAY-shuhss) (Latin) He Is Aflame with Greatness

Kohlmann (KOHL-mun) (German) He Is a Peaceful Dove

Vieira (vee-ay-EE-ruh) (Portuguese) He Is a Fragrant Olive Tree

Adonai (ad-doh-NYE) (Hebrew) He Rules Heaven

Allah (ahl-LAH) (Arabic) He Rules Heaven

Christ (KHRYST) (English) He Is Divinely Chosen

Christos (KHRIS-tohss) (Greek) He Is Divinely Chosen

Yahveh (YAH-vay) (Hebrew) He Rules Heaven

Yitzhak (YIT-zahk) (Hebrew) He Is God's Laughter

Yochanan (yo-KAN-nun) (Hebrew) His God Is Gracious

Yosef (YO-sef) (Hebrew) His Greatness Increases

Zachariah (zak-uh-RYE-yuh) (Hebrew) His God Remembers Him

Zebulon (ZEB-yoo-lahn) (Hebrew) He Exalts God

Ahmad (ah-MAHD) (Arabic) He Honors Us

Dawud (dah-WOOHD) (Arabic) He Is Greatly Beloved

Haman (hah-MAHN) (Arabic) He Is the Sacred One

Harun (hah-ROON) (Arabic) He Is the Lofty Mountain

Idris (EE-driss) (Arabic) He Is Faithful and Loyal

Ilyas (IL-yahss) (Arabic) His God Is the True God

Ishaq (EE-shahk) (Arabic) He Laughs with Joy

Israil (iss-rah-IL) (Arabic) He Surpasses Everyone

Jibril (jih-BREEL) (Arabic) He Is a Prophet of God

Nasara (NAH-sah-rah) (Arabic) He and His Companions Follow Jesus Christ

🕮 **Albert** (AL-burt) (English) He Is Brilliantly Aristocratic

Joseph (JO-suf) (English) His Greatness Increases

> *Albert Schweitzer (1875–1965) was a German-French musician who became a Nobel-Prize-winning physician. He and his wife Helen devoted their lives to healing the sick in Africa. Their first patient was Joseph, a Gabonese citizen.*

🕮 **Alfred** (AL-frud) (English) He Is a Small but Wise Counselor

Martin (MAR-tun) (English) He Is Powerfully Male

> *Alfred Nobel (1833–1896) was the Swedish inventor of dynamite, a substance used in warfare. In 1895, a remorseful Nobel established the Nobel Peace Prize. One of the prize's greatest recipients was African-American activist Martin Luther King, Jr.*

🕮 **Alois** (AH-lo-weess) (German) He Is a Renowned Warrior

Alphonse (al-FOHSS) (French) He Is Aristocratic

Amato (ah-MAH-toh) (Italian) He Is Greatly Loved

Ambroise (awm-BWAHZ) (French) He Is Immortal

Elliott (EL-lee-yut) (English) He Is the Little One Whose God Is the Only True God

Girolamo (zhee-ro-LAH-mo) (Italian) His Name Is Sacred

Madhav (mahd-HAHV) (Sanskrit) He Is Springtime

Otto (AHT-toh) (German) He Is Powerfully Successful

Sigmund (ZEEG-moon) (German) He Is Our Triumphant Defender

Vidus (VYE-dus) (Latin) He Is Life Itself

🕮 **Ambrose** (AM-brohss) (Latin) He Lives Forever

Athanasius (ath-uh-NAY-zhuhs) (Greek) He Lives Forever

Augustine (AW-gus-teen) (Latin) He Is Absolutely Magnificent

Basil (BAY-zul) (Greek) He Rules Humanity

Bellarmine (bel-ar-MEEN) (Latin) He Is a Beautiful Warrior

Chrysostom (kris-SAHS-tum) (Greek) He Speaks Eloquently

Gregory (GREG-ree) (Latin) He Is Always Alert

Jerome (jair-ROME) (Greek) His Name Is Sacred

Pius (PYE-yus) (Latin) He Is Respectful

Ramon (ruh-MOHN) (Latin) He Is a Wise Counselor-Protector

🕮 **Balthasar** (BAL-thuh-zar) (Hebrew) He Is the Divine Protector

Berrigan (BAIR-rih-gun) (Irish) His Birth Is a Miracle

Bienvenido (bee-en-veh-NEE-doh) (Spanish) He Is Welcome in Our Hearts

Brennan (BREN-nun) (Irish) He Descends from the One Who Understands Sadness

Claude-Jean (klode-ZHAW) (French) He Is Divinely Protected, and His God Is Gracious

Eusebio (yoo-SAY-bee-yo) (Italian) He Is Respectful

Francesco (fahn-CHESS-ko) (Italian) He Is the Nation of France

Garnet (GAR-net) (English) He Is a Sweet Pomegranate

Giulio (jee-OO-lee-yo) (Italian) He Is Youthful

Walsh (WALSH) (Irish) He Is the Nation of Wales

🕮 **Bartolomeo** (bar-tah-luh-MAY-yo) (Italian) He Descends from the One with a Furrowed Brow

Camillo (kuh-MEE-yo) (Italian) He Is the Youth Who Observes Sacred Ceremonies

Campbell (KAM-bul) (Scottish) His Mouth Is Unique

Charles-Pierre (shahl-pee-YAIR) (French) He Is a Rock-Solid Warrior

Heinrich (HINE-rish) (German) He Rules Our Home Magnificently

Jean-Martin (zhaw-mah-TAN) (French) He Is an Aggressive Male Whose God Is Gracious

Lorenz (LOR-rentz) (German) He Is a Laurel Wreath of Victory

Theodor (tay-oh-DOR) (German) He Is God's Divine Gift

Santiago (sahn-tee-AH-go) (Spanish) He Is the Blessed Saint James

Wilhelm (VIL-helm) (German) He Protects Humanity

🕭 *Benedict* (BEN-uh-dikt) (Latin) He Is Divinely Blessed

Callixtus (kul-LIX-tus) (Latin) He Is a Chalice of Sacred Wine

Evaristus (ev-uh-RISS-tus) (Latin) He Fills Us with Pride

Fabian (FAY-bee-yun) (Latin) He Is a Seed from Which Great Things Grow

Innocent (IN-nuh-sunt) (English) He Is Pure-Hearted

Lando (LAHN-doh) (Italian) He Is the Little One from the Renowned Land

Liberius (lye-BEER-ee-yus) (Latin) He Is Liberty

Marcellinus (mar-SEL-lih-nus) (Latin) He Is a Powerful Male

Sergius (SUR-zhee-yus) (Latin) He Serves Humanity

Urban (UR-bun) (English) He Lives in the Great Metropolis

🕭 *Berchmans* (BIRCH-munz) (German) He Is a Grove of Birch Trees

Corridan (KOR-rih-dun) (Irish) He Is a Sacred Poem

Courtois (koor-TWAH) (French) He Is Well-Mannered

Hoffman (HAWF-mun) (German) He Is the Man Who Farms the Land

Horacio (or-AH-see-yo) (Spanish) He Is a Person for all Seasons

Jakob (YAH-kub) (German) He Surpasses Everyone

Marquette (mar-KET) (French) He Is the Little One Who Is Marked for Greatness

McLaughlin (mac-LOF-lin) (Irish) He Descends from the One Who Is the Land of Lakes

Regis (RAY-zhiss, REE-jiss) (French) He Is a Majestic Monarch

Rubio (ROO-bee-yo) (Spanish) He Has Fiery-Red Hair

🕭 *Chang* (CHANG) (Chinese) He Eternally Flourishes

Li (LEE) (Chinese) He Stands Facing the Dawn

Chang Chung Chung (A.D. 150–A.D. 219) is revered as China's greatest physician. Chang's successor was Li Shizen, a pharmacologist.

🕭 *Chiune* (chee-YOO-nay) (Japanese) He Possesses a Thousand Lives

Sempo (SEM-po) (Japanese) He Is the Distant Shore

Chiune Sugihara (1900–1986) was a Japanese consul in Lithuania during World War Two who defiantly issued visas to thousands of Jewish refugees, that they might escape the Nazi death-camps. In 1985, Chiune was honored for his deeds by the state of Israel.

🕭 *Claude* (KLODE) (French) He Walks a Difficult Path

James (JAYMZ) (Hebrew) He Is Divinely Protected

In 1947, American physician Claude Beck (1894–1971) performed the world's first defibrillation—the use of electricity to restart a human heart. Claude invented his defibrillation machine with the help of colleague James Rand.

🕭 *Clive* (CLYVE) (English) He Is a Lofty Cliff

Duncan (DUNG-kun) (Scottish) He Is a Soldier Who Fights for Our Good Earth

Ingvar (ING-var) (Norwegian) He Is Our Greatest Warrior

Jean-Charles (zhaw-SHAL) (French) He Is the Mighty Soldier Whose God Is Great

Katharine (kat-uh-RAY-nuh) (German) She Is Pure-Hearted

Marlene (mar-LEEN) (English) She Is Love

Pascal (pass-KAL) (French) He Is the Easter Holiday and the Passover Holiday

Russ (RUSS) (English) He Is the Little One Who Has Fiery Red Hair

Satyendra (saht-ee-END-ruh) (Sanskrit) He Is the Lord of Truth

Sibel (SIB-bul) (Greek) She Is an All-Seeing Prophetess

🕭 *Confucius* (kun-FYOO-shuhss) (Chinese/Latin) He Is the Son of the Great Place of Beginning

Wei (WAY) (Chinese) He Is Powerful

Confucius (551 B.C.–479 B.C.) founded the philosophy of Confucianism, which focuses on morality. Confucius was revered by Chinese monarchs such as King Hui of Wei.

Domini (DOH-mih-nye) (Latin) He Is Our Lord and Master

Isa (EE-sah) (Arabic) His God Is Eternal Salvation

Jehovah (jeh-HO-vuh) (Hebrew) He Is All-Knowing

Jesu (ZHAY-soo) (Latin) His God Is Eternal Salvation

Jesus (hay-SOOS) (Spanish) His God Is Eternal Salvation

Josh (JAHSH) (English) He Is the Little One Whose God Is Eternal Salvation

Khristos (KREESS-tohss) (Greek) He Is Chosen by God

Yushua (YOO-shoo-wuh) (Arabic) His God Is Eternal Salvation

Yahweh (YAH-way) (Hebrew) He Is All-Knowing

Yeshua (YEH-shoo-wuh) (Hebrew) His God Is Eternal Salvation

Enrico (en-REE-ko) (Italian) He Rules Our Home Magnificently

Filippo (FIL-ip-po) (Italian) He Is a Friend of Horses

François (fraw-SWAH) (French) He Is the Nation of France

Franciscus (farn-SIS-kus) (Latin) He Is the Nation of France

Hubert (HYOO-bairt) (German) His Heart Shines Brightly

Louis-Antoine (loo-wee-an-TWAHN) (French) He Is the Blossoming Flower of War

Marcello (mar-CHEL-lo) (Italian) He Is Powerfully Male

Rolando (RO-lahn-doh) (Spanish) He Is from the Renowned Land

Rudolf (ROO-dolf) (German) He Is a Mighty Wolf

Ruggero (roo-ZHEH-ro) (Italian) He Is a Renowned Weapon

Hippocrates (hip-PAH-krah-teez) (Greek) He Possesses the Power of the Horse

Herodicus (heh-RAHD-ih-kus) (Greek) He Is a Heroic Melody

Hippocrates (c. 460 B.C.–C. 370 B.C.) was a founder of modern medical science, a Greek physician who developed the Hippocratic Oath, which states in part, "I will . . . never do harm to anyone." The physician Herodicus was one of Hippocrates's early teachers.

Jean-Jacques (zhaw-ZHAHK) (French) He Is the Little One Whose God Is Gracious

Johann (YO-hahn) (German) His God Is Gracious

Karel (KAH-rul) (Dutch) He Is a Mighty Soldier

Kaspar (KAHS-pahr, KAS-pur) (German) He Holds the Priceless Treasure

Korbinian (kor-BIN-yun) (German) He Is an Ebony-Black Raven

Ole (OH-luh, OH-lee) (Danish) He Descends from the Great Ancestors

Stephen (STEE-vahn) (Greek) He Is a Shining Crown

Václav (VAH-klahv) (Czech) He Is More Glorious than Others

Willis (WIL-lus) (English) He Is a Helmet of Protection

Winslow (WINZ-low) (English) He Is a Hill Owned by a Trusted Friend

Kofi (KO-fee) (Akan) He Arrived on a Friday

Ted (TED) (English) He Is a Gift from God

Kofi Annan (1938–) was the first African Secretary-General of the United Nations (UN). Annan received the Nobel Peace Prize in 2001, and currently serves on the board of the United Nations Foundation, established by billionaire Ted Turner.

Magnus (MAG-nus) (Latin) He Is Magnificent

Gallus (GAL-lus) (Latin) He Is a Great Bantam Rooster

Saint Magnus of Füssen, Germany, was an early Christian who may have preached the Gospel in conjunction with Saint Gallus (?–A.D. 754), a revered Irish priest.

Marinus (MAIR-ih-nuss) (Latin) He Is the Vast Ocean

Paschal (pass-KAL) (French) He Is the Sacred Easter Holiday and the Passover Holiday

Pelagius (pul-AH-zhee-yus) (Greek) He Is the Vast Ocean

Pontian (PAHN-tee-yun) (English) He Is the Little One Who Crosses the Sacred Bridge

Sabinian (suh-BIN-yun) (Latin) He Is Sabinium

Sylvester (sil-VES-tur) (English) He Is the Beautiful Woodlands

Valentine (VAL-en-tyne) (English) He Is Powerful and Energetic

Vitalian (vih-TAL-yun) (English) He Is the Little One Who Is Alive and Well

Zephyrinus (zuh-FEER-ih-nus) (Latin) He Is the Refreshing West Wind

Zosimus (ZO-sih-mus) (Greek) He Is Filled with Energy

⊕ **Muhammad** (muh-HAHM-mahd) (Arabic) He Is Praise-Worthy
Gabriel (GAY-bree-yul) (Hebrew) He Is God's Angelic Messenger
The Arab prophet Muhammad (c. A.D. 570–A.D. 632) is revered by one billion Muslims worldwide as the founder of the religion of Islam. Muslims believe that Muhammad received divine revelations from the archangel Gabriel, God's messenger.

⊕ **Nelson** (NEL-sun) (English) He Descends from the Champion
Desmond (DEZ-mahnd) (Irish) He Is from South Munster, Ireland
Nelson Mandela (1918–), a black South African crusader against his country's racist apartheid system, was imprisoned twenty-seven years. After his 1990 release, he was elected president in 1994. With his ally Archbishop Desmond Tutu, Mandela formed The Elders organization in 2007 to lead Africa toward liberty.

⊕ **Newton** (NOO-tun) (English) He Is the Shining New Town
Grace (GRAYSS) (English) She Is Grace and Beauty
John Newton (1725–1807) was an English sea-captain who kidnapped thousands of Africans and transported them to slavery in America—until a storm at sea caused him to embrace God. Eventually, he became a preacher and wrote the hymn Amazing Grace, *which states in part, "I once was lost, but now am found."*

⊕ **Ralph** (RAHLF) (Norwegian) He Counsels Us Like a Mighty Wolf
Nader (NAY-dur) (Arabic) He Is Precious
Ralph Nader (1934–) is a heroic Arab-American activist who has spent decades guarding American consumers from corporate fraud, beginning with the publication of his 1965 book Unsafe at Any Speed, *about defective cars.*

⊕ **Rune** (ROON) (Swedish) He Is Our Secret Religion
Ake (OH-kuh) (Swedish) He Is a Great Ancestor
Swedish physician Rune Elmqvist (1906–1996) invented history's first pacemaker, an electrical device implanted to keep diseased hearts beating. Rune's mentor was Dr. Ake Senning of the Karolinska University Hospital, Sweden.

⊕ **Salih** (sah-LEE) (Arabic) He Is Full of Greatness
Shuabib (swah-BEEB) (Arabic) He Is a Celestial Star
Sulayman (SOO-lay-mahn) (Arabic) He Is Peace
Suwa (SOO-wah) (Arabic) He Is Divine
Uzair (oo-zah-EER) (Arabic) He Is Ever-Present Asssitance
Yahud (yah-HOOHD) (Arabic) He Follows the Prophet Moses
Yahya (yah-HEE-yah) (Arabic) His God Is Gracious
Yunus (YOO-nus) (Arabic) He Is a White Dove
Yusuf (YOO-suff) (Arabic) His Greatness Increases
Zakariyah (zah-KAR-yuh) (Arabic) He Is Favored by God

⊕ **Siddhartha** (sid-DAR-thah) (Sanskrit) He Completes His Life's Work
Theravada (thair-uh-VAH-dah) (Sanskrit) He Is the Wisdom of Our Ancestors
Siddhartha Gautama (c. 563 B.C.–483 B.C.) was an Indian prince who, through meditation, became the Buddha, the "Enlightened One," founder of Buddhism. The largest group of Buddhists are the Theravada Buddhists, who stress logic and meditation.

⊕ **Wilberforce** (WIL-bur-forss) (English) He Is the One Whose Fortress Is in a Canyon
Gustavus (guh-STAH-vus) (Swedish) He Is the Weapon of the Gothic People
William Wilberforce (1759–1833) was a member of Parliament and the driving force behind Great Britain's movement to abolish slavery. With the help of people such as former African slave Gustavus Vassa (c. 1745–1707), a.k.a. Equiano, slavery was abolished throughout the British Empire in 1833.

⊕ **Zarathustra** (zair-uh-THOOS-truh) (Persian) He Is a Sacred Golden Camel
Zoroaster (zor-oh-ASS-tur) (Greek) He Is a Sacred Golden Camel
Zarathustra, called Zoroaster by the Greeks (c. sixth century B.C.), was the Persian visionary who founded the religion of Zoroastrianism, which stresses that people should concentrate their thoughts on truth and goodness.

GIRLS

🕭 **Albright** (ALL-brite) (German) She Shimmers with Magnificence

Billie (BIL-lee) (English) She Is the Little One Who Is a Helmet of Protection

Blair (BLAIR) (Scottish) She Dominates the Battlefield

Blythe (BLYTHE) (English) She Is Energetic and Joyful

Mallory (MAL-lur-ree) (English) She Is Strengthened by Misfortune

Marisol (MAHR-ee-sohl) (Spanish) She Is the Radiant One Who Is Love Itself

Mattea (mat-TAY-yuh) (Italian) She Is God's Divine Gift

Paola (pah-OH-lah) (Italian) She Demonstrates Humility

Shari (SHAIR-ree) (English) She Is the Little One Who Is a Fertile Plain Filled with Crops

Tipper (TIP-pur) (American/English) She Is the Little One Who Is a Swift Gazelle

🕭 **Anousheh** (ah-NOO-shee) (Persian) She Is as Sweet as Sugar

Azar (ah-ZAR) (Persian) She Is Blazing Fire

Farah (FAHR-ruh, FAIR-ruh) (Arabic) She Is Great Happiness

Fatemeh (FAH-tay-may) (Persian) She Is Modest

Mina (MEE-nuh) (Sanskrit) She Is the Little One Who Is a Divine Helmet of Protection

Nasrin (nahz-REEN) (Persian) She Is Our Fragrant Rose

Nazanin (NAZ-uh-neen) (Persian) She Is Elegant and Beautiful

Shirin (Sheer-REEN) (Persian) She Is as Sweet as Sugar

Simin (sih-MEEN) (Persian) She Is as Valuable as Silver

🕭 **Apple** (AP-pul) (English) She Is a Sweet Apple

Apricot (AP-rih-kaht) (English) She Is a Sweet Apricot

Berry (BAIR-ree) (English) She Is a Sweet Berry

Cherry (CHAIR-ree) (English) She Is a Sweet Cherry

Orange (OR-rinj) (English) She Is a Sweet Orange

Papaya (pah-PYE-yuh) (English) She Is a Sweet Papaya

Peach (PEECH) (English) She Is a Sweet Peach

Pear (PAIR) (English) She Is a Sweet Pear

Persimmon (pur-SIM-mun) (English) She Is a Sweet Persimmon

Plum (PLUM) (English) She Is a Sweet Plum

🕭 **Bay** (BAY) (English) She Is the Savory Bay Herb

Cassia (KASS-see-yah) (English) She Is a Fragrant Cassia-Spice Tree

Chicory (CHIK-ur-ree) (English) She Is the Flavorful Chicory Herb

Cicely (SIS-uh-lee) (English) She Sees Deeply Within Herself

Cinnamon (SIN-uh-mun) (English) She Is the Cinnamon Tree

Coriander (kor-ee-AN-dur) (English) She Is Fragrant Coriander (Cilantro)

Damiana (dahm-YAH-nuh) (Italian) She Is the Figlike Damiana Herb

Ginger (JIN-jur) (English) She Is Peppery Ginger-Spice

Juniper (JOON-ih-pur) (English) She Is the Spicy Juniper Berry

Meadowsweet (MED-oh-sweet) (English) She Is a Sweet Meadow-Flower

🕭 **Bess** (BESS) (English) She Is the Little One Favored by God

Diahann (dye-ANN) (American/French) She Is the Heavenly Life Source

Edie (EE-dee) (English) She Is the Little One Who Is a Prosperous Warrior

Gaye (GAY) (English) She Rejoices

Heather (HEH-thur) (English) She Is Fragrant Heather Flowers

Jami (JAY-mee) (American/English) She Is Divinely Protected

Joyce (JOYSS) (English) She Is Supreme

Mitzi (MIT-see) (German) She Is Our Little Beloved One

Raelene (ray-LEEN) (English) She Is a Gentle Mother Ewe

Uma (OO-muh) (Sanskrit) She Is Beautiful White Linen

🕭 **Betony** (BET-nee) (English) She Is the Mint-Fresh Betony Flower

Clary (KLAIR-ree) (English) She Is the Bright Clary Herb

Curry (KUR-ree) (English/Tamil) She Is the Fragrant Curry Tree

Marigold (MAIR-ih-gold) (English) She Is a Fragrant Marigold Flower

Mint (MINT) (English) She Is Refreshing Mint

Tulsi (TUL-see) (Sanskrit) She Is the Fragrant Tulsi Flower

Twinleaf (TWIN-leef) (English) She Is the Fragrant Twinleaf Flower

Vanilla (vuh-NIL-luh) (English/Spanish) She Is Sweet Vanilla Bean

Yarrow (YAIR-roh) (Welsh) She Is the Hardy Yarrow Flower

Yerba (YAIR-buh) (Spanish) She Is a Beautiful Herb

🔊 **Betty** (BET-tee) (English) She Is the Little One Favored by God

Carolyn (KAIR-uh-lin) (English) She Is a Mighty Soldier

Emily (EM-uh-lee) (English) She Is Powerfully Competitive

Emmeline (EM-muh-leen) (English) She Does Extraordinary Work

Grace (GRAYSS) (English) She Is Grace and Beauty

Nawal (nah-WAHL) (Arabic) She Is a Precious Gift

Raden (rah-DEN) (Javanese) She Has a Thunderous Spirit

Shamima (shah-MEE-muh) (Arabic) She Is a Bright Candle

Shirin (shur-REEN, SHEER-rin) (Persian) She Is as Sweet as Sugar

Unity (YOO-nih-tee) (English) She Is Unity

🔊 **Coretta** (kor-RET-tuh) (English) She Is Chaste and Pure

Winnie (WIN-nee) (English) She Is Our Fair Little Beauty

> African-American orator Coretta King (1927–2006) was the wife of civil rights activist Martin Luther King, Jr., and a leader in her own right. In 1986, Coretta met Winnie Mandela, wife of the liberator and future president, Nelson Mandela of South Africa.

🔊 **Davina** (DAH-vee-nah) (English) She Is Greatly Beloved

Elsie (EL-see) (English) She Is the Little One Favored by God

Jadwiga (yahd-VEE-ghuh) (Polish) She Is Aggressive

Josephine-Charlotte (zho-seh-feen-shar-LUT) (French) She Is a Beloved Little Warrior

Ljiljana (lil-YAN-nuh) (Croatian) She Is a Fragrant Lily Flower

Margrethe (mar-GRET-tuh) (Danish) She Is a Priceless Pearl

Maxima (MAH-hee-muh) (Spanish) She Is Supreme

Paz (PAHZ) (Spanish) She Is Peace

Severina (sev-ur-EE-nuh) (Croatian) She Strictly Adheres to Righteousness

Tanni (TAHN-nee) (English) She Is Tanned and Beautiful

🔊 **Delta** (DEL-tuh) (Greek) She Is the Place Where the River Meets the Ocean

Happy (HAP-pee) (English) She Rejoices

Jaclyn (JAK-lin) (English) She Is Divinely Protected

Kaye (KAY) (English) She Is Our Little Pure-Hearted One

Kristine (kris-TEE-nuh) (Danish) She Follows Christ

Nanci (NAN-see) (American/English) She Is the Little One Who Shimmers with Sunlight

Rena (REE-nuh) (English) She Is Born Again in Christ

Rhona (RO-nuh) (Scottish) She Is Rona Island, Scotland

Suzyn (SOO-zin) (American/English) She Is Our Fragrant Little Lotus Flower

Tami (TAM-mee) (American/English) She Is Our Beautiful Little Palm Tree

🔊 **Noni** (NOH-nee) (Hawaiian) She Is God's Divine Gift

Paprika (pap-REE-kuh) (Russian) She Is Our Spicy Little Pepper Plant

Passion (PASH-shun) (English) She Is Sweet Passion-Fruit

Primrose (PRIM-roze) (English) She Is First Rose of Spring

Rowan (RO-wun) (Irish) She Is the Tree with Sweet Berries

Rue (ROO) (English) She Is a Lovely Flower Bush

Senna (SEN-nuh) (English) She Is the Fragrant Senna Flower

Sorrel (SOR-rul) (English) She Is the Tangy Sorrel Plant

Sweetgrass (SWEET-grass) (English) She Is the Fragrant Herb Sweetgrass

Tansy (TAN-zee) (English) She Is the Golden Tansy Flower

🌸 **Rosa** (RO-zuh) (English/Spanish) She Is
Our Fragrant Rose

Johnnie (JAHN-nee) (English) Her God Is
Gracious

Rosa Parks (1913–2005) was an African American who advanced the civil rights movement by refusing to yield her seat on a segregated Montgomery, Alabama, bus. Her friend Johnnie Carr joined her and thousands of other protesters in the Montgomery Bus Boycott, which eventually ended segregation.

🌸 **Teresa** (tair-RAY-sah) (Polish) She Is a
Summer Harvest

Monica (MAH-nuh-kah) (Italian) She Counsels
Wisely

Mother Teresa (1910–1997) was a Catholic missionary in India. In 2003, the Vatican made Mother Teresa a saint due to her miraculous cure of Indian patient Monica Besra.

🌸 **Vera** (VEER-rah) (Latin) She Is Honest

Winifred (WIN-ih-fred) (Welsh) She Is
Beautifully Fair

Vera Brittain (1893–1970) was an English peace-activist whose 1933 Testament of Youth tells of the horrors of World War One. Vera's other acclaimed work, Testament of Friendship, describes her friendship with pacifist Winifred Holby.

BOYS AND GIRLS

🌸 **Abba** (AHB-buh) (Hebrew) He Is Our Wise
Patriarch

Barnet (bar-NET) (English) He Is a Courageous
Bear

Corrie (KOR-ree) (English) She Is Our Virtuous
Little Maiden

Gandhi (GAHN-dee) (Sanskrit) He Sells
Fragrant Perfumes

Hemingway (HEM-ing-way) (English) He
Guides Us to the Shape-Shifters

Hiram (HYE-rahm) (Hebrew) He Is a Cherished
Sibling

Longfellow (LONG-fel-lo) (English) He Is Our
Tall Friend

Priestley (PREEST-lee) (English) He Is the
Forest Owned by the Priests

Sophie (SO-fee) (Greek) She Is Our Wise Little
Scholar

Stanislaw (STAH-nee-slahv) (Polish) He Stands
Covered in Greatness

🌸 **Abijah** (uh-BEE-zhuh) (Hebrew) He
Resembles God

Adin (AY-din) (English) Her Star Burns
Brightly

Betsy (BET-see) (English) Her God Is
Abundance

Elihu (EL-ih-hyoo) (Hebrew) He Resembles
God

Josephine (JO-suh-feen) (English) Her
Greatness Increases

Lemuel (LEM-yoo-wul) (Hebrew) He Is Devoted
to God

Lydia (LIH-dee-yuh) (Greek) She Is Lydia

Parker (PAR-kur) (English) He Guards
Humanity's Gardens

Shields (SHEELDS) (German) He Is
Humanity's Protector

Zachariah (zak-uh-RIE-uh) (English) He Is
Favored by God

🌸 **Absalom** (AB-suh-lahm) (Hebrew) His
Father Is Peaceful

Erastus (uh-RASS-tuhss) (Greek) He Is Beloved
by All

Gerrit (GAIR-rit) (Dutch) He Rules with
Powerful Weapons

Gideon (GID-ee-yun) (Hebrew) He Is a Mighty
Woodsman

Harriet (HAIR-ree-yut) (English) She Rules
the Home

Judith (JOO-dith) (Hebrew) She Is a Woman
from Judea

Myrtilla (mur-TIL-luh) (English) She Is a
Fragrant Myrtle Tree

Paulina (po-LEE-nuh) (Latin) She Is Modest

Silas (SYE-luhss) (English) He Is the Little One
Who Is the Untamed Woodlands

Thaddeus (THAD-ee-yuhss) (English) He Is a
Precious Gift

🌸 **Acacius** (ah-KAY-shuhs) (Latin) He Is
Innocent

Anthony (AN-thuh-nee) (Latin) He Is a
Blossoming Flower

Apollonia (ahp-puh-LO-nee-yah) (Greek) She
Is Radiance

Barbara (BAR-brah) (Greek) She Is Our Divine
Voyager

Blaise (BLAYZ) (Latin) Her Speech Is Uniquely
Her Own

Catherine (KATH-uh-rin) (English) She Is
Pure-Hearted

Christopher (KRIS-tuh-fur) (English) He Follows Christ

Cyriacus (seer-ee-AH-kus) (Latin) He Is Our Revered Father

Denis (DEH-nis) (Latin) He Makes His Voice Heard

Dorothea (dor-uh-THEE-yah) (Latin) She Is God's Divine Gift

The fourteenth century canon of Catholic saints called the Fourteen Holy Helpers—including Acacius, Anthony, Apollonia, Barbara, Blaise, Catherine, Christopher, Cyriacus, Denis, and Dorothea—gained fame in Germany due to their miraculous healings. The Basilica of the Vierzehnheiligen, Germany, honors the Fourteen Holy Helpers.

🕮 **Adeline** (ahd-LEEN) (French) She Is Aristocratic

Arnie (AR-nee) (English) He Is Our Soaring Little Eagle

Atul (ah-TOOL) (Indian) He Has No Equal

Deepak (DEE-pak) (Sanskrit) He Energizes and Thrills Us

Dimitris (dim-EE-triss) (Greek) He Is Like Demeter, the Earth Mother

Gabriele (gay-bree-YEL) (Italian) He Is a Prophet of God

Gerhard (GHAIR-hart) (German) He Is a Powerful Weapon

Joseph-Ignace (zho-sef-ig-NAHSS) (French) He Is the Fiery One Whose Glory Increases

Moritz (MOR-ritz) (German) He Is a Dark Moor

Stanislaw (STAH-nee-slahv) (Polish) He Stands Covered in Greatness

🕮 **Agostinho** (ah-go-STEEN-yo) (Portuguese) He Is Absolutely Magnificent

Armand (aw-MAW, AR-mund) (French) He Is Aggressive

Bette (BET, BET-tee) (English) She Is the Little One Favored by God

Caspar (KAHS-pahr, KAS-pur) (Dutch) He Holds Priceless Wealth

Cesare (CHEZ-ah-ray) (Italian) He Is Gloriously Covered with Hair

Hélio (AY-lee-yo) (French) He Is the Radiant Sun

Lafayette (lah-fay-YET) (French) He Is Our Magical Little Fairy

Maxime (mahk-SEEM) (French) He Is Supreme

Navin (nah-VEEN) (Sanskrit) He Is Fresh and Unique

Nehemiah (nee-uh-MYE-yuh) (Hebrew) His God Comforts Him

🕮 **Alder** (ALL-dur) (English) He Is a Fragrant Alder Tree

Ash (ASH) (English) He Is the Little One Who Is a Meadow in the Ash-Tree Forest

Aspen (ASS-pen) (English) She Is a Fragrant Aspen Tree

Birch (BURCH) (English) He Is a Fragrant Birch Tree

Catalpa (kuh-TAL-puh) (Catawba/English) She Is a Fragrant Catalpa Tree

Cedar (SEE-dur) (English) She Is a Fragrant Cedar Tree

Cherry (CHAIR-ree) (English) She Is a Sweet Cherry from a Cherry Tree

Cypress (SYE-press) (English) She Is a Fragrant Cypress Tree

Ebony (EB-uh-nee) (English) She Is a Fragrant Ebony Tree

Kaya (KYE-yuh) (Japanese) She Is a Fragrant Kaya Tree

🕮 **Aldous** (ALL-duss) (English) He Has the Wisdom of the Elderly

Alterman (ALL-tur-mun) (Yiddish) He Is Not Ready to Depart

Asa (AY-suh) (Hebrew) He Is a Skilled Physician

Chamberlain (CHAYM-bur-lin) (English) He Is the Master of the Chambers

Channing (CHAN-ning) (English) He Is a Mighty Wolf

Dryden (DRY-den) (English) He Is a Dry Valley

Noeleen (no-el-LEEN) (English) She Is Christmas Day

Hobson (HAHB-sun) (English) He Descends from the One Who Is Brilliantly Renowned

Rand (RAND) (German) She Is Our Mighty Shield-Maiden

Springsteen (SPRING-steen) (Dutch) He Is Our Stepping-Stone to Glory

🕮 **Alia** (AHL-yuh) (Arabic) She Is the Vault of Heaven

Brandon (BRAN-dun) (English) He Is a Wheat-Covered Hill

Ernst (ERNST) (German) He Is Serious

Hana (HAH-nuh) (Arabic) She Is Happiness

Jean-Philippe (zhaw-fee-LEEP) (French) He Befriends Horses, and His God Is Great

Kim (KIM) (Korean) He Is Pure Gold

March (MARCH) (English) He Is the Fresh Spring Month of March

Quinn (KWIN) (Irish) She Descends from the Great Leader

Shakuntala (shah-KOON-tuh-luh) (Sanskrit) She Is a Beautiful Bird

Song (SONG) (Korean) He Is Complete

Arnulfo (ar-NOOL-fo) (Spanish) He Is a Soaring Eagle and a Mighty Wolf

Brendon (BREN-dun) (Irish) He Is a Majestic Monarch

Che (SHAY) (Spanish) He Is a Greeting of Friendship

Hedy (HAY-dee) (Dutch) She Is the Aggressive Little One

Mungo (MUNG-go) (Scottish) He Is Compassionate

Osamu (oh-SAH-moo) (Japanese) He Fills His Soul with Learning

Paolo (pah-OH-loh) (Italian) He Demonstrates Humility

Vladislav (VLAHD-ih-slahv) (Russian) He Stands Covered in Greatness

Wilbert (VIL-burt) (Dutch) He Is Shining Determination

York (YORK) (English) He Is York, England

Atkinson (AT-kin-sun) (English) He Descends from the First Man to Walk the Earth

Clive (CLYVE) (English) He Is a Lofty Cliff

Ely (EE-lye) (English) He Will Rise toward Heaven

Fuller (FULL-lur) (English) He Makes Beautiful Cloth

Henri (aw-REE) (French) He Rules Our Home Magnificently

Molly (MAHL-lee) (English) She Is Our Little Beloved One

Paula (PAW-luh) (English) She Shows Great Humility

Santayana (sahn-tah-YAH-nah) (Spanish) He Follows the Holy Saint Joan

Tenzin (TEN-zin) (Tibetan) He Follows the Scriptures

Thoreau (thor-RO, THOR-ro) (French) He Controls Thunder and Water

Avicenna (ah-vih-SEN-nuh) (Arabic) He Is the Father of Magnificent Descendants

Luna (LOO-nuh) (Greek) She Is the Moon

Arab physician Avicenna (c. A.D. 980–A.D. 1037) founded modern medical science. To honor Avicenna, scientists have named a lunar crater after him, an honor he would have enjoyed, since he fought to dispel the idea that the Moon—Luna in Latin—caused illness.

Benjamin (BEN-juh-min) (Hebrew) He Is Born in the South

Christie (KRIS-tee) (English) She Is Christ's Little Follower

Ellen (EL-lun) (English) She Is a Radiant Torch

Hans (HAHNZ) (Danish) He Is the Little One Whose God Is Gracious

Herbert (HUR-burt) (English) He Is a Brilliant Conqueror

Jefferson (JEF-ur-sun) (English) He Descends from the Peacemaker

MacArthur (mak-AR-thur) (Scottish) He Descends from the Mighty Bear of a Man

Schneider (SHNIDE-dur) (German) He Tailors Clothes Beautifully

Sherman (SHUR-mun) (English) He Shears Sheep of Their Beautiful Wool

Winston (WIN-stun) (English) He Is Contented and Rock-Solid

Bonner (BAHN-nur) (French/Irish) He Does Good Things for Others

Criswell (KRIZ-wel) (Scottish) His Life Is Centered in Christ

Freeman (FREE-mun) (English) He Is Born Free

Hafez (hah-FEZ) (Arabic) He Is Our Guardian Angel

Hamon (HAY-mun, HAM-mun) (English) He Is Our Glorious Home

Helmer (HEL-mur) (Norwegian) He Is a Mighty Helmeted Warrior

Jeane (JEEN) (English) Her God Is Gracious

Jonsson (JAHNSS-sun) (Swedish) He Descends from the One Whose God Is Gracious

Malachy (MAL-uh-kye) (Irish) He Is a Disciple of Saint Seachnall

Vaughan (VAWN) (Welsh) He Is Petite

Canyon (KAN-yun) (English) He Is a Deep Canyon

Grenadilla (gren-ah-DEE-yuh) (Spanish) She Is a Beautiful Grenadilla Tree

Jacaranda (jak-uh-RAN-duh) (Spanish) She Is a Beautiful Jacaranda Tree

Karri (KAIR-ree) (Irish/English) She Descends from the Darkly Handsome One

Lacewood (LAYSS-wood) (English) She Is the Beautiful Lacewood Tree

Laurel (LOR-rul) (English) She Is a Laurel Wreath of Victory

Maple (MAY-pul) (English) She Is a Sugary Maple Tree

Pear (PAIR) (English) She Is a Golden Pear

Sal (SAL) (Indian) She Is a Fragrant Sal Tree

Willow (WIL-lo) (English) She Is a Fragrant Willow Tree

🕊 **Cat** (KAT) (American) She Is Our Little Pure-Hearted One

Edi (ED-dee) (Slovene) He Is Our Wealthy Little Protector

Lis (LEESS) (Norwegian) She Is the Little One Favored by God

Nicu (NEE-koo) (Romanian) He Is Humanity's Little Triumph

Rad (RAHD) (Arabic) He Is Thunder and Lightning

Ran (RAHN) (Japanese) She Is a Fragrant Orchid

Sem (SEM) (Dutch) His Name Is Sacred

Shea (SHAY) (Irish) She Is as Noble as a Falcon

Tod (TAHD) (English) He Is a Cunning Fox

Wat (WAHT) (English) He Is Our Little Military Commander

🕊 **César** (say-ZAR) (Spanish) He Is Hirsute

Dolores (doh-LO-rayss) (Spanish) She Understands Sorrow

César Chávez (1927–1993) was a Mexican-American farm-worker unionist who cofounded the United Farm Workers of America (UFW) in 1962, in conjunction with the UFW's other cofounder, Dolores Huerta.

🕊 **Cho** (CHO) (Chinese) She Is a Beautiful Butterfly

Fu (FOO) (Chinese) She Is a Fragrant Lotus Flower

Haley (HAY-lee) (English) He Is a Meadow of Hay in the Woodlands

Jeremy (JAIR-uh-mee) (English) He is the One Whom God Uplifts

Lope (LO-pay) (Spanish) He Is a Mighty Wolf

Marla (MAR-luh) (English) She Is Our Little Beloved One

Maximiliano (max-uh-mill-YAH-no) (Spanish) He Is Supreme

Mikaela (mih-KAY-lah) (Norwegian) She Resembles God

Sho (SHO) (Japanese) He Flies High above the Clouds

Tatum (TAY-tum) (English) She Is the Homestead of the Famous Tate

🕊 **Christiaan** (KRIS-chun) (Afrikaans/Dutch) He Follows Christ

Denise (duh-NEES) (French) She Is God's Mountain

Christiaan Barnard (1922–2001) was a South African doctor who successfully performed history's first human heart transplant. The heart-donor for this historic operation was Denise Darvall, a woman who had lost her life one day earlier.

🕊 **Corazon** (kor-uh-ZONE) (Spanish) She Is Our Sacred Heart

Benigno (beh-NEEN-yo) (Spanish) He Is Our Compassionate Friend

Corazon Aquino (1933–) was the eleventh president of the Philippines, following a tumultuous election where President Ferdinand Marcos was deposed by "People Power" in response to the assassination of Corazon's husband, pacifist Benigno Aquino.

🕊 **Edwina** (ed-WEE-nuh) (English) She Is a Wealthy Companion

Heather (HEH-thur) (English) She Is Fragrant Heather Flowers

Jay (JAY) (English) He Is Our Divinely Protected Little Savior

Kittie (KIT-tee) (Hungarian) She Is Our Little Pure-Hearted One

Marianne (mair-ee-ANN) (French) She Is the Graceful, Beloved One

Mildred (MIL-drid) (English) She Is Gentle and Powerful

Nancy (NAN-see) (English) She Is the Little One Who Shimmers with Sunlight

Niles (NYE-yulz) (English) He Is a Great Victor

Nils (NILZ) (Norwegian) He Is Humanity's Triumph

Sheila (SHEE-luh) (Irish) She Sees Deeply Within Herself

🕊 **Erasmus** (ee-RAZ-mus) (Latin) He Is Greatly Beloved

Eustace (YOO-stuhs) (Latin) He Produces Much

Giles (JYE-yulz) (English) He Is a Powerful Young Goat

Katharina (kat-ah-REE-nah) (German) He Is Pure-Hearted

Leonard (LEH-nurd) (English) He Is a Noble Lion

Margaretha (mar-gah-REE-tah) (German) She Is a Priceless Pearl

Oswald (AHZ-wald) (English) His God Rules Humanity

Pantaleon (pan-TAYL-yun) (Latin) He Is a Noble Lion

Sebastian (seh-BAS-chin) (Latin) He Is Honorable

Sixtus (SIX-tus) (Latin) He Is the Sixth

Vitus (VYE-tus) (Latin) He Is Life Itself

Wolfgang (VULF-gahng) (German) He Is the Pathway of the Wolf

The fourteenth century canon of Catholic saints called the Fourteen Holy Helpers—including Erasmus, Eustace, Giles, Katharina, Leonard, Margaretha, Oswald, Pantaleon, Sebastian, Sixtus, Vitus, and Wolfgang—gained fame in Germany due to their miraculous healings. The Basilica of the Vierzehnheiligen, Germany, honors the Fourteen Holy Helpers.

☞ **Gamaliel** (guh-MAYL-yul) (Hebrew) He Is God's Great Gift

Jeremiah (jair-eh-MYE-yah) (Hebrew) He Is Exalted by God

Julia (JOOL-yuh) (Latin) She Is Beautifully Youthful

Lyman (LYE-mun) (English) He Is a Meadow in the Woodlands

Macon (MAY-kun) (English) He Is the Region of Maconnais, France

Oren (OR-run) (Hebrew) He Is an Enormous Pine Tree

Osborne (AHZ-born) (English) He Is the Master of the Bears

Pardee (par-DEE) (English) He Is God's Divine Gift

Person (PUR-sun) (English) He Is a God-Created Person

Sherman (SHUR-mun) (English) He Shears Sheep of Their Beautiful Wool

☞ **Godiva** (guh-DYE-vuh, guh-DEE-vuh) (English) She Is a Gift of God

Leofric (lee-AH-frik) (English) He Is the Power of the Lion

Lady Godiva (eleventh century A.D.) was an English aristocrat who, having failed to persuade her husband, Lord Leofric, to repeal taxes on the city of Coventry, accepted Leofric's promise that he would abolish the taxes if she rode a horse nude through the city. Godiva completed her ride and Leofric eliminated the taxes.

☞ **Jane** (JAYN) (English) Her God Is Gracious

Nicholas (NIK-uh-lus) (English) He Is Humanity's Triumph

American activist Jane Addams (1860–1935) was a revered pacifist. Jane shared the 1931 Nobel Peace Prize with academician Nicholas Butler, another renowned pacifist.

☞ **Jovita** (jo-VEE-tah) (Spanish) She Resembles the Ruler of Heaven

Faustinus (FAH-oh-stih-nus) (Latin) He Is Blessed with Good Fortune

Saint Jovita (?–A.D. 120) and Saint Faustinus (?–A.D. 120) were early Christians who endured persecution under the Roman Emperor Hadrian.

☞ **Mohandas** (mo-HAHN-dahss) (Sanskrit) He Serves a Beautiful God

Indira (in-DEER-rah) (Sanskrit) She Is Exceedingly Beautiful

Mohandas Gandhi (1869–1948) was one of history's greatest pacifists, whose nonviolent philosophy helped expel British forces from India in 1947. Indira Gandhi (no relation), daughter of Mohandas's ally Jawaharlal Nehru, became India's prime minister in 1966.

Name Pairs and Groups
from Educators, Philosophers, and Scholars

BOYS

 Adamnan (ah-DAHM-nun) (Irish) He Is the Little One Who Is the First Man to Walk the Earth

Einhard (INE-hard) (German) He Is an Invincible Sword

Grammaticus (grah-MAT-ih-kus) (Latin) He Is a Scholar

Jordanes (jor-DAN-nis) (Latin) He Is the River Jordan, Israel

Procopius (pro-KO-pee-yus) (Latin) He Advances Brilliantly

Regino (reh-JEE-no) (Latin) He Is a Majestic King

Svend (SVEND) (Danish) He Is an Energetic Youth

Symeon (SIM-ee-yun) (Hebrew) He Hears Everything Clearly

Usamah (oo-SAH-mah) (Arabic) He Is a Noble Lion

Yue (YOO-way) (Chinese) He Is the Silvery Moon

 Adhamh (AHD-dum) (Irish) He Is History's Greatest Man

Bahrey (BAIR-ree) (Amharic) He Is a Priceless Pearl

Dunlop (DUN-lop) (Scottish) He Is the Region of Dunlop, Scotland

Fabyan (FAY-bee-yun) (English/Latin) He Is the Seed from Which Great Things Grow

Geoffroi (zheh-FWAH) (French) He Is the Land of Peace

Hayward (HAY-wurd) (English) He Is the Warden of the Forest

Philippe (fee-LEEP) (French) He Befriends Horses

Sharaf (shah-RAHF) (Arabic) He Is Trustworthy

Templar (TEMP-lur) (English) He Is the Warrior Who Fights for the Temple

Vergil (VUR-jil) (Latin) He Is Pure and Chaste

 Alvin (AL-vin) (English) He Is the Companion of the Elfin People

Bernie (BUR-nee) (English) He Is Our Courageous Little Bear

Célestin (say-leh-STAN) (French) He Is the Heavenly Sky

Clifton (KLIF-tun) (English) He Is the City near a Lofty Promontory

Cosimo (KAH-zee-mo) (Italian) He Is Well-Ordered Decorum

Enoch (EE-nuk) (Hebrew) He Is Faithful

Marvin (MAR-vin) (English) He Is Gloriously Renowned to the Marrow of His Bones

Olivier (oh-LIV-ee-yay) (French) He Is a Fragrant Olive Tree

Seymour (SEE-mor) (English) He Is Saint Maur, France

Yaron (yuh-RAHN) (Hebrew) He Sings a Beautiful Melody

 Ampelius (am-PEE-lee-yoh) (Latin) He Is the Fruitful Grapevine

Eusebius (yoo-SEE-bee-yus) (Greek) He Is Courteously Respectful

Herodian (hair-OH-dee-yun) (Latin) He Is the Little One Who Sings of Courageous Deeds

Polybius (puh-LIB-ee-yus) (Greek) He Lives Forever

Priscus (PRISS-kuss) (Latin) He Is Honored

Sima (SEE-muh) (Sanskrit) He Is the Farthest Boundary of the Universe

Thallus (THAL-luss) (Latin) He Is a Blossoming Flower

Theodoret (thee-oh-DOR-ret) (Greek) He Is Our Little Present from God

Timaeus (tih-MAY-yus) (Greek) He Is Magnificent Honor

Zosimus (ZO-sim-muss) (Greek) He Lives and Prospers

🕮 *Amycus* (AM-uh-kus) (Latin) He Is Stainless and Pure

Gyrneus (JURN-nee-us) (Latin) He Runs in Great Circles

Amycus and Gyrneus were two of the Centauri, as the Romans called them—whose upper torsos were those of human males and whose lower bodies were those of horses. The Centauri were renowned for their skill as wise educators.

🕮 *Andrzej* (AHN-zhay) (Polish) He Is Powerful

Aubrey (AW-bree) (French) He Has the Power of the Magical Elfin People

Calestous (suh-LES-tus) (English/Latin) He Is the Heavenly Sky

Grayson (GRAY-sun) (English) He Descends from the Great Steward

Malcolm (MAL-kum) (Scottish) He Obeys the Teachings of Saint Columba

Morrie (MOR-ree) (English) He Is the Little Moor With a Dark Complexion

Nabil (nah-BEEL) (Arabic) He Is Aristocratic

Reiner (RAY-nur) (German) He Gives Wise Counsel to Warriors

Romano (ro-MAH-no) (Italian) He Is the Great Roman Empire

Vasant (vah-SAHNT) (Indian) He Is Springtime

🕮 *Angus* (ANG-ghuss) (Scottish) He Is Powerful

Antoine (aw-TWAHN) (French) He Is a Blossoming Flower

Dudley (DUD-lee) (English) He Is a Beautiful Meadow Belonging to Dudda

Erich (AIR-rikh) (German) He Rules Forever

Grenville (GREN-vil) (English) He Is the City

Jerzy (YAIRT-see, JUR-zee) (Polish) He Farms the Land

Milan (mil-LAHN) (Serbian) He Is Graceful

Nikolaes (nee-ko-LAY-yesh) (Dutch) He Is Humanity's Triumph

Sandeep (sahn-DEEP) (Sanskrit) He Is Flaming-Hot Fire

Vijay (vee-ZHYE, VEE-jay) (Indian) He Is Humanity's Triumph

🕮 *Apollinaris* (uh-pah-lih-NAIR-rus) (Greek) He Is the Source of all Light

Bab (BAHB) (Persian) He Is Heaven's Gate

Donatus (doh-NAH-tuss) (Latin) He Is Given to Us as a Sacred Gift

Ford (FORD) (English) He Gives Us a Safe Place to Cross

Kemal (keh-MAHL) (Arabic) He Is Absolutely Perfect

Mani (MAH-nee, MAN-nee) (Sanskrit) He Is a Priceless Gemstone

Nestorius (nes-TOR-ee-yus) (Latin) He Always Returns Home

Rasta (RAHS-tuh) (English/Ethiopian) He Is the World's Greatest Ruler

Ulrich (OOL-rikh) (German) He Is Wealth and Strength

Zion (ZYE-un) (Hebrew) He Is the Mighty Fortress and the Invincible Homeland

🕮 *Arne* (ARN, AR-nee) (Norwegian) He Is a Soaring Eagle

Warwick (WAR-rik) (English) He Is a Strong Fence Across Our Farmland

Arne Naese (1912–) is Norway's greatest philosopher, the creator of Deep Ecology, which views all life as equal to humanity. An adherent of Arne's philosophy is Australian writer Warwick Fox of the University of Tasmania.

🕮 *Barthold* (BART-holt) (German) He Is Our Brilliant Emperor

Finlay (FIN-lee) (Irish/English) He Is the Warrior Who Is Beautifully Fair

Hegel (HAY-ghel) (German) He Is a Soaring Eagle

Hume (HYOOM) (Scottish) He Is Our Blessed Homeland

Keating (KEE-ting) (Irish) He Descends from the One Who Is as Solid as Wood

Lindgard (LIN-gard) (English) His Estates Include Lime Trees and Hills

Louis-Sebastien (loo-ee-seh-BASS-tee-yen) (French) He Is a Renowned Warrior

Ludovico (loo-doh-VEE-ko) (Italian) He Is a Renowned Warrior

Prescott (PRESS-kot) (English) He Is the Cottage of the Holy Priest

Yu (YOO) (Chinese) He Is Priceless Jade

🖉 **Baruch** (bah-ROOK) (Hebrew) He Is Blessed by God

Gilles (ZHEEL) (French) He Is a Frisky Young Goat

Baruch Spinoza (1632–1677) was a Jewish-Dutch philosopher whose book Ethics *(1677) heralded the age of Enlightenment, where rationality replaced dogma. The twentieth century French philosopher Gilles Deleuze called Baruch, "the absolute philosopher."*

🖉 **Bennett** (BEN-net) (English) He Is Divinely Blessed

Carleton (KARL-tun) (English) He Is a Community of Free Persons

Colby (KOL-bee) (English) He Is Ebony-Black Charcoal

Drake (DRAYK) (English) He Is a Mighty Dragon

Drew (DROO) (English) He Is Our Powerful Little Man

Duke (DOOK) (English) He Is Our Great Leader

Hall (HAWL) (English) He Is the Great Manor Hall

Kenyon (KEN-yun) (English) He Has Revered Ancestors

Radcliffe (RAD-klif) (English) He Is a Beautiful Red Cliff

Reed (REED) (English) He Has Fiery Red Hair

🖉 **Benno** (BEN-no) (German) He Is a Mighty Bear

Bert (BURT) (Dutch) He Is Our Brilliant Little Aristocrat

Buz (BUZ) (Hebrew) He Looks Down from a Lofty Height

Elisha (ee-LYE-shuh) (Hebrew) His God Is Eternal Deliverance

Errol (AIR-rol) (Scottish) He Is Errol, Scotland

Gerardus (jur-AR-dus) (German) He Is a Bold Weapon

Godehard (GOTE-hart) (German) He Has a Good Heart

Hans-Martin (hahnz-MAR-tin) (German) He Is a Bold Little Male Whose God Is Gracious

Jean-Louis (zhaw loo-WEE) (French) He Is a Renowned Warrior Whose God Is Gracious

Vance (VANSS) (English) He Is a Vast Area of Wetlands Teeming with Life

🖉 **Bertrand** (BUR-trund) (English/French) He Is an Ebony-Black Raven

Aleksandr (al-ek-SAN-dur) (Russian) He Protects Humanity

Bertrand Russell (1872–1970) was a mathematician and peace activist who was awarded the Nobel Prize in Literature in 1950. Bertrand was an early supporter of the great Russian author and dissident Aleksandr Solzhenitsyn.

🖉 **Booker** (BOOK-kur) (English) He Crafts Fine Books

Theodore (THEE-oh-dor) (Greek) He Is God's Divine Gift

Booker T. Washington (1856–1915) was a remarkable African-American educator who founded the Tuskegee Normal and Industrial Institute for newly freed slaves, with the help of his great benefactor, President Theodore Roosevelt.

🖉 **Bradford** (BRAD-furd) (English) He Is a Ford Across a River

Brooks (BROOKS) (English) He Is a Land of Clear Brooks

Callahan (KAL-ah-hahn) (Irish) He Descends from a Great Warrior

Conway (KAHN-way) (Welsh) He Is Holy Water

Dalton (DAHL-tun) (English) He Is a Town in a Peaceful Valley

Graham (GRAM) (English) He Is a Grand Homestead on Gravelly Land

Gresham (GREH-shum) (English) He Is a Fine Homestead for Grazing

Murphy (MOOR-fee) (Irish) He Descends from the Sea Warrior

Reilly (RYE-lay) (Irish) He Is Supreme

Verner (VUR-nur) (Norwegian) He Safeguards the Army

🖉 **Christoph** (KREE-stuff) (German) He Carries Christ in His Heart

Fitzedward (fitz-ED-wurd) (American/English) He Is Our Little Son and Protector

Hartwig (HART-vig) (German) He Is a Courageous Warrior

Ignaz (EGG-nahtss) (Hungarian) He Is Blazing Fire

Ljubomir (LYOO-bo-meer) (Croatian) He Is Peace and Love

Nicolae (NEE-ko-lye) (Romanian) He Is Humanity's Triumph

Rajendra (rah-ZHEN-druh) (Sanskrit) He Is the King of Kings

Shelomo (SHLO-mo) (Hebrew) He Is Peace

Tamaz (tah-MAHZ) (Georgian) He Is a Precious Twin

Tanzan (tahn-ZAHN) (Japanese/Tibetan) He Obeys the Scriptures

⏁ **François-Louis** (fraw-swah-loo-WEE) (French) He Is Mighty France, Famed for Its Warriors

Hauser (HOW-zur) (German) He Is Hausen, Germany

Laughton (LAW-tun) (English) He Is a Prosperous Farm on a Hillside

Maitland (MAYT-lund) (English) He Is Hardened

Nikodim (nik-oh-DEEM) (Russian) He Is Humanity's Triumph

Rene (reh-NAY) (French) He Is Reborn in Christ

Spenser (SPEN-sur) (English) He Dispenses All We Need to Survive

Timofey (tee-mah-FYAY) (Russian) He Honors God

Trevelyan (treh-VEL-yun) (English) He Is a Grand Hillside Manor House

Winsor (WIN-zur) (English) He Is a Riverside Windlass (Lifting Machine)

⏁ **Frantz** (FRANSS) (German) He Is the Nation of France

Jean-Paul (zhaw-POLE) (French) He Is the Humble Little One Whose God Is Gracious

Caribbean-French psychologist Frantz Fanon was the anticolonial author of the seminal work The Wretched of the Earth *(1961), which contained a preface by France's premier philosopher, Jean-Paul Sartre, founder of Existentialism, the belief in happenstance.*

⏁ **Gareth** (GAIR-reth) (Welsh) He Is a Courageous Knight

Saul (SAWL) (Hebrew) He Is the One for Whom We Have Prayed

Gareth Evans (1946–1980) was a British logician at Oxford University from 1964–1967 and

author of such works as The Causal Theory of Names *(1973). One of Gareth's influences was American philosopher Saul Kripke, winner of 2001's Schock Prize in Logic and Philosophy awarded by the Swedish Royal Academies.*

⏁ **Karl** (KARL) (German) He Is a Mighty Warrior

Niels (NEELZ) (Danish) He Is Humanity's Triumph

Karl Popper is the creator of the concept of falsification—that ideas can be scientifically proven false. Karl rejected the pragmatic ideas of his friend Niels Bohr, the Danish physicist who won the 1922 Nobel Prize in Physics.

⏁ **Kurt** (KURT) (German) He Is Our Bold Little Advisor

Immanuel (im-mahn-yoo-WEL) (German) His God Is Eternal

Austrian-American logician Kurt Gödel (1906–1978) was a revered philosopher, the author of such works as 1931's On Formally Undecidable Propositions of Principia Mathematica and Related Systems. *Kurt was influenced by the German philosopher Immanuel Kant, a proponent of freedom of thought.*

⏁ **Lerone** (luh-RONE) (American) He Is the Ruler of the Land of the Yew Trees

Abraham (AY-bruh-ham) (Hebrew) He Is the Father of Nations

Lerone Bennett (1928–) is an African-American historian who has written scholarly works including 2000's Forced into Glory, *which examines the legacy of Abraham Lincoln, the nation's sixteenth president.*

⏁ **Marshall** (MAR-shul) (English) He Is a Law-Enforcer Riding a Horse

Derrick (DAIR-ik) (English) He Is God's Divine Gift

Marshall McLuhan (1911–1980) was a Canadian scholar whose seminal work Understanding Media *(1964) introduced the idea, "The medium is the message," meaning that how something is said trumps what is said. One of Marshall's disciples is Canadian sociologist-philosopher Derrick de Kerckhove.*

⏁ **Mortimer** (MOR-tih-mur) (English) He Is a Place of Peace

Max (MAHX) (German) He Is the Little One Who Is Supreme

Mortimer Adler (1902–2001) was an American philosopher who preached that philosophy

complements religion and science. With his colleague, philosopher Max Weismann, Mortimer established the Center for the Study of the Great Ideas in Chicago.

🌿 **Rolf** (RAHLF) (German) He Is Our Courageous Little Wolf

Willard (WIL-lurd) (English) He Is the Courageous One

Rolf Schock (1933–1986) was an American philosopher at Uppsala University, Sweden. In 1993, Sweden's Royal Academies founded the Schock Prize for Logic and Philosophy. The first recipient of the prize was American philosopher Willard Quine of Harvard University.

GIRLS

🌿 **Afsaneh** (ahf-sah-NAY) (Persian) She Is a Beautiful Story

Camila (kah-MEE-lah)(Spanish) She Observes Sacred Rituals

Elaheh (el-ah-HAY) (Persian) She Is a Divine Goddess

Farzaneh (far-SAH-nay) (Persian) She Is Knowledgeable and Wise

Jaleh (zhah-LAY) (Persian) She Is Morning Dew

Majgan (mahzh-GHAHN) (Persian) She Has Beautiful Eyelashes

Maryam (mar-ee-YAHM) (Persian) She Is Love

Nahid (nah-HEED) (Persian) She Is Immaculate

Roya (ROY-yuh) (Persian) She Is a Beautiful Dream

Saba (SAH-buh) (Arabic) She Is the Radiant Dawn

🌿 **Agnes** (AG-nus) (Greek) She Shimmers with Sunlight

Bethel (BETH-ul) (Hebrew) Her House Is God's House

Corona (kor-OH-nuh) (Latin) She Is a Shining Crown

Elmira (el-MYE-ruh) (English) She Is Aristocratic

Evelyn (EV-uh-lin) (English) She Is the Beloved One

Immaculata (im-mak-kyoo-LAH-tuh) (Latin) She Is the Immaculate Conception

Lesley (LESS-lee) (Scottish) She Is a Fragrant Garden of Holly

Marian (MAIR-ee-yun) (English) She Is the Beloved One Who Is Love Itself

Meredith (MAIR-eh-dith) (Welsh) She Is a Powerful Conqueror

Sophie (SO-fee) (Greek) She Is Our Wise Little Scholar

🌿 **Annas** (AHN-nuss) (Hebrew) Her God Is Gracious

Ayn (EYE-n, ANN) (American/Finnish) She Is Our Joy in Life

Eliot (EL-ee-yut) (English) Her Only God Is God

Hipparchia (hip-PAR-shuh, hip-PARK-yuh) (Greek) She Is a Majestic Friend of Horses

Leontium (lee-AHN-tee-yum) (Latin) She Is the Place of the Lionesses

Macaulay (muh-KAW-lee) (Scottish) She Descends from the Great Ancestor

Maddy (MAD-dee) (English) She Is the Little One from Magdala, Palestine

Michèle (mee-SHEL) (French) She Resembles God

Onora (uh-NOR-ruh) (Irish) She Is Honor Itself

Zhao (ZHAH-woh) (Chinese) She Is the Temple of Sunbeams

🌿 **Arete** (uh-REE-tee) (Greek) She Possesses Shining Integrity

Aristoclea (uh-ris-toh-KLEE-yuh) (Greek) She Speaks Magnificently

Bracha (BRAHK-khuh) (Hebrew) She Blesses Our Family

Damaris (DAM-uh-ris, duh-MAIR-ris) (Greek) She Is a Beautiful Calf

Émilie (ay-mee-LEE) (French) She Is Powerfully Competitive

Hélène (eh-LEN) (French) She Is a Radiant Torch

Mechthild (meh-TEELD) (German) She Is a Powerful Warrior

Nancey (NAN-see) (American/English) She Is the Little One Who Is Golden Sunlight

Philippa (PHIL-lih-puh) (English) She Befriends Horses

Raya (RYE-yuh, RAY-yuh) (Bulgarian) She Is Our Little Queen

🌿 **Freya** (FRAY-yuh) (Norwegian) She Is Aristocratic

Rachel (RAY-chul) (Hebrew) She Is a Gentle Mother Ewe

Freya Matthews, Australian environmentalist, has written such books as 2005's Reinventing Reality. *Freya's greatest influence was American*

biologist Rachel Carson, who, with her book
Silent Spring, helped create today's environ-
mental movement.

🖉 **Isabel** (IZ-ah-bel) (Spanish) Her God Is
Abundance

Eva (AY-vah) (Spanish) She Wants to Live
Chilean-American author Isabel Allende
(1942–) has written such acclaimed books as
1995's Eva Luna, tracing the life of a South
American orphan girl.

BOYS AND GIRLS

🖉 **Abbie** (AB-bee) (English) She Is the Little
One Whose Father Is Joyful

Edilberto (ed-el-BAIR-to) (Spanish) He Is
Aristocratic

Hiram (HYE-rum) (Hebrew) He Is a Cherished
Sibling

Hugo (HYOO-go) (English) He Has a
Compassionate Heart

Lamar (luh-MAR) (English) He Is the Blue
Ocean

Larkin (LAR-kin) (English) He Is a Laurel
Wreath of Victory

Meribeth (mair-ih-BETH) (American/English)
Her God Is Loving-Kindness

Myles (MYE-yulz) (English) He Is Graceful

Osman (AHZ-mun) (Arabic) He Is Our Soaring
Little Crane

Takashi (tuh-KAH-Shee) (Japanese) He Is Our
Faithful Child

🖉 **Abbott** (AB-but) (English) He Is the Leader
of a Great Monastery

Deane (DEEN) (English) He Is a Peaceful
Valley

Eliphalet (el-IH-fuh-let) (Hebrew) His God Is
Comforting

Elmer (EL-mur) (English) He Is Aristocratic

Increase (IN-kreess) (English) He Grows
Eternally Greater

Jared (JAIR-red) (Hebrew) He Descends from
the Mighty Ones

Lou (LOO) (English) She Is Our Renowned
Little Warrior

Modesto (mo-DES-toh) (Spanish) He Has
Humility and Self-Discipline

Naphtali (NAF-tuh-lee) (Hebrew) He Wrestles
with Greatness

Roderick (RAHD-rik) (English) He Is Mighty
and Renowned

🖉 **Agni** (AHN-yee) (Sanskrit) He Is Blazing
Fire

Anahata (ah-nah-HAH-tuh) (Sanskrit) She Is
Invincible

Bhakti (BAHK-tee) (Sanskrit) He Is Faithful to
His God

Hatha (HAH-thuh) (Sanskrit) He Is Powerful

Karma (KAR-muh) (Sanskrit) He Is Forceful
Actions and Deeds

Kriya (KREE-yuh) (Sanskrit) He Is Decisive
Action

Raja (RAH-zhah) (Sanskrit) He Is a Majestic
Prince

Tantra (TAHN-truh) (Sanskrit) She Is the
Strands of a Lovely Braid

Yantra (YAHN-truh) (Sanskrit) She Is the
Sacred Temple of the Body

🖉 **Aguilar** (AH-gwee-lahr) (Spanish) She Is a
Soaring Eagle

Bancroft (BANG-kroft) (English) He Is a Mighty
Fortess near a Riverbank

Burrows (BUR-rowz) (English) He Is a
Beautiful Hill

Castillo (kas-STEE-yo) (Spanish) He Is a
Mighty Castle

Corbett (KOR-bet) (English) His Hair Is
Beautifully Dark

Hilaire (hil-LAIR) (French) He Laughs with
Joy

Léopold (LAY-uh-pold) (French) He Is
Humanity's Courage

Lucien (loo-see-YAN) (French) He Is Radiance

Montagu (MAHN-tuh-gyoo) (English) He Is a
Lofty Mountaintop

Numa (NOO-muh) (Arabic) He Is Handsome

🖉 **Ahron** (ah-RONE) (Hebrew) He Is from the
Lofty Mountain

Allard (AL-lurd) (English) He Is Aristocratic

Altman (ALT-mun) (English) She Is the Nation
of Germany

Arrington (AIR-ring-tun) (Scottish) He Is
Harrington, Scotland

Barclay (BARK-lee) (Scottish) He Is a Beautiful
Birchwood Tree

Blainey (BLAY-nee) (Irish) He Is a Blossoming
Little Flower

Bond (BAHND) (English) He Farms the Land

Gisela (zhee-ZEL-lah) (German) She Serves
Humanity

Hanne (HAHN-nuh) (German) She Is Graceful

Yehuda (yeh-HOO-duh) (Hebrew) He Is Highly Praised

🐘 **Alistair** (AL-ih-stur) (Scottish) He Protects Humanity

Eugen (yoo-ZHEN) (Romanian) He Is Aristocratic

Grigol (gree-GUHL) (Georgian) He Is Always Alert

Marius (MER-ee-yuhss) (English) He Is Love Itself

Retha (REE-thuh) (English) She Is Our Priceless Little Pearl

Sybil (SIH-buhl) (English) She Is a Prophetess

Tanika (tuh-NEE-kuh) (American/English) She Is a Child Who Is Infinitely Lovely

Tormod (TOR-mud) (Norwegian) He Is Thunder and Lightning

Yehoshua (YAH-shoo-wuh) (Hebrew) His God Is Eternal Salvation

Yve-Alain (eev-ah-LEN) (French) He Is a Dynamic Jewel

🐘 **Arjun** (ar-ZHOON) (Indian) He Is Beautifully Fair

Boyd (BOYD) (Scottish) He Is Fair and Blond

Darlyne (dar-LEEN) (American/English) She Is Darling and Sweet

Hosea (ho-ZAY-yuh) (Hebrew) He Is Divine Redemption

Kemp (KEMP) (English) He Is a Triumphant Warrior

Les (LESS) (English) He Is the Little One Who Is a Fragrant Garden of Holly

Marleen (mar-LEEN) (English) She Is the Beloved One Who Is a Mighty Tower

Monroe (mun-RO) (Irish) He Is the Delta of the River Roe

Omer (oh-MAIR) (Hebrew) He Is Abundant Grain

Yaneer (yah-NEER) (Arabic) He Is Wholesome Dairy Products

🐘 **Austin** (AW-stin) (English) He Is the Little One Who Is Absolutely Magnificent

Trinity (TRIN-ih-tee) (English) She Is the Holy Trinity

Austin Farrer (1904–1968) was an English philosopher famous for the concept of double agency, where people act through their own volition, as well as through God's direction. Austin was a professor at Trinity College, Oxford, England, for twenty-five years.

🐘 **Ayesha** (aye-EE-shuh) (Arabic) She Is Full of Vitality

Gavan (GAV-in) (Scottish) He Is a White Falcon

Geir (GHEER) (Norwegian) He Is a Powerful Weapon

Hasan (hah-SAHN) (Arabic) He Has Striking Features

Ivane (EYE-vuhn) (Georgian) His God Is Gracious

Jacek (YAH-tsek) (Polish) He Is a Fragrant Hyacinth Flower

Jung (YUNG) (Chinese) She Is Pure and Chaste

Klaus (KLOWS) (German) He Is Humanity's Little Triumph

Nikoloz (NEE-ko-lohss) (Georgian) He Is Humanity's Triumph

Urvashi (oor-VAH-Shee) (Indian) She Captures Our Hearts

🐘 **Bobbi** (BAHB-bee) (English) She Is Beloved and Glorious

Braulio (brah-OO-lee-yoh) (Spanish) He Shimmers Brilliantly

Eliezer (el-YEE-zur) (Hebrew) His God Is an Ever-Present Help

Joanne (jo-ANN) (English) Her God Is Gracious

Johnnetta (jah-NEH-tuh) (American/French) She Is God's Graceful Little Messenger

Josue (JO-soo-way) (Spanish) His God Is Eternal Salvation

Leon (LEE-yahn) (Latin) He Is a Noble Lion

Maximilian (max-uh-MIL-yun) (German) He Is Supreme

Meyer (MYE-yur) (Yiddish) He Shimmers Brilliantly

Sven (SVEN) (Swedish) He Is an Energetic Youth

🐘 **Chandra** (SHAHN-druh) (Sanskrit) She Is the Silvery Moon

Cooper (KOO-pur) (English) He Makes Sturdy Barrels

Creighton (KRAY-tun) (English) He Is the Great Borderline

Devi (DEH-vee) (Sanskrit) She Is a Goddess

Emerson (EM-ur-sun) (English) He Descends from the Tireless Worker

Harvey (HAR-vee) (English) He Is Battle-Ready

Hunter (HUN-tur) (English) He Is a Skilled Hunter

Pace (PAYSS) (English) He Is Peace

Rani (RAH-nee) (Sanskrit) She Is a Majestic Queen

Rosalind (RAH-zuh-lind) (English) She Befriends Horses

☙ **Francis** (FRAN-sis) (English) He Is the Nation of France

Elizabeth (ee-LIZ-uh-beth) (English) Her God Is Abundance
   Francis Bacon (1561–1626) was an English philosopher whose 1623 book The New Atlantis *proposed the concept of a society founded on generosity and enlightenment. In 1596, Francis became Queen's Counsel for England's Queen Elizabeth I.*

☙ **Prabhat** (prah-BAHT) (Sanskrit) He Is the Radiant Dawn

Ananda (ah-NAHN-duh) (Sanskrit) She Rejoices
   Indian philosopher Prabhat Sarkar (1921–1990) is famed for introducing the world to Ananda Marga, a creed emphasizing selfless service as the path to fulfillment.

☙ **Sarah** (SAIR-ruh) (Hebrew) She Is a Majestic Princess

William (WILL-yum) (English) He Protects Humanity
   Sarah Grimké (1792–1873) defied nineteenth century laws by teaching slaves and women. Her essays advocating the abolition of slavery and suffrage for women were published in abolitionist William Lloyd Garrison's newspaper, The Liberator.

Name Pairs and Groups
from the World of Science, Mathematics, and Nature

BOYS

🐾 **Aarne** (AR-nee) (Finnish) He Is a Soaring Eagle

Alton (ALL-tun) (English) He Is a Town near a River Delta

Aurelio (or-EL-ee-yoh) (Spanish) He Is Pure Gold

Friedrich (FREED-rish) (German) He Rules Peacefully

Galo (GAH-lo) (Portuguese) He Is a Fighting Rooster

Geert (KAY-yurt) (Dutch) He Is a Powerful Weapon

Leopold (lay-oh-POLD) (Dutch) He Is Humanity's Courage

Lloyd (LOYD) (Welsh) He Is Gray and Wise

Olav (OH-lahv) (Danish) He Descends from Our Great Ancestors

Salvatore (sal-vah-TOH-ray) (Italian) He Resembles Our Savior, Christ

🐾 **Albert** (AL-burt) (English) He Is Aristocratic

Leo (LEE-yoh) (Latin) He Is a Noble Lion
  Albert Einstein (1879–1955) is history's greatest physicist and peace activist. Although Albert worked with physicist Leó Szilárd and others to create America's atomic bomb during World War Two, he later campaigned for peace.

🐾 **Alessandro** (al-ess-SAHN-dro) (Italian) He Protects Humanity

Luigi (loo-EE-jee) (Italian) He Is a Renowned Warrior
  Alessandro Volta (1745–1827) was the Italian inventor of the Voltaic Pile, history's first battery.

Alessandro was inspired by the work of Italian physicist Luigi Galvani.

🐾 **Alphaeus** (al-FEE-yus) (Greek) He Is Always Growing

Antonio (an-toh-nee-yoh) (Italian) He Is a Blossoming Flower

Augusto (oh-GOOS-toh) (Spanish) He Is Absolutely Magnificent

Domenico (doh-MEN-ee-ko) (Italian) He Reflects God's Greatness

Ernest (UR-nest) (English) He Is Serious

Hermann (HAIR-mahn) (German) He Is a Warrior

Kama (KAH-mah) (Sanskrit) He Is Divine Love

Kiyoshi (kee-YO-Shee) (Japanese) He Is Pure-Hearted

Luther (LOO-thur) (German) He Is Humanity's Invincible Army

Valentino (val-en-TEE-no) (Italian) He Is Vigorously Powerful

🐾 **Augustin-Jean** (aw-goo-stan-ZHAW) (French) He Is Magnificent and His God Is Gracious

Davy (DAY-vee) (English) He Is the Little One Who Is Beloved

Hammond (HAM-mund) (English) He Safeguards Our Home

Humphry (HUM-free) (English) He Is a Peaceful Warrior

Laszlo (LAHSS-lo) (Hungarian) He Judges Honorably

Laurens (LOR-renz) (Dutch) He Is a Laurel Wreath of Victory

Leigh (LEE) (English) He Is a Fragrant Meadow

Maxim (MAX-eem) (Russian) He Is Supreme

Mikhail (mee-KYLE) (Russian) He Resembles God

Petrus (PET-rus) (Dutch) He Is Rock-Solid

🖉 **Augustin-Louis** (aw-gus-tan-LOO-wiss) (French) He Is a Magnificent Warrior

Bhaskara (BAHS-kah-rah) (Sanskrit) He Shimmers with Brilliance

Birkhoff (BURK-hawf) (German) He Guards Our Estate

Eudoxus (yoo-DOX-suss) (Greek) He Appears Glorious

Euler (YOO-lur) (German) He Crafts Beautiful Pottery

Evariste (ay-vah-REEST) (French) He Fills Us with Pride

Fermat (FAIR-mat, FUR-mat) (French) He Speaks Brilliantly

Gauss (GAWSS) (German) He Raises Magnificent Geese

Godel (go-DEL) (German) He Is God's Glory

Napier (NAY-pee-yur) (English) He Keeps Linens Freshly Pressed

🖉 **Bailly** (BAY-lee) (English) He Enforces the Law as a Trusted Bailiff

Balandin (BAL-aw-dan) (French) He Is Energetic

Barnard (bar-NARD) (German) He Is Courageous

Beaumont (BO-mahnt) (English) He Is a Lofty Mountaintop

Bergman (BURG-mun) (Swedish) He Is the Man of the Mountain

Bettinus (BET-tih-nus) (Latin) He Is the Little One Who Is Divinely Blessed

Boris (BOR-riss) (Russian) He Is a Courageous Wolf

Boss (BAWSS-suh) (Swedish) He Is the Little One Who Wants to Live

Burckhardt (BURK-hart) (German) He Is Our Lion-Hearted Protector

Burnham (BURN-num) (English) He Is a Town near a River

🖉 **Bell** (BEL) (English) He Is a Melodious Bell

Watson (WAHT-sun) (English) He Descends from a Military Commander

Among his scientific achievements, American scientist Alexander Graham Bell (1847–1922) invented history's greatest communication device—the telephone. But Bell might never have succeeded without the assistance of engineer Thomas Watson.

🖉 **Bengt** (BENKT) (Swedish) He Is Divinely Blessed

Fritz (FRITZ) (German) He Is Our Peaceful Little Ruler

Gunter (GOON-tur) (German) He Is an Invincible Army

Hannes (HAHN-ness) (German) He Is the Little One Whose God Is Gracious

Hans-Emil (hahnz-ay-MEEL) (German) He Is the Little One Whose God Is Gracious

Harding (HAR-ding) (English) He Is Stout-Hearted

Lubos (LOO-bosh) (Czech) He Is Peace and Love

Moore (MOOR) (English) He Is a Dark Moor

Nicholson (NIK-ul-sun) (English) He Descends from Humanity's Great Victor

Tadeas (TAH-day-yahss) (Czech) He Is a Precious Gift

🖉 **Benjamin** (BEN-juh-min) (Hebrew) He Is Born in the South

Franklin (FRANK-lin) (English) He Is a Free Man

Benjamin Franklin (1706–1790) was an American Founding Father, who urged Congress to adopt the Declaration of Independence and sever political ties with Great Britain. Benjamin was also an accomplished scientist—discovering, for example, that lightning bolts are electricity discharges.

🖉 **Bharat** (bah-RHAT) (Indian) He Cannot Be Defeated

Erno (AIR-no) (Finnish) He Is Straightforward

Felix (FEE-lix) (Latin) He Is Favored with Good Fortune

Gore (GOR) (English) He Possesses a Three-Sided Farmstead

Josiah (jo-ZYE-yah) (Hebrew) He Is Divinely Favored

Nicolas (nee-ko-LAH) (French) He Is Humanity's Triumph

Owen (OH-wehn) (Welsh) He Is Aristocratic

Petri (PEE-tree) (Finnish) He Is Rock-Solid

Stirling (STUR-ling) (English) He Is as Excellent as the Stars

Walther (VAHL-tur) (German) He Commands the Military

🖉 **Buckminster** (English) He Is a Church in a Deer-Filled Forest

Nicholas (NIK-uh-lus) (English) He Is Humanity's Triumph

Buckminster Fuller (1895–1983) was an American inventor noted for designing the geodesic dome, i.e., triangles shaped into a hemisphere. Earth's largest geodesic dome is the Eden Project in Cornwall, Great Britain, designed by architect Nicholas Grimshaw.

🖉 **Carlos** (KAR-lohss) (Spanish) He Is a Mighty Warrior

Carlyle (kar-LYLE) (Scottish) He Is a Metropolis of Radiant Light

Chalid (kah-LEED) (Arabic) He Lives Forever

Fraser (FRAY-zhoor) (Scottish) He Is an Adventurous Explorer

Hiroshi (hee-RO-Shee) (Japanese) He Is Successful and Compassionate

Igor (EE-gor) (Russian) He Fights the Enemy with His Yew-Wood Longbow

Jafar (juh-FAR) (Arabic) He Is a Sparkling River

Jorge (HOR-hay) (Spanish) He Farms the Land

Makio (MAH-kee-yo) (Japanese) He Represents Our Hopes and Dreams

Masaru (MAH-sah-roo) (Japanese) He Is Humanity's Triumph

🖉 **Cepheus** (SEF-ee-yus) (Greek) He Is Ethiopia's Great King

Cetus (SEE-tus) (Greek) She Is the Ocean-Dwelling Leviathan

Circinus (SUR-sih-nus) (Latin) He Is a Reliable Compass

Eridanus (air-ih-DAY-nuss) (Greek) He Is the River Po, Italy

Hydrus (HYE-druss) (Latin) He Is a Towering Dragon

Octans (AHK-tunz) (Latin) He Is the Eighth Segment of Heaven

Phoenix (FEE-nix) (Greek) He Is Reborn in Fire

Sculptor (SKULP-tur) (English) He Sculpts Artistic Masterpieces

Taurus (TOR-russ) (Latin) He Is a Raging Bull

Tucana (too-KAHN-nuh) (Latin) She Is the Colorful Toucan Bird

The constellations Cepheus, Cetus, Circinus, Eridanus, Hydrus, Octans, Phoenix, Sculptor, Taurus, and Tucana illuminate the night sky.

🖉 **Dan** (DAN) (Hebrew) He Is a Wise Judge

Evgenii (yev-GAY-nee) (Russian) He Is Aristocratic

Grigory (gree-GOR-ree) (Russian) He Is Always Alert

Jean-Luc (zhaw-LUKE) (French) He Is Lucania, Italy, and His God Is Gracious

Osamu (oh-SAH-moo) (Japanese) He Fills His Soul with Wisdom

Paulo (pah-OO-lo) (Portuguese) He Demonstrates Humility

Ronaldo (ro-NAHL-doh) (Portuguese) He Rules by Wise Counsel

Rudolph (ROO-dolf) (English) He Is a Courageous Wolf

Takeshi (tah-KAY-Shee) (Japanese) He Is a Great Warrior

Toshiro (toh-SHEE-ro) (Japanese) He Is the Frosty Winter Season

🖉 **Darwin** (DAHR-win) (English) He Is a Devoted Friend

Herschel (HUR-shull) (Yiddish) He Is a Powerful Little Stag

English naturalist Charles Darwin (1809–1882) proposed his theory of evolution in 1859's On the Origin of Species—that beings with desirable traits evolve while others die out. Darwin rests in Westminster Abbey, London, near astronomer John Herschel.

🖉 **Edison** (ED-ih-sun) (English) He Descends from a Wealthy Protector

Tesla (TES-luh) (Serbian) He Is a Razor-Sharp Tool

Thomas Edison (1847–1931) was an American inventor responsible for innovations such as a practical electric lightbulb. Edison's contemporary, Serbian engineer Nikola Tesla, was called, "The man who invented the twentieth century," by biographer Robert Lomas.

🖉 **Galileo** (gal-ih-LAY-yoh) (Italian) He Is a Noble Lion from Gaul

Isaac (EYE-zik) (Hebrew) He Laughs with Joy

Italian scientist Galileo Galilei (1564–1642) perfected telescopes and observed that Jupiter has its own moons—proving that Earth was not the universe's center. Afterwards, English mathematician Isaac Newton (1643–1727) used Galileo's work to formulate his own laws of celestial motion.

Gian-Carlo (jee-ahn-KAR-lo) (Italian) He Is a Warrior Whose God Is Gracious
Norbert (NOR-burt) (German) He Is the Radiant North
Gian-Carlo Rota (1932–1999) was an Italian-American mathematician whose class in probability at the Massachusetts Institute of Technology (MIT) became legendary. Gian-Carlo earned MIT's Norbert Wiener Professorship, named after American mathematics professor Norbert Wiener.

Govind (go-VEEND) (Sanskrit) He Knows Where to Find Sacred Cows
Harold (HAIR-ruld) (English) He Commands the Military
Lars (LARZ) (Norwegian) He Is a Laurel Wreath of Victory
Olof (OH-lahf) (Swedish) He Descends from Our Mighty Ancestors
Orazio (or-AHSS-ee-yo) (Italian) He Is a Man for all Seasons
Poul (POLE) (Danish) He Demonstrates Humility
Shaun (SHAWN) (Irish) His God Is Gracious
Shin (SHEEN) (Japanese) He Is Genuinely Honest
Takeo (tah-KAY-yo) (Japanese) He Is Our Little Warrior
Yusuke (YOO-soo-kee) (Japanese) He Is Assisted by Spirits

Gregor (GREG-gohr) (Slovene) He Is Our Little Guardian
Gene (JEEN) (English) He Is Our Little Aristocrat
Gregor Mendel (1822–1884) was a German-Czech priest whose experiments with inherited traits helped establish the science of genetics. Mendel's research showed that inherited traits are passed from parents to offspring by molecules called genes.

Ister (ISS-stur) (Latin) He Is the Ister River, Scythia
Cephisus (SEF-uh-sus) (Latin) He Is the Cephisus River, Greece
Ister and Cephisus were two of the river-spirits, called the Flumina by the Romans, who personified every river in the world.

Peloreus (puh-LOR-ree-yus) (Latin) He Is a Towering Giant
Euphorbus (yoo-FOR-bus) (Latin) He Is Hearty

The Romans attributed volcanic eruptions to Gigantes, such as Peloreus and Euphorbus, who battled Jove, high king of Greek gods, and suffered defeat. Thereafter, the Gigantes were buried under mountains, which caused eruptions when they tried to escape.

Ptolemy (TAH-luh-mee) (Greek) He Is Warlike
Nicolaus (nih-ko-LAY-yus) (German) He Is Humanity's Triumph
Ptolemy (A.D. 83–A.D. 161) was the Roman-Egyptian astronomer whose erroneous conclusions—that the cosmos revolved about the Earth—were universally accepted until disproved by Polish astronomer Nicolaus Copernicus in 1543's On the Revolutions of the Heavenly Spheres (De Revolutionibus Orbium Coelestium).

Radovan (RAHD-oh-vahn) (Czech) He Greatly Rejoices
Jaroslav (YAR-uh-slahv) (Czech) He Is a Glorious Warrior
The Czech thinker Radovan Richta (1924–1983) proposed in 1963's Man and Technology in the Revolution of Our Day that civilization substitutes brain-work for muscle-work. Radovan's colleague at the Czechoslovak Academy of Sciences was Jaroslav Heyrovský, winner of the 1959 Nobel Prize in Chemistry.

René (ruh-NAY) (French) He Is Born Again in God
Gottfried (GAHT-freed) (German) He Is God's Sublime Peace
René Descartes (1596–1650) was a French philosopher-mathematician who invented the x- and y-coordinates system used to locate points in space. René influenced the work of German mathematician Gottfried Leibniz, coinventor of calculus.

Stephen (STEE-vun) (Greek) He Is a Shining Crown
Cambridge (KAYM-brij) (English) He Is the Bridge on the River Cam, England
Stephen Hawking (1942–) is a British physicist at Cambridge University, England. Stephen's disabilities have not prevented him from becoming a revered scientist who has sold millions of copies of his 2002 book A Brief History of Time.

Tycho (TYE-ko) (Greek) He Is Always on Target

Johannes (yo-HAHN-nus) (Danish) His God Is Gracious
Tycho Brahe (1546–1601) was a Danish astronomer who measured the movements of planets and stars. Tycho's assistant was German astronomer Johannes Kepler, who helped Tycho formulate his laws of planetary motion.

GIRLS

🌸 *Abella* (ah-BEL-luh) (Italian) She Is the Breath of Life
Alessandra (ah-lih-SAN-druh) (Italian) She Protects Humanity
Artemisia (ar-teh-MEE-see-yuh) (Greek) She Is the Heavenly Life Source
Constanza (kahn-STAN-zuh) (Spanish) She Is Loyal and Constant
Dorotea (dor-oh-TAY-yuh) (Italian) She Is God's Divine Gift
Elisabeth (el-LEE-zah-bet) (German) Her God Is Abundance
Hildegard (HIL-duh-gard) (German) She Is a War-Fortress
Jacobina (zhah-KO-bih-nuh) (Dutch) She Surpasses All Others
Martine (mar-TEEN) (French) She Is as Powerful as any male
Novella (no-VEL-luh) (Italian) She Is Truly New and Exciting

🌸 *Almira* (all-MEER-ruh) (English) She Is Aristocratic
Berta (BUR-tuh) (Polish) She Shines Gloriously
Carlotta (kar-LOT-tuh) (Italian) She Is Our Mighty Little Warrior
Carole (keh-RULL) (French) She Is a Mighty Warrior
Claudine (klo-DEEN) (French) She Walks a Difficult Path
Clemence (kleh-MAWSS) (French) She Is Compassionate
Fiammetta (fee-uh-MET-tuh) (Italian) She Is the Little Hot-Blooded One
Inge (ING-guh) (German) She Is the Little One Who Is Supreme
Irène (ih-REN) (French) She Is Springtime
Noemie (no-eh-MEE) (French) She Is Agreeable

🌸 *Arti* (AR-tee) (Mingrelian) She Is First
Beirt (BAIRT) (Irish) She Is Second
Dre (DRAY) (Pashto) She Is Third
Eman (ee-MAHN) (Marshallese) She Is Fourth

Koro (KOR-roh) (Nama) She Is Fifth
Koto (KOH-toh) (Erzya) She Is Sixth
Nana (NAH-nah) (Japanese) She Is Seventh
Pela (PEL-lah) (Tok Pisin) She Is Eighth
Teisha (tay-EE-shuh, TAY-shuh) (Hebrew) She Is Ninth
Zehn (SAYN, ZEN) (German) She Is Tenth

🌸 *Betsy* (BET-see) (English) She Is the Little One Favored by God
Daisy (DAY-zee) (English) She Is a Fragrant Daisy
Eva (AY-vuh) (Spanish) She Wants to Live
Florrie (FLOR-ree) (English) She Is the Little Flourishing One
Gladys (GLAH-diss) (Welsh) She Is a Mighty Nation
Grace (GRAYSS) (English) She Is Beauty and Grace
Janetta (juh-NET-tuh) (English) She Is the Little One Whose God Is Truly Gracious
Nellie (NEL-lee) (English) She Is a Radiant Little Torch
Rosa (RO-sah) (Spanish) She Is Our Fragrant Rose
Ruby (ROO-bee) (English) She Is a Priceless Ruby

🌸 *Bettie* (BET-tee) (English) She Is the Little One Favored by God
Consuelo (kohn-SWAY-lo) (Spanish) She Is Consoled by the Virgin Mary
Delphia (del-FEE-yuh) (English) She Is the Delphia Temple, Greece
Delvina (del-VEE-nuh) (American/Greek) She Is the Delphia Temple, Greece
Ettie (ET-tee) (English) She Rules Our Home Magnificently
Fannie (FAN-nee) (English) She Is the Little One Who Is the Nation of France
Flossie (FLAHSS-see) (English) She Is the Little One Who Flourishes
Leila (LAY-luh) (Arabic) She Is the Beautiful Dark Night
Martha (MAR-thuh) (Hebrew) She Rules Our Home Magnificently
Neva (NEE-vuh) (English) She Is the Little One Who Is a Woman of Her People

🌸 *Blossom* (BLAHSS-sum) (English) She Is a Fragrant Blossoming Flower
Clematis (kluh-MAT-tiss) (English) She Is a Fragrant Clematis Vine

Dahlia (DAHL-yuh) (Hebrew) She Is a Tree Bough That Never Breaks

Gardenia (ghar-DEEN-yuh) (English) She Honors the Scottish Scientist Alexander Garden

Hyacinth (hye-uh-SINTH) (English) She Is a Fragrant Hyacinth Flower

Nigella (nye-JEL-luh) (English) She Is a Lofty Champion

Pansy (PAN-zee) (English) She Is a Fragrant Pansy Flower

Petunia (peh-TOON-yuh) (Guarani) She Is a Fragrant Petunia Flower

Poppy (PAHP-pee) (English) She Is a Fragrant Poppy Flower

Primula (PRIM-yoo-luh) (English) She Is Dawn's First Flower

Camelia (kuh-MEEL-yuh) (English) She Honors German Missionary Georg Kamel

Clover (KLO-vur) (English) She Is Fragrant Clover

Columbine (KAH-lum-byne) (English) She Is a Peaceful Dove

Jessamine (JES-suh-min) (English) She Is a Fragrant Jasmine Flower

Laurel (LOR-rul) (English) She Is a Laurel Wreath of Victory

Lilac (LYE-lak) (English) She Is a Fragrant Lilac Blossom

Magnolia (mag-NO-lee-yuh) (English) She Honors French Naturalist Pierre Magnol

Peony (PEE-uh-nee) (English) She Honors the Greek Healer Paeon

Scarlet (SKAR-let) (English) She Has a Fiery Red Temperament

Violet (VYE-uh-let) (English) She Is a Fragrant Violet

Chiara (kee-AHR-ruh) (Italian) She Shimmers with Fame

Christiane (kriss-tee-AH-nah) (German) She Follows Christ

Gerty (GUR-tee) (English) She Is Our Powerful Little Weapon

Kirstine (KUR-steen) (Danish) She Is Christ's Little Follower

Leona (lee-OH-nuh) (English) She Is a Noble Lion

Lise (LEE-suh) (German) She Is the Little One Favored by God

Luise (loo-EE-zuh) (German) She Is a Renowned Warrior

Misha (MEE-shuh) (Russian) She Is the Little One Who Resembles God

Rosalyn (RAHZ-uh-lin) (English) She Is Our Fragrant Rose

Sulamith (SHOO-luh-meeth) (Hebrew) She Is Peace

Danica (DAHN-ih-kuh) (Slovene) She Is the Morning's Bright Star

Crystal (KRIS-tul) (English) She Sparkles Like Diamonds

> *American actress Danica McKellar (1975–) played Winnie Cooper on the American Broadcasting Corporation (ABC) television series* The Wonder Years. *But Danica is also an accomplished mathematician, author of* Math Doesn't Suck. *Danica's younger sister Crystal is a Yale-educated, Harvard-educated attorney.*

Dian (dye-YAN) (English) She Is a Heavenly Goddess

Mary (MAIR-ree) (English) She Is Love

> *American animal-behaviorist Dian Fossey (1932–1985) did important research into the lives of Rwanda's mountain gorillas. Dian was inspired by anthropologist Mary Leakey to study these gentle primates.*

Ellen (EL-lun) (English) She Is a Radiant Torch

Susan (SOO-zun) (English) She Is a Fragrant Little Lotus Flower

> *Famed educator Ellen Spertus teaches computer science at Mills College in Oakland, an institution cofounded in 1852 by educator Susan Mills.*

Émilie (ay-mee-LEE) (French) She Is Powerfully Competitive

Françoise (frahn-SWAHZ) (French) She Is the Nation of France

Giuseppa (jee-oo-SEP-puh) (Italian) Her God Is Abundance

Hertha (HUR-thuh) (German) She Is Powerfully Energetic

Lorenna (lor-REN-nuh) (Italian) She Is Lorraine, France

Louise-Anastasia (loo-EEZ-ahn-nuh-STAH-see-yuh) (Italian) She Is a Newborn Warrior

Nicole-Reine (nih-kul-REN) (French) She Is the Ruler Who Is a Triumph for Humanity

Olive (AH-liv) (English) She Is a Fragrant Olive Tree

Thomasia (toh-MAH-see-yuh) (Italian) She Is a Precious Twin

Williamina (wil-yuh-MEE-nuh) (American/German) She Protects Us

🕊 **Hypatia** (hye-PAY-shah) (Greek) She Is the Greatest

Eudocia (yoo-DOH-shuh) (Latin) She Is Glorious

The Greek philosopher Hypatia (c. 350 B.C.–415 B.C.) was history's first woman mathematician, the inventor of an early astrolabe, a navigational tool. Hypatia's successor was the lexicologist Eudocia Macrembolitissa, empress of Byzantium.

🕊 **Louise** (loo-WEEZ) (French) She Is a Renowned Warrior

Lesley (LES-lee) (English) She Is a Garden of Holly Trees

Louise Brown (1978–) was the world's first "test-tube baby," born through a process of in vitro (in the glass) fertilization, where human sperm was injected into a human egg-cell. The donor of Louise's egg-cell was her mother, Lesley Brown.

🕊 **Marissa** (muh-RISS-suh) (English) She Is Love, a Mighty Helmet of Protection

Lorraine (lor-RAIN) (English/French) She Is Lorraine, France

At the Mountain View, California, headquarters of the search-engine corporation Google, Marissa Mayer (1975–) is a respected manager who works with engineer Lorraine Twohill to develop services on behalf of Google's users.

🕊 **Mary** (MAIR-ree) (English) She Is Love

Dorothy (DOR-uh-thee) (English) She Is God's Divine Gift

Mary Leakey (1913–1996) was a pioneering British archaeologist who began her career under the tutelage of archaeologist Dorothy Liddell. Later, Mary met and married the pioneering anthropologist Louis Leakey.

🕊 **Yun** (YOON) (Chinese) She Is a Floating White Cloud

Jade (JAYD) (English) She Is Precious Jade

Yun Wang (1964–) is an astrophysicist at the University of Oklahoma, Norman, with expertise in the study of the theoretical matter called dark energy. Yun also writes poetry, which can be found in her masterwork, The Book of Jade.

BOYS AND GIRLS

🕊 **Aaronson** (AIR-run-sun) (Hebrew) He Descends from the Mountain-Man

Abell (AY-bul) (English/Hebrew) He Is the Breath of Life

Jana (YAH-nuh) (Czech) Her God Is Gracious

Kamil (kah-MEEL) (Czech) He Observes Sacred Rituals

Kyle (KYLE) (Scottish) He Is the Water Between Two Regions

Levy (LEE-vee) (Hebrew) He Is Bound to Us by Ties of Love

Milos (MEE-lohsh) (Czech) He Is the Little One Adored by God

Moreno (mor-REN-no) (Spanish) He Is the Moor with a Dark Complexion

Morrison (MOR-ih-sun) (English) He Descends from the Moor with a Dark Complexion

Tempel (TEM-pel) (German) He Is a Warrior Who Fights for the Glory of the Temple

🕊 **Abraham** (AY-brah-ham) (Hebrew) He Is the Father of Nations

Ali (AH-lee) (Arabic) He Is Magnificently Noble

Elwyn (EL-win) (English) He Befriends the Elfin People

Ian (EE-yun) (Scottish) His God Is Gracious

Jimmy (JIM-mee) (English) He Is the Divinely Protected Little One

Kenn (KEN) (Scottish) He Is the Handsome Little One

Meriwether (English) He Is Cheerful Weather

Patrick (PAH-trik) (Irish) He Is Aristocratic

Phoebe (FEE-bee) (Greek) She Is Radiantly Beautiful

Salim (sah-LEEM) (Arabic) He Is Divinely Protected

🕊 **Abu** (ah-BOO) (Arabic) He Is the Honored Patriarch

Hitoshi (hee-TOH-Shee) (Japanese) He Is Righteously Calm

Ivan (EE-vahn) (Russian) His God Is Gracious

Mikheil (mik-hay-YEEL) (Georgian) He Resembles God

Naoto (nah-OH-toh) (Japanese) He Is Genuinely Honest

Sadao (suh-DOW) (Japanese) He Is a Beautiful Mahogany Tree

Wlodzimierz (wah-JEE-mesh) (Polish) He Rules Peacefully

Wu (WOO) (Chinese) His Life Is a Well-Executed War

Yasuo (YAH-soo-woh) (Japanese) He Is the Peaceful Child

Zdenka (zuh-DEN-kuh) (Russian) She Is Sidon, Phoenicia

⌘ *Acamar* (AHK-uh-mar) (Arabic) He Is the River's Mighty Source

Adib (ah-DEEB) (Arabic) He Is a Courageous Wolf

Alhena (ahl-AY-nuh) (Arabic) She Is the Sign of the Master

Alula (uh-LOO-luh) (Arabic) She Is First Step of the Journey

Alya (AHL-yuh) (Arabic) She Is a Gentle Lamb's Wagging Tail

Arrakis (uh-RAK-kiss) (Arabic) He Dances Joyfully

Deneb (duh-NEB) (Arabic) He Is Long, Elegant Plumage

Glenah (GLEN-nah) (Arabic) She Is the Star-Bird's Colorful Wings

Hadar (hah-DAR) (Arabic) He Is Unmatched Greatness

Hamal (hah-MAHL) (Arabic) He Is the Refreshing Ram

⌘ *Adad* (ah-DAHD) (Akkadian) He Is Thunder and Lightning

Jaggy (JAG-ghee) (American/English) She Is the Beloved One Whose God Is Gracious

Page (PAYJ) (English) She Serves Humanity

Rip (RIP) (American/English) He Is the Little One Who Is a Narrow Forest-Meadow

Sax (SAX) (American/English) He Is a Sharp-Bladed Little Axe

Sha (SHAY) (American/Greek) She Is Destined

Tao (TAH-woh) (Chinese) He Is a Sweet Peach

Ula (OO-luh) (Arabic) She Is Majestic

Vesa (VAY-suh) (Finnish) He Is a Swiftly Growing Tree

Wai (WYE) (Chinese) He Is Extraordinary

⌘ *Adelina* (ah-duh-LEE-nuh) (Italian) She Is a Little Aristocrat

Asa (AY-suh) (Hebrew) He Is a Skilled Physician

Emiliano (eh-mee-lee-AH-no) (Spanish) He Is a Courageous Rival

Hendrikje (HEN-drih-kuh) (Dutch) She Rules Our Home Magnificently

Lydie (lee-DEE) (French) She Is Lydia

Maggie (MAG-ghee) (English) She Is Our Priceless Little Pearl

Maude (MAWD) (English) She Is a Powerful Warrior

Minnie (MIN-nee) (English) She Is Our Little Protector

Odie (OH-dee) (Hungarian) He Is the Little One Who Is Our Wealthy Protector

Ramona (rah-MO-nah) (Spanish) She Counsels Us Wisely

⌘ *Aden* (AY-din) (English) His Star Burns Brightly

Andrei (AHN-dray) (Russian) He Is Powerful

Benoit (ben-WAH) (French) He Is Divinely Blessed

Leonhard (lee-awn-HART) (German) He Is a Noble Lion

Lucretia (loo KREE-shuh) (Latin) She Is Pure Gold

Philibert (FIL-ih-bair, FIL-ih-burt) (French) He Is Incredibly Brilliant

Pierre-Simon (pee-air-see-MO) (French) He Is the Rock-Solid One Who Hears Everything

Tor (TOR) (Norwegian) He Is Thunder and Lightning

Urbain (oor-BAN, UR-bayn) (French) He Lives in the Metropolis

Vaclav (VAH-klahv) (Czech) He Adds Prestige to Our Lives

⌘ *Adhara* (ah-DAHR-rah) (Arabic) She Is Chaste and Pure

Altair (al-TAIR) (Arabic) He Flies above the Clouds

Aludra (ah-LOO-drah) (Arabic) She Is Chaste and Pure

Arista (ah-RIS-tah) (Latin) She Is Plentiful Harvests

Bellatrix (BEL-lah-trix) (Latin) She Is a Mighty Warrior

Betelgeuse (BEE-tul-jooss) (Arabic) He Is the Constellation Gemini

Lyra (LYE-rah) (Greek) She Is a Beautiful Harp

Rigel (RYE-jul) (Arabic) He Stands Proudly

Sirius (SEER-ee-yus) (Latin) He Is the Radiant Dog Star

Vega (VAY-gah) (Arabic) She Is a Soaring Eagle

The beautiful stars Adhara, Altair, Aludra, Arista, Bellatrix, Betelgeuse, Lyra, Rigel, Sirius, and Vega illuminate the night sky.

♫ **Adolf** (AH-dahlf) (German) He Is a Courageous Wolf

Dietrich (DEE-trish) (German) He Is God's Divine Gift

Erwin (UR-vin) (German) His Friends Are Courageous Boars

Gunar (GUN-nar, GOON-nar) (Norwegian) He Is the Warrior Who Is Battle-Ready

Josef (YO-sef) (Hebrew) His Greatness Increases

Lia (LEE-yuh) (Italian) She Is Humanity's Queen

Lorand (lor-RAWND) (Hungarian) He Is a Mighty Nation

Luba (LOO-buh) (Russian) She Is Our Little Beloved One

Miller (MIL-lur) (English) He Mills Wheat into Bread-Flour

Vasili (vah-SEE-lee) (Russian) He Rules Humanity

♫ **Adriaan** (ahd-ree-AHN) (Dutch) He Is Hadria, Italy

Antoni (AN-toh-nee) (Polish) He Is a Blossoming Flower

Cor (KOR) (Latin) He Is Our Vibrant Heart

Crimson (KRIM-zun) (American) She Is the Deep Red of the Human Heart

Leporis (LEP-rus) (Latin) She Is a Swift Rabbit

Navi (NAH-vee) (American/Latin) He Is God's Graciousness

Nicolo (NEE-ko-lo) (Italian) He Is Humanity's Triumph

Regor (REH-gor) (American/Latin) He Is the Invincible One

Willem (VIL-lum) (Dutch) He Protects Humanity

Wojciech (VOY-chek) (Polish) He Is the Warrior Who Safeguards Us

♫ **Ah** (AH) (Chinese) She Is the Delightful Little One

Arin (AIR-run) (Irish) She Is the Nation of Ireland

Ata (AH-tuh) (Arabic) He Is God's Divine Gift

Avi (AH-vee) (Hebrew) He Resembles God

Ber (BAIR) (Yiddish) He Is a Courageous Bear

Caid (KAYD) (American/English) He Is the Circle of Life

Cam (KAHM) (Vietnamese) She Is a Sweet Orange

Dao (DOW) (Laotian) She Is a Heavenly Star

Des (DEZ) (English) He Is the Little One Who Is South Munster, Ireland

Dev (DEV) (Sanskrit) He Is Divine

♫ **Aimé** (em-MAY) (French) She Is Greatly Beloved

Camille (kuh-MEEL) (English) She Is the Young One Who Performs Rituals

Germaine (zhair-MEN) (French) She Is a Beloved Friend

Henri (aw-REE) (French) He Rules Our Home Magnificently

Lazare (luh-ZAR) (French) His God Is an Ever-Present Help

Lucie (loo-SEE) (French) She Is Radiance

Marie-Clémentine (mah-ree-klaym-aw-TEEN) (French) She Is Compassionate

Marie-Louise (mar-ree-loo-WEEZ) (French) She Is Love, and Warfare

Mathilde (mah-TEELD) (French) She Is a Powerful Warrior

Octavie (ahk-tay-VEE) (French) She Is Eighth

♫ **Aki** (AH-kee) (Japanese) She Is the Beautiful Autumn Season

Chika (CHEE-kuh) (Japanese) She Scatters Fragrant Blossoms

Chinatsu (chee-NAHT-soo) (Japanese) She Is the Warm Summer Season

Chou (JO) (Japanese) She Is a Lovely Butterfly

Daichi (DYE-chee) (Japanese) He Is Our Marvelous Planet Earth

Hana (HAH-nuh) (Japanese) She Is a Fragrant Blossom

Haru (HAH-roo) (Japanese) He Is Golden Sunlight

Hinata (hee-NAH-tah) (Japanese) She Is Golden Sunlight

Hotaru (HO-tuh-roo) (Japanese) She Is a Brilliant Firefly

Kaede (KAY-dee, KYE-day) (Japanese) She Is a Sugary Maple Tree

♫ **Alban** (AHL-ban) (German) He Is Alba Longa, Italy

Aram (ah-RAHM) (Georgian) He Is Level-Headed

Bela (BEL-luh) (Hungarian) He Is Beautifully Fair

Elgar (EL-gur) (English) He Is a Weapon of the Magical Elfin People

Franck (FRAHNK) (French) He Is the Nation of France

Gaetano (ghye-TAH-no) (Italian) He Is Gaeta, Italy

Monteverdi (mohn-tay-VAIR-dee) (Italian) He Is a Beautiful Green Mountain

Rodion (roh-dee-YOHN) (Russian) He Sings of Conquests

Tikhon (TEE-khan) (Russian) He Is Always on Target

Tomaso (toh-MAH-so) (Italian) He Is a Precious Twin

🖉 **Amalia** (uh-MAHL-yah) (German) She Works Tirelessly

Arbella (ar-BEL-luh) (American/Scottish) She Is the One Upon Whom We Depend

Beatrice (BEE-uh-triss) (English) She Is a Great Voyager

Corinne (kor-REEN) (French) She Is Chaste and Pure

Fred (FRED) (English) He Is Our Peaceful Little Ruler

Johnson (JAHN-sun) (English) He Descends from the One Whose God Is Gracious

Lillian (LIL-ee-yun) (English) She Is the Little One Favored by God

Luce (LOOSS) (French) She Is Radiance

Yasu (YAH-soo) (Japanese) He Is Peaceful

Zora (ZOR-ruh) (Slovak) She Is the Radiant Dawn

🖉 **Amalie** (ah-mah-LEE) (German) She Works Tirelessly

Bernhard (BAIRN-hart) (German) He Is a Mighty Bear

Brook (BROOK) (English) He Is a Rushing Brook

Emmy (EM-mee) (Dutch) She Is the Little One Who Is Our Entire Universe

Hilbert (HIL-burt) (German) He Is Brilliant Warfare

Joseph-Louis (zho-sef-loo-WEE) (French) He Is the Warrior Whose Greatness Increases

Kepler (KEP-lur) (German) He Is Bohemia

Lagrange (luh-GRAYNJ) (French) He Is a Beautiful Farm

MacLaurin (mak-LOR-rin) (Scottish) He Descends from the One Wreathed in Victory

Stevin (STEE-vun) (English) He Is a Shining Crown

🖉 **Andre** (AHN-dray) (French) He Is Powerfully Male

Amil (ah-MEEL) (Indian) He Is an Important Statesman

Brett (BRET) (English) He Is Bretagne, France

Giuseppe (joo-SEP-pee) (Italian) His God Is Abundance

Ibrahim (ee-brah-HEEM) (Arabic) He Is the Father of Nations

Kirill (keer-REEL) (Russian) He Is Supreme

Marcelo (mar-SEL-lo) (Spanish) He Is Powerfully Male

Merieme (MEER-ee-yum) (Arabic) She Is Love

Tetsuya (tet-SOO-yuh) (Japanese) He Is Clever

Vasily (vah-SEE-lee) (Russian) He Rules Humanity

🖉 **Andy** (AN-dee) (English) He Is a Powerful Little Man

Haydn (HYE-dun) (German) He Battles Against True Believers

Henrik (HEN-rik) (Norwegian) He Rules Our Home Magnificently

Kilian (KIL-ee-yun) (Irish) He Is the Aggressive Little One

Lada (LAH-duh) (Czech) She Is Affectionate

Leoš (LAY-yohsh) (Czech) He Is a Noble Lion

Mihai (mee-HYE) (Romanian) He Resembles God

Modest (mo-DEST) (Russian) He Is Wonderfully Modest

Rabindranath (rah-BIN-drah-nath) (Sanskrit) He Is the Golden Sun

Verdi (VAIR-dee) (Italian) He Is Green Forests

🖉 **Antlia** (ANT-lee-yuh) (Latin) She Brings Earth, Wind, and Water

Aquarius (uh-KWAIR-ee-yus) (Greek) He Brings Water

Aquila (uh-KEE-luh) (Greek) She Is a Soaring Eagle

Ara (AIR-ruh) (Greek) She Is the Sacred Altar

Aries (AIR-reez) (Greek) He Is an Enchanted Ram

Auriga (or-EE-ghuh) (Greek) She Is a Heavenly Charioteer

Caelum (SEE-lum) (Latin) She Is a Divinely Inspired Chisel

Cassiopeia (kass-see-uh-PEE-yuh) (Greek) She Is a Majestic Throne

Centaurus (sen-TOR-rus) (Latin) He Is the Mighty One Who Slays Bulls

Corvus (KOR-vuss) (Latin) He Is the Night-Black Raven
The beautiful constellations Antlia, Aquarius, Aquila, Ara, Aries, Auriga, Caelum, Cassiopeia, Centaurus, and Corvus illuminate the night sky.

🐝 **Anton** (ahn-TOHN) (Dutch) He Is a Blossoming Flower
Astrid (ASS-trid) (Swedish) She Is a Radiant Goddess
Baltimore (BALL-tih-mor) (English/Irish) He Is Stately Mansions
Cori (KOR-ree) (Scottish) She Is a Hillside Teeming with Swift Animals
Eugénie (yoo-zhay-NEE) (French) She Is Aristocratic
Fernandus (fur-NAHN-duss) (Latin) He Is Peaceful and Brave
Gerty (GUR-tee) (English) She Is Our Mighty Little Weapon
Kleopatra (klee-oh-PAT-truh) (Greek) She Is Her Father's Glory
Mendel (MEN-del) (Yiddish) He Is the Little One Who Blesses Us
Torvald (TOR-vahld) (Norwegian) He Rules with Thunder and Lightning

🐝 **Aristarkh** (ahr-iss-TARK) (Russian) He Is the Source of all Greatness
Edmondson (ED-mun-sun) (English) He Descends from the Wealthy Protector
Frédéric (fray-dair-REEK) (French) He Rules Peacefully
Gerard (jur-RARD) (English) He Is a Powerful Weapon
Liisi (LEE-see) (Finnish) She Is the Little One Favored by God
Pol (POLE) (Irish) He Demonstrates Humility
Sylvain (seel-VAN) (French) He Is the Great Woodlands
Wesley (WES-lee) (English) He Is a Meadow in the Western Forest
Xaver (hah-VAIR) (German) He Is a Shining New Mansion
Zach (ZAK) (English) He Is the Little One Remembered by God

🐝 **Aristoteles** (air-ih-STAH-tuh-leez) (Greek) He Has the Best Ambitions
Bedrich (BAYD-rish) (Czech) He Rules Peacefully
Burkhardt (BURK-hart) (German) He Safeguards Us Courageously

František (FRAHN-tih-Shek) (Czech) He Is the Nation of France
Josephus (jo-SEE-fus) (Latin/Hebrew) His Greatness Increases
Locke (LAHK) (English) He Is the Great Land of the Lochs (Lakes)
London (LUN-dun) (English) He Is London, England
Mika (MYE-kuh) (Finnish) He Is God's Little Disciple
Samuil (sah-moo-WEEL) (Russian) His God Hears Him
Sokrates (SAH-kruh-teez) (Greek) He Is Powerful

🐝 **Baron** (BAIR-run) (English) He Is a Free, Invincible Warrior
Basilius (buh-SIL-ee-yus) (Latin) He Rules Humanity
Heng (ENG) (Chinese) He Is Eternally Faithful
Jethro (JETH-ro) (Hebrew) His God Is Abundance
Ken-Ichi (ken-EE-chee) (Japanese) He Vigorously Pursues Knowledge
Stephan (SHTEF-fahn) (German) He Is a Shining Crown
Valentinus (val-en-TEE-nus) (Latin) He Is Energetic
Yury (YOO-ree) (Russian) He Farms the Land
Zhang (ZHANG) (Chinese) He Flies on the Wings of Fortune
Ziga (ZEE-guh) (Slovene) He Is Our Defender

🐝 **Carina** (kah-REE-nah) (Latin) She Is a Ship's Balance and Equilibrium
Crux (KRUX) (Latin) He Is Christ's Heavenly Cross
Delphinus (DEL-fin-nuss) (Latin) He Is Delphi, Greece
Dorado (dor-AH-doh) (Spanish) He Is a Swift Swordfish
Gemini (GEM-ih-nye) (Latin) He Is a Precious Twin
Lynx (LINX) (Latin) She Is a Sharp-Eyed Lynx
Mensa (MEN-suh) (Latin) He Is a Beautiful Mesa
Pavo (PAH-vo) (Latin) He Is a Resplendent Peacock
Pictor (PIK-tur) (Latin) He Is a Great Artist's Easel
Volans (VO-lunz) (Latin) He Is a Shimmering Flying-Fish

The constellations Carina, Crux, Delphinus, Dorado, Gemini, Lynx, Mensa, Pavo, Pictor, and Volans illuminate the night sky. (Note: Mensa can mean "stupid" in Spanish.)

🐝 **Caroline** (KAIR-uh-line) (English) She Is a Powerful Warrior

William (WILL-yum) (English) He Protects Us

Caroline Herschel (1750–1848) was a German-English astronomer who was the first woman to discover a comet, in 1786. Caroline worked with her brother William Herschel, another famed German-English astronomer.

🐝 **Carolus** (KAIR-oh-luss) (Latin/German) He Is a Mighty Warrior

Evgeniya (eev-GAYN-yuh) (Russian) She Is Aristocratic

Georgy (gay-OR-ghee) (Russian) He Farms the Land

Joran (jo-RAHN) (Swedish) He Farms the Land

Kryštof (KRISH-toff) (Czech) He Carries Christ in His Heart

O'Connell (oh-KAHN-nul) (Irish) He Descends from the Courageous Wolf

Tomáš (toh-MAHSH) (Czech) He Is a Precious Twin

Winton (WIN-tun) (English) He Is a Vineyard of Wine-Grapes

Zdislava (zhee-SLAH-vuh) (Czech) She Brings Us Great Honor

Zoya (ZOY-yuh) (Russian) She Is Life Itself

🐝 **Chaim** (KHIME) (Hebrew) He Is Life Itself

Ada (AY-duh) (English) She Is Our Little Aristocrat

Chaim Weizmann (1874–1952) was a Russian-Israeli chemist and first president of Israel, who established the Weizmann Institute of Science in Rehovot. Scientists who have worked at the Weizmann Institute include Israeli crystallographer Ada Yonath.

🐝 **Christa** (KREES-tah) (German) She Is Christ's Little Follower

Dmitry (dih-MEE-tree) (Russian) He Is Like Demeter, the Earth Mother

Ellison (EL-ih-sun) (English) He Descends from a Gentleman

Hideo (hih-DAY-yoh) (Japanese) He Is a Marvelous Person

Ilan (ee-LAHN) (Hebrew) He Is a Towering Tree

Kalpana (kahl-PAH-nuh) (Sanskrit) She Is Our Dream of Success

Konstantin (KON-stun-teen) (Russian) He Is Dependably Constant

Liwei (lee-WAY) (Chinese) He Is Humanity's Triumph

Marla (MAR-luh) (English) She Is Our Little Beloved One

Pascale (pah-SKAH-lay) (Italian) He Is Easter and Passover

🐝 **Dawson** (DAW-sun) (English) He Descends from the Beloved One

Ferguson (FUR-ghuss-sun) (English/Irish) He Descends from the Powerful Man

Gaston (gas-TOW) (French) He Is Gascony, France

Ignacy (ig-NAH-see) (Polish) He Is Blazing Fire

Irmgard (URM-gard) (German) She Is the Little One Who Embraces the World

Matthias (muh-THYE-yuss) (Greek) He Is God's Divine Gift

Maynard (MAY-nurd) (English) He Is Powerfully Courageous

Per (PAIR) (Swedish) He Is Rock-Solid

Petr (PET-tur) (Czech) He Is Rock-Solid

Reuben (ROO-bayn) (Hebrew) Behold, He Is Our Glorious Son

🐝 **Dom** (DAHM) (English) He Is the Little One Sent by God

Eda (ED-duh) (Turkish) She Is Charmingly Courteous

Efi (EF-fee) (American/Scottish) She Is Our Beautiful Little Speaker

Eula (YOO-luh) (English) She Is Our Beautiful Little Speaker

Iana (ee-YAH-nuh) (Russian) Her God Is Gracious

Íde (EE-duh) (Irish) She Thirsts for Knowledge and Love

Ime (EE-may) (Ibibio) She Waits Serenely

Jax (JAX) (American/English) He Is the Little One Whose God Is Gracious

Jini (JEE-nee) (American/English) She Is God's Graceful Little Messenger

Lilo (LEE-lo) (German) She Is Our Beloved Little Warrior Whose God Is Abundance

🐝 **Eena** (EE-nuh) (English) She Is Unequalled

Jain (JAYN) (English) She Is Unequalled

Lora (LOR-ruh) (English) She Is Unequalled

Meena (MEE-nuh) (English) She Is Unequalled

Mo (MO) (English) He Is Unequalled

Para (PAIR-ruh) (English) She Is Unequalled

Patera (puh-TAIR-ruh) (English) She Is Unequalled

Peina (PAY-nuh) (English) She Is Unequalled

Pip (PIP) (English) He Is Unequalled

Yahn (YAHN) (English) He Is Unequalled

🐝 **Ellen** (EL-len) (English) She Is a Radiant Torch

Emma (EM-muh) (English) She Is Our Universe

Johanna (yo-HAH-nah) (German) Her God Is Gracious

Josefa (ho-SAY-fuh) (Spanish) Her God Is Abundance

Lovisa (lo-VEE-suh) (Swedish) She Is a Renowned Warrior

Mamie (MAY-mee) (English) She Is the Beloved One Who Is Love Itself

Mito (MEE-toh) (Japanese) She Is Fresh Water in the Rice Fields

Niwa (NEE-wah) (Japanese) She Is a Fragrant Garden

Sarah (SAIR-ruh) (Hebrew) She Is a Majestic Princess

Yone (YO-nay) (Japanese) She Farms the Land

🐝 **Geoffrey** (JEFF-ree) (English) He Is the Land of Peace

Guo (GWO) (Chinese) He Is Our Great Nation

Matsuo (MAHT-soo-woh) (Japanese) He Is a Sky-High Pine Tree

Nilakantha (nee-luh-KAN-thuh) (Sanskrit) He Is as Bright-Blue as Shiva

Pelageya (pel-AH-zhee-yuh) (Sanskrit) She Is the Blue Ocean

Rashid (rah-SHEED) (Arabic) He Is Divinely Protected

Solomon (SAH-lah-mahn) (Hebrew) He Is Peace

Stéphane (saty-FAHN) (French) He Is a Shining Crown

Toru (TOR-roo) (Japanese) He Is the Unconquerable Ocean

Viktor (VEEK-tohr) (Russian) He Is Humanity's Triumph

🐝 **Izar** (ee-ZAR) (Arabic) She Is the Garment That Preserves Modesty

Kaus (KAY-yus) (Arabic) He Is a Powerful Longbow

Kitalpha (kit-TAL-fuh) (Arabic) He Is a Divine Steed

Kurhah (KUR-rah) (Arabic) He Is a Fiery Steed

Lesath (leh-ZAHTH) (Arabic) He Is a Powerful Sting

Maasym (mah-SEEM) (Arabic) He Has a Supple Wrist

Markab (mar-KAHB) (Arabic) He Is the Divine Steed's Muscles

Matar (muh-TAR) (Arabic) He Brings Life-Giving Rain

Meissa (may-EE-suh) (Arabic) She Shimmers in Heaven

Merak (mair-RAHK) (Arabic) He Is Magnificent

🐝 **Janna** (JAHN-nah) (Swedish) Her God Is Gracious

Juro (JOO-ro) (Japanese) He Is Our Tenth Son

Kaoru (KAIR-roo) (Japanese) He Is the Breath of Heaven

Kenneth (KEN-neth) (Scottish) He Is Handsome

Liu (LYOO) (Chinese) He Is a Beautiful Willow Tree

Lyudmila (lyood-MIL-luh) (Russian) She Is Beloved by Humanity

Mikhail (meek-hah-YEEL) (Russian) He Resembles God

Minoru (mih-NO-roo) (Japanese) He Is Genuinely Honest

Shams (SHAHMZ) (Arabic) He Is the Golden Sun

Yoshio (YO-see-yo) (Japanese) He Is all Good Fortune

🐝 **Mac** (MAK) (Irish) He Is Our Powerful Descendant

Nat (NAT) (English) He Is the Generous Little One

Nic (NIK) (English) He Is Humanity's Little Triumph

Nio (NEE-yoh) (American/Greek) He Is New and Unique

Oasis (oh-AY-sis) (American/English) She Is Water in the Desert

Perl (PURL) (American/English) She Is a Priceless Pearl

Pim (PIM) (Dutch) He Is Our Little Protector

Pine (American/English) She Is a Lofty Pine Tree

Pio (PEE-yoh) (Italian) He Is Respectful

Ram (RAHM) (Hebrew) He Surpasses Everyone

🌙 **Madhava** (mahd-HAH-vah) (Sanskrit) He Is Springtime

Surya (soor-EE-yuh) (Sanskrit) She Is the Radiant Sun

Madhava (c. 1350–c. 1425) was an Indian mathematician who, according to researchers from the University of Manchester, may have discovered calculus centuries before English mathematician Isaac Newton. Madhava's achievements are recorded in a book of Indian astronomy, Surya Siddhanta.

🌙 **Marie** (mah-REE) (French) She Is Love

Pierre (pee-AIR) (French) He Is Rock-Solid

Marie Curie (1867–1934) was a Polish-French scientist who won the 1903 Nobel Prize for her achievments in physics, such as her discovery of the element radium. Marie's husband Pierre assisted in these momentous scientific discoveries.

🌙 **Mizar** (mee-ZAR) (Arabic) She Is the Garment That Keeps One Clean

Murzim (mur-ZEEM) (Arabic) He Is the Lion's Roar

Nashira (nah-SHEE-ruh) (Arabic) She Brings Good Fortune

Nihal (nee-HAHL) (Arabic) He Is the Source of Water

Pherkad (fair-KAHD) (Arabic) He Is a Strong Calf

Rastaban (RAHSS-tuh-bahn) (Arabic) He Is the Swift-Striking Serpent

Risha (REE-shuh) (Arabic) She Is a Life-Saving Rope

Sabik (SAH-bik) (Arabic) He Comes Before Others

Sadalmelik (sah-dahl-meha-LEEK) (Arabic) He Is a Brilliant Star

Sadr (SAH-dur) (Arabic) He Has a Muscular Chest

🌙 **Saiph** (sah-EEF) (Arabic) He Is a Razor-Sharp Sword

Shaula (SHAW-lah) (Arabic) She Is the Scorpion's Sting

Sirrah (seer-RAH) (Arabic) He Is the Steed's Heart

Tarf (TARF) (Arabic) He Is the Lion's Terrifying Gaze

Talitha (tuh-LEE-thah) (Arabic) She Is the Southern Star

Thuban (THOO-bun) (Arabic) He Is the Swift-Striking Serpent

Yed (YED) (Arabic) He Is the Hand That Seizes

Zaniah (zuh-NYE-yah) (Arabic) She Is the Vertex

Zaurac (ZOR-rahk) (Arabic) He Is Heaven's Graceful Sailboat

Zavijava (zah-vee-YAH-vah) (Arabic) She Is the Vertex

Name Pairs and Groups
from the World of Fine Arts

BOYS

 Agreus (AG-gree-yus) (Latin) He Is a Hunter
Nomius (NOME-ee-yus) (Latin) He Is Green
Pastures
Agreus and Nomius belonged to the group of nature-spirits the Romans called fauns, who were half-human and half-goat, and delighted mortals by playing on their panpipes.

 Aiden (AY-dun) (English/Irish) He Is the
Little One Who Is Flaming Fire
Agustin (ah-GOOS-tin) (French) He Is
Venerated
Angel (AYN-jul) (English) He Is God's Angelic
Messenger
Arjun (ar-ZHOON) (Indian) He Is Beautifully
Fair
Ethan (EE-thahn) (Hebrew) He Is Rock-Solid
Justin (JUS-tin) (Latin) He Is Righteous and
Just
Lewis (LOO-wiss) (English) He Is a Renowned
Warrior
Olexandr (oh-lex-AHN-dur) (Ukranian) He
Protects Humanity
Ryan (RYE-yun) (Irish) He Descends from a
Beloved King
Santiago (sahn-tee-AH-go) (Spanish) He Is the
Blessed Saint James

 Ainsley (AINZ-lee) (English) He Is a Hidden
Meadow
Clare (KLAIR) (English) She Is Clearly Famous
Ainsley Harriott (1957–) is a Jamaican-English chef who has created a line of gourmet products.

He is also known for his television series Ready, Steady, Cook, *produced by the Dutch company* Endemol. *Ainsley is married to English designer Clare Fellows.*

 Alejandro (al-eh-HAHN-dro) (Spanish) He
Protects Humanity
Alexandru (ahl-ex-AHN-droo) (Romanian) He
Protects Humanity
Arda (AHR-duh) (Arabic) He Is Warm and
Righteous
Erik (AIR-ik) (Norwegian) He Is an Ever-
Powerful Ruler
Iker (EE-kair) (Basque) He Blesses Us with His
Presence
João (zhoh-AH-woh) (Portuguese) His God Is
Gracious
Marc (MAHK) (French) He Is Powerfully
Male
Mattia (MAH-tee-yuh) (Italian) He Is God's
Divine Gift
Nikola (NEE-ko-lah) (Serbian) He Is
Humanity's Triumph
Théo (tay-YOH) (French) He Is the Little One
Given to Us by God

 Artem (AHR-tem) (Russian) He Is Artistic
Eetu (EE-too) (Finnish) He Is Our Wealthy
Protector
Georgi (gay-OR-ghee) (Bulgarian) He Farms
the Land
Jens (YENZ) (Danish) His God Is Gracious
Luka (LOO-kuh) (Croatian) He Is Lucania,
Italy

Mehdi (MED-dee) (Arabic) He Is the Righteous Path

Mikkel (meek-KEL) (Danish) He Resembles God

Muhammed (muh-HAHM-mehd) (Arabic) He Is Praise-Worthy

Narek (NAH-rehk) (Armenian) He Is Narek, Armenia

Uri (YOOR-ree, OOR-ree) (Hebrew) He Is Radiance

☺ **Bence** (BEN-say) (Hungarian) He Is a Mighty Conqueror

Enzo (EN-zo) (French) He Rules Our Home Magnificently

Giorgi (jee-OR-jee) (Georgian) He Farms the Land

Jakub (YAH-koob) (Polish) He Surpasses Everyone

Luke (LOOWK) (Greek) He Is Lucania, Italy

Matas (MAH-tahss) (Lithuanian) He Is God's Divine Gift

Mathéo (mah-TAY-yoh) (French) He Is God's Divine Gift

Mathias (muh-THYE-yuss) (Norwegian) He Is God's Divine Gift

Sem (SHEM) (Dutch) His Name Is Sacred

Yiannis (YAHN-nees) (Greece) His God Is Gracious

☺ **Berry** (BAIR-ree) (English) He Is the Little Fair-Haired One

Lennon (LEN-nun) (Scottish) He Descends from the Great Lover

Chuck Berry (1926–) is an African-American guitarist with a claim to having invented rock-and-roll, with such tunes as Johnny B. Goode. Beatles legend John Lennon said, "If you tried to give rock-and-roll another name, you might call it, 'Chuck Berry.'"

☺ **Edgar** (ed-GAIR) (French) He Is a Powerful Weapon

Henri (aw-REE) (French) He Rules Our Home Magnificently

Edgar Degas (1834–1917) was a French Impressionist who painted scenes of the lives of Parisian dancers. Edgar was emulated by French Impressionist painter Henri de Toulouse-Lautrec, who overcame handicaps to produce masterpieces.

☺ **Gilbert** (GIL-burt) (English) He Is a Shining Promise

Sullivan (SUL-lih-vahn) (Irish) He Descends from the Dark-Eyed One

British playwright William Gilbert (1836–1911), and his collaborator, composer Arthur Sullivan (1842–1900), created some of the nineteenth century's most memorable comic operettas, including The Pirates of Penzance.

☺ **Grant** (GRAHNT) (Scottish) He Is Magnificently Great

Nan (NAN) (English) She Is the Little One Who Shimmers with Sunlight

Grant Wood (1981–1942) was an American painter who created the 1930 masterpiece American Gothic, *showing a farmer holding a pitchfork, with his wife standing beside him. The model for the farmer's companion was Grant's sister Nan Wood Graham.*

☺ **Hieronymous** (heer-RAH-nuh-mus) (Greek) His Name Is Holy

Pieter (PEE-tur) (Dutch) He Is Rock-Solid

Hieronymous Bosch (c. 1450–1516) was a painter who used fearsome shapes to reveal humanity's wickedness. Hieronymous influenced Pieter Brueghel the Elder, another intensely moral painter.

☺ **Imhotep** (im-HO-tep) (Egyptian) He Journeys Peacefully

Zoser (ZO-sur) (Egyptian) He Lives Forever

Egyptian physician-architect Imhotep (2650 B.C.–2600 B.C.), whom the Greeks called Aesculapius, god of medicine, built history's first known colossal pyramid, the Step Pyramid of King Zoser in Saqqara, Egypt.

☺ **Jackson** (JAK-sun) (English) He Descends from the One Whose God Is Gracious

Cody (KO-dee) (Irish) He Descends from the Wealthy One

Jackson Pollock (1912–1956) was an American painter renowned for his dynamic painting methods, such as spilling paint onto huge canvases. Jackson was born in Cody, Wyoming, named after showman Buffalo Bill Cody.

☺ **Jin** (JIN) (Chinese) He Is Pure Gold

Wei (WAY) (Chinese) He Is a Tower of Strength

Jin of the Xia Dynasty ruled China from 1810 B.C. to 1789 B.C., and was responsible for creating the distinctive music called West Sound. One of Jin's artistic protegés, Fan, eventually became the ruler of the kingdom of Wei.

🅑 **Johann** (YO-hahn) (German) His God Is Gracious
Antonio (ahn-toh-nee-yoh) (Italian) He Is a Blossoming Flower
Johann Sebastian Bach (1685–1750) and Antonio Vivaldi (1678–1741) were giants of the Baroque music era, a time when melodies became increasingly intricate. Johann is known for such jewels as the Brandenburg Concertos, *while Antonio is known for such masterpieces as* The Four Seasons.

🅑 **Leonardo** (lay-oh-NAR-doh) (Italian) He Is a Courageous Lion
François (frahn-SWAH) (French) He Is the Nation of France
Leonardo da Vinci (1452–1519) is the quintessential fifteenth century Renaissance man and one of history's greatest painters. Leonardo ended his long productive life in a villa provided for him by the art-loving French ruler Francois I.

🅑 **Ludwig** (LOOD-vig, LOOD-wig) (German) He Is a Renowned Warrior
Franz (FRAHNZ) (German) He Is the Nation of France
Ludwig van Beethoven (1770–1827) is history's greatest classical composer, producing such gems as the Symphony No. 9 in D Minor (Ode to Joy). *Beethoven's tutor was classical composer Franz Joseph Haydn, the Father of String Quartets.*

🅑 **Matty** (MAT-tee) (English) He Is the Beloved One Given to Us by God
Arlen (AR-len) (English) He Is a Sacred Promise
Matty Groves is the main character in the seventeenth century English ballad Matty Groves, *which tells of the servant Matty, who betrays his master Lord Arlen by seducing Arlen's wife. Arlen slays the lovers, then himself.*

🅑 **Michelangelo** (mye-kul-AN-jah-lo) (Italian) He Resembles God's Angels
Lorenzo (lo-REN-zo) (Italian) He Is a Laurel Wreath of Victory
Michelangelo (1475–1564) was the artist-architect best known for painting uplifting biblical scenes on the ceiling of the Sistine Chapel in Rome, Italy. The Italian monarch Lorenzo de' Medici was one of Michelangelo's earliest patrons.

🅑 **Paul** (POLE) (French) He Demonstrates Humility

Pierre-Auguste (pee-AIR-oh-GOOST) (French) He Is Magnificently Rock-Solid
French painter Paul Cézanne (1839–1906) conveyed impressions of reality with careful strokes and subjective coloration, as in L'Estaque *(1885). Paul often allowed his studio to be used by colleague Pierre-Auguste Renoir, another Impressionist genius whose masterworks include* La Loge *(1874).*

🅑 **Pyotr** (PYO-tur) (Russian) He Is Rock-Solid
Vincenzo (vin-CHEN-zo) (Italian) He Conquers
Russian musician Pyotr Tchaikovsky (1840–1893) was a renowned composer of nineteenth century Romantic music, as exemplified by The Nutcracker Ballet. *Pyotr's greatest influence was the Italian composer of Bel canto operas, Vincenzo Bellini.*

🅑 **Raphael** (rah-fah-EL) (French) His God Heals the Sick
Donato (doh-NAH-toh) (Italian) He Is God's Divine Gift
Raphael (1483–1520) was a painter of the Italian Renaissance, who, with Leonardo da Vinci and Michelangelo, comprise a trio of revered masters. Raphael's works, such as Portrait of Pope Julius II, *exhibit realism and human compassion.*

🅑 **Rembrandt** (REM-brant) (Dutch) He Counsels Warriors
Christiaan (KRIS-tee-yahn) (Dutch) He Follows Christ
Dutch painter Rembrandt (1606–1669) was a master at painting light and shadow. The Dutch politician Constantijn Huygens advanced Rembrandt's artistic career, as well as the career of his own son, physicist and astronomer Christiaan Huygens.

🅑 **Salvador** (SAL-vah-dor) (Spanish) He Resembles Our Savior, Christ
Dada (DAH-dah) (Yoruba) He Has Beautiful Fleecy Hair
Salvador Dali (1904–1989) was a giant of surrealist painting, where the mind flows unimpeded—such as in 1931's The Persistence of Memory, *with its eerie images. Salvador has also been called the premiere painter of Dada, an anti-war artistic creed.*

🅑 **Vincent** (VIN-sunt) (English) He Is a Mighty Conqueror
Paul (PAHL) (Latin) He Demonstrates Humility

Dutch painter Vincent van Gogh (1853–1890) pioneered Expressionism, imparting ideas through visual distortion, as in Starry Night *(1889). Vincent's friend Paul Gaugin (1848–1903), was an Impressionist who painted Tahitian life-scenes, as in* Maternity *(1899).*

🖉 **Yves** (EEV) (French) He Is the Magnificent Yew Tree

Christian (KRIS-chun) (English) He Follows Christ

Yves Saint Laurent (1936–2008) was a French designer who made production clothing as opposed to custom pieces. Yves's mentor was French designer Christian Dior.

GIRLS

🖉 **Adelaide** (AD-uh-layd) (English) She Is Aristocratic

Adriana (ay-dree-AN-nuh) (Italian) She Is Hadria, Italy

Andrea (AN-dree-yuh) (Italian) She Is Powerful

Angel (AYN-jul) (English) She Is God's Angelic Messenger

Béatrice (bay-ah-TREESS) (French) She Is a Great Voyager

Dafne (DAF-nee) (Italian) She Is a Fragrant Laurel Tree

Elektra (ee-LEK-truh) (Greek) She Is Golden Amber

Fedora (feh-DOR-ruh) (Russian) She Is a Gift from God

Florencia (flor-EN-see-yuh) (Italian) She Flourishes

Genoveva (hen-oh-VAY-vuh) (Spanish) She Is Humanity's Greatest Woman

🖉 **Adele** (uh-DELL) (English) She Is Aristocratic

Aline (ah-LEEN) (French) She Is Our Little Aristocrat

Autumn (AW-tum) (Latin) She Is the One Who Is the Colorful Autumn Season

Charity (CHAIR-ih-tee) (English) She Is Generosity and Charity

Christina (kris-TEE-nuh) (German) She Follows Christ

Lavender (LAV-en-dur) (English) She Is Fragrant Lavender

Lilac (LYE-lak) (English) She Is a Fragrant Lilac

Madeleine (mad-LEN) (French) She Is the Biblical Land of Magdala

Pepita (peh-PEE-tah) (Spanish) She Is the Little One Whose Greatness Increases

Pierrette (pee-air-RET) (French) She Is the Little Rock-Solid One

🖉 **Aino** (ah-EE-no) (Finnish) She Is Our Universe

Anastasiya (ahn-nuh-STAH-see-yah) (Russian) She Is Reborn to New Life

Giulia (JOOL-yuh) (Italian) She Is Beautifully Youthful

Kamile (kah-MEE-luh) (Lithuanian) She Is the Young One Who Performs Rituals

Leonie (LAY-oh-nee) (German) She Is a Noble Lioness

Lisette (lee-SET) (French) She Is the Little One Favored by God

Milica (mil-EE-kuh, MIL-ee-kah) (Serbian) She Is Graceful

Ona (OH-nuh) (Lithuanian) She Is Graceful

Sanne (SAHN-nuh) (Dutch) She Is Greatness

Yekaterina (ee-kah-tah-REE-nuh) (Russian) She Is Pure-Hearted

🖉 **Amethyst** (AM-uh-thist) (English) She Is Golden Tranquility

Azure (AZH-zhur) (English) She Is the Heavenly Blue Sky

Burgundy (BUR-gun-dee) (English) She Is the Colorful Region of Burgundy, France

Carolina (kar-oh-LEE-nuh) (Spanish) She Is a Warrior with Rose-Red Armor

Cerise (sur-REESS) (French) She Is a Fragrant Cherry Blossom

Coral (KOR-rul) (English) She Is Shining White Coral

Cyan (sye-YAN) (English) She Is Blue-Green Peace

Indigo (IN-dih-go) (English) She Is Lovely Indigo-Blue Dye

Sienna (see-EN-nuh) (English) She Is Sienna, Italy

Spring (SPRING) (English) She Is the Fresh New Season of Springtime

🖉 **Ane** (AH-nuh) (Danish) She Is Graceful

Elif (el-LIFF) (Arabic) She Is First

Emily (EM-uh-lee) (English) She Is Powerfully Competitive

Florencia (flor-EN-see-yuh) (Italian) She Flourishes

Gabriela (gah-vree-EL-lah) (Spanish) She Is God's Angelic Messenger

Kayla (KAY-lah) (Yiddish) She Is a Laurel Wreath of Victory

Léa (lay-YAH) (French) She Is Our Queen

Nika (NEE-kuh) (Russian) She Is Humanity's Triumph

Valeriya (vah-LAIR-ee-yuh) (Russian) She Is Powerful

Wilma (VIL-mah) (German) She Protects Humanity

🎨 **Aoi** (ah-OH-yee) (Japanese) She Is a Fragrant Althea Flower

Arpita (ar-PEE-tuh) (Indian) She Brings Flowers

Darja (DAHR-yuh) (Czech) She Possesses Goodness

Eden (EE-den) (Hebrew) She Is a Paradise of Delights

Jessa (JESS-suh) (English) She Is the Little One Who Is a Great Sight to Behold

Layla (LAY-lah) (Arabic) She Is a Darkly Beautiful Evening

Mariam (MAIR-ee-yahm) (Arabic) She Is Love

Milena (mil-LAY-nuh) (Russian) She Is Graceful

Noa (NO-wuh) (Hebrew) She Is Blessed Tranquility

Tereza (tair-AY-zuh) (Czech) She Is a Summer Harvest

🎨 **Ave** (AH-vay) (Latin) She Is Hailed as Humanity's Greatest Woman

Blanca (BLAHNG-kuh) (Spanish) She Is Beautifully Fair

Concorde (ko-KORD, KAHN-kord) (French) She Is Peace and Concord

Liberdade (lee-bair-DAH-day) (Spanish) She Is Glorious Liberty

March (MARCH) (English) She Is the Fresh Springtime Month of March

Maris (MAIR-riss) (English) She Is the Blue Ocean

Masiwa (mah-SEE-wah) (Shikomor) She Is a Great Archipelago

Mila (MEE-luh) (Bulgarian) She Is Darling and Sweet

Renaissance (REN-uh-sahnss) (French) She Is Reborn in God

Tharana (thah-RAH-nah) (Persian) She Sings Sweet Melodies

🎨 **Candy** (KAN-dee) (English/Nubian) She Is Our Little Queen Mother

Caramel (KAIR-uh-mel) (Spanish) She Is Golden-Brown Sweetness

Delight (dee-LYTE) (English) She Is all Our Delight

Dulce (DOOL-say) (Spanish) She Is Sugary-Sweet

Maple (MAY-pul) (English) She Is a Sugary Maple Tree

Marzipan (MAR-zee-pan) (German) She Is the Sweet Bread Served in March

Pattie (PAT-tee) (English) She Is Our Beloved Aristocrat

Plum (PLUM) (English) She Is a Sweet, Purple-Red Fruit

Taffy (TAF-fee) (Welsh) She Is Greatly Beloved

Teja (TAY-yuh) (Slovene) She Is God's Sweet Pastry

🎨 **Donna** (DAHN-nuh) (Italian) She Is a Beautiful Lady

Liz (LIZ) (English) She Is the Little One Favored by God

Donna Karan (1948–) is an American designer whose clothing-line DKNY (Donna Karan New York) sells in stores worldwide under the auspices of Liz Claiborne, the $5 billion firm founded in 1976 by designer Liz Claiborne.

🎨 **Emerald** (EM-ur-ruld) (English) She Is a Priceless Green Emerald

Fern (FURN) (English) She Is a Living Forest-Green Fern Tree

Goldie (GOL-dee) (Yiddish) She Is the Little One Who Is Pure Gold

Ivory (EYE-vur-ree) (English) She Is a Beautiful Cream-White Color

Jade (JAYD) (English) She Is a Precious and Beautiful Green Gemstone

Lavender (LAV-en-dur) (English) She Is Fragrant Lavender

Misty (MIS-tee) (English) She Is the Fresh, Cool, Morning Mist

Myrtle (MUR-tul) (English) She Is a Fragrant Myrtle Tree

Olive (AH-liv) (English) She Is a Fragrant Olive Tree

Robin (RAH-bin) (English) He Is the Beloved One Who Is Radiant Glory

🕊 **Georgia** (JOR-juh) (English) She Farms the Land

Mabel (MAY-bul) (English) She Is the Adorable Little One

Georgia O'Keefe (1887–1986) was an American painter famed for her sensuous paintings of desert flowers, such as 1935's White Hollyhock and Little Hills. One of Georgia's wealthy supporters was Mabel Luhan, an American philanthropist.

🕊 **Isadora** (iz-uh-DOR-ruh) (Greek) She Is a Gift from the Goddess Isis

Eleonora (el-ee-uh-NOR-ruh) (Italian) She Is the Beloved One Who Is a Healer

Isadora Duncan (1877–1927) was an American dancer who revolutionized dance with her free-spirited movements. Her friend Eleanora Duse was a famed Italian stage-actress.

🕊 **Lin** (LIN) (Chinese) She Is a Forest Where Green Jade Is Found

India (IN-dee-yuh) (English) She Is India

Maya Ying Lin (1959–) is an American sculptress renowned for designing the Vietnam Veterans Memorial in Washington, D.C., a black granite wall featuring the names of every Vietnam veteran. Lin's youngest daughter is India Wolf.

🕊 **Mona** (MO-nah) (Italian) She Is the Little One Who Is My Revered Lady

Lisa (LEE-suh) (English) Her God Is Abundance

The sixteenth-century painting Mona Lisa *was painted by the Italian Renaissance master Leonardo da Vinci throughout his lifetime, and is the world's most recognizable portrait, currently appraised at $700 million.*

🕊 **Ruby** (ROO-bee) (English) She Is a Priceless Ruby

Saffron (SAF-frun) (English) She Is Fragrant Saffron Spice

Sapphire (SAF-fyre) (English) She Is a Priceless Blue Sapphire

Silver (SIL-vur) (English) She Is Priceless, Gleaming Silver

Sky (SKYE) (English) She Is the Beautiful and Heavenly Blue Sky

Tawny (TAW-nee) (English) She Is Tanned and Beautiful

Teal (TEE-yul) (English) She Is the Beautiful Blue-Green of the Seas

Terra (TAIR-ruh) (Greek) She Is Mother Earth

Venetia (ven-EE-shuh) (English) She Is the City of Venice, Italy

Wisteria (wih-STEER-ee-yuh) (English) She Honors the American Botanist Caspar Wistar

🕊 **Susannah** (soo-ZAN-nuh) (Hebrew) She Is a Fragrant Lotus Flower

Giorgio (JOR-jee-yo) (Italian) He Farms the Land

Susannah Constantine (1962–) is an English fashion designer and television personality, as seen on What Not to Wear, *produced by the BBC. Susannah's first boss was billionaire Italian fashion designer Giorgio Armani.*

🕊 **Yoshino** (YO-Shee-noh) (Japanese) She Is a River of Cherry Blossoms

Akari (ah-KAH-ree) (Japanese) She Is Radiance

Yoshino Aoki is a Japanese composer of video-game music such as the melodies heard in the game Mega Man X3. *In collaboration with musician Akari Kaida, Yoshino penned the score for the game* Breath of Fire III.

BOYS AND GIRLS

🕊 **Acosta** (ah-KOHSS-tuh) (Spanish) She Is the Beautiful Coast

Charles-Valentin (sharl-val-en-TAN) (French) He Is Energetic Warrior

Dimitri (dee-,MEE-tree) (Russian) He Is Like Demeter, the Earth Mother

Ilse (IL-suh) (German) She Is the Little One Favored by God

Lazar (luh-ZAR) (Russian) His God Is a Wondrous Help

Myriam (MEER-ee-yum) (Hebrew) She Is Love

Pierre-Laurent (pee-air-law-RAW) (French) He Is a Laurel Wreath of Rock-Solid Victories

Piotr (pee-OH-tur) (Russian) He Is Rock-Solid

Valery (vah-LAIR-ree) (Russian) He Is Valorous

Webster (WEB-stur) (English) He Is a Skilled Weaver

🕊 **Ad** (AHD) (Dutch) He Is the Little One Who Is Hadria, Italy

Alla (AH-luh) (Russian) She Is Reminds Us of Greatness

Di (DYE) (English) She Is the Little One Who Is the Highest Source of Life

Fantasia (fan-TAY-zhuh) (Italian) She Improvises Imaginatively

Marcia (MAR-shah) (Latin) She Is as Powerful as any Male

Ossia (OH-see-yuh, AH-see-yuh) (Italian) She Is a Peaceful Little Doe

Placido (PLAH-see-doh) (Italian) He Is Placid and Harmonious

Prima (PREE-muh) (Latin) She Is First

Symphony (SIM-fo-nee) (English) She Is Harmonious and Melodious

Una (OO-nuh) (Irish) She Is a Gentle Lamb

♫ **Amar** (uh-MAHR) (Sanskrit) He Lives Forever

Avraham (AHV-rah-hahm) (Hebrew) He Is the Father of Nations

Bautista (bow-TEES-tuh) (Spanish) He Honors Saint John the Baptist

Concepcion (kohn-sep-see-YONE) (Spanish) She Is the Immaculate Conception

Levi (LEE-vye) (Hebrew) He Is Bound to Us by Ties of Love

Moshe (MO-shay) (Hebrew) He Is the Great Son Who Rescues Us

Reyes (RAY-yess) (Spanish) He Is the Delegation of Three Kings Who Honored Jesus

Sharma (SHAR-muh) (Sanskrit) He Protects Humanity

Tal (TAHL) (Hebrew) He Is the Morning Mist

Zhou (ZHOH) (Chinese) He Is the Ship That Carries Our Dreams

Amar, Bautista, Concepcion, Avraham, Levi, Moshe, Reyes, Sharma, Tal, and Zhou are baby names artistically fashioned from surnames.

♫ **Amhran** (ahm-RAHN) (Irish) She Is a Harmonious Melody

Banner (BAN-nur) (English) He Is the Great Banner of Our Nation

Bravo (BRAH-vo) (Spanish) He Is Bold and Courageous

Denes (DAY-nesh) (Hungarian) He Makes Himself Heard Clearly

Eleutheria (el-yoo-THEER-ee-yuh) (Greek) She Is Glorious Liberty

Hatikvah (hah-TEEK-vah) (Hebrew) She Is Humanity's Hope

Jamaica (juh-MAY-kuh) (Arawakan) She Is Jamaica

Liberté (lee-bair-TAY) (French) She Is Glorious Liberty

Rivers (RIH-vurz) (English) She Is Countless Powerful Waterways

Tien (tee-YEN) (Vietnamese) She Is an Enchanting Sprite

♫ **Amity** (AM-ih-tee) (English) He Is Treasured Friendship

Arroyo (uh-ROY-yo) (Spanish) He Is a Rushing River

Bernabe (bair-nah-BAY) (Spanish) He Descends from the Prophet

Diamond (DYE-mund) (English) She Is a Sparkling Diamond

Harlan (HAR-lun) (English) He Is the Land of the Swift Hares

Heaven (HEH-vun) (English) She Is the Paradise Called Heaven

Merritt (MAIR-rit) (English) He Is Great Worthiness and Merit

Pasqual (pahss-KAHL) (Spanish) He Is the Easter Holiday and the Passover Holiday

Potter (PAHT-tur) (English) He Crafts Clay Pots

Rutherford (RUH-thur-furd) (Scottish) He Is Rutherford, Scotland

♫ **Antonin** (AHN-toh-neen) (French) He Is a Blossoming Flower

Viola (vye-OH-lah) (Latin) She Is a Fragrant Violet

Antonin Dvořák (1841–1904) was a Czech composer noted for his use of ethnic motifs to produce such masterworks as Symphony No. 9, From the New World *(1893). Antonin's favorite instrument was the viola, which he played brilliantly.*

♫ **Aretha** (uh-REE-thuh) (Greek) She Is Honest

Otis (OH-tiss) (English) He Is the Little One Who Is Successful

Aretha Franklin (1942–) is an African-American singer whose powerful voice, heard in songs such as Respect, *has earned her millions of fans.* Respect *was written by the great African-American songwriter Otis Redding.*

♫ **Atlas** (AT-luss) (Greek) He Becomes Legendary

Catarina (kaht-ah-REE-nuh) (Portuguese) She Is Pure-Hearted

Fe (FAY) (Spanish) She Is Devotion

Genevieve (zhaw-vee-YEV) (French) She Is Loyal to Her People

Hudson (HUD-sun) (English) He Descends from the High-Spirited One

Luis (loo-WEESS) (Spanish) He Is a Renowned Warrior

Monterey (mahn-tur-RAY) (Spanish) She Is the King's Mountain

Rio (REE-yoh) (Spanish) He Is a Rushing River

Tomás (toh-MAHSS) (Spanish) He Is a Precious Twin

Zona (ZO-nuh) (Greek) He Encircles Us with Love

🕊 **Bailey** (BAY-lee) (English) He Enforces the Law as a Trusted Bailiff

Chan (CHAHN) (Khmer) She Arrived on a Monday

Kerr (KAR) (Scottish) He Is the Fresh Earth

Marin (muh-RIN) (Spanish) He Is the Blue Ocean

Reid (REED) (English) He Has Fiery Red Hair

Roberts (ROH-bairtss) (Latvian) He Is Brilliantly Renowned

Ross (RAWSS) (Scottish) He Is a Lofty Cliff

Wallace (WALL-liss) (Scottish) He Is a Mysterious Stranger

Wright (RYTE) (English) He Is a Skilled Artisan

Young (YUNG) (Korean) He Is Boldly Courageous

Bailey, Chan, Kerr, Marin, Reid, Roberts, Ross, Wallace, Wright, and Young are baby names artistically fashioned from surnames.

🕊 **Bennie** (BEN-nee) (English) He Is the Little One Born in the South

Burt (BURT) (Dutch) He Is Our Brilliant Little Aristocrat

Dave (DAYV) (English) He Is the Little One Who Is Greatly Beloved

Felice (feh-LEESS) (Italian) She Is favored with Good Fortune

Lew (LOO) (English) He Is Our Renowned Little Warrior

Milton (MIL-tun) (English) He Is the Mill Town

Nacio (NAH-see-yo) (Spanish) He Is the Little One Aflame with Greatness

Nickolas (NIK-uh-lus) (English) He Is Humanity's Triumph

Rube (ROOB) (English) Behold, He Is the Little One Who Is Our Glorious Son

Thom (TAHM) (English) He Is Our Precious Little Twin

🕊 **Byrne** (BURN) (Irish) He Descends from the Ebony-Black Raven

Eder (AY-dur) (Basque) He Is Good-Looking

Fiala (fee-AH-luh) She Is a Fragrant Violet

Hartmann (HART-mahn) (German) He Is a Courageous Male

Koppel (KAHP-pul) (Yiddish) He Is Our Little Magnificent One

Laine (LAYN-nee) (Estonian) She Is an Unstoppable Tidal Wave

Lambert (LAHM-burt) (German) He Is the Shining Nation

Laurent (lor-RAW) (French) He Is a Laurel Wreath of Victory

Marek (MAH-rek) (Polish) He Is Powerfully Male

Mora (MOR-ruh) (English) She Is Love

Byrne, Eder, Fiala, Hartmann, Koppel, Laine, Laurent, Lambert, Marek, and More are baby names artistically fashioned from surnames.

🕊 **Claude** (KLODE) (French) He Walks a Difficult Path

Camille (kah-MEEL) (French) She Is the Young One Who Performs Rituals

French painter Claude Monet (1840–1926) was an artist who conveyed impressions of reality through his use of light and color, as in his masterpiece Impression, Sunrise *(1872–1873). Claude married model Camille Doncieux in 1870.*

🕊 **Colombo** (koh-LUM-bo) (Italian) He Is a White Dove

Doyle (DOYL) (Irish) He Descends from the Dark Stranger

Gallagher (GAL-ih-ghur) (Irish) He Descends from Our Immigrant Ally

Gil (GHEEL) (Spanish) He Is a Powerful Young Goat

Hagen (HAH-ghen) (Danish) He Is the Greatest Son in History

Marino (mah-REE-nuh) (Italian) He Is the Vast Blue Ocean

Murray (MOOR-ree) (Scottish) He Is the Region of Moray, Scotland

Pace (PAYSS) (English) He Is Peace

Romero (ro-MAIR-ro) (Italian) He Journeys to the Eternal City of Rome

Wojciecha (voy-SHEE-kah) (Polish) She Is the Warrior Who Safeguards Us All

Colombo, Doyle, Gallagher, Gil, Hagen, Marino, Murray, Pace, Romero, and Wojciecha are baby names artistically fashioned from surnames.

🕊 **Édouard** (ed-WAH) (French) He Safeguards Our Good Fortune

Berthe (BAIRT) (French) She Shines Gloriously

French painter Édouard Manet (1832–1883) was a pioneer of Impressionism whose practitioners filter reality through personal impressions. Édouard became the brother-in-law of Berthe Morisot, another great Impressionist.

🕊 **Felix** (FEE-lix) (Latin) He Is Favored with Good Fortune
Fanny (FAN-nee) (English) She Is the Little One Who Is the Nation of France
Felix Mendelssohn (1809–1847) was a German composer, beloved for such works as his ballet A Midsummer Night's Dream, featuring the Wedding March, heard in virtually all weddings. Felix's sister was Fanny Mendelssohn, a respected composer in her own right.

🕊 **Frans** (FRAHNZ, FRANZ) (Dutch) He Is the Nation of France
Judith (JOO-dith) (Hebrew) She Is a Woman from Judea
Frans Hals (c. 1580–1666) was a Dutch painter whose masterpieces, such as Jester with a Lute, show great empathy. One of the painters inspired by Hals was colleague Judith Leyster, who emulated his compassion in her paintings of Dutch women.

🕊 **Georges** (ZHORZH) (French) He Farms the Land
Carmen (KAR-men) (Spanish) She Is a Garden of Melodies
Georges Bizet (1838–1875) was a French composer adored for his opera Carmen (1875) about the lovely thief Carmen who seduces the soldier Don José. Opera America, a New York opera organization, lists Carmen as one of history's twenty most popular operas.

🕊 **Gordon** (GOR-dun) (Scottish) He Is a Lofty Hill
Maida (MYE-duh) (English) She Is Chaste and Pure
Gordon Ramsay (1966–) is a Scottish chef starring in several television programs, such as Hell's Kitchen, a cooking contest produced by London's Granada Productions. Gordon also owns successful restaurants worldwide, including London's esteemed Maida Vale.

🕊 **Hilda** (HIL-dah) (German) She Lives for Combat
Peter (PEE-tur) (Hebrew) He Is Rock-Solid
Hilda Paredes (1957–) is a Mexican-British composer trained under British composer Peter Davies at the Dartington School, Devon.

🕊 **Irving** (UR-ving) (Scottish) He Is Irving, Scotland
Kate (KAYT) (English) She Is Our Little Pure-Hearted One
Irving Berlin (1888–1989) was a Russian-American musician famed for such standards as 1918's God Bless America. Later, in the 1943 film This Is the Army, singer Kate Smith sang a version of God Bless America which helped immortalize Irving's patriotic hymn.

🕊 **Marc** (MAHK) (French) He Is Powerfully Male
Bella (BEL-luh) (Latin) She Is a Warrior
Marc Chagall (1887–1985) was a Russian-French impressionist painter who sought ways to express his personal impressions of reality, rather than using photorealism, in works such as 1917's Bella with White Collar, a depiction of his artist-wife Bella Rosenfeld.

🕊 **Marcel** (mar-SEL) (French) He Is Powerfully Male
Suzanne (soo-ZAHN) (French) She Is a Fragrant Lotus Flower
French artist Marcel Duchamp (1887–1968) fostered appreciation for modernism with works such as 1917's Fountain, a "found art" piece consisting of a urinal. Marcel's sister Suzanne Duchamp-Crotti was an accomplished painter in her own right.

🕊 **Maurits** (MAH-oh-ritz) (Dutch) He Is a Dark Moor
Jetta (JET-tuh) (Dutch) She Rules Our Home Magnificently
Maurits Cornelis Escher (1898–1972) was a brilliant Dutch mathematician-artist whose complex masterpieces have fascinated generations of art-lovers. Maurits married the talented Dutch artist Jetta Umiker in 1924.

🕊 **Micheline** (mish-LEEN) (French) She Is the Beloved One Who Resembles God
Louis (loo-WEE) (French) He Is a Renowned Warrior
Micheline Bernardini was an exotic dancer who caused an international sensation by modeling the world's first bikini in 1946, at the Piscine Molitor swimming club in Paris, France. The bikini was designed by French artist Louis Réard.

🕊 **Norman** (NOR-mun) (English) He Is a Norse Viking
Judy (JOO-dee) (English) She Is the Little One Who Is Judea
American painter Norman Rockwell (1894–1978) lauded democracy in works such as 1943's Four Freedoms. His final work was of American

singer Judy Garland, famed as Dorothy in 1939's The Wizard of Oz.

🕊 **Pablo** (PAHB-lo) (Spanish) He Demonstrates Humility

Dora (DOR-rah) (Spanish) She Is Our Little Present from God

Pablo Picasso (1881–1973) was a revolutionary Spanish artist who utilized distorted shapes and bold colors. He is best known for 1937's Guernica, showing the horrors of aerial bombing. Pablo's friend was the Croatian-French photographer Dora Maar.

🕊 **Sergei** (sair-GAY) (Russian) He Is a Servant of Humanity

Francesca (fran-CHESS-kah) (Italian) She Is the Nation of France

Russian composer Sergei Rachmaninoff (1873–1943) wrote melodies such as Piano Concerto No. 2 in C Minor (1901). Sergei's best opera is 1906's Francesca da Rimini.

🕊 **Yi** (YEE) (Chinese) He Is a Celebration of Honor and Joy

Mario (MAH-ree-yoh) (Italian) He Is Powerfully Male

Chen Yi (1953–) writes Baroque music in the style of Johann Sebastian Bach. Emigrating to New York in the sixties, Yi studied under Columbia University professor Mario Davidovsky.

Name Pairs and Groups
from the Ranks of Infamous Despots, Criminals, Gangsters, Outlaws, Law-Enforcement Heroes, and Legal Luminaries

BOYS

🕊 **Abdulla** (ab-DOOL-luh, ab-DUL-luh) (Arabic) He Is God's Loyal Servant

Adam (AD-dum) (Hebrew) He Is History's Greatest Man

Bartholomew (bar-THAH-luh-myoo) (Greek) He Has a Furrowed Brow

Bernard (bur-NARD) (German) He Is a Courageous Bear

Dirk (DURK) (Dutch) He Is Our Little Present from God

Hendrick (HEN-drik) (Dutch) He Rules Our Home Magnificently

Howell (HOW-wull) (Welsh) He Is Illustrious

Hugh (HYOO) (English) His Heart and His Courage Are Truly Great

Israel (IZ-ray-yul) (Hebrew) His God Triumphs Forever

Red (RED) (English) He Has Fiery Red Hair

🕊 **Afeni** (ah-FAY-nee) (Yoruba) She Is Lovely and Cherished

Colin (KAHL-lin) (Scottish) He Is an Innocent Youth

Francisco (frahn-SEES-ko) (Spanish) He Is the Nation of France

Horatio (ho-RAY-Shee-yoh) (Latin) He Is a Person for all Seasons

Nelson (NEL-sun) (English) He Descends from the Great Champion

Sam (SAM) (English) He Is God's Little Announcer

Slobodan (slo-bo-DAHN) (Serbian) He Is Freedom

Ted (TED) (English) He Is Our Little Present from God

Vojislav (VOY-slahv) (Serbian) He Is a Renowned Warrior

Zacarias (zahk-uh-REE-yus) (Spanish) He Is Favored by God

🕊 **Al** (al-FAHNS) (English) He Is Our Noble Little Leader

Eliot (EL-ee-yut) (English) His Only God Is God

> Al Capone (1899–1947) was an Italian-American mobster who, during the Great Depression, led a criminal enterprise headquartered in Chicago. Eliot Ness was the government agent who finally arrested him.

🕊 **Aten** (AT-tun) (Egyptian) He Is the Golden Sun-Disk

Bat (BAT) (English) He Is the Little One with a Furrowed Brow

Bullock (BULL-luk) (English) He Is a Powerful Bull

Camillus (kuh-MIL-luss) (Latin) He Observes Sacred Rituals

Mariano (mar-ee-AH-no) (Spanish) He Is Love Itself

Perry (PAIR-ree) (Welsh) He Descends from Our Homeland's Ruler

Price (PRICE) (Welsh) He Descends from a Dynamic Man

Reeves (REEVS) (English) He Comes from a Family of Law-Enforcers

Wiley (WYE-lee) (English) He Is Cunning

Wyatt (WYE-yut) (English) He Is a Courageous Warrior

🐾 **Brutus** (BROO-tus) (Latin) He Is a Massive Heavyweight

Tobias (toh-BYE-yahss) (Greek) His God Is Goodness

Brutus (85 B.C.–42 B.C.) assassinated Roman dictator Julius Caesar. And, although not an outlaw, British actor Tobias Menzies portrayed Brutus brilliantly in the HBO 2005–2007 television series Rome.

🐾 **Chance** (CHANSS) (English) He Is the Little One Who Is a Golden Opportunity

Ellis (EL-liss) (Welsh) He Is Compassionate

Emery (EM-uh-ree) (English) He Works Tirelessly

Gottlieb (GOT-leeb) (German) He Reveres the Lord

Hale (HAYL) (English) He Is a Peaceful Hideaway

McKenzie (muh-KEN-zee) (Irish) He Is Handsome

Piper (PYE-pur) (English) He Plays the Panpipes Beautifully

Steen (STEEN) (Danish) He Is Rock-Solid

Sterling (STOOR-ling) (Scottish) He Is Star-Bright

Wilmer (WIL-mur) (English) He Is Famously Determined

🐾 **Davis** (DAY-viss) (English) He Is Greatly Beloved

Gallagher (GAL-ih-ghur) (Irish) He Descends from the Compassionate Stranger

Graham (GRAM) (Scottish) He Is a Homestead Built on Solid Gravel

Hadley (HAD-lee) (English) He Is a Meadow Filled with Heather

Porter (POR-tur) (English) He Guards the Door

Shaw (SHAW) (Scottish) He Is a Mighty Hawk

Smith (SMITH) (English) He Smites Metal Powerfully

Spalding (SPAHL-ding) (Scottish) He Is a Beautiful Furrowed Farm

Winston (WIN-stun) (English) He Is Contented and Rock-Solid

Winthrop (WIN-thrup) (English) He Is Brotherhood and Love

🐾 **Helix** (HEE-lix) (Greek) He Is Helisson, Greece

Nyctimus (NIK-tuh-mus) (Greek) He Is Nyktimos, Greece

King Lycaon of Arcadia, Greece, had fifty sons. including the warriors Helix and Nyctimus. However, when Lycaon offended Zeus, high king of the gods, Zeus transformed Lycaon into a wolf and slew his sons. Their legacy was the fifty magnificent Greek cities they established.

🐾 **John** (JAHN) (Hebrew) His God Is Gracious

Melvin (MEL-vin) (English) He Is a Good Advisor

Depression-era outlaw John Dillinger (1903–1934) and his gang executed daring bank robberies from Indiana to Arizona. Dillinger's nemesis was Federal Bureau of Investigation (FBI) agent Melvin Purvis.

🐾 **Joseph** (YO-sef) (Russian) His Greatness Increases

Nikita (nih-KEE-tuh) (Russian) He Is Invincible

Joseph Stalin (1878–1953) led the Union of Soviet Socialist Republics during World War Two (1939–1945), slaying millions of political opponents. Joseph's equally ruthless successor Nikita Khrushchev was known as the Butcher of Ukraine.

🐾 **Phrixus** (FRIX-suss) (Latin) He Bristles with Hair

Elatus (ee-LAY-tus) (Latin) He Is Flexible

Phrixus and Elatus were two of the powerful Centauri, as the Romans called them—whose upper torsos were human and whose lower bodies were those of horses. The poet Ovid, in his Metamorphoses, *describes the lawless nature of many Centauri.*

🐾 **Robert** (RAH-burt) (English) He Is Brilliantly Renowned

Harry (HAIR-ree) (English) He Rules Our Home Magnificently

Butch Cassidy (Robert Parker) (1866–1908) and the Sundance Kid (Harry Longabaugh) (1867–1908) were outlaws in the American West. Both reportedly perished in Bolivia following an abortive robbery.

🐾 **Robin** (RAH-bin) (English) He Is the Beloved One Who Shines Gloriously

Marian (MAIR-ee-yun) (English) She Is the Beloved One Who Is Love Itself

Robin Hood of Sherwood Forest, England, was either a real person or a folk-hero conjured up by an oppressed populace. Robin was an outlaw, but one who robbed from the rich and gave to the poor. Maid Marian was the lovely woman whom Robin adored.

GIRLS

🕮 **Bathsheba** (bath-SHEE-buh) (Hebrew) She Descends from the Promise-Keeper
Blanche (BLAWSH) (French) She Is Beautifully Fair
Daisy (DAY-zee) (English) She Is a Fragrant Daisy
Elfriede (el-FREE-duh) (German) She Is the Power of the Elfin People
Griselda (gree-ZEL-dah) (Spanish) She Is a Gray-Haired Warrior
Jezebel (JEZ-uh-bel) (Hebrew) She Calls Forth Divine Powers
Lea (LEE-yuh) (German) She Is Humanity's Queen
Tillie (TILL-lee) (English) She Is Our Powerful Little Warrior
Tracie (TRAY-see) (English) She Is Thrace
Velma (VEL-mah) (German) She Protects Humanity

🕮 **Lizzie** (LIZ-zee) (English) She Is the Beloved One Whose God Supplies All
Emma (EM-muh) (English) She Is the Entire Universe
Lizzie Borden (1860–1927) was the daughter of Andrew and Sarah Borden of Massachusetts, who in 1892 were slain by an intruder; fortunately, Lizzie's sister Emma was away at the time. Lizzie's subsequent trial garnered huge publicity, eventually ending in an acquittal.

🕮 **Patty** (PAT-tee) (English) She Is Beloved and Aristocratic
Tania (TAHN-yah) (Russian) She Is Our Little Saint
Patty Hearst (1954–) is the daughter of the late newspaper tycoon William Hearst. After being kidnapped in 1974 by the Symbionese Liberation Army gang, Patty apparently sided with the kidnappers, taking the name Tania to honor Cuba's Tania the Guerilla.

BOYS AND GIRLS

🕮 **Antigone** (an-TIG-uh-nee) (Greek) She Is Against Unfair Compromise
Polynices (pah-lee-NYE-seez) (Greek) He Is War and Conflict
In the play Antigone by Sophocles (c. 496 B.C.–406 B.C.), Polynices of Thebes wars against King Creon and perishes. Creon says Polynices's body must remain unburied, but Polynices's sister Antigone defies the law, arguing that decency trumps edicts.

🕮 **Arden** (AR-den) (English) She Is as Lofty as Heaven
Art (ART) (English) He Is a Powerful Little Bear
Cal (KAL) (English) He Has a Beautiful Little Hairless Head
Earnest (UR-nest) (English) He Is Serious
Fee (FAY) (Dutch) She Is a Magical Fairy
Hùng (HUNG) (Vietnamese) He Is Courageous
Re (RAY) (Egyptian) He Is the Radiant Sun
Reg (REHJ) (English) He Is Our Wise Little Counselor
Sé (SHAY) (Irish) He Is a Soaring Hawk
Si (SYE) (English) He Is Our Quiet Little Listener

🕮 **Baker** (BAY-kur) (English) He Bakes Warm Bread
Deuce (DOOSS) (English/Latin) He Is Doubly Powerful
Doc (DAHK) (American/English) He Is a Little Physician
Emmett (EM-met) (English) He Is the Little One Who Is Our Entire Universe
Fisher (FISH-shur) (English) He Fishes for Wealth
Gregorio (greh-GOR-ee-yoh) (Spanish) He Is Always Alert
Longley (LONG-lee) (English) He Is a Long Meadow in the Forest
Riley (RYE-lee) (Irish) He Is a Meadow of Rye Grass
Simeon (SIM-ee-yun) (Hebrew) He Hears Everything Clearly
Texas (TEX-suss) (Caddoan/English) He Is a Trusted Friend from the Great State of Texas

✤ **Bonnie** (BAHN-nee) (Scottish) She Is
Exceedingly Pretty

Clyde (KLYDE) (Scottish) He Is the River Clyde,
Scotland

*American gangsters Bonnie Parker (1910–1934)
and Clyde Barrow (1909–1934) led a Depression-era gang of bank robbers. The public
idolized the gang because of the presence of the
popular, attractive Bonnie.*

✤ **Cameron** (KAM-ur-un, KAM-run) (Scottish)
His Nose Goes Its Own Way

Clayton (KLAY-tun) (English) He Is a
Community Built on Solid Clay

Dewey (DOO-wee) (Welsh) He Is Greatly
Beloved

Goddard (GOD-durd) (English) He Is God's
Courageous Warrior

Goodwin (GOOD-win) (English) He Is
Befriended by God

Harris (HAIR-riss) (English) He Rules Our
Home Magnificently

McKenna (muh-KEN-nuh) (Irish) He Is Created
in Fire

Norton (NOR-tun) (English) He Is from the
Northern City

Whitney (WHIT-nee) (English) She Is a
Beautiful White Realm

Zabel (zah-BEL) (Armenian) Her God Is
Abundance

✤ **Cassidy** (KASS-sih-dee) (Irish) He Descends
from the Fleecy-Haired Man

Cherokee (CHAIR-oh-kee) (Cherokee/English)
He Is the Great Cherokee Nation

Colbert (KOL-burt) (English) He Is a
Conqueror with a Gleaming Helmet

Cullen (KUL-len) (English) He Is Cologne,
Germany

Daly (DAY-lee) (Irish) He Descends from the
Magnificent Nation

Hardin (HAR-din) (English) He Is the Little
One Who Is Vigorously Courageous

Reno (REE-no) (Spanish) He Is the Little Dark-
Haired One

Starr (STAR) (English) She Is a Heavenly Star

Sundance (SUN-danss) (English) He Is the
Native American Sun Dance

Tiburcio (tih-BOOR-see-yoh) (Spanish) He Is
Tibur, Italy

✤ **Locusta** (lo-KYOOS-tah) (Latin) She Is
Lucania, Italy

Nero (NEE-ro) (Latin) He Is Hearty and
Powerful

*Locusta was a Roman botanist who became a
poisoner for hire. Her infamy was such that
when Emperor Nero (A.D. 37–A.D. 68) needed
to slay his rival Britannicus, he hired Locusta
for the task.*

Name Pairs and Groups
from Animé, Comic Books, and Video Games

BOYS

🎮 **Jonny** (JAHN-nee) (English) He Is Beloved and His God Is Gracious

Hadji (HAH-jee) (Arabic) He Is Our Spiritual Leader

The 1964–1965 cartoon television series Jonny Quest *followed the adventures of young Jonny Quest, his Indian friend Hadji, his brilliant father Benton Quest, bodyguard "Race" Banon, and the intrepid mutt Bandit.*

🎮 **Mario** (MAH-ree-yoh) (Italian) He Is Powerfully Male

Luigi (loo-EE-jee) (Italian) He Is a Renowned Warrior

In the video-game Super Mario Bros.*, first distributed by the Nintendo Entertainment System in 1985, brothers Mario and Luigi battle tirelessly to rescue Princess Toadstool from the nefarious King Bowser.*

🎮 **Neal** (NEEL) (Irish) He Is a Great Victor

Roy (ROI) (Scottish) He Is the Fiery Red King

American artist Neal Adams (1941–) is one of history's greatest comic artists, having made his mark on such titles as The Uncanny X-Men *published by Marvel Comics of New York. Many X-Men stories were written by the legendary Roy Thomas.*

🎮 **Riku** (REE-koo) (Japanese) He Is the Fertile Land

Sora (SO-ruh) (Japanese) He Is the Heavenly Blue Sky

Riku and Sora are two young warriors in the Kingdom Hearts video game series, created by Square Enix. Riku and Sora join characters from the Walt Disney Company in sword-wielding battles.

🎮 **Xavier** (ZAY-vee-yur) (English) He Builds a New House

Scott (SKAHT) (Scottish) He Is the Nation of Scotland

In the Marvel Comics universe, Charles Xavier is the founder of the team of supermutants called the X-Men. Charles's first X-Man was Scott Summers, known as Cyclops for his deadly eye-beams.

GIRLS

🎮 **Adriana** (ay-dree-AN-nuh) (Italian) She Is Hadria, Italy

Caitlin (KAYT-lin) (Irish) She Is Pure-Hearted

Elaine (ee-LAYN) (French) She Is a Shining Torch

Glynis (GLIN-nis) (Welsh) She Is a Peaceful Valley

Jenette (zhuh-NET) (American/French) She Is God's Graceful Little Messenger

Jenna (JEN-nuh) (English) She Is Our Fair Little Beauty

Jodi (JO-dee) (English) She Is the Little One Who Is Judea

Pia (PEE-yuh) (Italian) She Is Respectful

Rachelle (ruh-SHEL) (English) She Is a Gentle Mother Ewe

Tara (TAR-rah) (Irish) She Is the Divine Realm

243

🌸 **Alison** (AL-lih-sun) (English) She Is Our Little Aristocrat

Chynna (CHYE-nuh) (American) She Is China

Geneviève (zhaw-vee-YEV) (French) She Is Humanity's Greatest Woman

Jennie (JEN-nee) (English) She Is Our Fair Little Beauty

Joyce (JOYSS) (English) She Is Supreme

Leanne (lee-ANN) (English) She Is a Graceful Meadow

Paige (PAYJ) (English) She Serves Humanity

Shaenon (SHAH-nun) (American/Irish) She Is God's Graceful Little Messenger

Shary (SHAIR-ree) (American) She Is Darling and Sweet

Tavisha (tuh-VEE-shuh) (American/Scottish) She Is a Precious Twin

🌸 **Anina** (ah-NEE-nuh) (German) She Is the Graceful Little One

Bobbie (BAHB-bee) (English) She Is Our Glorious Little One

Devin (DEH-vin) (Irish) She Is a Swift-Running Deer

Fiona (fee-OH-nuh) (Scottish) She Is Beautifully Fair

Meloney (MEL-uh-nee) (American) She Is Darkly Beautiful

Ramona (rah-MO-nah) (Spanish) She Counsels Us Wisely

Renae (reh-NAY) (English) She Is Reborn in God

Rosario (ro-SAHR-ee-yo) (Spanish) She Is the Blessed Rosary

Samm (SAM) (American) She Is the Little One Whom God Hears

Tatjana (taht-YAH-nuh) (Serbian) She Is a Saint

🌸 **Ashly** (ASH-lee) (American) She Is a Meadow in the Ash-Tree Forest

Bettina (bet-TEE-nuh) (Italian) She Is the Divinely Blessed Little One

Erika (AIR-eeh-kah) (German) She Rules Forever

Federica (fed-ur-EE-kuh) (Italian) She Rules Peacefully

Hilda (HIL-dah) (German) She Lives for Combat

Holly (HAHL-lee) (English) She Is the One Who Is the Lovely Holly Bush

Lea (LEE-yah) (German) She Is Humanity's Queen

Rina (REE-nah) (Italian) She Is the Pure-Hearted Little One

Rivkah (REEV-kuh) (Hebrew) She Is the Little One Who Brings Us Closer

Yoko (YO-ko) (Japanese) She Is Sun-Bright and Ocean-Beautiful

🌸 **Beth** (BETH) (English) She Demonstrates God's Abundance

Bunny (BUN-nee) (English) She Is an Adorable Bunny Rabbit

Kristen (KRIS-ten) (English) She Follows Christ

Lynn (LIN) (Welsh) She Is a Clear Lake

Marjorie (MAR-jur-ree) (English) She Is a Priceless Pearl

Nicola (NEE-ko-lah) (Italian) She Is Humanity's Triumph

Queenie (KWEEN-nee) (English) She Is Our Majestic Little Queen

Selby (SEL-bee) (English) She Is a Farm in the Willow Groves

Tina (TEE-nuh) (English) She Is Christ's Little Follower

Wendy (WEN-dee) (English) She Is Beautifully Fair

🌸 **Carla** (KAR-lah) (Italian) She Is a Mighty Warrior

Christine (kris-TEEN) (French) She Follows Christ

Diane (dee-YAHN) (French) She Is the Heavenly Life Source

Dori (DOR-ree) (Hebrew) She Is Her Generation's Greatest

Hope (HOPE) (English) She Is Our Greatest Hope

Megan (MAY-gahn) (Welsh) She Is Our Priceless Little Pearl

Melinda (muh-LIN-duh) (English) She Is Darkly Beautiful

Trina (TREE-nuh) (English) She Is the Pure-Hearted Little One

Ulli (OO-lee) (American/Norwegian) She Is the Powerful Little One

Vanesa (vuh-NES-suh) (American/English) Her God Is Salvation

🌸 **Chen** (CHEN) (Chinese) She Is the Sunrise

Ichigo (ITCH-chee-go) (Japanese) She Is a Fragrant Strawberry

Ling (LING) (Chinese) She Is the Bell That Chimes on Time

Meena (MEE-nuh) (Sanskrit) She Is a Beautiful Sea-Creature

Merle (MURL) (English) She Is the Shimmering Ocean

Ming (MING) (Chinese) She Inscribes Love in Our Hearts

Mithra (MITH-rah) (Persian) She Is the Radiant Sun

Natsuki (NAHT-soo-kee) (Japanese) She Is a Moon-Child

Scottie (SKAHT-tee) (English) She Is the Little One Who Is the Nation of Scotland

Sera (SAIR-ruh) (English) She Is a Majestic Princess

❧ **Haruhi** (HAR-oo-hee) (Japanese) She Is Honey in the Springtime

Renge (RENG-gay) (Japanese) She Is a Fragrant Lotus Flower

> *Haruhi Fujioka is the heroine of the Japanese anime series* Ouran High School Host Club, *created by Bisco Hatori. Haruhi dresses like a boy to save money on uniforms while she repays a debt to Ouran High. Haruhi's friend Renge Houshakuji runs Ouran's Host Club, a student association.*

❧ **Lara** (LAH-rah) (Icelandic) She Is a Laurel Wreath of Victory

Jacqueline (JAK-kwuh-lin) (English/French) She Is Divinely Protected

> *English aristocrat Lara Croft is a character from Eidos Interactive's 1996 video game* Tomb Raider. *Lara's quest for hidden treasure is often thwarted by the seemingly immortal tycoon Jacqueline Natla.*

BOYS AND GIRLS

❧ **Ackerman** (AK-ur-mun) (English) He Proudly Farms His Acreage

Daisuke (DICE-kee) (Japanese) He Assists Us

Grant (GRAHNT) (Scottish) He Is Magnificent

Lee (LEE) (Chinese) He Stands against the Wind

McFarland (mak-FAR-lind) (Scottish) He Descends from the One with a Furrowed Brow

Mike (MYKE) (English) He Is God's Little Disciple

Teng (TENG) (Chinese) He Is an Invincible Dragon

Tiffany (TIF-fuh-nee) (English) She Proves God's Greatness

Vic (VIK) (English) He Is Humanity's Little Triumph

Yuri (YOO-ree) (Japanese) He Is a Fragrant Lily

❧ **Asuka** (ah-SOO kah) (Japanese) He Is Fragrant Perfume

Azazel (aw-ZAH-zul) (Hebrew) He Is Self-Sacrificing

Bryan (BRYE-yun) (Irish) He Is Aristocratic

Christie (KRIS-tee) (English) She Is Christ's Little Follower

Eddy (ED-dee) (English) He Is Our Little Protector

Jin (JIN) (Chinese) He Is as Good as Gold

Jun (JOON) (Chinese) She Is the Supreme Ruler

Lili (LI-lee) (German) She Is the Little One Favored by God

Michelle (mee-SHEL) (French) She Resembles God

Violet (VYE-uh-let) (English) She Is a Fragrant Violet

❧ **Brenda** (BREN-duh) (Norwegian) She Is a Mighty Sword

Buck (BUK) (English) He Is a Mighty Stag

Calvin (KAL-vin) (English) His Head Is Smooth and Hairless

Cathy (KATH-thee) (English) She Is the Pure-Hearted Little One

Garfield (GAR-feeld) (English) He Is a Three-Sided Farmer's Field

Hobbes (HAHBZ) (English) He Is Brilliantly Renowned

Kirby (KUR-bee) (English) He Is a Beautiful Community with a Church

Modesty (MAH-dus-tee) (English) She Is a Pure-Hearted Woman

Prince (PRINSS) (English) He Is a Royal Prince

Tracy (TRAY-see) (English) He Is Thrace

❧ **Clark** (KLARK) (English) He Studies and Learns

Lois (LO-wiss) (Greek) She Is Greatly Desired

> *Clark Kent is the alter ego of the mightiest hero in comic history—Superman, sole survivor of the doomed planet Krypton. Clark's true love Lois Lane is a reporter for* The Daily Planet *newspaper of Metropolis.*

❧ **Renton** (REN-tun) (English) He Is a Town of Compassion

Eureka (yur-EE-kah) (Greek) He Has
Discovered Greatness
   Eureka Seven *is an anime television series cre-*
   ated by the legendary Bones animation studio
   of Japan. Renton Thurston—operator of a
   mecha, or futuristic war-machine—offers moral
   support for Eureka, a troubled adolescent and
   fellow mecha-warrior.

Ⓐ **Riyoko** (ree-YO-ko) (Japanese) She Is a
   Jasmine-Scented Child
Napoleon (nuh-POH-lee-yun) (Italian) He
Descends from the Clouds
   Riyoko Ikeda (1947–) is a mangaka *or Japa-*
   nese comic-book illustrator. Her specialty is

sh'jo—*comics for young girls. One of Ryoko's*
finest works is Eikou no Napoleon, *chronicling*
the exploits of French conqueror Napoleon
Bonaparte.

Ⓐ **Shigeru** (Shee-GAIR-roo) (Japanese) He Is
   the Seventh Son
Zelda (ZEL-duh) (Yiddish) She Is the Little One
Who Is Good Fortune
   Japanese artist Shigeru Miyamoto (1952–) is
   the leading game-designer for the Nintendo
   Company. He has created such video games
   as The Legend of Zelda, *which follows the*
   exploits of the hero, Link, in his quest to protect
   Princess Zelda.

About the Author

Eric Groves, Sr., is the proud father of two beautiful children and a seventh-grade English teacher who has spent twenty years teaching students the beauty of English literature. A first-place winner on *Jeopardy!* (1984) and the holder of degrees in Law and English, Groves is the author of *Butt Rot and Bottom Gas: A Glossary of Tragically Misunderstood Words* (Quirk Books, 2007). Groves has also written *The Anti-War Quote Book* (Quirk Books, 2007), a timely collection of history's greatest, most unforgettable anti-war quotations; and *Divine Baby Names* (Sellers, 2008), a book of Greek and Roman names for the four million little gods and goddesses born annually in the United States.